Community Psychology

Linking Individuals and Communities

THIRD EDITION

BRET KLOOS
University of South Carolina

JEAN HILL
New Mexico Highlands University

ELIZABETH THOMAS
University of Washington Bothell

ABRAHAM WANDERSMAN
University of South Carolina

MAURICE J. ELIAS
Rutgers University

JAMES H. DALTON
Bloomsburg University

WADSWORTH
CENGAGE Learning

Australia • Brazil • Japan • Korea • Mexico • Singapore • Spain • United Kingdom • United States

Community Psychology: Linking Individuals and Communities, Third Edition, International Edition
Bret Kloos, Jean Hill, Elizabeth Thomas, Abraham Wandersman, Maurice J. Elias and James H. Dalton

Publisher/Executive Editor: Linda Schreiber-Ganster

Acquisitions Editor: Timothy Matray

Editorial Assistant: Lauren K. Moody

Media Editor: Lauren Keyes

Senior Marketing Manager: Elisabeth Rhoden

Marketing Coordinator: Janay Pryor

Marketing Communications Manager: Laura Localio

Content Project Management: PreMediaGlobal

Senior Art Director: Pamela Galbreath

Print Buyer: Rebecca Cross

Rights Acquisitions Director: Bob Kauser

Rights Acquisition Specialist, Image/Text: Roberta Broyer

Production Service: PreMediaGlobal

Cover Image: © VisionsofAmerica/Joe Sohm/ Digital Vision/Getty Images

Compositor: PreMediaGlobal

Library of Congress Control Number: 2011923313

International Edition:

ISBN-13: 978-1-111-72640-9

ISBN-10: 1-111-72640-X

Cengage Learning International Offices

Asia
www.cengageasia.com
tel: (65) 6410 1200

India
www.cengage.co.in
tel: (91) 11 30484837/38

Australia/New Zealand
www.cengage.com.au
tel: (61) 3 9685 4111

Latin America
www.cengage.com.mx
tel: +52 (55) 1500 6000

Brazil
www.cengage.com.br
tel: (011) 3665 9900

UK/Europe/Middle East/Africa
www.cengage.co.uk
tel: (44) 207 067 2500

Represented in Canada by Nelson Education, Ltd.
tel: (416) 752 9100 / (800) 668 0671
www.nelson.com

Cengage Learning is a leading provider of customized learning solutions with office locations around the globe, including Singapore, the United Kingdom, Australia, Mexico, Brazil, and Japan. Locate your local office at: **www.cengage.com/global**

For product information: **www.cengage.com/international**
Visit your local office: **www.cengage.com/global**
Visit our corporate website: **www.cengage.com**

Printed in the United States of America
1 2 3 4 5 6 7 15 14 13 12 11

To Suzanne, who has been an inspiration through her work to address injustice and a support through her love and care; and to my parents Richard and Kathleen Kloos, who provided me countless opportunities to learn and models of lives well lived.—B. K.

To Tom, who, although he still believes community psychology is just a form of sociology, has always been an amazing source of support in my work and my life; and to Mikaele, in the hope that her passion for social justice will continue to inform and inspire her life.—J. L. H.

To Chris, whose love and support bring me courage and great joy; and to my parents, Bo and Rubye Lynn Thomas, and my sister, Stephanie—with much love and gratitude to each of you. I am inspired by your wisdom, strength, and grace.—E. T.

To my wife Lois, whose love and wisdom make me happy and wiser; to my father Irving Wandersman and in memory of my mother Hadassah Wandersman, who saw great things in me and nurtured me.—A. W.

To my wife Ellen, with gratitude for her love and cherished support always; and to Agnes and Sol Elias, whose unwavering support has served as the springboard for my accomplishments—M. J. E.

To my wife Carolyn, whose companionship, love, and wisdom sustain me daily; to my sister Mary Hannah, who exemplifies courage; and to the memory of Heath and Sally Dalton, who taught by example the integration of faith and action—J. H. D.

Brief Contents

Contents

PART V   Promoting Community and Social Change

11   Empowerment and Citizen Participation   350

Foreword

Thriving, transforming, renewing, strengthening, sustaining—these pathways of growth require transitions for individuals, families, and communities. So it is with this textbook. With this edition, the original author team (Jim Dalton, Maurice Elias, and Abe Wandersman) passes to a new author team the tasks, joys, values, and living community of readers of *Community Psychology: Linking Individuals and Communities*.

Abe Wandersman continues as a member of the new author team, joining Bret Kloos, Jean Hill, and Elizabeth Thomas as authors. The two of us (Jim and Maurice) served as consultants and reviewers throughout this process. This third edition is itself a transition in progress; it reflects the perspectives and writing of the original author team and the new authors. Future editions will complete the transition as the new team assumes full authorship. That future is also linked to our history: Our book was itself the product of a transition from two editions of *Psychology and Community Change* (published in 1977 and 1984), written by Kenneth Heller, John Monahan, Richard Price, Shula Reinharz, Stephanie Riger, Abe Wandersman, and Tom D'Aunno.

Together with Abe, we chose the new author team carefully, with much discussion and deliberation. We wanted scholars committed to the values of community psychology. We sought authors who would provide fresh ideas and communicate the ever-changing nature of our field. We wanted engaging, creative thinkers and writers. We sought authors who would provide the structure that upper-level undergraduate students need and communicate the nuances and details that graduate students and practicing community psychologists require. We wanted a team who would work together, thriving on their agreements and their disagreements and learning from each other (as we have). We knew the challenges of a multiauthor textbook, and we sought authors who would produce a book with coherent themes and continuity of chapters.

Our new author team does all these things exceedingly well!

We are thankful for their commitment and skill and goodwill. Bret, Jean, Elizabeth, and Abe built on the strengths of our prior work and enhanced that work with their own fresh perspectives. Their work, like ours and like the work of community psychology pioneers before us, responds to contemporary social contexts and challenges.

Without question, the work of our new author team strengthens our textbook—deepening and broadening its coverage while incorporating new topics, perspectives, research findings, and narratives of real-life communities.

In this third edition, new and returning readers of our book will find an exciting, engaging, well-written textbook, with scholarly perspective and memorable narratives. We are confident that this textbook will engage you in transforming how you participate in the communities in which you live.

January 2011
James H. Dalton
Maurice J. Elias

Preface

We invite you to join us for this book's journey through the exciting field of community psychology! As a team of authors, we each came to community psychology because it engaged our minds, our values, and our lives. We hope this book does that for you.

To enliven the journey and to engage you actively in learning, we have included opening exercises, questions for reflection, and examples of social change, including stories from people practicing community psychology. We want to engage you in conversation about how we understand social issues and how to promote the well-being of persons in communities. We build on the strengths of our first two editions, which were praised by teachers and students for their exercises and applications. Community psychology is a way of thinking that can be applied to many life situations and communities. This textbook reflects that perspective.

We intend this book to be useful for upper-level undergraduate students and graduate students in psychology and related fields. We provide an overview of community-based research and action for community psychologists, citizens, and professionals in other fields. Community psychology's perspectives make contributions to the wider social science dialogue about social change and community-based research. We have colleagues who have used material from the book in social work, counseling, education, and public health courses. Finally, we seek to make conceptual contributions to community psychology, posing issues for scholars and activists in our field to consider and adding to the ongoing conversation that allows our field to evolve.

We wrote all our chapters after a wide-ranging examination of new developments in the field and extensive mutual feedback. Technology helped to make our extended discussions possible. For more than 18 months, the new author team had "meetings" nearly every week to review new developments in the field and develop this text; sometimes, we "met" more than once a week. The ability to teleconference with Skype across continents was very valuable to promoting dialogue. This edition benefits from multiple perspectives and varied experience of the author team while using a collaborative writing process to promote continuity between chapters. The Skype teleconferencing allowed us to challenge each others' perspectives, promote understanding, and develop consensus for the revisions. The founding authors helped us clarify and improve drafts of new material. Each chapter has a primary author whose perspective led our revision. Bret is the primary author for Chapters 2, 5, 8, and 14 and responsible for the coordination of this edition; Jean for Chapters 1, 6, 9, 10, and 12; Elizabeth for Chapters 3, 4, 7, and 11; and Abe for Chapter 13.

We wanted to include a special word about the book cover. The picture for the cover was created by David Asiamah, a graduate student in clinical-community psychology at the University of South Carolina. The sweet grass basket in the center of the picture is an important cultural item in South Carolina history and current culture. Woven by Gullah and Geechee Island descendants in the South Carolina low country, it is a tangible representation of preserving a unique culture and community. Today, these baskets are celebrated by Black and White Carolinians as a cultural treasure. We liked the image David created with other students, faculty, and staff because it underscores community psychology's mission to promote well-being and sense of community across age, gender, race, and other indices of diversity.

We also want you to know that we donate one-tenth of our royalties to the Society for Community Research and Action (SCRA), an international body of community psychologists and scholars in related fields. To learn more about SCRA or to become a member, see its website at http://www.scra27.org.

ACKNOWLEDGMENTS

This book would not have been conceived or written without the support of many individuals and of the multiple communities in which we live. Jean Ann Linney first conceived of writing a new community psychology textbook with an engaging pedagogy and continued to encourage us after other commitments precluded her continuing with it. Jon David Hague and Tim Matray, our editors at Cengage, helped us navigate the tremendous changes occurring in publication and production of textbooks and to prepare a text that could be delivered on multiple platforms. We thank Toshi Sasao for his thoughts and comments about preparing for a third edition and the emergence of global community psychology. We express our appreciation to several colleagues for their support and critical comments to improve this book: Rhonda Johnson, Colleen Loomis, Ken Maton, Jim Kelly, and Suzanne Swan. We want to recognize Elise Herndon for the material that she contributed to the second edition's Chapters 1 and 8. We retained and updated the presentation of some of this material in the third edition because it helps to illustrate key points from those chapters and was appreciated by reviewers. Our perspectives on community psychology have been strongly influenced by mentors, colleagues, and students. The new authors very much appreciate the examples of our mentors who introduced us to community psychology: Mark Aber, Leonard Jason, Thom Moore, and Julian Rappaport. We expect that they will recognize many of their influences in the book. We also thank many colleagues and students who have given us comments and suggestions in class, at conferences, on surveys, and by e-mail. Our students—Greg Townley, Betsy Davis, Laura Kurzban, Victoria Chien, and David Asiamah—have been especially patient in reading drafts, writing responses, and enduring our mistakes. We thank the blind reviewers of chapters for their feedback and encouragement that helped in preparing our final presentation. We also acknowledge the value of reading recent community psychology textbooks by other authors, especially those by Geoff Nelson and Isaac Prilleitensky; Murray Levine, Douglas Perkins, and David Perkins; Jennifer Rudkin; and John Moritsugu, Frank Wong, and Karen Duffy. All these make valuable contributions to the ongoing conversation of our field. Our reviewers' support and critiques were genuinely thoughtful and valuable.

The new authors want to acknowledge the gifts of vision, confidence, and generosity that Jim Dalton and Maurice Elias gave to us by recruiting us to be stewards for the future development of this textbook as a resource for community psychology. They have consistently been encouraging and helpful. It is a somewhat sobering responsibility to follow their lead, but we will strive to produce a text and supplementary resources that thoughtfully present community psychology in ways that engage students and current social issues. Bret thanks his community partners in social change efforts and his students for helping to challenge his thinking. He is especially grateful to community partners for demonstrating the value of perseverance and creativity in promoting sustainable social change. Jean thanks Jim, Mo, and Abe for their work on earlier editions of this book and for their amazing generosity in sharing that work with us. She also thanks her students and colleagues who have enthusiastically supported her community work, even when they did not really share her excitement. Elizabeth thanks her community partners at the family center for all that they have taught her about collaboration and building inclusive communities. She thanks her students for the energy and insights they bring to community-based learning and action research efforts. Abe thanks his students and former students for their valuable contributions to theory, research, and action that make community psychology valuable to our communities. He also thanks Bernadette Sanchez for her contributions on mentoring in Chapter 13. Maurice thanks his colleagues at the Collaborative for Academic, Social, and Emotional Learning (www.CASEL.org) and all our partners, whose sustained dedication to children and to the families, schools, and communities who nurture them inspires him to be a better community psychologist and teach others to do the same. Jim also especially thanks the members of the Millville (Pennsylvania) Meeting of the

Religious Society of Friends (Quakers), who have sustained him spiritually and cheerfully throughout the writing of this book. Finally, we deeply thank our families, whose love, patience, and support always nurture and enrich our lives.

January 2011
Bret Kloos
Jean L. Hill
Elizabeth Thomas
Abraham Wandersman
Maurice J. Elias
James H. Dalton

To Instructors

CHANGES IN THE THIRD EDITION: OVERVIEW

Observing changes in community psychology, the three new authors for the third edition were recruited to add new perspectives to the book: interdisciplinary collaboration, social, and cultural dimensions of health and feminist scholarship. We build on a strong foundation from the second edition. This edition uses the same framework of chapters and has worked to maintain the quality and scholarship established in the first two editions. Kenneth Maton's (2003) review in *Contemporary Psychology* praised our first edition as "well-written, innovative, and informative" (p. 186) and cited its attention to ecological context and to community psychology values as particular strengths. However, the book includes substantial revisions within this framework. In some cases, we have reorganized material and developed new approaches to presentation. We have added new theoretical and empirical developments in the field. In particular, we have expanded our presentations of cultural, feminist, and global community psychology perspectives and discussions of the social dimensions of health. We have also field-tested our chapters with students in our classes—undergraduates and graduate students—and have carefully considered their suggestions.

First, throughout each chapter, we have incorporated social and cultural diversity perspectives to a greater extent. As described in changes made to specific chapters, we have expanded conceptual frameworks and provided more examples of human diversity in our reviews of empirical findings, community change strategies, and contemporary debates. These additions include more examples from community psychology around the world and discussions of different perspectives on community psychology in different countries.

Second, we include greater emphasis on the people affected by community intervention. We have added sidebar features written in collaboration with community members who are actively involved in change efforts. These features are titled "Community Psychology in Action" and serve to provide more narratives for students to consider how they might "do community psychology" once they complete taking the course. Some of these examples highlight the work of community psychology practitioners; others emphasize the work of citizens responding to the needs of their communities; and a few come from long-standing community-university collaborations. We have also expanded the discussion of community psychology practice, paralleling developments in the Society for Community Research and Action since the second edition.

Third, we have increased the facilitative resources that can complement the book's content and enhance the classroom experience for students. For the first time, we include templates for PowerPoint slides for each chapter. The *Instructor's Manual* includes exercises and materials for student evaluation from the second edition. We have expanded the instructional materials based on discussions with our editors. We have included ideas about websites, videos, and the use of social media in teaching. In an effort to reduce the cost of the textbooks to students, we have moved some examples from the second edition to the *Instructor's Manual* for use as lecture enrichments. These changes respond to developments in the field of community psychology, technology, and patterns of college student learning.

We continue many conventions that students, instructors, and reviewers had found helpful about the previous editions. We begin each chapter with an outline and opening question to frame what is important and prepare for discussion. We cover core areas of the field and provide enrichment materials at the end of each chapter (e.g., chapter summaries, suggested readings, websites). We emphasize core conceptual areas for community psychology while bridging our work to other disciplines. We have included many links between chapters to help students review and retain the main points from chapters. We have retained many distinctive features of our first editions, which are seldom available in other community psychology texts. These include whole chapters on the development and practice of community psychology, research contexts and methods, concepts of community (including sense of community), concepts of human diversity, exemplary prevention programs, implementation of prevention programs, citizen participation, and program development and evaluation. We also retain our pedagogical focus and features, especially exercises to begin chapters and resources for enriching lectures with compatible examples developed specifically for the book.

CHANGES IN THE THIRD EDITION:
SPECIFIC CHAPTERS

The main goal of Chapter 1 is to get students to negotiate the cognitive shift to a community psychology perspective, and the chapter starts with an exercise designed to do exactly that. The exercise tells the story of Bessie Mae Berger, a 97-year-old homeless woman. Students are encouraged to switch from an individualistic view of the causes of homelessness to an ecological/structural view.

This shift in perspective is then reinforced through the example of Elaine (retained from the last edition), whose story illustrates how individual life is intertwined with community and macrosystem processes and how clinical treatment can be strengthened by understanding ecological levels of analysis and identifying community resources.

In Chapter 2, the focus has been modified to spotlight the development and practice of community psychology. While still presenting on overview of the field, we reorganized the chapter to parallel the subsequent chapters better and to include connections to the discussion of community psychology values. We have added a discussion of community psychology practice as part of the field's historical and ongoing development. Our view of community psychology's development is written from a North American perspective. However, we note parallels and differences in the development of community psychology in different countries and regions. Furthermore, we have added a section on international community psychology to provide students examples of the global range and scope of community psychology. We seek to present the field's history as part of ongoing development of community psychology across the world. We include our first "Community Psychology in Action" feature on the community psychology practice of José Ornelas, Maria Moniz-Vargas, and Teresa Duarte at the Associação para/o Estudo e Integração Psico-Social (Association for Study and Psychosocial Integration) in Lisbon, Portugal.

Chapters 3 and 4, the research methods chapters, include updated and expanded coverage of collaborative and participatory research. These include developments in feminist community psychology research and constructivist and critical approaches. Extended examples of research studies are used to illustrate how community psychology values can be realized through research (e.g., research examining women's experience of college conducted in a prison with incarcerated women as part of the research team; a study of a Cambodian American youth dance troupe that meaningfully addresses cultural aspects of adolescent identity; and an international study that includes ethnographic, participatory, GIS, and experimental methods to assess the effectiveness of community-based HIV awareness and prevention strategies). Chapter 3 contains our second "Community Psychology in Action" feature, highlighting a longtime partnership between researchers at the University of Illinois Chicago and El Valor, a community-based organization serving mostly Latinos with developmental disabilities across the life span and their families. Chapter 4 contains coverage of community case studies, experimental social innovation and dissemination, mapping physical and spatial environments, and integrating quantitative and qualitative methods as well as updated examples of community psychology studies. Ours is one of only two current community psychology textbooks to cover community research and methods in this depth.

Chapter 5 continues our presentation of fundamental ecological concepts of the field, which has been well received by our users. In this edition, we revised the order of presentation of concepts to emphasize the influence of ecological perspectives and social ecology on the field. We have retained the second edition's review of six approaches to understanding persons in context.

We have added discussion of the Harlem Children's Zone as an illustration of the importance of understanding persons and environments as well as persons in the context of their environments. The Harlem Children's Zone example allows us to emphasize the value of ecological perspectives for conceptualization and for social intervention. We have updated our discussion of the Fairweather Lodge with consideration of current efforts to expand use of this alternative model to mental health services used in 13 states across the United States. Our third "Community Psychology in Action" feature provides a narrative for how contemporary lodges can be understood to promote community psychology values: promotion of well-being, focus on strengths and collaboration, empowerment, and empirical basis.

In Chapter 6, we focus on the complex nature of communities and the role of community psychology theory and research in understanding them. While we present a nuanced picture of the state of communities in contemporary society, we have worked to maintain an excited, optimistic tone about the state of communities. We did not want to leave readers with the impression that modern communities were definitively in a state of decline. We discuss the issue of loss of community as a hypothesis rather than an accepted fact. As one aspect of this point, we tried to remove any insinuation that the communities that our students engage in are any way less "real" or "healthy" than the communities of previous generations. This chapter tries to emphasize the idea that communities are changing, not that they are necessarily declining. We added a discussion of the relationship between the physical and natural environment and community. We also significantly expanded on the research regarding community and the Internet. Our fourth "Community Psychology in Action" feature builds on several of these themes by presenting the story of Daniel Kent and Net Literacy, the nonprofit organization he started as a teenager. This story demonstrates the use of technology and building capacity and bridging relationships between teens and elderly members of their community.

In Chapter 7, we have expanded our discussion of dimensions of diversity receiving greater attention in community psychology and the intersectionality of these dimensions. We have updated sections on socialization and cultural practices to include developments in the scholarship of understanding racial and ethnic identity, including Whiteness. We have expanded our discussion of acculturation to include greater awareness of how communities can change and a more ecological understanding of the challenges and opportunities provided by immigration and cross-cultural contact. We have focused on attention to diversity issues in the practice of community psychology and have added a discussion on diversity and sense of community as values that may come into tension with one another in our work. Throughout, we continue to emphasize that there are many dimensions of human diversity and that every individual has a place on each dimension.

In Chapter 8, we spend more time developing and explaining the ecological model of stress and coping for two purposes. First, we wanted to make it more accessible to students and to make the connections between the organization of the chapter and the model more explicit. To that end, we present the model in simplified form and build up to the final model. Second, we want to introduce students to reading models and support their scientific literacy. Later chapters in this book also use models to present relationships between key concepts. We have updated empirical literature about stress and coping. While we continue to present three community-based resources for coping after the discussion of the model, we have reworked their presentation to include more examples of cultural and global perspectives on social support, mutual help, and spiritual-religious coping resources. Extended discussions of Elaine, U.S. reactions to 9/11, and reactions to Hurricane Katrina have been moved to the *Instructor's Manual*.

Chapters 9 and 10 present key concepts, exemplars, and issues of prevention and promotion, a distinctive strength of our first edition (Maton, 2003). Chapter 9 is a combination of Chapters 9 and 10 in the previous edition. It begins with the story of John Snow, the London cholera epidemic of 1854, and the birth of the public health model. The story is used to emphasize the paradigm shift inherent in a prevention perspective. Key aspects of prevention theory are presented. A major emphasis of the chapter continues to be the elucidation of factors known to increase the efficacy of prevention and promotion programs. The chapter includes an extended discussion of resiliency and risk and protective factors, along with a discussion of the cost-effectiveness of prevention programming. The chapter ends with the presentation of three examples of successful prevention/promotion programs (targeting HIV/AIDS, parenting, school bullying), which are used to illustrate the information presented in the first part of this chapter. Our updated Chapter 10 remains a groundbreaking analysis of the importance of implementation and context in preventive efforts. It is the only chapter of its kind in a community psychology textbook and has been praised by many users and in a published review (Maton, 2003). It is based on the assumption that all students in a class will be involved in implementing prevention and promotion programming at some point in their lives and is designed to present them with a sophisticated set of skills to support successful implementation. As Chapter 9 focuses on the elements necessary for program efficacy, Chapter 10 focuses on the factors that support program effectiveness, with the main point of this chapter being that successful programs must adapt to settings while retaining a commitment to core components. This chapter uses extended examples of social-emotional learning (SEL) programs and home visiting programs to illustrate the process of successful program implementation. In Chapter 10, we include our fifth "Community Psychology in Action" feature—this one by Amy Mart on her experience as a graduate student working with SEL programs.

Chapters 11 and 12 form a unit in their focus on how community and social change intertwine with individual lives. We have expanded Chapter 11's discussion of empowerment and citizenship by adding recent theoretical and empirical developments in empowerment and citizen participation. As both concepts are widely used and have various connotations, we discuss the context and limits of both concepts within community psychology. As we continue to emphasize the complexity of the concepts, we try to make them accessible as tools that students can use as they engage in various roles and relationships—not just as potential community psychologists—in trying to understand and improve the quality of life in our communities. Toward this end, we develop a focus on empowering practices as routine activities that may transform role relationships within settings. Through new examples, we examine the possibilities for helpers to approach their work as facilitators and partners and as teachers and learners. We attend more closely to how relational contexts across multiple levels serve as a foundation for empowering settings. In this chapter, we include our sixth "Community Psychology in Action," which features an example of empowerment through long-term action by residents of Sugar Creek, Missouri, and community psychologist Marci Culley to respond to environmental pollution in their community.

Chapter 12 reflects a multilevel, ecological perspective on empowerment and change in communities and societies, a perspective that emphasizes community psychology values as well as concepts and methods. Our goals are to help students understand how community and social changes are linked to their lives and to inspire them to personal involvement in efforts for community and social transformation that express their values. This revised chapter begins with the stories of three people who felt compelled to take action when they learned about problems in their communities. We have added a section of the use of technology in community and social change initiatives. This chapter also includes a significantly expanded discussion of social policy, focusing on crime policy and policies aimed at reducing poverty and homelessness. This chapter includes our seventh "Community Psychology in Action" feature, written by Lenny Jason. He describes his experience testifying in front of the U.S. Congress on public policy related to teenage smoking.

Chapter 13 opens with examples of how evaluation and program improvements are pervasive in everyday life and then expands and updates its coverage of how citizens can use evaluation methods to monitor and strengthen community programs, including an emphasis on empowerment evaluation. Only one other community psychology text contains a chapter on program evaluation, and no other text presents the distinctive perspective of our chapter, which integrates community program development with program evaluation and evaluation concepts with practical methods. We include our eighth "Community Psychology in Action" feature—this one on Greg Tolbert, CEO of the Boys & Girls Club of the Upstate (Spartanburg, South Carolina) and his perspective on empowerment evaluation.

Chapter 14 provides a summary for the book and a discussion about using these ideas in our lives. We seek to promote students' optimism for their own engagement in community and social change, and we add additional real-life, hopeful stories of such change. We have expanded discussions about how students may use concepts from this book as citizens or social service professionals. We adopt the points made by Kelly's (1971) qualities for the community psychologist to discuss what may be useful for citizens as well as for a career in community psychology. For students interested in community psychology, we expand our discussion of community psychology practice and community psychology training. Consistent with other chapters, we discuss the expanding awareness of feminist and cultural perspectives in the field. We consider effects of globalization on social issues as well as on community psychology itself. We have updated the examples used to conclude the second edition. It is interesting to note that these examples continue to provide inspiration and hope for the field. We include discussion of the Society for Community Research and Action's response to Hurricane Katrina as an example of how community psychologists can collaborate to use their expertise to respond to practical and policy needs of social problems. In our last "Community Psychology in Action" feature, Brad Olson provides an account of efforts to develop a resource for community responses to the aftermath of disasters that is accessible and available.

ALTERNATIVE ORDERINGS OF CHAPTERS

Community psychology course instructors have their own favorite ways to organize the concepts and themes of the field. In revising our third edition, we make it more convenient to arrange your own ordering of its chapters while still building on the core concepts of the field and fostering student recognition of interrelated strands among community psychology concepts. Some possible chapter orderings follow. All our suggestions use Chapters 1–2 to introduce the field, although some instructors may choose to rely on Chapter 1 alone.

After the introductory chapters, you may proceed directly to Chapters 5–7 (ecology, community, diversity). To highlight an empowerment perspective early, you may also use Chapters 11 (empowerment and citizen participation) and 12 (community social change) much sooner than they appear in the book. If your course has many clinically minded students (this includes graduate students in clinical or counseling psychology, but it is also the implicit focus of many undergraduates), enlarging their perspective to think ecologically and preventively may be an important goal. To engage their interest, you might assign Chapter 8 (coping) early to highlight the integration of clinical and community concepts. Alternatively, Chapters 8–10 (coping and prevention/promotion) can form an integrated unit on coping and prevention at some point in the course. Chapter 13 could be added to illustrate how local program evaluation can improve implementation and quality. However, full coverage of community psychology requires covering Chapters 5–7 and 11–12 at some point.

You may wish to assign Chapter 13 (program evaluation) following the research focus of Chapters 3–4 to illustrate how the logic of scientific thinking can be adapted to practical community program monitoring and improvement. Some instructors assign Chapters 3, 4, and 13 near the end of the course. After chapters on ecology, community, diversity, and empowerment, the emphases in Chapters 3, 4, and 13 on participatory research and cultural anchoring may have deeper meaning. Our students have found Chapter 13 useful for an evaluation component in papers proposing a community intervention.

These are only some of the possible orderings of chapters in this text. We encourage you to develop your own approach.

PEDAGOGY

Many instructors and students consider our engaging pedagogy to be a distinctive strength of our textbook. We remain committed to integrating pedagogy into the text to promote student reflection, insight, application, and action. We continue the first two editions' primary focus on advanced undergraduate students. This builds on the book's established success for this audience. However, through enrichment sections, updates of current research, and online discussion formats, we have developed this book to be a resource for graduate courses. Furthermore, with advances noted in this book, it can serve a third function as a record of advances in the field for community psychology professionals.

To this end, this book continues a pedagogy that engages students in a variety of contexts (e.g., urban/rural and traditional and nontraditional students). Although not all students will become community psychologists, our pedagogy assumes that many will have careers in human services and all can participate in civic life. Community psychology frameworks can assist critical review of social problem definitions and proposed solutions that they will encounter as citizens, community leaders, and professionals. Furthermore, as diversity in the United States and other countries increases and interaction across cultural boundaries becomes more common, the ability to take different perspectives and use new analytic frameworks presented in this book will assist the understanding of human problems and the pragmatic search for solutions.

Pedagogical tools include an emphasis on the outline for each chapter as an "advance organizer," boldface to highlight key terms, chapter summaries that point students to the principal themes and concepts in each chapter, and suggested readings and websites for further exploration. Each chapter begins with an opening exercise that is designed to immediately engage readers in the central questions and viewpoints presented in each chapter. Other exercises from previous editions have been moved to the *Instructor's Manual*. These are resources for you to use in class to foster student application of concepts individually, in small groups, or in whole-class discussions. Some involve out-of-class projects. Many of these have been featured in the Community Psychology Education Connection, which Maurice Elias and Jim Dalton founded in 1982 and which appears in *The Community Psychologist* newsletter for members of the Society for Community Research and Action. To learn more about SCRA or to become a member, see its website at http://www.scra27.org.

A new pedagogical tool included in this edition is the "Community Psychology in Action" feature, which presents stories of real people (community psychologists and others) doing community work. These stories were chosen to illustrate major points of the chapters and to instill in students an enthusiasm, energy, and optimism for community work.

About the Authors

I am an associate professor of psychology at the University of South Carolina at Columbia. I received my Ph.D. in clinical community psychology from the University of Illinois at Urbana-Champaign in 1999 and completed a postdoctoral fellowship at The Consultation Center and Yale University. I earned my bachelor's degree in music and psychology from St. Olaf College in Northfield, Minnesota. The importance of social and cultural factors on individual and community well-being was emphasized through studies in Thailand and Guatemala and work in Germany. A growing awareness of different perspectives on social issues and a commitment to social justice based in my faith community led me to community psychology.

I am interested in promoting adaptive functioning in community settings and meaning-making after major life disruptions. These interests developed through experiences with mutual assistance and self-help groups, settlement of immigrant groups, and the efforts of religious communities to address social justice needs of their communities. I have devoted the last 15 years to promoting opportunities for recovery and participation in community life for persons with diagnoses of serious mental illness. Over my career, I have used a variety of community psychology practice skills in several roles. Prior to coming to the University of South Carolina, I was the director of a supportive housing program for people who had been homeless and had mental health and substance abuse problems, an evaluation and program development consultant to community organizations, and the coordinator of the Connecticut Self-Help Network. I am also a community psychology researcher and have received funding from the National Institute of Mental Health, the Center for Mental Health Services/SAMHSA, and the National Institute for Disability Rehabilitation and Research to conduct research and develop programs related to the housing needs of persons with serious mental illness and co-occurring addictive disorders. My teaching and intervention interests include community psychology, social and cultural dimensions of health, homelessness, community intervention, service learning, and research methods.

When I was a child, my parents encouraged me to be an active member of the communities where I lived. Their example and encouragement have enriched my life and my work. As a citizen (and community psychologist), I continue to be involved in local issues but also promoting community and quality of life. I volunteer at nonprofits, sing in choirs, and coach soccer and basketball teams. Relationships built during these activities have helped sustain me and my work. I am particularly grateful for my family—Suzanne, Sarah, and Bonnie—for their commitments to social justice, for their faithful companionship, and for their patience during the hours when I was away working on this book.

Bret Kloos, Ph.D

I am a professor of psychology at New Mexico Highlands University. I received my doctorate in community/clinical psychology from DePaul University.

As a teenager, I knew I wanted to become a psychologist, but I was already skeptical regarding traditional clinical approaches to alleviating human suffering. Several experiences, including volunteering for a local crisis hotline, convinced me that the best way to support healthy functioning for people was through supporting healthy communities, although I did not phrase it that way at the time. It was while I was writing a paper on crisis lines in college that I first came across the term *community psychology* and realized that was what I was. I joined SCRA in my first semester as a graduate student, and that community has been an important part of my life. I have spent almost the whole of my career in a small rural town in the mountains of New Mexico, and my connection with my colleagues in SCRA has been a very important part of my life.

My clinical work always focused on adolescents, including teens living on the streets in Chicago and incarcerated boys in New Mexico, and my community work has followed this focus. I have worked on school-based prevention and promotion programs and headed a community-wide initiative based on the Communities That Care model. I am particularly interested in the role of sense of community as a foundational aspect of community well-being.

Living in New Mexico has allowed me to indulge my passion for mountains through hiking, skiing, and camping. I also love to cook (particularly with New Mexico green chili!) and garden. I only regret about this long-distance book project is that I have not been able to cook for my co-authors. However, I will continue to cook for my friends and family who supported me during this project.

Jean Hill, Ph.D

I am an associate professor and associate director for graduate education in the Interdisciplinary Arts and Sciences Program at the University of Washington at Bothell and editor emerita of *The Community Psychologist*. I received my Ph.D. in personality and social ecology from the psychology department at the University of Illinois at Urbana-Champaign in 1998. My undergraduate degree is in psychology from Georgetown University. At Georgetown, I also studied art history and developed a passion for community-based arts that I continue to explore in my life and work. Before and after graduate school, I worked in community mental health—first as a case manager at a group home for adults with schizophrenia and then as a program evaluator for a community mental health center after I earned my Ph.D. I really enjoyed that work but found that I missed teaching and community-based research with students. I returned to a university setting, with my first faculty position being at Hendrix College, a small liberal arts college in Conway, Arkansas.

As a young person growing up in a small town in Arkansas in the 1970s, I developed a keen interest in the issues facing that region, including poverty, lack of access to educational opportunities, and racial injustice. My parents were educators and encouraged me to strive to reach my potential. (They also made me a huge sports fan, mystery novel reader, and gardener.) Unlike many of my peers, I had the opportunity and support to take advantage of an excellent college education. I now take pride in helping other students realize their goals and visions.

I joined the University of Washington at Bothell faculty in 2002, and I teach courses in community and cultural psychology, research methods, psychology and the visual arts, and community-based program evaluation. As associate director for graduate education, I also advise students and provide oversight of graduate curriculum, policies, and planning in the cultural studies and policy studies master of arts programs.

I work with my students and community partners to examine social and cultural contexts for learning, adolescent engagement in community-based settings, and the potential of arts-based and participatory strategies for community research and action. As a teacher, I try to communicate my curiosity and love of learning.

I want students to think about learning as a process that enriches and enables valuable contributions they may make as individuals and as parts of communities. Toward these goals, I strive to teach in ways that foster active learning and encourage students to make connections between the classroom and other commitments.

My family, friends, and community support my work as a community psychologist; they challenge my thinking and encourage celebration of our life together. I am particularly grateful to my husband Chris, my son Thomas, and my parents and sister for all they do to enrich my life and work.

Elizabeth Thomas. Ph.D

I am a professor of psychology at the University of South Carolina at Columbia. I received my Ph.D. from Cornell University and my bachelor's degree from the State University of New York at Stony Brook. I perform research and program evaluation on citizen participation in community organizations and coalitions and on interagency collaboration. I am co-author of *Prevention Plus III* and co-editor of *Empowerment Evaluation Principles in Practice*. I have published many other books and articles and have served on a number of national advisory committees for prevention. I received the 1998 Myrdal Award for Evaluation Practice from the American Evaluation Association. In 2000, I was elected SCRA president and in 2005 received the SCRA Award for Distinguished Contributions to Theory and Research. In a project with the Centers for Disease Control and Prevention, I am working on the development of empowerment evaluation systems in the area of teenage pregnancy prevention.

I was born in a displaced persons camp in Germany, the son of two Holocaust survivors. I came to the United States at nine months of age and grew up in Brooklyn, New York. I date my quest to improve the quality of people's lives to age six, when my sister died from what I later understood was medical malpractice. Although the death of any child is a family tragedy, her death was all the more tragic because each child born to a Holocaust survivor is viewed not only as a precious treasure but as a living repudiation of Hitler and his racist beliefs.

Entering Stony Brook in 1967 was a transforming experience in my life. Stony Brook was a hotbed of social change being played out in the larger society. I changed my major from pre-med to psychology and looked to the social sciences for a career. I also met Lois Pall at Stony Brook, and we married shortly before we began graduate study in psychology at Cornell. Lois was a source of personal support and intellectual growth at a time when I was struggling "to learn how to think." At Cornell, I majored in social/personality psychology but cobbled together a broad curriculum by also studying child and family psychopathology, social organization and change, and environmental psychology. When I took my first teaching job at George Peabody College, Bob Newbrough introduced me to the new field of community psychology.

I am very grateful to my wife Lois and sons Seth and Jeff for attempting to keep me real and grounded and for loving me. My linkages with family, extended family, community, and society are what life is all about.

Abe Wandersman, Ph.D

I am a professor of psychology at Rutgers University. I received my doctorate from the University of Connecticut and my B.A. from Queens College, City University, New York. Starting in 1979, I co-developed the Social Decision Making/Social Problem Solving Project, which received the 1988 Lela Rowland Prevention Award from the National Mental Health Association and has been recognized as a model program by the U.S. Department of Education's Expert Panel on Safe, Disciplined, and Drug-Free Schools, the National Association of School Psychologists, the Character Education Partnership, and other national groups.

Currently, I am a member of the Leadership Team of the Collaborative for Academic, Social, and Emotional Learning (CASEL) and a Trustee of the Association for Children of New Jersey and the H.O.P.E. Foundation. With colleagues at CASEL, I am the senior author of *Promoting Social and Emotional Learning: Guidelines for Educators*, published by the Association for Supervision and Curriculum Development and circulated to over 100,000 educational leaders in the United States and internationally; I wrote a document commissioned by the International Bureau of Education and UNESCO; and I collaborated on related works that can be found at www.CASEL.org. I have written numerous books and articles on prevention and have served in various capacities for SCRA, most recently working as part of a team establishing practice journal for the field.

Born in the Bronx, New York, I was taken to Yankee Stadium many times at an early age and imprinted as a lifelong fan. This has generalized to other sports, particularly college basketball. Another impassioned pursuit is Jewish education and its attendant commitment to making the world a better, more socially just place for all—something shared deeply with my wife Ellen and children Sara and Samara. As a family, we feel a deep sense of mission about closing the gaps that seem to be growing in our society and worldwide. For these and related reasons, the field of community psychology has been deeply fulfilling for me—personally and professionally.

Maurice J. Elias, Ph.D

I am a professor of psychology at Bloomsburg University in Pennsylvania. I grew up in Floyd, Virginia, and received a bachelor's degree from King College in Tennessee and a doctorate from the University of Connecticut. With Maurice Elias, I developed the Community Psychology Education Connection, a resource for teachers of community psychology course that now appears in *The Community Psychologist*. At Bloomsburg, I have played leadership roles in the Task for Racial Equity, which works for social change on issues of human diversity and social justice. I also work with the Frederick Douglass Learning Community, which brings together first-year Bloomsburg University students of varied racial and ethnic backgrounds to live together in a residence hall, take courses together, and build a shared community. I originally became interested in community psychology because it seemed related to strengths and limitations of community that I experienced while growing up in a small rural town as well as to concerns of social justice that I developed while growing up in the South during the years of the civil rights movement and Great Society antipoverty programs. During college, my involvement in a faith-based community service learning experience in inner-city Newark, New Jersey, deepened these interests. I met Maurice on my first day of graduate school at UConn. Although we came from very different backgrounds, we became lasting friends and colleagues. Abe and I met later and became friends at a biennial conference of the Society for Community Research and Action (SCRA).

The happiest outcome of graduate school for me was meeting my wife Carolyn, whose mix of genuine love, companionship, and Connecticut Yankee practicality made this book possible. Carolyn and I have two children, Craig and Julia, and are active in the Friends (Quaker) Meeting in Millville, Pennsylvania. By the time you read this, we hope to have returned to one of our favorite hobbies: hiking the Appalachian Mountains.

Janes H. Dalton, Ph.D

Community Psychology

Linking Individuals and Communities

1

Introducing Community Psychology

HIRB/Index Stock/PhotoLibrary

WHAT IS COMMUNITY PSYCHOLOGY?

Welcome to community psychology!

Humans seek communities. Relationships with others are a central part of human existence. People cannot live in complete isolation from each other; individual lives and community life are intertwined. This book is about the many ways in which that intertwining occurs.

Community psychology is different from other fields of psychology in two ways. First, community psychology offers a different way of thinking about human behavior. We focus on the community contexts of behavior. That shift in perspective (which is the first thing we will discuss in this chapter) leads to the second difference: an expansion of the definition of what are appropriate topics for psychological study and intervention. Community psychologists are interested in effective ways to prevent problems rather than treat them after they arise. The field emphasizes promoting healthy functioning for all members of a community rather than intervening when problems develop for a few of those members. And they focus their research on factors at the neighborhood, community, and societal level that support or impede healthy development rather than internal psychological processes or biological factors.

In this chapter, we will discuss the shift in perspective that is central to community psychology and the values of the field. In Chapter 2, we present the historical context that gave rise to the field. Chapters 3 and 4 deal with the research methods that underlie community research and how those methods derive from the basic values of the field. Chapters 5 through 8 present some underlying concepts of the field and the theories and research related to them. These chapters present the field's approach to understanding communities. Chapters 9 and 10 present a major focus of intervention in community psychology: the prevention of disorder and the promotion of wellness. Chapters 11 and 12 focus on intervention at the community and society levels, and Chapter 13 presents some theories, models, and skills used to develop, evaluate, and improve those interventions. In the final chapter, we talk about some challenges and opportunities facing the field.

At the beginning of each chapter in this book, we present an opening exercise that is designed to help you explore these two aspects of community psychology. The exercise might present an opportunity for a shift in perspective or an expansion of what it means to engage in psychology. In many of the chapters, we also present stories of "Community Psychology in Action," focusing on the personal stories of people doing community work.

While we hope that at the end of this book some of you will consider further education in community psychology, we realize that for many of you, this may be your only formal involvement with the field. However, it is our firm belief that all of you will—at various times in your life—be involved in initiatives that will benefit from the theories, research, and skills we present in this book. While the number of people who formally identify themselves as community psychologists may be relatively small, the influence of the field is much larger than those numbers would suggest. Community psychology theories and research are reflected or directly cited in the work of public health experts, social workers, sociologists, public officials, and other psychologists. Snowden (1987) wrote about the "peculiar success" of community psychology; its approaches are widely adopted, but as a field, it is not well known.

We hope that you finish this book with several accomplishments: a better understanding of community psychology; increased skills for working effectively in diverse contexts and communities; a greater appreciation of the intertwining of individual, community, and society; a greater awareness of your own values; a willingness to consider with respect the many sides of community and social issues; and a passionate engagement in changing your communities and society for the better. We came to community psychology because it engaged our minds, our values, and our lives. We hope this book does that for you.

OPENING EXERCISE: MUSICAL CHAIRS

She's 97 years old and homeless. Bessie Mae Berger has her two boys, and that's about all. She and sons Larry Wilkerson, 60, and Charlie Wilkerson, 62, live in a 1973 Chevrolet Suburban they park each night on a busy Venice street. Bessie spent her young adulthood in Northern California and worked as a packer for the National Biscuit Co. until she was in her 60s. Charlie worked in construction and as a painter before becoming disabled by degenerative arthritis. Larry was a cook before compressed discs in the back and a damaged neck nerve put an end to it. Twenty-six years ago, he began working as a full-time caregiver for his mother through the state's In-Home Supportive Services program. That ended about four years ago, when the owner of a Palm Springs home where they lived had to sell the place. At the same time, the state dropped Larry and his mother from the support program, he said. The three have tried at various times since to get government-subsidized housing. But they have failed, in part because they insist on living together. (Pool, 2009)

On one night in January 2009, an estimated 643,067 people were homeless in the United States (U.S. Department of Housing and Urban Development [HUD], 2010). Of those people, only 63% were in shelters or other types of transitional housing. The remaining 37% were living on the street, in their cars, or other places where people are not meant to live. Increasingly, homelessness in the United States is affecting families, including those with children. Consider the news stories you have heard about the problem of homelessness or perhaps the homeless people you have met yourself. Why do you think these people are homeless? Take a minute to list what you think are the top three contributing causes to homelessness.

If you are like many people, you listed such things as substance abuse, mental illness, and domestic violence—problems affecting the lives of the people who become homeless. These are indeed contributing factors. But they are not the primary factor. All these variables are more common among persons who do not become homeless than among those who do (Shinn, Baumohl, & Hopper, 2001; Shinn, 2009). The single most important factor contributing to the problem of homelessness in the United States has nothing to do with the character of the individuals who become homeless. It is a lack of affordable housing in our communities.

The best predictor of the extent of homelessness in a community is the ratio of available, affordable housing units to the number of persons and families seeking them (Shinn, Baumohl, & Hopper, 2001; Shinn, 2009). This finding has been repeatedly supported by the Hunger and Homelessness Survey conducted yearly by the U.S. Conference of Mayors. Lack of affordable housing is always the most frequently cited reason for family homelessness—even above poverty (U.S. Conference of Majors, 2009).

Listing factors such as substance abuse, mental illness, and domestic violence as the main causes of homelessness represents an *individualistic* perspective, focused on how homeless persons and families are different from those with housing. While this viewpoint is an important one, as individual factors do matter, we are going to ask you to consciously make a perceptual shift and to analyze problems in living through a *structural* perspective as well. Using this perspective requires you to think about how organizations, neighborhoods, communities, and societies are structured as systems and how those systems impact the lives of individuals and families. In community psychology, this is generally presented as taking an *ecological* perspective, and that is how it will be discussed in this book.

This shift in perspective can be made clear by viewing homelessness as a game of musical chairs (McChesney, 1990). In any community, there is a finite number of affordable housing units—just as there is a finite number of chairs in a game of musical chairs. And in both situations, there are more people than there are available chairs (or housing units). While individual variables do influence who becomes chairless (or homeless), these are not the defining factors in the game. These factors determine who gets the available seats and who is left standing *but not how many chairs are available*. The game is structured from the beginning to ensure that someone is left without a chair.

A study of solely individual-level variables in homelessness misses this larger reality. A social program for homelessness that focuses only on such factors as treating individual mental disorders or promoting job-interviewing skills may reshuffle which persons become homeless and which do not, but it does nothing about the availability of housing. This illustrates the difference between first-order and second-order change, which we will discuss later in this chapter. Addressing community or societal problems such as homelessness requires a shift in perspective—from an individualistic perspective to a structural/ecological one. Within this broader perspective, community psychologists have much to contribute (e.g., Shinn, 1992; Shin, 2009; Toro, 1999).

We will revisit the issue of homelessness and what we can do about it in Chapter 12. For now, we would like you to know that after the publication of Pool's article in the *Los Angeles Times*, Bessie Mae Berger and her sons obtained housing from a nonprofit organization: the Integrated Recovery Network.

> "The formulation of a problem is far more often essential than its solution."
>
> ALBERT EINSTEIN

The shift from an individualistic to a structural/ecological perspective is related to another issue we would like you to consider in this class: **problem definition**. As we are sure you have learned in other psychology courses, human beings are rarely content to just observe something. We want to understand it, and we will, almost automatically, construct some sort of explanation. These personal explanations then become the basis for how we define social problems. If you view an issue through an individualistic perspective, your definition of the problem will center on individual-level variables.

As the quote from Einstein indicates, the issue of problem definition is not an incidental one. How we define a problem shapes the questions we ask, the methods we use to answer those questions, and the way we interpret those answers. And all those things affect the types of interventions we will consider.

How we define a problem has such far-reaching effects that social scientists have declared problem definition to be an ethical issue (O'Neill, 2005).

Assumptions we make about a problem determine how we define the problem, which in turn determines the ways we approach and try to solve it. This may be particularly true when we are not consciously aware of the assumptions we are making. Our cultural background, personal experiences, education, and biases (and sometimes the biases that came with our education) help shape those assumptions, which may actually prevent effective responses to the problem. Our assumptions can thus become the real problem. If we ignore how problems are framed, the viewpoint through which we derive our definitions, we will be imprisoned by those frames (Seidman & Rappaport, 1986). In this book, we hope to broaden your thinking about framing problems and the process of problem definition. Community psychologists think outside the traditional boxes of psychology to define problems and generate interventions at many levels.

Actually, there are no truly individual problems or interventions. Everything that humans do takes place in social contexts: in a culture, a locality, a setting (such as a workplace, school, playground, or home), and in a set of personal relationships. For example, a child matures within many social contexts. When a client arrives for a psychotherapy session, he or she brings a personal set of life experiences (in social contexts), as does the therapist. They form a relationship that is rooted not only in who they are as persons but also in cultural, gender, social, economic (e.g., who pays for treatment, and how does that affect it?), and other contexts. Even the atmosphere of the waiting room, interpreted in cultural terms, makes a difference.

In this chapter, we will first discuss how community psychology involves a shift of perspective from the viewpoint of most of psychology. We then elaborate on the community psychology perspective by describing some of its basic assumptions about persons, contexts, and two types of change. We offer a definition of community psychology and then discuss two conceptual frameworks central to the field: ecological levels of analysis (multiple layers of social contexts) and seven core values of the field. This chapter is the first of two that introduce and define community psychology in Part 1 of this book. In Chapter 2, we trace the historical development of and current practice in community psychology.

COMMUNITY PSYCHOLOGY: A SHIFT
IN PERSPECTIVE

We hope that the problem of homelessness is a clear example of how a shift from an individual perspective to a structural/ecological perspective changes how we define a problem and what types of interventions we consider. Next, we will provide an example of how to apply this shift to a problem that we are sure you have been taught to understand at an individual or perhaps a family level: depression. In this example, we hope to provide a more detailed analysis of how individual and social problems are intertwined.

Elaine: Multiple Contexts of Clinical Depression

"Elaine" (a pseudonym) telephoned a counseling center to ask if they had anyone on staff like Dr. Kevorkian, the physician known for assisting suicide. Her husband was terminally ill, and Elaine wanted to end his life and then hers. Under the circumstances, she reasoned, everyone would be better off. When seen at the center, Elaine felt no pleasure in life, could not eat or sleep, and lacked energy to do even simple tasks. She met the diagnostic criteria for major depressive disorder in the *DSM-IV-TR* (American Psychiatric Association, 2000). Although Elaine's problems seem like a simple case of depression, examining the contexts of her problems reveals important stressors, resources, and avenues for interventions (Wandersman, Coyne, Herndon, McKnight, & Morsbach, 2002).

Elaine's family and community contexts seemed bleak. Her husband had responded to his illness by extensive alcohol abuse and impulsive spending. When a major flood damaged their home, he spent the government disaster grant instead of making repairs. The only family income was his disability payments, too little to pay the debts, and which would end with his death. Although the family was in danger of losing its home, her husband did not want Elaine to work, drive, or become involved in financial affairs. Elaine had no friends or support outside the family. She lived in a rural area with no neighbors within walking distance, and she could not drive. She had no history of employment, had left school at age 15, and had few marketable skills. Her rural Southern U.S. community was geographically dispersed and offered few community services.

Intervention: An Ecological Approach   Staff at the counseling center took a contextual, ecological approach to shift their focus from clinical treatment alone. Staff developed a plan to address multiple stressors: medication and counseling for Elaine, family home visits, help identifying and using community resources for financial assistance, promoting better communication with the medical system treating her husband, and encouraging Elaine to seek wider sources of support. Elaine benefitted from this approach. Elaine and her husband began attending a nearby church and made supportive friends. With her son's help, Elaine learned to drive, broadening her sources of support. The family's money problems did not disappear, but together, they were managing them better. With family life improved, Elaine's "sunny disposition" and coping skills returned, and medication was discontinued (Wandersman et al., 2002, p. 22). These approaches shifted perspective from focusing only on Elaine's personal and family situation to promoting involvement with community resources.

Potential Community and Macrosystem Approaches   While an ecological approach can change how professionals intervene, community psychology's shift of perspective leads to further reaching questions: What can communities do to prevent or lessen the suffering of people like Elaine? How many cases like Elaine's go unnoticed, and what is the cost to society? Can we afford to train and employ enough professionals to treat everyone with psychological problems? Is clinical treatment the only effective intervention? What other interventions might be helpful? As a field, community psychology is dedicated to offering practical and conceptual approaches to intervention so citizens, psychologists, and decision-makers can address health needs and resources at community and societal levels, not just focus on individual cases.

Wider social forces cannot be ignored in cases like Elaine's. Economic decisions by powerful others have hit U.S. communities hard, as jobs have disappeared while executives and investors benefit. Global and local economic forces help create many personal and family difficulties as well as limit public and private funding for community services. Also, while Elaine's family members contributed to their personal and financial problems, wealthier people with similar failings have far more resources for dealing with such problems. Inequalities of wealth and opportunity are growing in many societies, including the United States. This inequality is associated with poorer health and other negative outcomes for everyone, not just those with low incomes (American Psychological Association, 2010; Kawachi & Kennedy, 2006; Lott & Bullock, 2001).

Gender beliefs and practices, from family to society, created a context in which Elaine became the overburdened caretaker in her family. She had no sources of outside support and little voice in family decisions, while the men did little work but exercised control. Like many women in her circumstances, Elaine had not been encouraged to pursue education, make connections outside the family, make financial decisions, or even drive.

How can psychologists address issues such as these? In this book, we will discuss a number of responses to this question. Here is an overview:

- *Prevention/promotion programs* reduce the future likelihood of problems—for example, by strengthening protective factors and reducing risk factors in individuals, families, schools, organizations, and communities.

- *Consultation* focuses on roles, decision making, communication, and conflict in organizations to promote employee job satisfaction or effectiveness of human services, social change organizations, or schools.

- *Alternative settings* arise when traditional services do not meet the needs of some populations (e.g., women's centers, rape crisis centers, and self-help organizations for persons with specific problems). In Elaine's situation, a women's center and self-help groups for persons in recovery from addictions or coping with disabilities would have been helpful. For instance, Liang, Glenn, and Goodman (2005) discussed Reaching Out About Depression, a community program for women based on a feminist model. It pairs women advocates with low-income women coping with depression, providing personal support and advocacy based on feminist concepts and sharing power in relationships.

- *Community organizing* at grassroots levels helps citizens organize to identify local issues and decide how to address them. *Community coalitions* bring together citizens and community institutions (e.g., religious congregations, schools, police, business, human services, government) to address a community problem together instead of with separate, uncoordinated efforts.

- *Participatory research*, in which community researchers and citizens collaborate, provides useful information for action on community issues. *Program evaluation* helps to determine whether community programs effectively attain their goals and how they can be improved.

- *Policy research and advocacy* includes research on community and social issues, efforts to inform decision-makers (e.g., government officials, private sector leaders, mass media, the public) about courses for action, and evaluation of the effects of social policies. Community psychologists are engaged in advocacy regarding homelessness, peace, drug abuse, positive child and family development, and other issues. One goal of this book is to introduce you to tools for advocacy, as a citizen or professional, at levels from local to international.

Any reader of this book is quite likely to participate in community initiatives such as these in the future, whether as a community psychologist, clinical counseling psychologist, or another health professional, educator, researcher, parent, or citizen. One goal of this book is to give you tools for doing so.

Understanding diverse cultures, including your own, may require another shift of perspective. Cultural traditions of individuals, families, and communities provide personal strengths and resources for effective action. Community psychology emphasizes understanding each culture's distinctiveness while not losing sight of that culture's core values and shared human experiences. A further goal of this book is to provide you with some tools for learning about and working in diverse cultures.

PERSONS, CONTEXTS, AND CHANGE

The shifts of perspectives that we have described involve underlying assumptions about two questions. How do problems arise? How can change occur? Every day, each of us acts on our own assumed answers to these questions. Next, we describe some assumptions among community psychologists about these questions.

Persons and Contexts

Some of our most important assumptions about problems concern the importance of persons and contexts. Shinn and Toohey (2003) coined the term **context minimization error** to denote ignoring or discounting the importance of contexts in an individual's life. Context (a term we will use throughout this book) refers to the encapsulating environments within which an individual lives (e.g., family, friendship network, peer group, neighborhood, workplace, school, religious or community organization, locality, cultural heritage and norms, gender roles, social and economic forces). Together, these make up the structural forces that shape the lives of individuals. Context minimization errors lead to psychological theories and research findings that are flawed or that hold true only in limited circumstances. These errors can also lead to therapy interventions or social programs that fail because they attempt to reform individuals without understanding or altering the contexts within which those individuals live.

A key concept of social psychology is the fundamental attribution error (Ross, 1977)—the tendency of observers watching an actor to overestimate the importance of the actor's individual characteristics and underestimate the importance of situational factors. When we see someone trip on a sidewalk, we often think "how awkward" or wonder if the person has been drinking. We seldom look to see if the sidewalk is flawed. Context minimization is similar but refers to contexts and forces that include those beyond the immediate situation. Cultural norms, economic necessities, neighborhood characteristics, and the psychological climate of a workplace are examples. Contexts influence our lives at least as much as individual characteristics do. This is not to say that personal characteristics do not matter or that individuals are not responsible for their actions but to recognize the impacts of contexts. Community psychologists seek to understand people within the social contexts of their lives and to change contexts in order to promote quality of life for persons.

Consider the multiple contexts that influence a child in a first-grade public school classroom. The personalities of teacher and students certainly influence the classroom context; the curriculum and routine ways that the teacher engages with students are also important. But also consider the relationships of the school principal, faculty, and staff with the child and his or her family. The class occurs in a physical room and school in a wider neighborhood and community, which can support or interfere with learning. Relationships between administrators, school board, and citizens (and taxpayers) certainly influence the classroom environment, as do community, state, and national attitudes and policies about education. These contexts have important influences beyond simple effects of the individuals involved. Actions to improve learning for students in that first-grade classroom will need to change multiple contexts (see especially Weinstein, 2002a).

Persons and Contexts Influence Each Other   Community psychology is about the *relationships* of persons and contexts. These are not one-way streets. Contexts affect personal life, while persons, especially when acting together with others, influence and change contexts. Riger (2001) called for community psychology to appreciate how persons respond to contexts and how they can exercise power to change those contexts.

Persons influence context when citizen efforts in a neighborhood lead to improved police coverage, neighboring connections among residents, assistance for battered women, affordable housing, or when citizens act to reduce pollution by a neighboring factory. Persons who share a problem or illness influence context when they form a mutual help group to support each other. Community psychology seeks to understand *and* to improve individual, community, and societal quality of life. One of our goals for this book is to whet your appetite for involvement in community and social action in ways that draw on your personal strengths and community resources.

Reading This Book "In Context"   In reading this book, we expect that, at times, you will disagree with or recognize limitations to what we write. Respectful disagreement is important in community psychology. Community psychologist Julian Rappaport playfully yet seriously proposed Rappaport's Rule: "When everyone agrees with you, worry" (Rappaport, 1981, p. 3). Diversity of views is a valuable resource for understanding multiple sides of community and social questions.

As you read this book, identify your specific life experiences that lead you to agree or disagree, and identify the social contexts of those experiences. If possible, discuss these with your instructor, a classmate, or in class. It is our observation that many disagreements in communities and societies are based on differing life experiences in different contexts. It is important to discuss those experiences with respect and to understand them. That discussion can deepen your own and others' learning.

What Is Community Psychology? A Definition

At first, the ideas of community and psychology can seem contradictory. Community suggests the idea of persons coming together in some shared endeavor or at least geographic proximity (e.g., groups, neighborhoods, and larger structures). Psychology has traditionally concerned individual cognition, emotion, motivation, behavior, development, and related processes. In Western cultures, individual and community often have been considered opposing interests. Is community psychology an oxymoron—a contradiction in terms?

A paradox exists when two seemingly contradictory ideas turn out, upon further analysis, to be interrelated, not contradictory (Rappaport, 1981). That is true of individual and community, which are intertwined in a number of ways (Shinn, 1990). Community psychologists see quality of life for individuals, for communities, and for societies as inextricable.

Keeping in mind the diversity of community psychologists' interests and personal views, we offer this definition of the field: **Community psychology concerns the relationships of individuals with communities and societies. By integrating research with action, it seeks to understand and enhance quality of life for individuals, communities, and societies.**

Community psychology is guided by its core values of individual and family wellness, sense of community, respect for human diversity, social justice, empowerment and citizen participation, collaboration and community strengths, and empirical grounding. We elaborate on these core values later in this chapter.

Let us unpack this definition. Community psychology concerns the multiple relationships between individuals, communities, and societies. We define community broadly. An individual lives within many communities and at multiple levels: family, networks of friends, workplace, school, voluntary association, neighborhood, and wider locality—even cultures. All these exist within larger societies and ultimately within a global context. The individual must be understood in terms of these relationships, not in isolation. This means that community psychology is actually interdisciplinary, drawing on the concepts and methods of many other disciplines, including public health, community development, human development, anthropology, sociology, social work, geography, and other fields. The principal professional society for the field in the United States is the Society for Community Research and Action, in recognition of this interdisciplinary focus. Similar organizations represent community psychology in Europe, the Americas, Africa, Australia, and Asia.

Community psychology's focus is not on the individual or on the community alone but on their linkages (as in the title of this book). The field also studies the influences of social structures on each other (e.g., how citizen organizations influence the wider community). But unlike sociology, community psychology places a greater emphasis on individuals and their complex of interactions with the social structure.

Community psychology is also committed to developing valid psychological knowledge that is useful in community life. In the community psychology perspective, knowledge is constructed through action. The community psychologist's role has often been described as that of a **participant–conceptualizer** (Bennett et al., 1966, pp. 7–8), actively involved in community processes while also attempting to understand and explain them, as aptly summarized in these statements:

> If you want to understand something, try to change it. (Dearborn, cited in Bronfenbrenner, 1979, p. 37)
>
> There is nothing so useful as a good theory. (Lewin, cited in Marrow, 1969)
>
> If we are afraid of testing our ideas about society by intervening in it, and if we are always detached observers of society and rarely if ever participants in it, we can only give our students ideas about society, not our experiences in it. We can tell our students about how society ought to be, but not what it is like to try to change the way things are. (Sarason, 1974, p. 266)

Community psychology research is intertwined with community and social action. Findings from research are used to build theory *and* to guide action. For example, a program developed in a high school setting to prevent youth violence can generate greater knowledge of the problem, of adolescent development, of the local school and community, and of how to design future prevention programs. Moreover, community psychology research and action are collaborative, based on partnerships with the persons or communities involved.

Community psychology research and action are rooted in the seven core values listed in our definition. To elaborate on our definition, we next turn to discussing first-order and second-order change, surveying the levels of relationships and social contexts within which we live, and then to detailing those seven core values.

Structural Perspectives and First-Order and Second-Order Change

Developing a comprehensive understanding of the problem of homelessness introduced at the beginning of this chapter requires a conceptual shift from an individual-level perspective to a structural perspective. This perceptual shift may be particularly difficult for those of us who were raised in the American cultural tradition of individualism. This tradition holds that America, from its founding, has offered equal opportunities for all, so what we make of our lives solely depends on individual talent and effort. While we do not discount the importance of individual knowledge, skills, and effort (and, in fact, actively work to develop programs to increase these attributes in individuals, as you will see in Chapters 9 and 10), we believe that the role of structural forces in human behavior has been undervalued in psychology as a whole. One of the major skills we want you to take away from this class is the ability to look at a problem and ask yourself, "What structural factors influence this problem or behavior? How could those be modified to improve the lives of individuals and families?"

One of the first major studies demonstrating the importance of structural forces was a study of crime and juvenile delinquency in Chicago in the first half of the 20th century. Two sociologists, Clifford Shaw and Henry McKay, looked at official sources of juvenile delinquency rates (arrests, adjudications, etc.) in Chicago neighborhoods during three time periods: 1900–1906, 1917–1923, and 1927–1933. This was a period of rapid change in Chicago: successive waves of immigration by different ethnic groups, increased industrialization, sharp increases in population density, and high levels of mobility. What they found was that, over time, rates of juvenile delinquency remained high in inner city neighborhoods, even though almost the entire population of the neighborhoods had changed! Even when the ethnic makeup of a neighborhood completely changed (due to existing immigrant groups moving to more desirable neighborhoods and new immigrant groups moving in), the high rates of juvenile delinquency persisted. Shaw and McKay concluded that it was structural factors in the neighborhoods (poverty, overcrowding, and the social disorganization that accompanies rapid change) that were causing the high crime rates, not the characteristics of the individuals who lived there (Shaw and McKay, 1969). The theory they developed, Social Disorganization Theory, is still an influential theory in the field of criminology, but the general point about the importance of structural forces has important implications well beyond that field. Their research also illustrates the difference between first-order and second-order change.

Writing of the family as a social system, Watzlawick et al. (1974) distinguished between two kinds of change. **First-order change** alters, rearranges, or replaces the individual members of a group (the neighborhood in Shaw and McKay's research). This may resolve some aspects of the problem. However, in the long run, the same problems often recur with the new cast of characters, leading to the conclusion that the more things change, the more they remain the same. Attempting to resolve homelessness by counseling homeless individuals without addressing the supply of affordable housing represents first-order change. You may help that individual, but the social problem will persist because you have not addressed all the reasons that homelessness exists.

Try a thought experiment suggested by community psychologist Seymour Sarason (1972) to analyze the educational system. Criticisms of schools, at least in the United States, often focus blame on individuals or collections of individuals: incompetent teachers, unmotivated or unprepared students, or uncaring parents or administrators. Imagine changing every individual person in the school: firing all teachers and staff and hiring replacements, obtaining a new student population, and changing every individual from the school board to the classroom—yet leaving intact the structure of roles, expectations, and policies about how the school is to be run. How long do you think it will be before the same issues and criticisms return? Why? If you answer "not long," you are seeing the limits of first-order change. It is sometimes enough, but often, it is not.

A group is not just a collection of individuals; it is also a set of relationships among them. Changing those relationships, especially changing shared goals, roles, rules, and power relationships, is **second-order change** (Linney, 1990; Seidman, 1988). For example, instead of preserving rigid lines between bosses who make decisions and workers who carry them out, second-order change may involve collaborative decision making. Instead of rigid lines of expertise between mental health professionals and patients, it could involve finding ways that persons with disorders may help each other in self-help groups. The point is not that specific interventions need to always be used but rather that the analysis of the problem takes into account these set of relationships and contexts as possible contributing sources of the problems. Here are some more detailed examples.

Reaching Higher: **Second-Order Change in Schools**   How can schools create "contexts of productive learning" for all students (Sarason, 1972)? Currently, in the United States, the No Child Left Behind law seeks to reform schools by relying on standardized testing and drastic penalties for students and schools that fail. This represents first-order change within the assumptions and roles of the existing system. The law links a specific outcome, test scores, to a potentially drastic shift in resources and authority. This is first-order change because it ensures that schools will change the way they function, even if the exact nature of those changes cannot be predicted and may actually be harmful.

Articulating a different approach to improving student learning, Rhona Weinstein began her 2002 book *Reaching Higher* with the story of "Eric" (pseudonym), a 10-year-old who had never learned to read. Tests showed no learning disability, but years of tutoring had been no help.

> A visit to his classroom, however, provided more of the story. Eric was a member of the lowest reading group, which was called the "clowns." Among its members were the sole ethnic minority child, a nonreader, an overweight child, and so on. Comparing the climate of the highest and lowest ability reading groups was exceedingly painful. In the highest group, the pace was lively, the material interesting, and the children active. In the lowest group, the work was repetitive, remedial, and dull. Upon following the children out to recess, I found that the friendship patterns matched the reading group assignments, but that the members of the lowest reading group stood alone and isolated, even from each other.
>
> So I suggested changing the context for learning instead of trying to change the child—that is, that Eric be moved up to the middle reading

group. I also insisted on a contract specifying that he remain there for a three-month trial and that I would provide extra tutoring and psychological help to support his learning. A lengthy battle ensued. In a classic catch-22, both Eric's teacher and the principal asked for proof that Eric was capable of handling the material in the middle reading group. I argued that we would not have proof until the educational context was changed and Eric's anxiety about learning was relieved. I finally won approval. Eric was promoted to the middle reading group and slowly but surely began to read and participate in classroom life. By the end of the school year, he had reached grade level in his reading skills and he had friends. He proudly showed them off to me, his arms linked with theirs, as I walked the school halls.

... But I kept thinking about the other Erics left behind in the lowest reading groups.... (Weinstein, 2002a, pp. 2–3)

Weinstein's experience with Eric inspired her to study and create better contexts for learning in schools. She learned that students from many backgrounds experience poor contexts for learning. For example, her twin sons, one with a visual problem from birth complications, were treated very differently in their public schooling. After only two months of first grade, the principal told Weinstein and her husband that their son with the visual problem would never be "college material like his brother" (Weinstein, 2002a, p. 19). School professionals began offering exciting classes and learning opportunities for the "talented" son but not for the "learning-disabled" son. Parents and son had to fight this disparity throughout his schooling. With determined parental support for each son to learn in his own way, both eventually excelled in school and college.

Weinstein and her associates (Weinstein, 2002a, 2002b; Weinstein, Gregory, & Strambler, 2004) have shown how teachers can use a wider range of techniques to teach and motivate all students, enabling them to become active learners. This leads to gains in their educational achievement. To broaden their skills, teachers need their own contexts of productive learning: administrative and peer support and opportunities to experiment and learn. That will require changes in school systems' routines and in public beliefs to support the view that every child can learn if taught appropriately. All these steps change role relationships, representing second-order change.

Oxford House: Second-Order Change in Recovery from Substance Abuse

Traditional professional treatments for substance abuse have high recidivism rates. Methods that rely more on persons in recovery helping each other offer promising alternatives. One example is 12-step groups, such as Alcoholics Anonymous. Another is Oxford House, a network of residential settings (Ferrari, Jason, Olson, Davis, & Alvarez, 2002; Jason, Ferrari, Davis, & Olson 2006; Suarez-Balcazar et al., 2004).

Many recovery homes (halfway houses) are located in areas of higher crime and drug use, have crowded and time-limited accommodations, and impose rules that limit resident initiative and responsibility. Some of these limitations reflect the reluctance of the larger society to support or have day-to-day contact with persons in recovery. In contrast, Oxford Houses offer more spacious dwellings in lower-crime residential neighborhoods. Residents are required to be employed, pay rent, perform chores, and remain drug-free. The resident may chose whether to be involved in professional treatment, mutual help groups (e.g., 12-step programs), or both. Separate Oxford Houses exist for women and men. Each house is governed democratically, with leaders chosen by residents but without professional staff. Current residents vote on applications of prospective residents to join the house; a resident who returns to drug use or who is disruptive can be dismissed by a similar vote. The new resident joins a community in which there is support, shared responsibility, and shared decision making.

Oxford Houses represent second-order change because they alter the usual roles of patient and staff, making persons in recovery more accountable for their own behavior and for each other in a context of equality, support, and shared community. Evaluations indicate positive outcomes and reduced recidivism.

Listening Partners: Second-Order Change Among Women   The Listening Partners Program blended feminist and community psychology principles to provide peer groups for young mothers in Vermont (Bond, Belenky, & Weinstock, 2000). Its participants were low-income European American women living in isolated rural circumstances, although many of its principles could be extended to other groups.

In Listening Partners, groups of young mothers meet weekly with local women leaders. Groups empower women to construct personal stories of their lives and strengths, learn from and support each other, and develop skills in addressing problems. Leaders minimize status distinctions between leader and participant (altering role relationships). Evaluations showed that women in Listening Partners groups (compared to a control group) strengthened qualities of "developmental leadership" in their lives, families, and communities. As one participant described her progress:

> I think a lot more about things and whether or not they can be changed. If they can, then I try to think of [things] I can do to change them. If they can't be changed, then I try to think of ways of dealing with them.... Now I care about other people and myself. I have a new self-assuredness—that I can do it right and that I have rights. (Bond, Belenky, & Weinstock, 2000, p. 720).

Listening Partners involves second-order change because it addresses societal injustice and enables changes in role relationships in women's lives, promoting individual growth within the bonds of community.

Limits of Change in Social Contexts   Even second-order change does not "solve" community and social problems. Attempts to resolve community and social issues represent a problem resolution process rather than problem solving. Every resolution creates new challenges and perhaps problems: unintended consequences, altered alignments of human or material resources, or new conflicts involving human needs and values. This is not a reason to give up. The process leads to real improvements if communities and societies carefully study both history and likely future consequences (Sarason, 1978).

For example, the school reforms discussed previously will create challenges (Elias, 2002; Sarason, 2002, 2003a; Weinstein, 2002a, 2002b). Creating contexts of productive learning for all will surely meet resistance—some of it legitimate. Resources are limited in schools and communities. Questions will include: Who benefits from the inequities and shortcomings of the educational system as it exists now? Who will benefit from proposed changes? Is there any common ground for compromise? Where will the necessary money, skills, and leadership come from? What will happen over time? These and other questions are critical aspects of community change.

ECOLOGICAL LEVELS OF ANALYSIS IN COMMUNITY PSYCHOLOGY

As individuals, we live within webs of social relationships. Urie Bronfenbrenner (1979) originated a concept of levels of analysis (describing levels of social contexts) that is influential in developmental psychology and community psychology. Our discussion of ecological levels is partly based on Bronfenbrenner's approach, but our frame of reference is the community, not just the developing individual. Thus, we differ in some details from his approach. Historically, community psychology has used ecological levels as a way of clarifying the differing values, goals, and strategies for intervention associated with each level of analysis (Rappaport, 1977a; Rappaport, 1977b; Seidman & Rappaport, 1974). In addition, this approach helps us focus on the interactions between systems (see also different concepts of ecological levels in Maton, 2000; Moane, 2003; Nelson & Prilleltensky, 2010).

Thinking in terms of ecological levels of analysis helps to clarify how a single event or problem has multiple causes. For example, factors that contribute to a child's problems in school may include forces at multiple levels. Powerful adults at school, locality, national, and global levels make policy decisions that affect the quality of education the child receives. Family members, friends, and teachers have a great impact, but even their thinking and values are influenced by the school system, locality, cultural, societal, and even global levels.

Thinking in terms of ecological levels of analysis also helps to illustrate multiple answers to an important question for community psychology: What is a community? While originally tied to place or a locality, "community" has come to refer to sets of relationships among persons at many levels—whether tied to place or not. Thus, a classroom, sorority, religious congregation, online community, or cultural group (e.g., the Mexican American community) may be considered a community.

Figure 1.1 illustrates our typology of ecological levels of analysis for community psychology. The most **proximal**, closest to the individual and involving the most face-to-face contact, are closer to the center of the diagram. The more

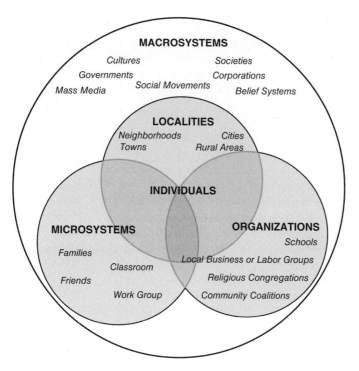

FIGURE 1.1   Ecological Levels of Analysis for Community Psychology

distal systems, less immediate to the person yet having broad effects, are toward the outside of the diagram. As you can see in the diagram, some of these systems overlap; for example, some organizations, such as small businesses or community groups, are so small that they have many of the psychosocial qualities of microsystems. The examples in italics in Figure 1.1 are illustrative and do not represent all groups at each level.

Bronfenbrenner (1979) described the webs of relationships surrounding the individual by using the metaphor of the Russian nesting doll. A nesting doll is egg-shaped and contains a succession of smaller dolls. When opened, each doll reveals a smaller doll inside. The nesting doll metaphor calls attention to how the smallest doll exists within layers of larger dolls—just as each individual exists within layers of contexts. Figure 1.1 is based on this metaphor: Proximal systems are nested within broader, more distal systems. However, the nesting doll metaphor is incomplete, omitting the relationships among levels. Individuals, societies, and the levels between them are interdependent, and their contributions to behavior and social problems may overlap in different ways. Indeed, community psychology is based on that interdependence.

Individuals

Consider the individual person, nested within the other levels. The person chooses his or her relationships or environments to some extent and influences them in many ways; likewise, they influence the person. Each person is involved in systems at multiple ecological levels (e.g., family and friends, workplace, and neighborhood). Much research in community psychology concerns how individuals are interrelated with social contexts in their lives. For example, a special journal issue examined the human costs of underemployment (Dooley & Catalano, 2003).

Community psychologists and others in related fields have developed individually oriented preventive interventions to increase personal capacities to address problems in communities. These interventions have been documented to be effective in reducing such problems as difficulties in the social and academic development of children, adolescent behavior problems and juvenile delinquency, adult physical health and depression, HIV/AIDS, difficulties during family transitions such as parenting and divorce, and family violence (we will discuss these in detail in Chapters 9–10). Many preventive approaches promote social-emotional competence, skills for adapting to challenging contexts, and ecological transitions from one context to another, such as entering school or becoming a parent (Weissberg & Kumpfer, 2003).

Microsystems

Microsystems are environments in which the person repeatedly engages in direct, personal interaction with others (Bronfenbrenner, 1979, p. 22). They include families, classrooms, friendship networks, scout troops, athletic teams, musical groups, residence hall wings, and self-help groups. In microsystems, individuals form interpersonal relationships, assume social roles, and share activities (Maton & Salem, 1995).

Microsystems are more than simply the sum of their individual members; they are social units with their own dynamics. For example, family therapists have long focused on how families function as systems beyond their individual members (Watzlawick et al., 1974). Members have roles, differential power in making decisions, reactions to the actions of other members, etc. Microsystems can be important sources of support for their members and also sources of conflict and burdens.

The concept of a **setting** is important in community psychology. In this psychological usage of the term, setting is not simply a physical place but is an enduring set of relationships among individuals that may be associated with one or several places. A chapter of a self-help group is a setting, even if its meeting place changes. Physical settings such as playgrounds, local parks, bars or coffee shops may provide meeting places for microsystems. The term *setting* is applied to microsystems and to larger organizations.

Individuals in different contexts use microsystems in different ways. For example, one study at a predominantly European American university found that family support was more important during the first year of college for African American students, who had fewer peers on campus, while peer support was more important for European Americans, who had more peers available (Maton et al., 1996).

What are the most important microsystems in your life? Are these microsystems part of wider settings, such as a neighborhood, university, or business?

Choose one microsystem. What resources does it provide for you? What challenges or obligations does it present?

Name something that you would like to change about one of the microsystems in your life. Why?

Organizations

Organizations are larger than microsystems and have a formal structure: a title, mission, bylaws or policies, meeting or work times, supervisory relationships, and so on. Organizations studied by community psychologists include human service and health care settings, treatment programs, schools, workplaces, neighborhood associations, cooperative housing units, religious congregations, and community coalitions. These are important forms of community in that they affect who people associate with, what resources are available to them, and how they define and identify themselves. Employed persons often introduce themselves by where they work.

Organizations often consist of sets of smaller microsystems. Classes, activities, departments, staff, administrators, and boards make up a school or college. Departments, shifts, or work teams make up a factory or restaurant. Religious congregations have choirs, religious classes, and prayer groups. Large community organizations usually work through committees. However, organizations are not simply the sum of their parts; the dynamics of the whole organization, such as its organizational hierarchy and its informal "culture," are important.

In turn, organizations can be parts of larger social units. A local congregation may be part of a wider religious body or a retail store part of a chain. A neighborhood association offers a way for citizens to influence city government. The largest organizations (e.g., international corporations, political parties, or religious denominations) are macrosystems, which are discussed later.

What are the most important organizations in your life?

Do you participate in these organizations through smaller microsystems? Are these organizations part of larger localities or systems?

Choose one organization. What resources does it provide for you? What challenges does it present?

Name something that you would like to change about an organization in your life. Why?

Localities

Although the term **community** has meanings at many levels of analysis, one prominent meaning refers to geographic localities, including rural counties, small towns, urban neighborhoods, or entire cities. Localities usually have governments, local economies, media, systems of social, educational and health services, and other institutions that influence individual quality of life.

Localities may be understood as sets of organizations or microsystems. Individuals participate in the life of their shared locality mainly through smaller groups. Even in small towns, individuals seldom influence the wider community unless they work alongside other citizens in an organization or microsystem. An association of neighborhood residents is an organization, while the entire neighborhood is a locality. That neighborhood may also host microsystems of teen friends, adults who meet for coffee, and parents and children who gather at a playground. However, a locality is not simply the sum of its citizens, microsystems, or community organizations. Its history, cultural traditions, and qualities as a whole community surround each of those levels.

Neighborhoods are important in individual lives, and community and developmental psychologists have begun to study them. A research review (Shinn & Toohey, 2003) concluded that neighborhood conditions (in both urban and rural areas) are linked to children's health, personal distress, academic achievement, employment opportunities, behavior problems, delinquency, teenage childbearing, and being a victim of violence. Parenting strategies that are adaptive in safer neighborhoods differ from strategies adaptive in riskier neighborhoods (Gonzales, Cauce, Friedman, & Mason, 1996). Among adults, neighborhoods affect fear of crime, anxiety, depression, and sense of community (Shinn & Toohey, 2003).

An example of the linkage between organizations and localities is the recent emergence of community coalitions, comprised of representatives of various community groups and organizations and formed to address wider community issues such as drug abuse or health concerns.

What localities are important in your life?

Describe a locality that you live in or have lived in. What are its strengths? Limitations? What would you change about it if you could? What organizations are important in this locality? How is it affected by larger social forces?

Macrosystems

Macrosystems are the largest level of analysis in our system. While Figure 1.1 portrays only one macrosystem, in fact individuals, microsystems, organizations, and localities are all continually influenced by multiple macrosystems. Macrosystems include societies, cultures, political parties, social movements, corporations, international labor unions, multiple levels of government, international institutions, broad economic and social forces, and belief systems. Community psychology's perspective ultimately needs to be global.

Macrosystems exercise influence through policies and specific decisions, such as legislation and court decisions, and through promoting ideologies and social norms. Ideals of individual autonomy greatly influence U.S. culture and the discipline of psychology. Mass media communicate subtle forms of racial stereotyping and cultural expectations for thinness, especially for women. Macrosystems also form contexts within which the other levels function, such as the economic climate affecting businesses. But systems at other levels can influence macrosystems through social advocacy or through actions such as buying locally grown foods.

An important level of analysis that we include under macrosystems is the population. A population is defined by a broadly shared characteristic (e.g., gender, race, ethnicity, nationality, income, religion, sexual orientation, or having a physical or mental disability). Populations can be the basis of a broad form of community (e.g., the Jewish community, the gay community). However, not all individuals within a population will identify with it as a community.

Many studies in community psychology concern more than one level of analysis. For instance, a recent study of children in Head Start programs investigated neighborhood-, family-, and individual-level factors related to educational success. The researchers found that neighborhood-level factors (including the number of families of low or high socioeconomic status and the number of homes in which English was a second language) had significant *direct* effects on the cognition and behavior of children in Head Start (Vanden-Kiernan et al., 2010). These direct neighborhood-level effects were not mediated by such family-level factors as family structure, income or ethnicity, and family processes (e.g., amount of social support available to parents, parents' involvement in their children's education). What this means, for example, is that living in a neighborhood marked by concentrated poverty had a significant negative effect on the cognitive and behavioral development on children, even if those children lived in a two-parent home with good income and parents who were highly involved in their education. The negative neighborhood-level effects were strong enough to overwhelm any positive effects the children received from their parents. We will discuss the strong effects of neighborhood context on child development in Chapter 5.

Levels of Intervention

Ecological levels of analysis are helpful tools in shifting perspective about "where to look" to promote change. Systematically examining an issue across levels of analysis can uncover multiple contributing factors to that issue. However, examining social issues across levels of analyses is not sufficient to promote change; that is, understanding "where" to look is only the first step of the community psychology shift in perspective.

One way in which levels of analysis can help suggest appropriate points of intervention is through the concept of mediating structures. Peter Berger and John Neuhaus (1977) were sociologists who developed a strategy to promote well-being for individuals and communities through the development of **mediating structures**. Central to this theory is that society can exert stressful conditions on individuals, some of whom have difficulty coping with these stressors. However, a strategy of promoting the development of mediating structures focuses on settings that can assist individuals coping with society's stressors. In our ecological levels of analysis framework, these might be organizations (e.g., schools, mutual help groups, barbershops/beauty parlors) or less formal settings. Community psychologists have been interested in the potential of settings that can serve as mediating structures—many of which are under-utilized resources in communities already. In some cases, they focus on creating new alternative settings that better meet the needs of the individuals affected by the focal concern.

"What to change" and "how to change" are crucial components of any change strategy. In the coming chapters, we will elaborate on "how" and "what" to change. For this introduction of the community psychology perspective, we emphasize two related points that need to be paired with any consideration of ecological levels of analysis: problem definition and selecting interventions that are linked to ecological levels of analysis.

The focus of any change effort requires a problem definition to organize resources and action. In the example of homelessness presented earlier, if homelessness is defined as a problem with the person only (e.g., addiction, mental health, lack of job skills) or problem of the environment only (e.g., lack of affordable housing), the selected interventions will be quite different (e.g., a treatment for an individual deficit or creating a program to create access to affordable housing). It is critical to examine how a problem is framed and how this dictates interventions. By focusing on a single level of analysis (e.g., individual problems), the intervention strategy is constrained to individual change efforts and will be ineffective in addressing homelessness if aspects of the problem at higher levels of analysis are not addressed (e.g., access to safe, affordable housing). Too often, levels of analysis might be examined for an issue, but the change strategy ignores or does not match this analysis. In North America, many problems are framed at an individual level of analysis. However, from a community psychology perspective, addressing such issues as homelessness or joblessness will require multiple interventions at different levels of analysis. If interventions are not implemented at multiple levels of analysis, they will likely fail to be effective at addressing the issue.

Furthermore, there are three ways that we may fall short of addressing issues even if we examine multiple levels of analyses. First, it may be that action is necessary but not taken (e.g., additional resources for treatment of homeless persons or affordable housing are not committed). Second, it may be that action is taken where it should not be (e.g., arresting homeless persons for sleeping on the street; how does this prevent homelessness?). Third, and perhaps more common, action is taken at the wrong level of analysis (e.g., the only action taken is passing city ordinances to limit panhandling or loitering—observable individual level behaviors of some homeless persons that are troubling to many community members). In community psychology terms, this is referred to as an **error of logical typing** (Watzlawick et al., 1974; Rappaport, 1977). While panhandling and loitering can be problematic, focusing change efforts on this individual level of analysis likely will not reduce homelessness. These efforts may also not reduce behaviors perceived to be problematic; rather, these behaviors will likely be moved to different locations as the root causes for homelessness have not been addressed.

How do community psychologists decide to frame problem definitions? How can you choose which levels of analysis need to be included in an intervention strategy? In the next section, we present core values of community psychology that help guide these decisions.

SEVEN CORE VALUES IN COMMUNITY PSYCHOLOGY

Our personal values about relationships, accountability, social change priorities, and our personal political world view all shape our priorities and agenda for community work. (Bond, 1989, p. 356)

Our work always promotes the ends of some interest group, even if we do not recognize that explicitly. (Riger, 1989, p. 382)

Awareness of values is crucial for community psychology. But what exactly do we mean by values? Values are deeply held ideals about what is moral, right, or good. They have emotional intensity; they are honored, not lightly held. Values may concern ends (goals), or means (how to attain goals), or both. They are social; we develop values through experiences with others. Individuals hold values but so do families, communities, and cultures. Values may be rooted in spiritual beliefs or practices but can also be secular. Many values conflicts involve choices about which of two worthy values is more important in a given situation (Nelson & Prilleltensky, 2010; O'Neill, 1989; Rudkin, 2003; Schwartz, 1994; Snow, Grady, & Goyette-Ewing, 2000).

In community psychology, discussions of values are useful for several purposes. First, values help clarify choices for research and action. Even defining a problem is a value-laden choice, strongly influencing subsequent action (Seidman & Rappaport, 1986). Public definitions of community and social problems reflect the worldviews of the powerful and help to maintain the status quo. Attending to values can lead to questioning those dominant views. For community psychologists, deciding whether to work with a particular organization or community requires attention to values. Sometimes, the community psychologist may conclude that his or her values do not match those of a setting and choose not to work in that setting (Isenberg, Loomis, Humphreys, & Maton, 2004).

Second, the discussion of values helps to identify when actions and espoused values do not match. Consider a community leader who helps to found a neighborhood social center to empower teens who are gay, lesbian, bisexual, or questioning their sexuality. The leader decides how to renovate the space and plans programs, allowing the youth themselves little say. Despite the leader's intent, this actually disempowers the youth (Stanley, 2003). The leader "talks the talk" but does not "walk the walk."

Or consider an alternative high school that seeks to empower students, their families, and teachers (Gruber & Trickett, 1987). But when decisions are to be made, the teachers have sources of day-to-day information and influence that students and parents lack; teachers thus dominate the discussion. Despite the espoused values of all involved, the organizational practices do not empower students and families. The problem is not individual hypocrisy but an organizational discrepancy between ideals and actual outcomes.

Third, understanding a culture or community involves understanding its distinctive values. For instance, Potts (2003) discussed the importance of Africanist

TABLE 1.1   Seven Core Values in Community Psychology

Individual and family wellness	Empowerment and citizen participation
Sense of community	Collaboration and community strengths
Respect for human diversity	Empirical grounding
Social justice	

values in a program for middle school African American youth. Native Hawai'ian cultural conceptions of health are closely tied to values of *'ohana* and *lokahi*, family and community unity, and of interdependence of the land, water, and human communities. A health promotion program in Native Hawai'ian communities needs to be interwoven with these values (Helm, 2003).

Fourth, community psychology has a distinctive spirit (Kelly, 2002a)—a shared sense of purpose and meaning. That spirit is the basis of our commitment and what keeps us going when obstacles arise (Kelly, 2010). It is thoughtful but also passionate and pragmatic, embodied in research and action.

In our experience, the spirit of community psychology is based on seven core values, listed in Table 1.1. We begin with the value most closely linked to the individual level of analysis, proceeding to those more closely linked to community and macrosystem levels. This order is not a ranking of these values' importance. Our discussion of these seven values is influenced by, yet different from, the discussions of values by Isaac Prilleltensky and Geoffrey Nelson (2002; Nelson & Prilleltensky, 2010; Prilleltensky, 1997, 2001). These seven values, based on our experiences, are just one way of summarizing the field's values. Each individual and working group within the field must decide what values will be central to their work. Our discussion here is intended to promote the discussion of these values and the issues they raise for community life. As Bond (1989) and Riger (1989) asserted in quotations at the beginning of this section, community psychology will be guided by some set of values and serve someone's interests, whether we realize it or not. Better to discuss and choose our values and how to put them into action.

Debi Starnes, a community psychologist, provided examples of how she has applied each value in her leadership on the Atlanta, Georgia, city council (Starnes, 2004). These examples illustrate how one committed person can make a difference by speaking out and working cooperatively with others.

Individual and Family Wellness

Wellness refers to physical and psychological health, including personal well-being and attainment of personal goals (Cowen, 1994, 2000a, 2000b, 2000c). Indicators of wellness include symptoms of psychological distress and such measures of positive qualities as resilience, social-emotional skills, personal well-being, and life satisfaction. These and similar indicators are often outcome criteria for community psychology interventions.

Strengthening families can promote individual wellness. Community prevention programs that focus on child development often address parent and family functioning. However, individual and family wellness are not synonymous. For example, when violence or other exploitation of family members is ongoing, preserving the family conflicts with the individual wellness of those victims.

Individual/family wellness is also the focus of clinical psychology and related fields. Community psychology goes beyond, yet complements, clinical methods by placing individual wellness in the context of ecological levels of analysis. One of the events leading to the founding of community psychology in the United States was a study showing that professional clinical treatment for all who need it would be prohibitively expensive and impossible in practice (Albee, 1959). (Albee's analysis is even more believable now in the current health care climate.) Clinical care is valuable but not available to all and often not to those who need it most (U.S. Department of Health and Human Services, 1999, 2001).

To promote individual/family wellness, community psychologists have studied and developed community interventions focused on the prevention of maladaptive behavior, personal and family problems, and illness; promotion of social-emotional competence and of health; social support networks and mutual help groups; intervention programs in such nonclinical settings as schools and workplaces; and advocacy for changes in social services, laws, policies, and programs to promote physical and mental health.

In her work on the Atlanta City Council, Starnes promoted the value of individual and family wellness by heading an action group that produced policies and programs for homeless persons and families. This led to developing services along a continuum of care: emergency shelter care, transitional housing, self-sufficient housing for living independently, job training, supportive housing for homeless persons with serious mental illness, and a resource opportunity center and management information system that coordinated services among 70 agencies serving the homeless. These services also helped cut costs they diverted homeless persons from emergency rooms and jails. (Starnes, 2004, p. 3)

Starnes's efforts benefit homeless persons and families and the community at large. Prilleltensky (2001) proposed the concept of **collective wellness** to refer to the health of communities and societies. Cowen's (1994, 2000c) descriptions of wellness include concepts of empowerment and social justice. Certainly, individual and community well-being are interwoven, and collective wellness is an attractive general principle. It is involved with the next five values that we discuss.

Sense of Community

Sense of community is the center of some definitions of community psychology (Sarason, 1974). It refers to a perception of belongingness, interdependence, and mutual commitment that links individuals in a collective unity (McMillan & Chavis, 1986; Sarason, 1974). For example, community psychologists have studied sense of community in neighborhoods, schools and classrooms, mutual help groups, faith communities, workplaces, and Internet virtual environments (e.g., Fisher, Sonn, & Bishop, 2002; Newbrough, 1996). Sense of community is a basis for community and social action as well as a resource for social support and clinical work.

The value of sense of community balances the value of individual/family wellness. The emphasis in Western cultures and in their fields of psychology is on the individual, which in its worst forms can foster selfishness or indifference to others (Bellah, Madsen, Sullivan, Swidler, & Tipton, 1985; Sarason, 1974). Building a sense of community goes beyond individualism to a focus on interdependence and relationships. From a community psychology perspective, quality of life for individual and community ultimately depend on each other.

Yet sense of community is not always positive. It can involve distancing "insiders" from "outsiders." It can be bolstered by ignoring or attacking diversity within a community, creating injustice or a deadening conformity. It is not a cure-all. In especially risky neighborhoods, withdrawal from the community may be adaptive for adults or children (Brodsky, 1996). Thus, this value must be balanced with other values, especially social justice and respect for diversity.

In her work in Atlanta, Starnes (2004, p. 4) promoted this value through several initiatives. Atlanta has become a leader in replacing large, concentrated public housing units with attractive, well-built, mixed-income communities. Starnes was considered naïve for championing the mixing of middle-income and lower-income residents, but the first project in her district was such a success that six more similar public housing communities have been rebuilt. These have increased feelings of community across social class lines. In addition, Starnes helped initiate Community Redevelopment Plans for seven Atlanta neighborhoods affected by the 1996 Olympics development. Finally, she helped initiate new Quality of Life zoning and building ordinances requiring street planning and housing features that encourage neighboring. For instance, those ordinances promote having services within walking distance and having front porches and sidewalks so that people can see each other and chat more.

Respect for Human Diversity

This value recognizes and honors the variety of communities and social identities based on gender, ethnic, or racial identity, nationality, sexual orientation, ability or disability, socioeconomic status and income, age, or other characteristics. Understanding individuals-in-communities requires understanding human diversity (Trickett, 1996). Persons and communities are diverse, defying easy generalizations and demanding that they be understood in their own terms.

This is not a vague respect for diversity as a politically correct attitude. To be effective in community work, community psychologists must understand the traditions and folkways of any culture or distinctive community with whom they work (O'Donnell, 2005a). That includes appreciating how the culture provides distinctive strengths and resources for living. Researchers also need to adapt research methods and questions to be appropriate to a culture. This is more than simply translating questionnaires; it involves a thorough re-examination of the aims, methods, and expected products of research in terms of the culture to be studied (Hughes & Seidman, 2002).

Respect for diversity does not mean moral relativism; one can hold strong values while also seeking to understand different values. For example, cultural traditions differ in the power they grant to women; religious traditions vary in their teachings about sexuality. Respect for diversity also must be balanced with the values of social justice and sense of community—understanding diverse groups and persons while promoting fairness, seeking common ground, and avoiding social fragmentation (Prilleltensky, 2001). To do that, the first step is usually to study diversities in order to understand them. A related step is to respect others as fellow persons, even when you disagree.

Starnes (2004, p. 5) described how she promoted respect for diversity in Atlanta by strengthening affirmative action policies, insurance coverage for domestic partners in gay and lesbian couples, and related ways of addressing past and present discrimination (matters of both social justice and respect for diversity). The housing initiatives discussed above involved promoting neighboring and community ties among diverse groups. Starnes represents a district with plenty of socioeconomic, racial, and other forms of diversity, and her job requires considerable cultural competence to represent her constituents. Starnes also pointed out that Atlanta now has women in a majority on City Council and as mayor, city attorney, and chief operating officer (playfully known as "chicks in charge"). A familiar experience in community organizations is that most of the volunteers and local leaders are women, and women are now assuming leadership roles in a variety of larger contexts.

Social Justice

Social justice can be defined as the fair, equitable allocation of resources, opportunities, obligations, and power in society as a whole (Prilleltensky, 2001, p. 754). It is central to some definitions of community psychology (Nelson & Prilleltensky, 2010; Rappaport, 1981).

Social justice has two meanings especially important here. **Distributive justice** concerns the allocation of resources (e.g., money, access to good quality health services or education) among members of a population. The community mental health movement that arose in the United States in the 1960s was a distributive effort to provide mental health services to more citizens. Who determines how such resources are distributed? That is the question of **procedural justice**, which concerns whether processes of collective decision making include a fair representation of citizens. Thus, distributive justice concerns the outcomes of a program or social policy, while procedural justice concerns how it is planned and implemented (Drew, Bishop, & Syme, 2002; Fondacaro & Weinberg, 2002).

Psychology's record of support for social justice in the United States has been mixed. It has sometimes been at the forefront of social justice struggles, as in the involvement of psychologists Mamie and Kenneth Clark and others in research cited in the 1954 school desegregation case *Brown vs. Board of Education*. However, psychological research and practice has also had the effect of supporting sexism, racism, and other injustices, for instance in the area of intelligence testing (Gould, 1981; Prilleltensky & Nelson, 2002). The tradition of liberation psychology, rooted in Latin America, and the related fields of critical psychology and feminist psychology exemplify psychological pursuit of social justice (Bond, Hill, Mulvey, & Terenzio, 2000a, 2000b; Martin-Baro, 1994; Montero, 1996; Prilleltensky & Nelson, 2002; Watts & Serrano-Garcia, 2003).

A social justice perspective is often most concerned with advocacy: for social policies (e.g., laws, court decisions, government practices, regulations) and for changes in public attitudes, especially through mass media. But it can also guide clinical work with members of oppressed populations and research on psychological effects of social injustice or changes in social policy.

Social justice involves concern for wellness of all persons and an inclusive vision of community and recognition of human diversity. Procedural justice is especially related to values we present next: citizen participation in making decisions and genuine collaboration between psychologists and community members.

In practice, the pursuit of social justice must be balanced with other values and with inequalities in power that are difficult to change (Prilleltensky, 2001). For instance, psychologists who have worked with survivors of state-sponsored violence in Guatemala and South Africa have found that pursuing full accountability of perpetrators of past violence and greater power for survivors (social justice) must be balanced with other aims: individual healing (wellness), community and national reconciliation (sense of community), and the realities of who continues to hold power in communities and society (Lykes, Terre Blanche, & Hamber, 2003).

In Atlanta, Starnes (2004, pp. 4–5) and other Council members are addressing their concern with social justice through sponsoring a city living wage policy, which would raise the minimum wage for employees of city services and of contractors serving the city. When business representatives told her that she did not understand the "ripple effects" of that policy, she replied that she did indeed understand ripple effects, and that was why she proposed the raise! Starnes also helped pioneer a system of community courts using principles of restorative justice for nonviolent crimes, such as cleaning up graffiti and performing community service. In a related initiative, arrested prostitutes are now offered help through treatment and services for the homeless. Recidivism and costs have decreased. The housing reforms, affirmative action policies, and services for the homeless discussed above also promoted social justice.

Empowerment and Citizen Participation

Fundamental to a community psychology perspective is the consideration of power dynamics in individual relationships, organizations, and communities. Empowerment is aimed toward enhancing the possibilities for people to control their own lives (Rappaport, 1981, 1987). Empowerment is a process that works across multiple levels and contexts; it involves gaining access to resources and exercising power in collective decision making. Citizen participation is a strategy for exercising this power. It emphasizes democratic processes of making decisions that allow all members of a community to have meaningful involvement in the decision, especially those who are directly affected (Prilleltensky, 2001; Wandersman & Florin, 1990). Grassroots citizen groups, neighborhood organizations, and community-wide prevention coalitions promote citizen participation. Citizen participation also refers to the ability of a community to participate in decisions by larger bodies (e.g., macrosystems) that affect its future. Empowerment and citizen participation are related to the concept procedural justice (Fondacaro & Weinberg, 2002; Rappaport, 1981; Zimmerman, 2000).

Citizen participation does not automatically lead to better decisions. Sometimes, citizens do not consider the rights and needs of all individuals or groups, and empowerment has been used to justify the strengthening of one group at the expense of another. Thus, this value must be balanced with values of sense of community, social justice, and respect for diversity. This can lead to conflict among competing views and interests. However, simply avoiding conflict by limiting opportunities for meaningful citizen participation is often worse for those values than promoting free debate.

Atlanta is divided into 24 neighborhood planning units. Proposed city policies (e.g., zoning) are sent to these groups for discussion and input. Starnes (2004, p. 4) referred to these sessions as "raucous democracy," but that passionate involvement of citizens means that their voices are heard, that elites find it difficult to make decisions in private, and that citizens and neighborhoods have a say in decisions that affect them. Starnes herself is a former chair of one of these groups. The community development plans growing out of the Olympics (mentioned earlier) also brought citizens and professional planners together as partners in making decisions.

Collaboration and Community Strengths

Perhaps the most distinctive value of community psychology, long emphasized in the field, involves *relationships* between community psychologists and citizens and the *process* of their work.

Psychologists usually relate to community members as experts: researchers, clinical or educational professionals, and organizational consultants. That creates a hierarchical, unequal relationship of expert and client—useful in some contexts but often inappropriate for community work. Psychologists also traditionally address deficits in individuals (e.g., diagnosing mental disorder), while community psychologists search for personal and community strengths that promote change. Community psychologists do have expertise to share with communities. However, they also need to honor the life experiences, wisdom, passionate zeal, social networks, organizations, cultural traditions, and other resources (in short, the community strengths) that already exist in a community. Building on these strengths is often the best pathway to overcoming problems (Maton, Schellenbach, Leadbeater, & Solarz, 2004).

Furthermore, community psychologists seek to create a collaborative relationship with citizens so community strengths are available for use. In that relationship, both psychologist and citizens contribute knowledge and resources, and both participate in making decisions (Kelly, 1986; Prilleltensky, 2001; Tyler, Pargament & Gatz, 1983). For example, community researchers may design a study to meet the needs of citizens, share research findings with citizens in a form that they can use, and help use the findings to advocate for changes by decision-makers. Developers of a community program would fully involve citizens in planning and implementing it.

Collaboration is best pursued where psychologist and community share common values. Thus, it is crucial for community psychologists to know their own values priorities and to make careful choices about with whom to ally in the community. It also means that differences in views that emerge must be discussed and resolved fairly.

Community psychologist Tom Wolff was engaged by a community health coalition to work with local citizens to plan health initiatives. He held an evening meeting open to all citizens. At such a meeting, one might expect to discuss community health education campaigns, the need for a community clinic, early screening programs, or mutual help groups. Instead, the most important need identified by many citizens was for street signs! Wolff barely contained his amazement. Yet recently in this community, emergency medical care had been delayed several times, with serious consequences, because ambulances could not locate residences.

Wolff duly noted this concern, then sought to turn the conversation to matters fitting his preconceptions. However, the local citizens would not have it; they wanted a plan for action on street signs. When that need had been met, they reasoned, they could trust the health coalition to work with them on other issues. Wolff then shifted to working with the citizens to get the municipality to erect street signs. Instead of pursuing his own agenda, he worked with citizens to accomplish their goals. His actions illustrate the values of citizen participation and collaboration. (Wolff & Lee, 1997)

In Atlanta, Starnes (2004, p. 4–6) noted how her work as an elected official often involves listening to and mediating between competing interests whose advocates hold strong emotional views. She cited a pressing need in government for community psychologists with mediation skills. Starnes uses her community psychology process and collaborative skills every day, and has a lively appreciation of the strengths of her constituents and of the city at large.

Empirical Grounding

This value refers to the integrating research with community action, basing (grounding) action in empirical research findings whenever possible. This uses research to make community action more effective and makes research more valid for understanding communities. Community psychologists are impatient with theory or action that lacks empirical evidence and with research that ignores the context and interests of the community in which it occurred.

Community psychologists use quantitative and qualitative research methods (we discuss both in Chapter 4). Community psychologists prize generating knowledge from a diversity of sources, with innovative methods (Jason, Keys, Suarez-Balcazar, Taylor, & Davis, 2004; Martin, Lounsbury, & Davidson, 2004).

Community psychologists believe no research is value-free; it is always influenced by researchers' values and preconceptions and by the context in which the research is conducted. Drawing conclusions from research thus requires attention to values and context, not simply to the data. This does not mean that researchers abandon rigorous research but that values and community issues that affect the research are discussed openly to promote better understanding of findings.

Starnes (2004, p. 5–6) has advocated basing decisions of Atlanta government on empirical evidence whenever possible. She admitted that she had only mixed success. Yet methods abound for using research evidence to inform government decisions, evaluate community programs, and assist neighborhood associations. Moreover, Starnes noted that community problems and decisions are growing more complex, requiring more knowledge and analytical ability and providing a challenge for community psychologists.

CONCLUSION: VALUES IN CONTEXT

No discipline commands unanimity among its members, and community psychologists in particular can be a skeptical, questioning lot (recall Rappaport's Rule). These core values therefore must be understood in terms of how they complement, balance, and limit each other in practice (Prilleltensky, 2001). For example, individual wellness must be balanced with concern for the wider community. Collaborating with local community members is a time-consuming approach that can slow the completion of research. Promoting a local sense of community or cultural identity does not necessarily promote a wider concern for social justice. Community life and a wise community psychology require accommodations among these values rather than single-minded pursuit of one or two.

Moreover, such abstract ideas as individual/family wellness, social justice, respect for diversity, and sense of community can mean very different things to different persons or in different contexts. These seven core values must be elaborated and applied through example and discussion. As you read this book, seek a way to discuss values questions respectfully with others. Part of the appeal of community psychology is that values issues are "on the table" to be discussed.

CHAPTER SUMMARY

1. Community psychology concerns the relationships of individuals with communities and societies. By integrating research with action, it seeks to understand and enhance quality of life for individuals, communities, and societies. Community psychology emphasizes collaboration with community

members as partners in research or action. Community psychologists are *participant-conceptualizers* in communities, engaged in community action and in research to understand that action.

2. Compared to other psychological fields, community psychology involves a shift in perspective. The focus of community psychology is not on the individual alone but on how the individual exists within a web of *contexts*—encapsulating environments and social connections. Persons and social contexts influence each other. Discounting the influence of social contexts is the *context minimization error.*

3. *First-order change* alters or replaces individual members of a group or community; *second-order change* alters the role relationships among those members. Examples of second-order change include changing schools to provide contexts of productive learning for all students, changing systems for recovery from substance abuse, and empowering young mothers. For social and community issues, problems are not "solved" but changed. Every action creates new challenges, but these can be an improvement over time.

4. Community psychologists study *ecological levels of analysis. Individuals* interact within such *microsystems* as families, friendship networks, classrooms, and small groups. Microsystems often are nested within such *organizations* as schools and workplaces. Microsystems and organizations may exist in specific *localities*, such as neighborhoods. All these systems exist within such *macrosystems* as societies and cultures. Microsystems are the most *proximal* (closest) level to individuals, while macrosystems are the most *distal*—but all influence individual lives. A *setting* is an enduring set of relationships among individuals that may be associated with one or several physical places. It may apply to microsystems or to organizations.

5. Values are important in community psychology. They help clarify issues and choices in research and action, facilitate questioning of dominant views of social issues, and promote understanding how cultures and communities are distinctive.

6. Community psychology is based on seven core values: *Individual and family wellness; sense of community; respect for human diversity; social justice; empowerment and citizen participation; collaboration and community strengths;* and *empirical grounding. Distributive justice* concerns whether resources in society are allocated fairly, while *procedural justice* includes whether decision-making processes are inclusive. These seven core values are interrelated. Pursuit of one value, without consideration of the others, leads to one-sided research and action.

RECOMMENDED READINGS

Rappaport, J. & Seidman, E. (Eds.). (2000). *Handbook of community psychology.* New York: Kluwer/Plenum.

Shinn, M. & Toohey, S. M. (2003). Community contexts of human welfare. *Annual Review of Psychology, 54,* 427–460.

Trickett, E. (2009). Community psychology: Individuals and interventions in community context. *Annual Review of Psychology, 60,* 395–419.

RECOMMENDED WEBSITES

Society for Community Research and Action:
http://www.scra27.org

> Website of the international professional body of community psychology. Information on SCRA mission and goals, membership benefits, interest groups, listservs, graduate schools and job opportunities in community psychology, conferences, and activities (including those for students). Useful for students, citizens, and community psychologists.

The Social Psychology Network: Community Psychology:
http://www.socialpsychology.org/community.htm

> The community psychology page of the Social Psychology Network website. Information on journals, books, careers and graduate programs, service learning, teaching resources, and other topics. Useful for students, citizens, and community psychologists.

2

The Development and Practice of Community Psychology

HIRB/Index Stock/PhotoLibrary

OPENING EXERCISE

In Chapter 1, we presented community psychology as offering an alternative paradigm for how community challenges might be defined and addressed. In the coming chapters, we emphasize how an understanding of contextual factors can improve efforts to address problems and improve communities. In this chapter, we present the foundations of how community psychology action and research are carried out. Before we present how community psychology understands community phenomena and social intervention, we first need to put the field into historical context and describe the practice of community psychology. Like other fields of study and human institutions, community psychology has stories about why, where, when, and how it developed. The stories that a group tells about itself communicate its values and purposes. Briefly consider what stories are told about the founding of your country? What values do they communicate? How are they different from other countries' stories?

Now consider the founding of a new field of research and action focused on linking individuals and communities. Why did psychologists believe that they needed to develop a new field? To understand what community psychologists do, it is helpful to understand how the field developed. For example, there must be reasons why community psychologists emphasize prevention and health promotion as major modes of intervention. Similarly, why do community psychologists emphasize a link between research and action in their practice? Examining the historical links between the development of community psychology and its contemporary practice will reveal that some contextual factors were instrumental in building a new field and others were helpful in articulating a new direction for psychology.

The viewpoints we present here are not the only ways to view the history of community psychology and its practice. Indeed, our goal is to stimulate you to think about the field critically—for yourself and in dialogue with others. Based on our experience, we focus on community psychology in the United States but also recognize its international roots and that it is now a global field.

COMMUNITY PSYCHOLOGY AS A LINKING SCIENCE AND LINKING PRACTICE

Community psychology can be viewed as a *linking science and practice* (Stark, 2009). As a linking science, community psychology looks for relationships among factors across micro to macro levels of analysis to construct a more comprehensive understanding of what can influence an individual's health and well-being. As a linking practice, community psychology brings together multiple stakeholders, some of whom are often overlooked, to address community issues (Community Psychology Vision Group, 2006).

Consider the first chapter's description of community psychology's shift in perspective about how psychology can be helpful in addressing human problems. Community psychology explicitly connects its core values to different ways of defining social problems. It uses conceptual tools (e.g., ecological levels of analysis) to show how problem definitions are related to approaches for intervention. Furthermore, as the core values of collaboration and empowerment suggest, community psychology is deliberate in thinking about how psychologists and persons interested in social change can work together to address community-based challenges. The metaphor of linking helps to understand the purpose and scope of the field and helps describe what community psychologists do. This is why we have titled our book *Community Psychology: Linking Individuals and Communities*.

Community psychology in the United States is usually considered to have originated at a conference of psychologists in Swampscott, Massachusetts, in 1965. Psychologists attending this conference were interested in linking their training and resources to addressing community problems. They proposed creating a new field to support these efforts. Yet the story does not start there. The Swampscott Conference was nested in the historical and cultural context of mid-20th-century U.S. society and psychology. U.S. psychology was greatly influenced by European-trained psychologists and the events of two world wars. In fact, community psychology was evolving in many locations before its first conference, and it has continued to grow. We must go back before the beginning (Sarason, 1974) to set the stage. First, we consider two characteristics of psychology that led psychologists to look for new models to conduct research and interventions: an overly individualistic focus and limited interest in cultural understandings on human behavior.

INDIVIDUALISTIC SCIENCE AND PRACTICE
IN PSYCHOLOGY

> If [early psychologists] had put not one but two or three animals in a
> maze, we would have had a more productive conception of human
> behavior and learning. (Sarason, 2003b, p. 101)

Psychology, especially in the United States, has traditionally defined itself as
the study of the individual organism. Even social psychologists have studied primarily the cognitions and attitudes of individuals. The tradition of behaviorism,
which does emphasize the importance of environment, has seldom studied
cultural-social variables. Psychodynamic, humanistic, and cognitive perspectives
have focused on individuals rather than on persons in their environments. This
stance has had considerable benefits but also limitations that led to the emergence
of alternative viewpoints, including those of community psychology.

Individualistic Practice

Professional psychological practice also focuses primarily on individuals. The psy-
chometric study of individual differences has long been linked to testing in
schools and industry. Individuals are measured, sorted, and perhaps changed,
but the environments of school and work seldom receive such scrutiny. In addition, much of Western psychotherapy is based on the assumptions of individual
primacy. The client focuses inward to find new ways of living that yield greater
personal happiness. Concern for others is assumed to automatically follow from
this concern for self (Bellah, Madsen, Sullivan, Swidler, & Tipton, 1985). This
approach is often helpful for those whose lives are in disarray. However, it may
overlook interpersonal, community, and social resources for recovery. As a general philosophy of living, it emphasizes self-fulfillment and says little about commitment to others. An individualistic perspective frames the ways we picture
ourselves, the discipline of psychology, and our communities and society.

However, changing settings, communities, or society is often necessary to
improve quality of life for individuals. Our point is not that individually based
research, testing, and psychotherapy are useless but that psychology relies heavily
on individualistic tools when others are also needed. Community psychology
seeks to identify and work with those other tools.

Psychology did not have to develop with so much focus on the individual.
Two prominent early psychologists, John Dewey and Kurt Lewin, defined psychology as the study of how individuals are related to their sociocultural environment
(Sarason, 1974, 2003b). In developing psychological practice, Lightner Witmer's
Psycho-Educational Clinic—the first psychological clinic in the United States—
opened in Philadelphia in 1896. Concerned with educational problems of children,
Witmer asserted that every child can learn. He altered teaching methods to fit the
needs of each child and worked collaboratively with public schools, anticipating
later themes of community psychology (Levine & Levine, 1992). Despite these
examples, later psychological practice focused on individual disorders and on professional assessment and treatment, primarily with adults. Kurt Lewin and Marie Jahoda

fled Europe with the rise of the Nazi Germany. They encouraged others to ask new research questions focused on social relations and contextual factors related to health, and they demonstrated how research could be used as an active force to improve the social world. It should be noted that at these formative stages for psychology in the United States, ideas and examples from Europe were influential on persons interested in studying individuals in relation to their social environments. Witmer had studied for his Ph.D. in Germany, and Lewin and Jahoda brought their ideas to the United States as they escaped Nazi persecution a generation later. These early developers of psychology laid the groundwork that would later be picked up by U.S. psychologists interested in forming the field of community psychology.

Psychology in Cultural Perspective

For most of its history, psychology has been primarily conceptualized, researched, and practiced by European and European American men, often with research participants from the same background. When women were studied directly, it was often within a theoretical framework based on male experience. The experiences of persons of differing racial and ethnic backgrounds were seldom a focus of study until recently and often within a northern European or North American cultural framework. This approach to psychological inquiry assumed that individuals are largely independent of each other and that research findings were largely universal across contexts and people. As we will discuss in more detail in Chapter 7, contemporary discussions of cultural influences on behavior, interdependence in relationships, and the relationships of individuals to communities are important for community psychology, although they have been secondary concerns or ignored by much of the field of psychology (e.g., Miller, 1976; Sarason, 1974, 1994; 2003).

In a classic challenge to traditional ways of thinking about psychology, Kenneth Gergen (1973, p. 312) argued that from a cross-cultural perspective, many psychological concepts would seem very different. High self-esteem—prized in Western, individualistic cultures—could be considered an excessive focus on oneself in cultural contexts that emphasize interdependence among group members. Similarly, in many world contexts, seeking to control events and outcomes in one's life might communicate a lack of respect for others. Social conformity, something to be resisted in the worldview of Western individualism, could be interpreted in a collectivist cultural context as behavior cementing the solidarity of an important group. This is not to say that individualistic concepts are mistaken, simply that they are not universal.

Power and control are psychological concepts especially influenced by individualistic thinking (Riger 1993; van Uchelen, 2000). Psychologists often have focused on whether an autonomous individual can exercise control over his or her circumstances. Believing that you hold such internal control, in general, is often associated with measures of psychological adjustment in individualistic contexts (Rotter, 1966. 1990). This approach assumes an independent self with a clear boundary between self and others. While applicable in individualistic contexts, such a view does not hold in contexts where interdependence is prized: in non-Western cultures or in close-knit communities in Western cultures (van Uchelen, 2000). Individuals in those contexts assume that to exert control, they must cooperate with others. This weakens the psychological distinction between "internal" and "external" control. Moreover, feminist thinkers (e.g., Miller, 1976; Riger, 1993) have noted that psychological conceptions of control often equate pursuit of one's goals or interests with dominating others. But greater control of one's circumstances can often be pursued through cooperation (Shapiro, Schwartz, & Astin, 1996; van Uchelen, 2000).

These examples are only a few of the issues for which cultural awareness is needed in psychology. Many areas of the discipline, including community psychology, are now beginning to study individuals within cultural and social contexts. Yet as we shall see in this and later chapters, this is not always easily put into practice.

Community psychology represents both a reaction to the limitations of mainstream psychology and an extension of it. The field developed through this tension and continues to experience it today. To understand further how the field has developed in the United States, we briefly consider events in U.S. society during the mid-20th century.

THE FORMATIVE CONTEXTS OF
COMMUNITY PSYCHOLOGY

During the 1930s and 1940s, most countries of the world were confronted with a disastrous economic depression and involvement in World War II, which had wide-ranging effects on social life. While fighting and casualties were limited on U.S. territory, the social forces of the depression and war shaped community life in ways that had not been expected. Women entered the paid workforce in unprecedented numbers. Many of them were laid off at war's end, but their competence had been established and helped fuel later feminist efforts. African Americans and other persons of color served their country and returned home less willing to tolerate racial discrimination. American troops of Japanese ancestry earned recognition for bravery, while at home, Japanese Americans were incarcerated in detention camps. Anti-Semitism, openly practiced in academia and elsewhere, lost influence in the wake of the Holocaust. Social forces and the importance of environmental factors in people's lives were accepted as major influences and thus the focus of study and intervention.

Similarly, large-scale interventions were seen to be effective during the 1930s and 1940s. Roosevelt's New Deal created social safety net structures that continue to this day (e.g., Social Security). The social policy established by the postwar G.I. Bill sent many veterans to college and broadened the focus of universities and helped to spur economic development. Government policy was seen as an active force in promoting individual and community well-being. If the government could organize a response to win a world war fought on three different continents, what could it not do (Glidewell, 1994)? In terms of health care, the U.S. government responded to widespread psychological problems among returning combat veterans by funding the expansion of clinical psychology; this was an instrumental step in establishing the modern field of clinical psychology. There was a widespread belief that we can improve society with policy and resources. Similarly, countries in Western Europe began exploring ways that they might cooperate economically and politically, resulting in the creation of the European Union and a common currency. Many countries created new initiatives to address human needs and avoid the pain and suffering inflicted by economic crisis and war.

These events set in motion important changes in societies from the 1950s to the 1980s that have led to the emergence of community psychology across the world (Wilson, Hayes, Greene, Kelly, & Iscoe, 2003). We will describe five forces that influenced this emergence. (Admittedly, this framework oversimplifies the many factors involved.) All five forces reflect increasingly community-oriented thinking about personal, community, and social problems: (a) interest in preventive perspectives, (b) reforms in mental health systems, (c) developments in group dynamics research and action, (d) movements for social change and liberation, and (e) an undercurrent of optimism about social change efforts. (See Levine, Perkins, & Perkins [2005] for a detailed alternative account of these origins.) The relative importance of each factor varies by national context. For our discussion, we begin with examples from the United States, where community psychology first gained prominence as an academic discipline and field of practice.

Preventive Perspectives on Problems in Living

No mass disorder afflicting humankind has ever been eliminated or brought under control by attempts at treating the affected individual. (Albee & Gulotta, 1997, pp. 19–20)

The first of these forces involved the development of a preventive perspective on mental health services—influenced by the concepts of the discipline of public health. Public health is concerned with preventing illness more than with treating it. Prevention may take a variety of forms: sanitation, vaccination, education, early detection, and treatment. Moreover, public health takes a population perspective, focusing on control or prevention of disease within a community or society, not merely for an individual. As implied in the quotation, long-term successes in controlling such diseases as smallpox and polio have come from preventive public health programs, not from treating persons already suffering from the disease. Treatment is humane but does not lead to wider control of disease. Responding to a greater need for mental health services after World War II, a few psychiatrists began applying public health perspectives that emphasized environmental factors in mental disorder. They proposed early intervention for psychological problems and community-based services as primary modes of intervention rather than isolation in hospital settings. Furthermore, they wanted to use community strengths to prevent problems in living (Caplan, 1961; Klein & Lindemann, 1961; Lindemann, 1957). This new approach emphasized the importance of life crises and transitions as the points of preventive intervention for mental health services. Rather than waiting for full-blown disorders to develop, the mental health clinics could develop education about coping and support for the bereaved to have a preventive effect.

The public health prevention model was also applied to programs that addressed the mental health needs of children in schools. In 1953, in St. Louis County, Missouri, psychologist John Glidewell joined Margaret Gildea to establish programs in schools and with parents designed to prevent behavior disorders in children (Glidewell, 1994). In 1958, in Rochester, New York, Emory Cowen and colleagues began the Primary Mental Health Project in the elementary schools of Rochester, New York, seeking to detect early indicators of school maladjustment in students and intervene before full-blown problems appeared (Cowen et al., 1973). These innovative programs involved collaboration with community members that helped to initiate second-order change. They also evaluated their efforts with empirical research. Thus, they helped forge the community psychology values of wellness, community collaboration, and empirical grounding.

Although not within a public health framework, another early program in schools was noteworthy. Seymour Sarason and colleagues at the Yale Psycho-Educational Clinic began collaborating with schools and other institutions for youth in 1962. (Sarason took the clinic's name from Lightner Witmer's early clinic mentioned previously.) Working alongside school staff, the clinic staff sought to understand "the culture of the school" and to identify and foster "contexts of productive learning" to promote youth development. The clinic focused on understanding and changing settings, not just individuals, by taking an ecological approach that foreshadowed important community psychology themes (Sarason, 1972, 1995).

While prevention initiatives represented important innovations, they encountered sharp resistance by advocates of traditional clinical care and did not yet enter the mainstream of either psychiatry or clinical psychology (Strother, 1987).

Reforms in Mental Health Systems

> They had more patients than beds, more patients than blankets. It was run like a feudal estate that turned money back to the state every year.... One of our group documented all these things and brought it to the state legislature, which had a special session and appropriated more money for all the state hospitals.... This is an example of how, if you take action, good things can happen. (Edgerton, 2000)

A second force leading to the emergence of community psychology involved sweeping changes in the U.S. system of mental health care. These began with World War II and continued into the 1960s (Levine, 1981; Sarason, 1988). After the war, a flood of veterans returned to civilian life traumatized by war. The Veterans Administration (VA) was created to care for the unprecedented numbers of veterans with medical (including mental) disorders. In addition, the National Institute of Mental Health (NIMH) was established to coordinate funding for mental health research and training. Both of these federal administrations decided to rely heavily on psychology (Kelly, 2003).

These events led to a rapid expansion of the field of clinical psychology and continue to influence it today. Clinical training became a specialized program within university psychology departments. Clinical skills were primarily learned in medical settings (often in VA hospitals, working with adult male veterans). This medical approach to psychology was codified at the Boulder Conference in 1948. Its emphasis on individual psychotherapy was a product of the needs of the VA and the treatment orientation of a medical model. The environmental perspective of Witmer's and other early psychological clinics—another possible pathway for the new field—was largely overlooked and became an important missed opportunity (Humphreys, 1996; Sarason, 2003b).

Also emerging in the postwar society was a movement for reform in the quality of mental health care (Levine, 1981; Sarason, 1974) and reducing the reliance on large mental health hospitals. Journalistic accounts and films documented inhumane conditions in psychiatric hospitals, and citizen groups advocated reform. Advances in psychotropic medication made prolonged hospitalization less necessary, strengthening reform efforts. Over the past 50 years, the number of regional mental hospitals has been greatly reduced throughout most industrialized countries, as many have been closed and deemed not worth reforming (Kloos, 2010). Between 1972 and 1982, the number of hospitals with more than 1,000 psychiatric beds was reduced by 50–80% in Denmark, England, Ireland, Italy, Spain, and Sweden (Freeman, Fryers, & Henderson, 1985). Similar patterns occurred in North America and Australia (Carling, 1995; Newton et al., 2000). With so many large mental hospitals closing, new models of care were needed.

In 1961, the federally sponsored U.S. Joint Commission on Mental Illness and Mental Health recommended sweeping changes in mental health care (Joint Commission, 1961). In one of the commission's studies, psychologist George Albee (1959) reviewed recent research that documented surprisingly high rates of mental disorders, compared this with the costs of training clinical professionals, and concluded that the nation could never afford to train enough professionals to provide clinical care for all who needed it. Albee and others called for an emphasis on prevention. Psychologist Marie Jahoda headed efforts to broaden thinking about mental illness by defining qualities of positive mental health—a forerunner of current concepts of wellness, resilience, and strengths (see Box 2.1). Jahoda also

---

B o x 2.1   Marie Jahoda: A "Foremother" of Community Psychology

The work of social psychologist Marie Jahoda foreshadowed and influenced today's community psychology. In 1930, Jahoda and her associates formed an interdisciplinary team to research the psychological effects of unemployment (Jahoda, Lazarsfeld, & Zeisel, 1933/1971). They studied Marienthal, an Austrian village where the principal workplaces closed as worldwide economic depression deepened. Their study was the first to connect unemployment with psychological experiences, which ranged from resignation and despair to practical coping and hardy resilience. The research team focused on studying the community as well as individuals and used documents, questionnaires, interviews, individual and family histories, and participant and nonparticipant observation. They collaborated as partners with community members and found practical ways to serve the community. They sought to understand Marienthal in its own terms, not to test hypotheses for generalization to other locales. Their research has influenced much later work, including community psychology research today (Fryer & Fagan, 2003; Kelly, 2003). When fascists took power in Austria, Jahoda was jailed and then allowed to

emigrate to Britain; she also lived in the United States (Unger, 2001).

Partly because of her research on resilience and strengths among Marienthal families, in the 1950s, the U.S. Joint Commission on Mental Health asked Jahoda to lead an interdisciplinary committee to define positive mental health—not simply as absence of mental disorder but as the presence of positive qualities. The group's report identified criteria of positive mental health, including a strong personal identity, motivation for psychological growth, pursuit of values, resilience under stress, independent choices and actions, empathy, and adequacy in love, work, play, and interpersonal relations. Jahoda and associates concluded that positive mental health is a value-laden concept influenced by social context. For example, they argued that for Western cultures, autonomy is a key component of positive mental health but that it may be less important elsewhere (Jahoda, 1958; Jahoda, in Kelly, 2003). The report defined qualities of persons but not of conditions that might foster mental health. Yet it was an important advance, foreshadowing current concepts of community psychology and positive psychology.

advocated identifying conditions that inhibited personal mental health and altering those conditions through prevention and social change (Albee, 1995; Kelly, 2003). However, in their final report, most Joint Commission members remained committed to individualized professional treatment (Levine, 1981).

As a response to the Joint Commission report, the NIMH proposed a national system of community mental health centers (CMHCs; Goldston, 1994; Levine, 1981). With the support of President Kennedy, whose sister suffered from a mental disorder, and through timely advocacy by members of Congress, the NIMH, and the National Mental Health Association, Congress passed the Community Mental Health Centers Act in 1963. CMHCs were given a different mandate than traditional psychiatric hospitals, including care for persons with mental disorders in the community, crisis intervention and emergency services, consultation with community agencies (e.g., schools, human services, and police), and prevention programs (Goldston, 1994; Levine, 1981). Indeed, in many countries, community mental health centers were founded with the charge of developing care for serious mental health problems within the community contexts where people lived rather than at remote hospitals (Kloos, 2010). The implementation of the CMHC approach led directly to discussions that resulted in the emergence of community psychology.

Group Dynamics and Action Research

Kurt Lewin was not concerned with research topics considered "proper" within psychology, but with understanding interesting situations.... Lewin was a creative person who liked to have other people create with him. (Zander, in Kelly, 2003; Zander, 1995)

A third force influencing the development of community psychology originated in social psychology: the group dynamics and action research traditions that began with Kurt Lewin (Kelly, 2003; Marrow, 1969; Zander, 1995).

Lewin spent much of his career demonstrating to laboratory-based psychologists and to citizens that social action and research could be integrated in ways that strengthen both. He is known for asserting "there is nothing so practical as a good theory" (Marrow, 1969). Lewin was a founder of the Society for the Psychological Study of Social Issues (SPSSI), long an important voice in U.S. psychology. During the 1940s, as a Jewish refugee from Nazi Germany, he became interested in how the study of group dynamics could be used to address social and community problems.

The first community problem with which the Lewin action research team became involved was not primarily a mental health issue. The team was asked to help develop methods to reduce anti-Semitism in Connecticut communities and it began conducting citizen group discussions (Marrow, 1969, pp. 210–211). The insistence of citizens that they be included when psychologists analyzed these discussions and their disagreement with those psychologists' views led Lewin's team to focus on group dynamics and to the creation of training group methods (T-groups; Bradford, Gibb, & Benne, 1964). After Lewin's death, his students and others founded the National Training Laboratories (NTL) in Bethel, Maine, a center for professionals and citizens to learn about the dynamics within and between groups in everyday life (Marrow, 1969; Zander, 1995). The NTL workshops (still offered

---

B o x 2.2   Exemplary Early Settings in Community Psychology

Community psychology emerged not simply from individuals but from trailblazing *settings,* many of them where psychologists and citizens worked together. We chose four early settings for a closer look: the Wellesley Human Relations Service, the Community Lodge, the Yale Psycho-Educational Clinic, and the Primary Mental Health Project. We have described their work elsewhere in this chapter. Here, we focus on their personal-emotional meaning and how they involved collaboration with citizens, appreciation of community strengths, and second-order change in role relationships. Those themes appear especially clearly in interviews with early community psychologists conducted by James Kelly and students (excerpted in Kelly, 2003).

The Wellesley Human Relations Service was founded at the request of community leaders. While other mental health professionals asserted their special knowledge of mental disorders and treatment, Erich Lindemann, the service's first leader, stressed the importance of learning from citizens and enabling them to take responsibility for the mental health of their community. Donald Klein (1995) described preparing for a meeting with community leaders in which he planned primarily to inform them of what the service could do for their community. "No, no," Lindemann told him, "it's what we can learn *from them* that's important."

Even in interviews conducted decades later, key interpersonal qualities come through when Don Klein and Jim Kelly discuss their years with the Human Relations Service: a certain gentleness, an appreciation of community strengths and of listening carefully, an attention to personal relationships. These are rooted in part in Lindemann's leadership style, Klein's experiences with the National Training Laboratories (based on Lewin's group dynamics work), and the experience

of working alongside citizens as partners in Wellesley (Klein, 1995; Kelly, 1997, 2003).

The Community Lodge went further, creating a setting that empowered men with psychological disorders. George Fairweather and colleagues at a VA hospital began by seeking to improve group therapy with their patients. Their experiences and research eventually led them to finding that a group of men with serious psychological disorders—working together and helping each other in their own daily lives—could live together successfully outside the hospital. The success of the Community Lodge contradicted many professionals' assumptions about the capabilities of persons with mental disorders. Its success was principally due to the emergence of unrecognized strengths and mutual support among its participants. Fairweather's folksy, commonsense style and facilitative-consultative role supported that emergence.

An important point in any community partnership comes when citizens assert control. Fairweather later described the poignant moment when the first lodge members thanked him for his efforts but also stated "it's time for you to go." Fairweather termed this a "horrible moment for a professional," yet he understood and accepted their decision. The lodge had become its own community, and the presence of a professional, however well-intentioned and supportive, would hinder its future development. The original lodge and others have enjoyed sustained success (Fairweather, 1994; Kelly, 2003).

Seymour Sarason described the Yale Psycho-Educational Clinic as having three aims: to understand the "culture of the school" and how that often inhibits productive learning, to gain that understanding experientially through performing services in schools, and to model for university students the everyday practical

---

today) focus on the development of skills for working in groups and communities. They are not therapy or support groups and are not clinical in orientation. Instead, they embody the social–psychological concern with group dynamics. This approach ran counter to the prevailing individualism and laboratory focus of psychology and involved a collaborative partnership of professionals and citizens.

Several early community psychologists (Don Klein, Jack Glidewell, Wil Edgerton) worked with NTL, thus linking the group dynamics and action research tradition with innovations in prevention and community mental health (Edgerton, 2000; Glidewell, 1994; Klein, 1995). The Lewinian focus on action research, in collaboration with citizens, was a forerunner of community psychology research today. The importance of personal relationships and group process can be seen in three exemplary early settings in community psychology, profiled in Box 2.2.

involvement of their faculty in schools (Sarason, in Kelly, 2003). These goals indicate a willingness to step outside the usual research methods, to ask open-ended questions and learn from rigorous analysis of personal experience, and to take risks to promote learning.

At the outset, Sarason and his colleagues were not entirely sure what they were looking for or what roles and findings might evolve in their work. Murray Levine described his first job at the clinic as being to "go out to the schools and find a way to be useful." A smiling Sarason later told students how he applied for grants to support the clinic but was unable to specify exactly what he meant by "culture of the school" or what research methods he would use to study it. His proposals were rejected twice. But the clinic's approach eventually led to influential books, papers, and concepts that permeate community psychology today. Clinic staff analyzed their experiences intensively in Friday staff meetings. These involved deep, wide-ranging scrutiny of personal experiences and events at the school, asking tough questions about their meaning (Levine, in Kelly, 2003; Sarason, 1995; Sarason, in Kelly, 2003).

The Psycho-Educational Clinic experience was deeply personal for its staff and students. Many influential community psychologists testify to the clinic's importance in their lives. Rhona Weinstein's innovative work in schools began there (we described her work with "Eric" in Chapter 1). Sarason intervened on her behalf when her application was rejected by those at Yale who did not desire to admit women (Weinstein, 2005). Murray Levine still carries his key to the old clinic building, a token of his personal attachment to the people there (Levine, in Kelly, 2003).

Emory Cowen has been described by George Albee as "the tallest oak in the forest of prevention" (Albee, 2000, xiii). Much of his stature came from the Primary Mental Health Project (PMHP) and the Center for Community Study (now the Children's Institute) that Cowen founded and headed at the University of Rochester.

Cowen and colleagues (Cowen, Hightower, Pedro-Carroll, Work, Wyman, & Haffey, 1996; Cowen, in Kelly, 2003) have described how PMHP grew from several mental health revelations of the 1950s: that we lack enough personnel to help all children in need; that early identification of young children with academic, behavioral, or emotional problems and prompt intervention would forestall later, more intractable problems; and that paraprofessionals building positive relationships with at-risk children and helping them learn key coping skills could accomplish at least as much as professional services. In 1963, Cowen and his team developed the role of Child Associates—paraprofessionals working under professional supervision in schools, providing support and tangible assistance to children. Cowen and his teams of colleagues and students built PMHP from a pilot project in a single school to over 2,000 schools worldwide. The Center for Community Study broadened its focus over the years to include action research on such topics as social problem-solving skills training in schools, preventive services for children of divorce, and child resilience. Its work in prevention and Cowen's (1994, 2000a) concept of wellness helped shape community, developmental, clinical, and school psychology. Many influential community psychologists worked with Cowen on PMHP or other projects; an edited volume honored his conceptual contributions and innovative community work (Cicchetti, Rappaport, Sandler, & Weissberg, 2000).

Movements for Social Change and Liberation

I am sure that we all recognize that there are some things in our society, some things in our world, to which we should never be adjusted.... We must never adjust ourselves to racial discrimination and racial segregation. We must never adjust ourselves to religious bigotry. We must never adjust ourselves to economic conditions that take necessities from the many to give luxuries to the few. We must never adjust ourselves to the madness of militarism, and the self-defeating effects of physical violence. (King, 1968, p. 185)

A fourth force influencing the development of community psychology in many countries involves movements for social change and liberation. For U.S. community psychology, the civil rights and feminist movements most directly influenced psychology, but the peace, environmental, antipoverty, and gay rights movements were also important. These movements are associated in the popular mindset with the 1960s, although all had much longer historical roots. They reached a crescendo during the 1960s and early 1970s, bringing their grievances and ideals to national attention.

The ideals of these social movements had several commonalities (Kelly, 1990; Wilson et al., 2003). One was the challenging of hierarchical, unequal role relationships between Whites and people of color; men and women; experts and citizens; persons of heterosexual and homosexual orientations; and the powerful and the oppressed. Youth often assumed leadership: College students sat in at segregated lunch counters, participated in Freedom Rides through the segregated South, led antiwar protests, and organized the first Earth Day. Values common to these movements match well with some core values of community psychology: social justice, citizen participation, and respect for diversity (Wilson et al., 2003).

Another commonality of these social movements was that they sought to link social action at the local and national levels. Advocates in each movement pursued change in local communities and nationally. "Think globally, act locally" became a familiar motto. The movements advocated changes at each of the ecological levels that we delineated in Chapter 1. For example, the various groups in the civil rights movement used different approaches. For decades, the NAACP (National Association for the Advancement of Colored People) employed policy research and legal advocacy in the courts. Other organizations used community-mobilizing approaches: time-limited mass demonstrations that attracted media attention (Birmingham and Selma campaigns, Freedom Rides, the March on Washington). Less-recognized local people pursued long-term community organizing for voter registration and other aims, an approach that generated fewer famous names but many enduring community changes (Lewis, 1995; Payne, 1995). Women, including Ella Baker, Fannie Lou Hamer, and Septima Clark, often were local leaders (Collier-Thomas & Franklin, 2001). All these coincided with the emerging power of national television to portray social conflicts to national audiences. It became more difficult to deny the existence of racism (Wilson et al., 2003).

A few psychologists played a policy advocacy role in the civil rights movement. The research of Kenneth and Mamie Clark, African American psychologists, was cited in the 1954 Supreme Court desegregation decision in the case of *Brown vs. Board of Education*. The Clarks' research, which originated in Mamie Clark's master's thesis, compared children's reactions to dolls of differing skin colors to measure the self-esteem of African American and European American children. Advocacy and research, including court testimony, by Kenneth Clark and members of SPSSI was important in the NAACP lawsuits against segregated schools (e.g., Clark, 1953; Clark, Chein, & Cook, 1952/2004). However, the reaction of the professional psychological establishment was mixed. Other psychologists testified to defend segregation. Clark later came to believe that the social science advocacy that led to the 1954 Court decision had underestimated the depth of racism in the United States (Benjamin & Crouse, 2002; Keppel, 2002; Lal, 2002).

The feminist movement has shared many goals with community psychology and continues to challenge the field (Gridley & Turner, 2010). In 1968, psychologist Naomi Weisstein gave an address with the spirited title "Psychology Constructs the Female: Or the Fantasy Life of the Male Psychologist" (Weisstein, 1971/1993). Weisstein's paper has been described as an "earthquake … shaking the foundations of psychology" (Riger, in Kelly, 2003)—a formative event for many women in community psychology and women's studies. Weisstein questioned whether psychology at the time knew anything about women at all, especially after years of research that systematically excluded women or interpreted their responses from men's perspectives. Moreover, she emphasized the importance of social context in shaping choices and acts and the ways in which contexts constrained women's choices. Her critique was one of many roots of feminist scholarship that has transformed concepts and methods of inquiry in many disciplines, including community psychology. Moreover, Weisstein and others in the women's movement were activists in their communities, founding settings to support women's development and advocating for social change (Dan, Campbell, Riger, & Strobel, 2003). Although there are substantial common values between feminism and community psychology, there are differences, principally that feminism arose as a social movement willing to take risks (Mulvey, 1988), whereas community psychology originated as an academic discipline.

As the social change movements of the 1960s progressed, many psychologists became convinced that citizen and community action was necessary to bring about social change on multiple fronts and that psychology had a role to play (Bennett et al., 1966; Kelly, 1990; Sarason, 1974; Walsh, 1987). In 1967, Martin Luther King Jr. addressed the American Psychological Association, calling for psychologists to study and promote youth development, citizen leadership, and social action, especially among African Americans (King, 1968). But the vision of a socially involved psychology was not widely supported in the field. King's speech was arranged by activist psychologists, including Kenneth Clark, over the objections of APA leaders (Pickren & Tomes, 2002).

Undercurrents of Optimism

We had just won a huge war, the biggest ever. And we had started from way back—we had been about to get whipped. If we could do this, we could do anything, including solving all the social problems of the U.S.: race relations, poverty…. There was a sense of optimism … a messianic zeal…. We believed that we could change the world, and we felt that we had just done it.

Solving social problems is sobering…. To win wars, you kill people and destroy things. To solve social problems, you must build things, create things. (Glidewell, 1994)

Glidewell's remarks illustrate a fifth force that provided underlying support for previous forces we have described: optimism about the ability to find solutions for social problems. That optimism is very American in nature (Kelly, 1990; Levine & Levine, 1992; Sarason, 1994) and supported the emergence of community psychology.

In 1965, the Johnson Administration initiated a collection of federally funded Great Society programs, popularly known as the War on Poverty. These included educational initiatives such as Head Start, job training and employment programs, and local community action organizations. Federal funders of community mental health and of the War on Poverty looked to the social sciences, including psychology, as a source of scientific solutions to social problems. This attitude grew out of a very American faith in science and technology—based on experiences in World War II and the Cold War and gaining clearest expression in the space program. That faith has since been replaced by a more sober sense of the real but limited utility of social science for social change, reflected in Glidewell's remarks.

COMMUNITY PSYCHOLOGY: DEVELOPING AN IDENTITY

As a new field, community psychology had to distinguish itself from other fields, such as clinical psychology, social psychology, sociology, and community mental health. As an emerging field, it needed to develop new conceptual frameworks for linking individual well-being with higher levels of analysis. It needed to propose new ways of conducting research and interventions. A focus on social community and change has helped to orient these developments. Thus, community psychology expanded its scope of potential foci for intervention. Poverty, lack of resources, and organizational functioning were seen as important targets for intervention. As the field developed its own identity, it proposed new ways of defining problems and new kinds of interventions. In the United States and several European countries, it first had to distinguish itself from developments in community mental health.

The Swampscott Conference

In May 1965, 39 psychologists gathered in Swampscott, Massachusetts to discuss training psychologists for new roles in the CMHC system (Bennett et al., 1966). Most of the group described themselves as atypical psychologists because their involvement in community work had transformed their interests and skills (Bennett et al., 1966). Many were forging new connections between academic researchers, mental health professionals, and citizens. At Swampscott, they took over a conference called to design a training model for community mental health and made it a founding event for the new, broader field of community psychology.

The new field would focus on "psychological processes that link social systems with individual behavior in complex interaction" (Bennett et al., 1966, p. 7).

It would not be limited to mental health issues or settings and would be distinct from community mental health, although the two would overlap.

Conferees agreed on the concept of *participant–conceptualizer* to describe the role of a community psychologist. This is someone who would act as a community change agent as well as conduct research on the effectiveness of those efforts. They discussed activities for a new community psychology: consulting with schools and community agencies, developing prevention programs, advocating for community and social change, and collaborating with citizens. Notice that they were distinguishing themselves from activities of clinical psychology (e.g. assessment, testing, and therapy). They also called for interdisciplinary collaboration and humility in the face of complex community dynamics (Bennett et al., 1966).

Swampscott was an energizing turning point for its participants and for those who soon flocked to the emerging field. Many had felt isolated in traditional academic and clinical settings and rejoiced to find colleagues with similar visions and values. "We found each other!" is a common memory among Swampscott participants (Klein, 1987). Thirty years later, describing the impact of Swampscott to a student audience, Donald Klein spontaneously smiled, drew himself up, and with enthusiasm in his eyes and voice asserted, "[T]he excitement of the conference is still as if it happened yesterday" (Klein, in Kelly, 2003).

Establishing a Field of Community Psychology

After Swampscott, U.S. community psychology gradually developed its own distinctive identity and diverged from community mental health. During the 1970s, community psychologists created many conventions necessary for founding and sustaining a new discipline. These included founding training programs and federal initiatives to fund community psychology research and intervention (Cowen, 1973). Many universities were expanding at this time, and community psychology provided an academic discipline that could help address the social issues so prominent in public discourse. As a new field, textbooks had to be written, which helped shape the field's identity (Revenson & Seidman, 2002) and are still influential (e.g., Heller & Monahan, 1977; Rappaport, 1977; Levine & Perkins, 1987). The perspectives of this new field's research and intervention were not always well received or well understood in existing academic psychology journals. In 1973, two new journals were founded that continue to serve as records of the best community psychology research in the United States and for some international authors: the *American Journal of Community Psychology* and the *Journal of Community Psychology*.

During this formative period in U.S. community psychology's development, several key conceptual frameworks and clarification of values were proposed that have become cornerstones of the field. Initially, community psychologists had some difficulty in charting a new path consistent with the vision of their new perspective. Emory Cowen's (1973) *Annual Review of Psychology* chapter "Social and Community Interventions" (the first devoted to this topic) observed that less than 3% of community mental health research articles had a prevention focus. Nonetheless, he called for more emphasis on *prevention*, which had been expected given early adoption of public health perspectives to psychology. Cowen identified a number of interventions, principally dealing with child or youth development, and often focused on disadvantaged populations and collaboration with local citizens, which we discuss in Chapters 9 and 10. Second, James Kelly, Edison Trickett, and others proposed that ecological concepts could enhance the understanding of how individual coping or adaptation varied in social environments (e.g., schools) with differing psychosocial qualities (Trickett, Kelly, & Todd, 1972; Kelly, 1979a). This approach suggests understanding how environments and individuals are interrelated and will be presented in greater detail in Chapter 5. Third, Seymour Sarason published another early critique of the field: *The Psychological Sense of Community* (1974). He proposed that community psychology abandon its individualistic focus on mental health services and embrace a broader concern with the "*psychological sense of community*." As we discuss in Chapter 6, he argued that community psychology should focus broadly on the relationships between individuals and their communities rather than just on the psychological adjustment of individuals.

Fourth, Julian Rappaport (1977) made persuasive arguments that the field of community psychology needs to focus on its values to guide research and social action. In summarizing the first 10 years of the field's development, Rappaport proposed valuing *human diversity, collaboration, social justice*, and *strengths* rather than deficits as unifying concepts that are needed to guide the field's value in *empirical* investigation of social problems. A few years later, Rappaport (1981) extended these ideas to argue that an emphasis on a community's *self-determination* and *empowerment* were as vital to the field of community psychology as *prevention* (see Chapter 11). Finally, in her presidential address to the professional community psychology organization, Barbara Dohrenwend (1978) proposed an influential framework for an *ecological model of stress and coping* that integrated many of the emerging themes in community psychology and provided a guide for intervention (see Chapter 8 for a discussion). Many of these concepts are now familiar notions but were innovations at the time. These advancements were critical in helping community psychologists define the field, articulate its core values, and distinguish it from community mental health.

COMMUNITY PSYCHOLOGY IN SHIFTING SOCIAL CONTEXTS

As it has developed a distinctive identity, community psychology also has coped with changing social and political contexts. The contexts and conditions that helped to create community psychology in the 1960s and 1970s began to change in the 1980s, requiring community psychologists to examine the relevance of their field as societies changed and to adapt to those changes. Many countries with active fields of community psychology, including Australia, Britain, Canada, Germany, New Zealand, and the United States, became more socially conservative in the 1980s. Over time, countries have elected leaders that are identified as more liberal or conservative, although what is considered liberal or conservative has shifted. In this section, we consider how ongoing economic, political, and social forces have shaped contemporary community psychology.

In the 1980s in the United States, the community-social perspective on social issues that helped create community psychology was supplanted by strongly biomedical views. Coming from politics, medicine, and science, national discussions changed in how they defined problems, consideration of which problems were important, and support for which interventions were seen as being worthy of funding. These critical changes were propelled in part by genuine advances in biomedical research and treatment. However, the pendulum swing was also the result of social forces. As society and government became more conservative, funding agencies called for psychological research on biomedical causes of mental disorders rather than social causes, and researchers' interests followed suit (Humphreys & Rappaport, 1993).

Federal attention also shifted from mental health to substance abuse. Social factors associated with mental health had been a particular emphasis of the progressive social era. In the 1980s, President Reagan declared a War on Drugs. It focused on causal factors for drug abuse within the individual, such as genes, illness, and willpower. It also greatly expanded the use of police and prisons while shifting attention and resources away from mental health. The federal prison population doubled during the Reagan administration; most of the increase was in drug offenders (Humphreys & Rappaport, 1993).

With these different forces defining and prioritizing social problems differently, research followed this trend. Psychological journals for the years 1981–1992 contained 170 articles for drug addiction and personality and only three references for drug addiction and poverty; similar findings appear if similar index terms are searched. Likewise, primary federal funding for research on homelessness was provided by the Alcohol, Drug Abuse, and Mental Health Administration, not the Department of Housing and Urban Development. Research thus focused on the subgroup of homeless persons with substance abuse and mental disorders rather than on affordable housing and employment—issues that affected all homeless persons (Humphreys & Rappaport, 1993; Shinn, 1992).

After declining during the 1960s and remaining largely steady during the 1970s, the proportion of children living in poverty rose after 1980. In the early 1990s, it returned to mid-1960s levels (U.S. Census Bureau, 2005). Homelessness became a visible problem in many U.S. cities. The focus of community psychology practice shifted and began to address these issues more than explicit mental health interventions (Levine, Perkins, & Perkins, 2005).

In the United States at least, this generally conservative period has persisted into the 21st century, with some variations in intensity, and with either political party in power. This poses challenges and opportunities for community psychology. Many citizens and opinion leaders fail to recognize the impact of complex social and economic forces on personal life. Faced with many voters suspicious of government, elected officials continue to cut taxes and slash funding for many community and social programs, unlike the 1950s. Community programs that are growing tend to focus on helping individuals and families change and have emphasized a microsystem level of analysis more than higher levels of analysis. For example, involvement in self-help groups and spiritual small groups (not dependent on government funding) has burgeoned (Kessler, Mickelson, & Zhao, 1997; Wuthnow, 1994) while comprehensive, integrated mental systems have not (New Freedom Commission, 2003). Problem definitions that are not socially conservative also have difficulty obtaining funding. Community programs involving sexuality (e.g., teen pregnancy, HIV prevention, or sexual orientation) are especially controversial. Before we discuss how community psychologists respond to these shifts in public perspective, we must consider some lessons to be drawn from the history we have already described about the relationships of community psychology and its social contexts.

Defining Social Issues in Progressive and Conservative Eras

Murray Levine and Adeline Levine (1970, 1992), a community psychologist and a sociologist, wrote a classic historical analysis of how social and political forces in the United States have shaped public beliefs about social problems and helping services. Their historical work concerned services to children and families in the early 20th century, but their analysis also fits several trends in the history of community psychology.

Levine and Levine proposed a simple hypothesis. In times that are socially and politically more progressive, human problems will be conceptualized in environmental terms (e.g., community or societal). Progressive times are not necessarily associated with one political party but are marked by optimism about the possibility of lessening social problems as varied as poverty, drug abuse, crime, psychological disorders, and the educational and behavioral problems of children. In the common sense of a progressive period, social causes of such problems will be emphasized, and community or social interventions will be developed to address these. Persons are to be helped by improving their circumstances or resources, giving them greater freedom and choice in their lives. Not all political progressives will endorse an environmental view, but a progressive trend in society overall tends to strengthen it.

During more politically conservative times, the same problems will be conceptualized in individualistic terms, emphasizing individual causes. The common sense of the era will locate problems within the biological, psychological, or moral makeup of the individual. These individual deficits must be remedied by changes in the individuals themselves, and programs to help them will seek to change the individuals (and perhaps families). This will enhance their ability to cope with environmental circumstances. Conservative times are not necessarily tied to one political party but to pessimism about whether social problems can be lessened or to the belief that individual changes are more important than wider social change. Not all social conservatives will endorse an individualistic view, but a conservative trend in society overall tends to strengthen it.

Social forces influence how a problem is defined and what is done to address it. They also define what research is considered worth doing (and worth funding) and how that research is applied in practice. As we have noted, community psychology in the United States arose in the 1960s—a progressive time that emphasized social and economic root causes of social problems. As we just described, since the 1980s, individualistic thinking has dominated research and funding in the United States on such topics as mental health, drug abuse, and homelessness. Psychological research and practice cannot be insulated from such swings in social-political public thinking.

The differences between more progressive and more conservative periods and between individualistic and environmental perspectives are not absolute (Levine & Levine, 1992). In any historical period, both perspectives are voiced, and some historical periods are difficult to categorize as one or the other. Moreover, the worldview of individualism—focused on individual happiness and autonomy—often outweighs other American ideals (Bellah et al., 1985). A focus on individuals becomes more dominant in more conservative times, yet is powerful even in progressive times.

Both individualistic and environmental perspectives hold truth; neither completely accounts for personal and social difficulties. Recall that the ecological levels of analysis cover a range of perspectives. Environments (including macrosystems) *and* personal factors and choices shape our lives. But progressive and conservative advocates articulate very different goals for social policy and community life, and these often reflect differences along the lines we are discussing. As Levine and Levine showed, the political contexts of the time influence which of those ideas are more widely accepted.

Addressing Social Issues and Equality

To illustrate the importance of problem definitions and community contexts, we consider a classic example from community psychology's formation. While the field developed, much effort was invested in examinations of how social issues are defined and addressed, particularly issues associated with inequality. Today, community psychologists continue to examine how people understand social issues and how interventions are carried out.

Blaming the Victim   Psychologist William Ryan's 1971 book *Blaming the Victim* provided a classic critique of individualistic thinking about social problems. It had widespread impact and was important in the development of community psychology. When we assume that such problems as poverty, drug abuse, educational failure, crime, or unemployment are caused by deficits within individuals, we ignore such larger macrosystem factors as economic conditions, discrimination, or lack of access to good quality health care. In terms of our ecological levels of analysis presented in Chapter 1, we focus only on one level and ignore the potential factors at other levels of analysis. Even if we assume that personal deficits are caused by one's family or by "cultural deprivation," we still locate the deficit within the person and still ignore larger factors. Coining a now-popular term, Ryan (1971) called this thinking *blaming the victim*.

For example, in a community with underfunded schools, in neighborhoods where violence is common, and where many students do poorly on standardized tests, are we to blame the individual students or their parents or something about their community's culture? (All of these can be ways of blaming victims.) Alternatively, we could ask: Why are schools in some communities underfunded? How can the larger society help fund better education for all? What can be done to make all children safe? What community resources could be involved? Are the tests really valid measures of learning, and who decided to use them? These questions address social conditions at multiple ecological levels (see Weinstein, 2002a). The social justice values of community psychology call for us to examine social problems at multiple ecological levels. The pragmatic value of empirical findings leads us to systematically examine multiple ecological levels to account for what contributes to a situation. Focusing on only one level of analysis violates both of these values and will likely be ineffective. An issue unaddressed at one level of analysis usually does not disappear because it is overlooked.

Ryan also questioned whether researchers, policymakers, or others who have never directly experienced a social problem (e.g., poverty) have the best viewpoint for analyzing it. They (often, we) tend to have a middle-class perspective that is not an accurate understanding of poverty's everyday realities. For someone who grew up with the blessings of family and access to community resources, success in school and life may seem largely due to personal characteristics or effort (especially if he or she does not recognize how important those blessings are). However, for persons in poverty and other oppressive conditions, success is heavily influenced by social and economic factors; sadly, the effects of their personal efforts are limited by those factors. Many of the programs that Ryan criticized were "liberal" social and educational programs. These can blame victims, especially if they focus on individual, family, or "cultural" deficits of program participants but fail to address economic and sociopolitical roots of social problems.

Certainly, it is true that personal effort and responsibility do count in life. Nor is every person with a problem necessarily a victim; the term "victim" has been trivialized and stretched far beyond Ryan's original usage (see Sykes, 1992, for a critique). But Ryan drew attention to how social conditions and problem definitions can create or worsen seemingly personal problems. He wanted us to examine how we are trained to ignore those conditions. For Ryan, improving the quality of community life means addressing social and economic root causes.

Fair Play and Fair Shares: Contrasting Definitions of Equality   These individualistic and environmental perspectives correspond to Ryan's discussion of two differing definitions of the cherished American value of equality (1981, 1994). The **Fair Play** definition of equality seeks to assure rules of fairness in competition for economic, educational, or social advancement. The central metaphor is that of a competitive race, with everyone starting at the same place and rules of the contest treating all individuals similarly. If the rules of the race are fair, Fair Players accept great differences in the outcome of the competition, assuming that those differences are caused by individual merit, talent, or effort. "The Fair Player wants an equal opportunity and assurance that the best get the most" (Ryan, 1994, p. 28).

A Fair Play orientation often leads to agreement with statements such as "The most important American idea is that each individual would have the opportunity to rise as high as his talents and hard work will take him" (Ryan, 1994, p. 29). Examples of Fair Play social policies include basing educational and employment decisions on test scores and flat rates of taxation (all income groups are taxed the same percentage).

Ryan (1981, 1994) described an alternative perspective of **Fair Shares**, which focuses on fairness of procedure but is also concerned with minimizing extreme inequalities of outcome. Adopting a Fair Shares perspective does not preclude Fair Play rules, but it goes beyond them to consider other factors. The central metaphor of the Fair Shares perspective is a family or community taking care of all of its members. For example, Fair Shares involves limiting accumulation of wealth so everyone has some minimum level of economic security. While achieving absolute equality is impractical, a Fair Shares approach seeks to avoid extreme inequalities (Ryan, 1994).

Fair Sharers tend to agree with such statements as "For any decent society, the first job is to make sure everyone has enough food, shelter, and health care" and "It simply isn't fair that a small number of people have enormous wealth while millions are so poor they can barely survive" (Ryan, 1994, p. 29). Examples of Fair Shares social policies include universal health care, enriching educational opportunities for all students (not just the gifted), affirmative action in college admissions and employment, and progressive taxation (in which persons with higher incomes pay a higher percentage).

Ryan (1981, 1994) emphasized that although both perspectives have value, Fair Play thinking dominates American discussions of equality and opportunity. Yet Fair Play presumes that all participants in the race for economic and social advancement begin at the same starting line and that we only need to make sure the race is conducted fairly. In fact, few citizens really believe that all persons share the same economic or educational resources, the same chances of employment in well-paying jobs, or the same starting line for advancement. In the United States, as in many countries, a very small proportion of the population controls a very large proportion of the wealth. In our view and in the view of many community psychologists, some methods of strengthening Fair Shares seem necessary to set up truly Fair Play.

Bottom-Up and Top-Down: Contrasting Approaches to Social Change

Whatever our theories about causes of a community or social problem, we can address that problem in either of two ways. Both are important for citizens and community psychologists to understand; both were involved in the social initiatives of the 1960s.

Bottom–up approaches originate at the "grassroots"—among citizens rather than among professionals or the powerful. They reflect attempts by ordinary people to assert control over their everyday lives. They reflect the experiences and ideas of people most affected by a community or social problem (Fawcett et al., 1995). **Top-down** approaches are designed by professionals, community leaders, or similar elites. These may be well intentioned and grounded in research findings but also inevitably reflect the life experiences, worldviews, and interests of the powerful and usually preserve the existing power structure (perhaps with some reform). They also often overlook the strengths of a community (Kretzmann & McKnight, 1993).

Professional mental health care represents a top-down approach; self-help groups tend to use a bottom-up approach. Centralizing decisions in city hall offices is a top-down approach; enabling neighborhood associations to make local decisions is a bottom-up approach. Relying only on psychologists or other professionals to design a program to prevent drug abuse is a top-down approach; involving citizens in making decisions about that program is a bottom-up approach.

Neither approach is always best. Values of social justice, empowerment, citizen participation, collaboration, and community strengths are linked to bottom-up approaches. Yet outside resources (funding, expertise) are often easier to acquire with a top-down approach, which may also better apply research findings on effective programs elsewhere. The two approaches can complement each other, such as when mental health professionals and mutual help groups collaborate or when psychologists and citizens collaborate on research that assists the community.

Opposing Viewpoints and Divergent Reasoning

Social issues involve opposing viewpoints. In many cases, opposing views can both be true (at least, both hold some important truth). Already in this book, we have discussed several such oppositions: persons and contexts; first-order and second-order change; potential conflicts among community psychology core values; individualistic and environmental perspectives on social issues; progressive and conservative viewpoints.

Recognizing important truths in opposing perspectives forces us to hold both in mind, thinking in terms of "both/and" rather than "either/or" (Rappaport, 1981). (This thinking has roots in the dialectical philosophies of Hegel and Marx but is not identical to either system.) Rappaport (1981) advocated **divergent reasoning** for community psychology: identifying multiple truths in the opposing perspectives; recognizing that conflicting viewpoints may usefully coexist; and resisting easy answers. This is *not* to say that attempts to address social problems are useless. But the best thinking about social issues takes into account multiple perspectives and avoids one-sided answers.

Dialogue that respects both positions, rather than debate that creates winners and losers—can promote divergent reasoning. A good metaphor for this process, often suggested in feminist theory (Bond, Belenky, & Weinstock, 2000; Reinharz, 1994) is a frank yet respectful conversation among multiple persons. It involves boldly setting out one's views in one's own voice but also careful listening to others and recognizing that many positions hold some truth. Divergent reasoning recognizes conflict between differing perspectives as a path to knowledge. It is not a search for complete objectivity but a process of learning through dialogue. In community psychology, that conversation is often multisided, not simply two opposing poles.

Divergent reasoning also involves questioning the status quo or commonly accepted view of an issue (Rappaport, 1981). In discussing a social issue such as poverty, there is often a dominant, widely accepted view and an opposing pole that is largely ignored. The dominant view serves the interests of the powerful by defining the issue and terms of debate. Psychology has often adopted or been co-opted by dominant views rather than questioned them (Gergen, 2001; Humphreys & Rappaport, 1993; Riger, 1993; Ryan, 1971, 1994; Sarason, 1974, 2003b). Often, this happens as psychologists and citizens think solely in individual terms, ignoring the importance of contexts (Shinn & Toohey, 2003). Questioning the status quo often involves listening carefully to the voices of persons who have direct experience with an issue, especially those whose views have been ignored. For example, research that investigates the experiences and perspectives of persons with mental disorders can illuminate their strengths and focus on their rights to make decisions in their own lives as well as their needs for treatment and support (Rappaport, 1981).

Finally, divergent reasoning requires humility. No matter how strong your commitment to your own viewpoint, it is likely to be one-sided in some way, and there is likely to be some truth in an opposing view. Remember Rappaport's Rule: "When everyone agrees with you, worry."

Community Psychology Responses to Political Contexts

Despite differences in how problems are defined and prioritized, opportunities for community psychology research and action exist in conservative or progressive social times and locations. Sarason (1976) articulated the "anarchist insight" (with which many conservatives agree) that government interventions for social problems may undermine the sense of community and mutual aid among citizens. Lappe and DuBois (1994) and Wolff (1994) noted that many conservatives and progressives agree that social problems must be addressed at the community level, where many community psychologists are engaged.

Some very influential perspectives in community psychology are related to conservative as well as to progressive thinking. For instance, Sarason's (1974) concept of sense of community and Rappaport's (1981) concept of empowerment are both locally focused and reflect a skeptical view of top-down government interventions. Progressives will likely engage community psychologists' problem definitions that emphasize structural factors and levels of analysis. Interestingly, conservative or progressive views can be at odds with community psychologists who challenge the status quo and current power structures in their efforts to promote social change. When the values of community psychology can be addressed in a locality or particular political context, collaboration is quite possible. However, there are many instances where political views are narrowly individualistic, victim-blaming perspectives (Levine & Levine, 1992; Rappaport, 1981; Ryan, 1971, 1994) or when political views emphasize one set of values to the exclusion of others (e.g., liberty while overlooking justice). Such views often fail to understand or appreciate human diversity and often keep money and resources in affluent communities rather than using them where there are pressing needs.

Furthermore, what one means by empowerment can differ greatly from what most community psychologists mean by those terms (see Chapter 11). Prilleltensky and colleagues have emphasized the role of critical reflection in community psychology work and suggest that it is helpful to seek a balance of classic Western values of liberty, fraternity, and justice as contexts and conditions change (Nelson & Prilleltensky, 2010). In conservative or progressive locales, indeed, in all of our work, community psychologists of any political persuasion need to be explicit about their values, understand differing values, support their claims with research findings, search for common ground with those who differ, and engage in divergent reasoning about promote well-being and community life.

Training for Community Psychology

As the field emerged, the shift in perspective of community psychology required new models of training. Universities needed to create undergraduate and graduate courses in community psychology. Prevention of psychological problems and promotion of social competence, especially in schools, represented one important theme at the first conference on training held in Austin, Texas, in April 1975 (Iscoe, Bloom, & Spielberger, 1977). A second theme concerned social advocacy to address such issues as poverty, racism, and sexism. Austin's conference participants were more diverse than Swampscott's, reflecting a third theme of emerging diversity. Swampscott's participants were all White and included only one woman. At the Austin conference, the perspectives of women and persons of color were voiced to a degree that had not happened before, although these groups were concentrated among students and junior professionals, not among senior professionals who were slower to engage these perspectives (Mulvey, 1988). Reports from working groups of Blacks, Hispanics, and women called for translating espoused values of the field into tangible changes in training, research, and action (Iscoe et al., 1977; Moore, 1977). Currently, there are master's-level training programs in community, counseling-community, or clinical-community (e.g., Canada, Egypt, Italy, New Zealand, South Africa, the United Kingdom, and the United States) and doctoral programs in community, interdisciplinary studies, social-community, or clinical-community (e.g., Australia, Canada, New Zealand, Portugal, Puerto Rico, and the United States).

As we have previously discussed, the development of community psychology led to a divergence of community mental health and community psychology training over the past 40 years. While community mental health remained focused on mental health services, community psychology expanded its focus to schools, workplaces, neighborhoods, community development, and advocacy for social change. Individual/family wellness remained an important concern of community psychology, but the field gradually began to focus on other values as well, such as sense of community, social justice, respect for diversity, and citizen participation. We discuss current training opportunities in greater detail in Chapter 14.

WHAT DO COMMUNITY PSYCHOLOGISTS DO?

As part of developing a new field, community psychologists examined the roles and skills required to promote social change and work at different ecological levels. As you might guess, this has involved active roles in community settings and adopting models of professional relationships that expanded on those taken by clinicians. In 2010, the Community Psychology Practice Council of the Society for Community Research and Action developed a statement to help advertise the unique skills and perspectives of community psychologists to prospective employers (Ratcliffe & Neigher, n.d.); this statement is included with a longer discussion of community practice in Chapter 14.

Community psychologists work collaboratively with others to help strengthen systems, provide cost-effective services, increase access to resources, and optimize quality for individuals, private and governmental organizations, corporations, and community groups. Community psychologists build on existing strengths of people, organizations, and communities to create sustainable change.

The professional roles of community psychologists range from consultants, trainers, and grant writers to human service managers and program directors, to policy developers and evaluators, and to educators and professors. Today, community psychologists work at social service agencies, in private policy organizations, and in government departments or institutes (e.g., Center for Disease Control and Prevention). Many have their own consulting businesses, and a large number work at colleges and universities. Over the course of a career, a community psychologist may work in several different capacities. For example, since I (Bret) completed my doctoral training, I have had many different professional roles. I have worked as a program director for a housing program for persons who were homeless. I was a coordinator of a statewide self-help network. I have been an evaluation and program development consultant to human service programs. I have been a researcher on large, federally funded grants and small local initiatives. I have served on boards of nonprofit organizations and citizen committees. During my career, I have also worked in a wide variety of settings. I have worked in a mental health center, a nonprofit agency, and a university. I regularly collaborate with state departments of mental health, human services agencies, community organizers, and community coalitions.

Many community psychologists work in multiple settings where their perspectives and skills are helpful. We will highlight the work of community psychologists and others involved in social action in most of our chapters with sidebar features where you can learn about their work. We call this feature "Community Psychology in Action." Box 2.3 presents the experiences of community psychologists in Portugal who have used their academic training to create an alternative setting to address the needs of persons with mental illness and their family members that were not sufficiently well addressed by existing resources.

Community psychology promotes training in a wide range of skills required to engage in social change. Each community psychologist develops skills particularly suited to her or his social change interests. Wolfgang Stark outlined a useful framework for thinking about skills needed for community psychology (Stark, 2009). Some of these skills are *design skills* in formulating evaluation and research questions, developing programs and policy, analyzing social conditions, and planning intervention. Some of these skills are *action skills*, such as consulting,

---

B o x 2.3   Community Psychology in Action

Social and Political Change in the Mental Health System in Portugal

Jose Ornelas, Maria Moniz-Vargas, and Teresa Duarte
Associação paralo Estudo e Integração PsicoSocial (AEIPS)
(Association for Study and Psychosocial Integration)

The mental health system in Portugal during the '80s was structured around large psychiatric hospitals or wards integrated in general hospitals, and institutional facilities managed by religious congregations. In 1987, through a small grant provided by the State Mental Health Department, we began to organize group meetings with people in the community who were discharged to the community of Olivais in Lisboa. Our group created a nongovernmental organization named *Association for the Study and Psychosocial Integration* (AEIPS) to implement a community-based service system, which has involved over 750 mental health services users to date.

Drawing upon values and concepts from community psychology, we sought to promote opportunities for social integration of people with mental illness, accessibility to individualized housing, professional alternatives, and participation in community life as any other person. We wanted to create settings that would allow people with histories of psychiatric treatment to choose the location where they would live, work, study or socialize. In the housing area, we have helped create a range of options by providing group or individualized opportunities with tailored professional intervention focused on the maintenance of the housing, even in crisis situations. Currently, one of the most relevant and recognized services provided by our organization is the supported employment program. It is a system to assist people with the experience of mental illness to work in the open labor market. The program promotes opportunities to reach the labor market, and actively participate in society, and emphasizes the diversity of employment options depending on a person's interest, educational background, or specific training. The model is one person working in one company. The supported education program is focused on opportunities to return to school for this group that often has unfinished degrees. In creating opportunities to address the concerns of persons with mental illness, we seek to support the transformation of individual's lives by emphasizing processes of building (or renewing) social support systems and participating in community life.

The main lesson that we have learned over the past 25 years is that applying an empowerment paradigm to mental health services requires consistent attention and measurement of processes and results. While this new perspective has helped us to see how we needed to create new settings to address the interests of persons with mental illness to participate in community life, we realized that we need to collaborate with stakeholders (mental health services consumers, families and professionals) at all ecological levels to promote individual, family, and community well-being.

---

community organizing, community development, coalition building, conducting evaluation, and research. Finally, community psychologists need well-developed *social skills*, both those that people develop naturally (e.g., active listening, rapport building, and conscientiousness) and those that may require specialized training (e.g., group facilitation and conflict resolution).

Recent initiatives by community psychology practitioners are bringing more expertise and focus to the development of practice skills useful in community psychology. As we discuss in greater detail in Chapter 14, a Summit on Community Psychology Practice was held in 2007 that has promoted a rich dialogue within the field. You can read about these developments in *The Community Psychologist*, which is published by the U.S. community psychology professional organization: the Society for Community Research and Action. A link to the website is included at the end of this chapter.

THE GLOBAL CONTEXTS OF COMMUNITY PSYCHOLOGY

Distances between diverse cultures, communities, and persons are shrinking. Communication media, travel, trade, cultural exchange, and, sadly, exploitation and violence are becoming increasingly global in scope. Here, we briefly present how community psychology has developed in different countries. Given the emphasis on understanding context in community psychology, it is not surprising that the priorities and development of community psychology varies by national context.

Unique Development in Different Contexts

The 1970s and early 1980s saw the emergence of community psychology across the world. The origins and the focus of social change efforts differed by national contexts. In South Africa, opposition to apartheid was a unifying force. In West Germany, social movements for women and the environment played important roles. In Australia, New Zealand, and Canada, similar social movements were central to efforts to organize a new perspective on psychology as well as disenchantment with purely clinical concepts of human strengths and problems. Today, community psychology is a burgeoning international field. Learning from and working with indigenous peoples is a focus in several countries—for instance, the Maori in New Zealand, Aboriginal peoples in Australia, and Mayan peoples in Guatemala (Glover, Dudgeon, & Huygens, 2005; Lykes, Blanche, & Hamber, 2003; Wingenfeld & Newbrough, 2000). The *Journal of Community and Applied Social Psychology* carries articles from an international array of community psychologists. Training programs and practitioners now exist across Latin America, Europe, Japan, New Zealand, Australia, Israel, South Africa, Canada, and the United States. There is not space in this chapter to review community psychology in each country. We have selected a few to give you an idea of community psychology's diversity.

Community Psychology in North America

Canada has a four-decade history of community psychology that shares in many of the contexts that were formative for the field in the United States but have developed uniquely Canadian features. Nelson, Lavoie, and Mitchell (2007) suggest that there have been six main areas of emphasis in Canada: values and ethics, community mental health, health promotion and prevention, social network intervention, promotion of inclusion, and community economic development. Several universities offer training programs in French and English. Conferences and journals are published with translations in both languages.

Mexico has also had a community psychology tradition for over 30 years at several universities (Montero, 2007). Several community psychologists have developed interventions working with indigenous communities, documenting cultural traditions, and collaborating to preserve cultural traditions and to respond to poverty and infrastructure needs in rural areas. In 2010, Universidad Iboamericana in Puebla, Mexico hosted the third International Conference on Community Psychology.

Community Psychology in Latin America

During the 1970s, community psychology developed among psychologists throughout Latin America—largely independent of North American trends (Comas-Diaz, Lykes, & Alarcon, 1998; Montero, 1996). The Latin American movements for community psychology and liberation psychology grew out of social psychology and social change movements rather than from clinical psychology. In some countries (e.g., Chile, El Salvador, and Guatemala), these trends were a response to repressive government regimes and overt conflict. These developments were influenced by liberation theology, which combined many values of Christianity and Latin American liberation struggles. At the community level, liberation theology and psychology emphasized empowerment of citizens and struggle against injustice (Martin-Baro, 1994). Another influence was the approach of Brazilian educator and activist Paulo Freire (1970/1993), who focused on new methods of education as means of raising consciousness of the impact of social conditions on personal lives and as beginning points for social transformation. Freire focused on practical, local initiatives for social change.

A distinctive Latin American social-community psychology emerged, more explicitly concerned with social critique and with liberation than North American community psychology at the time. It emphasized democratic participation, social justice, concepts of power and ideology, and social change and established a presence in Venezuela, Colombia, Brazil, Argentina, Chile, Cuba, and other countries (Montero & Varas Diaz, 2007). Much of the work in Latin America is not well known in the United States because of language barriers; however, the ideas have been influential, particularly in liberation psychology.

Community psychologists from Puerto Rico have been particularly influential in the development of social-community psychology. Having established a training program for 35 years, Puerto Rican community psychologists have developed textbooks (Serrano-Garcia, Figueroa-Rodríguez, & Pérez-Jiménez, 2008), conducted large-scale federally funded research projects, and produced over 100 graduates in the past three decades (Montero & Varas Diaz, 2007). As a field, it has had to defend its viewpoint in contrast to other subfields in Puerto Rico, with a particular emphasis on producing psychologists that are "interested and committed to intervention in research, promoting interventions simultaneously with research projects" (Montero & Varas Diaz, 2007, p. 71).

Community Psychology in Europe, Australia, and New Zealand

Community psychology in Europe, Australia, and New Zealand is quite varied in emphasis. In Portugal and Spain, the fields emerged as fascist regimes were pushed out of power in the 1970s. In northern Europe and Australia, development of community psychology paralleled developments in the United States and Canada of extending community mental health and eventually branching out into other areas (Reich et al., 2007). Community psychologists in New Zealand have made collaboration with Maori peoples a keystone of their work that extends to examining its philosophy of science to its methods for intervention (Robertson & Masters-Awatere, 2007). The development of community psychology in Australia and New Zealand draws upon influences from Europe through shared cultural history. However, contemporary expressions of community psychology emphasize the realities of their location in the Asia-Pacific region.

Italy has a rich history of community psychology research and intervention. The development of community psychology emerged as a new, decentralized model for health services was being implemented. The perspectives of community psychology were helpful in defining new roles for psychologists, promoting self-help groups and changing the culture of health care. Promoting and measuring sense of community have been particular concerns in Italy, as has working for action that results in a balance of individual efficacy, collective resources, and well-being. Italian community psychologists have been active in promoting European views of community psychology, hosting conferences and serving as leaders in European professional networks (Franscescato, Arcidiacono, Albanesi, & Mannarini, 2007).

To date, there is not a single European community psychology. However, the professional society—the European Congress on Community Psychology—holds regular conferences and exchanges across countries. Jose Ornelas, Maria Moniz-Vargas, and other community psychologists in Lisbon, Portugal, hosted the second International Community Conference on Community Psychology, which included training institute courses by community psychologists from around the world to promote this perspective in Portugal.

Community Psychology in Africa and Asia

Community psychology practitioners have been active in Africa and Asia for 30 years, but formally organized programs are more recent. In Ghana, Cameroon, Egypt, and South Africa, psychologists have been drawn to perspectives of community psychology to address the shortcomings of traditional psychological approaches. In South Africa, community psychology's focus on liberation and social justice was resisted by psychologists during the apartheid years. There was more interest and support for community psychology in English-speaking universities than Afrikaans. While community psychology is still not recognized as its own discipline in South Africa, it has become a valuable resource for clinical psychologists who now have a compulsory community service requirement due to changes in health care laws (Bhana, Petersen, & Rochat, 2007). Two journals and edited books have been developed to feature community psychology. An interesting discourse for a global community psychology is emerging in South Africa about the need to adapt North American and European conceptualizations of community psychology to be relevant in poor areas of Africa. Seedat (1997) has been particularly active in articulating the tensions between northern hemisphere community psychology and that of the southern hemisphere.

In Japan, a professional society was organized in 1998. Much work has focused on school settings and promoting adaptation of students. Although much of Japanese community psychology has paralleled that in North America, Japanese community psychologists are working to develop cross-cultural models to enhance understanding of community psychology perspectives in Japan (Sasao & Yasuda, 2007). In Hong Kong and India, community psychology is an emerging discipline (Reich et al., 2007), although there are long helping traditions and histories of addressing social conflict. Developments throughout Asia and Africa will enrich community psychology throughout the world as critics of current practice and innovators for their cultural contexts.

Moving Toward a Global Community Psychology

Since the last edition of this book, several important developments mark the emergence of efforts to create global understandings of community psychology. As noted previously, an important book documented the development and practice of community psychology in 37 countries on six continents (Reich, Riemer, Prilleltensky, & Montero, 2007). In 2006, the first International Conference on Community Psychology was hosted in Puerto Rico. This was an exceptional site for bringing together community psychologists from different traditions and different countries. Puerto Rico's unique history as a leader of community psychology in Latin American and many connections with U.S. community psychology were instrumental in linking community psychology traditions from different countries. The second international conference was held in Lisbon, Portugal, in 2008, demonstrating the vibrancy of community psychology in Europe. At the third international conference in Puebla, Mexico, in 2010, international exchanges continued to build on the rich traditions of community psychology in different countries while struggling to articulate what a global community psychology might be. A fourth conference is planned for Barcelona, Spain, in 2012, where new conventions for presentations and cross-cultural exchange will aim to support the development of global understandings of community psychology.

CONCLUSION

"The major job was getting people to understand that they had something within their power that they could use, and it could only be used if they understood what was happening and how group action could counter violence...." (Baker, p. 2)

"When those of us working in this field in the early 1960s began, we were innocent of the questions as well as of the answers. Now at least we are developing an intellectual framework within which diverse experiences make some sense. We can at least ask questions that are more meaningful than ones we were able to ask 40 years ago. (Levine, Perkins, & Perkins, 2005, p. 9)

Developing during the 1960s, U.S. community psychology was shaped by the civil rights movement and a conviction that addressing social conditions and engaging community members as citizens were important aspects of improving individual and community well-being. Ella Baker's quote helps to capture the spirit of the period, as she worked with the Southern Christian Leadership Conference and the Student Nonviolent Coordinating Committee. In this chapter, we discussed how the contexts of these important periods of community psychology's development have shaped its perspective, practices, and values. We also discussed how changing contexts have an impact on the continuing development of the field around the world.

As the Levine, Perkins, and Perkins quote illustrates, community psychology is still maturing as a field. It has made important contributions to understanding and intervening with social issues. However, even the most experienced community psychologist is still a student of relationships between individual and community life at many ecological levels. Every generation of students builds on the experiences of prior generations as they reinvent community psychology in new contexts.

CHAPTER SUMMARY

1. Psychology in the United States has been strongly influenced by individualism and defined itself as the study of the individual, with little attention to social context. Psychological practice is also individualistic, which is useful in many ways but one-sided and limited.

2. Community psychology emerged in the United States in the mid-20th century. Among the many forces that led to this development, we identified five important ones: (1) a preventive perspective; (2) reforms in mental health care; (3) action research and group dynamics; (4) social change movements, such as civil rights and feminism; and (5) optimism about solving social problems. The Swampscott Conference in 1965 identified community psychology as a new field.

3. During the 1960s and 1970s, community psychology in the United States diverged from community mental health. This development parallels community psychology in other countries. Changes in the mental health system and the limitations of government social programs influenced this. Blaming the victim occurs when social problems or programs are defined by focusing only on individual causes, not social factors. Top-down approaches to change are designed by the powerful, while bottom-up

approaches reflect the ideas of ordinary citizens. Both have advantages and limitations.

4. During the 1970s, conceptual frameworks appeared for the field: prevention, an ecological perspective, sense of community, social justice, valuing human diversity, self-determination and empowerment, and multiple interventions to promote coping. These developments continue to be influential in community psychology.

5. In the 1980s, in the United States and many Western countries, the sociopolitical context grew more conservative. The Levine and Levine hypothesis predicts that, in politically progressive times, environmental explanations of social problems will be favored, leading to programs to change community environments. In conservative times, individualistic explanations of social problems will be favored, leading to programs to change individuals. These are also related to two definitions of equality. Fair Play—a more conservative view—defines fairness in terms of rules for fair competition for economic success. Fair Shares—a more progressive view—defines fairness in terms of providing basic necessities for all.

6. For community psychology, thinking about social issues requires divergent reasoning: understanding how opposing viewpoints may both hold truth, responding to such conflicts with "both/and" rather than "either/or" thinking, being open to dialogue with those who hold different views, and questioning the status quo while searching for viewpoints that are not being voiced or recognized.

7. Political eras and political contexts of different locations can provide challenges and opportunities for community psychology. Areas of common ground between the field and conservative views include skepticism about top-down programs and a focus on local decision making. Progressives have common ground with community psychology's structural critiques of social problems. However, community psychologists may have differences with progressive or conservative leaders when those leaders are more interested in maintaining the status quo rather than addressing the issues of concern to community members.

8. Training in community psychology includes many options for both master's- and doctoral-level training. These include community psychology, clinical-community psychology, counseling-community psychology, and interdisciplinary approaches to community research and action. While still evolving, the training is more closely realizing the values of the field than when it was founded.

9. Community psychologists practice in a wide array of settings and professional roles. They may work in nonprofit organizations, government agencies, companies, start their own businesses, or work in education. The professional roles include consultants, program developers, policy specialists, community organizers, community developers, and evaluation specialists.

10. Community psychology is now an international field. Community social psychology emerged in Latin America with a distinctive social change focus. Empowerment, feminist, liberation, and critical perspectives have become important perspectives, and collaborative, participatory research methods have emerged.

RECOMMENDED READINGS

Revenson, T., D'Augelli, A., French, S., Hughes, D., Livert, S., Seidman, E., Shinn, M., Yoshikawa, H. (Eds.) (2002). *A quarter century of community psychology: Readings from the American Journal of Community Psychology*. New York: Kluwer/Plenum. [Classic articles from community psychology's history, with four essays on the development of the field.]

Ryan, W. (1971). *Blaming the victim*. New York: Random House [especially first chapter]. Or: Ryan, W. (1994). Many cooks, brave men, apples, and oranges: How people think about equality. *American Journal of Community Psychology, 22,* 25–36.

Reich, S.M., Riemer, M., Prilleltensky, I. & Montero. (2007). *International community psychology: History and theories*. Springer: New York.

RECOMMENDED WEBSITES

Global Journal of Community Psychology Practice:
http://www.gjcpp.org/en.

Society for Community Research and Action:
http://www.scra27.org.

SCRA Community Psychology Practice Council:
http://www.scra27.org/practice.

The Community Psychologist:
http://www.scra27.org/resources/scrapublic/tcp

RECOMMENDED VIDEODISC

Kelly, J.G. (Director/Producer) (2003). *Exemplars of community psychology* [DVD]. Society for Community Research and Action. Available through: SCRA Membership Office, 4440 PGA Blvd #600, Palm Beach Gardens, FL 33410, info@scra27.org, 561-623-5323. Excerpts from interviews of pioneering community psychologists and others on the early development of the field in the United States. Their personal stories often reveal sources of ideas, support, emotion, and conflict not addressed in print.

3

The Aims of Community Research

HIRB/Index Stock/PhotoLibrary

OPENING EXERCISE

Isn't it a pleasure when you can make practical use of what you have learned? (Analects of Confucius, cited in Reid, 1999, p. 90)

> My department colleagues asked me, "Where have you been? We haven't seen you in three days!" I told them I had been out collecting data. "Oh? In whose laboratory?" [they asked]. "In St. Louis County," I said. "It's a great laboratory." (Glidewell, 1994)

Jack Glidewell evaluated one of the first preventive mental health interventions in schools during the 1950s. As he asserted, communities offer rich opportunities for research. This is an ancient concern: The Chinese sage Kung Fu Tzu (known in the West as Confucius) spent his life seeking to integrate knowledge with action and community governance (Reid, 1999).

Community psychology has taken up this action research tradition, though it was introduced to us much later by Kurt Lewin (remember our discussion in Chapter 2). We use action research to pursue answers to questions about how individuals shape ecological contexts and how ecological contexts impact individuals. As we discussed in Chapter 1, community psychologists value empirical answers to our questions; we are impatient with theory or action that lacks evidence based in systematic observation and measurement. We base our action in research findings, and we use research to understand the impact of our actions. Our community research aims to provide useful knowledge for decision making, planning, and action at multiple levels—from local action and community change efforts to state, federal, and international policymaking.

Glidewell's work evaluating school-based prevention programs in St. Louis County provided useful knowledge for action at multiple levels. Yet it represented a departure from much mid-20th century research in psychology and clearly surprised his colleagues. Why do you think Glidewell's colleagues were surprised? Take a minute to think about the shift in perspective that Glidewell's community-based research represented for psychology. How do you think research conducted in community settings would be different from research conducted in the laboratory? What new challenges might you face conducting research in community settings?

Glidewell's colleagues most likely conducted their research in university classrooms and designated lab spaces (some with the famous white rats running through mazes). And laboratories are, of course, useful settings because they offer the researcher a great deal of control. The laboratory psychologist largely controls the choice of phenomena to study, the perspective from which to study it, the methodology, the treatment of participants during the procedure, the format in which those participants provide data, the analysis of data, the interpretation of findings, and the reporting of results. That control promotes clarity of conclusions and the production of some forms of knowledge. Of course, the researcher must make all these choices within accepted ethical limits. But the degree of control granted the psychological researcher in the laboratory is great.

However, while many individuals (e.g., students in introductory psychology courses) are willing to briefly participate in a laboratory experiment, few citizens are willing to cede control in the settings where they and their families live every day (e.g., school, work, family, neighborhood, or mutual help group). The settings that are most significant for community psychology research are also the most important to their inhabitants.

In this chapter, we present a different view of control: *sharing* control with community members can *enhance* the knowledge gained from community research. Well-designed community research, conducted within a collaborative relationship with a community, can yield insights not available in the laboratory. Sharing control does not mean giving it up. In a collaborative relationship, both community members and researchers plan and implement research. In this chapter, our goal is for you to better understand and respect the interests of communities as well as the methods for community psychology research.

This chapter is the first of two on community research. In Chapter 4, we describe specific methods for community psychology research. By reading both chapters, we hope that you learn how community research becomes richer by embracing and seeking to understand the complexities of community life.

Questions for Conducting Community Inquiry

Research can support or harm persons in communities, so values are involved in every step of that research. Community psychology is committed to the value of research; along with action, it is central to our identity. All community psychologists are engaged in some form of inquiry whether we identify ourselves primarily as researchers or practitioners. Across a variety of settings and types of engagement, we strive for rigor and excellence by using the very best strategies and methods to answer our research questions. Yet our research questions are grounded in the way that we define problems and priorities for inquiry. Further, each community research project must resolve larger questions about the relative priority of several other values: citizen participation and collaboration, social justice, respect for human diversity, and searching for community strengths. These issues can be summarized in this general question: Who will generate what knowledge, for whom, and for what purposes?

Seymour Sarason (1972) spoke about the important time *before the beginning* of a community initiative. In that period, the persons involved become aware of a problem or challenge to be addressed, trying to make sense of the problem and what to do about it. This concept also fits well with the early stages of a research project—well before a design is chosen and data collected. Important, overarching issues for community psychology research can be summarized in terms of the following four questions. After summarizing these questions, we will take up each in detail in the rest of this chapter.

1. What Values and Assumptions Do We Bring to Our Work?   Community psychology researchers need to be clear on their fundamental values and their assumptions about research and its relation to community and social action. Researchers need this clarity before approaching a community to conduct research, although their ideas about these issues will also be influenced by their experiences with community members.

2. How Can We Promote Community Participation and Collaboration in Research?   The most distinctive quality of community psychology research is its process of conducting research within a participatory, collaborative relationship with citizens and communities. That distinctive approach developed from the practical experiences and careful reflection of community psychologists and researchers in related fields. They grapple with questions such as these: Specifically, how can researchers and citizens collaborate in planning and conducting research? How can that collaboration be empowering and productive for both? How can respectful relationships between researchers, community members, and research participants be best created and maintained?

3. How Do We Understand the Cultural and Social Contexts of This Research? Community research always occurs within a culture—perhaps more than one. Often, the cultural assumptions and experiences of researchers differ from those of community members, so an early task is for researchers to deepen their knowledge of the community with whom they seek to work. Community researchers may also seek or need to address questions of human diversity beyond culture (e.g., gender, sexual orientation, ability-disability, and social class). A related concern is whether the research will take account of strengths of the individuals, communities, and cultures studied.

4. At What Ecological Levels of Analysis Will We Conduct This Research? Community researchers make decisions, explicitly or implicitly, about the level(s) of analysis they will focus on. The history and practices of psychology draw attention to individual processes, but community psychology draws our attention to social systems at higher levels. Such choices of focus are better made explicitly.

WHAT VALUES AND ASSUMPTIONS DO WE BRING TO OUR WORK?

Recall the discussion of homelessness in Chapter 1: Unrecognized assumptions about problems often prevent resolution of those problems. Similarly, unrecognized assumptions influence researchers' choices of what phenomena to study, from what perspective, and within what framework of methods and values. Those assumptions can concern one's most basic ideas of what constitutes social-scientific knowledge and how it can best be used. We begin with a contrast between three different views of what constitutes knowledge and how to obtain it.

Three Philosophies of Science for Community Psychology Research

A philosophy of science refers to one's beliefs about what scientific knowledge is, through what methods it is obtained, and how it is related to action. You may never have thought of yourself as having a personal philosophy of science, but your ideas about research and how to do it (perhaps as you learned it in prior psychology or other social science courses) reflect a philosophy of science. We will now discuss three general philosophies of science for community psychology research and compare them briefly in Table 3.1. Each is actually a family of related approaches, not a single school of thought. Riger (1990, 1992), Campbell and Wasco (2000, pp. 779–783), and Nelson and Prilleltensky (2005, pp. 239–248) provide succinct overviews, and our summary here especially relies on these sources.

T A B L E   3.1   Three Philosophies of Science for Community Psychology Research

Philosophy of Science	Epistemology	Methodology
Postpositivist	Knowledge is built through shared understanding, using rigorous methods and standards of the scientific community.	Emphasis is placed on understanding cause and effect relationships, hypothesis-testing, modeling, and experimental methods.
Constructivist	Knowledge is created collaboratively in relationships between researchers and participants.	Emphasis is placed on understanding contexts, meanings, and lived experiences of participants; qualitative methods.
Critical	Knowledge is shaped by power relationships and location within social systems.	Emphasis is placed on integrating research and action, attending to unheard voices, and challenging injustice using a variety of methods.

In psychology, **positivism** has been the dominant philosophy of science. Positivism has assumed many forms, but a few common elements important in psychology are these: pursuit of objectivity and value-free neutrality in research, an ultimate goal of understanding cause and effect relationships, hypothesis testing with control of extraneous factors to clarify cause and effect, and measurement as the source of data. Positivist science seeks to construct generalized laws, based on research findings, which are applicable to many circumstances. If you have taken prior courses in psychological research methods, what you learned there was influenced by positivism.

This vision of research (admittedly oversimplified here as an introduction) has come under increasing criticism. No observer is value-free; for example, one is always a member of a culture and influenced by it. Moreover, the particular qualities of cultures, historical circumstances, and settings limit the "generalizability" of research findings from one context to another (Gergen, 1973, 2001). These and other critiques have led to **postpositivist** epistemologies that recognize that no researcher is truly objective yet seek to reduce biases and build shared understandings as much as possible. Postpositivist approaches in community psychology adapt experimental methods, hypothesis testing, and psychological measurement to community settings.

Constructivist (sometimes termed *contextualist* or *postmodernist*) philosophies of science take a different approach (Campbell & Wasco, 2000; Gergen, 2001; Kingry-Westergaard & Kelly, 1990; Montero, 2002; Nelson & Prilleltensky, 2005; Tebes, 2005; Trickett, 2009). Instead of pursuing the ideal of value-free objectivity, constructivists assume that knowing occurs in a relationship and is a product of a social connection between researcher and research participant. This emphasis on knowing through connection, collaboration, and mutual understanding is a particular emphasis of qualitative research and of some feminist researchers (see Campbell & Wasco, 2000; Riger, 1992; Stein & Mankowski,

2004). Constructivist approaches seek to understand a particular social context and what it means to the people who experience it (e.g., what having schizophrenia means for the person and their family; Stein & Wemmerus, 2001). Testing hypotheses about causes and effects becomes less important. For these purposes, qualitative research methods, such as interviewing, often provide the best techniques. Of course, the viewpoint of the researcher can still influence findings. The idea is not to eliminate researcher bias, which constructivists consider impossible, but to put the assumptions of the researcher on the table to be discussed and evaluated. This puts responsibility on researchers to make their assumptions explicit, and to describe carefully the relationships in which research was conducted, reporting faithfully the words and ideas of research participants.

Critical philosophies of science take a third position, related to contructivism yet distinct from it (Campbell & Wasco, 2000; Nelson & Prilleltensky, 2005). They assume that knowledge is shaped by power relationships created and maintained by social institutions and belief systems. They ask questions about who has the power to state what is true, and who is able to define the nature of research relationships. Critical approaches put responsibility on the researcher to recognize and question one's own position in social systems and how this affects research. The gender, race, ethnicity, social class, and other social positions of the researcher and research participant strongly influence what they experience in everyday life because these positions reflect greater or lesser degrees of social power. Critical researchers also take an activist stance, conducting research that can lead to challenging injustice. Critical community research may use specific research methods drawn from either postpositivist or constructivist approaches. Some feminist and liberation approaches to community psychology reflect a critical philosophy of science. Of course, an activist stance influences research choices and findings, so (as with constructivist approaches) this puts responsibility on the researchers to make their assumptions and viewpoints explicit.

Thus, "before the beginning" of research, postpositivist, constructivist, and critical philosophies of science have different aims. They are based in different ideas of the roles of researcher and research participant, different conceptions of how to use research, different ideas about how to deal with researchers' values and assumptions, and even different conceptions of what is "knowledge." Much useful community research has postpositivistic features, especially the use of measurement and experimentation modified to fit community settings. Constructivist approaches have become influential in community psychology in the last two decades, especially fitting the field's emphasis on a collaborative researcher-community relationship. Critical approaches also have become influential—in part because they call attention to integrating research and action and to the importance of social systems. All three philosophies of science are useful in community psychology research, and a study may incorporate elements of more than one of these three philosophies.

For example, imagine that you wanted to develop a study that examines the impacts of a neighborhood on children's lives (Nicotera, 2007). You might draw on multiple measures, including those developed out of each of the three frameworks. The study might measure structural characteristics favored by postpositivists, such as census data that provide demographic information and reveal the social and economic composition of the neighborhood. But you might also be concerned that census data alone leaves out social process measures of the neighborhood more often brought to the fore by constructivists. These measures would help to focus on how the residents of the neighborhood understand the neighborhood. In other words, "What is it really like to live there?" This might lead you toward residents' perceptions of norms, opportunities, barriers, dangers, and available resources. A critical focus would also be useful, helping you think about power, how different stakeholders might define the neighborhood differently (e.g., what areas are safe, what resources are available, etc.), and how children's perceptions should be included as well as adults. Our main point here is not that you should measure everything; instead, it is to show how each perspective guides research questions and strategies. No perfect research design exists; there are always trade-offs in conducting research. But we advocate that community researchers make their choices explicit in planning their research.

Problem Definition in Research: Taking a Stand on Social Issues

Community researchers must decide how their research will relate to action. A postpositivist approach to social problems seeks concrete, pragmatic, generalizable answers supported by research findings. It applies (with modifications) the scientific methods and findings of psychology to society in terms often defined by policymakers and funders. Much social science research assumes this stance, which dominated the early development of community psychology.

Some aspects of this approach are useful. For example, how does a nation or a community prevent the spread of AIDS, or improve child health, or reduce violence in schools? Community research can identify causes of these problems, develop programs or social policies to address those factors, and evaluate their effectiveness. The U.S. Institute of Medicine approach to prevention science involves such a process: conducting research on factors that lead to health or behavior problems, using that knowledge to develop prevention programs, testing their effectiveness in controlled studies, and then disseminating the most effective programs for replication in other settings (Mrazek & Haggerty, 1994). We will have the opportunity to further discuss the benefits and limits of this prevention science approach in Chapters 9 and 10.

For now, however, we will point out that the usefulness of such research depends in part on social consensus in definition of problems, causes, and appropriate responses (Price, 1989). That consensus around problem definition and solution often does not exist. Even with public health problems that are clearly defined and for which causal factors are understood (e.g., the diagnosis and transmission of HIV infection), there is often great controversy about prevention methods (e.g., needle exchange or education about condoms). Conflicts mushroom when citizens cannot even agree on the definition of the problem and its causes, as with many issues of sexuality, child and family problems, and drug use, for instance. A research team may use what they believe are commonsense definitions of problems and solutions, only to have their findings rejected by those who disagree with their premises. Price (1989) described his own experience in testifying before Congress about community programs for reducing teen pregnancy, preventing child abuse, and coping with marital separation, only to receive the response that such programs undermined the institution of marriage and family values. Thus, Price (1989, p. 157) argued that many social dilemmas are better understood as social conflicts than as social "problems" to be "solved" (see also Sarason, 1978). Those conflicts involve competing assumptions and values and are no less present today.

Does such conflict mean empirical research on social and community issues is useless? Price argued not. Instead of seeking to be "value-neutral," researchers can acknowledge that social issues involve multiple positions, each with different value assumptions, different definitions of the problem, different theories about its causes and effects, and different interventions to prevent or treat it. Researchers can point out when the empirical evidence overwhelmingly favors particular problem definitions over others as well as the likelihood that multiple, divergent, community-based solutions may be most effective in addressing any complex problem (Miller & Shinn, 2005; Rappaport, 1981; Wandersman et al., 2008). Researchers must still be intellectually honest, recognize the value of opposing views, use defensible methods, and be willing to present findings that turned out contrary to their assumptions (Nelson, Prilleltenskys, & MacGillivary, 2001, p. 671). Yet boldly and explicitly stating one's premises and values actually can improve research by clarifying the assumptions on which it is based.

With whom does a community researcher stand? One's personal values are the most important guide. Another guideline is to look for whose viewpoints are missing in the debate over a social issue (Freire, 1970/1993; Price, 1989; Rappaport, 1981; Riger, 1990). Discussion of social issues is often dominated by the powerful, who define the problem and set the terms of debate (Caplan & Nelson, 1973). Their ideas become the conventional wisdom about the problem. Thus, an important role of community researchers is to identify a community whose views are being overlooked and to conduct research that helps bring attention to the experiences and views of persons in that community. This provides broader knowledge of the issue and may also identify community strengths and resources. This approach can be termed **attending to unheard voices**.

The metaphor of **voice** comes from feminist thinkers (Belenky, Clinchy, Goldberger, & Tarule, 1986; Reinharz, 1994; Riger, 1990). In their view, positivist methods and theories in psychology obscured and distorted women's experiences and knowledge. Women's voices—their words, intuitions, and insights—have not been clearly heard or understood. This obscuring of voices has also happened to other groups not well represented among researchers (e.g., persons of color, low-income persons, and those with physical or mental disabilities). Students in schools are seldom asked for their experiences and views in research on teaching and learning (Weinstein, 2002a). Reinharz (1994) noted that researchers cannot "give" voice to excluded groups or individuals; voice is something one develops oneself. Yet researchers can create ways to listen to and learn from voices of diverse persons and help bring their voices into psychology's knowledge base.

Attending to unheard voices involves beginning research from the standpoint of the less powerful individuals within social systems—the people who are most affected by the practices of social system(s) (e.g., global economy, workplace, mental health services, school system, or university) but who have the least control over those practices. Study the issue through their experiences, from their point of view, to understand the multiple social systems that affect them. That knowledge can then be used to advocate for social change to improve their lives and perhaps the quality of life for the whole community or society. Rappaport (1981) advocated this approach in his early discussions of empowerment. It is especially consistent with critical philosophies of science (Nelson & Prilleltensky, 2005).

Many forms of feminist community psychology (e.g., Bond, Hill, Mulvey, & Terenzio, 2000a, 2000b; Salina, Hill, Solarz, Lesondak, Razzano, & Dixon, 2004) illustrate research that takes a stand. Feminist researchers are often explicit about values and premises, attend to unheard voices, and conduct valid scholarly research that supports an activist approach to social change. They also call attention to how multiple ecological levels are intertwined, examining how macrosystems, organizations, and interpersonal forces are connected to oppression and liberation of women (recall the feminist slogan: "The personal is political"). Feminist community researchers often show how their own life experiences influence their perspectives, seek to be explicit about their assumptions, and aim to learn from others' perspectives. Research becomes a process of personal development and interpersonal bonding, not simply an intellectual undertaking—a distinctively feminist theme.

Cris Sullivan and associates worked with community women's advocates and survivors of domestic violence to develop a program in which paraprofessional advocates worked with women with abusive partners. The researchers "took a stand," based in feminist values and analysis, but also used randomized experimental designs with representative samples. Their studies demonstrated that battered women involved in the advocacy relationship reported less violence, more social support, and better perceived quality of life than those in a control group (Bybee & Sullivan, 2002; Sullivan, 2003).

Community researchers can take a stand in many community contexts. Participatory community researchers also work collaboratively with citizens in communities and attend to unheard voices (Jason, Keys, Suarez-Balcazar, & Davis, 2004; Langhout & Thomas, 2010). For example, consider a middle-class community that develops a program to prevent drug abuse among its youth. The program funders require evaluation of the program's effectiveness. In a positivist approach, the evaluation researchers would maintain a neutral stance, distant from the program, making most or all of the choices about the evaluation research. In contrast, empowerment evaluation methods (see Chapter 13) focus on working with the program, helping to clarify its goals and initial planning, providing feedback on how it is actually implemented, and evaluating its outcomes. Important voices to consider would include the community's youth.

This approach creates a partnership that continually improves program quality over time, instead of issuing a one-time verdict on program effectiveness from an outsider's perspective (Fetterman, 2002). Both approaches have value; our point here is that taking a stand (in this case, empowerment evaluation) is a legitimate approach, generating knowledge not provided by an outside evaluation.

HOW CAN WE PROMOTE COMMUNITY PARTICIPATION AND COLLABORATION IN RESEARCH DECISIONS?

The first time I ever did research, I'll never forget it…. I went through eleven organizations; they all turned me down. So Baake called some guy … and said will you be kind to Chris Argyris and let him come into your bank and interview some people…. So I went in and interviewed fifty people, did my study…. And I went and gave the people some feedback, and they said "We like this. Would you come in now and do a total bank study?" Which I did…. I got almost diametrically opposed data. And I had interviewed twenty-five of the same people that I interviewed before…. I had nineteen of them come into a room, and I said "You can tell me what's going on." They said "Professor, it ain't so difficult. Four weeks ago, it was be-kind-to-Chris week. So some of us answered the questions in a way, who cares, and some said what the hell, it's not threatening, tell the truth. Now you come back as a consultant/researcher. Those of us who are now frightened distort the data, and those who think they might get some help give you the truth." (Argyris, quoted in Kelly, 1986, p. 583)

It is clear from this anecdote that the quality and usefulness of research data depend on the context in which they are collected and especially on the relationship between researcher and research participants. When the researcher's position, power, and purposes changed, so did the nature of what employees told him. Argyris was performing organizational research, but similar issues pervade community psychology research.

One metaphor for the researcher-community relationship is that of guest and host (Robinson, 1990). Research is conducted by guests in a host community; among the good manners that might be expected of such guests are full disclosure of their intent and methods, seeking permission for their activities, respect for host wishes and views, and meaningful thanks for hospitality. Researchers receive the gift of cooperation by the community in providing data; reciprocating that gift involves providing products of that research in a form useful to the community. Another metaphor for this relationship is a collaborative partnership, with both parties having some degree of choice and control and with open communication, compromise, and respect regarding those choices. Each partner brings unique resources to the shared work. Participatory community research is not a "noble sacrifice" by researchers; it involves rewards and costs for researchers and community members (Isenberg, Loomis, Humphreys, & Maton, 2004).

These metaphors imply a concern for the long-term interests of the community. The partnership metaphor especially involves participation by community members in planning and conducting research. The approaches we will discuss here have been termed **participatory community research**, **participatory action research**, **action research**, **collaborative research**, and **community science** (Jason et al., 2004; Kelly, Ryan, Altman, & Stelzner, 2000; Reason & Bradbury, 2001; Tolman & Brydon-Miller, 2001; Trickett & Espino, 2004; Wandersman, Kloos, Linney, & Shinn, 2005). Many of these are intellectual descendants of Lewin's action research efforts in the 1940s.

Many researchers have exploited communities as "pockets of needs, laboratories for experimentation, or passive recipients of expertise" (Bringle & Hatcher, 2002, pp. 503–504). The metaphor of "data mining" fits the approach of researchers who conduct community research that benefits the researchers but not the community studied. To extend the metaphor of guests and hosts, researchers have not been particularly good guests. Reciprocity has not been the norm for much research conducted by academic researchers working in community settings. Those communities are understandably reluctant to cooperate with future researchers. As community psychologists, we have to keep this history in mind, making sure that we do not repeat these patterns and that we follow through on commitments to create useful research products for our host communities. While collaborative methods are not a panacea, they do address issues of control and avoiding exploitation.

These control-related issues become even more important if the research involves an intervention or action program. The problem to be addressed, the specific objectives of the intervention, and how it is implemented and evaluated, are all issues to be decided. Long-term commitment by researchers is needed if the intervention is to be incorporated into the everyday life of the setting (Primavera, 2004). The practice of conducting collaborative research involves values, emotions, personal relationships, and resolving conflicts. Researchers need not only an intellectual understanding of the issues involved, but also social-emotional insight and skills.

Genuinely collaborative research often leads to personal change for citizens and researchers (Foster-Fishman et al., 2005). Cultural misunderstandings, power differentials, divergent values, and other factors create challenges, yet also can lead to richer understandings and better research (Jason et al., 2004; Primavera & Brodsky, 2004; Sarason, 2003a). This is a key point. In collaborative research practice, we are often able to gain key insights into community processes and learn things that we would not have otherwise known using more traditional approaches to research (Chirowodza et al., 2009).

In this section, we review specific approaches to facilitating researcher-community partnership and citizen participation in research decision making at each stage of community research: before the beginning, defining the topic, collecting data, interpreting and reporting findings, and actions based on findings.

At each step, we present approaches that maximize participation by community members. We do not advocate that these methods are useful or appropriate in every context. Community research varies along a spectrum from minimum to maximum community participation, and participation may be understood as a process in which capacity is built over time (Bess, Prilleltensky, Perkins, & Collins, 2009). Each community and research project requires a different matching of researcher and citizen roles (Pokorny et al., 2004). For further reading, we especially recommend several resources (Bond, Hill, Mulvey, & Terenzio, 2000b; Bringle & Hatcher, 2002; Brodsky, 2001; Fisher & Ball, 2003; Hazel & Onanga, 2003; Hughes & Seidman, 2002; Jason et al., 2004; Kelly, Ryan, Altman, & Stelzner, 2000; Langhout & Thomas, 2010; Nelson et al., 2001; Primavera & Brodsky, 2004; Tolan et al., 1990; Wandersman et al., 2005).

Partnership "Before the Beginning"

The research partnership begins with entry of researchers into the community. Entry issues include the following: Who are the researchers, what institutions support or fund them, and what are their purposes? Are researchers invited into the community? By whom and under what terms? Who are the community representatives, and are they representative of the community? Who will benefit from research in this community?

The resources of researchers and the host community must be assessed. From researchers, these may include funding for programs or staff positions for community members. To build true collaboration, both sides will need to devote time and effort and decide how to share control. Not every community needs or wants the same resources from researchers: an economically oppressed community may look for economic resources, while in a more affluent community, the need may be for emotional support and respect for persons with chronic illness (Nelson et al., 2001). Community members also offer resources, such as practical knowledge of the community and culture, social networks, and access to community settings.

Interdependence of researchers and citizens must be built through interpersonal relationships. That involves plenty of informal face-to-face contact, getting to know each other without the barriers of expertise and titles. It also involves commitments for a longer period of time than a traditional research and/or intervention project might assume. For community researchers, important interpersonal skills include accurate self-awareness of one's emotions and of how one appears to others, self-disclosure in the process of building trust, and clear communication of aims, viewpoints, and values. Having community members explain their community and culture to researchers in an atmosphere of learning and respect is valuable. Humility and willingness to learn are essential. Volunteer community service and informal socializing with community members can be helpful. It is important for researchers to recognize differences in social status, power, culture, and life opportunities between researchers and community members, and to acknowledge how those can limit the perspectives of researchers (we will discuss this more in the section on culturally anchored research).

Researchers may need to demystify the images many citizens hold about research. To promote effective communication within the team, researchers must be willing to find a vocabulary that is commonsensical yet not condescending. Language communicates power, and the use of words such as "empirical" can alienate citizens. Researchers also need to learn from community members' experiential, cultural, "insider" knowledge.

Research Decisions

One option for making research decisions is to create a community research panel, comprised of representatives of community organizations and other citizens, which allows researchers to communicate and negotiate with community members. It also improves the ability of researchers to understand the cultural characteristics of the community and provides a way for the community to hold researchers accountable. Instead of creating a new panel, researchers can establish a formal relationship with an existing body in the community (e.g., a tribal council or neighborhood association).

Another model for research decision making is to include community stakeholders as part of the research team itself. For example, Michelle Fine and her colleagues (2003) worked with incarcerated women to study the impact of college education on women's self-understandings and lives while in prison, the prison environment, and the world outside the prison. A small group of women in prison enrolled in a college-level research methods course and learned to become interviewers and analysts. They joined the research team and shared difficult decisions about the research process as it unfolded. As persons holding insider knowledge and as skilled researchers, they were able to document a process of women's transformation in which "individuals move from being passive objects to active subjects—critical thinkers who actively participate in their lives and social surroundings; who take responsibility for past and future actions; who direct their lives, networks, and social actions in the world" (p. 186).

In both models, a community research panel working with professional researchers as well as a research team comprised of university-community partners, research is planned collaboratively. Some examples of issues to negotiate include whether to use a control group (which does not receive a promising program), whether observers of mutual help group meetings are acceptable, the format and questions for questionnaires, and even where original data will be kept and how its confidentiality can be assured.

These and similar decisions have trade-offs. For example, lack of a control group may limit the evaluation of a program's effectiveness. Open-ended interviews fit the folkways of many communities better than standardized questionnaires but make it more difficult to develop reliable, valid measurements and use a large sample. Negotiating methodological or practical decisions with the community takes time and involves compromise. But the traditional psychological paradigm, in which researchers make these and other choices in the interest of experimental control, is also limited. Many community questions simply cannot be studied with traditional methods. Moreover, genuine collaboration with community members can increase the validity of measurement, as researchers craft more appropriate methods and research participants take the research more seriously. (Have you ever completed a survey hurriedly because you had no investment in the results?) Studies with mutual help groups that involved the group as a genuinely collaborative partner have had very high response rates (Isenberg et al., 2004). Creating a positive relationship with a community affords returning there for future studies. The trade-offs must be considered in each study and community.

A participatory approach can involve experimental methods. The research on advocacy with battered women conducted by Sullivan (2003) and associates (described earlier in this chapter) involved women's shelters, community advocates, and survivors of abuse in decisions about all aspects of the research, including the development of assessment questions and measures. The most difficult decision involved whether to use an experimental design—randomly assigning women to the advocacy program or to a control group that received the usual shelter services. The community members resisted the randomization at first, but eventually were convinced of its fairness and of the value of carefully evaluating the actual effects of the program.

Another step in the community-researcher partnership is interpretation of results. One useful step is to present results to the community research panel or other community members, asking for their interpretations. Researchers and citizens can consider such questions as: Are these results surprising? Is further refinement of methods needed? How can these results be useful to the community? How might they harm the community? For example, if a community needs assessment identified high rates of adolescent risk behaviors or substance abuse, how will this be understood? And what will be done with these results? Will they be used to further stigmatize a community or to leverage additional resources?

Interdependent relationships grow from reciprocity, in which each partner moves from a focus on satisfaction of one's own interests, to focusing on outcomes that benefit both partners over the long term in an atmosphere of trust (Bringle & Hatcher, 2002). Affirming shared values and long-term aims fosters this development, especially when conflicts arise. That does not mean an end to conflicts, but it builds a climate in which to resolve them. It is also important to share credit for successes and work together to address challenges and conflicts. Important interpersonal skills for making collaborative research decisions include providing interpersonal support, asserting and accepting disagreement, avoiding defensiveness, sharing power, and recognizing and managing conflicts. Close monitoring and discussion of these issues fosters relationship development. Primavera (2004) described the ebb and flow of relationships in a university-community partnership for a family literacy program, concluding that "if there is gold to be found in community research and action, it lies in the *process* of our work (p. 190)." Again, how we make research decisions is just as important as the decisions that we make.

In Chapter 1, we discussed the Oxford House movement, in which persons in recovery from substance abuse live together and promote each other's recovery without professional supervision. This nationwide movement began in a Chicago recovery home without any researcher or professional involvement.

Over more than a decade, Oxford House and a research team from DePaul University have developed a collaborative partnership that has benefitted both. The DePaul team entered the relationship with an interest in innovative models of recovery and believed that involving Oxford House members in all phases of the research would enhance its validity and practical value. Oxford House members and researchers meet weekly for an open exchange of ideas and monitoring ongoing research; these meetings are open to any Oxford House member. Likewise, Oxford House meetings, even when sensitive topics are discussed, are open to researchers. Both partners worked to promote trust in the relationship. The research began with student researchers attending Oxford House activities and conducting interviews with residents to learn about the process of recovery at Oxford House from the residents' perspective. This qualitative research became the basis for later quantitative studies, including a randomized experiment comparing Oxford house to other substance abuse recovery conditions, such as outpatient treatment. After 24 months, those in the Oxford House condition compared with the usual-care condition had significantly lower substance use, significantly higher monthly income, and significantly lower incarceration rates (Jason, Olson, Ferrari, & Lo Sasso, 2006).

Research design and assessment instruments were discussed thoroughly and approved by Oxford House representatives. In grant-supported studies, the staff who recruited participants and collected data were current or former Oxford House residents, approved by Oxford House representatives and the research team. The partnership has built the capacity of the research team to understand and measure the utility of the Oxford House approach while also building the capacity of Oxford House staff to perform their own ongoing evaluation and program development. Researchers have become advocates for Oxford House and worked with the movement in establishing new houses for women with children (Suarez-Balcazar et al., 2004).

Research Products and Impact

Research typically generates scholarly reports such as journal articles, books, conference presentations, and the like. These further the researchers' careers but usually do little for the community.

Important questions concern products of research: Who is actually benefitting from this research? Will researchers share their findings with community members in a form useful to them? Did citizens gain knowledge, skills, funding, or other resources to pursue their own goals? Have the researchers and the community members built an ongoing alliance for future collaborations? Even broader issues arise when macrosystems are also considered: Will the research methods or findings promote social justice? Will research products accurately portray the strengths of the individuals, communities, or cultures studied? How can the research inform future decisions by citizens, communities, organizations, governmental bodies, or other groups? How can the research speak directly to policymakers at local, regional, and national levels? Refer to Box 3.1 for a Community Psychology in Action feature describing a partnership that has focused on research processes and products that benefit all involved.

B o x 3.1   Community Psychology In Action

Research Collaborations in Which Everyone Wins
Yolanda Suarez-Balcazar,
University of Illinois at Chicago, Professor and
Gloria Curtin, El Valor, Vice-President for Disability Services

While we get ready to begin a research meeting the students and I admire the art work created by El Valor's clients; colorful large Mexican dolls made of papier mache and picture frames decorated with dried flowers are displayed all around the conference room. El Valor is a community-based organization serving mostly Latinos with developmental disabilities across the lifespan and their families. El Valor is located in a working-class Latino neighborhood in Chicago, home of a Mexican Arts Museum, and bordering the University of Illinois-Chicago (UIC) campus on its south side. El Valor was founded by a Latina immigrant mother of a child with a developmental disability who could not find services for her child at the time. The Spanish word "valor" means "courage," which the founder used to communicate the will and power of Latinos with disabilities and their families that allow them to succeed.

The goals of our collaboration, which has expanded for over 15 years, include to facilitate the empowerment of individuals with disabilities, their families, and that of staff members serving them, and to foster a positive partnership that benefits El Valor's participants and their families, and UIC researchers and students.

During years of working together we have been able to foster a strong collaboration in which each partner is willing to work towards benefiting the other. As such, Yolanda has participated in United Way program reviews while Gloria has spoken at classes taught at UIC. We both have supported each other in grant writing activities. Most fascinating, we, including faculty from UIC and staff from El Valor, recently sponsored an exchange between EL Valor and another partner agency, the Ann Sullivan Center in Lima Peru (CASP), an internationally-recognized research, demonstration, and educational community integrated program that serves individuals and families with a variety of developmental disabilities. A family and staff member from CASP spent a week at El Valor, in May of 2010, learning about EL Valor's aging-in-place research model program while the CASP family trained EL Valor's families using their family empowerment model. In September of 2010, a family and staff from El Valor, two university researchers and one student spent a week at CASP, sharing their aging-in-place research model and learning about CASP's successful consumer and family empowerment model. This has been one of our long-term goals, miles and countries away from each other. We have been studying the CASP's family empowerment model, a which focuses on training family members to work with their member with a disability on functional, productive behaviors and tasks that would lead to independence and employment (e.g., cooking, baking, sorting, counting, etc.). As Gloria says "our plan is to be able to replicate the CASP family empowerment model at El Valor in Chicago" (See photo of the research collaborators in Figure 3.1).

To report results of studies on citizen participation in block associations in Nashville neighborhoods, Chavis, Stucky and Wandersman (1983) and a citizens' panel developed workshops for block association leaders. Community members and researchers led these workshops. Researchers discussed their research in common-sense terms, presented their results, and asked for feedback and interpretations by the citizens. Participants broke into small groups, listed priority problems for their neighborhood, and devised action plans. The workshops enriched the researchers' understanding of their results and facilitated action by the community. Adaptations of this approach have been adopted widely in community research (Jason et al., 2004).

Examples of additional research products might include reader-friendly newsletters for citizens, opinion essays or letters to the editor in newspapers,

Yolanda Suarez Balcazar

F I G U R E 3.1 From left to right: First row: Student, CASP parent, EL Valor parent, CASP participant, dean of the college, Yolanda Suarez-Balcazar, Gloria Curtin, and El Valor staff. Back row: Student, two UIC faculty, and CASP staff.

articles in popular magazines, interviews on broadcast media, expert testimony in legislative hearings or in court, advocacy reports or visits to policymakers, teaching formal or informal courses, contributing to community art projects, and developing educational videos, role-plays, skits, or other performances (Stein & Mankowski, 2004). While conducting interviews on the psychological effects of unemployment, Fryer and Fagan (2003) used a handheld computer to calculate eligibility for government entitlements and programs (for those who were willing to share the financial information needed). This was the first time those benefits had been helpfully explained to many participants. In a project aimed at understanding and enhancing children's experience of an elementary school, the research team (including community psychologists, university students, and elementary school students) created a mural as one of the ways to share their research findings and create change (Langhout, personal communication, see Figure 3.2). The elementary student researchers named the mural "We Are Powerful," and they offered the following inscription: "We hope our mural themes of community, education, and diversity will help all feel like this is a place for them and will inspire all to see they have the power to change their community." In each of these examples, collaborative research teams moved from simply having good intentions to intentionally trying to make a difference (Smith, 2006).

Prilleltensky (2003, 2008) proposed that community psychology research be evaluated not only in terms of methodological (often positivist) forms of validity,

Regina Langhout

F I G U R E 3.2 "We Are Powerful" mural created by team of elementary school student researchers.

but also in terms of two other criteria, which are part of his concept of psycho-political validity. First, does the research account for the influence of macrosystem and other social forces, especially social injustice, on the lives of individuals and communities? Were these forces measured or studied in the research and discussed with community members? Second, does the research promote the capacity of research participants and community members to understand macrosystem forces and to become involved in liberating social change? For example, did citizens gain skills for understanding injustice, articulating their views, forming alliances, resolving conflicts, gaining power, making decisions, and similar capacities for advocating their community's interests?

Pursuing these aims involves careful thinking not only "before the beginning" but also about what happens "after the ending." Throughout our research, we should be thinking not only about the benefits of our research, but also about how our research might be problematic. This reflexive practice helps us attend to possible unintended consequences and *iatrogenic*, or harmful, effects of the research.

Limitations of Participatory Approaches

Participatory, collaborative community research methods have limitations. Not all community psychology research need be participatory. For example, naturalistic assessment of community physical environments or analyses of archival data do not require participatory methods (although a collaborative approach can enhance the research, e.g., Chirowodza et al., 2009; Kuo, Sullivan, Coley, & Brunson, 1998; Perkins & Taylor, 1996).

Participatory methods are time-consuming and risky for citizens, who often must master new roles that can be empowering but also take time, effort, and skill development. The extent of that commitment should be chosen by the citizens, with the support and respect of the other members of the research team. Moreover, participation by some citizens in research decisions opens them to criticism by other community members displeased by the methods or findings. The research team may need to navigate these situations carefully. For example, this may mean respecting the wishes of community panel members for private rather than public involvement (Chataway, 1997). In another case, it may mean building a safe and supportive environment for citizen researchers to take small steps toward political action (Bess, Prilleltensky, Perkins, & Collins, 2009).

The university environment presents obstacles to participatory research by faculty and students. Many graduate programs need more training for the sensitivity, communication, and negotiation that conducting research with full citizen participation involves, especially across cultural boundaries (Hazel, 2007; Julian, 2006; Nelson et al., 2001). Moreover, universities often demand publications more quickly than participatory community research allows in forms not useful to communities.

Although participatory methods level to some extent the hierarchical, unequal relationship between researchers and community members, some power differentials seem inherent in conducting research. Using participatory methods does not magically erase these differentials, which must be acknowledged and dealt with. Even participatory research may have unintended negative consequences for the community. Researchers must be vigilant regarding the process and actual outcomes of their work (Bond, 1990; Burman, 1997; Isenberg et al., 2004).

Terms such as *participatory* and *collaborative* have multiple meanings, which can be divergent or even contradictory (Trickett & Espino, 2004). We have emphasized the commonalities of a number of participatory-collaborative approaches, but further reading is best focused on the diversity of different approaches (see resources we have cited).

Participatory approaches provide specific ways to enact core community psychology values and embody the Swampscott ideal of the *participant-conceptualizer*, who is actively involved in community processes while also attempting to understand and explain them. They represent a distinctive contribution of community psychology to academic research and to communities.

HOW DO WE UNDERSTAND THE CULTURAL AND SOCIAL CONTEXTS OF THIS RESEARCH?

All research, even a laboratory study, occurs within a culture, perhaps more than one. Understanding diverse cultures, populations, and settings is essential for community psychology. It is especially important that community researchers study a variety of cultures and communities, especially those that have been ignored by mainstream psychology. Researchers also need to understand how they themselves are affected by culture. In this section, we will focus on a few specific cultural issues in conducting research. We leave for Chapter 7 a larger analysis of cultural and related concepts for understanding human diversity.

Four Methodological Issues Involving Culture

Cultural assumptions influence every research decision. Yet psychologists have only recently considered how these assumptions limit the meaning and interpretation of our research findings (Sue, 1999; Tebes, 2000; Bond & Harrell, 2006). Recently, cultural variables have been included in many studies without adequate reflection about what is meant by these constructs, why they may be important for a given study, and how they are to be measured or assessed.

For example, suppose a study finds that Latino/a adolescents dropped out of school more often than European American teens—a seemingly simple empirical effect. But such a finding is useless, even harmful, as a basis for designing social policy or prevention programs unless important conceptual questions are answered. Were confounds such as socioeconomic status, effects of stereotyping and discrimination, access to educational opportunities, and first language (English or Spanish) controlled in this study? Is this difference due to factors within Latino cultures or to external economic forces or discrimination? Which Latino/a ethnicities (e.g., Mexican American, Puerto Rican, Cuban, Dominican) were represented in the sample? How might these specific ethnic groups differ from each other? How many Latino/a adolescents were recent immigrants or longer-term U.S. residents? Are cultural factors best understood in a "between group" study that compares two ethnic or cultural groups or by "within group" studies that focus on one culture? These questions illustrate the methodological issues we describe next (see Bernal, Trimble, Burlew, & Leong, 2003; Hughes & Seidman, 2002).

How Is Cultural or Ethnic Identity Assessed?   These and similar concepts are often assessed with simple "box-checking" based on the participant's self-reported choice among a limited set of categories. For example, on a questionnaire, "Asian American" may be the only available category for Americans of Japanese, Vietnamese, Indian, and other ancestries (the category is even wider if Pacific Islanders are included). Related issues include: Is there a coding scheme for multiethnic or biracial responses? Are one's first language, birthplace and parents' birthplaces, and length of residence in the country assessed? What is the extent of one's personal identification with an ethnic or cultural tradition? If researchers rely on simple box-checking, even with more specific boxes to check, they assess only the surface of ethnocultural identification, not its deeper reality (Frable, 1997; Trimble, Helms, & Root, 2003). Deeper identification rather than simple categorization also may be an issue for concepts such as sexual orientation, ability-disability, and religion or spirituality.

Assumptions of Population Homogeneity   A related issue concerns accurately understanding the diversity within every culture. An assumption of population homogeneity (Sasao & Sue, 1993) categorizes all members of a cultural group as alike and overlooks differences among them. Research in social categorization suggested that this results from the cognitive tendency to think about members of one's cultural in-group in more detail than persons outside it (Kelly, Azelton, Burzette, & Mock, 1994). Thus, people understand members of their own culture in complex ways—as individuals and as members of various groups or categories. But people think more simplistically about members of other cultures or communities and tend to categorize them in more general terms. This is ethnocentrism, although often inadvertent. It also reflects lack of detailed knowledge and experience with phenomena we wish to understand in the communities where they occur. Forming a collaborative relationship with community members helps to counteract assumptions of population homogeneity.

For example, Hamby (2000) found considerable differences in cultural gender norms among the 512 recognized American Indian cultural communities in the United States (e.g., Seneca, Zuni, and Apache). Also important are differences between generations of immigrant groups (e.g., first generation immigrants from Mexico, second and third generation Mexican-Americans) as well as gender, socioeconomic, or other differences within ethnic or racial categories (Goodkind & Deacon, 2004; Hughes & Seidman, 2002). In studies of alcohol use among Americans of Japanese ancestry, findings from samples in Hawaii differed from those on the mainland (Sasao & Sue, 1993). At the individual level, some members of an ethnic population may consider their ethnicity a very important aspect of their personal identity, while others do not. Characteristics such as gender make a great deal of difference in worldview and life experiences in any culture.

Assumptions of Methodological Equivalence   A third issue concerns the equivalence of research methods across cultures (Burlew, 2003; Hughes & Seidman, 2002). Such assumptions can occur even when cultural differences are not the topic of research or recognized by researchers. Linguistic equivalence of questionnaires or other measurement instruments is the simplest example. Tanaka-Matsumi and Marsella (cited in Hughes et al., 1993) found that the English clinical term *depression* and the closest Japanese translation *yuutsu* were not equivalent. When asked to define them, U.S. citizens described internal states such as "sad" and "lonely," whereas Japanese described external states such as "dark" and "rain." Careful checks on translation can reduce but not eliminate such problems. Some measures may simply be inappropriate for some cultural groups. For example, Coppens, Page, and Thow (2006) describe the problem of using self-esteem measures with teens engaged in a Cambodian dance group. The self-esteem measures were based on Western understandings of selfhood and self-esteem as a protective factor in youth development, while both the teens, whose families were recent immigrants to the United States, and the dance group were rooted in an interdependent, non-Western cultural tradition.

Issues of scale equivalence refer to whether choices on questionnaires or other measures mean the same thing across cultures. Hughes and Seidman (2002) cited evidence that African American and Hispanic participants were more likely to use the extremes of Likert scales, whereas European American respondents were more likely to use the intermediate areas of such scales. More generally, the quantitative approach of Western psychology is unfamiliar in many cultures. Goodkind and Deacon (2004) discussed how they developed qualitative and quantitative methods for research with two groups of refugee women: Hmong women from Laos and Muslim women from the Middle East, Afghanistan, and Africa. Combining qualitative and quantitative approaches proved to be most effective, as both approaches had strengths and limitations. Survey methods emphasizing forced choice responses were sometimes experienced as silencing but also allowed for longitudinal analysis over time. Qualitative interviewing required overcoming extensive language and translation barriers but allowed for listening to often unheard voices and rich understanding of refugee women's experiences.

Between-Group and Within-Group Designs   A between-group design compares two or more cultural groups, for instance African Americans and European Americans, on variables specified by the researchers. Its strength is that such a comparison can yield knowledge of differences between cultures. One major drawback is that the researchers' own cultures will affect their design, assessment, and interpretation of differences. Also, the equivalence of procedures, setting, and measurements in both cultures is difficult to assure. Finally, without a deep understanding of both cultures, it is difficult to avoid interpreting differences as a deficit or weakness in one of the cultural groups. Thus, between-group studies are vulnerable to producing results that "blame cultures" for problems rather than considering cultural strengths and effects of such external factors as economic and political forces.

Researchers using a within-group design study a cultural group in more depth on its own terms. Comparisons and differences between cultures are not the focus. This approach fosters understanding of why distinctive cultural practices exist. In addition, subgroups within the culture (e.g., based on socioeconomic status or length of U.S. residence) can be understood more clearly. Population-specific psychologies study psychological aspects of specific cultures or cultural groups (e.g., African, Mexican, Polish or Japanese) (Kim & Berry, 1993; Potts, 2003). A review of studies in a major community psychology journal found that between-group studies were more likely to emphasize deficits of a culture or population, while within-group studies more often emphasized strengths (Martin, Lounsbury, & Davidson, 2004). However, between-group comparative studies focusing on distinctive cultural practices and community strengths are possible when research teams include members of each group studied and rely on strong communication between insiders and outsiders of each cultural community (Rogoff, 2003).

Conducting Culturally Anchored Research

What can researchers do to recognize issues of culture and respond to them?

The first steps begin with oneself. Cultivate an understanding of how your own culture and experiences have shaped your own worldview. In addition, adopt a "stance of informed naivete, curiosity, and humility" in learning about another culture: an awareness of your own limited knowledge and a genuine willingness to learn (Mock, 1999). Recognize that this learning will be an ongoing process.

This learning cannot be cultivated in isolation. Seek experiences and personal relationships that promote learning about your own culture and the culture in which you seek to do research. Those experiences may be informal socializing or attending community celebrations and events or more structured interviews with interested community members. What you do may be less important than how you do it, with respect and willingness to listen.

Create safe settings for discussion where researchers and citizens can personally explore difficult issues of culture and power: how one's own culture influences and limits one's worldview; strengths of different cultural worldviews and values; personal effects of social injustice and oppression; how to plan research to promote empowerment of community members; and access to resources that are wanted by the host community. Examples include the following.

Susan McMahon and Roderick Watts (2002) studied ethnic identity among urban African American youth. For this study, McMahon, a European American woman, worked with Watts, an African American man. McMahon examined her own cultural background and how it shaped her own identity, spent much time talking about her interests with African Americans in the school and community, conducted observations and focus group interviews to test measures for validity and cultural equivalence, and sought to understand how economic and sociopolitical barriers affect the lives of African American youth (Keys et al., 2004, p. 189).

James Kelly and his associates (Kelly et al., 1994; Kelly et al., 2004; Tandon et al., 1998) pursued a long-term research project on the nature of leadership in an African-American community in Chicago, collaborating with a panel of community leaders there. Those local leaders, with the support of the researchers, actually designed the interview used in the research. The researchers' original conceptions of leadership focused on personal qualities of individual leaders. However, the leaders on the panel articulated a collective definition of leadership based on their experiences in working together and consistent with their African heritage. They used the metaphor of making soup to describe the importance of individual contributions and group experiences. The research team's perspective, rooted in the individualism of psychology, was expanded by this encounter with different cultural assumptions. These examples highlight the value of learning through extensive communication between "insiders" and "outsiders" of multiple communities (Rogoff, 2003).

One valuable way to learn about cultures is to study its narratives—the shared stories that express important values, historical events, folkways, and emotions. Gary Harper and associates collaborated with Project VIDA, a community-based organization in Little Village, a Mexican American neighborhood in Chicago (Harper, Bangi et al., 2004; Harper, Lardon et al., 2004). Project VIDA conducts HIV prevention programs for adolescent Latinas and for Latino gay, bisexual, and questioning youth. Harper and associates read Latino/a magazines and newspapers, especially those for Latina adolescents. They visited Little Village repeatedly, learning about cultural murals and the neighborhood's decorative gateway, shopping and eating locally, attending (and dancing at) cultural events, and meeting Project VIDA staff and Little Village residents. They sought to learn stories associated with Mexican culture, Little Village, and individuals involved with Project VIDA. Meetings with project staff began with sharing of food and personal stories—a reflection of Mexican culture. The study itself used individual and group interviews to elicit stories from adolescent participants and program staff about culturally based expectations that can promote or hinder HIV prevention among Latino/a adolescents.

Gerald Mohatt, Kelly Hazel, and associates (2004) also drew on narratives in research on sobriety in Alaska Native communities. They took a strengths perspective by studying personal stories of pathways to sobriety. They developed a collaborative research relationship with a coordinating council composed mostly of Native Alaskans while also negotiating steps of the research with a number of Native Alaskan tribal boards and village councils. Tribal Elders rejected the idea of monetary payment for participation, saying that their participation was not for sale and that many persons would participate to contribute to the community. Institutional review boards required that tapes of interviews be destroyed after the research, but Elders also rejected this notion, pointing out the usefulness of tapes for future prevention activities. The researchers developed procedures for each participant to choose whether to receive payment or donate it to charity and to choose whether to allow retention of tapes with confidentiality assured. When recruitment of participants greatly outpaced all expectations (152 persons volunteered for an initial study requiring only 36 participants), the Elders insisted that each volunteer be interviewed to respect their willingness to help. Researchers developed a briefer interview process for this purpose. Researchers also had to forge compromises between federal funders who desired quantitative methods, and Native preference for qualitative interviews that allowed them to tell their own stories. The patience of Native representatives and the research team was rewarded with a rich archive of interviews that expressed cultural strengths and provided a basis for sobriety promotion in Native communities.

An Example: The Akwesasne Study

Santiago-Rivera, Morse, Hunt, and Lickers (1998) reported on the process of building a collaborative partnership between university-based researchers and the Mohawk Nation of Akwesasne, a community located along the St. Lawrence River between the United States and Canada. Their work illustrates many aspects of the participatory approach and of culturally anchored research.

The Mohawk Nation of Akwesasne faces serious environmental contamination from outside corporations' dumping pollutants (e.g., fluorides, cyanide,

PCBs) into the land, water, and air. Ms. Katsi Cook, a Mohawk midwife and community leader, headed efforts to obtain support for a study, funded by an external grant, of the effects of PCB exposure on the health of Akwesasne citizens. Santiago-Rivera and colleagues became involved as part of that study.

The researchers and their Mohawk hosts worked through a process developed by the Akwesasne Task Force on the Environment, a Mohawk group. The researchers found that they had to adapt their communication style to facilitate dialogue with community members. They limited use of scientific vocabulary. They spent much time listening to the experiences and views of many community members and sought education in Mohawk beliefs, customs, and language, as well as the history of the community. Mohawk beliefs about their spiritual relationship with the land made environmental contamination a deeply emotional and spiritual matter. Customs regarding interpersonal relationships affected every aspect of data collection and research planning. The researchers had to sufficiently learn Mohawk culture to gain the trust of their community partners.

Akwesasne Task Force members had many questions for the Santiago-Rivera research team: How will this benefit us? How will you assure confidentiality of data? Will you follow a research protocol and methods that we approve? Who will own and keep the data? Who will be employed with the research grant money?

Researchers and the Akwesasne Task Force worked together to assess the cultural appropriateness of all measurements and materials and to field-test all methods and materials in a small pilot study with Akwesasne citizens. Those participants also discussed their concerns about measurements with the research team and suggested changes. The researchers and task force negotiated roles for carrying out research, including hiring and training Mohawk staff for data collection and supervisory responsibilities. All original data would remain in the Akwesasne community, an Akwesasne committee would review all research to assure that it had followed agreed-on procedures, and an Akwesasne Task Force member would be coauthor of any published reports.

The researchers and community also devised workable means of resolving disagreements. The Mohawk method is to do this by discussion and consensus. The researchers had to adjust their schedules and styles to participate in this approach; balancing the time needed for consensus and the reporting deadlines of the granting agency was a problem. However, the commitment of the Akwesasne and the researchers led to successful resolutions of these issues and completion of research that benefitted both parties.

AT WHAT ECOLOGICAL LEVELS OF ANALYSIS
WILL WE CONDUCT THIS RESEARCH?

For any study, the researchers choose the ecological level(s) of analysis. Questions about ecological levels are actively debated in community psychology. The challenge for a community psychologist is addressing the interrelationships among these differing levels of analysis, not just studying one level in isolation. For example, in a study of protective factors for adolescent resistance to drug use, variables across multiple levels should be considered. These may include individual needs and strengths, such microsystem factors as family and peer influences, neighborhood characteristics, cultural values and resources, economic factors, and political influences on drug laws and enforcement.

Examples of the Importance of Considering Levels of Analysis

Phenomena such as social support for seniors and supported housing for persons with serious mental illness can be viewed through different "lenses" at different ecological levels. Let us consider the following examples.

Supported Housing Environments   How do we understand the ecology of persons living with and recovering from serious mental illness? How do key contexts for living, such as housing, impact well-being? Wright and Kloos (2007) addressed these questions, with particular attention to multiple levels of analysis. They used survey data and observations to examine the specific conditions that served as risk and protective factors for general well-being in persons living in supported housing (persons living independently with a housing subsidy and mental health services that residents choose to utilize). They looked across apartment-level, neighborhood-level, and community-level factors by using self-report measures that examined residents' perception of housing and neighborhood, observer-rated qualities of apartments and neighborhood, and census-tract data. Neighborhood characteristics, particularly the residents' perceptions of belonging, acceptance, and community tolerance, were most predictive of differences in well-being. Wright and Kloos caution that neighborhood characteristics stood out in part because there was less variability in the quality of housing, but their findings show that neighborhood variables were just as important to the residents as the quality of their individual apartments. Many people typically think of the apartment level as the most proximate and most important level for well-being, but it could be that the social qualities of the neighborhood are "closer" in some ways to one's sense of home than the qualities of the apartment itself. The findings point to the importance of social relationships and individuals' overall sense of comfort in their neighborhood. They suggest that supported housing programs focus not just on quality control in terms of the physical conditions of an apartment and its safety but also on increasing tolerance for diversity and disability in neighborhoods as well as increasing opportunities for social contact between neighbors.

Social Support Networks   Do senior citizens receive support from individuals only or do microsystems and organizations also provide support beyond that from individuals? Felton and Berry (1992) conducted a study of social support networks among senior citizens at a hospital geriatric clinic. Their interview questions, following standardized, often-used procedures, asked respondents to name individuals who provided important support to them. Yet Felton and Berry's respondents provided some initially puzzling answers. Although asked about individuals who provided support, many respondents gave answers like "all my nieces and nephews," "my grandchildren," and "the people at my senior center." Almost one-third of the respondents named such groups, not an individual, at least once. In total, about 10% of the support sources listed were groups. When interviewers asked for clarification, most respondents insisted that they meant a group and that it was the group as a whole, not particular individuals, who provided support. (Notice that Felton and Berry then listened to and reported the words of these respondents, whose ideas did not fit the original measurement procedure.)

What do we make of this finding? Social support has usually been understood and measured as a process occurring between two individuals. This has kept much of the research on social support at the individual level (Felton & Shinn, 1992). Yet clearly social support also occurs in groups (Maton, 1989), especially in microsystems. Those groups provide support and a sense of community even when the individual members change. Maton (1989) found that highly supportive religious congregations, mutual help groups, and senior centers provided significant aid to members facing a variety of stressors. In fact, the sense of belonging within such an organization or microsystem (social integration) may be as important as social support from individuals (Felton & Shinn, 1992).

How Can Ecological Levels Be Studied?

How can researchers study the characteristics of levels beyond the individual, such as microsystems, organizations, and communities? These cannot solely be studied by administering individual measures familiar to psychologists. Individuals within a classroom, organization, or even locality may be interdependent members of a community, which complicates statistical analysis and interpretation (Shinn & Rapkin, 2000). Community psychology seeks to answer questions about the effects of larger ecological units on individual lives. Following are a few ideas—a suggestive but not exhaustive list.

In Chapter 5 we describe the idea of measuring the social climate of a setting (Moos, 1984, 1994, 2003). In a number of studies, Moos and associates measured the psychological characteristics of environments such as classrooms and mental health treatment settings. They did this by using questionnaires to ask individuals about their perceptions of qualities of the environment, which are summed to measure constructs such as supportiveness of relationships among setting members, how task-oriented the setting is, and how clear the goals and rules of the organization are. These are subjective ratings based on individual judgments. When scores are combined for everyone in the setting, the mean level of perceived supportiveness for a classroom, for example, can be used to compare it to other classrooms. However, this approach has limitations. For example, an overall mean level of perceived supportiveness among employees in a workplace does not reveal if there are systematic differences in perceptions between female and male employees (Shinn, 1990; Shinn & Rapkin, 2000).

More objective measures of a small group or organization can be provided by independent outside observers (Shinn, 1990). Roberts et al. (1991, 1999) used trained independent observers to conduct behavioral observations of a self-help group. Their studies yielded important findings about social support exchanged in such groups.

An intermediate approach uses key informants to provide information on an organization or community. Allen (2005) studied the effectiveness of community coordinating councils by interviewing and surveying members and leaders. Chesir-Teran (2003) suggested methods for measuring heterosexism in high schools—through surveys, interviews, physical observations, and archival records.

Another approach is to identify and count changes in a community as a whole. Fawcett and associates have developed a variety of such measures (Fawcett et al., 1995). Examples include a new high school peer-helping program to reduce drug abuse, a new radio station policy prohibiting the glamorization of drug use, and the creation of training courses for clergy in drug abuse prevention efforts for their congregations. Speer, Hughey, Gensheimer, and Adams-Leavitt (1995) used archival data to measure the impact of community advocacy organizations. Over a three-year period, they counted the number of stories in major metropolitan newspapers on two such organizations and the number of ideas emphasized by each group that appeared in these stories. Such measures are especially useful in longitudinal studies of community change.

Finally, we might approach complex social settings and contexts as systems (Foster-Fishman & Behrens, 2007; Helm & Flaspohler, 2008). Recall, for example, our discussion earlier in this chapter of a study that examines the impacts of a neighborhood on children's lives. We suggested that multiple measures might be used to understand the neighborhood context, including demographic census data and different stakeholders' perceptions of problems, opportunities, and resources in the neighborhood. We might also think about the neighborhood (and the children in the neighborhood) as part of a system with boundaries, ecological layers, niches, organizations, and actors (Foster-Fishman, Nowell, & Yang, 2007). For example, we might begin by asking how to determine the boundaries of the neighborhood. What would children who live in the neighborhood tell us about this (or show us on a guided tour or draw for us on a map)? How would we reconcile the perspectives of children with the perspectives of their caregivers and other stakeholders in the neighborhood as well as the boundaries created by elementary school catchment areas, service delivery systems, public transportation routes, and census tracts? A focus on ecological systems might not make our jobs as researchers easier, but it may help us to focus on dynamic, multilayered contexts and second-order, participatory strategies.

In Chapter 5, we describe in greater detail a number of ecological concepts that community psychologists use to think about these issues (for useful reviews, see also Linney, 2000; Shinn & Rapkin, 2000; Trickett, 2009). Multiple ecological levels are embedded in the name "community psychology." Researchers in the field choose ecological level(s) of analysis for every study, even if only by default. Research is improved by making those choices explicit and by addressing factors at multiple ecological levels.

CONCLUSION

Our format of four questions for community research may seem to imply that a research team answers these four questions in a sequence. Actually, these choices are interdependent and not necessarily sequential. It is not unusual for an existing partnership with a community organization to influence the researcher's choice of phenomenon, perspective, and level of analysis for a study. Or a researcher may study her own culture or population—often within an existing relationship with a specific community. What is certain is that all four questions are involved in community research, whether explicitly chosen by the researcher or implicitly assumed without reflection. Community research always occurs within a culture and a community, always concerns levels of analysis, and always studies a phenomenon from a particular framework of values. Our purpose in this chapter has been to help you become more aware of these questions, and thus more capable of making explicit, reasoned choices in performing community research. In the next chapter, we turn to specific research methods.

CHAPTER SUMMARY

1. Communities provide useful settings for research. Conducting community research involves explicitly answering four questions: What values and assumptions do we bring to our work? How can we promote community participation and collaboration in research decisions? How do we understand the cultural and social contexts of this research? At what ecological levels of analysis will we conduct this research? These four questions involve aspects of a larger question: Who will generate what knowledge, for whom, and for what purposes?

2. Three philosophies of science underlie much community psychology research. These concern definitions of science, scientific knowledge, proper research methods, and how to use research findings. *Positivist* views emphasize objectivity, measurement, experimentation, hypothesis-testing to discover cause and effect, and generalizing findings to other settings. *Post-positivist* views, a later development of positivism, assume that no researcher is truly neutral but seek to minimize bias with measurement and experimentation. *Constructivist* views emphasize a connection between researcher and participant, the particular setting where research occurs, and understanding participants' experiences and their meaning to participants,

not just causes and effects. *Critical* views emphasize how social forces and belief systems influence researchers and participants and researchers' responsibility for integrating research with social action. Each philosophy of science has advantages and limitations. Our main point is to encourage explicit decisions by researchers about values and philosophy of science.

3. Social issues also affect community research. A positivist approach defines social problems and seeks to test solutions with scientific research. A problem with this is that social issues are often conflicts between competing perspectives offering different definitions of the issue. Community researchers can address controversial issues by taking a stand, conducting research that provides information from overlooked or missing perspectives. *Attending to unheard voices*, the views and strengths of persons who are affected by social issues and policies but who hold little power, is one such approach.

4. We described *participatory, collaborative community research* processes: "before the beginning" of research, making research decisions, and products of research. Developing a *community research panel* is one way to involve citizens in these decisions; community members may also become part of the research team itself. *Psychopolitical validity* concerns whether the research process empowered citizens to become involved in liberating social change to benefit their communities. Participatory research involves trade-offs. Each researcher-community partnership will have its own level of optimal involvement.

5. Understanding the cultural and social contexts of a community is important. Four research issues involve culture: (a) how cultural and ethnic identity are assessed; (b) challenging assumptions of *population homogeneity*, that everyone is similar within a cultural group; (c) *methodological equivalence* of research methods and measures across cultures; and (d) whether it is more valuable to study differences between cultural groups or study one cultural group in detail (*between-group* or *within-group* studies).

6. Much community research concerns multiple ecological levels of analysis. We illustrated how thinking in levels-of-analysis terms helps to understand community contexts for well-being and social support networks. We gave suggestive examples of how ecological levels above the individual may be studied.

7. The four questions for community research are not a sequence but are interrelated. We advocate making explicit choices about each question.

RECOMMENDED READINGS

Bond, M., Hill, J., Mulvey, A., & Terenzio, M. (Eds.). (2000a, 2000b). Special Issues: Feminism and community psychology [Parts I and II]. *American Journal of Community Psychology, 28*(5, 6).

Hughes, D., & Seidman, E. (2002). In pursuit of a culturally anchored methodology. In T. Revenson, A. D'Augelli, S. French, D. Hughes, D. Livert, E. Seidman, M. Shinn, & H. Yoshikawa, (Eds.), *Ecological research to promote social change: Methodological advances from community psychology* (pp. 243–255). New York: Kluwer/ Plenum.

Jason, L., Keys, C., Suarez-Balcazar, Y., Taylor, R., & Davis, M. (Eds.). (2004). *Participatory community research: Theories and methods in action.* Washington, DC: American Psychological Association.

Primavera, J., & Brodsky, A. (Eds.). (2004). Special issue: Process of community research and action. *American Journal of Community Psychology, 33*(3/4).

RECOMMENDED WEBSITES

American Journal of Community Psychology
http://www.springer.com/psychology/community+psychology/journal/10464

Journal of Community Psychology
http://onlinelibrary.wiley.com/journal/10.1002/(ISSN)1520-6629

Journal of Community and Applied Social Psychology
http://onlinelibrary.wiley.com/journal/10.1002/(ISSN)1099-1298

4

Methods of Community Psychology Research

J. Stan Mason

OPENING EXERCISE

What specific methods do community psychologists draw upon in answering research questions?

In this chapter, we discuss qualitative and quantitative community research methods, introducing each approach in its own terms. Pause for a moment to think about your own experience with research methods. What classes have you taken that inform your perspective on research methods? Have you participated in research projects before? What do you think makes for good research? Reflect also on what you have learned about community psychology so far. How do you think community psychology methods reflect the values and goals of the field? How do they contribute to knowledge in the field?

Here, we highlight specific methods, with summaries of their strengths and limitations and examples of actual studies. We also examine how qualitative and quantitative methods can be integrated in a single study. Our overall themes are these:

- Qualitative and quantitative methods yield complementary forms of useful knowledge.

- Choice of methods must depend on the questions to be answered in the research.

- Both qualitative and quantitative methods can be used in participatory-collaborative community research of the type we discussed in Chapter 3.

- Multiple methods often strengthen a specific study.
- Contextual and longitudinal perspectives often strengthen community research.
- Community psychology is best served by a diversity of forms of knowledge and methods of research.

QUALITATIVE METHODS

Let us begin with a study that illustrates the power of a detailed analysis of meaningful human experience found in qualitative methods. Catherine Stein and Virginia Wemmerus (2001) studied how a sample of families of adults with schizophrenia responded to their family members' illness. They interviewed 22 individuals from six families, including the family member with schizophrenia. (Studies of families with members who have schizophrenia seldom include the ill family member. One goal of this study was to attend to their perspectives.) This sample is small and limited in diversity; more studies are needed. Yet the authors' use of qualitative methods yielded a rich, compelling account of family life not provided by other studies and led to actions beyond a research report (Stein & Mankowski, 2004).

Stein and Wemmerus interviewed all participants, asking open-ended questions about their perceptions of the onset and course of the schizophrenia, the impact of that illness on the family, family caregiving efforts, and expectations for the future. The researchers' "passionate listening" allowed participants to "think out loud" about the meaning of their experiences and to share hurt, vulnerabilities, and strengths. The experience led the researchers to consider how society (including themselves) contributes to the pain of coping with schizophrenia and to consider the hopes, strengths, and active coping of families and persons with schizophrenia (Stein & Mankowski, 2004, p. 28).

Stein and Wemmerus reported their findings in terms of a life course perspective: the ways in which schizophrenia had interrupted what families considered "a normal life" for their family member in early or middle adulthood; the losses and grief that ensued; the efforts of the person with schizophrenia and his or her family to recover or achieve the social roles of "a normal life" (e.g., daily activities, work, social life, and intimate relationships); and their expectations for the future. These excerpts convey participants' efforts to live socially valued roles and suggest the immediacy and emotional impact of attending to unheard perspectives:

> From Martin's mother, describing the onset of his illness: "Well, mothers are supposed to fix things. And all I could do was, you know, try to get help.... It's devastating to understand that [your child has] a lifelong illness and it's going to be hard for him, a lot harder for him than it is for me, and it's devastating for me."
> From Martin's sister: "Martin's not fine in any sense of the term, but he's doing fine. He's living independently, he can go do his own shopping, he can go to the doctor's, and he can drive a car."

From Donna, who was a wife, mother of two, and a teacher when her schizophrenia began: "I never dreamed when [my children] were born that I'd get that sick, and have [my children] move away and live with my brother. That was hard. Very hard."

From Mary, who has coped with schizophrenia for 11 years: "This Thanksgiving was different. I had my own Thanksgiving here with my husband. And it turned out to be a success. We had a couple and a single person. We had our own turkey, sweet potatoes, lima beans, gelatin salad and the couple brought a pumpkin pie. My first Thanksgiving since I've been married." (Stein & Wemmerus, 2001, pp. 734–735, 738–739; names are pseudonyms)

In reading these remarks, if you experience some of their anguish, longing, courage, pride, and other feelings, that illustrates the power of qualitative methods. Stories of meaningful life experiences are not easily forgotten.

The researchers' commitment to understanding the role of the ill family member in family life led to uncovering a striking finding: When family members were asked about their preparations for future caregiving with their ill family member, none of the six families had discussed those issues with that person, despite abundant evidence of the families' caring involvement (Stein & Wemmerus, 2001, p. 740). That omission did not result simply from family dynamics but from societal attitudes about persons with schizophrenia, and it suggests that more active efforts are needed by both families and the mental health system to include persons with mental illness in decisions about their lives and care.

This research led to a publication and to Stein's developing a course in which clinical psychology graduate students learn about schizophrenia through being paired with persons coping with the illness. Through shared learning activities, these persons teach the future clinicians about daily coping with the illness (Stein & Mankowski, 2004). Disseminating this type of research to persons who make decisions and set policies has also proven useful. Sharing less-often told, yet meaningful life stories, helps stakeholders to connect with one another and see one another's needs and strengths more fully.

Common Features of Qualitative Methods

Qualitative methods have a long history in psychology (Maracek, Fine, & Kidder, 1997; Stewart, 2000). The clinical case history is a qualitative method. Other examples include Dollard's (1937) study *Caste and Class in a Southern Town* and Rosenhan's (1973) infiltration of psychiatric units by pseudo-patients, "On Being Sane in Insane Places." *Women's Ways of Knowing* (Belenky, Clinchy, Goldberger, & Tarule, 1986) advocated the importance of qualitative approaches for understanding women's experiences.

Qualitative approaches are useful for examining situations, processes, and contexts that have not been studied in detail. They give voice to perspectives that have not been fully articulated in existing research. Thus, some community researchers use qualitative approaches in initial exploration and theory development stages of a project, generating hypotheses that can be later tested in quantitative research.

But qualitative approaches also stand on their own, providing detailed analysis of complex, dynamic, and meaningful lived experiences across a variety of social and cultural contexts (Camic, Rhodes, & Yardley, 2003). This detailed analysis of meaningful human experience in particular contexts is essential for advancing scientific knowledge in community psychology (Tebes, 2005). Qualitative research includes a diversity of methods, but most of them share the common features listed below.

1. **Contextual meaning.** The principal aim of qualitative research is to understand the meaning of a phenomenon for persons who experience it in the contexts of their lives. This involves allowing persons to "speak in their own voices" as much as possible, although interpretation by researchers is also involved. Contextual understanding represents a form of "insider knowledge," although it is generated in part by discussions with outsiders (researchers).

2. **Participant-researcher collaboration.** Contextual meaning is created within personal, mutual relationships that evolve over time between research participants and researchers. These methods are thus especially apt for collaborative research with community members and for understanding diverse social and cultural contexts. Participatory approaches (as discussed in Chapter 3) extend modes of collaboration, so participants contribute directly as members of the research team.

3. **Purposeful sampling.** The researcher develops a richly layered understanding of a particular community group or setting. The sample of persons included in the research is usually small to facilitate the level of detail needed. Researchers may also rely on their own experiences as sources of information.

4. **Listening.** As much as possible, the researcher sets aside preconceptions and attempts to understand the persons or setting on their terms, in their language and context. Attentiveness, asking open-ended questions, and providing freedom for interviewees to structure their own responses are preferred over standardized questionnaires (which often reflect researchers' preconceptions or theories).

5. **Reflexivity.** Researchers also seek to be reflexive: stating their interests, values, preconceptions, and personal statuses or roles as explicitly as possible—both to the persons studied and in the research report. They also re-examine those assumptions in light of what they learn from the research participants. This makes potential biases and assumptions as transparent as possible.

6. **Thick description.** Qualitative data in psychology are usually in the form of words. The researcher seeks specific "thick description" of personal experiences, detailed enough to provide convincing evidence of realism. This also affords later checking for significant details and patterns. Other researchers can also use these detailed notes or transcripts to check the validity of analysis and interpretation.

7. **Data analysis and interpretation.** The processes of data collection, data analysis, and interpretation overlap, and the researcher moves back and forth among them. Analysis often consists of identifying (coding) repeating themes or separating and comparing distinct categories or stages. For example, a researcher may use a question-ordered matrix (Sonn & Fisher, 1996, p. 421) in which questions form the columns, individual interviewees the rows, and answers by each participant the entries in each cell. This framework promotes comparison of responses. Researchers can test the validity of themes or categories by collecting and analyzing more data. Multiple coders and checks on inter-coder agreement are used to strengthen reliability.

8. **Checking.** Usually after several rounds of refinement through data collection and analysis, the researcher may check themes and interpretations by presenting them to informants or other community members for correction, clarification, and interpretation. Participatory methods allow community members to critically evaluate themes and challenge interpretations during the analysis process.

9. **Multiple interpretations.** It is possible to have multiple interpretations or accounts of a topic. However, an account should be internally consistent and compelling in terms of its realism and thick description. Yet tensions and competing perspectives that arise from within a participatory research team can also provide compelling evidence.

10. **Generalization.** Generalization of findings is less important than understanding meaning among the persons sampled. Researchers may generalize findings by identifying converging themes from multiple studies or cases.

(Useful resources include Brodsky, 2001; Brydon-Miller & Tolman, 1997; Camic, Rhodes, & Yardley, 2003; Cosgrove & McHugh, 2000; Denzin & Lincoln, 1994; Langhout, 2003; Miles & Huberman, 1994; Miller, 2004; Miller & Banyard, 1998; Rapley & Pretty, 1999; Rappaport, 1990, 1993, 1995, 2000; Reinharz, 1994; Riger, 1990; Stein & Mankowski, 2004; Stewart, 2000; Tolman & Brydon-Miller, 2001.)

Acts of Qualitative Research   How do qualitative researchers conduct a study? Catherine Stein and Eric Mankowski (2004) identified four essential steps in qualitative study (they focus on qualitative interviewing). They termed these *acts* that progress and build on one another over time, like acts in a play.

Act One, **asking**, involves identifying the persons to be included in the study and making explicit the researchers' assumptions and values. This involves our first two questions for community research in Chapter 3: What values and assumptions do we bring to our work? And how can we promote community participation and collaboration in research? (Note that *asking* here does not involve interviewing, which comes in the next step.)

For Stein and Mankowski, qualitative research is directly connected to social justice and social change and explicitly taking a stand. They noted that qualitative methods can be used not only to attend to unheard voices of marginalized groups but also to understand and critique the conceptions of privileged groups.

Either approach can promote social change. For example, Stein and Wemmerus (described earlier) studied families of persons with schizophrenia, including the often ignored views of ill family members. On the other hand, Mankowski studied men's support groups and intervention groups for men who battered women. Many but not all of their experiences reflected the power of their gender roles.

Rebecca Campbell and associates described how they designed recruitment flyers to offer a safe, respectful setting for interviewing women who were survivors of rape and circulated these in community locales frequented by women (Campbell, Sefl, Wasco, & Ahrens, 2004). Research participants attested to the power of these flyers in their decision to participate in the study, feeling safe, respected, and able to share personal experiences in ways that would help other women.

Act Two, **witnessing**, concerns how researcher and participant create knowledge through developing relationships. The researcher poses open-ended questions, the participant describes experiences and ideas, and the researcher provides an attentive, empathic, affirming audience. Participants' words are recorded in some way. In the Campbell et al. (2004) study of rape survivors, interviewers formed an emotional bond with participants that facilitated participants' ability to tell their stories and (for many) the experience of some healing of their trauma by participating in the interview.

Witnessing requires that the researchers put aside their own preconceptions as much as possible and be open to the words and experiences of the participants. Moreover, their relationships may lead to transformation for both researcher and participant. Both researchers and participants may get more than they expected in terms of intensity of the experiences, personal revelations, and motivation or accountability for engaging in personal, community, or social change (see also Campbell, 2002; Stewart, 2000).

Act Three, **interpreting**, is analysis of the information gathered in asking and witnessing, making wider sense of patterns in the experiences of participants. This act raises the question: Whose story is this? Is the primary purpose to communicate the experiences and voices of participants (their stories) or to classify, analyze, or critique those experiences (the researcher's story)? Also, is there one underlying story or many stories among participants? The researcher creates meaning by "transforming 'participant stories' into 'research stories'" (Stein & Mankowski, 2004, p. 22). That meaning must explain the participant stories, so reflexivity, checks on interpretation, and acknowledgment of multiple possible interpretations are needed.

For example, in the Stein and Wemmerus (2001) study of families that include a person with schizophrenia, the researchers recorded and transcribed all interviews with participants and independently read each repeatedly to identify themes in the participant comments. They then discussed and agreed on themes and excerpted quotations that reflected each. Themes concerned similarities and differences among families and among individuals within families. To test the reliability and coherence of their findings, the researchers then had two assistants match the excerpted quotations with the themes. Further discussion among researchers and assistants led to refinement of theme categories and eventually to agreement on several key themes (Stein & Wemmerus, 2001, p. 732). The participants' words and experiences did not always fit the researchers' preconceptions, which required refinement of themes (Stein & Mankowski, 2004).

Stein and Mankowski argued that researchers have legitimate authority to make interpretations that challenge participants' views, but that such interpretations are best made explicit so others can evaluate them. Brodsky and colleagues (2004) describe negotiating agreement on interpretations among members of a research team.

Act Four, **knowing**, involves the products of qualitative research and whether these are used to further the interests or capacities of research participants. This includes not only academic research reports but also other arenas. Stein developed the innovative course we discussed earlier, in which graduate students were paired with persons with schizophrenia, teaching the future clinicians about everyday life with schizophrenia. Mankowski developed a YMCA class, regional conferences, and radio appearances to promote men's discussion of sexism and dismantling sexist roles.

While these four acts form a sequence, some moving back and forth among them is characteristic of qualitative research. Each specific qualitative research method conducts each act in somewhat different ways, and researchers can shape each act to the circumstances in their study.

As emphasized throughout this section, qualitative methods are very useful for attending to unheard voices of marginalized groups and reducing (but not eliminating) power differentials between researcher and participant. They also afford a deeper, contextual understanding of a culture, community, or population. However, they do not simply express the views and voices of participants. The assumptions and interpretations of the researcher are always involved, even with open-ended questioning and discussion (Miller, 2004; Rapley & Pretty, 1999).

The grounding of qualitative research in researcher-participant relationships is both a strength and source of potential limitations. These relationships not only generate knowledge, but may also lead to friendship or to meaningful personal change and social action. However, dilemmas may arise as the researcher moves from witnessing to interpreting. Participants may find their views described or critiqued in ways they do not like and feel betrayed in proportion to the degree of trust that they had established. Researchers may be reluctant to analyze or critique the views of persons with whom they are now personally connected. Even with informed consent at the outset, and participant checking of interpretations later, problems may arise. Participatory approaches to research decisions facilitate discussion of such dilemmas (Jason, Keys, Suarez-Balcazar, Taylor, & Davis, 2004; Langhout & Thomas, 2010; Paradis, 2000).

We next discuss four types of qualitative methods: participant observation, qualitative interviews, focus groups, and case studies. These are only some of the available qualitative methods. (The following sources present other qualitative methods, including discourse analysis, conversation analysis, and concept mapping: Campbell & Salem, 1999; Cosgrove & McHugh, 2000; Denzin &

Lincoln, 1994; Miller & Banyard, 1998; Rapley & Pretty, 1999; Stewart, 2000; Tandon, Azelton, Kelly, & Strickland, 1998.)

Participant Observation

Many community researchers, especially if they conduct participatory research, perform at least some participant observation. It is a key component of ethnographic research in anthropology and other social sciences. For some studies, participant observation is the primary method. Both words in its title are important. Participant observation involves careful, detailed observation, with written notes, interviews or conversations with citizens, and conceptual interpretation. It is not just a description or a memoir. Yet it is also participation, as the researcher becomes a member of a community or a collaborator in its efforts, an actor in community life. This provides at least some of the experiential insider knowledge of community members, while the researcher also strives to maintain something of the outsider perspective.

Strengths and Limitations Participant observation is the method of choice for a researcher seeking maximum insider knowledge and depth of experience in a community. The participant observer knows the setting thoroughly and can communicate its essence vividly. This method also maximizes the researcher-community relationship and affords thick description of many aspects of community life.

However, that depth of knowledge comes at a price. First, the focus on one setting necessarily means that generalizability to other settings is a problem. This can be reduced by visiting other settings—usually in less depth but long enough to discern the applicability of one's findings.

A second issue concerns whether the researcher's experiences and records are representative of the setting and its dynamics. The participant observer relies at least in part on field notes as data, often supplemented by other methods, such as interviews. The researcher's notes, analysis, and interpretation can be affected by selective observation, selective memory, and selective interpretations. Findings can also be affected by an unrepresentative sample of informants or of situations studied (e.g., observations of formal meetings but not informal caucuses or personal contacts). Researchers need to explicitly report their value commitments relevant to the study, and whether they took sides in a controversy, so readers can judge the effects of these choices on data collection and interpretation.

Another problem is that the researcher is influencing (at least weakly, but perhaps strongly) the phenomena or community under study. Field notes and interpretations should explicitly indicate the extent of the researcher's influence on the actions of others so the impact of the researcher's participation can be assessed.

A final limitation is the role conflict created by playing both participant and observer roles (Wicker & Sommer, 1993). An ethical and personal problem concerns what the researcher tells the members of the community about the research. For example, the more forthrightly the researcher speaks about taking field notes, the more suspicious or less revealing the community members may be. On the other hand, research ethics, truthfulness, and norms of neighborliness require that some explanation of one's research intent and methods be made. Playing a role that is both an insider and a researcher can be stressful. Striking a balance between these is an important part of gaining entry, forming a relationship, and seeking to benefit the community.

A Participation Observation Study Caroline Kroeker (1995, 1996) used this method to study the community functioning of peasant agricultural cooperatives in Nicaragua.

> The main portion of the research was done through 7 months of participant observation in one agricultural cooperative in Nicaragua, and four follow-up visits. I lived in the cooperative, observing formal and informal meetings. I shared their living conditions and food, in exchange for assisting in the education of the children and in a peer adult education program. By living among them, I was able to integrate, listen, engage in many conversations, ask questions, and determine subtle feelings and meanings. The notes of the cooperative's meetings, conversations and observations were supplemented by documents and observations of processes and interactions in the village and in the town close to the cooperative. The research also included a general study of other cooperatives in Nicaragua through a literature review, interviews of key informants, and visits to 15 cooperatives around the country. (Kroeker, 1995, p. 754)

These sources of data provided thick description of the cooperative as a community. To analyze her data, Kroeker (p. 754) categorized the information she had collected, identified patterns and causal links, and developed interpretations of their meaning. This was a reiterative process involving several repetitions of data collection and analysis. She identified alternative interpretations of her findings and weighed the evidence for each interpretation.

Kroeker's (1995, 1996) reports presented themes, including the importance of consciousness-raising and development of skills in citizen participation, and the difficulties of strengthening these in a context where such citizen leadership had not been possible (and where many outsiders still did not believe it workable). One of her principal findings was the importance of "accompaniment," a process of mentoring and support for emerging leadership skills that Kroeker herself was able to provide to the cooperative members. This role encouraged local leaders. Kroeker's willingness to work in collaborative, empowering ways with cooperative members benefitted the cooperative and enriched her findings.

Qualitative Interviewing

Interviewing a sample of individuals has become a popular qualitative research format in community psychology. The interview is often open-ended or minimally structured to promote participants' describing their experiences in their words. Samples are usually small to facilitate interviewing and analysis in depth. The researcher is not necessarily a participant in the community under study but usually does assume a role of collaboration or extended contact with interviewees.

Strengths and Limitations   Qualitative interviewing allows flexible exploration of the phenomenon of interest and discovery of aspects not anticipated by the researcher. It is based in a strong relationship between researcher and participant. It involves attending to the voices of participants and thick description of their experiences. It can challenge the researcher's preconceptions and affords contextual understanding of a community, culture, or population.

Interviewing has several advantages over participant observation. Data collection can be more standardized, limiting biases of selective perception, memory, and interpretation. Interviews can be recorded and transcripts prepared so analysis can be based on participants' actual words. Analysis can also be standardized and performed by multiple, independent raters, not just the interviewer, which increases reliability and validity. The interviewer can develop a relationship with the setting and participants that is mutual and trusting yet with less role conflict than participant observation. Of course, all these also mean that the insights developed from interviews are less direct than those from participant observation.

These advantages require intensive study of a small sample, which means that generalizability of findings is often limited. Also, the time required for research interviews may subtly exclude participants in marginalized groups or demanding circumstances (Cannon et al., cited in Campbell & Wasco, 2000). Differences of interpretation between participants and researchers do create challenges (Stein and Mankowski, 2004).

The Stein and Wemmerus (2001) study of families that include a person with schizophrenia, described earlier, provides an example of a qualitative interviewing study.

Focus Groups

A focus group discussion is an interview with a group. It generates thick description and qualitative information in response to questions or discussion topics posed by a moderator. Using focus groups, researchers can assess similarities and differences among individuals and allow participants to elaborate on ideas and themes by reacting to each other, not just to an interviewer. Hughes and DuMont (1993) offered an introduction to the use of focus group research methods in community psychology.

In focus group research, the group, not the individual, is the unit of analysis: The sample size is one for each group. Individual comments are not independent of other group members; indeed, one of the purposes of the focus group is to elicit discussion. Each group is usually composed of 6–12 participants who share some characteristic of concern to the researchers—for example, the same race, gender, culture, or age, similar occupations, or the same health problem.

This homogeneity helps to promote free discussion and ability of participants to be able to identify with each others' experiences. A group of strangers is preferred to minimize the effects of prior personal contacts. Multiple focus groups are needed to provide broader information and to compare populations (husbands vs. wives, for example). However, as with qualitative interviewing, samples are seldom representative of a large population. The goal is to generate contextual understanding.

The moderator's responsibilities include creating an environment conducive to free discussion, speaking in language comfortable to all participants, ensuring that all members participate, eliciting both agreement and disagreement, and balancing between being nondirective and covering all topics of interest to the researchers. The moderator uses a discussion guide that includes topics to be discussed and that moves from general topics to specific phenomena relevant to the research. Analysis of focus group data is similar to the process of analyzing individual qualitative interviews.

Strengths and Limitations   These are similar to qualitative interviewing. However, focus groups have several advantages over other qualitative methods. Researchers can structure discussion and learn about topics of interest and personal experiences of others more easily than with participant observation. Compared to individual interviews, focus groups allow greater access to shared knowledge and mutual discussion. They also allow researchers to observe social interaction among group participants, perhaps revealing behavioral patterns unavailable in individual interviews. However, a focus group moderator has less flexibility to ask for elaboration, control changes of topic, or learn about individuals in depth than an interviewer of individuals. Focus groups are not a good approach for understanding an individual's unique experiences and cannot simply be used as a substitute for individual interviewing. Focus groups are especially useful for gaining cultural understanding. They also can help explore a topic or test questionnaires prior to quantitative studies.

Studies Using Focus Groups   Hirokazu Yoshikawa and associates (2003) used focus groups to understand the experiences and lessons learned by frontline peer educators in a community agency conducting HIV prevention programs in communities of Asian/Pacific Islanders in New York City. These workers knew their communities and cultures well and were rich resources for understanding effective, culturally anchored techniques for disseminating information and influencing behaviors that often transmit HIV. The researchers convened focus groups for workers with different populations (youth, gay/bisexual/transgender persons, women, heterosexually identified men). Their protocol questions concerned "success stories" of effective outreach and behavior change and how the peer educators adapted their techniques to different ethnic groups, populations of different immigration and socioeconomic statuses, and in ethnic, mainstream U.S., and gay communities. Yoshikawa et al. developed categories of responses, refining these through reviews of interview transcripts until they had inter-judge agreement on matching respondent comments to categories. For example, categories concerned cultural norms about sexuality, contexts where peer educators focused their outreach, specific strategies used for that outreach, and specific risk and protective behaviors. The results showed the influence of culture, social oppression, and immigration status on HIV-related behaviors and effective, culturally appropriate methods of addressing these.

Additional examples emphasize the role of focus groups in defining key concepts and practices from participant perspectives. Hughes and DuMont (1993) convened focus groups to learn how African American parents socialize their children to deal with racism. Dumka, Gonzales, Wood, and Formoso (1998) used focus groups with families in four cultures in their locality (African Americans, European Americans, Mexican Americans, and Mexican immigrants) to learn about parenting adolescents in these cultures. Lehavot, Balsam, and Ibrahim-Wells (2009) conducted focus groups with ethnically diverse lesbian and bisexual women to understand their perspectives on the meanings and functions of "community." In each of these studies, focus groups helped develop and refine measures for later quantitative studies.

Case Studies

The case study method, usually conducted on individuals in clinical psychology, can be applied to an organization, locality, or change process (Bond & Keys, 1993; Mulvey, 2002; Evans, Hanlin, & Prilleltensky, 2007). Community psychologists also can study an individual in relation to the settings in that person's life (Langhout, 2003). They may conduct multiple case studies so comparisons can be made. For example, Wasco, Campbell, and Clark (2002) interviewed eight advocates who worked with rape victims, about how the advocates coped with the emotional trauma encountered in their work, and about personal and organizational resources that promoted coping. Neigher and Fishman (2004) used multiple case studies to describe planned change and evaluation in five community organizations.

Case studies provide a bridge connecting qualitative and quantitative approaches. A case study may rely on any or all of the qualitative methods we have described. It may also use qualitative **archival data** (i.e., from archives or records) such as minutes of group meetings, organizational policy manuals, or newspaper stories. Archival data can also be quantitative records such as police statistics, records of attendance at programs, or quantitative evaluations of whether a program attained its goals. Case studies also can use other quantitative measures, such as questionnaires. Later in this chapter, we will describe case studies using both qualitative and quantitative methods. In Chapter 11, we will return to a community case study of a hazardous waste dispute (Culley & Hughey, 2008).

Strengths and Limitations   Like participant observation, a case study can examine in depth a single person, setting, or locality. Case studies are excellent for understanding the nuances of cultural, social, or community contexts. They can afford thick description and contextual understanding. By using multiple data sources, subjective biases can be checked. The longitudinal focus of most case studies is also useful. Although case-study researchers cannot study causes and effects with experimental control, they can identify complex patterns of causation in natural settings.

Their focus on a single case is also the principal limitation for case study methods. Generalizability of findings to other settings is uncertain. Researchers can include multiple case studies in one analysis, but that may weaken some of the strengths described here. Sometimes, description and analysis of one case is the goal, not generalization to other cases. Involvement in the setting or locality studied may create insider-outsider role conflicts, as discussed earlier.

The use of archival records presents both advantages and problems. Written records can provide information on meetings or other events not attended by the researcher and remembered imperfectly by interview informants. Archival records can also document events in the history of an organization or community. However, researchers who review archival data may not discover the processes that they are most interested in. For example, conflict and compromise preceding a group decision are usually omitted or sparingly recorded in meeting minutes.

A Case Study Using Qualitative Methods   Anne Brodsky (2003, 2009) used a variety of qualitative methods to study the Revolutionary Association of the Women of Afghanistan (RAWA). Her book, *With All Our Strength*, describes the history, philosophy, actions, resilience, and sense of community shared by the members of this remarkable Afghan women's movement. Since 1977, RAWA has advocated forcefully yet nonviolently for women's and human rights and for a democratic, secular government in Afghanistan. It is outspoken and independent of the various invading armies, Afghan warlords, and governments during this period. Founded in 1977 by a 20-year-old college student, RAWA promotes indigenous feminist values that defy both traditional Afghan patriarchal values and the stereotypes of Afghan women widely held in the outside world. RAWA members (all volunteers, all women) publish advocacy materials and maintain a website, document and publicize abuse and atrocities, aid women suffering from many forms of trauma, distribute humanitarian assistance, conduct literacy and educational classes for women and girls, work with men who share their goals, hold protest rallies in Pakistan, and conduct international outreach (Brodsky, 2003, pp. 2–3). These activities have generated such fierce opposition that RAWA is a clandestine, underground organization that nonetheless engages in public actions. While RAWA's struggle is ongoing, it has made a difference in Afghan life and offers a vision for the future that continues to inspire Afghan women and men.

Brodsky was especially interested in how RAWA acted and sustained itself as a community. She was also interested in their shared resilience in the face of vigorous and violent opposition and of many setbacks and losses, including the assassination of Meena, RAWA's founder (Brodsky, 2003). Her use of a research framework and methods based in feminist qualitative research fits well with the feminist philosophy of RAWA, with the need to take Afghan culture and context into account, with the need to attend to emotions in RAWA members and in the researcher, with the fact that RAWA is a clandestine organization and that a participatory-collaborative research relationship was necessary, and with the goal of empowering RAWA and other feminist organizations through the research (pp. 7–9).

Brodsky used multiple qualitative methods (2003, 2009). She has been very involved with RAWA's outreach in the United States for several years. For this research, Brodsky visited Pakistan and Afghanistan in 2001 and 2002, beginning prior to September 11, 2001, and the U.S.-led war in Afghanistan. She interviewed more than 100 members and supporters of RAWA—women and men—in Afghanistan and Pakistan. Interviews often lasted 2–3 hours, and many persons were interviewed more than once. Brodsky also conducted group interviews and spent many hours in participant observation and informal conversations with RAWA members, visited 35 RAWA projects in 10 localities in Pakistan and Afghanistan, and reviewed archival records and sources. Most of her interviews were conducted in Dari, an Afghan language, with Tahmeena Faryal, a translator, key informant, and collaborator who was a RAWA member. Brodsky knew the language well enough to serve as a check on accuracy of translation but remained in many ways an outsider (see Brodsky & Faryal, 2006, for further discussion of the challenges and rewards of their insider-outsider collaboration).

Brodsky's findings are rich and contextual. She examines the strong sense of community for members and supporters of RAWA in the context of the other Afghan communities to which they also belong, including extended families and villages. She finds in RAWA a positive sense of community that is consistent with its feminist ideals and practices but also with the collective orientation of Afghan culture that makes it difficult, if not impossible, for women to choose not to be part of a community. Resilience in the face of trauma and violent opposition is another theme. These themes are expressed in the ongoing commitment of RAWA members to their ideals and the emotional caring and practical support offered among RAWA members. Two interview excerpts express these themes and illustrate the power of qualitative methods.

> From a member who joined RAWA in a refugee camp: "I found everything; I escaped out of my grief and sadness. There were classes, the handicraft center, and I found these people serving the rest of the people of Afghanistan and going toward the lightness…. [B]y lightness I mean education…. RAWA giving education, hope and enables us to serve our people." (Brodsky, 2003, p. 245)
>
> From a member who compared the freedoms afforded women inside and outside of RAWA: "In [RAWA] I have all my rights and what I believe. I have education, go outside … talk to anyone I want. I have the same rights as men. But not in my village. My father would say nothing. But I have male cousins that are my age who I can't talk with. Here I talk to men and it is fine…. When I go to my village I just stay in the house. And I can't go out without a scarf or talk to boys. They will kill me. I think here if a member really believes in a right she can do it." (2009, p. 182)

Two Concluding Issues

We conclude this section by discussing two overarching issues for qualitative methods: how they elicit narratives and meaning and how they address the criteria of reliability, validity, and generalizability.

Narratives in Qualitative Research   Qualitative methods often tap narratives. Narratives have a plot, or sequence of events, and meaningful characters and settings. They may be individual stories or cultural myths. They provide insights into psychological themes and convey emotions and prized values in memorable ways (Rappaport, 1993, 1995, 2000; Thomas & Rappaport, 1996). For example, the Stein and Wemmerus (2001) study elicited narratives from the lives of families of persons with schizophrenia. Harper, Lardon, Rappaport, Bangi, Contrerars, and Pedraza (2004) illustrated the power of narratives—in written texts, oral histories, murals, songs, poems, and many other forms—to convey Mexican American cultural meanings. Lehrner and Allen (2008) showed how the narratives of advocates underlie and support different understandings of domestic violence. Some advocates' narratives framed domestic violence as a problem that must be addressed by social change efforts, while others drew upon a more person-centered frame and suggested individual-level, therapeutic solutions.

Rappaport (2000) defines **narratives** as being shared by members of a group. A community or setting narrative communicates events, values, and other themes important to the identity and sustainability of that group. Cultural myths and traditions also are narratives. **Personal stories** are individuals' unique accounts, created to make sense of their own lives. Personal identity is embedded in a life story. Qualitative research methods can be designed to elicit shared narratives or personal stories or both. Both are studied in anthropology, sociology, and cognitive, personality, and developmental psychology (Rappaport, 1993, 1995, 2000). They can be analyzed for descriptive details and abstract themes. Looking across personal stories and shared narratives is an excellent opportunity to examine persons in context across multiple levels of analysis. They are one of the best ways to attend to unheard voices and to understand a culture or community.

Reliability, Validity, and Generalizability   Students educated in the thinking of positivistic, quantitative methods may wonder about the reliability, validity, and generalizability of qualitative methods. It is important to remember that the aims of qualitative methods are different than much quantitative research. In a qualitative study, sensitivity to participants' interpretations is more important than standardization. Yet many qualitative methods use scientific criteria analogous to the reliability and validity criteria of a more positivist approach (Lincoln & Guba, 1985).

For qualitative methods, reliability is sometimes demonstrated by inter-rater reliability among multiple readers who are coding or categorizing verbal data. Reliability may also be demonstrated by evidence of the *dependability* of researchers, who have developed a deep understanding of a particular context.

Generalizability of findings to other persons or populations is more limited than with larger studies but is usually not the aim of the qualitative study. However, the thick description generated by qualitative research allows readers to understand more fully the persons and contexts being studied and to compare them with other samples. The reader is then able to decide whether the findings have *transferability*, proving useful in other contexts.

Qualitative research addresses validity in part by **triangulation**—the use of different methods to understand the same phenomenon. These can be interviews and personal observation, the use of several informants who can be expected to have different viewpoints, the use of multiple interviewers, or the use of quantitative measures along with qualitative information. Triangulation in qualitative studies is analogous to the use of multiple measures of a variable in quantitative research. In addition, the thick, detailed description of experiences in qualitative research offers convincing realism and allows for judgment of validity, or *credibility*, of the study. Moreover, the connection of researcher and participant in qualitative studies allows clarifying and elaborating of the meaning of participant responses to questions, an issue of validity overlooked in standardized questionnaires.

A common goal of qualitative research is not only to provide intellectual evidence of validity but also **verisimilitude**, eliciting a personal experience in a reader similar to the original experiences of the research participant. For example, recall the quotations earlier in this chapter from families of persons with schizophrenia or the Afghan women of RAWA (Stein & Wemmerus, 2001; Brodsky, 2003). If you experienced the emotional power of their words, that is verisimilitude.

"Whether numbers or words, data do not speak for themselves."
(Marecek et al., 1998, p. 632)

As this quotation emphasizes, bias affects qualitative and quantitative methods. Choices of what to study and of how to interpret findings are matters of theory and values—whatever the method. **Reflexivity** (discussed earlier in this chapter and in Chapter 3), including explicit statements of the researcher's perspective, are useful in any study. Regardless of method, multiple interpretations of complex phenomena will arise because diverse persons and groups have different perspectives. Both qualitative and quantitative methods can illuminate those perspectives.

QUANTITATIVE METHODS

We now turn to methods that emphasize measurement, statistical analysis, and experimental or statistical control. They address different purposes and questions than qualitative methods. Quantitative methods are historically based in a positivist philosophy of science but can be used effectively within contemporary frameworks for scientific practice (Tebes, 2005). Quantitative methods are particularly useful in helping us describe and model the multileveled influence of environmental factors on individual health and well-being (Luke, 2005). While general differences certainly exist between qualitative and quantitative approaches, they are not a simple dichotomy.

Common Features of Quantitative Methods

A great diversity of quantitative methods exists. However, most quantitative methods in community research share some common features. We do not wish to repeat all of what you may have learned in previous methodology courses, so the list below focuses on features that offer clear contrasts with qualitative methods and highlights how quantitative methods can be adapted to community research.

1. **Measurement and comparisons.** The principal aim of quantitative methods is to analyze measurable differences along variables and the strength of relationships among those variables. They facilitate understanding variables, predicting outcomes, and understanding causes and effects. Quantitative research can generate "outsider knowledge" that affords comparisons across contexts.

2. **Numbers are data.** Although some variables are categorical (e.g., an experimental program compared to a control group), the purpose is almost always to study their relationship to measured variables. While researchers using qualitative methods look for patterns in words and narratives, researchers using quantitative methods seek patterns in numbers.

3. **Cause and effect.** One important objective is to understand cause-effect relationships. This can then lead to the prediction of consequences and inform social action to promote desirable changes. Experiments and similar methods are often used to evaluate the effects of social innovations, programs, or policies. Even nonexperimental quantitative studies identify empirical relationships that can eventually lead to knowledge of causes and effects and to social innovation.

4. **Generalization.** Another important objective is to derive conclusions that can be generalized at least to some extent across contexts, settings, and communities (e.g., empirical findings showing that a prevention program or social policy is effective in many communities).

5. **Standardized measures.** Standardized measurement instruments are preferred to ensure reliable, valid measurement. The flexibility and contextual sensitivity of qualitative methods are lost, but the comparability of findings across studies and control of extraneous variables are increased.

Next, we discuss four specific types of quantitative methods in community psychology research: quantitative description, randomized field experiments, nonequivalent comparison group designs, and interrupted time-series designs. These are only some of the available quantitative methods for community research. (These sources present others: Langhout, 2003; Luke, 2005; Revenson et al., 2002; Shadish, Cook, & Campbell, 2002.)

Quantitative Description

Quantitative description methods include a variety of procedures—e.g., surveys, structured interviews, behavioral observations of community settings, epidemiological studies, and use of social indicators (i.e., census data, crime and health statistics). They are quantitative but not experimental, and they do not involve manipulation of an independent variable. They can be used for such purposes as the following:

- To compare existing groups (e.g., women's and men's perceptions of crime)
- To study associations between survey variables (e.g., correlation of family income with health or changes over time in adolescent sexual attitudes)
- To measure characteristics of community settings (e.g., measure the frequency of emotional support and giving advice in mutual help groups)
- To conduct epidemiological studies to identify factors predicting the presence or absence of an illness (e.g., behaviors that increase or decrease the risk of HIV infection)
- To study relationships between geographic-spatial and social environments (e.g., the correlation between density of liquor stores and crime rates in neighborhoods)

Statistical analyses may include correlation, multiple regression, path analysis and structural modeling, and even *t* tests and analyses of variance to compare naturally occurring groups. These studies may be cross-sectional, sampling only one point in time, or longitudinal, sampling repeatedly over time.

Quantitative description usually samples more individuals than either qualitative studies or experiments. This facilitates statistical analysis and generalizability. To enable a study of this breadth, these methods rely on previous knowledge and/or exploratory research to determine which variables to study, how to measure them, and whom to sample. As we mentioned earlier, qualitative research is very useful for this.

Correlation and Causation   Early undergraduate education in psychology typically contrasts correlation and causation. Just because two factors are associated statistically does not mean that one causes another. The causation could just as easily run in the opposite direction than what you think (B causes A rather than A causing B). Or the causal factor may be a "third variable" that determines both correlated variables (C causes both A and B).

However, under some conditions, nonexperimental designs can be used to identify causal patterns and test causal hypotheses. The simplest case involves precedence in time: If the change in A is correlated with the change in B but A consistently precedes B, a causal interpretation (A causes B) is more warranted (although a third variable still may be involved). A theoretical model, based on prior knowledge of relationships among A, B, C, and other related variables, strengthens causal inference from nonexperimental data. Such causal inference relies on logic models and/or statistical control of extraneous variables, not experimental control.

Community Surveys Surveys of community samples, using standardized questionnaires or other measurements, are quantitative description methods. For example, Fleishman et al. (2003) conducted longitudinal surveys of well-being in a large, multiethnic, nationally representative U.S. sample of HIV-infected persons. Using the statistical method of cluster analysis, they identified four coping styles among the respondents: active-approach, distancing, blame-withdrawal, and passive. Although they could not determine causes and effects with precision, the longitudinal design did reveal some patterns. When levels of emotional distress in earlier surveys were statistically controlled, the correlation of blame-withdrawal coping with lower emotional well-being was no longer statistically significant. This suggests that the degree of prior distress, not coping style, influenced later well-being. In contrast, the passive group had the lowest levels of symptoms, and (having less to cope with) the least active coping style, yet higher well-being.

A disturbing finding of this survey was that members of several more socially marginalized groups (women, racial/ethnic minorities, and injection drug users) had less social support than men, whites, and those who had not used injection drugs. This suggests a need for more understanding and support for HIV-infected persons in these groups among health professionals and society (Fleishman et al., 2003, p. 201).

Community surveys can focus on organizations as the unit of analysis. Community coalitions bring together representatives of various segments of a locality to address an issue such as domestic violence (Allen, 2005; Allen, Watt, & Hess, 2008) or promoting positive youth development (Feinberg, Greenberg, & Osgood, 2004). Feinberg et al. conducted structured interviews with representative of 21 local Communities That Care coalitions and derived quantitative measurements from them. Results indicated the importance of community readiness and internal functioning of the coalition as a group for perceived coalition effectiveness. Allen surveyed and interviewed representatives of 43 local domestic violence coalitions, finding that perceived effectiveness was most related to having an inclusive climate of share decision-making, and active membership participation.

Epidemiology These methods are useful for community research concerned with health and mental health. Epidemiology is the study of the frequency and distribution of disorders, and of risk and protective factors for these. Epidemiology is usually a precursor to more experimental studies of causal factors of these disorders and is essential to practical planning of prevention and treatment. Epidemiology is most often used in the discipline of public health but is also used in the social sciences (e.g., Mason, Chapman, & Scott, 1999).

Two basic epidemiological concepts are incidence and prevalence. **Incidence** is the rate of *new* occurrences of a disorder in a population within a specific time period (usually a year). It is thus a measure of the frequency of the onset of a disorder. **Prevalence** is the rate of *existing* occurrences of a disorder in a population within a time period. It includes new cases and continuing cases of the disorder that began before the time period studied. Both concepts are usually expressed as rates (e.g., the number of cases per thousand persons in the population). The incidence–prevalence distinction is important for community psychology. Prevention is more concerned with incidence—the frequency of new cases. Prevalence—the rate of existing cases—is relevant to mutual help or mental health services policy.

When incidence and prevalence rates have been determined for a population, epidemiological research is focused on identifying risk and protective factors. **Risk factors** are associated with increased likelihood of a disorder. These may be causes of the disorder or simply correlated with it. Exposure to stressors or lack of coping resources are examples of risk factors. **Protective factors** are associated with lesser likelihood of a disorder; they may counteract or buffer the effects of the disorder's causes or simply be correlated with other factors that do so. Personal or cultural strengths and support systems are protective factors. Note that we will discuss risk and protective factors more fully in Chapter 9 when we focus on the prevention of disorders and promotion of health.

Mapping Physical and Social Environments   The increasing availability of geographical information systems (GIS) methods offer a rich new resource for studying relationships between physical-spatial aspects of communities and their psychosocial qualities (Chirowodza, van Rooyen, Joseph, Sikotoyi, Richter, & Coates, 2009; Luke, 2005). GIS methods can be used to plot onto a map any data available for spatial locations. Archival data sources can include census information on population density or average household income, or social indicators such as neighborhood crime rates or density of liquor stores. Community survey data can also be entered in GIS databases if associated with respondents' residences (Van Egeren, Huber, & Cantillon, 2003). GIS data and the resulting maps can be used for quantitative statistical analysis or for visual searching for spatial patterns (a more qualitative approach). For example, in a study of Kansas City neighborhoods, Hughey and Whitehead (2003) found lack of access to high-quality food statistically related to rates of obesity, and density of liquor outlets related to rates of violent crime. GIS also can be used to track changes in localities over time.

Strengths and Limitations   Quantitative description methods have a number of strengths. Standardized measurement affords statistical analysis and large samples that provide greater generalizability. These methods can be used to study variables that cannot be manipulated in an experiment. Epidemiological research can be used to identify risk and protective factors and evaluate the outcome of preventive efforts.

Finally, these studies often identify factors that can be targeted for social or community change, even without experimental knowledge of specific causes and effects. For example, one need not know all the cause-effect relationships for youth violence in order to identify risk and protective factors and to initiate change efforts.

However, these methods have several limitations. They rely on prior knowledge to select and measure variables and populations. Also, except for GIS approaches, the knowledge provided by these studies is usually "decontextualized"—gathered from individuals but not associated with existing settings, communities, or cultures. This can increase breadth of sampling but limits knowledge of these contextual factors. The study of causes and effects is limited, as we have discussed.

The focus of epidemiological research on disorders also limits its utility for community psychology (Linney & Reppucci, 1982). Community psychology is concerned with overall psychological well-being, including but not limited to disorders. When mental disorders are studied, difficulties of accurate diagnosis and measurement make its epidemiology more difficult than that of physical disease. Also, community psychology's focus on promotion of strengths includes identifying protective factors for disorders but goes beyond that to concern the development of positive qualities.

Experimental Social Innovation and Dissemination

Fairweather's (1967) concept of experimental social innovation and dissemination (ESID) is the community research approach closest to the classic laboratory experiment. Yet it also involves explicit awareness of social values and the gritty world of community action. ESID is an enduring contribution to community psychology (Hazel & Onanga, 2003; Seidman, 2003). Fairweather's Community Lodge program (described in Chapter 2) was the prototype for this approach (Fairweather, Sanders, Cressler, & Maynard, 1969).

Experimental social innovation is based on careful groundwork "before the beginning." The social or community problem is carefully defined, the goals of an experimental innovation (e.g., community program or social policy) and to address that problem are specified, and the innovation itself planned.

A hallmark of Fairweather's experimental social innovation is evaluating the effects of the innovation in an experimental design. Researchers conduct a longitudinal study in which the innovation is implemented and compared with a control or comparison condition. In experimental terminology, the independent variable is the comparison of the social innovation to a control condition. Dependent variables are measurements of the outcomes of the program. If effective, the findings and knowledge of how to implement the innovation are then disseminated to other communities and decision-makers (Hazel & Onanga, 2003). The ESID method addresses the ethical imperative that the effects of social actions be evaluated and the practical imperative that effective solutions are shared widely. In Chapter 10, we will return to a discussion of program dissemination and the challenges faced in "scaling up" an effective social innovation.

Here, we will discuss three research methods as forms of experimental social innovation: randomized field experiments, nonequivalent comparison group designs, and interrupted time-series designs.

Randomized Field Experiments

This is the most rigorous form of experimental social innovation. Participants (individuals or settings) are randomly assigned to experimental or control groups. These are compared at a pretest before the implementation of the experimental social innovation, at which time they are expected to be equal on measures of dependent variables. They are compared again at posttest(s), when they are expected to differ because of the effects of the innovation. Follow-up posttests can continue over several years.

The experimental social innovation represents the experimental condition. The control condition can often be "treatment as usual" under existing policy or practices. For example, in Fairweather's Community Lodge study (Fairweather et al., 1969), men in a psychiatric hospital were assigned to either the Community Lodge program or to the usual treatment and aftercare procedures for the hospital. Another experimental approach is to compare two different innovations with each other, such as two contrasting prevention programs in a school (Linney, 1989). A third approach is to provide the experimental innovation to members of the control group after the posttest. They serve first as a control group and then receive the innovation, minimizing ethical problems with their not receiving it originally.

A key issue is the method of assignment to experimental and control conditions. If this is random, many confounding variables are controlled. These include individual differences in personality, coping skills, social support networks, and life experiences that may affect their responses to the innovation. Confounds also include differences between groups in demographics such as gender, age, race, culture, and family income. In the laboratory, random assignment is taken for granted, but in the community, it must be achieved by collaboration and negotiation with community members (Sullivan, 2003).

Strengths and Limitations   Randomized field experiments are unsurpassed for clarity of cause-effect interpretation (e.g., for testing effects of a social innovation). With greater control over confounding factors, researchers can make more confident interpretations of its effects. Moreover, if experimental studies demonstrate the effectiveness of a social innovation, advocacy for it can be more effective. For example, randomized field experiments have helped to document the effects of many preventive interventions and increase the credibility of prevention efforts generally (Weissberg, Kumpfer, & Seligman, 2003).

However, experiments require substantial prior knowledge of the context to propose social innovations worth testing and to choose measurements. A useful sequence might be to conduct qualitative studies to understand the context and key variables, then quantitative descriptions to specify risk and protective factors and refine measurements, then developing an experimental social innovation and conducting an experiment to evaluate its effectiveness. Even during the experiment, qualitative or individualized quantitative methods are helpful to understand differences in outcomes and whether these were due to the intervention (Lipsey & Cordray, 2002).

The intrusiveness of experiments also raises issues of control in community settings. Permission is needed to collect quantitative data (often in multiple waves) and to randomly assign participants to experimental conditions. Those decisions must be explained and negotiated with community members.

Evaluating Advocacy for Women with a Randomized Field Experiment   Cris Sullivan (2003) described how she worked with community survivors of domestic violence and staff in women's advocacy centers to consider such questions as: What community resources do battered women need to prevent further abuse? How can understaffed women's advocacy settings address these issues and empower battered women (Sullivan, 2003, pp. 296–297)?

Sullivan and her community collaborators then worked together to design the Community Advocacy Project, an innovation in which university students were trained as advocates for battered women (beyond the usual training for volunteers in women's shelters). These advocates were trained for one semester in a practicum course, then during a second semester worked with community women to devise individualized safety plans for each woman and to help carry out those plans. The latter involved advocating directly with community agencies and resources needed to carry out those plans and working with the women to empower them to devise and implement their own future plans (pp. 298–299).

The researchers and community collaborators decided to evaluate the project with a randomized field experiment. This was not an easy decision. The needs of battered women were so immediate, and the prospect of project effectiveness so intuitively obvious, that they were reluctant to assign some women to a control group. Eventually, the community members were convinced by these arguments: At the time of the research, there were not enough resources to offer the advocacy program to all women; the program sounded promising but was unproven and could even be counterproductive (as a woman established her own life, the batterer might become more violent to reassert control); an experiment was the best way of determining its effectiveness; the fairest method of assigning women to the advocacy or control conditions was randomization. The project became the experimental condition, and the usual shelter services comprised the control condition. Community members also participated fully in creating and choosing measures of program effectiveness (p. 297).

At the conclusion of the intervention and in follow-up assessments over two years, battered women who worked with student advocates in the Community Advocacy Project were less likely than women in the control group to experience further violence, were less depressed, had more social support and better perceived quality of life, and reported greater success in obtaining needed resources. Sullivan is conducting studies with an expanded form of the project and helped obtain funding for expanded shelter staffing to provide expanded advocacy and to train volunteers for expanded advocacy (pp. 300–301).

Evaluating a Crisis Residential Program for Adults with Psychiatric Disabilities with a Randomized Experiment   Thomas Greenfield, Beth Stoneking, Keith Humphreys, Evan Sundby, and Jason Bond (2008) used a randomized experimental design to evaluate the effectiveness of a crisis residential program managed by mental health consumers. The program served as a treatment alternative for adults in acute psychiatric crisis.

Consumer-managed services, like the crisis residential program studied in this experiment, have a long history that is closely related to the development of community psychology. Remember, for example, the Community Lodge, in which male veterans with severe mental disorders lived in a community setting and supported one another with minimal professional supervision. Other forms of consumer-managed services now include advocacy organizations, clubhouses, and mutual help groups (which we will discuss in greater detail in Chapter 8). While support for these consumer-managed services is widespread, few resources are dedicated to sustaining them. And there have been few controlled studies that demonstrate the effectiveness of this type of service for those who are in crisis.

This experiment compared outcomes for psychiatrically disabled adults who were randomly assigned to either the experimental condition, an unlocked crisis residential program emphasizing client decisions and involvement in recovery, or to the usual care condition: a locked inpatient psychiatric facility that was professionally staffed and working from a medical model of treatment. Participants in this study were facing civil commitment in California. They were assessed by a psychiatrist as gravely disabled or a threat to themselves, but they were not considered a threat to others.

The findings indicated that those who were randomly assigned to the unlocked crisis residential program had greater reduction of symptoms, including psychoticism, depression, and anxiety. Level of functioning outcomes, including problematic behavior and living skills, were not significantly different for the two groups, but participants assigned to the crisis residential program were significantly more satisfied with services, including staff and program, medications and aftercare, day/night availability, and facilities.

Given the lower costs of the crisis residential program ($211 per day, compared to $665 per day for the traditional inpatient treatment) and the outcomes demonstrated in the study, the researchers argued for expansion of these less restrictive, consumer-run services (Greenfield et al., 2008).

Nonequivalent Comparison Group Designs

For a variety of reasons, many settings simply cannot support random assignment to experimental and control conditions. For example, seldom can a school randomly assign some children to an innovative classroom and others to a control classroom. Even if they did, the students may mix at lunch or recess so much that the independence of experimental and control conditions is greatly reduced. Providing the innovation to all students in a grade and comparing their outcomes to another school or to students in a previous year means, of course, that assurance of equivalence between groups is lost. Comparing a sample of schools rather than a sample of individuals (making the unit of analysis the school, not the individual) may be prohibitively expensive.

Yet many of the strengths of the experiment can be retained if researchers are creative about working around such obstacles. Using a nonequivalent comparison group is a common approach.

Nonequivalent comparison group designs are used whenever assignment to experimental or comparison condition is something other than random. For example, different classrooms within a school or different schools within a region may serve as experimental and comparison conditions. Assignment to classroom or choice of school is not random, but the classes or schools may be similar. The choice of comparison group is critical to generating interpretable results. In schools, student socioeconomic status, race, gender, and age are examples of variables to equate as much as possible in the two groups. Teacher demographics, school size, and curriculum also need to be similar (Linney & Repucci, 1982).

Strengths and Limitations   Using an existing group as a comparison condition is practical and less intrusive than randomized experiments. However, the control of confounding factors is much weaker, and clarity of interpretation and confidence in conclusions is decreased. Researchers in this situation must collect as much data as possible on factors that may confound the comparison. This allows them to document the similarity of the two conditions or to use those variables as statistical controls. For example, researchers may be able to show that the average family income of the experimental and control conditions was similar or control effects of family income statistically. The ultimate goal is to weaken or eliminate plausible competing explanations for findings.

Evaluating School Reforms with a Nonequivalent Comparison Group   Rhona Weinstein and associates used qualitative and quantitative methods to study how teacher expectations and school curriculum policies affect student performance. Weinstein described this multiyear program of research in *Reaching Higher* (Weinstein, 2002a; Weinstein et al., 1991). They implemented practical reforms to enhance learning for students not considered capable of college preparatory courses in an urban California high school. Our concern here is with the empirical evaluation of that intervention, conducted with a nonequivalent comparison group design. It used both quantitative and qualitative methods.

"Los Robles High School" (a pseudonym), a midsized urban school in an aging, run-down building, drew students from both wealthier and lower-income areas. Over two-thirds of the students but only one-fifth of the teachers were members of ethnic minority groups. School student achievement scores were below the state median, yet the school also ranked high in the number of graduates admitted to the selective University of California system. The school staff culture held a bimodal view of the students: Some were very talented and hard-working, others were not, and little could be done to change this. Weinstein and her team discovered that students assigned to "lower track" curriculum in ninth grade, based on tests that often underestimated their strengths, were assigned to classes that did not prepare them for college. These classes were often taught with uninteresting materials and teacher-centered methods that did not generate discussion. Students in this track were disproportionately African

American (68%). In contrast, classes for honors students were often discussion-oriented and used challenging yet interesting materials. Similar situations are all too common in U.S. schools (Weinstein, 2002a, pp. 209–211).

Weinstein and her team implemented an ongoing series of workshops with some teachers (volunteers) of reputedly lower-ability ninth-grade classes. Workshops focused on the importance of challenging and motivating students to higher performance, involving all students more actively in classroom learning, involving parents, and using more challenging yet interesting materials (often from the honors curriculum). Teachers met and discussed their efforts to alter teaching strategies and classroom climate. Weinstein's team worked with them to devise responses to obstacles. A year of these workshops showed positive results, but also the need for training more teachers and for curriculum reform and administrative changes. These became the next goals of the project (pp. 211–227).

A team of school staff and university researchers worked collaboratively to plan the research evaluating project effectiveness. Qualitative analysis of meeting records indicated positive shifts in teacher expectations, teaching strategies, and curriculum policy. The research also used a quantitative comparison of grades and other records for 158 students involved in classes in the project (the experimental group) and grades and records for a demographically similar group of 154 students from the previous two years' classes (the nonequivalent comparison group). Analyses statistically controlled prior differences between students in achievement. Project students attained higher overall grades and had fewer disciplinary referrals than comparison students in the first year of the project. They also were less likely to leave the school in subsequent years. The project's effects on grades ebbed after one year. This also suggests the need for curriculum reform and wider teacher training to spread the positive changes throughout the school.

These outcomes cannot be as confidently attributed to the project as in a randomized design. Possible confounding differences between the experimental group and comparison group could have included subtle changes in the student body between comparison and experimental years, events during the experimental year that altered student performance, or changes in teacher grading practices (Weinstein et al., 1991). But there were many qualitative signs of project effectiveness. For the first time, "lower-track" students were excited about school, despite challenging readings and writing assignments (Weinstein 2002a, p. 228). These are promising findings that suggest directions for genuine school reform.

Interrupted Time-Series Designs

Another approach is the use of interrupted time-series designs. In the simplest case, this involves repeated measurement over time (a time series) of a single case (an individual, organization, locality, or another social unit). In an initial baseline period, the participant or setting is monitored as measurements of dependent variables are collected. This provides the equivalent of a control condition. Then, the social innovation (e.g., program, policy) is introduced while measurement continues. Data collected in the baseline period are compared to data collected during or after the innovation was implemented. This is termed an *interrupted* time-series design because the innovation interrupts the series of measurements. This approach combines time-series measurement with an experimental manipulation, providing a useful design for small-scale experimental social innovation when a control group is not available.

Strengths and Limitations   Time-series designs are practical. They also afford understanding of change over time in a specific context, such as one community, while standardizing measurement and minimizing extraneous confounds.

However, a time-series design with one group is still open to a number of external confounds (Linney & Reppucci, 1982). These include seasonal or cyclical fluctuations in the variables measured. An example is that the number of college students who seek counseling rises as final exams approach. If seeking counseling is used as a dependent variable in a time-series study, researchers must take this seasonal rise into account. A further confound concerns historical events that affect the variables measured. An example is negative national publicity about tobacco use at the same time as implementation of a local anti-tobacco prevention program for youth. If youth tobacco use drops, the publicity may have been the real cause, not the local prevention program. Finally, findings from a single case or community, even over a long time period, may not generalize to other communities.

A key issue for time-series designs is the number and timing of measurements in the baseline and experimental periods (Linney & Reppucci, 1982). Social innovations may have gradual or delayed effects difficult to detect in a short time-series design. Seasonal or cyclical fluctuations (confounds) in the dependent variable may be detected if the time series is long enough.

Multiple-Baseline Designs   This is a form of interrupted times-series design that reduces the problems of external confounds and generalizability. Think of this design as a set of time-series studies, each conducted in a different community and compared to each other. The experimental social innovation is implemented at a different time in each community so effects of an external historical factor (happening at the same time for all communities, such as national publicity about tobacco use) will not be confounded with the innovation. If measures of the dependent variable show a change soon after the implementation of the innovation, at a different date in each community, confidence can be stronger that the innovation caused this effect. This also provides some evidence of generalizability. In effect, the design tests whether findings from one community can be replicated in other communities within a single study (Biglan, Ary, Koehn et al., 1996; Watson-Thompson, Fawcett, & Schultz, 2008).

The multiple-baseline design combines the strengths of the interrupted time-series and nonequivalent comparison group designs. However, the multiple communities studied are still nonequivalent (assignment of individuals to them is not random), and differences among them still exist that complicate interpretation. However, it is a very useful way to combine repeated measurement, contextual study of a single community, and replication across communities.

A Community-Level Multiple-Baseline Study   Can a community intervention emphasizing positive reinforcement reduce tobacco sales to youth in multiple communities? Anthony Biglan and colleagues addressed this question. They studied whole localities, using multiple-baseline, time-series methods (Biglan et al., 1996). They analyzed the antecedents and consequences of illegal sales of tobacco products to youth by retail merchants, devised an intervention, and evaluated its effectiveness in a multiple-baseline design in localities in rural Oregon.

In each town, the research team and local community members organized a proclamation by community leaders opposing tobacco sales to minors. Community members then visited each merchant to remind them of the proclamation and to give the merchant a description of the law and signs about it for posting. A key element was intervention visits to merchants by teen volunteers seeking to purchase tobacco products. If the clerk asked for identification or refused to sell, the volunteer handed the clerk a thank-you letter and a gift certificate donated by a local business (positive reinforcement). If the clerk was willing to sell, the volunteer declined to buy and gave the clerk a reminder statement about the law and proclamation. The researchers periodically provided feedback to merchants about their clerks' behavior in general (but not about individual clerks). In addition, in newspaper articles, ads, and circulars, community members publicly praised clerks and stores who had refused to sell (again providing reinforcement).

Measurement of intervention effectiveness was conducted with assessment visits to stores by teens seeking to purchase tobacco. These measurement visits were separate from the intervention visits and did not provide reinforcement of refusals to sell or reminders of the law. Teens simply asked to buy tobacco and then declined to buy if a clerk was willing to sell. Over 200 volunteer youth—males and females, aged 14–17—participated as testers. Attempts to buy were balanced by gender.

Researchers measured the effectiveness of the intervention by locality, not by individual store, because they had implemented a community intervention. The dependent variable was the proportion of stores in a community willing to sell tobacco to youth in assessment visits by youth. The researchers studied four small towns; all had fewer than 6,000 residents, mostly European American.

Biglan et al. collected baseline assessments in each community before implementing the intervention and then compared those data to similar assessments during and after the intervention. They conducted up to 16 assessment periods in each town. They used multiple-baseline techniques by conducting the intervention at one time in two communities and later in the other two.

In two communities, Willamina and Prineville, clerks' willingness to sell during assessment visits clearly decreased following the intervention. These differences were statistically significant. The intervention occurred at different times in these two communities, indicating that the intervention, not an extraneous factor, caused the reduction. In Sutherlin, a third town, willingness to sell decreased but not immediately after the intervention began. In Creswell, the fourth town, baseline willingness to sell was somewhat lower than elsewhere, and the intervention did not make a significant difference. Unknown local community factors influenced the intervention's effectiveness.

The generalizability of these findings may be limited because the sample was only a small number of relatively similar localities. In addition, it is not clear which element of the intervention accounted for its success (e.g., community proclamation, reinforcement of clerk refusals to sell, feedback to merchants, or the combination of these). Yet the intervention package, in most communities, was effective in reducing retail clerks' willingness to sell tobacco to youth. Biglan et al. noted that preventing sales in one community does not necessarily mean youth will not use tobacco, because they may obtain it from adults or in other communities. However, both behavioral analysis and common sense suggest that the more difficult it is to obtain tobacco, the less likely that youth will begin to use it.

INTEGRATING QUALITATIVE
AND QUANTITATIVE METHODS

Qualitative and quantitative methods can be used in a single study to offer the advantages of both perspectives and overcome the limitations of each (Lipsey & Cordray, 2000; Maton, 1993). We next discuss three examples that illustrate the benefits of multiple methods to study communities, interventions, and social change.

Combining Participatory Methods and GIS Mapping
to Understand Community

Researchers combined ethnographic, participatory, and GIS methods as part of a randomized controlled study on the effectiveness of community-based HIV awareness and prevention strategies within 48 communities in Zimbabwe, Tanzania, South Africa, and Thailand (Chirowodza, van Rooyen, Joseph, Sikotoyi, Richter, & Coates, 2009). Prior to intervention in each of the communities, the multilingual and transnational team of researchers needed to work with members of each of the communities to identify 1) community boundaries, 2) how the community was defined socially and geographically, 3) where to deliver services, and 4) individuals, groups, and community networks with whom to partner in delivering services. GIS technologies were used to generate maps of the geographic area and relevant community sites. Yet, in order to identify and define community resources, ethnographic and participatory methods were needed to complement and extend the GIS technologies.

For example, participatory mapping and transect walks were used in a rural community in South Africa so community members could describe the community as they experienced it. Facilitators worked with community teams to create maps, usually on the ground outdoors with natural materials, such as sticks, leaves, and stones. Community members identified such features as community landmarks, infrastructure, transport routes, places for livelihood and dwelling, and boundaries. Maps were transferred to charts by community members for record keeping. Transect walks were then conducted with community members serving as guides to explore key community networks and resources in greater detail.

The participatory process complemented and challenged quantitative descriptions generated by outsiders. Multiple methods illuminated key differences between the mental maps of communities, maps generated by government surveys, and census data. A multimethod approach more effectively named community boundaries, challenges, strengths, and resources than any one research method alone.

A Mixed-Method Evaluation of Peer Support for Early Adolescents

Louise Ellis, Herbert Marsh, and Rhonda Craven (2009) integrated quantitative and qualitative methods to evaluate a peer support program in Australia for schoolchildren making the transition to adolescence and high school. The peer support program is one that was widely implemented in Australia, with over 1,600 schools adopting the program in New South Wales (including the metropolitan region of Sydney). The program was offered as a set of 12 once-a-week sessions in which high school seniors (who received initial and ongoing training and support) worked with small groups of seventh grade students. The groups discussed and practiced goal setting, decision making, problem solving, and developing support networks.

The quantitative component of the evaluation included a sample of 930 students from three high schools. In the first year of the longitudinal study, all seventh grade students were assigned to the within-school, baseline control group. Researchers collected data at three points from the beginning to the end of the school year. In the second year, new seventh grade students from the same three schools participated in the peer support program. As with the control group, data was collected at three points from the beginning to the end of the school year. Surveys measured the students' self-concept (e.g., physical abilities, relationships, and academic abilities), personal effectiveness (e.g., self-confidence and leadership), coping, and perceptions of bullying.

Results for the experimental group were compared with the control group and with the experimental group's own baseline data. Multilevel path analysis indicated that the program enhanced psychological well-being and adjustment and that some benefits emerged after time elapsed at the end of the program and were stronger over time. Researchers found this "sleeper effect" surprising, given the steady loss of benefits once many interventions have concluded.

The qualitative component, designed to privilege the personal perspectives of participants, included open-ended questionnaires and focus groups with seventh-grade student and peer support leaders. Content analysis showed themes that were not fully named or examined in the researcher-designed surveys. For example, the strongest finding that emerged was that the program helped strengthen student connectedness and understanding of others. Students also emphasized how the program helped them deal with difficult situations and fostered a sense of possibility for their own futures. Mixed methods strengthened the study, providing complementary evidence and allowing for participants' voices to be included.

Participatory Action Research on the Impact of Mental Health Consumer-Run Organizations

Researchers in Ontario, Canada (Janzen, Nelson, Hausfather, & Ochocka, 2007), worked with stakeholders to conduct a mixed method, participatory action research project focusing on consumer-run mental health organizations that offered mutual support but also advocated for social change. The organizations, called Consumer/Survivor Initiatives (CSIs) in Ontario, focused on multiple levels in their work for systems change. They worked to impact local services (e.g., mental health and health services, planning bodies), policy (e.g., provincial ministry of health, mental health umbrella organizations), and society (e.g., public, media, educational institutions). The purpose of the research project was to assess the kinds of work that CSIs in Ontario were doing and to evaluate changes in local services, policies, and society due to the work of the CSIs.

The participatory action research approach included a number of components. CSI members were included in developing the study proposal. Fourteen CSI members were hired, trained, and supported as co-researchers. A stakeholder steering committee was formed and guided each step of the study. The research team also provided ongoing feedback to CSIs in popular, accessible formats.

The evaluators used quantitative and qualitative components to achieve triangulation of findings. They used quantitative methods to get at breadth and causal impacts. They developed a tracking tool—a spreadsheet that logged all the systems-level activities and outcomes of the CSIs over a 25-month period. Researchers found a total of 665 events over the 25 months of the study, and the most frequently used strategy for social change was community planning—ahead of public education, political advocacy, and action research strategies.

The research team utilized qualitative methods to get in-depth insights into the experiences of CSI members and organizations as a whole. These methods included key informant interviews and focus groups. These methods proved more effective for pinpointing outcomes of CSI social change activities, such as successfully advocating for increased subsidized housing units and hiring peer support workers in a local hospital.

Interestingly, the participatory component of the evaluation became an intervention in itself, as those involved in the research had the opportunity to engage in regular reflection on systems change. The CSI researchers and steering committee developed a common language for talking about the important work they were doing. Their reflexivity helped them think about how they could be more strategic and collaborative in the future. For example, the steering committee developed a 20-minute professionally produced DVD for CSIs to use in advocacy, education, and planning. They also held a series of regional workshops with CSIs to explore further action together. Participatory processes and mixed methods helped to capture the impact of the CSIs but also extended their impact.

CONCLUSION

Table 4.1 summarizes the distinctive features, strengths, and limitations of the qualitative and quantitative methods described in this chapter. That summary is simplified to save space, so remember that each set of methods has nuances and can be applied in many ways. There is plenty of room for creative imagination in designing community research.

Six themes run through this chapter. First, qualitative and quantitative methods tap different sources of knowledge and complement each other. As you probably noticed, the limitations of one are often the strengths of the other. No single approach provides a royal road to knowledge. A second theme is that much can be gained by integrating qualitative and quantitative approaches in one study to provide differing perspectives. Third, a longitudinal perspective often enhances community research. Studying changes over time reveals the workings of communities in ways not available in cross-sectional analysis.

Fourth, both qualitative and quantitative approaches can be used within a participatory-collaborative partnership with community members. Many studies we have described embody this theme. Fifth, no one method is best for every research question. Community researchers would be wise to respect and know how to use both qualitative and quantitative methods. Ideally, the nature of the research question to be studied would play an important role in choosing methods. Realistically, every community researcher cannot be equally competent with qualitative and quantitative methods; some specialization is to be expected. Yet the student of community psychology needs to be familiar with both approaches to knowing. The sixth and overarching theme is that community psychology as a field is best served by a diversity of forms of knowledge and methods of research.

It is important to think of our two research chapters as a unit. Chapter 3 concerned the importance of social values in community research, of participatory, collaborative research in partnership with community members, and of sensitivity to cultural and social contexts and multiple ecological levels. Chapter 4 illustrates specific methods for conducting community research along those lines, to provide knowledge useful to a community and to the world beyond it.

T A B L E 4.1   **Comparison of Community Research Methods**

Method	Distinctive Features	Strengths	Limitations
Qualitative Methods			
Participant observation	Researcher "joins" community or setting as a member, records personal experiences and observations	Maximum relationship with community, thick description, contextual understanding	Generalizability limited; sampling and data collection not standardized, researcher influences setting studied, potential role conflict
Qualitative interviewing of individuals	Collaborative approach, open-ended questioning to elicit participant' understandings in her or his own words, intensive study of small sample	Strong relationship with participants, thick description, contextual understanding, flexible exploration of topics, more standardized than participant observation	Generalizability limited, less standardized than quantitative methods, interpretation may create role conflict
Focus group interviewing	Similar to qualitative interviews, but conducted with a group to elicit shared views	Similar to qualitative interviews but allows group discussion, especially useful for cultural understanding	Similar to qualitative interviews, except less depth of understanding of individual
Case studies	Study of single individual, organization or community over time (can use qualitative and quantitative methods)	Understanding setting in depth, understanding changes over time, thick description, contextual understanding	Generalizability limited; less standardized than quantitative methods, limitations of archival data, interpretation may create role conflict
Quantitative Methods			
Quantitative description	Measurement and statistical analysis of standardized data from large samples, without experimental intervention	Standardized methods, generalizability, study of variables that cannot be experimentally manipulated	Reliance on prior knowledge, often decontextualized, limited understanding of cause and effect; epidemiology focuses on disorder
Randomized field experiments	Evaluation of social innovation, random assignment to experimental and control conditions	Standardized methods; control of confounding factors, understanding of cause and effect	Reliance on prior knowledge, difficulty in obtaining control groups in community settings, generalizability limited
Nonequivalent comparison group designs	Similar to field experiments, without random assignment to conditions	Standardized methods, some control of confounds, practicality	Reliance on prior knowledge, less control of confounds than randomized experiments, generalizability limited
Interrupted time-series designs	Longitudinal measurement of one or more settings before and after intervention; may use multiple-baseline design	Measurement in context, practicality, longitudinal perspective	Reliance on prior knowledge, less control of confounds than randomized experiments, generalizability limited (multiple-baseline better)

CHAPTER SUMMARY

1. Community research methods can be divided into *qualitative* and *quantitative* methods, largely on the basis of whether the data studied are in verbal or numerical form. Each method has characteristic strengths and limitations. Qualitative methods often provide knowledge of what a psychological or community phenomenon means to those who experience it. Quantitative methods often provide knowledge useful in making statistical comparisons and testing the effectiveness of social innovations or programs.

2. Qualitative methods have a long history in psychology. In this chapter, we described 10 common features of these methods. They usually involve intensive study of a small sample. The goal is to understand *contextual meaning* for the research participants, in their own terms, through a personal *participant-researcher relationship*. The researcher uses open-ended questions and listens carefully to participants' language to generate *thick description* of participants' experiences. Data are usually words. Data analysis often involves interpretation of themes or categories in participant responses, often refined through checking of interpretations with participants. Multiple interpretations are acceptable. Stein and Mankowski described four acts of qualitative research: *asking, witnessing, interpreting,* and *knowing.*

3. We discussed four qualitative methods: *participant observation, qualitative interviewing* (of individuals), *focus group interviewing,* and *case studies.* Qualitative methods often tap shared *narratives* and *personal stories* of individuals. Qualitative methods address reliability, validity, and generalizability differently than quantitative methods. Validity for qualitative methods often concerns *triangulation, verisimilitude,* and *reflexivity.*

4. Quantitative research emphasizes *measurement, comparisons, cause-effect* relationships, *generalization* across multiple contexts, and often experimentation. Data are numbers. *Standardized measurements* with established reliability and validity are preferred. Statistical analysis is the dominant method of analysis.

5. Quantitative description includes a variety of methods involving measurement but not experimental manipulation of variables (e.g., community surveys, epidemiology, and use of geographical information systems). While correlation is not causation, description can sometimes be used for conclusions about causes. In epidemiology, important concepts include *incidence, prevalence, risk factor,* and *protective factor.*

6. In community research, an important use of experimental methods is *experimental social innovation,* in which social innovations are tested for effectiveness. Methods include *randomized field experiments, nonequivalent comparison group designs,* and *interrupted time-series designs,* the latter sometimes in a *multiple-baseline* format.

7. Qualitative and quantitative methods can be integrated in a single study or in multiple related studies to offer the advantages of both approaches.

8. Table 4.1 summarizes the distinctive features, strengths, and limitations of eight specific qualitative and quantitative methods often used in community research. Six themes of this chapter are summarized in the "Conclusions" section.

RECOMMENDED READINGS

Hazel, K. & Onanga, E. (Eds.). (2003). Experimental social innovation and dissemination [Special issue]. *American Journal of Community Psychology, 32* (4).

Revenson, T., D'Augelli, A., French, S., Hughes, D., Livert, D., Seidman, E., Shinn, M., & Yoshikawa, H. (Eds.). (2002). *Ecological research to promote social change: Methodological advances from community psychology.* New York: Kluwer Academic/Plenum.

Stein, C. & Mankowski, E. (2004). Asking, witnessing, interpreting, knowing: Conducting qualitative research in community psychology. *American Journal of Community Psychology, 33,* 21–36.

RECOMMENDED WEBSITES

American Journal of Community Psychology
http://www.springer.com/psychology/community+psychology/journal/10464

Journal of Community Psychology
http://onlinelibrary.wiley.com/journal/10.1002/(ISSN)1520-6629

Journal of Community and Applied Social Psychology
http://onlinelibrary.wiley.com/journal/10.1002/(ISSN)1099-1298

5

Understanding Individuals Within Environments

HIRB/Index Stock/PhotoLibrary

This chapter is the first of four chapters that present longer discussions of key concepts in community psychology. All concern understanding the links between contexts and individuals. In this chapter, we cover major ways of understanding environments and individuals' functioning within environments. Chapter 6 will cover concepts of community, Chapter 7 discusses ways of understanding human diversity, and Chapter 8 provides a contextual perspective on stress and coping.

OPENING EXERCISE

In everyday experience, we often talk about places where we feel comfortable, where we feel more stressed, or where we do not fit in. These might be work-places, schools, a group of friends, or a neighborhood. Often, we do not fully realize how much these places can affect us until we notice feeling uncomfortable.

Like a fish swimming in water, we take the contexts of our lives for granted. As we discussed in Chapter 1, we tend to minimize contextual factors and overlook ecological levels of analysis. Community psychologists try to understand the importance of contexts for people's lives and work to change the environments to be more supportive.

Most of us tend to notice aspects of environments most clearly when we are new to a setting. Take a moment to remember your first visit to the college or university you now attend. What do you recall about the college as a setting—about its atmosphere and its "feel" for you as an individual? Did you sense that people like you live, study, or work here or did you feel different in some important way? Think about how and where you carry out tasks of student life. On your campus, where is a place you like to socialize? A quiet place to study? A place and person you would seek for help with a personal problem?

Now take a longer view. How has this college environment affected you as an individual? Have you changed since you started or returned to college? How have your experiences in this environment shaped your learning, personal development, friendships, vocational plans, and personal well-being? How would you be different if you studied on a different campus?

These questions reflect the concepts community psychologists and others have developed to understand the interactions between persons and environments in everyday life, such as adjusting to college. This study of persons in ecological context has been a central theme for community psychology. At the 1965 Swampscott conference that organized community psychology in the United States, participants identified a central focus for the new field: "the reciprocal relationships between individuals and social systems" (Bennett et al., 1966, p. 7).

An interest in understanding environmental influences on individuals is common among many disciplines, including anthropology, public health, social work, and sociology. For over a century, ecological context has been implicitly recognized as important for understanding human behavior. At the turn of the 20th century, Lightner Witmer and the staff of the early child development clinics did their work in the settings where children lived and went to school and made changes in those settings to help children learn. The Chicago School of sociology documented the importance of neighborhood and city environments for personal life (e.g., Park, 1952). Social psychologist Kurt Lewin argued that behavior is a function of person *and* environment (Lewin, 1935). Theories of personality proposed by Murray (1938), Rotter (1954), and Bandura (1986) emphasized the interaction of person and situation, although applications of their concepts focused on individuals. Even scientists studying genetic contributions to behavior argue that is important to understand how environments interact with individual factors (Rutter, Moffat, & Caspi, 2006). However, the specific ways that contexts and individuals interact are not well understood. Psychology has focused on individual variables, devoting much less attention to environmental factors. Other disciplines have focused on understanding variables related to the environment but have not understood well how they link to processes that affect individuals. As a linking science, community psychology seeks to understand environmental factors and their connections to well-being.

In this chapter, we examine major approaches used in community psychology for understanding ecological context. Second, we illustrate how understanding contexts can inform research and action regarding the interplay of neighborhood, family, and personal life. Finally, we highlight two exemplary community programs that changed ecological contexts to improve the well-being of individuals and families.

CONCEPTUAL MODELS OF ECOLOGICAL CONTEXT

To understand interactions between environment and individuals, community psychologists typically focus on specific contexts where people interact and experience everyday life. In research terms, the unit of analysis is conceptualized as an environmental *setting*. The settings of interest might be physical (e.g., a school) or social (e.g., a team) and can be nested within levels of analysis (e.g., microsystem, organizational, or locality). As you read about these six models for understanding ecological context and how context factors can affect individuals, note how each model conceptualizes environmental settings, and keep in mind the levels of analysis that we introduced in Chapter 1. Some of the models can be used at multiple levels; others fit one or two levels best.

Four Ecological Principles

Community psychology's foundational framework for understanding context uses ecological metaphors to examine social environments and their physical settings. Adapting concepts from the biological field of ecology, James Kelly, Edison Trickett, and colleagues proposed four key ecological principles in understanding human environments: *interdependence, cycling of resources, adaptation, and succession* (Kelly, 1966, 1979a; Trickett, 1984; Trickett, Barone, & Watts, 2000; Trickett, Kelly, & Todd, 1972). These are principles about characteristics of settings, not of individuals. For example, workplaces differ in the extent of interdependence among workers, in what resources are exchanged, and in what processes are needed to adapt to the setting. Of course, these factors can influence individual life greatly in schools, families, workplaces, and other settings. This framework guides where and how to observe environments. Let us look at these principles in greater detail.

Interdependence   As with biological ecosystems, any social system has multiple related parts and multiple relationships with other systems. Changes in one of these parts can affect the others; they are interdependent (Trickett, Kelly, & Todd, 1972). For a public school, interdependent components include students, teachers, administrators, secretaries, janitors and other staff, parents, board members, and district taxpayers. Actions or problems of any of these groups can affect everyone else. State and national governments and local and international economies can also affect local schooling.

Consider the ecology of a family as another example. If one family member gets the flu, everyone else is affected in one way or another. If a young child is sick, an older member of the family will likely miss work or school to stay at home with the sick child. Others in the family may also become ill. If the primary caregiver gets the flu, meal preparation, washing, transportation, and a host of other daily operations for every other member of the family are affected. The change may be temporary, with the family system returning to its previous state after a few days. Other changes may last longer, such as having an ailing grandparent join the household.

A corollary of the principle of interdependence is that any change in a system will have multiple consequences—some of them unanticipated and perhaps unwanted. Similarly, change efforts within a system may be thwarted because concerns of interdependent components of the system were not addressed. For instance, a teacher may introduce cooperative learning techniques in a classroom, only to face resistance from students, principals, parents, or other teachers if the wider culture strongly endorses individual competition in education.

Cycling of Resources   The second ecological principle is closely related to interdependence. It specifies that any system can be understood by examining how resources are used, distributed, conserved, and transformed (Trickett, Kelly, & Todd, 1972). Community psychologists are also interested in how settings' members define and exchange resources. *Personal resources* include individual talents, knowledge, experiences, strengths, or other qualities that can address challenges in a setting. Social resources occur in relationships among members of the setting, including shared beliefs, values, formal rules, informal norms, group events, and shared sense of community. Even physical aspects of a setting are resources: a library with rooms for group study, quiet nooks for individual study, and a place to take a break. From an ecological perspective, social settings have many more resources than are commonly recognized. Community psychologists can help to define and utilize resources that have been overlooked (e.g., students at a school for an antibullying program).

What resources are important for a family? Time, nurturance, attention, emotional support, and money are some examples. By examining the availability and use of resources, one can begin to characterize family priorities and connections. You may not recognize how a family member can be a resource until you encounter a stressful life event that he or she has lived through and can advise you about. Similarly, a quiet person who understands others well is a valuable resource for a group but may be overlooked among more outspoken members. An implication of Kelly's approach is to search any environment (family, organization, or neighborhood) for resources (tangible or intangible) that can contribute to individual or system well-being.

Stack's (1974) classic study of a low-income African American community highlighted the importance of understanding patterns of resource sharing. In The Flats (a public housing community with limited financial resources), residents shared furniture, child care, food stamps, and money beyond their own families. For example, a member of the community loaned furniture to a neighbor for an extended period of time, and that neighbor had previously cared for her child while she was looking for work out of town. To an outsider without an ecological perspective, this exchange of resources may seem risky for families with little money, but it made sense to those within the system. However, by examining patterns of resource use within this community, it was recognized that resources were allocated to those who needed them; today's provider may be tomorrow's recipient. Stack's detailed study documented the value of an ecological perspective in recognizing the interdependence of the community members and their cycling of resources.

Adaptation   The third ecological principle concerns the transactions between person and environment. This is a two-way process; individuals cope with the constraints or demands of an environment, and environments adapt to their members (Trickett et al., 1972). For example, recall how you adapted to the demands of your first job. To adapt, you probably learned new skills without losing your unique identity. Some jobs require changes in appearance, changes in relating to people, or changes in schedules. Environments also adapt to their members. Think about the changes in a family triggered by such events as the birth of a child, a parent starting a new job, or children moving away from home. At a higher level of analysis, an organization that does not respond to the needs of its members will find it difficult to retain member involvement or attract new members. For individuals and social systems to survive, they need to adapt to each other (Kelly et al., 2000).

Social settings also adapt to the larger environments in which they are nested (Kelly et al., 2000). For instance a local school system adapts yearly to changes in the requirements and funding of local, state, and national government as well as to changes in the student makeup of the schools. Changes in technology, the economy, and cultural ideas about education also affect local schools.

A further implication of the adaptation principle is that every environment demands different skills. Skills students need are somewhat different from those for factory workers or homemakers or police officers. For example, consider the role of neighborhood contexts in parenting. Effective parenting in dangerous neighbor-hoods is more directive, setting more rules and firmer limits, than effective parenting in safer neighborhoods (Gonzales, Cauce, Friedman, & Mason, 1996).

Succession   Settings and social systems change over time. Interdependence, resource cycling, and adaptation must be understood in that perspective (Trickett et al., 1972). This principle applies to families, organizations, and communities. How many times have you heard that "you have to work at keeping a relation-ship healthy"? Over time, patterns of partner interdependence, the cycling of resources, such as emotional support, and the adaptation of each partner to the other can change without their noticing. The nature of the relationship changes over time. With successful adaptation and cycling of resources, the relationship continues and may deepen. If adaptation is difficult over time or needed resources are not available or utilized, perhaps partners drift apart. You can see succession in these relationship "settings" when there is a divorce, at the start of new relationships, and when children make decisions about their life commitments based on their parents' experiences.

An implication of understanding succession in settings is that psychologists need to understand a system's history before they plan an intervention in that system. In trying to make a neighborhood a safer place, what have people tried to do in the past? What worked? How did the problems develop? Psychologists should also carefully consider the likely consequences of the intervention, including possible unintended consequences. How can the community continue the intervention after the formal involvement of the psychologist ends? We discuss these considerations more in the prevention and promotion chapters (9 and 10).

The tremendous growth of mutual help (self-help) groups in responding to personal needs since the 1970s illustrates these ecological principles. Mutual help has become an important element in mental health care, largely without professional planning or intervention. Mutual help organizations have been recognized for their contributions addressing addictions, violence against women, and coping with chronic illnesses. Their primary purpose is to strengthen individual adaptation of members and to create a setting where members can have their needs met. Interdependence is encouraged, often including individual contacts outside the group meetings. Social support, information, and other resources are exchanged. The members who have gone through the same experiences themselves are resources for each other that are often overlooked by helping professionals. Persons who often think of themselves as needing resources can have the uplifting experience of providing resources to others. The way that a local self-help group maintains itself—especially after its founders move on—is a matter of succession. We discuss mutual help in greater detail in Chapter 8.

Contributions of This Approach   These four ecological principles provide distinctive, useful concepts for describing the dynamics of social environments. They address aspects not emphasized in other approaches to understanding context (e.g., interdependence and succession). Kelly et al. (2000) argued that ecological concepts can guide the development of preventive interventions in community settings. Furthermore, Kelly, Trickett, and associates (e.g., Kelly, 1979; Tandon et al., 1998; Vincent & Trickett, 1983) have applied the ecological principles to the conduct of research and psychological intervention in the community. An ecological approach to research emphasizes establishing an interdependent relationship between researchers and host community, identifying and cultivating community members who can be resources for the research, and anticipating unintended effects of research or intervention. The writings of Kelly and associates eloquently express values of genuine interdependence with community members and appreciation of community resources. This perspective underlies many of the aims of community research we discussed in Chapter 3.

Social Climate Dimensions

A second major framework for understanding environments emphasizes how people experience and understand settings. Rudolf Moos and colleague argued that many psychological effects of environments are best assessed in terms of persons' perceptions of the environment and the meaning people attach to it (e.g., Moos, 1973, 2003). Moos and colleagues developed a *social climate* approach to assess shared perceptions of a setting among its members and have created several scales to measure social climate in settings (e.g., Moos, 1973, 1994, 2002). Perceptions of social climates can affect social relationships and organizational functioning. Studying social climates of settings has been important for understanding how individuals cope and identifying which aspects of settings can help promote well-being (Holahan, Moos, & Bonin, 1997; Moos & Holahan, 2003). The social climate approach to understanding environments is based on three primary dimensions that can characterize any setting: how they organize social *relationships,* how they encourage *personal development,* and their focus on *maintenance* or *change* in the setting (Moos, 1994).

Relationships   This dimension of settings concerns mutual supportiveness, involvement, and cohesion of its members (Moos, 2002). The social climate approach looks for evidence of relationship qualities in each setting. For example, the Classroom Environment Scale, which measures high school classroom environments, contains subscales on the extent to which students are involved in and participate in class, the extent of affiliation or friendship they report among classmates, and the amount of support they perceive from the teacher (Moos & Trickett, 1987). The Family Environment Scale (Moos & Moos, 1986) includes subscales on how cohesive and how expressive the members perceive their family to be and the extent of conflict they perceive. Coworker cohesion and supervisor support can be measured in work settings (Moos, 2002). These constructs are conceptually related to Kelly's principles of interdependence and cycling of resources just discussed.

Personal Development   This dimension of settings concerns whether individual autonomy, growth, and skill development are fostered in the settings (Moos, 2002). For example, the Ward Assessment Scale (Moos, 1974) includes a subscale about how much a psychiatric treatment ward focuses on helping patients address their particular health needs. The Classroom Environment Scale contains a subscale on competition among students (Moos & Trickett, 1987). The Family Environment Scale (Moos & Moos, 1986) includes subscales concerning the independence accorded individual family members and the family's emphasis on achievement, intellectual-cultural pursuits, recreation, and moral-religious concerns. In work settings, worker autonomy and pressure on workers are measured (Moos, 2002). These environmental demands are related to Kelly's principle of adaptation.

System Maintenance and Change   This dimension of settings concerns settings' emphasis on order, clarity of rules and expectations, and control of behavior (Moos, 2002). The Classroom Environment Scale contains subscales concerning the extent to which class activities are organized and orderly, the clarity of rules, the strictness of the teacher, and the extent to which innovative activities and thinking are welcomed (Moos & Trickett, 1987). The Ward Assessment Scale (Moos, 1974) examines who makes decisions in the health care unit and whether rules are explicit. The Family Environment Scale (Moos & Moos, 1986) includes scales on the extent of control exerted by parents. In work settings, such variables as managerial control and encouragement of innovation are measured (Moos, 2002). These are conceptually related to adaptation and succession in Kelly's framework.

The social climate approach assumes that settings will vary on how much they emphasize relationships, personal growth of setting members, or maintenance in setting practices. Persons in a setting complete surveys to report their perception of these dimensions of that setting. Their responses are aggregated to form a profile of the shared perceptions of this particular environment (Moos, 1994, 2002). Furthermore, patterns of responses across the three dimensions can be compared among setting members and between different settings.

Use of Social Climate in Research and Community Practice

Social climate approaches have been used for research on settings at the microsystem and organizational levels of analysis, including workplaces, university residence halls, psychiatric inpatient settings, correctional settings, supported community living facilities, military units, and classrooms (Moos, 1994). Social climate scales can be useful in consultation and program development (Moos, 1984). A consultant may compare the perceptions of different stakeholders in a setting, such as teachers and students completing the Classroom Environment Scale. Differences in perceptions and common views can be used to start a discussion about how to improve a classroom or school. Similarly, a consultant may have setting members complete two forms of a social climate scale: the Real Form to report current setting functioning and the Ideal Form to report how they desire the setting to be. The consultant then presents the aggregated group scores on both forms, and the group discusses how to change the environment to become more like the shared ideal profile.

Social climate scores have been statistically related to measures of individual well-being, such as job satisfaction and psychological adjustment (Repetti & Cosmas, 1991). For instance, high school classrooms that emphasize competition and teacher control but not teacher support and student involvement have greater absenteeism (Moos, 1984). Juvenile delinquency treatment programs higher on support, autonomy, and clarity of expectations have lower rates of recidivism (Moos, 1975). Treatment settings perceived as less supportive by clients and/or staff and that lack clear rules and procedures have higher dropout rates (Moos, 1984). Of course, these are generalizations across many settings; for example, social climate scales also can be used to study a particular juvenile treatment program.

Generalizing across many studies and settings, Moos (2003) identified three general themes of how understanding social climates can improve well-being. First, a setting that emphasizes a balance of personal relationships, personal development, and setting organization often promotes setting performance, individual performance, and individual well-being. Second, highly structured settings and communities often promote cohesion but can foster conformity and inhibit minority views and personal growth. Third, the quality of personal relationships often affects how much long-term influence that a setting has on individuals.

Contributions and Limitations of This Approach   Social climate scales measure important aspects of settings, such as supportiveness, clarity of expectations, and individual growth. Social climates influence important individual outcomes. They connect subjective perceptions with setting characteristics in a way that other approaches do not. The conceptual value and ease of use of social climate scales has fostered research and practical applications in a variety of settings, generating a rich literature of empirical findings.

The chief limitation of the social climate scale approach to understanding environments is that individuals or subgroups within the setting may see its social climate differently. For example, Raviv, Raviv, and Reisel (1990) reported differences in levels of satisfaction between teachers and students in the same classroom. Trickett, Trickett, Castro, and Schaffner (1982) found differences between students and independent observers in rating the qualities of schools. These discrepancies suggest social climate measures are influenced by one's personality or social role in the setting, not just by the setting's overall characteristics. For example, if the mean score (for a sample of setting members) is midway on a social climate scale (e.g., supportiveness), it could mean at least two things. It may indicate unanimous perceptions of medium supportiveness or it may reflect two polarized camps of setting members—with one group perceiving a very supportive setting, while the other perceives a very unsupportive setting. For example, the same environment may generate quite different perceptions among women and men. Thus, social climate scores should be examined carefully for variation among individuals or subgroups in the setting (Moos, 2003; Shinn, 1990).

Social Regularities

Settings typically create predictable relationships among their members, and those qualities persist over time regardless of the individuals involved. Edward Seidman (1988, 1990) proposed that settings be understood in terms of these *social regularities*, defined as the routine patterns of social relations among the elements (e.g., persons) within a setting (Seidman, 1988, pp. 9–10). Seidman's focus is not on individual personalities but on relationships between individuals. The patterns of social relationships in communities can affect distribution of resources, access to opportunities, and authority to address social issues.

Think back over your schooling for a moment. Who asks most of the questions in the school or college classroom? If your answer is the teacher, you have noticed a social regularity (Sarason, 1982; Seidman, 1988). Why is this so predictable, despite the diversity of teachers and students and levels of education? Both teachers and students often focus on attributes of persons (e.g., boring teachers, lazy students). Instead, might this regularity have to do with assumptions (of teachers and students) about the roles and relationships of teachers and students, and about how learning takes place? Perhaps even about power in the classroom?

To discover social regularities, search for patterns of behavior that reveal roles and power relationships among setting members (e.g., teacher-student, therapist-client, employer-employee, parent-child). Roles are enacted in a specific setting in ways that affect power, decision making, resources, and inequalities (Seidman, 1988).

A historical social regularity is that U.S. schools have been a sorting mechanism for separating students by achievement or test scores and then preparing them for different roles in society. Segregated schools once also sorted students by race. When the courts mandated an end to segregation, communities brought Black and White students into the same schools. Yet both research and commonsense observation reveal that in many schools, a new form of sorting takes place. On the basis of (mainly White) staff perceptions of their abilities and on test scores that may not fairly measure those abilities, Black (and often Latino/Latina and Native American) students are assigned disproportionately to classes and curricula that limit their ability to apply for college and their future attainments (Linney, 1986; Seidman, 1988; Weinstein, 2002a, 2002b). By sorting on this basis, school systems have continued (in modified form) the historic U.S. social regularity of racial separation. The new form of sorting is often unintentional rather than accomplished segregation by law. Nonetheless, it has similar effects on students' lives and opportunities.

A final example of a social regularity concerns professional psychotherapy and mutual help for persons with mental disorders (Seidman, 1988). In a professionally conducted therapy group, members may fall into more passive "patient behavior," even when the professional seeks to promote active support among members. By contrast, in a mutual help group conducted by members, all of whom who have experienced the same problem, members exchange helping and are expected to give and receive help. In studies comparing the social climates of professionally conducted groups with peer-led groups, members of peer-led groups rated their groups as more cohesive and as fostering more independence (Toro, Rappaport, & Seidman, 1987; Toro et al., 1988). These differences in group member participation are rooted in the social regularities of who is perceived to have authority to address needs of group members.

Contributions and Limitations   The concept of social regularities calls attention to role relationships and power that the other approaches do not address explicitly. It also offers a way of understanding why it often seems that the more things change in a setting, the more they remain the same. If settings change the actors (e.g., new teachers or principal in a school) but not the fundamental social regularities of how a school functions and who makes decisions, it will only promote *first-order change*. Often, attempts to change a setting—such as a school—are undermined by social regularities that are not changed, such as decision-making power and role relationships. Only if those social regularities are altered is the system itself changed (Linney, 1986; Seidman, 1988), resulting in *second-order change*. These aspects of settings and relationships will be discussed more in Chapters 7 and 11. Identifying social regularities requires rich understanding of a setting that takes time and resources. Sometimes, a social climate survey will be cheaper and quicker. Methods for investigating social regularities include naturalistic observation, case study, and ethnographic approaches. Interpretation of results can be limited, as it can be hard to know how a detailed understanding of one setting applies to other settings. However, once particular regularities are identified, quantitative methods may be used.

Ecological Psychology and Behavior Settings

Roger Barker and colleagues developed a comprehensive approach to understanding settings and environments (Barker, 1968). The theory and methodology of Barker's ecological psychology has been important in the formation of environmental and community psychology. The development of ecological psychology is an interesting story of participatory and collaborative research. In 1947, Roger and Louise Barker, Herbert Wright, and colleagues began studying the lives of children in a town they referred to as "Midwest" (actually Oskaloosa, Kansas). The Barker family moved to Midwest to live and, with their colleagues, opened the Midwest Field Station. In this small town, they aimed to understand children's lives in ecological context (Barker, 1968; Barker & Wright, 1955; Barker et al., 1978). After earning the trust and cooperation of Midwest residents, they and their associates began careful, systematic, naturalistic observations of all aspects of children's everyday lives. Barker (1978, p. 3) referred to this method as studying the "stream of behavior" rather than breaking that stream into bits and choosing only some bits to understand apart from the whole. They soon discovered that they could not study children's lives in context without including the whole town.

> The truth is that we soon became overwhelmed with individual behavior. We estimated that the 119 children of Midwest engaged in about one hundred thousand behavior episodes daily.... We sampled behavior in such divergent places as the drugstore, the Sunday School classes, the 4-H Club meeting, and the football games.... At this point, we stopped focusing exclusively on the behavior of individuals and saw for the first time a thing that is obvious to the inhabitants of Midwest, namely, that behavior comes in extraindividual wave patterns that are as visible and invariant as the pools and rapids of Slough Creek, west of town. The Presbyterian worship services, the high school basketball games, and the post office, for example, persist year after year with their unique configurations of behavior, despite constant changes in the persons involved. These persisting, extraindividual behavior phenomena we have called the standing behavior patterns of Midwest.
> (Barker & Wright, 1978, pp. 24–25)

Barker and colleagues studied this community in great depth over many years and eventually a similar English town ("Yoredale") and other settings. They observed physical and social environments where community life was created and sustained. They were interested not in individual personalities but in patterns of behavior characteristic of a setting regardless of which individuals were there (Barker, 1965, 1968; Barker et al., 1978; Barker & Schoggen, 1973; Barker & Wright, 1955). Their work has been extended by others (e.g., Schoggen, 1989; Wicker, 1979).

Behavior Settings   Barker (1968) developed this concept as the primary unit of analysis for ecological psychology. A behavior setting is defined by having a place, time, and a standing pattern of behavior. Thus, the behavior setting of a third-grade class in Midwest involved meeting weekdays in one classroom at the school and then proceeding through a program involving predictable teacher and student behavior—largely regardless of which individuals were present. The drugstore behavior setting had wider time boundaries and more turnover of "inhabitants" (customers and staff) but occurred in a single place and involved standing behavior patterns, again regardless of which individuals were present. Some behavior settings were embedded within larger behavior settings, such as classes within a school. Others stood alone, such as a service station. Some occurred only occasionally, such as a wedding or talent show, whereas others were daily events. Barker (1968, p. 106) and colleagues identified 884 behavior settings in Midwest in 1963–1964; almost all could be grouped into five categories: government, business, educational, religious, and voluntary associations.

It is important to note that a behavior setting is not simply a physical place. The sanctuary of the Methodist church in Midwest was a physical setting but not a behavior setting. Instead, several behavior settings occurred within it, each with a time and standing behavior pattern (e.g., worship services, choir practices, and weddings). In contrast, many small retail shops comprised a single behavior setting. The physical setting and the behavior setting are synomorphic, or matched, in their structure. For example, the seats in a lecture hall face the speaker, while seats in a committee meeting room face each other. Each makes possible the enduring behavior pattern of the setting.

From Barker's perspective, persons in a behavior setting are largely interchangeable; the same patterns of behavior occur irrespective of the specific individuals. Barker further hypothesized that behavior settings have rules—implicit or explicit—that maintain the standing behavior pattern (Barker, 1968, pp. 167–171). These rules can be seen in specific behavior patterns:

- **Program circuits**, such as an agenda for a meeting or routines, guide the standing behavior pattern.
- **Goal circuits** satisfy goals of individuals, such as a customer purchasing an item or a member participating in a worship service.

The rules also incorporate control mechanisms to channel or limit individual involvement:

- **Deviation-countering circuits** involve training individuals for roles in the behavior setting and correcting their behavior to improve role performance.
- **Vetoing circuits** occur when individuals are excluded from the behavior setting.

The purpose of ecological psychology is to identify behavior settings and to understand the physical features and social circuits that maintain them.

A baseball game provides an illustration (Barker, 1968). The game is a behavior setting—a standing pattern of behavior—occurring at a given time and place. The field defines the physical environment alone but reveals little about the game. Similarly, we would not be able to understand the game or individual players' acts by focusing on each player in isolation (the common individual-level focus of psychological research). For example, imagine a film showing the first base player alone, without the context of the field or of plays not involving the first baseman. Very little could be learned about what this player is doing and why, and it would be quite difficult to predict that player's behavior. By observing the context of the entire behavior setting, the program circuits or rules become clearer. So do the relationships among players during the game. Barker (1968) suggested that it is the combination of the physical field, game time, and the standing patterns of behavior among players (and fans) that constitute the behavior setting of a baseball game.

Identifying behavior settings, as initially performed in Midwest, was an exceedingly lengthy process. Barker and colleagues spent over a year in an exhaustive description of the behavior settings in Midwest (Barker & Wright, 1955). Behavior setting methodology has been applied in schools, churches, mutual help groups, and work settings (Barker & Gump, 1964; Luke, Rappaport, & Seidman, 1991; Oxley & Barrera, 1984; Schoggen & Schoggen, 1988; Wicker, 1969).

Underpopulated Settings A second contribution of Barker's ecological approach has been the study of "manning" theory (Barker, 1968). Schoggen (1989) adopted the terms "*underpopulated*" and "*optimally populated*" settings.

In a classic study, *Big School, Small School*, Barker and Gump (1964) compared involvement of students in extracurricular activities (one form of behavior settings) in large and small high schools in Kansas (enrollments ranged from 35 to over 2,000). In the smaller schools, they found greater levels of student involvement in performances and in leadership roles and higher levels of student satisfaction and attachment to school. There existed a slightly greater number of opportunities for involvement in larger schools. But students in smaller schools were twice as likely to participate in active ways and on average participated in a wider variety of activities. Barker and Gump also found that students in smaller schools perceived more responsibility to volunteer for activities. They often reported a sense that even if they were not talented in a particular activity, their help was needed. The larger schools had higher rates of uninvolved, "marginal" students with little sense of commitment to the school or social connection with school peers or staff.

Studies in a variety of settings have established that the critical factor is the ratio of the number of roles available in a behavior setting compared to the number of individuals available to play those roles (Wicker, 1979, 1987). An optimally populated setting has as many or more players than roles. Settings easily recruit enough members to fill their roles; other students are marginalized or left out. Barker theorized that vetoing circuits (behaviors that screen out potential members) would be especially common in these settings because there are plenty of replacements available (1968, p. 181). A large school will probably have tryouts for athletic teams, musical groups, dramatic productions, and so on; only the most talented will be able to participate. Barker and Gump (1964) found that larger schools contained more optimally populated settings.

Alternatively, an underpopulated setting has more roles than members. That increases member sense of responsibility for maintaining the setting and offers them the chance to develop skills they otherwise might not have learned. It may also increase the diversity of persons participating in the setting, attracting unused resources. For example, a shy person who otherwise would not try out for a school play is pressed into service, developing social skills or perhaps revealing hidden talents. In addition, members of an underpopulated behavior setting would engage in deviation-countering circuits rather than vetoing circuits. They would invest time and effort in teaching the skills needed for a role in the setting rather than excluding the person. This strategy makes sense if members are needed to play roles necessary for maintaining the setting. Barker and Gump (1964) found that smaller schools contained more underpopulated settings. Of course, members in an extremely underpopulated setting will "burn out"; the setting may even be disbanded. Yet moderate understaffing may lead to positive outcomes for individuals (greater skill or personal development) and setting (greater commitment among members).

These concepts fit the organizational strategies of GROW, a mutual help organization for persons with serious mental illness. GROW began in Australia and was studied by community psychologists as they introduced its organization in the United States. GROW deliberately limits the size of local chapters, creates leadership roles for all members, and maximizes member sense of responsibility for group functioning. These methods promote member personal development and mutual commitment and illustrate the practical benefits of an underpopulated behavior setting (Luke et al., 1991; Zimmerman et al., 1991).

Contributions and Limitations of This Approach   Ecological psychology has generated an enduring body of concepts and research and influenced the development of other ecological perspectives in community psychology. The concepts of *behavior setting* and *underpopulated* settings represent two especially important contributions.

One limitation is that Barker and associates focused on behavior—largely overlooking cultural meanings and other subjective processes. A second limitation is that behavior setting theory focuses on how behavior settings perpetuate themselves and mold the behavior of individuals. This is one side of the picture, but it underplays how settings are created and changed and how individuals influence settings (Perkins, Burns, Perry, & Nielsen, 1988). Having originally been developed in a small-town setting, an emphasis on stability rather than change is understandable yet limited in scope. Third, the effects of underpopulated and optimally populated settings have not always been replicated in later studies, and their relationship to individual adjustment and behavior appear more complicated than behavior setting theory suggests (Perkins et al., 1988). (See Schoggen, 1988, for a defense of behavior setting concepts on these points.)

Activity Settings

Clifford O'Donnell, Roland Tharp, and Kathleen Wilson (1993) developed the concept of activity settings. While similar to ecological psychology in focusing on settings, activity setting theory takes subjective experiences and cultural-social meanings into account. O'Donnell and colleagues were influenced by the Russian developmental theorist Lev Vygotsky, by the contextualist epistemologies that we described in Chapter 3, and by working in Hawaiian and Pacific cultural contexts.

An activity setting is not simply a physical setting and not just the behavior of persons who meet there but also the subjective meanings that develop there among setting participants, especially intersubjectivities: beliefs, assumptions, values, and emotional experiences that are shared by setting participants. Key elements of an activity setting include the physical setting, positions (roles), people and the interpersonal relationships they form, time, and symbols that setting members create and use. Intersubjectivity develops over time as persons in the setting communicate, work together, and form relationships. They develop symbols, chiefly language but also visual or other images, to express what they have in common. This perspective calls attention to cultural practices used in the settings and meanings that members attach to them.

For example, in many spiritual settings, sacred written works and vocabulary, visual art, and music are important symbols whose meaning is both intensely personal and widely shared. In political rallies, particular colors, music, topics, and stories are used to connect current circumstances to historical precedents. Much of what is important about any culture is intersubjective, widely understood within the culture yet difficult to communicate to outsiders. Even within one culture, families and organizations develop intersubjective uses of language and gestures that outsiders cannot understand and that reflect important insider attitudes.

Contributions and Limitations of This Approach   Activity setting theory offers a broader conception of social settings than ecological psychology. It has been used to study child development, juvenile delinquency, education, and community interventions. Like social regularities and ecological psychology, it requires time and resources to gather the necessary data. Also, there are few conventions to comparing activity settings across contexts. However, an activity setting approach underscores the importance of subjective meaning in understanding links between individuals and their contexts. It is especially useful in working in settings that require crossing cultural boundaries, as O'Donnell and associates have shown in their work in Hawaii, Micronesia, and elsewhere

(O'Donnell, Tharp, & Wilson, 1993; O'Donnell & Yamauchi, 2005; Gallimore, Goldenberg, & Weisner, 1993).

Environmental Psychology

Environmental psychology examines the influence of physical characteristics of a setting (especially built environments) on behavior (Timko, 1996; Winkel, Saegert, & Evans, 2009). Environmental psychology in the United States arose at about the same time as community psychology. Its founders were primarily social psychologists interested in the physical environment and behavior. But both fields emphasize a shift of perspective from individual to individual-in-environment, and they overlap in several ways (Shinn, 1996b). Both fields emphasize research conducted in field settings and application of their concepts to social action.

Environmental Stressors   A major focus of environmental psychology is the study of the psychological effects of environmental stressors, such as noise, air pollution, hazardous waste, and crowded housing (Rich, Edelstein, Hallman, & Wandersman, 1995; Winkel, Saegert, & Evans, 2009). For example, the psychological effects of two notable incidents from the late 1970s have been researched intensively and longitudinally. At Love Canal, near Niagara Falls, New York, residents discovered in 1977 that they were living above a chemical waste dump when birth defects began appearing. The effects of that disaster and of citizen activism in response were studied by Adeline Levine and associates (Levine, 1982; Stone & Levine, 1985). The Three Mile Island nuclear plant near Harrisburg, Pennsylvania, had a serious accident in which radiation was released in 1979; the stressful effects of this accident on nearby residents have been studied over time (Baum & Fleming, 1993). In both cases, uncertainty about the levels of actual exposure to radiation or toxic substances and inconsistencies in public statements by industry and government officials exacerbated the stressful effects of the event (see also Wandersman & Hallman, 1993). After the Three Mile Island incident, blood pressure remained elevated, immune system functioning depressed, and symptoms of posttraumatic stress more common among nearby residents than in comparison samples. These effects did not dissipate for nearly 10 years (Baum & Fleming, 1993).

Environmental Design   Environmental psychologists also study the psychological effects of architectural and neighborhood design features. Examples include studies of enclosed workspaces, windows, and aspects of housing design (Sundstrom, Bell, Busby, & Asmus, 1996). For a personal example, consider arrangement of furniture in indoor spaces on your campus or in your workplace. The psychology department of one of the authors remodeled common space in the department offices to redirect traffic flow and conversation areas away from working staff. Students and faculty responded by regularly moving chairs to resemble the old arrangement, presumably to recreate the social spaces. In the department of another author, a common area for students has some seats in a circle, a few student carrels, snack machines and faculty mailboxes nearby, and is located between the hallway and psychology department offices. This creates a social space in which faculty and students can encounter each other outside of class as well as a corner for study when the space is quiet. Yet the competition for space on campus is keen, and periodically, this social space must be vigorously defended against administrative attempts to use it for offices.

The New Urbanism movement in residential architecture and neighborhood design encourages community. Plas and Lewis (1996) studied Seaside, Florida, a community designed along New Urbanist lines, with building codes that require front porches and low picket fences for each house, a town design with walkways to the town center and beach, and limited automobile access. Businesses are accessible on foot from anywhere in the community. These features encourage neighboring and are based on study of older, established towns and neighborhoods with a strong sense of community (e.g., Jacobs, 1961). Surveys, interviews, and naturalistic observation in Seaside indicated that these features did encourage neighboring contacts and sense of community (Plas & Lewis, 1996).

However, studies in other locales show that physical design does not always promote sense of community as intended (Hillier, 2002). For instance, in the 1960s, planners of the new town of Columbia, Maryland, put all mailboxes for a block together to encourage neighboring, but the new residents demanded mailboxes at their houses. In addition, a convenience store was planned within a short walk of every house, but residents preferred to drive a few minutes to larger stores in the town center, and the convenience stores failed (Wandersman, 1984, p. 341). Part of the problem may have been contextual: The principles used by the Columbia planners are useful in urban neighborhoods and small towns, where walking to corner stores is familiar, but Columbia is a suburb where residents expect to drive to supermarkets. As we will talk about in Chapter 11, citizen participation in planning is also important (Jacobs, 1961).

Contributions   By emphasizing the importance of the physical environment, environmental psychology complements the more social perspective of the other approaches. Although its focus is different from that of community psychology, there are significant areas of overlap.

Key concepts from the six ecological frameworks are listed in Table 5.1.

Comparing the Perspectives: An Example

To compare these six perspectives, consider a play to be performed by students in a high school setting.

A high school play is a behavior setting. It has boundaries of time (for practices and performances) and space (an auditorium or theater). It has a standing pattern of behavior: During the performances, actors, audience, and others behave in predictable ways and locate themselves in predictable places. These behavior patterns indicate the program circuit or agenda: to perform a certain play to entertain an audience.

TABLE 5.1 **Key Ecological Concepts for Community Psychology**

Ecological Principles (Kelly):	interdependence; cycling of resources; adaptation; succession
Social Climate Dimensions (Moos):	relationship; personal development; system maintenance and change
Social Regularities (Seidman):	patterns of power relationships, decision making, and access to resources in settings
Ecological Psychology (Barker):	behavior setting; optimally populated; underpopulated settings
Activity Settings (O'Donnell et al.):	intersubjectivity
Environmental Psychology	environmental stressors; environmental design

If the setting is underpopulated, having fewer participants than roles or functions to be filled, the principles of ecological psychology would predict that setting members (director, cast, and crew) would seek to recruit additional help and be likely to take on extra roles or tasks. They would engage in more deviation-countering circuits, teaching needed skills and keeping members involved. A person with no drama experience may be pressed to join the cast or crew, developing new skills or revealing hidden talents. In contrast, if the setting is optimally populated, vetoing circuits are likely; a member who cannot learn a role or task can be easily replaced. There will be auditions for parts, and only the best actors will be accepted. Other students will become marginalized. If many students seek to be involved in the play, the staff could create the benefits of underpopulated settings by having two casts of different actors perform the play on alternate nights or stage a second production with different actors (Wicker, 1973).

Performing a play is not just following a literal script; it involves recreating a world on stage that involves the relationships among actors and seeks to engage the audience. Actors seek an intangible "chemistry" between themselves and with the audience. That intersubjectivity is the focus of activity setting theory (O'Donnell, Tharp, & Wilson, 1993). Engaging theater communicates intersubjective meanings through words, gestures, set, costumes, lighting, and perhaps music. The bonding that occurs among actors and crew during the long hours and shared work of a production also creates intersubjectivities.

How could the high school play be described in terms of Kelly's ecological principles? By working together, students and faculty build interdependent ties. This provides a basis for the exchange of such resources as encouragement, instruction (especially from the director), and socializing. In addition, the play has interdependent relationships with other settings within the school. Its existence allows students who are not outstanding in other areas (e.g., academics, athletics) to feel connected with others, contribute to school life, and perhaps to shine, thereby becoming recognized for their work (Elias, 1987). The play is also a way for the school to connect with and be recognized in the community.

Resources may be cycled between the play and the school as a whole. In a school in which drama is prized, money, facilities, student interest, and overall support will be plentiful; in one that does not prize drama, the play will receive little of these. Availability of resources also depends on the strength of interdependent relationships built between the drama faculty and administration, parents, school board members, and others. In turn, the play may generate a flow of resources from the community to the school. For example, families, friends, and businesses may contribute such resources as props, costumes, food for intermission, and encouragement.

Adaptation for students involved in the play will involve learning skills in performance, set design, lighting, and so on. All members may have to help in publicizing and managing the production. These skills may also have adaptive value in the larger environments of school or community—for example, in future employment. In addition, the play will occur within a pattern of succession. It may be the first such production or the latest in a line of successful, well-attended productions; the latter may have more resources available but also place higher expectations on the cast and crew.

To apply Moos's social climate dimensions, members of the production (including director, actors, and crew) could complete questionnaires about their perceptions of the production environment. If they generally agree that play members were actively involved and supported each other well and believe the director was supportive, scores will be high on Relationship dimension scales. Questions on that dimension might also assess conflict among members. The Personal Development dimension would concern whether participating in the play provided them opportunities to develop skills or experience personal growth. System Maintenance and Change items would measure their perceptions about how organized the production was, how much control the director exerted, the clarity of expectations for members' performance, and how much creativity was valued.

If different perceptions of the group social climate occur among subgroups (e.g., director, actors, stage crew; men and women), discussion could focus on what events and processes led to those differences. Using both the Real and Ideal forms of a social climate scale would afford comparisons between the current group functioning and the visions of an ideal group held by all or by subgroups. Conclusions about social climate could be used in planning the next production.

What social regularities (Seidman, 1988) and role relationships are involved here? One concerns the roles of director and actors. The director, usually a faculty member, will assume a powerful role. Choosing the play, making casting decisions, coaching actors, and assuming responsibility for the quality of performance are all functions that the director may perform. With inexperienced actors, that assumption of power may make sense. However, each of these functions could be shared with experienced actors to promote their skill development and personal growth. Such altering of social regularities could also mobilize resources such as hidden leadership talents among the students. It changes the usual role relationship in schools but promotes the educational and perhaps artistic value of the production. (Indeed, using students as directors and in other authority roles seems more common in drama than in other areas of many schools.) The concept of social regularities calls attention to power and resources predictably invested in social roles in the setting and how these may be changed to promote the development of individuals or settings.

Finally, an environmental psychologist would examine how the physical environment can be manipulated to promote the artistic themes of the play. The stage set, lighting, sound, and costumes are not merely backdrops but artistic elements that help create mood and reflect the progress of the plot. Audience participation could be promoted by altering the room or seating. Actors in character could meet patrons at the door and create an atmosphere of immersion in the play. A play involves the creation of a believable world on stage that engages the audience by using artistic elements that parallel the concerns of environmental psychology.

THE IMPORTANCE OF UNDERSTANDING CONTEXTS FOR INTERVENTION

As you probably gathered from the overview of different approaches to understanding environmental contexts, community psychologists use these frameworks to identify potential areas for intervention. From a community psychology perspective, a better understanding of what contributes to problems forms the basis of choosing where to intervene. Note that community psychologists do not believe that interventions that change environmental conditions of settings are necessarily sufficient to address social issues. Rather, they place an emphasis on understanding environmental factors of social problems because they are so often overlooked. If the ecological context of social issues is left unaddressed, the interventions chosen will likely be limited in their effectiveness. In the remainder of this chapter, we illustrate how ecological thinking influences community research and action. Next, we discuss research on how neighborhood contexts intertwine with family lives and interventions to improve neighborhood quality of life.

Research: Neighborhoods, Families, and Individuals

Neighborhoods provide one example of relationships between ecological contexts and the lives of individuals and families. From an ecological viewpoint, all neighborhoods have their strengths and local resources as well as problems and limitations. Community psychologists seek to understand the complexity of neighborhoods and of how they are related to family and personal life. Some of this research supports what may seem intuitive; neighborhoods with more problems are stressful and contribute to problems in adaptation for individuals. However, some of the research has demonstrated that much of what we assume about the relationships of neighborhood factors may be wrong or at least oversimplified.

For example, Gonzales, Cauce, Friedman, and Mason (1996) studied predictors of grades in school for a sample of urban African American adolescents. They examined factors about family support for students, family income, parents' past schooling, and neighborhood conditions (e.g., occurrence of crime, gang activity, and violence). Somewhat surprisingly, not only were worse neighborhood conditions one of the variables that predicted poorer academic achievement, but neighborhood risk was a stronger predictor of grades than such family characteristics as parent education, family income, and number of parents living in the home. From the standpoint of interventions, the researchers found that neighborhood risk made a difference in what kind of parenting style was associated with higher grades. In lower-risk neighborhoods with better conditions, teens whose parents were *less* restrictive had higher grades; this is consistent with many studies in developmental psychology. But in higher-risk neighborhoods, teens whose parents were *more* restrictive had higher grades.

Studies of pregnant mothers provide another example. Women in higher-crime Baltimore neighborhoods had a risk of poor pregnancy outcomes (e.g., premature birth, low birth weight) that was 2.5 times higher than those in lower-crime areas. Moreover, while providing prenatal care and education about pregnancy reduces the risk of poor pregnancy outcomes, this reduction in risk was much less for women living in neighborhoods with high poverty rates and high unemployment than for women in other neighborhoods (Caughey, O'Campo, & Brodsky, 1999). This finding indicates that for women in high-poverty neighborhoods, providing access to prenatal care may not be enough. In Baltimore, the Healthy Start program develops jobs in the community and works to improve housing quality as well as providing prenatal care (Caughey et al., 1999). These problems are also rooted in macrosystem forces, requiring policy changes by governments and corporations.

Understanding Neighborhood Research   Before describing other research on neighborhood contexts, we must make a few introductory points.

There are many challenges in studying neighborhoods. First, there is little consensus on an exact definition of a neighborhood in social sciences; it is larger than an urban block and smaller than a city. Neighborhoods have somewhat fluid boundaries (Shinn & Toohey, 2003; Nicotera, 2007). A small town may have the qualities of a single neighborhood. Nevertheless, most of us have a rough, intuitive idea of neighborhood.

Second, there is much diversity in the ecologies of neighborhoods. There can be many differences between neighborhoods in how resources are organized, exchanged, and shared. Generalizations about the effects of neighborhoods on its residents can have many exceptions. Even within a single neighborhood, there may be different areas. Within one Baltimore neighborhood, areas varied greatly in income, rates of home ownership, and unemployment. "Blocks of vacant, boarded-up public housing projects are only a few blocks from streets of well-maintained homes with well-manicured lawns and gardens" (Caughey, O'Campo, & Brodsky, 1999, p. 629).

Third, neighborhoods are dynamic settings that are continually adapting. While a neighborhood may appear stable, it may in fact be in the process of gaining or losing in population, jobs, or quality and affordability of housing stock. Its ethnic mix or average income level may be changing. It may be in transition from a neighborhood whose residents live there for decades to a neighborhood with higher resident turnover or vice versa. Of course, individuals and families also are continually changing, as members mature and their actions and attitudes change over time. Thus, while many of the characteristics that we will describe may seem to be stable, they are actually snapshots that capture one point in ongoing change. Research on links between neighborhood qualities and individual functioning is in its early stages and has many complexities (Shinn & Toohey, 2003).

In our consideration of how neighborhoods can affect individual functioning, we will distinguish between **neighborhood risk processes**—which are statistically correlated with such problematic individual outcomes as personal distress, mental disorders, or behavior problems—and **neighborhood protective processes**—which are strengths or resources associated with positive individual outcomes. Protective processes may offset or buffer the impact of risk processes. Risk and protective processes may be different in different neighborhoods.

We also distinguish between **distal** processes—which are broader in scope and indirectly affect individuals—and **proximal** processes—which affect individuals more directly and immediately. Proximal and distal are not absolute categories but differ along a continuum. We will consider structural neighborhood processes (more distal), neighborhood disorder and physical-environmental stressors (both more proximal), and protective processes (proximal and distal). Our coverage is based on two seminal reviews by community psychologists (Shinn & Toohey, 2003; Wandersman & Nation, 1998) that outline how neighborhoods may impact individuals and families.

Distal Socioeconomic Risk Processes   These involve social and economic or physical characteristics of a neighborhood as a whole that are correlated with individual problems. For example, mental health and behavioral problems, delinquency, cardiovascular disease, and pregnancy problems are, on average, more common in neighborhoods where many residents have low incomes (Stimpson, Ju, Raji, & Eschbach, 2007; Menec, Shooshtari, Nowicki, & Fournier, 2010). Another distal social process is residential turnover: in neighborhoods with higher turnover, juvenile delinquency is more common.

Distal socioeconomic processes are not limited to cities. In a study in rural Iowa, community disadvantage (computed from community rates of unemployment, receiving of government assistance, and proportion of population with less than high school education) predicted rates of conduct problems among adolescent boys, while the proportion of single-parent households in the community predicted conduct problems among adolescent girls (Simons, Johnson, Beaman, Conger, & Whitbeck, 1996).

It is important to note that these neighborhood-level statistics do not mean that low-income or single-parent families themselves are to be blamed for such problems; recall our discussion of blaming the victim in chapter 2. Economic macrosystem forces (e.g., unemployment) are often the root causes, but this is not the only way to understand those neighborhoods. As we will note shortly, low-income neighborhoods and families may also have protective processes at work.

Risky Physical Environments   Socioeconomic root processes also create hazardous physical environments, which have more direct (proximal) effects on individuals and families. Residents of low-income neighborhoods are more likely to breathe polluted air and drink polluted water. They endure higher levels of traffic noise, which has been shown to limit academic learning in children, and higher exposure to lead, which limits cognitive development. Their neighborhoods have more hazardous traffic crossings and higher child pedestrian injury rates. Low-income neighborhoods often lack sources of healthy food: supermarkets are often hard to find, yet convenience and liquor stores are abundant. A growing literature documents how physical environments can impact nutrition, physical activity, and obesity (Berrigan & McKinnon, 2008). Housing is often of lower quality, presenting many health hazards. Overcrowded housing is also associated with psychological distress in children (Evans, 2004). As noted earlier, health interventions in low-income neighborhoods are less effective if such environmental problems are not addressed (Caughey et al., 1999).

Neighborhood Disorder   Another more proximal approach focuses on processes of neighborhood violence and incivilities. For example, about one-quarter of U.S. urban youth witness a murder in their lifetime. Exposure to violence is associated with posttraumatic stress disorder (PTSD), depression, and other distress, aggression, and behavior problems (Shinn & Toohey, 2003; Kim & Ross, 2009).

Incivilities are noticeable signs of neighborhood disruption that raise fears of crime (Dahl, Ceballo, & Huerta, 2010). Physical incivilities include abandoned or dilapidated buildings, litter, vandalism, and graffiti. Social incivilities include public drunkenness, gang activities, and drug trade. Perkins and Taylor (1996) reported that residents of U.S. city blocks with more incivilities (especially physical ones) tended to have greater fears of crime, more depression, and more anxiety than those in neighborhoods with fewer incivilities. Neighborhood disorder also leads to restrictive parenting and even withdrawal from the community by parents concerned for their own and their children's safety (Gonzales et al., 1996; Brodsky, 1996).

Protective Processes   Not every neighborhood with statistical risk factors has higher levels of individual problems or distress. This observation leads to inquiring about what protective processes neighborhoods may have (Dupéré & Perkins, 2007). Distal protective processes may include having a larger proportion of long-term residents and owner-occupied housing in a neighborhood (Shinn & Toohey, 2003). In addition, more proximal processes can be protective, such as relationships and sense of community among residents. For instance, in Baltimore neighborhoods that had higher levels of community organization (e.g., more voters registered, greater participation in community organizations), women had a much lower risk of problems with pregnancy than women in neighborhoods with low levels of such organization. Risks were also lower in neighborhoods with more community services, businesses, and health care (Caughey et al., 1999). In another study of low-income urban U.S. neighborhoods, those where social ties and support among residents were stronger had lower levels of child maltreatment than neighborhoods where these supports were weaker (Garbarino & Kostelny, 1992).

The interactions among macrosystem, neighborhood (i.e., locality), microsystems (e.g., family or peer group), and individual factors are considerably more complicated than what we have presented here. For example, Roosa, Jones, Tein, and Cree (2003) presented a model of neighborhood influences on children and families designed to guide prevention programs. Additional factors in their model include the importance of children's and parents' perceptions of the neighborhood, the importance of peer groups for adolescents and how these interact with neighborhood forces, and ways that prevention programs can enhance families' coping with the impact of neighborhood problems.

Promoting Neighborhood Quality of Life

These protective processes suggest avenues for community interventions. Community health and prevention programs and clinical interventions can link families with such community resources as jobs and child care. Community-level interventions have included working with neighborhood associations, efforts to create jobs and improve housing quality and affordability, and policy advocacy to address wider social issues (Kloos & Shah, 2009; Maton, Schellenbach, Leadbeater, & Solarz, 2004; Wandersman & Nation, 1998).

For example, consider this example of how citizen participation and cooperative housing initiatives for low-income residents in New York City addressed their concerns about building and neighborhood quality (Saegert & Winkel, 1990, 1996). When city government seized buildings from absentee landlords for unpaid taxes, it helped finance sale of the buildings to cooperatives of low-income tenants, who then managed the buildings. Cooperative housing was rated higher in management quality, safety, freedom from drug activity, and resident satisfaction than city-owned housing or buildings owned by private landlords (Saegert & Winkel, 1996, p. 520). Effective citizen leaders emerged, particularly among women and elderly residents, who worked to improve conditions (Saegert, 1989). Similarly, Alaimo, Reischl, & Allen (2010) studied the community gardening experiences of over 1,900 residents of Flint, Michigan, and found that those residents who were more involved in efforts to beautify neighborhoods reported more positive social connection and neighborhood social capital. Interestingly, those involved in gardening and beautification reported more positive connections than those who reported neighborhood involvement but not being involved in collective gardening. The actions of promoting neighborhood well-being appear to have a benefit for personal well-being as well as the community.

In urban neighborhoods in Nashville and in New York City, citizen block associations have had significantly positive impacts on the block physical environment. In longitudinal studies, improvements (on private as well as public properties) were more common on blocks with block associations (Wandersman & Florin, 2000). Also, recall that pregnancy problems are less likely in neighborhoods with more participation in community organizations and more community services (Caughey et al., 1999). These findings from quantitative research and case studies indicate that community development interventions can be effective. (We discuss these in more detail in Chapter 12.) But for neighborhoods to thrive, wider social issues also need to be addressed (Caughey et al., 1999; Maton, Schellenbach, Leadbeater, & Solarz, 2004).

CREATING AND ALTERING SETTINGS

As discussed previously, ecological frameworks can be used to improve environmental conditions that affect functioning. However, changing existing settings is usually not very easy, even when one can identify the contextual variables that need to be addressed. Settings, social systems, and individuals within them generally resist change and try to preserve the status quo. For example, we have had evidence for 40 years that secondhand smoke is bad for health, but it took nearly that long to pass laws that restrict smoking in public buildings. The concepts of interdependence, adaptation, and social regularities suggest some ways in which changing environmental conditions might happen. In the face of such resistance, community psychologists sometimes take a different approach to improving individual and family well-being. They stop trying to change the existing settings and work to create a new and different setting, which community psychologists refer to as an **alternative setting**. Alternative settings are not necessarily designed to replace current settings but rather to provide conditions and resources that support the functioning of people for whom the current options do not work.

Next, we describe two exemplary environmental interventions that created or changed community settings to promote the well-being of their inhabitants. The first example creates alternative places to live and work for persons being discharged after long-term mental health hospitalizations. The second is an effort to prepare children growing up in poor families, living in distressed neighborhoods, and who have fewer educational resources to compete academically and occupationally with students from upper-class neighborhoods with many educational advantages. In both of these examples, the existing approaches to deal with problems were not sufficient to address the concerns of individuals involved. Rather than creating new programs to address each need, the leaders of the interventions decided that more comprehensive approaches were necessary. Leaders decided that they needed to change the environments to support the development and functioning of those who they wanted to help.

The Community Lodge: Creating an Alternative Setting

The Community Lodge movement exemplifies an alternative setting approach to change. Based on the classic study (Fairweather, 1979, 1994; Fairweather et al., 1969), the first Community Lodge was created to address the unmet needs of persons with psychiatric disabilities when they left state hospitals. It was an important early influence on community psychology and community mental health (we described it briefly in Chapter 2). Yet some of its principal elements have never been widely adopted in mental health systems. These main elements happen to be the aspects that continue to pose the most interesting challenges to social regularities of mental health care.

The Community Lodge idea began in a Veterans Administration psychiatric hospital in the 1950s. After working in psychiatric hospital care for some time, Fairweather and others recognized that the context of the hospital did not promote the aim of independent community living for persons with serious mental illness. In hospital settings, the patient has few opportunities for decision making and autonomy. "Good behavior" usually means following orders. In contrast, once discharged, the individual needs to take initiative, make independent decisions, and form supportive relationships with others. Fairweather's group developed inpatient group treatments that promoted the ability of men (veterans) with even the most serious mental disorders to participate in group decisions and to prepare for living outside the hospital. However, even those treatments had limited value once patients left the hospital; people returned to the hospital at too high a rate after too short a period in the community. Fairweather and associates realized that the problem was a lack of a supportive community setting and a set of roles that could meet the needs of these ex-patients following their release from the hospital. Altering regularities within the hospital was simply not enough.

Fairweather and associates then created an alternative setting in which patients released from the hospital moved together to a residence in the community (Fairweather, 1979, pp. 316–322, 327–333). An old motel was leased and refurbished for their lodge. After visiting the new lodge several times, the members were discharged from the hospital and moved in. After several trial and error experiences, lodge members became self-governing. They developed lodge rules that, for example, made it acceptable to discuss symptoms of mental illness with other lodge members but not with neighbors. The researchers were surprised that some of the previously most seriously ill persons became active members of the community. With consultation, lodge members established a janitorial and gardening business and eventually became economically self-supporting. Finally, they felt confident enough that lodge members ended their professional relationship with Fairweather, although infrequent social contacts continued (Fairweather, 1994). Fairweather and colleagues conducted rigorous experimental designs to promote the adoption of the lodge model in community mental health systems (Fairweather, 1994; Hazel and Onaga, 2003).

Although this innovation in mental health care has not changed community mental health systems broadly, it was widely disseminated as an alternative setting. Currently, 10 states in the United States have Community Lodges (Coalition for Community Living, 2010). The programs actively work together to promote the ideals first demonstrated by Fairweather and the first lodge members to create alternative supports where the setting is part of the local neighborhood and supports the autonomy and development of the residents (Haertl, 2005). The Fairweather model is receiving renewed research attention as the programs across several states work to support each other and promote the model (Haertl, 2007).

Community Lodges have several distinctive features—all involving changed role relationships that are usually found in mental health care. The most important and surprising one is that lodge residents govern themselves. Professionals serve as consultants and have a collaborative role that seeks to maximize members' autonomy (Haertl, 2007). Ideally, the professional role will not be needed. Lodge members assume responsibility for monitoring each other for taking medication, behaving responsibly within and outside the lodge, and related issues. Lodges decide for themselves, as a group, whether to admit new members or to dismiss members (Fairweather, 1979, 1994). For more description of a lodge, see Box 5.1.

In controlled studies using volunteers randomly assigned to a lodge or to ordinary psychiatric aftercare, Fairweather (1979) and Fairweather et al. (1969) demonstrated that lodge members, although similar to the control group on background variables, relapsed less often, spent fewer days in the hospital when they did, and spent more days employed than the controls. These differences persisted for five years of follow-up studies. Moreover, the Community Lodge method was less expensive than traditional community aftercare. Recent studies have documented that lodge members had a 90% reduction in hospitalization rates over a year compared to their preadmission records (38 days compared to five days a year) (Haertl, 2007). Furthermore, their annual earned income rose 515% five years after completing occupational training compared to their prelodge involvement, although it is still represents a limited annual income of $6,708 (Haertl, 2007). By demonstrating the effectiveness of community-based housing and economic ventures, the Community Lodge studies have demonstrated the possibility of expanding mental health care in communities. But its key element—self-government by lodge members—has seldom been adopted (Fairweather, 1979). Perhaps that is because it undermines a social regularity many professionals believe is essential for helping persons with mental illness: professional supervision and control. As Fairweather has often pointed out, the Community Lodge findings indicate otherwise. Proponents of Community Lodges are working to establish a new research base that will allow the lodges to be considered an evidence-based practice that is promoted by federal agencies as a viable alternative in mental health systems and policy (Haertl, 2007). Chapters 10, 12, and 13 provide more details about how program implementation research and evaluation can be used to help establish policy.

B o x 5.1   Community Psychology in Action

Embracing the Fairweather Model
Kristine Haertl, Ph.D., OTR/L
St. Catherine University, St. Paul, MN

"You aren't lonely here"; "We care for each other"; "It's like a family." These quotes were all expressed by lodge members during focus group interviews researching the unique aspects of the Fairweather Model.

As I drove up to the duplex in a quiet suburban neighborhood, I noticed two cars and a motorcycle in the driveway. The vehicles were owned by lodge members—all of whom were able to afford them through work at the organization's large corporate janitorial and mail room services. Although the five lodge members carpooled to work, the vehicles provided autonomy on weekends and during events away from the lodge. While some used their own vehicles, others use the public transit system. Each lodge also has a van, and members are given training opportunities in order to serve as drivers.

During my visit, two of the members were making dinner for the group while others planned a shared evening outing. As we sat down to dinner and began the interview, one of the clients became delusional and agitated, claiming his belt was gone and disappeared forever. Rather than intervene, I watched as a lodge peer said, "Don't worry, Jack.* I believe it is on your bed. We can check later." This insightful response from his peer calmed the member down, and dinner proceeded as planned. This example of mutual peer support is integral to the peer culture that often occurs within the lodge. Members support each other throughout all phases of health and wellness.

As a former employee and long time board member of a large mental health Fairweather organization (Tasks Unlimited), I've witnessed the powerful effects of the environment on health, wellness, and recovery. Within Fairweather programs, the lodge is the central housing model incorporating shared resources, work, chores, and support. The concept of interdependence is integral to the supportive culture offered by the lodge, and members have extensive decision-making power in house functions. In working with various mental health programs, I've noticed that the Fairweather Lodge treats individuals as community participants rather than patients (such as those in medical expert based models). Often, group-living environments are time-limited, and the emphasis is on short-term stays.

In Fairweather programs, individuals can make the lodge a home for life. For example, Mary*—a woman with schizophrenia—had been in and out of state and county hospitals for decades. She entered Tasks Unlimited in her 40s through a Fairweather program offered at the state hospital that eventually transitioned to the community. Mary found that she thrived in the group living environment, enjoyed the work offered by the organization, and later took leadership roles in the lodge (including maintaining the weekly house budget). With the supportive environment, she developed many friendships, was afforded opportunities for numerous activities and various trips, and remained at the program and out of the state hospital for over 30 years. Atypical from most mental health residential houses, she was able to live nearly all her adult life in a quality environment until her death of natural causes in her mid-70s.

The support and comprehensive services enabled Mary to transition from years in the state hospital to decades out of the hospital and in a nice home with friends, productive work, and numerous recreational opportunities. The affordance of quality peer-based living is an important residential option. Concepts of interdependence and productive meaningful engagement in daily activities are central to the Fairweather Model. This holistic approach to developing a peer supportive culture has impressive outcomes in providing long-term quality residential, psychiatric, vocational, and recreational services through Fairweather programs.

* assumed names

The Harlem Children's Zone: Social Change
Through Creating Alternative Settings

Geoffrey Canada had worked for a New York City social service agency dedicated to addressing the needs of young children and their families for over 25 years. Located in Harlem on the north end of Manhattan, the clients that the agency served were severely affected by the increase in drug trade and violence that swept many urban neighborhoods in the United States with the introduction of crack cocaine in the 1980s. During this time, many social service agencies developed new programs to address the growing need of the children, but each new effort seemed to be too little, too late, although many well-designed efforts used current advances in the science of child development. Canada and his colleagues decided that the environmental conditions where these children lived, their neighborhoods, home environments, and community expectations and resources for parenting needed to be addressed if they were ever going to address the children's academic, social, and developmental needs. That is, they decided that a piecemeal program services approach would never be able to accomplish their goals of helping children develop academically and socially. With so many challenges in their lives, these children faced seemingly insurmountable odds for being competitive in modern work places or having greater choice in jobs, careers, and life paths. Such opportunities and such options are all too often not available to children growing up in distressed neighborhoods.

Numerous school reforms, social programs, and changes in welfare policy of the 1990s and earlier decades had not addressed the needs of these families or changed living conditions. In the late 1990s, there were 3,000 children living in a 24-block area of central Harlem. More than 60% of these children grew up in households with annual incomes below the poverty level (e.g., $16,700 for a family of four). Furthermore, more than 75% were performing below grade level in reading and math (Tough, 2008). Schools were not educating the children. Parents were too often underemployed and limited in their education. The staff at the agency that would become the Harlem Children's Zone asked themselves how a program—or even a series of programs—could possibly help these children catch up academically. They were driven to find a way to support these families and give their children a chance to break "the cycle of generational poverty for the thousands of children and families it serves" (Harlem Children's Zone, n.d.).

The Harlem Children Zone was founded to create supportive settings for child development and parenting in a dedicated geographic area. Canada and his colleagues decided to develop a comprehensive approach to address child development in a limited geographic area: 99 square blocks in Harlem. Programs alone were not sufficient to produce changes in children's well-being. Harlem Children's Zone leadership decided that they needed to create alternative settings in this geographic area as well as support skill development of individuals. They also decided that they needed to address the needs of many children across all ages—from prenatal classes for parents to day care, preschool, elementary school, middle school, high school, and college. To do this, they had to change the way that services were organized and delivered.

The Harlem Children's Zone broke the social regularity of services waiting for people come to appointments and had dedicated staff go find parents, build relationships with them, and recruit them to come to prenatal classes. They included incentives for attendance and developed interactive, culturally appropriate programming. They adapted early childhood programs into preschool that actively worked with parents and children to increase literacy skills. Developmental psychology research had found that children in impoverished areas tended to have fewer books read to them and to be exposed to less language. However, rather than blaming parents, staff found ways to nurture parent-children reading. The Harlem Children's Zone created several settings dedicated to supporting parents' and children's participation in these activities. With a new wave of school reforms in New York, they started an elementary charter school and then expanded over time to open a middle school and high school. To support children's development further, they also addressed common health conditions in the neighborhood (e.g., asthma, diabetes) and promoted the development of social skills that can impact children's learning (e.g., peacemaking, community pride, occupational training). Instrumental to realizing this comprehensive vision, the Harlem Children's Zone built relationships with New York City business people who believed in the Harlem Children's Zone's mission and vision. This type of programming required millions of dollars from individuals and the strategic use of public programs to fund its initiatives. Over a period of 10 years, the Harlem Children's Zone developed many program components and evaluated what was effective in terms of promoting participation and improving children's test scores.

In 2010, the Harlem Children's Zone served more than 10,000 children and 7,400 adults with a fiscal year 2010 budget in excess of $75 million (Harlem Children's Zone, n.d.). The Harlem Children's Zone's Baby College for parents of infants and toddlers reported 86% of them improved the frequency of their reading to children to more than five times a week. The Harlem Children's Zone's preschool initiative, Harlem Gems, reported increased school readiness; 73% of students tested as "advanced" or "very advanced"—up from 35%—and no students were listed as very delayed. All the third-grade students in the Harlem Children's Zone's Promise Academy tested at or above grade level on math, outperforming the New York state average. For English and language arts, more than 84% of students met or exceeded the state average. At the Promise Academy High School, 93% of ninth-graders passed the statewide algebra exam. These rates of school performance are outstanding for any community but are astounding for neighborhoods that have the challenges described. Furthermore, more than 90% of high school students were accepted into college (Harlem Children's Zone, n.d.). Given their successes, Harlem Children's Zone leaders are documenting their approach and beginning efforts to replicate it in other communities.

A hallmark of each program is an effort to foster skill development and build *strengths* of children and parents in a *collaborative, empowering* manner. The Harlem

Children's Zone is focused on both *preventing* poor academic outcomes and *promoting* positive youth development. An emphasis on *social justice* focused their attention on a geographic area that had few apparent resources and great challenges. Through the Harlem Children's Zone's sustained work and an *ecological perspective*, parents and families are recognized as resources to be cultivated and necessary components of their children's development rather than being blamed for the children's academic shortcomings. The comprehensive, integrated programming seeks to build a *sense of community* among families and students. Although based in research, the programming engages families in parenting practices and educational routines that are complementary to their cultural practices. Most of the students are African American or Latino. That is, their approach to engaging parents *valued diversity* of experience rather than assuming that there was only one way to reach these parenting and youth development goals. However, the standard by which all the efforts are judged is the *empirical* bottom line of children's performance academically. As indicated by the italicized words in this paragraph, the expressed values of the Harlem Children's Zone closely mirrors the values of community psychology.

CONCLUSION: PROMISE AND CHALLENGES
OF CHANGING ENVIRONMENTS

The Harlem Children's Zone and the Fairweather Lodge examples demonstrate the potential of using an ecological perspective to promote the well-being of individual and families. Environments can be sources of problems for individuals and also offer resources for negotiating challenges in individual and community life. Rudolf Moos (2002, 2003) spent his career developing frameworks and measures for understanding the role that environmental factors can play in well-being. He identified four enduring questions about the relationships of individuals and ecological contexts that summarize the complexity of these relationships. These questions are helpful considerations for anyone interested in changing environmental conditions of their neighborhoods or community.

How are contexts both powerful and fragile in their influences on individuals? Neighborhoods, community settings, treatment settings, families, and other contexts can be powerful. Cohesive settings especially exert influence on members' attitudes and actions. But that power is also risky; for example, cohesion and loyalty can become paramount, and differences can be labeled as deficits. "Any setting that is powerful enough to produce constructive personal change is also powerful enough to elicit self-doubt, distress, even suicidal behavior" (Moos, 2003. p. 8). The risks of promoting cohesion and the power of settings must be understood and considered. Building settings that truly respect diverse members and views is challenging.

Yet the impacts of settings on individual lives also can be fragile, in the sense that when persons leave the setting, its influence often wanes. Research amply demonstrates that while treatment settings, prevention programs, and other community changes may have short-term effects on individuals and communities, these changes are difficult to sustain over the long term. It is critical to find ways to create environments that sustain positive changes.

Many persons also endure traumatic effects of powerful environments, yet find ways to overcome that trauma and in fact to grow and to develop new strengths. What qualities of both persons and environments support this growth? Moos (2003) notes that clinical case studies can identify personal and environmental processes in such transformations. Community psychologists can study what aspects of community settings support individual development.

How can we understand ecological contexts as dynamic systems that change over time? Communities, settings, and other contexts have their own histories, which must be understood as an ongoing story of adaptation to shifting conditions. While the concepts we have presented in this chapter may give the illusion of stability in environments, these contexts are actually works in progress, changing over time. Families change as their members mature. Neighborhoods change as their social and cultural makeup, economic resources, and institutions evolve. Community organizations often begin in a period of energetic efforts and optimism but often evolve into predictable, structured forms or disband. We still only partially understand how these changes are related to internal forces within the environment and to external influences, such as relations with other settings and macrosystem forces.

How can we clarify the mutual relationships between individuals and contexts? Studying the characteristics of environments is challenging, given that many of their most psychologically important qualities are subjective (as with the Moos social climate scales). Methods exist for aggregating these into variables describing environments, yet there is still much to be worked out (Moos, 2003; Shinn & Rapkin, 2000). Moreover, the relationships between environments and individuals are reciprocal. Persons certainly select and influence contexts as well as being influenced by them. Teasing out causal patterns is difficult.

How are ecological contexts influenced by culture, ethnicity, gender, and other social processes? Communities, neighborhoods, settings, and other contexts differ in their cultural, historical, and social characteristics. This is important not only for explaining ecological contexts but also for developing them. For example, to create effective community settings for helping individuals overcome alcohol abuse, cultural and spiritual resources, ways of involving individuals, and shared ritual practices would be different among European Americans in an East Coast suburb and among Native Alaskans in rural Western villages (Hazel & Mohatt, 2001; Mohatt et al., 2004). A cultural perspective for community psychology will be needed (O'Donnell, 2005a).

Concepts of ecological context are central to community psychology. In many ways, the entire field is about understanding how contexts and individuals influence each other. In that sense, the remaining chapters of this text elaborate and extend this chapter.

CHAPTER SUMMARY

1. Ecological context consists of the physical and social aspects of environments that influence individuals. Persons and contexts influence each other. Community psychologists seek to understand the interplay of ecological context and individual life and to find ways to create or alter contexts to enhance individuals' quality of life.

2. Kelly and associates proposed four ecological principles for describing contexts in community psychology. *Interdependence* refers to the extent of interconnections among persons and among settings. *Cycling of resources* calls attention to how tangible and intangible resources are defined, created, exchanged, and conserved. *Adaptation* refers to the demands made on individuals by the setting and how individuals cope with those demands. Settings also adapt to the individuals within them and in relationships with other settings. *Succession* refers to how settings are created, maintained, and changed over time.

3. Moos developed the idea of measuring the *social climate* of environments through the perceptions of their members. In Moos's approach, social climates have three basic dimensions: *Relationship*, *Personal Development*, and *System Maintenance and Change*. Social climate scales have been related in research to many measures of setting qualities and individual functioning.

4. Seidman developed the concept of a *social regularity*, a predictable pattern of social behavior in a setting—often a role relationship, such as teacher-student. Social regularities involve differences in power between the roles, how decisions are made in the setting, and how resources are distributed among members.

5. Barker's ecological psychology was developed to study social behavior in everyday context. Barker and associates proposed the concept of *behavior setting*, comprised of a physical place, time, and program or standing pattern of behavior. Behavior settings have *program circuits*, agendas for the setting, and *goal circuits* to satisfy individual needs. They employ *vetoing circuits* to exclude some persons and *deviation-countering circuits* to teach individuals the skills needed to participate in the setting.

6. Barker and associates also proposed the concepts of *underpopulated* and *optimally populated settings*. Optimally populated settings engage only some persons by using *vetoing circuits* to exclude others. Somewhat underpopulated settings require participation from many inhabitants to fill needed roles and thus contribute to greater skill development and mutual commitment. They develop skills and involvement with *deviation-countering circuits* rather than vetoing.

7. O'Donnell and associates proposed the concept of *activity setting* that takes subjective experiences of setting participants into account more than

behavior setting concepts. Activity settings are based on *intersubjectivities* or shared assumptions and meanings among participants in a setting.

8. Environmental psychology concerns the relationships between the physical environment and individual or social behavior. Topics related to community psychology include environmental stress and environmental design of workspaces and neighborhoods.

9. We described an example of how a high school play could be analyzed from each of the six ecological perspectives in this chapter.

10. Neighborhood factors influence family and individual quality of life. In fact, neighborhood stressors may outweigh family and individual factors in importance. We defined neighborhood *risk and protective processes*—both *proximal* (forces directly affecting individuals and families) and *distal* (larger forces whose effects may be indirect). These included distal socioeconomic factors, risky physical environments, neighborhood disorder, and such protective processes as neighborhood strengths and resources.

11. Community psychologists are especially concerned with how smaller settings can be altered to improve individuals' quality of life. We described two examples: the Community Lodge, an *alternative setting* for persons with serious mental illness—and the Harlem Children's Zone, which altered social regularities of many settings in a neighborhood to support children's education and development.

12. Moos identified four enduring questions about ecological contexts, about the power and fragility of settings, how settings are dynamic and ever-changing, how individuals and environments are related, and how these relationships are affected by cultural and other social processes.

RECOMMENDED READINGS

Kelly, J. G. (2006). *Becoming ecological: An expedition into community psychology*. New York: Oxford University Press.

Linney, J. L. (2000). Assessing ecological constructs and community contexts. In J. Rappaport & E. Seidman (Eds.). *Handbook of community psychology*. New York: Kluwer Academic.

Moos, R. (2003). Social contexts: Transcending their power and their fragility. *American Journal of Community Psychology, 31*, 1–14.

Shinn, M. & Toohey, S. M. (2003). Community contexts of human welfare. *Annual Review of Psychology, 54*, 427–460.

Tough, P. (2008). *Whatever it takes: Geoffrey Canada's quest to change Harlem and America*. New York: Mariner Books.

RECOMMENDED WEBSITES

Harlem's Children Zone:
http://www.hcz.org/home

The Coalition for Community Living—Supporting the Fairweather Lodge Programs:
http://theccl.org/Fairweather.htm

American Community Gardening Association:
http://www.communitygarden.org/

6

Understanding Community

J. Stan Mason

OPENING EXERCISE

Take a look at the following quotes. What do you think these people are talking about? Are they all talking about the same thing? Try to make some guesses about who these people are and what kinds of settings they are referring to.

"I mean I can talk to them and they are there to help me when I need to talk to someone…For example…my father is very close to dying right now… they have all talked with me about it and have been a great deal of comfort to me."

"…people walk through there all the time … and I get to know them. I've probably met hundreds of people who go through there who speak to me every morning and evening and I've made some quite good friends amongst some on the street."

"We have encountered so many good people and we feel at home here. In the church, too, there are very good people, there is a lot of help given and very good people…. They offer us the things we need but treat all of us equal."

"Yeah, like when we were at meetings, they always asked our opinion. That was kind of fun being able to give your opinion when you have only been there a month. I thought that was great."

All these quotes are from qualitative studies of people's perceptions of community. The first quote is in reference to an online gaming community (Roberts, Smith, & Pollock, 2002, p. 236); the second is from a person talking about walking his dog in his town in Western Australia (Wood, Giles-Corti, Bulsara, & Bosch, 2007, p. 48); the third quote is from a Latina immigrant in the United States (Bathum & Baumann, 2007, p. 172); and the fourth quote is from a study of adolescents and their involvement in community organizations (Evans, 2007, p. 699).

Community psychology has a clear focus on communities. Communities are the ecological level at which we conduct the majority of our research and interventions. They are what the field is about. In this chapter, we will explore the question of what makes a community. Where do we find them? What forms do they take? We will also be exploring the relationships that people have with their communities. Community psychologists believe that people have emotional relationships with their communities, and we believe that the quality of those affective relationships has important implications for well-being and happiness. We call that affective relationship *sense of community*.

> I have never met anyone—young or old, rich or poor, black or
> white, male or female, educated or not—to whom I have had any great
> difficulty explaining what I meant by the psychological sense
> of community. (Sarason, 1974, p. 1)

This quote is from the book *The Psychological Sense of Community* by Seymour Sarason. In that book, Sarason set the tone for how community psychologists think about the relationships between individuals and communities. Sarason defined community as "a readily available, mutually supportive network of relationships on which one could depend" (p. 1). Sarason argued that the "absence or dilution of the psychological sense of community is the most destructive dynamic in the lives of people in our society." Its development and maintenance is "the keystone value" for a community psychology (p. x). He applied the term **community** to localities, community institutions, families, street gangs, friends, neighbors, religious and fraternal bodies, and even national professional organizations (pp. 131, 153).

Look back at the quotes at the beginning of this section. Do you think those people all felt a sense of community?

WHAT IS A COMMUNITY?

Ferdinand Tönnies was a German sociologist who lived from 1855 to 1936. This was a period of rapid and extensive social change as Western countries became increasingly urban, industrial, and technological. Tönnies was fascinated with the question of how those societal-level changes impacted human relationships, particularly at the community level. Tönnies (1887/1988) proposed a famous distinction between *Gemeinschaft* and *Gesellschaft* relationships. *Gemeinschaft* is often translated as "community." It refers to relationships that are multidimensional and are valued in their own right, not just as a means to an end. When you do something for someone or spend time with someone solely because you value that person and your relationship with him or her, that is a *Gemeinschaft* relationship. Small towns are often described as being dominated by *Gemeinschaft* relationships. The members of the communities know each other in many different roles and work to maintain those relationships. There is a shared sense of obligation to each other—not for any specific reason but because of the shared relationships.

Gesellschaft is often translated as "society" and refers to relationships that are based on a specific transaction. The relationship is instrumental in the sense that the participants view the relationship fundamentally as a means to an end, not as something that has value in its own right. This is a relationship you engage in solely because you expect to benefit in some way from the interaction, and the same is true for the other person. So, your relationships with your family and friends are *Gemeinschaft* relationships, while your relationship with the guy who runs the register at the grocery store where you shop is a *Gesellschaft* relationship.

Tönnies recognized that all our lives involve both types of relationships, but he believed that it is *Gemeinschaft* relationships that define communities. And an amazing number of historians, social scientists, and philosophers have been agreeing with him ever since. Look again at Sarason's definition of a community as "a readily available, mutually supportive network of relationships on which one could depend" (Sarason, 1974, p. 1). He is essentially saying a community is a setting defined by *Gemeinschaft* relationships.

We do not mean to imply in this discussion that there is one, easily recognized definition of community. That is far from the truth. Discussion of these issues is complicated by the variety of meanings of the term *community*. Its emotional connotations grant it power as a metaphor but make it difficult to define for research. Community can refer to varying ecological levels—from microsystems to macrosystems. But that diversity of meaning is not necessarily bad. It allows for creative exploration of conceptions of community at multiple levels.

Types of Communities

Definitions of community in sociology and in community psychology distinguish between two meanings of the term: community as locality and community as a relational group (e.g., Bernard, 1973; Bess, Fisher, Sonn, & Bishop, 2002).

Locality-Based Community   This is the traditional conception of community. It includes city blocks, neighborhoods, small towns, cities, and rural regions. Interpersonal ties exist among community members (residents); they are based on geographic proximity, not necessarily choice. When residents of a locality share a strong sense of community, individuals often identify themselves by their locality, and friends are often neighbors. In many nations, political representation, public school districts, and other forms of social organization are delineated by locality.

Relational Community   These communities are defined by interpersonal relationships and a sense of community but are not limited by geography. Internet discussion groups are communities completely without geographic limits. Mutual help groups, student clubs, and religious congregations are defined by relational bonds.

Although relational communities may be based only on friendships or recreation (e.g., sports leagues, sororities), many are organizations bound by a common task or mission. Workplaces, religious congregations, community organizations, chambers of commerce, labor unions, and political parties are examples.

Locality-based and relational communities form a spectrum rather than a dichotomy. Many primarily relational communities are seated in a locality (e.g., universities, religious congregations). An Internet discussion group where the members have never actually met each other face-to-face anchors the purely relational pole of the continuum; a town or neighborhood represents the opposite locality-based pole. How do the communities discussed in the quotes at the beginning of this chapter vary along this continuum?

Levels of Communities

Communities exist at different ecological levels. As discussed in Chapter 1, these include:

- Microsystems (e.g., classrooms, mutual help groups)
- Organizations (e.g., workplaces, religious congregations, civic groups)
- Localities (e.g., city blocks, neighborhoods, cities, towns, rural areas)
- Macrosystems (e.g., the Filipino community, political parties, nations)

Moreover, communities are related across levels. Classrooms exist within a school, which often draws its population from a specific locality. Macrosystem economic and political forces influence workplaces, schools, community programs, and families. Improving community and individual life often involves change at multiple levels, even macrosystems.

If communities exist at different levels, what is the smallest group that can be usefully called a community? Could your immediate family or your network of friends be considered a community? Certainly, these have some of the psychological qualities of communities. However, we previously argued that for conceptual clarity, connections with families and friends should be considered social networks, not communities (Hill, 1996). We defined community as a larger grouping of individuals who may not know all the other members but who share a sense of mutual commitment. In this chapter, we exclude immediate families and immediate friendship networks from our discussion of communities as a way to focus our discussion.

Who Defines Communities?

Certainly, communities define themselves, but it is important to recognize that this may require a struggle and that external systems (e.g., government planners, political forces) may be involved. For example, Sonn and Fisher (1996) studied the sense of community among "Coloured" South Africans, a racist category created by apartheid laws. Despite this artificial, externally-imposed categorization, "Coloured" South Africans managed to build shared ideas and commitments that helped them resist racist oppression and that persisted even among those who emigrated to Australia. In Australia itself, discussion of the Aboriginal "community" has often been in terms defined by European Australians in government and academia. Thus, it is phrased in Western concepts and often fails to recognize diversity among indigenous Australian peoples (Dudgeon, Mallard, Oxenham, & Fielder, 2002; Lee, 2000). This also occurs in dominant views of Native Americans and other dispossessed groups. Finally, concepts of what it means to be Australian (or any other national identity) are socially constructed and challenged over time (Fisher & Sonn, 2002).

In a 2001 study of neighborhood boundaries for families and children, census-tract definitions of neighborhoods in Cleveland, Ohio, often did not match residents' own drawings of neighborhood maps. Measures of social indicators such as rates of crime and teen childbearing differed depending on whether census or resident maps were used. This would greatly affect both community research and community programs that use census data (Coulton, Korbin, Chan, & Su, 2001). One interesting development in this area is the use of new technologies, such as GIS (geographic information system software), which can be used to allow community members to self-identify the geographic boundaries of their communities. These technologies may make it easier for researchers to identify member-defined local communities (Lohmann & McMurran, 2009).

SENSE OF COMMUNITY

Very important to community psychologists is the strength of bonding among community members, which Sarason (1974) termed the **psychological sense of community.** He defined it as

> the perception of similarity to others, an acknowledged interdependence with others, a willingness to maintain this interdependence by giving to or doing for others what one expects from them, the feeling that one is part of a larger dependable and stable structure (p. 157).

David McMillan and David Chavis (1986) reviewed research in sociology and social psychology on the sense of community and group cohesion. Their definition of sense of community resembled Sarason's:

> a feeling that members have of belonging, a feeling that members matter to one another and to the group, and a shared faith that members' needs will be met through their commitment to be together. (McMillan & Chavis, 1986, p. 9)

Four Elements of Sense of Community

What are the specific qualities of sense of community? McMillan and Chavis identified four elements: membership, influence, integration and fulfillment of needs, and shared emotional connection. These elements help translate the overarching theme of a sense of community, which characterizes Sarason's thinking, into measurable constructs for research and specific objectives for action. In their formulation, all four elements must be present to define a sense of community. No one element is the root cause; all strengthen each other. Our description of these elements is based primarily on McMillan and Chavis (1986) and McMillan (1996). The elements are summarized in Table 6.1.

Think of a community to which you belong as you read about these four elements.

Membership   This is the sense among community members of personal investment in the community and of belonging to it (McMillan & Chavis, 1986, p. 9). It has five attributes. The first attribute, boundaries, refers to the necessity of defining what includes members and excludes nonmembers. For a locality, this involves geographic boundaries; for a relational community, it may involve personal similarities or shared goals. Boundaries may be clearly or obscurely marked, and they may be rigid or permeable. They are necessary for the community to define itself. Ingroup-outgroup distinctions are pervasive across cultures (Brewer, 1997). Other qualities of sense of community depend on having boundaries.

T A B L E 6.1   Elements of the Psychological Sense of Community

Membership
  Boundaries

  Common symbols

  Emotional safety

  Personal investment

  Sense of belonging

  Identification with community

Influence
  Mutual influence of community on individuals—and individuals on community

Integration and Fulfillment of Needs
  Shared values

  Satisfying needs

  Exchanging resources

Shared Emotional Connection
  Shared dramatic moments, celebrations, rituals

SOURCE: Based on McMillan and Chavis (1986) and McMillan (1996).

Common symbols help define boundaries, identifying members or territory. Examples include the use of Greek letters among campus sororities, colors and symbols among youth gangs and sports teams, religious imagery, university decals on automobiles, characteristic slang expressions and jargon, and national flags and anthems (Fisher & Sonn, 2002).

In a community with clear boundaries, members experience **emotional safety**. This can mean a sense of safety from crime in a neighborhood. More deeply, it can mean secure relationships for sharing feelings and concerns. Emotional safety in that sense requires mutual processes of self-disclosure and group acceptance (McMillan, 1996).

A member who feels safe is likely to make **personal investment** in the community. McMillan (1996) refers to the latter as "paying dues," although it is often not monetary. Investment indicates long-term commitment to a community, such as home ownership in a neighborhood, membership in a religious congregation, or devotion of time to a charity organization. It can also involve taking emotional risks for the group.

These acts deepen a member's sense of **belonging and identification** with the community. The individual is accepted by other community members and defines personal identity partly in terms of membership in the community. Individuals may identify with being a resident of a neighborhood, adherent of a religion, member of a profession or trade, student in a university, or member of an ethnic group.

Influence   The second element refers both to the power that members exercise over the group and to the reciprocal power that group dynamics exert on members. McMillan and Chavis (1986, pp. 11–12) based their discussion of influence in part on the group cohesiveness literature in social psychology. Members are more attracted to a group in which they feel influential. The most influential members in the group are often those to whom the needs and values of others matter most. Those who seek to dominate or exercise power too strongly are often isolated. The more cohesive the group, the greater is its pressure for conformity. However, this is rooted in the shared commitments of each individual to the group, not simply imposed on the individual. (It does, however, indicate a disadvantage of a strong positive sense of community that we will discuss later.) Thus, the individual influences the wider group or community, and that community influences the views and actions of the person.

Integration and Fulfillment of Needs   While influence concerns vertical relations between individuals and the overall community, integration concerns horizontal relations among members. Integration has two aspects: shared values and exchange of resources. Shared values are ideals that can be pursued through community involvement: e.g., worship in a religious community, improving educational quality may be the shared value of a parent-school group.

The second concept refers to satisfying needs and exchanging resources among community members. McMillan (1996) referred to this as a "community economy." Individuals participate in communities in part because their individual needs are met there. Needs may be physical (e.g., for safety) or psychosocial (e.g., for emotional support, socializing, or exercising leadership). Integration is similar to interdependence and cycling of resources in Kelly's ecological perspective (see Chapter 5).

Shared Emotional Connection   McMillan and Chavis considered this the "definitive element for true community" (1986, p. 14). It involves a "spiritual bond"—not necessarily religious-transcendent, and not easily defined, yet recognizable to those who share it. Members of a community may recognize a shared bond through behavior, speech, or other cues. However, the bond itself is deeper, not merely a matter of behavior. Shared emotional connection is strengthened through important community experiences, such as celebrations, shared rituals, honoring members, and shared stories (Berkowitz, 1996; McMillan, 1996; Rappaport, 2000).

Questions and Issues for Defining Sense of Community

In community psychology, sense of community has been defined and used in a diversity of ways, raising a number of questions and issues. These illustrate the strengths and limitations of the concept.

Elements of Sense of Community   Are the four McMillan-Chavis elements the best way of describing the basic elements of sense of community? Empirical research has established the validity and importance of the overall sense of community construct, but findings have been inconsistent concerning the independence and validity of the four McMillan-Chavis elements. Some studies have generally confirmed them (Bateman, 2002; Obst & White, 2004) or validated them but also found additional dimensions (Obst, Zinekiewicz, & Smith, 2002). Some researchers found the four elements so highly intercorrelated that they focused only on the overall construct of sense of community (Mahan, Garrard, Lewis, & Newbrough, 2002). Other studies found different dimensions of sense of community (Chipuer & Pretty, 1999; Hughey, Speer, & Peterson, 1999; Long & Perkins, 2003).

These inconsistencies may be due in part to problems in the existing measures of sense of community. Existing quantitative scales often lack the richness of examples found in the original Sarason and McMillan-Chavis descriptions (Bess et al., 2002; Chipuer & Pretty, 1999; McMillan, personal communication, August 25, 2003). Qualitative research methods can be useful but also have limitations (Brodsky, Loomis, & Marx, 2002; Rapley & Pretty, 1999).

Perhaps sense of community is contextual, varying in different cultures and communities. If that is true, the McMillan-Chavis model (or any other single framework) might describe the basic elements in some communities, but other communities would require different conceptualizations. Indeed, that is one way to interpret some of the findings just discussed. Moreover, sense of community seems contextual to many community psychologists (Hill, 1996; Bess et al., 2002). For instance, Hughey, Speer, and Peterson (1999) found new dimensions of sense of community among members of locality-based organizations in a U.S. city. New conceptual frameworks may be especially needed in cultures markedly different from the Western ones—for example, among Australian Aboriginal groups (Bishop, Coakes, & D'Rozario, 2002; Dudgeon et al., 2002).

A related question: Is sense of community primarily a cognitive-emotional construct or does it include such related behaviors as acts of neighboring and citizen participation in decision making? The idea of "sense" of community refers to thinking and emotions: e.g., a feeling of belongingness, of emotional safety, a shared emotional connection. Should measures of sense of community include items concerning those actions (as in Chavis, Hogge, McMillan, & Wandersman, 1986)? Or are they separate concepts to be measured separately (Perkins & Long, 2002)? For our introductory purposes, we will discuss the behaviors of neighboring and citizen participation as separate concepts. However, note that McMillan argues that the cognitions, emotions, and actions of sense of community cannot be separated (personal communication, August 25, 2003).

Levels of Sense of Community   Is sense of community simply in the eye of the beholder—the individual's perception of the wider community? Or is it a characteristic of a community as a whole? Most studies have measured sense of community with questionnaires for individuals—analyzed at the individual level. However, in samples of high school and university students, Lounsbury, Loveland, and Gibson (2003) found that personality variables (e.g., extraversion, agreeableness) accounted for up to 25% of the variance in how much sense of community students perceived in their school or college. In contrast, a study of residential blocks in urban neighborhoods found substantial agreement among residents of each block in their reports of sense of community there as well as significant differences in sense of community between blocks (Perkins & Long, 2002). These shared perceptions of community seem to go beyond individual personality differences.

Both personal and neighborhood factors contribute to perceptions of sense of community (Long & Perkins, 2003). It also seems likely that their relative importance would vary in different contexts. For example, shared sense of community may develop more strongly in residential neighborhoods where individuals may remain for a longer time than in high school or college. The residential street blocks studied by Perkins and Long, although urban, also may be smaller communities than a university.

Sense of community is a rich concept. At this point in its development, it is probably better to study it in a variety of ways: with the McMillan-Chavis model and other frameworks, at individual and community levels, with qualitative and quantitative methods, while remaining sensitive to contextual differences.

Concepts Related to Sense of Community

Sense of community is conceptualized as the affective component of our relationship with our communities. But that affective component is related to and perhaps built on specific behaviors and connections. Some of these concepts include neighboring, place attachment, citizen participation, and social support.

Neighboring   Perkins and Long (2002, p. 295) define this as informal contacts and assistance among neighbors. In their view, it involves specific behaviors, while sense of community is strongly emotional and cognitive. It also refers to personal interaction among neighbors, not to participation in neighborhood associations. For instance, in a study of neighboring, Unger and Wandersman (1983, p. 295) asked residents of city blocks, How many of the people on this block would you:

- Know by name?
- Feel comfortable asking to borrow some food or a tool?
- Feel comfortable asking to watch your house while you are away?
- Feel comfortable asking for a ride when your car is not working?

Neighboring often occurs between persons who are not close friends, but acquainted sufficiently to pass on information and news, recognize mutual interests as neighbors, and provide limited assistance. These contribute to integration and fulfillment of needs. But they can occur to some extent even in neighborhoods with little sense of community and between neighbors who feel little connection to the wider community. Neighboring thus overlaps with sense of community but can be understood as distinct from it (Prezza, Amici, Roberti, & Tedeschi, 2001).

Place Attachment   Seldom studied by community psychologists but important for locality-based communities, this refers to emotional bonding to a particular physical environment and usually to the social ties one has there (Perkins & Long, 2002, pp. 296–297). Environments may vary in scale: a room, a building, a street corner's public space, a neighborhood or college campus, or a hometown or region. A research team's meeting room described by Brodsky et al. (2004) is also an example of the importance of place. Neighborhood sense of community is anchored in places there. Even sense of community for an ethnic or national group is often related to a geographic place as well as a society or culture (e.g., Sonn, 2002). These remarks by a geographer express the emotional and social power of places:

> Our lives are full of events that take place, in place.... Places are socially constructed; at the same time they have a physicality and an ecological history.... Places are charged with energy; they are full of stories that anchor the memories that shape our individual and collective identities. (Flad, 2003)

Citizen Participation As we discussed in Chapter 1, this is having a voice and influence in community decision making. It involves community decisions, not simply community service. Sense of community is a strong predictor of citizen participation in neighborhood associations (Perkins & Long, 2002; Saegert & Winkel, 2004; Wandersman & Florin, 2000). However, citizens may participate in community decisions even if they do not share a strong positive sense of community, so citizen participation can be considered distinct from sense of community. We will discuss citizen participation in detail in Chapter 11.

Social Support This is help provided by others to promote coping with stress. Social support and sense of community overlap but also differ. Certainly, a group with a strong sense of community will provide social support; this is one aspect of integration and fulfillment of needs. However, the community in which one feels a sense of belongingness may be much larger and less intimate than the immediate network of persons who provide support for coping with a specific stressor. Also, sense of community is not solely a resource for coping but also related to other important processes, including citizen participation. In Chapter 8, we will discuss social support in detail.

Mediating Structures Some groups and organizations connect individuals or smaller groups with a larger organization, locality, or society. Joining them provides a sense of community for the individual and a practical way to participate in the larger community or society. These intermediate communities link differing ecological levels and are called **mediating structures** (Berger & Neuhaus, 1977). For example, parent-teacher associations, civic clubs, political advocacy groups, and neighborhood associations all offer ways to become involved in wider communities and can give collective voice to their members' views about community issues. They mediate between individuals and the wider community. In a university, student clubs, residence hall organizations, and student governments are mediating structures.

THE IMPORTANCE OF COMMUNITY

So, what good is a sense of community? Why is it important? Certainly, social scientists have long argued that strong communities are essential for well-functioning societies. Durkheim (1893/1933) expressed the dominant view when he stated that it is because of our membership in communities that we adhere to social norms. This is the belief that our conscience lies in our bonds to other people. If community membership means nothing to us, then community norms and sanctions have no influence over our behavior.

Individuals also seem to benefit from strong communities. Research has demonstrated repeatedly that a positive psychological sense of community is correlated with a number of positive outcomes for individuals. A positive sense of community has been shown to correlate with adolescent identity formation (Pretty, 2002; Pretty, Andrews, & Collett, 1994, Pretty et al., 1996), individual well-being, mental health, recovery from substance abuse (e.g., Farrell, Aubry, &

Coulombe, 2004; Ferrari et al., 2002; Pretty et al., 1996; Prezza et al., 2001), and neighboring (e.g., Farrell et al., 2004; Garcia et al., 1999; Perkins & Long, 2002; Prezza et al., 2001).

Sense of community has also been linked with positive outcomes for communities, such as members believing that working with others to take community action can be effective (e.g., Perkins & Long, 2002; Peterson & Reid, 2003; Speer, 2000), and participation in neighborhood groups and religious institutions (e.g., Brodsky, O'Campo, & Aronson, 1999; Hughey et al., 1999; Perkins & Long, 2002). Finally, some correlates of a positive sense of community have national implications, such as voter participation (Brodsky et al., 1999; Davidson & Cotter, 1989, 1993; Xu, Perkins, & Chow, 2010). These positive outcomes for communities and societies are often discussed in terms of a concept related to sense of community: social capital.

Social Capital

> If the crime rate in my neighborhood is lowered by neighbors keeping
> an eye on one another's homes, I benefit even if I personally spend
> most of my time on the road and never even nod to another resident
> on the street. (Putnam, 2000, p. 20)

In this quote, the political scientist Robert Putman is referring to the concept of social capital. This concept was first developed by the sociologist Pierre Bourdieu, who originally used it to explain class-related differences in children's educational outcomes (Bourdieu, 1998). Bourdieu's point was that children of the upper class in France did not just depend on their education to succeed, but they also had access, through their parents, to an extended array of powerful social networks. For example, when they were looking for a job or starting a business, there was a wide group of people, some of whom they may have never met, who could be counted on to help them. A person may have significant social capital even if he or she does not personally own a large amount of economic capital (monetary wealth).

James Coleman took Bourdieu's concept and extended it to include the idea that it was not just the members of the upper class who benefitted from social capital (Coleman & Hoffer, 1987; Field, 2003). His research on educational attainment of children living in poverty in 1960s America found that children who attended Catholic schools had better educational outcomes than their counterparts in public schools. Coleman attributed this to school and community norms that encouraged involvement in school, and he theorized that those norms, along with the relationships that developed in those schools, were a form of social capital. This difference in educational attainment was particularly striking for those children coming from the most economically disadvantaged families. In short, he concluded that the availability of social capital was particularly important for children with very limited access to economic capital. (It should be noted that this research was done in the 1960s. Research on public vs. private school outcomes in 21st-century America is much less clear-cut.)

Bourdieu and Coleman saw social capital as being fostered and developed through societal structures (class or schools), but each discussed the *benefits* of social capital primarily in terms of individuals. Robert Putman further extended the concept by explicitly discussing social capital as a community construct (Field, 2003; Putman, 2000). As is clear in the quote at the beginning of this section, Putman believes that social capital varies by communities (and societies); some have a lot of social capital and some have very little. And when communities have a great deal of social capital, their members benefit. Putman said:

> by 'social capital' I mean features of social life—networks, norms and trust—that enable participants to act together more effectively to pursue shared objectives. (Putman, 1996, p. 56)

Putnam is especially concerned with face-to-face associations that strengthen relationships and communication about community life. This may be formal—through community organizations—or informal—through friendships, neighboring, and other social contacts. Both types of association increase social capital (Putnam, 2000).

Pamela Paxton (1999) has attempted to operationalize this definition by suggesting that social capital includes two components: *objective associations* (an observable network structure that links individuals) and a positive *subjective/ emotional tie* characterized by reciprocity and trust. Paxton summarizes this definition by saying that social capital is built through associations (an objective component) and trust (a subjective component). We will return to Paxton's research later in this section.

Bonding and Bridging   This is a key distinction (Putnam, 2000, pp. 22–23). **Bonding** refers to creating and maintaining strong social-emotional ties—usually in groups of similar persons that provide belongingness, emotional support, and mutual commitment. These internal ties underlie a sense of community and shared identity. Their limitations are often a lack of diversity of members or views and an exclusion of outsiders.

By contrast, **bridging** refers to creating and maintaining links between groups or communities. Bridging ties reach out to a broader set of persons than bonding and involve links among people whose life experiences may be very different. Bridging ties are especially useful when diverse groups face a common challenge and need to work together.

Bridging relationships often have what Granovetter (1973) termed the *strength of weak ties*. These are relationships between persons who are not close friends but sufficiently acquainted to recognize mutual interests, pass on information about the community, and act together when needed. A person may bridge by cultivating relationships with people in two different factions, groups, or communities. A community coalition to promote positive youth development may bridge by bringing together persons from diverse parts of the locality, such as schools, religious congregations, police, recreation groups, diverse racial or ethnic communities, and youth themselves. Bridging links can also help a group obtain access to key decision-makers in a locality in order to make their

---

B o x 6.1   Community Psychology in Action

Daniel Kent and Net Literacy

Net Literacy is a student-founded nonprofit where high school and college students comprise 50% of the board of directors and are responsible for all the actual volunteering services. Twenty-five hundred student volunteers have provided over 200,000 hours of community service, have increased access to over 150,000 Americans, donate $4,500 to schools and nonprofits each year, and have been recognized by two American presidents.

Senior Connects is one of Net Literacy's five core programs. It is an intergenerational program where student volunteers teach senior citizens computer and Internet skills in senior centers, community centers, and independent living facilities. Senior Connects believes that highly motivated youths can make a difference in the communities where they reside.

Friendly high school student volunteers teach senior citizens, many of which are technophobic and have had negative experiences trying to learn computer and Internet skills. The "magic" developed by the volunteers include developing senior-friendly training manuals that contain large fonts, few technical terms, and many descriptive pictures. Students spend a portion of each of the 8–12 training sessions to learn each senior citizen's broadband value proposition—or what makes it important and compelling for each senior to be able to enjoy the full richness that broadband offers. Some seniors are interested in being able to e-mail friends and family, others pursue their hobbies online, and others appreciate access to news, health care information, and online entertainment. The students teach seniors on a one-to-one basis rather than a one-to-many basis and build relationships with the senior citizens that they are helping. Some seniors "adopt" the student volunteers, and as the seniors progress through the digital divide, the students cross the intergenerational divide. More about the Senior Connects program is at www.seniorconnects.org and more about Net Literacy is at www.netliteracy.org.

---

concerns heard (Bond & Keys, 1993; Hughey & Speer, 2002). Bonding ties alone seldom accomplish these objectives.

Daniel Kent was working specifically to develop bonding and bridging relationships when he formed Senior Connects, a youth-run nonprofit organization that sent high school and college students into assisted living programs to help elderly residents get connected to the Internet. One of his first pupils, Helen Lenke, said:

> Now we don't have to sit around waiting for the undertaker. [Daniel] and his aids were patient, respectful, kind and successful in teaching us with a simple formula of his own to write e-mails, play poker, bridge, watch the news, search for bargains on the Internet, find pictures of my family receiving honors as professors of law and medicine and so much more. (Neilsen, n.d.)

See Box 6.1 to read more about Daniel and his organization.

The strengths of bridging links are their reach or breadth of contacts, access to a diversity of views and resources, and ability to support wider community collaboration. However, they seldom offer the sense of community that occurs in bonding groups. Both serve to strengthen social capital. Some relationships or groups can have elements of both. For example, a community coalition that brings together persons across lines of social class and race yet builds a sense of shared community is both bridging and bonding.

Social capital can result in important benefits at multiple ecological levels, and unfortunately, it is a form of capital that is often overlooked. Some of the clearest examples of the benefits of social capital involve individuals and families, but even these are often discounted or not even recognized. For example, when discussing the economic difficulties faced by residents of small, rural towns in northeastern New Mexico, and particularly the problems with finding jobs in those communities, prominent politicians have suggested that those people who could not find jobs in their hometowns should leave and move to where there are jobs. It has even been suggested that it was time to "let the small towns of northern New Mexico die." This is a perfect example of the ways in which the importance of social capital can be ignored. Yes, those people could move to Albuquerque (the largest city in the state) to find jobs, increasing their income (economic capital). But what about the loss in social capital such a move would bring? Suppose you are a single mother with two children. If you get a job in your hometown, the chances are you will have family members and friends who can help with child care. But if you move 200 miles away for that job, you will need to pay for day care, resulting in a serious decrease in the amount of your income you will have available for other expenses. Yes, you may earn more in the city, but the loss of social capital might actually result in a decrease in quality of life for you and your children.

Social capital also results in benefits at the community level, as is clear in the quote from Putman at the beginning of this section. Let us go back to our New Mexico example. Many of the small towns of northern New Mexico are particularly beautiful communities in the Rocky Mountains. But New Mexico is rich in such ecological resources as oil, gas, and minerals, and some of these communities are under strong economic and political pressure to allow development of those resources. It takes a great deal of social capital for a small, poor community to insist on responsible development of these resources. If the members of your community are moving to urban centers to find jobs, the town's social capital is decreased, and the ability of the community to play a positive, strong role in the development of the region is lessened.

Finally, social capital has extremely important benefits at the level of societies and nations. There are many researchers and social commentators, such as Putman, who believe that social capital is fundamental to the maintenance of a democracy. Pamela Paxton, who we mentioned earlier in this section, has done research that supports this hypothesis. She analyzed two international data sets —one including 41 countries and one including 101 countries. She concluded that there is a reciprocal relationship between social capital and democracy. Countries with higher levels of democracy generated more associations and higher levels of generalized trust over time. The reciprocal relationship is demonstrated by the finding that high numbers of associations and levels of trust in a country supported the development of a democratic system of government (Paxton, 2002).

Can you see how both those relationships would hold true? Countries with totalitarian governments but a relatively large number of associations actually had spaces and relationships that allowed for discussion of and planning for political change. People who wanted to change those governments had the opportunity to meet with others who felt the same way. In the other relationship, democratic governments tend to support the development and maintenance of voluntary organizations—in many cases, actually providing funding for those organizations. And democratic governments also tend to foster generalized trust among their citizens (Paxton, 2002).

Community Psychology and Social Capital   Community psychologists have begun to adopt the concept of social capital. For example, Perkins and Long (2002) propose a psychological definition of neighborhood social capital composed of four elements: sense of community, neighboring, citizen participation (covered earlier in this chapter), and sense of collective efficacy (the belief that neighbors acting together can improve community life). They analyzed data from a study of New York City neighborhoods, finding these four elements to be generally interrelated. Sense of community was significantly related to all three other factors.

One concern with this concept is that an emphasis on local social capital (or local sense of community) can lead to underestimating the importance of macrosystem factors. Corporate decisions, losses of federal funding for effective programs such as Head Start, and other macrosystem forces do affect community life. Strengthening local social capital is certainly important for addressing community problems. But in many communities, local resources cannot do it all. Broader social change is also important to address social problems and injustices.

THE COMPLEX REALITIES OF COMMUNITIES

It should be clear by now that the role communities play in our lives is a complex one. It is tempting to view the concept of community and, in particular, sense of community in a simplistic, romanticized way. In reality, communities overlap, are sometimes in conflict, and may actually have negative impacts for their members and societies. In this section, we will discuss some of those complex realities.

Strong communities do not come without their costs. If you think back to McMillan and Chavis' four elements of sense of community, these costs become obvious. A sense of community involves a personal investment, which almost always involves some kind of obligation. Your communities expect things from you, and those community obligations often "cost" you personal resources, such as your time. Membership in a community means you are acknowledging that a community can influence your behavior, your beliefs, and even your personal identity. While social scientists may have emphasized the positive aspects of community, these costs have not been ignored. It is understood that communities can sometimes painfully restrict individual development and freedoms. Can you think of a time in your life when you felt you had to distance yourself from a community for your own well-being?

> I don't go out here. I don't start things with people. I don't bother people. I go home, I close my door, I lock my door, I stay in my house. Don't bother me and I won't bother you. Don't bother my kids, I won't bother you. (Brodsky, 1996, p. 357)

What is this woman talking about? Does it have anything to do with sense of community? So far, we have discussed sense of community in positive terms. Sense of community exists when individuals feel positively about their communities. But does individual perception of sense of community vary only from neutral to highly positive or can it be negative? Psychological sense of community is negative when a person feels strongly negative about the wider community (Brodsky, Loomis, & Marx, 2002). Thus the person may resist community involvement, concluding it will be harmful.

The quote is from a study conducted by Anne Brodsky (1996) with 10 resilient single mothers who were living and raising daughters in an urban U.S. neighborhood with high rates of crime and violence. These women were nominated as especially resilient, effective mothers by two sources in their daughters' elementary schools. All were parenting at least one child and working full-time or part-time. Some were also pursuing education or taking care of other family members. Their views of their neighborhood in general were decidedly negative. They drew a strong boundary between family and neighborhood:

> And when you come into my house it's totally different.... It's my world.... when you close that door, leave that world out there. (Brodsky, 1996, p. 351)

Physical and emotional safety, a key characteristic of sense of community in the McMillan–Chavis model, seldom existed in their neighborhood. These mothers also shared few values with many others in the neighborhood. The neighborhood did have some positive resources for parents, and these women were involved in some of them (e.g., resident council, school), especially where involvement directly benefitted their children. But this involvement did not alter their views of the neighborhood at large. Their strength as persons and mothers involved resistance to neighborhood forces, not sense of community (Brodsky, 1996).

The adaptive value of a negative psychological sense of community is not limited to this sample (Brodsky, Loomis, & Marx, 2002). For example, consider a community with limited acceptance of diversity, where conformity pressures are strong. Persons who are not accepted there may strengthen their well-being by distancing themselves from the community and seeking settings where they are accepted.

Brodsky's findings thus raise the question: Is a strongly positive sense of community always "good for you"? Does it always promote individual well-being or resilience under stress? Community psychologists and others may romanticize the idea of sense of community. In many circumstances, it is true that a strongly positive sense of community benefits the individual. But it is also clear from Brodsky's findings that sometimes a negative psychological sense of community better promotes well-being.

Even social capital is not always a completely "good" thing. Putman talked about the fact that inner-city gangs possess social capital, but the ways in which they choose to use that social capital are not beneficial to the rest of us (Putman, 2000). And in his original writings on social capital, Bourdieu (1972/1977) was explicitly talking about the ways in which social capital supported the maintenance of class differences. There is a great deal of evidence supporting the idea that it is easiest to build social capital in groups that are homogenous in nature. We tend to develop associations with—and trust people more—when they are like us. Paxton has done research demonstrating that counties with higher levels of **connected** associations (whose members tend to belong to more than one organization) have higher levels of generalized trust than do countries with high levels of **isolated** associations (whose members tend to belong to only that one organization) (Paxton, 2007). Thus, social capital at the national level can actually be *negatively* affected by a large number of associations if those associations are largely isolated. This is true even though those associations might display high levels of social capital within themselves. It just does not translate to the national level.

Multiple Communities in a Person's Life

Individuals belong to many communities (Hunter & Riger, 1986). These multiple memberships can play a role in strengthening identity. We form multiple identities as members of multiple communities, such as student, employee, family member, and neighbor. Sometimes, these multiple commitments compete for our time and energy or conflict in important ways. A student may experience a sense of belonging to the college in which she is enrolled and to her hometown or neighborhood, with friends in both, yet neither of these communities may appreciate her loyalty to the other. Individual adult life is often filled with multiple identities in multiple communities and the balancing of commitments among them. On the other hand, some communities in our lives revitalize us, providing resources and energy for involvement in other communities. Spiritual and mutual help communities can have this effect but so can an exercise class or musical group. The key to understanding multiple community membership is the role of each community in a person's life. Individuals choose how committed they are to the various communities in their lives (Hunter & Riger, 1986). Community psychology is only beginning to study how these multiple communities interact (Brodsky et al., 2002).

Our membership in communities changes continually over our lives, as does the relative importance of the communities to which we belong. As we grow older, we may see ourselves making more conscious choices about our community connections. For example, we may actively decide to distance ourselves from a community that has been important to us but which no longer feels supportive. Young adults who are lesbian or gay may find themselves choosing to distance themselves from their childhood neighborhood communities if those communities do not support their sexual orientation. There may even be times during our lives when we do not feel a need for a sense of community and do not feel particularly engaged with any community in our life—instead focusing on family relationships. These changes in community relationships and in our need for sense of community are another area that has not received significant attention in the research to date.

Conflict and Change Within a Community

The psychological sense of community has a virtuous sound, stimulating as it does visions of togetherness and cooperation uncluttered by conflict, controversy, and divisiveness. Such visions are hard to resist, but they must be resisted because they are illusory (Sarason, 1974, p. 11).

Because members of a community also participate in other communities and have multiple identities, relationships between communities can be complex and interacting. Often, these interacting communities reflect the diversity of the people involved. So, you may identify yourself as a member of your college community and also as a member of the community of gay students or biology majors (or both) at your college. This identification as gay or as a biologist probably extends beyond your college to include communities in your town or state or even national communities. This diversity can be a strength for a community but only if it is recognized and valued (Trickett, 1996).

An emphasis on the similarities without attending to the differences in a community is what Wiesenfeld (1996) termed the *myth of "we"* in a community. Romanticizing sense of community, without recognizing diversity within a community, supports the myth of "we."

An example of the myth of "we" occurred among residents of four southeastern U.S. cities in response to Hurricane Hugo (Kaniasty & Norris, 1995). After the hurricane, these communities seemed to unite to help each other. Overall, citizens who suffered greater loss and personal harm received greater amounts of social support from others. A sense of "we" did exist within these communities. However, some groups received less support, especially if they suffered greater harm: African-Americans, persons with less education, and unmarried persons. In action, the sense of "we" did not include the entire community. Similar patterns have occurred following other disasters in the United States (Kaniasty & Norris, 1995).

Relationships among diverse communities can create conflict. But that is where constructive community change often begins (Wiesenfeld, 1996). For example, the societal transformations of the civil rights movement and the women's movement in the United States began with some communities, especially African Americans and women, attempting to change their local communities and the nation as a whole.

Without attention to these complex interrelationships among communities, and the conflict and change that can result, sense of community can become a static concept, supporting an unjust status quo instead of showing the way to constructive social change (see Fisher & Sonn, 2002; Rudkin, 2003). Ignoring conflict, stifling dissent, or excluding specific groups eventually undermines a community, while constructive resolution of conflict can strengthen it.

A community has changed, is changing, and will change again. (Sarason, 1974, p. 131)

Change is inevitable for communities. Sense of community is ultimately a process. For instance, Loomis, Dockett, and Brodsky (2004) found that it rose among students at one university in response to an external threat and then subsided later. Fisher and Sonn (2002) thoughtfully discuss conflict and change regarding what it means to be an Australian. Similar issues arise in communities at many levels: What does it mean to be a member of this community? How does that reflect the diversity within this community? How do we respond to the challenges of ongoing change?

A danger of strengthening sense of community is the potential that it may increase conflict between communities, especially if they encourage prejudice or hostility toward others. Sense of community may be strong in communities that scapegoat outsiders or in privileged communities that deny problems of poverty and injustice or in groups whose values are repugnant to many others, such as neo-Nazi or vigilante groups or youth gangs (McMillan & Chavis, 1986, p. 20; Sarason, 1974). Exclusion can be extremely painful when the person involved greatly values the community from which he or she is excluded. Recently, I (Jean) cut my waist-length hair extremely short. One of my students who is Diné (a member of the Navajo nation) was very taken aback. He told me that when he was a teenager, he had cut his hair, and as a result, some very important members of his community declared that he was "dead" to them. Even 20 years later, this feeling of exclusion from a community that he very much valued was still easily triggered by the sight of my newly cut hair.

These issues concern the relationships between communities. Communities influence other communities, are influenced by them, and are influenced by macrosystems (Hughey & Speer, 2002; Hunter & Riger, 1986). However, those complex relationships are not explicitly addressed in the four McMillan–Chavis elements of sense of community, which focus on the internal dynamics of a community. McMillan and Chavis (1986) concluded with a call for building "free, open, accepting" communities "based on faith, hope, and tolerance" and using sense of community "as a tool for fostering understanding and cooperation" (p. 20). Their model has been used to pursue those important values. However, because it focuses on the internal dynamics of communities, it does not provide explicit conceptual guidance for that pursuit.

For a practical example of these issues, imagine that you are approached for help with community development by a neighborhood organization whose members are all European Americans. You soon learn that their underlying aim is to exclude persons of color (especially African Americans and Latinos/as) from moving into their neighborhood. Unless those exclusionary aims are changed, strengthening sense of community within the neighborhood would have racist effects (Chavis, personal communication, October 1987). This dilemma reflects a potential conflict between core values of community psychology: sense of community in one neighborhood versus social justice and respect for human diversity (and, ultimately, individual wellness of all). An ethical response would be to decline to work with the organization unless it genuinely renounced its exclusionary aims.

The issues that we have just discussed involve balancing sense of community as a value with other values. Newbrough (1995) argued that traditional concepts of community do not address issues of justice and equality. He proposed a concept of the just community, whose members would seek to balance values of community, individual liberty, and equality (social justice)—within the community and in relations with the wider world. His view raises such questions as: How much concern does a community have for other communities? For its own diverse subcommunities and individual members? How is that concern expressed in action?

ARE COMMUNITIES DECLINING?

Remember Ferdinand Tönnies, the German sociologist who developed the concepts of *Gemeinschaft* and *Gesellschaft* relationships? Tönnies lived during a time of unprecedented change in Western societies. He believed that preindustrial agrarian towns and villages were characterized by *Gemeinschaft* relationships, resulting in strong communities. He also believed that modern Western society, characterized by isolating urban settings and increasingly specialized employment, not only promoted *Gesellschaft* relationships but actively undermined *Gemeinschaft* relations. His view was an early statement of the theme of loss of community.

This theme has been prominent in art, literature, film, and social criticism ever since. Examples of this theme are too numerous to document here but include the development of the idea of *anomie* by Émile Durkhm in 1893 and Robert Nisbet's book *The Quest for Community* in 1953. These ideas build on Tönnies' beliefs that modern, industrialized society resulted in an increased sense of alienation among individuals.

In the book *Bowling Alone* (2000), Robert Putnam marshaled broad evidence to argue that community ties and civic engagement in the United States have been steadily declining for 30-40 years. His research found declines in involvement in civic associations, political participation, religious congregations, charitable giving, and even trust in fellow citizens. Public opinion polls have found that individuals' sense of alienation from their communities is at the highest levels ever measured, while reported trust in others is at the lowest levels ever measured. Active involvement in local community organizations has also steadily declined over the last 30 years. These declines are especially serious for organizations that provide volunteer services for youth development and persons in need because government services for these populations also are being slashed. Informal neighboring and social visiting also are declining, although not as sharply as other indicators. Many forms of citizen participation in government have weakened over 30 years: voting, signing petitions, writing letters to the editor, and volunteering for a political party or campaign (Berkowitz, 1996; Putnam, 2000).

Putnam also attempted to explain the causes of this decline. He investigated numerous potential causal factors, including generational differences in civic engagement, the rise of television, suburban sprawl and commuting, and increased work time and strain. While he found evidence that all these factors contributed to his perceived decline, he placed particular emphasis on television as the main culprit.

The evidence that Putnam cited is not the whole picture. Many researchers disagree with Putman's conclusions regarding a decrease in civic engagement. For instance, Paxton analyzed some of the same data as Putman (from the General Social Surveys) but found little indication of a change in social capital in the United States between 1975 and 1994. She found that numbers of memberships in various associations remained stable, time socializing with neighbors decreased slightly, and time socializing with friends increased slightly (Paxton, 1999). She agreed with Putman that there was evidence of a decline in trust toward both individuals and institutions, but she found that levels of trust varied widely by year. These variations appeared to correlate with national events. For example, trust in religious organizations went down the year that a prominent religious leader (television evangelist Jim Bakker) was publicly involved in a sex scandal. Likewise, trust in political institutions decreased during the Watergate scandal. Taken together, these effects looked like an overall decline in trust, but Paxton argues that they would be more accurately interpreted as temporary responses to specific events.

Other data also point to high levels of civic engagement. In the United States, participation in mutual help groups has increased strongly (Kessler, Mickelson, & Zhao, 1997). Two out of every five U.S. adults are involved in a small group that provides caring for its members, a category that includes not only mutual help but also religious study and prayer groups (Wuthnow, 1994). In 2009, 26.8% of adults in the United States did some sort of volunteer work, a slight increase over the previous year (U.S. Bureau of Labor Statistics, 2010). Community service is growing among youth and retirees. Youth are increasingly involved in citizen advocacy. "E-activism", using online resources to engage citizens for action, is growing rapidly, often with youthful leadership (Kamenetz, 2005). In 2008, 61.8% of eligible voters participated in the U.S. presidential election, continuing a trend of increasing voter participation for the last three presidential elections (McDonald, 2010, 2008a, 2008b).

Other researchers have argued that Putman's conclusions might be unique to the United States. For example, declines in organization membership in Britain were found to vary widely by types of organization. While evidence suggested large declines in women's organizations, this was balanced by increases in membership among environmental organizations (Hall, 1999). Another study of time use in Great Britain found that parents in the late 1990s spent more time with their children than they did in the 1960s and more time socializing and more time playing sports with others than they had in previous decades (Gershuney & Fisher, 1999).

Even when we can point to demonstrable changes in community, social scientists are far from unanimous in the view that these changes represent an invariable decline. Durkheim (and others) discussed the role of social regulation and integration in insulating individuals from *anomie*. He felt that complex industrialized societies needed to develop new ways of promoting regulation and integration, not that they were incapable of it. He hypothesized the need for a collective consciousness to hold societies together. The sociologist Travis Hirschi (1969) also discussed the role of integration and regulation in healthy human development and, like Durkheim, did not feel that these tasks were beyond the capabilities of modern communities.

If these ideas of regulation, integration, and bonding seem to reflect McMillan and Chavisz' four elements of sense of community, you are right. We hope that throughout this chapter we have given multiple examples of these elements being present in diverse communities in modern society. Next, we will discuss how we can use the information in this chapter to build strong communities.

BUILDING COMMUNITIES

One of the major points of this chapter is that in recent decades, we have become very conscious of the communities around us and how our actions can strengthen or weaken them. The information presented in this chapter has very clear implications regarding how we can construct strong communities. Once again, think about the four elements of sense of community proposed by McMillan and Chavis. If you want to build a strong community, you should ensure that the members define the community for themselves through the development of recognizable community boundaries. The members should develop a set of common symbols, celebrations, and narratives that describe and reflect the meaning they assign the community. The members should set norms that support a sense of personal safety and that ensure all members have a level of influence over the community.

The Physical and Natural Environments

In addition to the elements of sense of community, the ways in which we construct our physical environment can work to support or destroy community. There are not many studies of changes in sense of community over time, but one of them demonstrates the negative effects of building a freeway through a community (Lohmann & McMurran, 2009). Sense of community was measured before and after the construction of a freeway through a Los Angeles suburb. Residents in neighborhoods adjacent to the freeway reported a decrease in sense of community over time compared to the rest of the city. At least part of this decrease is probably related to the fourfold increase in noise levels in their neighborhoods after the freeway was built.

Architects have long understood that how we construct buildings has a direct effect on how the residents interact and on the development of sense of community. A clear example of this can be found in the history of public housing projects in the United States. Low-income public housing in the United States started after World War II. The initial projects were designed as groups of small housing units—sharing a common entry point. During the 1960s, new low-income housing was dominated by high-rise apartment buildings. This turned out to have serious negative effects for those communities.

Think about this in terms of neighboring. Neighboring develops because you see the same small group of people every day. Neighboring behaviors are negatively affected by high-rise apartment buildings. When people do not interact with each other, it is impossible for a sense of community to develop. People did not feel a sense of connection to the buildings they lived in, and they did not feel safe there. This lead to high levels of violence and vandalism, and some of these public housing projects, such as the Robert Taylor Homes in Chicago, became synonymous with urban decay in America (Bradford, 2001). In the 1990s, public planners recognized their mistake and began to replace the high-rise buildings with low-rise apartment buildings and single-family units. But even with all their problems, some residents did develop communities in these high-rise public housing projects, and their displacement from the places that have been their homes for generations has been extremely difficult (Venkatesh, 2002).

Architecture and freeway construction are aspects of the "built" environment that can affect sense of community. In addition to the built environment, there is a growing body of evidence that connection to the natural world is an important element of communities. Children living in urban public housing were shown to engage in twice as much play, have twice as much access to adults, and to engage in more creative play when their outdoor spaces were rated as high in trees and grass versus low in trees and grass (Taylor, Wiley, Kuo, & Sullivan, 1998). Research has also found lower levels of both property and violent crime in inner-city neighborhoods with relatively high levels of trees, grass, and other plants. This relationship held true even though residents were randomly assigned to the buildings and such factors as the size and occupancy rate of the buildings were controlled for. As the researchers concluded, "the greener a building's surroundings were, the fewer crimes reported" (Kuo & Sullivan, 2001).

Unfortunately, this connection between the natural environment and sense of community is not yet widely recognized and, like the history of high-rise apartment buildings, has been largely ignored. The second study cited here was conducted in the Ida B. Wells public housing project in Chicago. This project was built in the 1940s and initially consisted of low-rise buildings surrounded by trees and grass. Over time, much of the green space surrounding many of the buildings was paved, and the trees died. At the time this research was conducted, some of the buildings had mature trees and grass around them, while others were surrounded by pavement. Even though the residents were randomly assigned to their apartments and were subject to the same levels of poverty and unemployment, there were about 50% fewer crimes reported in the buildings surrounded by trees compared to the buildings surrounded by pavement (Kuo & Sullivan, 2001).

This research hypothesized two major mechanisms through which the presence of plants and trees improves community functioning. The first is on the personal level. There is a growing body of evidence that interaction with green spaces reduces "mental fatigue," increases self-control, and decreases aggressive behavior. People feel calmer and more relaxed when they get to spend time around trees, shrubs, and grass. The other mechanism is at the community level. When people have access to common spaces with a high level of landscaping, they are more likely to spend time in those spaces. This then leads to an increase in neighboring practices and informal surveillance of the community (Kuo, Sullivan, Coley, & Brunson, 1998).

These are just two examples of ways in which the built environment and the natural environment can affect a sense of community—particularly in geographically based communities. But what about relational communities? We now turn to two extended examples of communities and community building: spiritual communities and online communities.

Spirituality, Religion, and Communities

The beauty of the religious and spiritual impulse, at its best, is the humility, person-affirmation, service-orientation, and mainstream culture-challenge which it can engender, along with a glimpse of the reality that we all are part of a larger whole, each of us (and each subgroup) valuable, necessary, and interdependent. (Maton, 2001, p. 611)

Spiritual communities play important roles in community life. Their holistic perspectives integrate spiritual, emotional, cognitive, and social aspects of personal life (Mattis & Jagers, 2001). Sarason (1993) noted that sense of community throughout history has often been tied to a sense of the transcendent—of spiritual experience beyond oneself and one's immediate world. He asked whether modern forms of community could be sustained without that sense of transcendence. Because of its holistic significance for human and community development, some assert that "spirituality is integral to community psychology as a human science" (Dokecki, Newbrough, & O'Gorman, 2001, p. 499).

In this section and throughout this book, we define **spirituality** inclusively as beliefs, practices, and communities associated with a personally meaningful sense of transcendence, beyond oneself and one's immediate world. This includes but is not limited to religious traditions worshipping a supernatural deity (Hill, 2000; Kloos & Moore, 2000b). While over 90% of U.S. poll respondents believe in God or a higher power, many of them do not associate themselves with religious institutions, and a sizable minority consider themselves spiritual but not religious (Hill, 2000; Pargament & Maton, 2000). Hill (2000, pp. 145–146) defined spirituality as a sense of connection to the human and natural worlds and awe at mysteries beyond our comprehension. Additional definitions of spirituality include "exploring what it means to be fully human" (McFague, cited in Dokecki et al., 2001, p. 498) and the "search for the sacred" (Hill & Pargament, 2003, p. 65), while Rasmussen, following theologian Paul Tillich, defined religion as concerning "ultimate meaning in universal life experiences" (Moore, Kloos, & Rasmussen, 2001, p. 490). As with concepts of community, definitions differ, but this can be a strength if carefully understood. Community psychologists are concerned with spirituality as expressed in communion with others, not simply individual belief or practice. We use the inclusive term **spiritual communities** to refer to religious or spiritual or faith-based institutions, organizations, or settings.

Spiritual communities differ in whether they focus on matters of belief, spiritual experience, or action. Some are primarily concerned with personal salvation; others with broader spiritual growth, community bonding, social service ministries, or prophetic calls for social justice. Many differences are subtle (Kress & Elias, 2000). Examples of spiritual communities studied by community psychologists have included:

- Afrocentric spiritual perspectives (Myers & Speight, 1994)

- Spirituality in Native American cultures (Hazel & Mohatt, 2001; Walsh-Bowers, 2000)

- Women's spirituality (Molock & Douglas, 1999; Mulvey, Gridley & Gawith, 2001)

- Twelve-step mutual help groups (Humphreys, 2000)

- Communities within Judaism, Christianity, Islam, and Buddhism (Abdul-Adil & Jason, 1991; Dockett, 1999; Dokecki et al., 2001; Kress & Elias, 2000; Mattis & Jagers, 2001; Stuber, 2000)

In the United States, poll respondents have more confidence in religious institutions than any other social institution. Over one third of volunteer activity is based in religious congregations, and congregations contribute more money to community causes than corporations do (Pargament & Maton, 2000). Spirituality and religion have played important roles in survival of oppressed groups. Spiritual beliefs, practices, and communities provide important resources for finding meaning in living and coping with stressors. They comprise important forms of community, contribute important resources to society, and often advocate for social justice. Their importance is increasingly recognized in community psychology (e.g., Hill, 1996, 2000; Kloos & Moore, 2000a, 2000b, 2001; Mankowski & Rappaport, 2000a; Maton & Wells, 1995; Pargament, 1997; Pargament & Maton, 2000).

However, the impact of religious and spiritual traditions is not always positive. History reveals many examples of religious exclusion and oppression. Research has indicated that some especially religious U.S. college students are more prejudiced than other students against African Americans, women, gay men, lesbians, and others (Hunsberger, 1995; Pargament, 1997, p. 352; Waldo et al., 1998). Like other communities, religious and spiritual traditions and local congregations can have positive and negative effects on persons, communities, and societies (Brodsky, 2000, 2003; Martin-Baro, 1990; Pargament, 1997; Ventis, 1995).

How Are Spiritual Communities Involved in Community Life?   Spirituality serves five important community functions (Kloos & Moore, 2000b; Pargament & Maton, 2000). First, it helps meet primary human needs for finding meaning in everyday life (Frankl, 1959/1984; Pargament, 1997). Spirituality provides solace in the face of uncontrollable circumstances and guides active coping with controllable ones. A sense of transcendence provides a way to understand one's life, while spiritual values provide guides for living.

Second, spiritual communities provide sense of community and meet primary human needs for belonging. Many can be described in terms of the four McMillan-Chavis elements. They provide a sense of membership through common rituals and symbols, including rites of passage for membership. These rituals also foster identification with the community. Emotional safety is provided through small-group and one-to-one sharing. The formation of a religious identity can be an important social identity—fostered by multiple religious contexts (Kress & Elias, 2000).

Spiritual communities also foster mutual influence and integration and fulfillment of needs. Shared spiritual practices influence individual decisions. In turn, many spiritual settings provide opportunities for members' participation in leadership and decision making (Maton & Salem, 1995). Members of a spiritual community help meet each other's interpersonal, economic, psychological, and spiritual needs. Finally, spiritual communities foster emotional and spiritual bonds based on a deeply shared sense of spiritual transcendence. Small groups, religious education classes, and shared worship foster community (Wuthnow, 1994).

Third, spiritual communities provide important community services. Religious involvement among teens and adults has been shown in research to protect against risky behavior and promote well-being (Kloos & Moore, 2000a; Kress & Elias, 2000; Steinman & Zimmerman, 2004). Spiritual communities offer supports for families, parents, and marital partners, including workshops, small-group meetings, and counseling. Many other community services have religious-spiritual bases—from soup kitchens to Habitat for Humanity. The Caroline Center, operated by sisters of a Roman Catholic order, provides job training and an important community for low-income Baltimore women (Brodsky & Marx, 2001). Twelve-step mutual help groups are common and effective forms of healing (Humphreys, 2000). Programs to promote sobriety in Alaska Native communities involve indigenous Native spiritual concepts (Hazel & Mohatt, 2001).

Fourth, spiritual communities are especially valuable for members of oppressed, disenfranchised populations who lack resources and power in society. For example, these have included Native Americans, African Americans and other peoples of color, gay and lesbian individuals, the economically oppressed, and women (Hazel & Mohatt, 2001; Mattis & Jagers, 2001; Potts, 1999; Rappaport, 2000).

Fifth, some spiritual communities challenge forces in mainstream culture. In Western cultures, these communities help to counterbalance mainstream values of individualism and materialism through concern for the public good, for the disenfranchised and for social justice, and for values of compassion and service. Social advocacy, one way that spiritual perspectives challenge mainstream culture, includes public positions taken by nationwide religious institutions and community-level efforts by local faith-based groups (Maton, 2000; 2001). For example, the U.S. civil rights movement involved many faith-based social change initiatives. Community organizing for social justice, based in faith communities, has achieved substantive community changes (Putnam & Feldstein,

2003; Speer, Hughey, Gensheimer, & Adams-Leavitt, 1995). "Basic ecclesial communities" are small spiritual groups that meet for worship, interpersonal support, reflection on spiritual ideals, and taking collective action for social justice and community development (Dokecki et al., 2001; Trout, Dokecki, Newbrough, & O'Gorman, 2003). Not surprisingly, many examples of faith-based advocacy arise among members of oppressed populations.

Of course, some spiritual communities focus on individual salvation or spiritual development or on community-building within the congregation, having little impact on wider community life. But when one considers all spiritual communities, these five functions are important contributions to communities and societies.

Narratives, Identity, and Meaning-Making in Spiritual Communities   Spiritual communities explicitly work to provide the shared emotional connection identified by McMillan and Chavis as being central to sense of community. One of the most effective ways these communities accomplish this goal is through the development of narratives (stories). Spiritual and religious narratives express important ideals and build spiritual bonds (Mankowski & Rappaport, 2000a; Rappaport, 2000). The narrative of Passover and the Exodus in Jewish tradition, the ministry, death, and resurrection of Jesus in Christian tradition, and Muhammad's encounters with the angel, call to prophecy, and ascension into heaven in Islamic tradition are examples. Numerous parables in these and other faiths are ways of teaching through narratives.

Spiritual narratives provide resources for individuals seeking to understand their own life experiences. This is especially important at life transitions or when a person or group is demeaned in dominant cultural narratives. For college students questioning their beliefs or struggling with choices, a campus ministry that interprets such questioning as a basis for growth thus provides a positive way of understanding one's own experiences (Mankowski & Thomas, 2000). To an alcoholic who has "hit bottom," 12-step principles offer a community narrative that explains his or her descent into alcoholism and offers a path to recovery validated by other group members' experiences (Humphreys, 2000). To persons wounded by past trauma, many spiritual settings provide narratives of healing and redemption. To spiritual gay men and lesbians, a congregation that offers a positive, strengths-based perspective on their sexuality and spirituality provides a safe haven and a place for spiritual growth. To persons experiencing serious mental illness, a mutual help group offers a focus on strengths and practical coping (Rappaport, 2000).

Spiritual narratives are vessels that carry meaning and values, communicating them to individuals and supporting their personal growth (Stuber, 2000). Meaning-making in spiritual communities can lead to personal and social transformations. Kenneth Maton, a community psychologist long involved in research with spiritual communities, argued for their importance in developing the strong sense of community necessary to engage in social change:

> …without incorporating the religious and spiritual domains of the larger community, prevention, empowerment-oriented, and other social action efforts stand little hope of mobilizing the resources, building the scale, and

challenging mainstream culture in the ways necessary to make any truly substantive difference in our social problems. (Maton, 2001, p. 610)

Online Communities

The World Wide Web is about 20 years old at the time of this writing. The first paper describing the basics design of the Web was published in 1989 and the first website was established on the Internet in 1991. According to the latest statistics available (June 2010), 77.4% of the population in North America currently uses the Internet—an increase of 146% from December 2000 (Internet World Stats, 2010). Internet usage is increasing at an even faster rate in other regions of the world. In the Middle East, the percentage of the population that uses the Internet increased 1,825% from 2000 through 2010, and in Africa, the increase was 2,357%. This represents an incredibly rapid pace of technological change.

In some respects, the most recent edition of this book is closely tied to the Internet. The authors live in South Carolina, New Mexico, Washington, Pennsylvania, and New Jersey. Close collaboration on the book was made possible through frequent conference calls via Skype and even more frequent use of e-mail. This use of the Internet to facilitate relationships over geographic distance is an undeniable benefit of the Internet age.

But as with all technological changes that impact how humans interact with each other and the world around them, the possibility of negative effects from the amazingly rapid growth of the Internet must be considered. One of the earliest studies of the effects of the Internet on human interactions involved purchasing computers and Internet connections for 73 households that were not previously connected to the Internet. After two years, the researchers concluded that increased use of the Internet was correlated with decreased interactions with family members, smaller social networks, and slight increases in reported loneliness and depression (Kraut et al., 1998). These findings seemed to support the pessimistic predictions regarding the Internet's effect on human relationships. However, in a three-year follow-up study of the same households, the researchers found that the negative effects found in the original study had disappeared. And data from a new sample found that Internet use was associated with positive effects on social interaction and psychological well-being (Kraut et al., 2001).

So, in the space of three years (from 1996 when the first study ended, to 1999 when the second study ended), the researchers reversed their conclusions about the effect of Internet use on human relationships. But even the positive effects found in the second study did not hold for all the participants. Participants classified as extroverts and those with more social support tended to have positive outcomes from Internet use, while those classified as introverts or those with less social support tended to have negative outcomes (Kraut et al., 2001).

One of the clearest findings in the research is that people tend to use the Internet to strengthen existing relationships rather than for establishing new ones. The research seems to show that the Internet is used as a supplementary form of communication with friends, colleagues, and family and can result in a strengthening of those relationships (Ellison, Steinfield, & Lampe, 2007; Lee &

Kuo, 2002; Lenhart, Madden, & Hitlin, 2005). This strengthening of relationships can also extend to organizations. For example, research has found that teens' Internet use tended to not only strengthen their already existing friendships but also their connection to school (Lee, 2009).

One example of this use of the Internet to strengthen existing relationships is CaringBridge, an online community started in 1997. CaringBridge allows people experiencing a critical illness or accident to maintain connections with family and friends (www.caringbridge.org). If you have ever had to deal with the critical illness of a family member yourself, you know about the time and energy involved in staying in constant communication with everyone who wants updates on the situation. CaringBridge allows you to develop a free website on which you can post updates for all your family and friends. For people who are isolated at home or in the hospital during recovery, this allows an easy way for family and friends to supply emotional support (a bonding activity). It also allows families to communicate specific needs to a wide variety of people. So, a family faced with building a ramp into its home for a member who will be using a wheelchair can suddenly learn that a friend has a friend who can donate the concrete (a bridging activity).

What about societal-level effects? If Internet use is decreasing the quantity and quality of social interactions overall, that will impact the social capital available to communities and nations. If the Internet is strengthening social interactions, and particularly if it is strengthening both bonding and bridging relationships, that will result in an increase in social capital, which will in turn strengthen communities and nations. The issue of social capital and the Internet has just begun to be explicitly examined. Perhaps the best publicized use of the Internet to develop social capital was the Obama campaign's development of a social networking site (my.barackobama.com) during the 2008 presidential election in the United States. This site successfully recruited and organized thousands of volunteer campaign workers around the country (Dickinson, 2008). Other examples include TakingITGlobal.org and YouthNoise.org, which both have the stated aim of supporting people around the world in local efforts to address such issues as poverty, AIDS, environmental concerns, and human rights (Raynes-Goldie & Walker, 2008). Even general social networking sites have been shown to be correlated with increases in measures of social capital. One study found small but positive relationships between the intensity of Facebook use and social trust, civic engagement, and political participation among college students (Valenzuela, Park, & Kee, 2009).

What about the ability of the Internet to help develop new relationships? Can relational groups that exist only on the Internet develop into communities? Take another look at the first quote at the beginning of this chapter:

> "I mean I can talk to them and they are there to help me when
> I need to talk to someone...For example...my father is very close to
> dying right now... they have all talked with me about it and have been
> a great deal of comfort to me." (Roberts et al., 2002, p. 237)

This quote is from a member of an online gaming community. But obviously this individual is not talking about games or entertainment. He is talking about the relationships he has developed and the support he has received from his community. An online community may be said to exist when "people carry on public discussions long enough, with sufficient human feeling, to form webs of personal relationships in cyberspace" (Rheingold, 2000). Some online communities are tied to an existing locality and build community ties among citizens there (e.g., craigslist.org). A mainly relational online community can arrange local events where members meet personally, such as the meetups hosted by the political organization MoveOn.org. Other online communities are purely relational, with membership that can be worldwide.

Roberts et al. (2002) interviewed a sample of individuals in online gaming environments. Most believed that their gaming site had a positive sense of community. Respondents' comments fit each of the four McMillan-Chavis elements of sense of community. Boundaries are enforced by membership requirements for site members and for the fictional characters they create. These communities have mechanisms for excluding members whose online behavior does not match community norms and a common symbol system. In the sites studied, there are offices and decision-making procedures allowing mutual influence, and mutual helping occurs (online and in person) that represents integration. Site users reported strong shared emotional connection. Roberts et al. concluded that these online environments were a relational community with a shared sense of community.

There is research indicating that Internet use is correlated with a generalized sense of community. Among Internet users in Australia who were aged 55 years or older, there was a positive correlation between Internet use, sense of belonging to an online community, sense of community, and general well-being (Sum, Mathews, Pourghasem, & Hughes, 2009). Generalized sense of community in this study was measured through such questions as, "The world is becoming a better place for everyone" and "I have something valuable to give to the world." Sense of online community was measured by such questions as, "The Internet has allowed me to communicate with all kinds of interesting people I otherwise would never have interacted with" and "I feel I belong to an online community on the Internet." These statements are clearly related to sense of community.

In online mutual help groups, individuals with a shared problem or concern (such as breast cancer or problem drinking) help each other online. This facilitates support among persons unable to attend face-to-face mutual help groups and those who feel especially stigmatized, out of place, or reluctant to attend in person. Some of the largest sites on the Internet (in terms of number of visitors) are support groups. Research indicates that helping in online mutual help settings resembles helping in face-to-face groups. We will discuss this form of support in more detail in Chapter 8.

Online communities have several advantages for community building. They can transcend geographic distance and social status boundaries. They offer choice for individuals in finding a community and sense of belongingness. The lack of nonverbal communication can be an advantage; stereotypes related to appearance are lessened when race, social class, attractiveness, age, and even gender are unclear. This can facilitate more democratic relationships and power sharing. Lack of nonverbal cues can also be a disadvantage; the communication of emotion is more difficult and easily misunderstood. The anonymity of much online communication is a strength and a drawback; it can allow heavily stigmatized individuals to self-disclose and form supportive relationships but can also lead to exploitation, mistrust, and rudeness ("flaming") (see the Center for Safe and Responsible Internet Use, csriu.org). Boundaries for membership and behavioral rules must somehow be established for online communities as they are for face-to-face groups and localities. Online communities represent an important new form of community, which can be linked with existing communities or create new ones (Putnam, Feldstein, & Cohen, 2003; Rudkin, 2003).

CONCLUSION

Concepts of community lie at the heart of community psychology but also involve the questions, issues, and values we have discussed. This chapter is only an introduction to the use of these concepts. In later chapters, we will discuss in detail other forms of community, such as mutual help groups (Chapter 8), and related topics, such as human diversity (Chapter 7), citizen participation in communities (Chapter 11), and community and social change (Chapter 12).

CHAPTER SUMMARY

1. Social scientists have been interested in the concept of community for more than 150 years. One of the earliest discussions of community was from the sociologist Tönnies, who distinguished between *Gemeinschaft* and *Gesellschaft* relationships.

2. We defined *locality-based* and *relational communities*. Communities exist at different ecological levels: microsystems, organizations, localities, and macrosystems. The question of who defines communities is an important one. Some communities must struggle for the right to define themselves.

3. *Sense of community* was first proposed as a key concept for the field by Sarason (1974) and defined in more specific terms by McMillan and Chavis (1986). They identified four elements of sense of community: *membership, mutual influence* between individual and community, *integration and fulfillment of needs* among members, and *shared emotional connection*. The elements and their attributes are listed in Table 6.1. Research on sense of community demonstrates its importance.

4. Questions remain about the sense of community concept. Does it have the four McMillan-Chavis elements or others or does it vary in each community? Does it exist as both an individual cognition and a characteristic of a community?

5. Concepts related to sense of community include *neighboring, place attachment, citizen participation, social support*, and *mediating structures*. Mediating structures provide links between individuals and larger communities or society.

6. A positive psychological sense of community has been shown to have positive outcomes for both individuals and communities. Strong communities often display high levels of *social capital*. Social capital refers to connections among citizens and reciprocity and trust based on them. It may be *formal* or *informal* and involve *bonding* or *bridging*. Research on social capital demonstrates its importance for community life and society.

7. Communities—and our relationships with them—are complex. A person can have a *negative psychological sense of community* and have *multiple psychological senses of community* for the multiple communities in one's life. The *myth of "we"* overlooks diversity in a community. Sense of community changes over time. Newbrough's concept of the *just community* balances community, freedom, and equality (social justice).

8. For as long as social scientists have been writing about communities, there have been concerns that communities in modern society are in decline. There is evidence supporting this position (summarized by Putman, 2000), but this evidence is open to opposing interpretations. There is also evidence supporting an increase in some measures of community. At this point, the question of whether communities are in decline has not been conclusively answered.

9. In addition to the aspects of community mentioned so far, there is strong evidence that the structure of the *physical and natural environments* have powerful effects on social interactions and the development and maintenance of communities.

10. Religious and spiritual communities represent an important form of community. We defined *spirituality* more broadly than religion; *spiritual communities* include both. These fulfill five functions in communities: providing meaning, sense of community, community services, resources for the oppressed, and challenges to mainstream culture. Shared narratives in spiritual communities promote these.

11. The Internet is definitely affecting communities in industrialized countries and will continue to do so. Although there were initial concerns that increasing use of the Internet would result in a decline in community, research now suggests that most people use the Internet to strengthen existing relationships. Research also shows that true online communities can develop, which demonstrate all the elements of sense of community proposed by McMillan and Chavis (1986).

RECOMMENDED READINGS

Sarason, S. B. (1974). *The psychological sense of community: Prospects for a community psychology.* San Francisco: Jossey-Bass.

McMillan, D. W. & Chavis, D. M. (1986). Sense of community: Definition and theory. *Journal of Community Psychology, 14,* 6–23.

7

Understanding Human Diversity in Context

HIRB/Index Stock/ PhotoLibrary

OPENING EXERCISE

What is human diversity? Let us begin by doing a simple exercise to place yourself in the "diversity of contexts" of your life (Trickett, 1996). Describing yourself with different indices of diversity will not reflect all of what makes you a unique individual, but the exercise may help you understand some of the cultural and social forces that influence you every day. We encourage you to discuss your thoughts about these questions with a class-mate or friend:

- What is your gender? How does this influence, for example, your everyday behavior, your career planning, or your approach to emotions, friendships, or intimate relationships?

- What is your culture or nationality? What is your first language? How do these factors affect your values, career planning, family relationships, and friendships?

- How do socioeconomic factors affect your life? How did they affect the nature and quality of education in your home community, your choice of college, or your experiences in college? Has a need to hold a time-consuming job or another economic stressor interfered with your schooling?

- What is your sexual orientation? How does your orientation affect your everyday life, friendships, career plans, and other choices?

- How would you describe your race and ethnicity? How does it influence your life, interactions with strangers or friends, life planning, choice of college, and friendships? How many meaningful relationships do you have with others of a different race or ethnicity?

We could write similar questions about physical or mental ability/disability, rural/suburban/urban background, or other forms of diversity. Consider these and other forms of diversity that are important in your life.

It should not be surprising to you now that community psychologists view diversity not simply as a discussion of individual differences; instead, we consider diversity of people in different contexts and between contexts. Depending on the context, we emphasize different dimensions of diversity. A community psychology approach encourages us to view multiple dimensions of diversity in the different contexts in which we live. Now consider these questions for integrative reflection:

- Which of these dimensions of human diversity are most important for understanding your experiences in college? Which dimensions are important for people to understand you at work? Which dimensions do you need to consider in understanding your classmates and coworkers' perspectives?

- How would you characterize your network of friends in terms of these dimensions? How would you characterize your sources of support—the people to whom you would turn in a crisis?

Every person is involved when we discuss human diversity. We sometimes encounter among U.S. students the assumption that "diversity" means the study of people other than a White, middle-class, heterosexual norm. Yet each person has a culture, a race, a gender, a sexual orientation, and a place somewhere on each dimension of human diversity. And each person interacts with others, who have their own unique diversity profile. Focusing on these multiple dimensions and their intersections, it becomes clear that diversity is an important part of understanding differences and similarities *between* individuals and communities, but also variation *within* communities. Each community has diversity, and we cannot assume that all members of a group share a similar lived experience. One goal of this chapter is to give you more tools for examining your location, and others' locations, on each dimension of human diversity.

Fruitful discussions of diversity take the perspective of pluralism—that no culture or group represents the norm. Every person, culture, or group has a place on each dimension, but none is superior. Each must be understood in its own terms. This perspective does not define differences as deficits but searches for cultural, community, and human strengths revealed in human diversity

(Trickett, Watts, & Birman, 1994; Trickett, 2009). This, of course, does not mean that all ways of doing things are fine or that one should refrain from drawing any comparisons or conclusions. Instead, a pluralistic perspective requires that one understand the value and meaning of differences and that value judgments are well informed. It also means that there is likely not just one best way to do things.

As you may recall from the first chapter, respect for human diversity is a core value of community psychology. Discussions of diversity are woven throughout this book, as the consideration of diversity issues is integral to all community research and action. It is critical to effective work as a community psychologist. Yet this chapter represents an opportunity to think more deeply about *how* we take diversity into consideration as we enter into collaborations, define problems, identify strengths, design interventions, and conduct research.

In this chapter, we introduce community psychology conceptions of human diversity. First, we briefly describe some of the dimensions of that diversity. Second, we discuss how persons are socialized into cultural communities, and we use the example of individualism-collectivism to illustrate this process. Third, we examine acculturation and social identities. Fourth, we discuss concepts of oppression and liberation that explicitly address power in social relationships and social inequities. Finally, we consider what cultural competence means for community psychologists.

Throughout this chapter, we emphasize the theme that understanding human diversity means studying the lives of others and ourselves from a pluralistic perspective while also recognizing how our own values affect our perspective. The meaning of this chapter depends on one's context and experiences. As a team of authors, we invite you to engage the ideas here, measure their meaning against your own experiences, and seek broader experiences that educate you further in issues of human diversity that are integral to community life.

KEY DIMENSIONS OF HUMAN DIVERSITY FOR COMMUNITY PSYCHOLOGY

The dimensions we discuss here certainly do not cover all the forms of human diversity, but they do represent concepts frequently addressed in community psychology research and action. Our definitions are brief, designed only to provide an orienting overview. Our major point is that human diversity has multiple intersecting dimensions, including dimensions not listed here.

Culture

"Cultural diversity" has become a buzzword as the world's societies have become more interdependent. The term *culture* has been stretched to refer not only to ethnic and cultural groups but also to nation-states, religious groups, racial groupings, and corporations (Betancourt & Lopez, 1993).

What is culture, and how are cultures diverse? While anthropologists and other social scientists have not settled on a single definition of culture, certain key elements are identifiable (Lonner, 1994). These key elements typically include meanings and experiences shared by a group and communicated across generations. It does not explain anything to say "Astrid behaves in a certain way because she is Swedish" (Lonner, 1994, p. 234). To understand cultural influences on Astrid's actions in a certain situation, we need to specify a Swedish cultural element that shapes her choices and actions in that situation. That element must be reflected in other aspects of Swedish culture. These might include a behavioral norm taught to children, a tradition reflected in literature or in religious or political documents, a concept for which Swedish language has a word, a folk saying, or a routine cultural practice. Culture is often expressed in what adults seek to transmit to children through family socialization practices and formal schooling. Shared language, social roles, and norms for thinking, feeling, and acting are cultural expressions important to psychologists (Kitayama & Marcus, 1994; Rogoff, 2003; Triandis, 1994). In multicultural societies with heterogeneous populations, boundaries between cultural groupings are often somewhat fluid. In all societies, cultures are dynamic and change over time. Culture is an essential dimension for community psychologists to study (O'Donnell, 2005a).

Community psychologists look for the impact of culture on the ecologies of communities across multiple levels of analysis (Trickett, 2009). That is, cultural influences can be seen in the functioning of individuals and families, organizational practices, and norms of local communities and societies. Community psychologists have sought to understand how settings have layers of cultural influences that impact the composition, functioning, and interactions of its members. A contextual, ecological understanding of cultural influences on communities seeks to understand how cultural influences structure community norms and processes for how decisions are made, how conflict is addressed, and how resources are distributed (Bond & Harrell, 2006). To fully understand the cultural context of settings requires historical and sociopolitical data that can track patterns of change over time.

Race/Ethnicity, Gender, and Social Class

Race, ethnicity, gender, and social class have been the dimensions of diversity most often discussed in community psychology research and social action in the United States. As a reflection of the contexts in which community psychology has developed, these dimensions of diversity have been centrally involved in defining and addressing social issues. In other locations (e.g., community psychology in Asia or Africa) or in the future (e.g., community psychology in North America in 30 years), different dimensions of diversity may be emphasized.

Race Race has long occupied a quasi-biological status in Western psychological thought (Zuckerman, 1990). That quasi-biological definition of race has often provided an intellectual basis for assumptions of racial superiority. For example, biological and psychological racist assumptions supported Nazi theories of Aryan superiority, colonialist theories of European superiority, restrictive U.S. immigration laws, and histories of slavery and segregation in the United States and apartheid in South Africa. The damage done to human lives by thinking of race in biological terms makes it particularly important to define race carefully.

Psychologists, anthropologists, and biologists have concluded that biological race differences are not meaningful (American Anthropological Association, 1998; Betancourt & Lopez, 1993; Helms, 1994; Jones, 2003; Smedley & Smedley, 2005). Human racial groups are biologically much more alike than different. Research from the Human Genome Project found a remarkable amount of genetic similarity among human beings: 99.9% at the DNA level. Leaders from the project concluded, "Those who wish to draw precise racial boundaries around certain groups will not be able to use science as a legitimate justification" (Collins & Mansoura, 2001). Furthermore, most genetic variation exists *within* socially defined racial groups rather than *between* them. Racial differences—as in IQ scores or educational achievement—are attributed to historical, social, and economic variables rather than biological differences. In an influential review of the literature on race, genetics, and intelligence, Sternberg, Grigorenko, and Kidd (2005) conclude that "the statement that racial differences in IQ or academic achievement are of genetic origin is, when all is said and done, a leap of imagination (p. 57)."

Yet race does have psychological and social meaning in many societies: as a socially constructed set of categories related to inequalities of status and power (Jones, 2003; Smedley & Smedley, 2005). Sternberg and colleagues (2005) suggest that while the link between IQ and genetics is a leap of imagination, it is one that is used to justify existing social stratification. Even as racial categories shift over time and across locations, race remains important because racism makes it so. In most contexts within the United States, Whites are privileged to not have to pay as much attention to race as members of other ethnic groups, as they tend to encounter far less racial prejudice and discrimination, whereas persons of color are more frequently made acutely aware of their race. That difference in life experiences and perspective reflects a powerful set of social dynamics. Racial distinctions in U.S. life are based on a history of slavery and segregation and the assumptions of White supremacy that were used to justify them. Today's differences in sociopolitical and economic power are maintained by persistent (often unrecognized) versions of those assumptions of superiority (Sue, 2004).

Race is not simply ethnicity. Race is "socially defined on the basis of *physical* criteria" (Van den Berghe, cited in Jones, 1997, p. 347). That is, people make racial distinctions based on assumptions about observable physical qualities, such as skin color. As we discuss further in the next section, ethnicity is "socially defined on the basis of *cultural* criteria" (Van den Berghe, cited in Jones, 1997, p. 358) such as language, national origin, customs, and values, having little to do with physical appearance.

An example of the significance of race for those of different ethnic or national backgrounds is that in the United States, persons of largely African ancestry include at least three groups: those with long ancestries in the United States dating primarily back to enslavement, those of Afro-Caribbean background, and recent immigrants from various parts of Africa. Yet all share experiences associated with racism in the United States.

No terminology is entirely satisfactory to describe the racial diversity of U.S. and many other societies. Use of almost any terminology and definition of race reflects and perpetuates racial oppression in some way (see Birman, 1994; Helms, 1994; and Jones, 1997, on concepts of race, ethnicity, and similar terms). Yet community psychology, at least in the United States, cannot ignore race, despite the drawbacks of our vocabulary for discussing it (Griffith, Childs, Eng, & Jeffries, 2007; Suarez-Balcazar, 1998; Trickett et al., 1994).

Ethnicity   Ethnicity can be defined as a social identity, based on one's ancestry or culture of origin, as modified by the culture in which one currently resides (Helms, 1994; Jones, 1997). The term is related to the Greek *ethnos*, referring to tribe or nationality. Ethnicity is defined by language, customs, values, social ties, and other aspects of subjective culture. In psychological research, it may refer to a simply demographic category, cultural qualities shared by a group or population, or ethnic identity—the extent to which an individual incorporates ethnicity into one's sense of self (Birman, 1994). It is important to know which is meant in a given study or social context.

Some broad categories often used in U.S. research combine multiple ethnicities. Hispanic or Latino/Latina may refer to persons of Puerto Rican, Cuban, Dominican, Mexican, Spanish, or many other ancestries. Many ethnicities and nationalities exist among Asian Americans. Native Americans represent a diversity of tribal and cultural traditions.

Ethnicity is also not simply nationality; for example, India is a very multiethnic nation, and even seemingly racially homogeneous countries—such as Japan—have multiple ethnic groups. In North America, ethnicity often involves an interaction of at least two cultures. Being Chinese American is not simply being Chinese but is defined by the interaction (including conflict) of Chinese and U.S. cultural contexts (Sasao & Sue, 1993).

Gender   Perceived differences between females and males provide a distinction that has been the basis of socially constructed concepts and definitions of "sexual" differences. Gender refers to our understanding of what it means to be female or male and how these categories are interpreted and reflected in attitudes, social roles, and the organization of social institutions. For example, how are parenting responsibilities divided? Which jobs do people consider appropriate for men?

Gender is not simply a demographic category but represents important psychological and social processes, including the distribution of resources and power (Gridley & Turner, 2010; Mulvey, Bond, Hill, & Terenzio, 2000). The lived experience of gender includes expectations for male and female behavior as well as potential consequences for those who act outside of these gendered expectations (Fields, Swan, & Kloos, 2010; Mankowski & Maton, 2010). During the past 40 years, many have written about or protested limitations in social opportunity that they have encountered with gender norms (e.g., jobs considered inappropriate for one gender, lower rates of pay). Increasingly, community psychologists are developing awareness of the experiences of people who identify themselves as transgender—living and presenting themselves in the opposite gender of their sex at birth (Paxton, Guentzel, & Trombacco, 2006). Within a community psychology framework, gender is an important aspect of one's identity and has an impact on how social problems are defined and addressed.

Social Class   While this dimension may be defined primarily in terms of income or material assets (socioeconomic status [SES]), it is usually used to state, either explicitly or implicitly, where one belongs in society. Thus, as a composite concept that also includes occupational and educational status, it typically includes assumptions about a person's prospects for the future, occupational aspirations, and even where one may live. Note that in research, income or educational level may also be studied alone.

Social class comprises a key dimension for community psychology. While often studied only as a demographic descriptor, social class actually marks differences in power, especially economic resources and opportunities (Nelson & Prilleltensky, 2010). It influences identity and self-image, interpersonal relationships, socialization, well-being, living environment, educational opportunities, and many other psychological issues (American Psychological Association, 2006; Bradley & Corwyn, 2002; McLoyd, 1998). Psychologists have only belatedly attended to psychological issues related to social class (Lott & Bullock, 2001; Ostrove & Cole, 2003).

Dimensions of Diversity Receiving Greater Attention in Community Psychology

The dimensions of diversity discussed in this next section represent areas of growing awareness and increased focus in community psychology. These are emerging and generative areas of research and action, driven in part by an increasingly diverse set of researchers and practitioners in community psychology and related fields.

Ability/Disability   Most persons will experience a physical or mental disability at some time in their lives. However, we often overlook the discrimination and barriers to participation in community life that many persons with disabilities face. While disabilities have implications for physical or cognitive functioning, community psychologists focus on the social experience of ability and disability (White, 2010). A disability creates life experiences different from those of fully "able" persons. Some persons with disabilities describe feeling invisible or being avoided by others who feel awkward in their presence. Many face negative judgments about their capabilities based solely on assumptions about their disability, which is often not based in fact or knowledge about the individual's abilities. A tendency in society to discriminate based on ableism leads to many barriers for participation in community life as a valued and contributing member. White has defined ableism as "a non-factual negative judgment about the attributes and capabilities of an individual with a disabling condition" (White, 2010, p. 432). Several community psychologists focus their work on challenging ability-based stigma, limits to opportunity, and accessibility challenges for persons with physical and mental disabilities (e.g., Fawcett et al., 1994; McDonald, Keys, & Balcazar, 2007; Kloos, 2010).

Sexual Orientation This is best understood as a spectrum from exclusively heterosexual to exclusively homosexual, with intermediate points. It refers to an underlying orientation, involving sexual attraction, romantic affection, and related emotions. Due to widespread social pressure to be heterosexual, some-times enforced with violence, outward social behavior does not necessarily cor-respond to an underlying orientation elsewhere along the spectrum (Gonsiorek & Weinrich, 1991; Rivers & D'Augelli, 2001). Sexual orientation is distinct from gender identity—one's sense of being psychologically male or female, and from gender role, one's adherence to social norms for masculinity and femininity (e.g., dress or appearance). Being gay, lesbian, or bisexual is a social identity important for many persons (Frable, 1997), and the importance of this dimension is increas-ingly recognized in community psychology (D'Augelli, 2006; Harper, 2010; Lehavot, Balsam, & Ibrahim-Wells, 2009; Schneider & Harper, 2003; Wilson, Harper, Hidalgo, Jamil, Torres, & Fernandez, 2010).

Age Children, adolescents, and younger and older adults differ in psychological and health-related concerns, developmental transitions, and community involve-ment. Similarly, aging also brings changes in relationships and power dynamics for families, communities, workplaces, and societies (Gatz & Cotton, 1994; Cheng & Heller, 2009). Community psychology has begun to attend to how age structures the available roles and channels for meaningful participation in communities, focusing on how children and adolescents are included as stake-holders in decision-making as well as how aging adults are afforded opportunities to contribute their talents and skills in communities (Cheng, Chan, & Phillips, 2004; Liegghio, Nelson, & Evans, 2010).

Spirituality and Religion Spirituality and religion concern community psy-chology because of their importance for personal well-being and the importance of spiritual institutions and communities (Pargament & Maton, 2000; Kelly, 2010). As we noted in Chapter 6, we use the inclusive terms *spirituality* and *spiritual* to refer to religious traditions and to other perspectives concerned with tran-scendence. Spirituality and religion often interrelate with culture and ethnicity. It is impossible to understand many cultures without understanding their religious institutions and spiritual practices. Yet religion and spirituality are not simply cul-tural. Moreover, many religions and spiritual traditions are multicultural, and many cultures contain multiple religious and spiritual communities. These inter-relationships can be complicated. Birman (1994) discusses the dilemmas faced by Jewish refugees from Russia to the United States. In Russia, they were consid-ered a nationality (connoting ethnicity) and sometimes considered a physically distinctive race. Judaism as a religion was not important to many. In the United States, their Jewishness was often perceived in religious terms, and their nationality was considered to be Russian, which astounded many of these immigrants.

Localities Differences among localities affect individual lives in many ways, creating differences in life experiences that comprise a form of human diversity. Localities are often said to differ along a dimension of rural/suburban/urban communities. An example of how locality affects personal life or community action is that rural areas are often marked by geographic dispersion, limited access to health care and other human services, and stable, insular social networks that can make it difficult to be different or for newcomers or outsiders to establish trust (Bierman et al., 1997; Muehrer, 1997). Transportation is a challenge for almost any community innovation.

In contrast, diversity and change are hallmarks of urban life. Skills in understanding multiple forms of human diversity, in establishing new interpersonal relationships, and in adapting to changing circumstances are important in urban life. Relationships between the physical environment and personal life are also different. Finally, disadvantaged urban and rural areas have far fewer economic resources than many suburban and affluent urban ones. This shapes the resources available for schools, human and health services, and key community institutions and organizations.

This is not to say that all urban, rural, or other communities, or their individual members, are alike. Each locality is distinctive, and people have different levels of engagement with the places they live, work, and play. The categories that we have discussed are only general guides to a richness of local and particular communities. In Chapter 5, we looked at how neighborhoods serve as an important context for individual development and quality of life as well as citizen action. In Chapter 6, we examined localities and their relationship to sense of community. We described individual, family, and cultural connections to particular localities in terms of place attachment, or sense of place. However conceptualized, life experiences in differing localities comprise one form of human diversity.

Social Inequities

Community psychology's value on social justice often leads to an examination of social conditions and opportunities within community settings. Social inequality within and between communities may not be thought of as diversity on an individual level of analysis but becomes clearer when diversity is examined at multiple levels of analysis. Social inequities occur when the lack of social and economic resources available to particular groups lead to reduced opportunities for education, health care, or work. In more extreme cases, a group's reduced social status can lead to group members having their property rights, voting rights, freedom of speech and assembly, and citizenship challenged. In the United States, disparities in rates of disease have received increasing attention (Lounsbury & Mitchell, 2007; Weber, 2010). These "health disparities" are often attributed to socioeconomic factors, but recent research is highlighting the social aspects of health disparities due to racism and history of racism (Gone, 2007; Griffith et al., 2007; Williams & Jackson, 2005). For example, even when level of income is comparable, African Americans have higher rates of heart disease and hypertension (Braveman, Cubbin, Egerter, & Pamuk, 2010).

The point here is that inequities exist in relationships, not in abstract principles. That is, from a community psychology viewpoint, a lack of opportunity for education, work, or housing for a particular community or group needs to be compared to the overall availability of those opportunities within a locality and between localities. Community psychologists may investigate the consequences of different social conditions for individuals' education attainment, disparities in disease and health, and a variety of social issues. Community psychologists may also focus on addressing social inequities in their intervention work as a primary means of promoting well-being and adaptive functioning for individuals of the group identified as experiencing the inequities. Addressing social inequities can be a powerful way of linking the well-being of individuals and communities (Griffith et al., 2007; Kim & Lorian, 2006).

Intersectionality

The dimensions briefly discussed previously—while important for community psychology—reflect only some forms of human diversity. Other important dimensions include nationality and generational differences in immigrant families. Discussion of these dimensions provides a beginning point for consideration of human diversity in communities, yet none can fully describe a person, specific population, or community. In addition, these dimensions are not independent of each other. The meanings of culture, race, and ethnicity especially converge. Human diversities are complex; languages often fail to reflect that complexity.

In any given situation, many forms of diversity may be psychologically important. A helpful tool for conceptualizing the interaction of different dimensions of diversity is **intersectionality** (Ostrove & Cole, 2003; Weber, 2010). Developed most prominently in feminist scholarship, intersectionality theory can help guide investigations of how several dimensions overlap. More importantly, it is used to investigate multiple injustices associated with social inequities—for example, how racism, sexism, and classism burden low-income women of color. Social myths often confuse issues and perpetuate stereotypes, especially of race and social class. For example, when we say "welfare recipient," we seldom think of low-income Whites (Ostrove & Cole, 2003). Similar to investigating phenomena at multiple levels of analysis, an intersectionality framework supports systematic investigation of how dimensions of diversity can affect power, opportunity, and functioning (Weber, 2010). Community psychologists also emphasize how intersectionality can help identify multiple dimensions of strengths, resources, and points of intervention (e.g., spirituality, cultural resources, and peer support networks). Moreover, a person may form multiple identities that help to negotiate participation in different community settings (e.g., based on his or her race, sexual orientation, and spirituality). In the following section, we examine participation in different community settings more closely.

EXPERIENCE OF CULTURE AND DIMENSIONS OF DIVERSITY: SOCIALIZATION IN CULTURAL COMMUNITIES

Whether we like it or not, we come to resemble the people who raised us in many ways. How could it be otherwise? Our families and cultural communities are the place where we learn language, values, and skills in getting along in the world. We learn what is considered smart, beautiful, efficient, and good. We learn what types of people to trust and who to stay away from. We learn how and when to express different emotions, how to be polite and show respect, and how to disagree. We learn how to make sense of differences in the way people and groups are valued in a society. While we mature and develop the capacity to become our own persons with our own values and ways of being in the world, this early and ongoing cultural socialization process is key to understanding part of what makes us the same and different from one another. It also helps us understand why we feel so comfortable in some contexts and so uncomfortable in others.

In this section, we will examine one key dimension of this cultural socialization process: individualism-collectivism. Remember, however, that this is just one example of how cultural patterns shape who we are and how we understand ourselves. There are many others to explore. Then, we will examine acculturation and identity development processes as they relate to community psychology.

Individualism-Collectivism: A Spectrum of Cultures

To increase employee productivity, a Texas corporation told its employees to look in the mirror and say "I'm beautiful" 100 times before coming to work. For much the same purpose, a Japanese supermarket in New Jersey told its employees to begin each work day by telling another employee that he or she is beautiful. (Markus & Kitayama, 1991, p. 224)

All cultures, in one way or another, negotiate some mixture of individual identity and collective identity. (Dudgeon, Mallard, Oxenham, & Fielder, 2002, p. 255)

Consider one way of living in which parents wish to impart these lessons to their children: Develop high self-esteem, take initiative to succeed as individuals, and resist peer pressure. However, in a different way of living, the same characteristics might be considered an excessive focus on self and lack of respect for others. That second way emphasizes cooperation and supportive relationships.

What the first way considers conformity, the second way views as teamwork (Gergen, 1973; Greenfield et al., 2003).

The first way of living described here emphasizes individual self-reliance, assertion, competition, and achievement. Important tasks of growing up include developing an independent self, with a sense of one's unique identity and strong, clear boundaries between oneself and others. Dependence on others is to be avoided.

The second way of living emphasizes security and harmony within groups. Individual achievement is to be attained through group success. Growing up includes cultivating an interdependent self, with a more open boundary between self and others. Identity is defined in terms of relationships with others and membership in communities. Being ostracized by others is to be avoided. These different ways of understanding the self have implications for personal health and well-being. Kitayama and colleagues (2010) found that Americans reported more well-being when they had more control in their lives, while Japanese reported more well-being when they experienced less conflict and had less strain on their relationships.

Cultural psychologists describe cultures embodying the first way of living as individualistic and cultures embodying the second way as collectivistic. Of course, no culture or community can be entirely one or the other. As noted in the second quotation that opened this section, all cultures and persons balance individual independence and collective interdependence (Dudgeon et al., 2002). Also, while collectivistic practices clearly go back much further in human history than individualistic ones, collectivistic cultures are not just traditional, "primitive," or less economically developed. For example, Japan is an economically developed society with many collectivistic norms, interwoven with growing individualistic practices (Markus & Kitayama, 1991; Reid, 1999). Individualism-collectivism is better understood as a spectrum along which cultures and communities vary (Greenfield, Keller, Fuligni, & Maynard, 2003; Kagitçibasi, 1997; Kim, Triandis, Kagitçibasi, Choi, & Yoo, 1994). It is one useful way for understanding the diversity of cultures, as long as you remember that it is a broad theme with many exceptions.

For example, differences in family life may reflect these patterns of an individualism-collectivism spectrum. Parents in Puerto Rico, Mexico, Nigeria, Cameroon, Japan, and China emphasize responsibility to others—especially family and elders—more than independence, assertion, and self-esteem. German, Dutch, and some other European American parents do the opposite (Greenfield et al., 2003). Certainly, there is diversity among parents within and among these societies, and parents in all societies value both independence and interdependence in their children to some extent. But a broad group difference emerged in what parents fostered more strongly in their children.

Such differences in worldviews can become practical conflicts that play out in communities around the world. As community researchers and practitioners, it is important for us to be aware that even as fellow community members may share values related to child development, individual wellness, healthy relationships, and thriving families, these ideals may have different meanings and different ways of being realized in practice.

Individualism-collectivism helps us understand some aspects of how people define themselves and their relationships to others across cultures, but it has limitations (Brewer & Chen, 2007). First, there is variation along the individualism-collectivism spectrum even within a culture (Lavee & Ben Ari, 2008). Second, all cultures change over time, and world cultures are becoming more interdependent and their differences less clear-cut. Many more collectivistic cultures are incorporating individualistic practices, particularly in work settings as global capitalism expands. Furthermore, in any country, there are typically many layers of cultural influence (e.g., immigration, regional differences). The worldwide reach of Western media and cross-cultural personal contacts also increase the interweaving of differing cultures, complicating easy generalizations (Fowers & Richardson, 1996; Hermans & Kempen, 1998; Tyler, 2001).

It is easy to oversimplify another culture by viewing it only in contrast to one's own. For example, Australians and others of European descent tend to view Aboriginal peoples—who have lived in Australia for at least 40,000 years—as a uniform "community" or culture, despite the diversity of indigenous Australian peoples. (Even the single term *Aboriginal* contributes to this.) This easily leads to romanticizing indigenous peoples as unselfish and primitive (i.e., the opposite of Western cultures) (Dudgeon et al., 2002; Lee, 2000). Similar conceptions influence European American views of Native Americans, who represent a diversity of cultures. Thinking in terms of dichotomies misunderstands another culture as an exotic "other"—a simple opposite of the familiar, not as diverse persons and communities to be understood in their own terms (Tyler, 2001).

Identity Development and Acculturation

One ever feels his two-ness,—an American, a Negro; two souls, two thoughts, two unreconciled strivings; two warring ideals in one dark body, whose dogged strength alone keeps it from being torn asunder.

The history of the American Negro is the history of this strife,—this longing to attain self-conscious manhood, to merge his double self into a better and truer self. In this merging he wishes neither of the older selves to be lost.... He simply wishes to make it possible for a man to be both a Negro and an American. (DuBois, 1903/1986, p. 365)

In this famous passage, W. E. B. DuBois addressed a conflict of two identities that he could not easily reconcile. His African ancestry and American experience promised mutual enrichment, but forces of oppression prohibited their merging. DuBois himself eventually left the United States because racism prevented an integration of these two identities.

Our focus on broad cultural socialization patterns does not fully address how individuals resolve such questions. Further elaboration is needed to focus on a person's multiple social identities and how they develop over time. These social identities are based on race, ethnicity, gender, sexual orientation, religion and spirituality, or other social or cultural distinctions that influence one's sense of "who I am" and "who I will become." For example, African American parents in the United States must help their children make sense of a devalued racial status by using racial socialization processes to help their children function effectively and experience self-worth in the face of prejudice and discrimination (White-Johnson, Ford, & Sellers, 2010). We will examine two theories that have influenced how community psychologists think about social identities: identity development and acculturation.

Psychologists have proposed models of social identity development for Americans of African, Asian, Latino, and White ancestry and status; U.S. ethnic minorities in general; feminists; and gays, lesbians, and bisexuals (e.g., D'Augelli, 1994; Helms, 1994; Phinney, 1990; Rickard, 1990). These models focus on how social identities develop—usually in late adolescence and early adulthood. They assume a sequence of stages (Frable, 1997; Helms, 1994; Phinney, 2003; Trimble, Helms, & Root, 2003).

Most begin with a stage of unexamined identity, in which the person identifies with mainstream cultural ideals, ignoring or denying their social group status (e.g., racial, ethnic, gender, or sexual orientation). That is challenged by life experiences that make one's social group status salient; this may involve experiencing or witnessing discrimination or perceiving oneself to be in a minority status.

The person begins to explore his or her social or cultural status and heritage, forming a new identity around these themes. This often involves a period of **immersion** in activities and groups of one's own social group. This stage may begin with anger about discrimination and oppression by dominant groups but tends to lead to a focus on the strengths of one's social group or cultural heritage.

The individual internalizes the newly formed social identity, strengthening commitment to the social group, before emerging into **transformed relations** with mainstream culture. For example, for gay men and lesbians, the experiences of "coming out" to others are important developmental steps at this stage (Rosario, Hunter, Maguen, Gwadz, & Smith, 2001).

Social identities are especially salient for oppressed groups, as they explore the realities of oppression and seek strengths in their own heritages (Birman, 1994; Helms, 1994; Phinney, 2003; Varas-Diaz & Serrano-Garcia, 2003). Yet members of privileged groups also develop social identities as they become aware of human diversity, social boundaries, and injustices (e.g., White identity development; Helms, 1994).

Identity development models have some limitations (Frable, 1997). A person may not go through all the stages or may not go through them in order or may repeat stages. This suggests that the stages are better understood as states, different ways of viewing the world, but not necessarily in a developmental sequence. These models also may be difficult to apply to individuals who identify as multiethnic. It is also important to recognize the intertwining of multiple social identities within a single person (e.g., gender, social class, and spirituality) (Frable, 1997; Hurtado, 1997).

Newer social identity models address such limitations. For example, Sellers, Smith, Shelton, Rowley, and Chavous (1998) proposed and validated a model of

African American racial identity that focuses on multiple dimensions of racial identity rather than a hierarchy of stages. It recognizes that the salience of racial identity is influenced by situational and larger contextual factors and that an individual may hold multiple social identities. It focuses on the cultural, historical, and personal experiences of African Americans and on multiple ideologies and worldviews among that population.

Many studies have established that higher levels of perceived racial or ethnic discrimination are associated with greater distress, depression, and impaired functioning among African Americans, Latinos, and Asians (e.g., Sellers & Shelton, 2003; Williams & Williams-Morris, 2000; Alegria et al., 2004). What has not been clear is how the potential negative health effects of discrimination might be addressed or even prevented. So, racial identity researchers have begun to investigate how racial and ethnic identity may act as a buffer from developing psychosocial problems. For example, in samples of African American youth, stronger ethnic-racial identity has been correlated with more active coping with stressors and fewer aggressive acts (Caldwell, Kohn-Wood, Schmeelk-Cone, Chavous, & Zimmerman, 2004; McMahon & Watts, 2002).

In a series of longitudinal studies of African American adolescents and young adults, the centrality of racial identity (i.e., the importance a person places on his or her racial identity) was a protective buffer when study participants experienced racism and was associated with less alcohol use (Sellers et al., 2003; Caldwell et al., 2004). Yet the context of these perceived experiences of racism played an important role. When African American adolescents reported more perceived discrimination experiences, they appeared to be at risk for developing more negative images of African Americans themselves and for developing expectations that non–African Americans would hold more negative views of them as African Americans (Seaton, Yip, & Sellers, 2009). Interestingly, expectations of negative views of African Americans were associated with the reporting of more discrimination experiences, acting as a risk factor for the adolescents (Sellers, Copeland-Linder, Martin et al., 2006). However, recognizing racism was also a necessary step in preparing these adolescents to cope with racism (Sellers et al., 2006).

Having a well-developed positive racial identity also appeared to protect students from racist experiences. African American college students with a well-formed racial identity had lower levels of depression (Yip, Sellers, & Seaton, 2006), and African American adolescents reported better functioning and well-being when they had positive racial identities (Seaton, Sellers, & Scottham, 2006). Future research will focus on understanding the process by which identity develops and the content of the identities that individuals hold (Scottham, Cooke, Sellers, & Ford, 2010).

Many identity development models explicitly address issues of oppression while making sense of lived experiences. The models help to explain some dynamics of relations between social groups, especially in high school and college. Tatum (1997; 2004) answered a question often asked by White students, "Why are all the Black kids sitting together in the cafeteria?" She used developmental theories to describe how African American students (and, by extension, other subordinated groups) sitting together are often in a stage of **immersion**: responding to experiences (often discriminatory) that made their racial status salient and exploring the resources and strengths of their peers and heritage.

Research about the importance of one's ethnic and racial identity for psychosocial functioning for racial and ethnic minorities has started to identify potential strategies for coping. However, research on White or European American identity has only recently began to take shape. Theorists and advocates have written about what it means to be White in the U.S. and Canada, such as the relative privilege of White persons and the guilt that some White persons have expressed about racial discrimination (e.g., Spanierman, Todd, & Anderson, 2009). Central to this discussion is the argument that most White persons do not report or have to cope with the same types or frequency of racial discrimination as ethnic minorities.

In attempts to address racism, some persons have suggested that a strategy of being "color blind" can avoid racism or discrimination based on racism. Interestingly, the few studies that have examined color blindness have suggested that there are costs of holding these views. For example, in two separate studies, White college students who reported not observing racial differences by being "color blind" reported more negative attitudes toward persons of other racial or ethnic groups on average than those that recognized racial differences (Carter, Helms, & Juby, 2004; Spanierman, Neville, Liao et al., 2008). The findings suggest that a strategy of looking past "color" may be more akin to avoiding racial issues rather than addressing them and thus has costs for its proponents.

An alternative research program is developing to understand the costs of racism to White persons. Todd, Spanierman, and Aber (2010) investigated the emotional responses that White college students had to their perceived Whiteness. They focused on understanding students responses to interviews and essays about how they experience and address racism; in particular, they focused on students' (a) potential for empathy with other racial groups, (b) guilt about White privilege, and (c) racial fear of non-Whites. Their findings suggest that having higher racial fear was associated with more negative emotional responses and distress when discussing how to address racism and White privilege. Conversely, those who had more empathy for persons of different racial backgrounds reported more positive emotions. White guilt was associated with negative emotions, but having more or less guilt was not related to reduced stress when discussing racism and White privilege (Todd, Spanierman, & Aber, 2010). This area of research is only developing, but it holds promise for identifying better ways that racism and discrimination might be addressed, particularly in classrooms.

Acculturation Models

- A student leaves her native South Korea to attend graduate school in Canada.

- A young Diné (Navajo) man must choose between career advancement that would mean leaving his home reservation, weakening ties to his family and culture, or staying home in jobs that will mean less income and prestige.

- An African American student must choose whether to attend a predominantly African American college or a predominantly White one.

- An Asian American and a Mexican American—college friends—talk a lot about how to balance a future career with loyalty to their families. They realize that they are experiencing differences between mainstream U.S. cultural trends and their own cultural backgrounds.

- Families from several villages leave a civil war in their home country and immigrate to the same city in the United States.

These examples pose a number of questions—three of which we take up here: To what extent do persons continue to identify or maintain relationships with their culture of origin? To what extent do they identify or maintain relationships with the host or dominant culture? How do communities change when they receive persons from other cultures?

Acculturation refers to changes in individuals related to the contact between two (or more) cultures that the person experiences (Birman, Trickett, & Buchanan, 2005; Sonn & Fisher, 2010). Culture here is used in a general sense that may also refer to ethnicity, nationality, race, or other dimensions of diversity. Although psychological acculturation research and interventions have focused primarily on the individual, community psychologists have emphasized an understanding of acculturation as a process that affects individuals and host communities (e.g., Birman, 1994; Dinh & Bond, 2008). Contact between cultural groups usually involves change by each of them to some extent, although differences in political and economic power can complicate the interaction. Individuals are nested in communities, and a two-way process of group contact is required to understand acculturation (Birman, 1994). For some, more than two cultures are involved. In this section, we present the more traditional, person-centered models for understanding acculturation and then show how community psychology's interest in context is expanding research and action focused on acculturation.

A terminological note: In some fields, **acculturation** has meant identification with the dominant or host culture and loss of ties to one's culture of origin. Following Berry (1994, 2003) and Birman (1994), we will term that loss of one's host culture as **assimilation**. Also, **enculturation** refers to developing within one's culture of origin, not involving change through relations with another culture (Birman, 1994).

Psychological Acculturation In psychological theories, person-centered understandings of acculturation may be behaviorally expressed, for example, in choices of language, clothing, food, gender roles, child-rearing strategies, or religious affiliation. It may also be internally expressed: One's personal identity, values, emotions, aspirations, and spirituality are grounded in culture. Berry (1994) proposed a model of psychological acculturation to describe experiences of immigrants adjusting to a new (host) culture; it can be extended to address other subordinated, minority, or indigenous groups. Berry's model assumes that in psychological acculturation, the individual identifies with one or the other

TABLE 7.1   Four Acculturative Strategies

	Identification with Dominant Culture	
Identification with Culture of Origin	Stronger	Weaker
Stronger	Biculturality	Separation
Weaker	Assimilation	Marginality

Note: Strategies blend into each other. Thus, we have labeled identification with each culture in relative terms: *stronger* and *weaker*.
SOURCE: Berry (1994, p. 126).

culture, with both, or with neither. This leads to the four strategies listed in Table 7.1 and subsequently described (Berry, 2003; LaFromboise, Coleman, & Gerton, 1993). You should understand these four strategies as blending into each other, not as simple, sharply demarcated categories.

Separation   Individuals pursue this strategy if they identify with their culture of origin, develop language and skills primarily for participating in that culture, live primarily within communities of that culture, and/or interact with the dominant culture only in limited ways (e.g., work or other economic exchanges). Separation has been a recurrent theme (and one adaptive strategy) in the histories of African Americans, French-speaking Canadians, Native Americans, and immigrants to many countries who live and work in their own ethnic communities. (Separation is not the same as segregation. If members of the dominant culture act in this way while reserving political, economic, and social power for their group, segregation is a more appropriate term.)

Assimilation   On the other hand, if individuals give up identifying with their culture of origin to pursue identification with the language, values, and communities of the dominant culture, they are assimilating. Assimilation is an acculturation strategy used by some immigrants, refugees, and similar groups in a new host culture. The idea of the "melting pot" for immigrants to the United States has usually meant assimilation to the dominant Anglo American culture.

Some form of behavioral (but not internal) assimilation may be the only strategy available under powerful systems of oppression. In such circumstances, some members of a subordinated population may be able to "pass" as a member of the dominant group. However, passing can exact a psychic price because it involves keeping secrets and maintaining a divided identity. Furthermore, assimilation may be impossible for individuals and groups who differ from the dominant cultural group in obvious ways, such as skin color. The first stage of many ethnic and racial identity development models involves attempts to assimilate by persons of color, who abandon it when they are rebuffed by discrimination (Phinney, 2003).

Marginality   This occurs if individuals do not or cannot identify with either their culture of origin or with the dominant culture. This strategy may not be chosen but can result from loss of contact with one's culture of origin combined with exclusion from the dominant culture. It appears to be the strategy usually associated with the greatest psychological distress (Berry & Sam, 1997; Vivero & Jenkins, 1999). Note that this involves not only being marginalized by a dominant culture (something that may also happen with separation) but also loss of contact or participation with one's culture of origin.

Integration and Biculturality   If individuals identify or participate in meaningful ways with both their culture of origin and the dominant culture, they are using a strategy that Berry (1994) termed **integration**—a strategy others consider **bicultural** (Birman, 1994; LaFromboise et al., 1993). It deserves a longer description in the section below.

Bicultural Competence

LaFromboise et al. (1993) defined eight characteristics of bicultural competence, summarized in Table 7.2.

The first two characteristics concern aspects of one's identity. A **strong individual identity** is crucial. This involves self-awareness and the ability to distinguish one's values and choices from others. A **strong cultural identity**—based on integration with one's culture of origin—is also crucial. This identification with one's cultural roots is a resource for the development of bicultural competence, providing a secure base from which to explore and learn about the second culture. Identification with one's culture of origin is also an emphasis of identity development models (Birman, 1994). Without identification with at least one culture, a person may possess knowledge and skills of two cultures but not be deeply identified with either. That state resembles biculturality in behavior but emotionally is more like marginality.

Three further characteristics are cognitive and emotional. The first involves sufficient **knowledge of both cultures**: cultural beliefs, social institutions, and

T A B L E 7.2   Characteristics of Bicultural Competence

Identity Factors

Strong individual identity

Strong cultural identity

Cognitive/Emotional Factors

Knowledge of both cultures

Positive attitude toward both cultures

Sense of bicultural efficacy

Social/Behavioral Factors

Communication competence in both cultures

Behavioral skills in both cultures

Social support networks in both cultures

SOURCE: LaFromboise et al., 1993, pp. 402–409.

everyday social norms. The individual may find ways to integrate differing values or need to know how and when to conform one's behavior to one culture or the other. The second characteristic is **having positive attitudes about both cultures**—being able to recognize strengths in each and holding both in positive regard. The third is a sense of **bicultural efficacy**, the belief or confidence that one can live satisfactorily within both cultures without compromising one's cultural and personal identity. (Note that conditions of oppression can make the latter two aspects difficult.)

LaFromboise and colleagues cite studies showing that many Native American children developed greater knowledge of the dominant Anglo American culture as they moved through school while also maintaining allegiance to tribal interpersonal norms. In universities in which Anglo American norms were dominant, bicultural Native American students knew more about strategies for academic achievement than Native American peers immersed mainly in their tribal culture. But the bicultural students were also more likely to enroll in courses and participate in cultural activities based on Native American cultures.

Bicultural competence also involves three social/behavioral factors. **Communication competence** in the languages of both cultures and a **repertoire of behavioral skills** in both cultures are necessary. For example, studies of Latino/Latina and Native American college students in the United States indicate that possessing academic and social skills for both the dominant culture and the culture of origin promoted personal adjustment to college (LaFromboise et al., 1993).

Finally, bicultural competence involves cultivating **social support networks** within both cultures. (LaFromboise terms this *groundedness*.) These networks promote learning bicultural skills and attitudes and provide emotional support for persisting in the face of cultural conflicts and obstacles. Such networks are stronger if they include both bonding ties (e.g., family, friends) and bridging ties for information and contacts.

There are many ways to be bicultural. Some involve strong identification with one's culture of origin and behavioral participation in the dominant culture but not deeper identification with it (Birman, 1994; Ortiz-Torres et al., 2000). This may especially fit the experiences of members of social groups faced with persistent discrimination. For others, particularly immigrant groups, a bicultural strategy may involve identification with both one's culture of origin as well as a deepening identification over time with the dominant culture (Birman, 1994; Phinney, 2003).

The Need for a Contextual Perspective in Acculturation

Two ancient stories from Jewish tradition—also familiar to Muslims and Christians—illustrate the value of acculturation strategies other than biculturality for a small cultural group within a powerful, oppressive society. Joseph, a Jew sold into slavery in Egypt by his brothers, assimilated to Egyptian society, rose to power, and became the instrument for preserving Jewish culture in a time of famine. Years later, Moses, a Jew reared by Egyptian royalty with little knowledge of his cultural heritage, learned about that heritage and then led a separatist movement and exodus from Egypt. In different ways, both Joseph and Moses helped preserve their culture. (Adapted from Birman, 1994, p. 281)

What is the most adaptive psychological acculturation strategy? As with Joseph and Moses, that depends on the context (Birman, 1994; Trickett, 1996; 2009).

Bicultural integration is not necessarily common. For example, in a study of adolescents whose families had immigrated from Latin America to Washington, D.C., most adolescents were highly involved in Hispanic culture and social networks (separation) or in wider American culture and networks (assimilation); few were highly involved in both (Birman, 1998). Among a sample of New York City residents of Puerto Rican ancestry, only about one-fourth were bicultural. About one-third were predominantly involved in Puerto Rican culture (separation), one-fourth were involved predominantly in U.S. culture (assimilation), and the remainder uninvolved in either culture (marginality) (Cortes, Rogler, & Malgady, 1994). Many members of immigrant groups in the United States pursue bicultural strategies—particularly family members born in the United States—but not all do (Phinney, 2003).

Bicultural integration is also not necessarily adaptive; findings on acculturation and personal adjustment for adolescents and for adults are mixed (Birman et al., 2002; Phinney, 2003). From an intersectional perspective, gender, social class, sexual orientation, religiosity, family dynamics, and the qualities of the setting can have an impact on the effects of particular acculturation strategies. A study of adolescents from the former Soviet Union in two U.S. communities found a number of differences between communities in the dynamics of acculturation and adaptation for these youth (Birman, Trickett, & Buchanan, 2005). Both social identity development and acculturation are far more complex processes than we have portrayed in our introduction here. For community psychologists, acculturation must be understood as related to multiple ecological levels (Trickett, 2009) and examine changes in host settings as well as individuals (Dinh & Bond, 2008).

How do neighborhoods, towns, and regions change with the influx of new residents? What specific qualities of communities or community settings promote appreciation of other communities and cultures and a wider sense of unity and affirmative diversity (Jones, 1994; Kress & Elias, 2000)? Smith (2008) examined community adaptations in Utica, New York, a city that has experienced a tremendous amount of immigration and resettlement of refugees during the last 20 years. One in six residents was born outside the United States. Given some rhetoric about immigration, such a wave of immigration might have been feared as "destroying the community" and "taking away jobs." While Utica had some resources for assisting immigrants (e.g., refugee social service agencies) and a history and social norms of helping immigrants (e.g., high levels of volunteering, many citizens whose parents or grandparents were immigrants), such a large influx over a short period of time required many adaptations.

Smith described clusters of adaptation in Utica, where newcomers actually helped reclaim and improve decaying neighborhoods and where some employers were grateful for a hardworking labor force to help a city that had lost much of its population. In the areas of education and health care, local organizations and institutions appeared to make many accommodations for new residents who left Bosnia, Burma, Somalia, and the Sudan. In the areas of housing and employment, there were fewer adaptations in policies and practices to make interaction more accessible. Smith observed that there are fewer formal roles for social service personnel in housing and employment domains of public life and likely fewer resources dedicated to helping with adaptations for new residents.

Utica has experienced challenges to its accommodation of such a large wave of immigrants. From interviews conducted with community leaders in Utica, there were substantial challenges with transportation, the need for translators in several languages, and different cultural expectations of immigrants for participation in health care, school, and urban life. Smith (2008) noted that there appeared to be more intergroup conflict among refugee populations than between refugee groups and U.S.-born Uticans. While Smith's study focused on one community, it helps to illustrate how a community psychology framework can be applied to understanding acculturation and immigration. Community psychologists are working to develop knowledge about greater understanding of community processes and how to support communities' adaptation efforts (Tseng & Yoshikawa, 2008).

CONCEPTS OF LIBERATION AND OPPRESSION

Whenever you feel like criticizing anyone, he told me, just remember that all the people in this world haven't had the advantages that you've had. (Fitzgerald, 1925/1995, *The Great Gatsby*, p. 5)

Consider these facts about U.S. society:

- Women who worked full-time in 2008 earned only 80% of the income of men who worked full-time (Bureau of Labor Statistics, 2009).
- Median household income in 2008 for Whites was $55,530, for Hispanics was $37,913 (68% of the White median), and for Blacks was $34,218 (62% of the White median) (U.S. Census Bureau, 2009).
- Inequality of household income is increasing steadily. From 1979–2009, incomes (adjusted for inflation) rose 95% for the highest-earning 5% of the population and 281% for the top 1%, while gains for the lower four-fifths of the population were much lower. Because of this trend, there is now "greater income concentration at the top of the income scale than at any time since 1928" (Center on Budget and Policy Priorities, 2010, p. 4).
- Upward economic mobility is decreasing; compared to earlier periods, fewer people are now moving from lower-income groups into higher ones (Inequality.org, 2004; Scott & Leonhardt, 2005).

- Wealth (net worth, not yearly income) is highly skewed. The wealthiest 1% of the population controls 34.6% of the nation's private assets, and the next 19% owns 50.5%. This means that 80% of American households own only 15% of the nation's private wealth (Wolff, 2010).

- "From 1990 to 2005, CEOs' pay increased almost 300% (adjusted for inflation), while production workers gained a scant 4.3%" (Domhoff, 2010).

- Large income gaps between rich and poor are correlated with lower life expectancy for the entire population, not just the poorest (American Psychological Association, 2010).

- In 2008, about one in every six U.S. residents and about one in every 10 children had no health insurance. Among Blacks and Hispanics, these figures are much higher (U.S. Census Bureau, 2009). Illness is more common among those with the lowest incomes (American Psychological Association, 2010).

- The rate of child poverty in the United States is higher than in 16 developed countries (Lott & Bullock, 2001).

- Growing up in sustained poverty places children at higher risk of many problems and illnesses (Bradley & Corwyn, 2002; McLoyd, 1998). Many low-income families are resilient, but they face daunting money-related challenges.

These and similar differences among persons and families do not result from cultural factors. They are better understood in terms of power and access to resources. To understand such differences, concepts of liberation and oppression are needed (e.g., Bond, Hill, Mulvey, & Terenzio, 2000; Fanon, 1963; Friere, 1970/1993; Martin-Baro, 1994; Miller, 1976; Nelson & Prilleltensky, 2010; Watts & Serrano-Garcia, 2003).

Oppression: Initial Definitions

Oppression occurs in a hierarchical relationship in which a dominant group unjustly holds power and resources and withholds them from another group (see Prilleltensky, 2008; Tatum, 1997; Watts, Williams, & Jagers, 2003). The more powerful group is termed the **dominant** or **privileged group**; the less powerful is the **oppressed** or **subordinated group**. Oppressive hierarchies are often based on ascribed characteristics fixed at birth or otherwise outside personal control (e.g., gender or race).

For example, oppressive systems in the United States create a privileged group of White persons and subordinate groups of all others, including African Americans, Latinos/Latinas, Asian Americans, and Native Americans. Similarly, men, persons without physical or mental disabilities, heterosexuals, and those with economic power and resources are privileged. Oppressive systems may also create intermediate groups. For example, South African apartheid and British colonialism in India created classes such as "coloured" South Africans and "Anglo Indians"—subordinated by the dominant class but more privileged than the lowest classes (Sonn & Fisher, 2003, 2010). Class privilege operates along a continuum in many Western societies; middle classes are more privileged than those with lowest incomes, but they are still less powerful and often manipulated by the wealthy. In U.S. history, some immigrant groups were only gradually accepted by dominant Anglo American groups. Racial privilege in the United States today often has different effects among diverse persons of color.

Resources controlled by a dominant or privileged group may include economic resources, status and influence, sociopolitical power, interpersonal connections among elites, the power to frame discussion of conflicts (often exerted through media and educational systems), representation in political and corporate offices, and even inequalities in marriage and personal relationships. Perhaps most insidious are ideologies and myths to convince members of subordinated groups that they actually are inferior (McDonald, Keys, & Balcazar, 2007). This sense of inferiority is termed **internalized oppression**.

Members of privileged groups are granted resources, opportunities, and power not by their own efforts but by oppressive systems (McIntosh, 1998). Members of a privileged class may not recognize or consent to this, but they are granted the privileges anyway. In the United States, many White persons oppose racial discrimination, but they are privileged by systems that reliably produce these effects. Similar statements apply to individuals in other privileged groups, such as men, the wealthy, and heterosexuals.

Subordinated groups are denied access to much power and many resources, without their consent. However, they are not powerless. They may resist injustice in many ways—direct and indirect. The strengths of their cultural heritage may provide resources for doing this. Subordinated groups may also develop ways of coping with oppression and protecting themselves. For example, women who are victims of battering often learn to interpret the nuances of their partners' moods (Tatum, 1997). Persons with disabilities may remove themselves from oppressive environments. They may also create new narratives about themselves that challenge or reframe dominant cultural narratives discounting their capabilities and potential (McDonald, Keys, & Balcazar, 2007). The subordinated group may comply overtly with oppressors yet create personal identities revealed only with other members of their group, as "coloured" South Africans did under apartheid (Sonn & Fisher, 1998, 2003).

Oppressive systems have long historical roots. Those systems, not individuals currently living within them, are the sources of injustice (Prilleltensky & Gonick, 1994; Freire, 1970/1993). For example, to dismantle sexism, **patriarchy** (the system of unearned male power) is the opponent, not individual men. In fact, patriarchy harms men as well as women—for example, by the emotional restriction and costly competitiveness of masculine role expectations. Of course, the harm is less for a privileged group than for subordinated groups. Watts (2010) referred to this phenomenon when he wrote about the need for men "to slay Frankenstein." He suggested that oppressive masculinity is like the creature that Dr. Frankenstein created but could not control. While one may empathize with Dr. Frankenstein's struggles, one may also find him particularly well suited for confronting the harmful creature. In using this evocative metaphor, Watts points out how men are agents and targets of oppressive masculinity. He shows how dismantling oppression may liberate privileged and oppressed from a system that dehumanizes both (see also Friere, 1970/1993; Mankowski & Maton, 2010).

In complex societies, multiple forms of oppression exist. Steele (1997) summarized evidence that in the United States, even the best African American students are affected by racial stereotypes and even the most mathematically talented women are similarly affected by stereotypes about women's mathematical ability. Moreover, the same individual can be privileged by one system while subordinated by another. In the United States, Black men are oppressed by racism and privileged by sexism; White women are oppressed by sexism and privileged by racism; working-class and low-income White men are oppressed by socioeconomic classism, while privileged by racism and sexism.

Oppression: Multiple Ecological Levels

The power relationships of the larger society are often mirrored at multiple ecological levels in macrosystems, communities, organizations, microsystems, and individual prejudices (James et al., 2003; Prilleltensky, 2008).

"Breathing Smog": Social Myths   Oppressive hierarchies are sustained in part by widely accepted myths that rationalize them (Freire, 1970/1993; Prilleltensky & Nelson, 2002; Watts, 1994). Blaming the victims of macrosystem economic forces is one example (Ryan, 1971). As a result, members of dominant groups and even subordinated groups often fail to recognize how systems of oppression are creating injustices. Tatum (1997) likened this process to "breathing smog." After a while, one does not notice it; the air seems natural.

One example of "smog" can be a false reading of differences in educational attainment or income. Values of individualism channel our thinking to interpret these as the result of individual effort or ability. This bias is so well established among people in Western nations that it is known as the "fundamental attribution error" in social psychology. While individual efforts do matter a great deal, it is also true that oppressive systems reward effort and ability among members of the privileged group while often ignoring the same qualities among members of the subordinated group. Recognizing that injustice, especially for members of the privileged group, would call into question cherished beliefs about individual freedom—something that many persons would rather not think about. So, when Whites earn more than other racial groups or men earn more than women, we are predisposed to interpret those differences in individual terms, ignoring broader factors. Rice (2001) reviews studies that indicate such social myths especially harm women in poverty.

In fact, an oppressive system often works best when a few members of an oppressed group break through to enjoy the privileges of the dominant group. They may be *tokens* accepted only to improve public relations, or perhaps they are the best at assimilating the values and behaviors of the dominant class. Their success seems to offer a lesson about the importance of individual effort, but it obscures a review of social conditions across levels of analysis. In addition, research shows that these token individuals are often placed in a bind—being held to higher performance standards than members of the privileged group (Ridgeway, 2001).

The Role of Mass Media   Print media, television, movies, radio, and the Internet comprise a very influential macrosystem. The presence and status of women, persons of color, and other oppressed groups have increased in U.S. mass media in the last half century. Yet mass media continue to provide misleading images of oppressed populations.

Often, the poor are simply ignored in mainstream news; Wall Street and economic-corporate news are headlined, while unemployment is sporadically mentioned, and economic inequality seldom covered. When news stories do cover poverty, they frequently ignore such macrosystem factors as low wages and high housing costs. Although U.S. drug users and dealers are most often European American men, in news and crime shows, they most often appear as urban African American and Latino men. Low-income women also are portrayed negatively (Gilliam & Iyengar, 2000; Bullock, Wyche, & Williams, 2001). Gilens (1996) investigated coverage of poverty in major U.S. news magazines, finding that while African Americans comprised less than one-third of persons living in poverty, every person pictured in news magazine stories about the "underclass" was African American. This bias had real effects: Public opinion polls cited by Gilens showed that U.S. citizens consistently overestimated the proportion of the poor who are Black.

Institutional Oppression: Workplaces   Organizational policies can have discriminatory effects, even when administered by well-meaning individuals. For example, reliance on standardized test scores in college admissions can exclude otherwise promising students of color and those who are economically disadvantaged.

The multiple barriers—or *labyrinth*—that women face in organizations is another example (Eagly & Carli, 2007). Studies of work communication show that in mixed-sex groups, men talk more, make more suggestions, use more assertive speech and gestures, and influence group decisions more often. These acts indicate the use of power in a group, and studies indicate that both women and men accept male leaders who use them competently. But when women use these actions to lead assertively, the response is often different. Many men and even women feel discomfort, and emotional backlash is more likely to occur, even if not voiced openly. For example, assertive women managers are more likely to be considered hostile than equally assertive men (Heilman, 2001). The source of discomfort is that assertive women contradict subtle, socially constructed (and unjust) expectations about who can legitimately exercise these forms of power (Carli, 1999, 2003; Ridgeway, 2001; Rudman & Glick, 2001). In other words, assertive women are challenging hierarchical systems of oppression. The discomfort and backlash even among other women indicates that an established system of power and roles is involved, not simply men.

Reviews of psychological research also indicate that women's work performance and leadership, even when identical to men's, is still often rated less positively (Carli, 2003; Crosby, Iyer, Clayton, & Downing, 2003; Eagly & Carli, 2007; Heilman, 2001). When men and women submit otherwise identical résumés for jobs, men's résumés are often evaluated more positively (Ridgeway, 2001). Even when undergraduate students were asked in several studies to hire a student for a campus job, both men and women raters preferred men over equally qualified women (Carli, 1999).

Pager (2003) conducted a field experiment to test the roles of race and criminal record in hiring. Four male testers answered advertisements for entry-level positions in the Milwaukee area in 2001. Two were White, one presenting credentials with no criminal record, the other presenting otherwise identical credentials but also reporting a (fabricated) felony conviction for selling cocaine and serving 18 months in prison. Two other testers were Black, with the same credentials and manipulation of criminal background. Testers appeared in person to apply for positions; they rotated which individual presented evidence of a criminal record. The pairs applied for a total of 350 jobs. Very few employers actually checked applicants' references; most seemed to accept their self-reports. The dependent variable was the rate of job offers or callbacks for further interviews from employers.

The results showed that Whites received callbacks or offers more than twice as often as Blacks. In fact, Whites reporting a felony drug conviction were more likely to receive callbacks or job offers than Blacks with no criminal record at all. Similar studies in other U.S. localities have found similar racial discrimination (Crosby et al., 2003; Pager, 2003).

Many social-psychological studies show that individuals who believe themselves free of prejudice nonetheless can behave in discriminatory ways (Jones, 1997, 1998). The widespread discrimination documented by Pager (2003) and others is an institutional and societal issue, not simply an individual matter.

Institutional Oppression: Schools   In the United States, schools are often believed to be the pathway to racial integration and to upward economic mobility. For some, this is true. But they often simply perpetuate existing race and class differences (Condron, 2009; Fine & Burns, 2003; Hochschild, 2003; Lott, 2001). One reason is residential racial segregation. In addition, reliance on local funding of schools and great disparities of wealth between school districts create much richer opportunities for some students than others. Within schools, tracking of students, largely based on test scores, shunts students of color and those from lower-income families disproportionately into lower-quality classes that do not prepare them for college or competitive jobs (Lott, 2001; Weinstein, 2002a). Further, teachers and schools may not adequately consider many students' and their families in terms of the knowledge and resources they bring to the classroom (Gonzalez, Moll, & Amanti, 2005).

Intergroup Relations and Individual Prejudices   Research on intergroup relations in social psychology demonstrates that as humans, we often hold positive attitudes about our in-group (who we see as similar to ourselves) while stereotyping and even holding prejudices about out-group members (those we see as different). This is an important insight for community psychology, as it reminds us that we are likely to approach a problem and attempt to solve it with an **ethnocentric** understanding or definition of the problem, believing that our own way is best. Examining these ethnocentric assumptions and collaborating across groups are key components of cultural competence, to which we will turn later in this chapter.

Members of both dominant and subordinated groups thus may hold stereotypes and prejudices about the other group. However, an insight of the liberation perspective is that not everyone's stereotypes and prejudices have the same effects. If a person is in a more powerful role (e.g., employer, teacher, police officer, or elected official), his or her biases have greater effects on others. Members of privileged groups have more influence in their organizations, communities, and societies. Members of the subordinated group are not free of prejudices, but theirs are less powerful because their subordinated status limits their influence. For example, in U.S. society, both Whites and persons of color are likely to hold at least some stereotypes and prejudices toward the other. Yet White persons as a group dominate economic, political, and social institutions (e.g., access to employment, housing, education, mortgages and loans, favorable mass media coverage, and political power). The biases of powerful Whites become part of an interlocking set of social arrangements that perpetuate this control of resources—in short, a system of racism (Jones, 1997). All Whites—even those who oppose racism—benefit from this system; inevitably, they are privileged by it. Similar dynamics perpetuate other forms of oppression.

Table 7.3 summarizes principles of the liberation perspective.

The Liberation Perspective: A Call to Action

> Liberation in its fullest sense requires the securing of full human rights
> and the remaking of a society without roles of oppressor and oppressed.
> (Watts, Williams, & Jagers, 2003, p. 187)

The liberation perspective is not just an intellectual analysis; it is a call to action. It explains injustices and names an opponent: the oppressive system. It also provides an orientation for something positive to work toward. The aim is to change the system, to emancipate both the privileged and the oppressed (Friere, 1970/1993). First-order change in this context would mean the currently oppressed group simply replaces the currently privileged group in power—a reshuffling within the oppressive system. Second-order change dismantles the oppressive system and its inequalities. That is the aim of liberation.

Members of subordinated groups usually understand the system of oppression better than those who are privileged by it. Frequent participation in relationships where one is privileged dulls the awareness of the privileged person, making injustices seem natural (breathing smog). But the same encounters can lead to insights by the subordinated. For example, European Americans are seldom forced to confront the existence of racism, while members of other racial groups have perhaps daily experience with it. This means that liberatory efforts need leaders from the

TABLE 7.3   Assumptions and Concepts of the Liberation Perspective

1. Oppression occurs in a hierarchical relationship in which a dominant group unjustly holds power and resources and withholds them from another group.

2. The more powerful group is the dominant or privileged group; the less powerful is the oppressed or subordinated group. A person's group membership is often determined by birth or other factors beyond one's personal control.

3. Resources controlled by a dominant group may include economic resources, status and influence, sociopolitical power, interpersonal connections, and the power to frame public discussion of issues.

4. The oppressive system grants unearned privileges to members of the dominant group—regardless of whether they recognize or consent to them.

5. The oppressed group resists oppression—directly or indirectly—with the power they have.

6. Multiple forms of oppression exist. An individual may be privileged by one form of oppression and subordinated by another.

7. Oppression involves multiple ecological levels: macrosystems, localities, organizations, interpersonal relationships, and individual prejudices.

8. Social myths rationalize an oppressive system. Tatum (1997) likened this process to "breathing smog": After a while, the workings of the oppressive system seem natural.

9. Because they experience its consequences directly, members of the oppressed group often understand an oppressive system better than members of the dominant group.

10. Any individual may have prejudices, but those of the dominant group are more damaging because they interlock with the power of oppressive systems.

11. Liberation theory is a call to action to work collectively to dismantle oppressive systems.

12. Oppression dehumanizes both oppressor and oppressed. To truly dismantle it, those who oppose it must aim to liberate both the oppressed group and the dominant group from the oppressive system.

SOURCES: Freire (1970/1993); Miller (1976); Nelson & Prilleltensky (2005); Olsson, Powell, and Steuhling (1998); Prilleltensky and Gonick (1994); Tatum (1997); Watts (1994); and Watts & Serrano-Garcia (2003).

subordinated group to sustain awareness of where the real issues lie. Liberation also needs commitment from persons in privileged groups to work toward addressing oppression. Paulo Friere (1970/1993), an important theorist of liberation, holds that three resources are needed for dismantling oppression. The first is critical awareness and understanding of the oppressive system. Second is involvement and leadership from members of the subordinated group. Third is collective action; solely individual actions are difficult to sustain against powerful opposition.

Contributions and Limitations of the Liberation Perspective

The liberation and cultural perspectives are complementary. Liberation concepts call attention to the workings of power—often obscured in a cultural perspective. A liberation perspective orients community psychology practice to challenge oppressive conditions *and* to emphasize and support the capacities for oppressed people to take action against problematic conditions that hinder their well-being (Montero, 2007; Prilleltensky & Nelson, 2010). A liberation perspective helps community psychology work toward its values of social justice, empowerment, collaboration and focus on strengths, and fostering individual and collective well-being.

A potential limitation of the liberation perspective is that by emphasizing the different positions of privileged and subordinated groups, it may underestimate the diversity within each of those groups. For example, not all women are identical in resources, power, or viewpoint nor do all Mexican Americans speak with one voice. A second possible limitation is that in its emphasis on social systems, liberation theory can portray members of subordinated groups merely as victims, unless their cultural strengths and resistance to oppression are explicitly recognized.

A third challenge can arise when liberation concepts are used in action. Oppression creates conflict between dominant and subordinated groups. That conflict is often based on real, undeniable injustices. Yet the ideal of liberating both the oppressor and the oppressed may be difficult to sustain in the heat of that conflict. Discussion may be dominated by blaming of individuals or groups rather than blaming social myths and practices. Intergroup conflict research shows that addressing these obstacles requires commitment to developing shared goals and to addressing injustice (Jones, 1997). The long-term value of liberation concepts lies in how well they lead to Friere's (1970/1993) vision of liberating both oppressor and oppressed.

ATTENDING TO DIVERSITY IN THE PRACTICES OF COMMUNITY PSYCHOLOGY

In this book, we view human diversity as both a challenge to address and an asset for improving community psychology work. The concepts in this chapter have a number of implications for community psychology. We first discuss cultural competence among community psychologists and organizations. We next build on our discussion of collaboration that we began in Chapters 2 and 3. Finally, we consider cultural appropriateness of community programs.

Cultural Competence Across Levels of Analysis

Community psychologists seek to understand communities by working within them, which often requires competence for working across cultural boundaries. Definitions and descriptions of cultural competence for community researchers and practitioners vary (e.g., Balcazar et al., 2009; Castro, Barrera, & Martinez, 2004; Guerra & Knox, 2008; Harrell, Taylor, & Burke, 1999; Sasao, 1999) but often contain the following elements (note that several elements parallel the characteristics of bicultural competence described earlier):

- Knowledge of and respect for the characteristics, experiences, beliefs, values, and norms of the cultural group with whom one is working

- Interpersonal-behavioral skills for working within the culture

- Supportive relationships within the culture with whom one is working and in one's own culture

- "[A] professional stance of informed naïveté, curiosity, and humility" (Mock, 1999, p. 40) involving awareness of one's limited knowledge and a commitment to learn

- Awareness of how one's own culture and experiences have shaped one's worldview

- A viewpoint that developing of cultural competence is an ongoing process, not an achievement.

These qualities involve not only cognitive knowledge and behavioral skills but also attitudes. Particularly important are a curiosity about other cultures, a genuine respect for the strengths of a cultural tradition, and a willingness to address differences in privilege and personal experiences with power. However, from a community psychology perspective, cultural competence cannot only be conceptualized as an individual level of analysis issue. When community psychologists begin working with people in a new setting, knowing the history of their concerns, challenges, and past social change efforts is critical to being culturally sensitive community psychology practice (Guerra & Knox, 2008; Trickett, 2009). Furthermore, reflexive community psychology practice requires examining your own culture as well as the people with whom you are doing the work. Community psychologists working to promote cultural competence will often focus on collaborating with organizations rather than working with individuals alone. For example, Balcazar, Suarez-Balcazar, and colleagues have developed a training model for supporting cultural competence (Balcazar et al., 2009) that emphasizes the importance of organizational context as well as individual attitudes and practices in promoting competence.

The model begins at the individual level focused on the following training elements: (1) *desire to engage*, referring to the individual's willingness to participate and learn about cultural diversity; (2) *development of critical awareness* of personal biases toward others who are different in any dimension of cultural diversity; (3) *knowledge* of the multiple factors that can influence diversity and *familiarization* with selected characteristics, histories, values, beliefs, and behaviors of members of diverse cultural groups; and (4) *development and practice of skills* for working effectively with other individuals from diverse cultural backgrounds.

In addition, cultural competence is facilitated or hindered by a fifth critical element: the degree of *organizational support* for cultural competence where the service providers work. Organizations have different levels of readiness for training and for discussing issues that may raise conflict. Through their policies, allocation of resources for training, and willingness to change organizational practices, organizations communicate powerful messages to their members about the importance of cultural competence. The researchers found that individual attitude and knowledge change were possible; however, they also examined organizational practices for changes (e.g., changes in outreach materials that were culturally sensitive and accessible in different languages). They concluded that "[c]ultural competence is a complex process that requires both individual and organizational willingness and commitment to change" (Taylor-Ritzler et al., 2008, p. 89). Viewing it as a process, cultural competence takes time and requires continual adaptation and awareness of the multiple factors.

Negotiating Collaborative Interventions and Research

As implied previously, we do not think that it is possible to become an expert on every dimension of diversity. Furthermore, it may be problematic to view oneself as an expert on dimensions of diversity if that leads one to stop inquiring about diversity and human experience. As community psychologists, approaching intervention and research as collaborations can be very helpful in representing multiple perspectives necessary for these activities to be considered successful by the different stakeholders involved in a project. First, additional information from multiple perspectives can assist in decisions about how to carry out an intervention. Second, information from multiple perspectives can lead to asking different kinds of questions and gathering different indices of success. When working across dimensions of diversity, challenges for communication and understanding can arise. For example, recall from Chapter 4 our discussion of Brodsky and Faryal's (2006) account of a U.S. researcher and Afghan woman who conducted research with an Afghan woman's humanitarian and advocacy organization. Because of the social pressures against women's organizing activities at the time, norms of secrecy and caution limited how interviews and other data could be collected—lest they threaten the well-being of the woman or the organization. The project leaders concluded that collaboration does not mean equal contribution on a project or project components—rather, that "a diverse set of skills of both parties are necessary" for the project to be successful (p. 318).

The experience of this project highlights that the human diversity of community psychologists or anyone involved in conducting research or implementing human services is important to consider. Addressing diversity challenges on professional and personal levels will be important for much community work. Furthermore, negotiating collaborations can place an extra burden on persons considered "insiders" who are working across dimensions of diversity on a project (Gone, 2006). The community's trust with insiders and their social position within the group may be challenged or they may come to be viewed as an outsider more closely related to the project than the community. Knowledge of past intervention or research efforts, the consequence of these activities, and the self-articulated needs of these communities are necessary for working across boundaries of difference in community settings.

When Values of Diversity and Community Conflict

As we discussed in Chapter 6, sense of community is a core value of community psychology and one of the most widely used and studied constructs in community psychology. However, sense of community can become problematic when it conflicts with another core value—the value of human diversity. Several commentators have noted that sense of community can come into conflict with diversity because it tends to emphasize group member similarity and appears to be higher in homogeneous communities (e.g., Caughy, O'Campo, & Muntaner, 2003; Farrell, Aubry, & Coulombe, 2004; Obset & White, 2005).

Townley, Kloos, Green, and Franco (2011) have argued that systematic consideration of a community-diversity dialectic is needed in much community psychology work to identify and address the inherent tension between sense of community and a value in diversity. Reviewing how understanding of diversity figured in their own work on housing environments and well-being, they found that cultural perspectives were required to interpret findings from research on community life in Uganda after displacement in war, experiences of Latino immigrants in the U.S. South, and experiences of persons diagnosed with severe psychiatric disorders integrating into neighborhoods. Townley and colleagues found that the values of diversity or community varied for individuals in settings depending on the cultural context. While conflict in community psychology values can be viewed as being problematic, it might be better viewed as a community-diversity dialectic that is an inherent tension and opportunity in multicultural societies. As community psychologists, it is critical to understand the manner in which individuals function and achieve a sense of community within diverse environments; each initiative will involve its own unique balancing of these values. Considering a community-diversity dialectic in community intervention and research leads us to re-examine our own understanding of the context of our work, of our collaborative relationships, and of potential outcomes (helpful and problematic) in diverse settings.

When Culture and Liberation Conflict

Culture, we believe, cannot become a haven for oppression, but must instead be a space where respect for diversity and participation in the development of new values leads all of us closer to health, dignity, and freedom. (Ortiz-Torres, Serrano-Garcia, & Torres-Burgos, 2000, p. 877)

When cultural traditions contribute to oppression and conflict with liberatory aims, how can this conflict be addressed or resolved? The values and practices of some cultures victimize women overtly or prescribe restrictive social roles for them. (Note that this benevolent sexism is often interpreted as honoring or protecting women.) Many traditional collectivistic cultures grant greater authority to men, some elders, or members of higher castes. Individualistic cultures offer much individual freedom but can tolerate great inequalities and undermine concern for the dispossessed.

Bianca Ortiz-Torres, Irma Serrano-Garcia and Nelida Torres-Burgos (2000) addressed these issues in an article titled "Subverting Culture." As part of an HIV prevention initiative, their aim was to promote the capability of Puerto Rican women to negotiate use of safer-sex precautions with male sex partners. This capacity-building goal conflicts with two cultural values. *Marianismo* defines the culturally feminine role in many Latino/a cultures: a vision of the ideal woman as chaste and virginal, nurturant with men yet obedient to them, based on the Christian image of the Virgin Mary. It leads to sexuality being a topic for only private conversation and often to young women knowing little about their own sexuality. By extolling virginity, *marianismo* can be protective against risky sexual behavior. However, its role in suppressing discussion and understanding of sexuality and its emphasis on obedience to men also leave many women less knowledgeable and powerful in sexual situations. *Machismo* defines the masculine role, emphasizing virility and sexual prowess. In sexual situations, the *marianismo-machismo* combination grants men greater power than women, for whom the contradictory cultural expectations are more difficult (e.g., being chaste vs. pleasing one's partner).

In focus groups and individual interviews, Latina college students (in Puerto Rico and New York City) reported emotional and interpersonal obstacles to discussing safer sex, negotiating with lovers for condom use, nonpenetrative sexuality, and other self-protective actions. Fears of rejection, feelings of hurt and anxiety, men's assertion that these actions demonstrated a lack of trust, and women's own love for their partners were obstacles mentioned by participants. These are universal concerns, but in the context of *marianismo-machismo* values and roles, they are especially powerful.

However, no culture is completely static or unchanging. Women's movements in many cultures have challenged traditions and practices that victimize and disempower women. Moreover, women disadvantaged by cultural values often also have cultural resources. In the Ortiz-Torres et al. study, these included social support from other women, the impact of women's movements within the culture, and contact with different gender roles in other cultures. Ortiz-Torres et al. conclude that feminist community psychologists inside Latino/a culture can work to promote sexual education and open discussion of women's sexuality, to challenge values and practices that harm women, and to build women's personal negotiating skills and social support. These efforts can use traditional *marianismo* conceptions of abstinence and of protecting women so they can build families and serve others. But they can also advocate condom use, nonpenetrative sexuality, and women's power to make decisions and to negotiate as equals in sexual situations.

Three key conclusions emerge about conflicts between culture and liberation. The first is that cultural values often contain contradictions. Such cultural values as *marianismo* and *machismo* have long histories but so do values for protecting Latina women. Similarly, to oppose cultural norms underlying men's violence against women among some Southeast Asian immigrant communities in the United States, women's activists advocated for traditional Southeast Asian cultural values of protecting women (Silka & Tip, 1994, p. 518).

A second point is that cultures are continually evolving in response to external and internal conditions, including contacts with different cultures and diversity within the culture. Efforts for cultural transformation enter a stream of ongoing changes in a culture.

Finally, to be legitimate, cultural transformation needs to be initiated from inside the culture by its own members. Ortiz-Torres and her colleagues developed their intervention as cultural insiders. Similarly, Afghan women initiated the Revolutionary Association of the Women of Afghanistan (RAWA) to advocate for women's and wider human rights in their own nation (Brodsky, 2003). For outsiders to impose their conceptions on a culture raises many questions of social justice.

Designing Culturally Anchored Community Programs

Culturally sensitive or appropriate community programs must address many aspects of the culture for which they are designed. These are best developed in genuine collaboration with members of the local culture and community. Writing from a health promotion perspective, Resnicow and colleagues (1999) proposed a useful distinction for describing cultural issues in designing community programs, borrowed from linguistics: the surface structure and deep structure of a community program.

Surface structure involves observable aspects of a program: race, ethnicity, and gender of its staff; language(s) used; choice of cultural elements, such as food or music; and setting. These elements are important, but surface structure alone may not be enough to make a program effective. For example, Sasao (1999) found that simply having Asian American staff in a clinical service for Asian Americans did not resolve all cultural differences between therapists and clients. As another example, simply being a Black psychologist is not enough to secure the trust of a Black community; that trust must be built (Jordan, Bogat, & Smith, 2001).

Deep structure involves core cultural beliefs, values, and practices. The deep structure of a culture requires historical, psychological, and social knowledge of the culture. For example, some Latino/Latina and African cultural beliefs emphasize supernatural causes for illness as well as natural causes (Resnicow et al., 1999). These multiple explanations of illness will affect willingness to report symptoms, choice of indigenous healers or Western health professionals, and many health-related behaviors. A health promotion outreach program for these populations must address those issues. The sexuality intervention for young Latinas that we described earlier illustrated deep structural elements, addressing values of *marianismo* and *machismo* (Ortiz-Torres et al., 2000). Deep structural cultural programs may appeal most to persons pursuing separation or bicultural strategies, not those seeking assimilation or who are marginalized. Effectiveness of culturally sensitive programs needs to be evaluated in research (Resnicow et al., 1999). (For additional examples of culturally anchored programs, see Harper et al., 2004; Helm, 2003; Jumper-Thurman, Edwards, Plested, & Oetting, 2003; and Potts, 2003).

Alaska Native Spirituality and Sobriety   Alaska Native indigenous communities are using their cultural heritages to create community climates of sobriety, helping individuals and communities prevent and promote recovery from substance abuse (Hazel & Mohatt, 2001; Mohatt et al., 2004). These provide an example of culturally anchored community initiatives, developed by community members, which address both surface and deep structure.

Alaska Native peoples are diverse, yet they share some common cultural elements, especially spiritual perspectives, that offer rich resources for the Native sobriety movement and community sobriety initiatives. Common spiritual elements include beliefs in a Creator, the spirituality of all living beings, the intermingling of the spiritual and material worlds, and the importance of personal awareness of spiritual forces. These offer rich resources for community sobriety initiatives.

Native leaders summarized cultural elements related to sobriety in four interrelated realms of living. Persons and communities promote sobriety in the *physical* realm by using Native healing and traditional foods; by participation in Native cleansing rituals, dancing, singing, and other arts; and by subsistence gathering and hunting. In the *emotional* realm, individuals foster sobriety by experiencing joyful and painful emotions, connecting with family and community, and practicing forgiveness. In the *cognitive* realm, they can learn and take pride in cultural legends, history, and practices; learn the culture's language; and take responsibility for self, family, and community. Sobriety in the *spiritual* realm involves opening one's eyes to the spiritual world, connecting with ancestors, meditation, prayer, and using dreams and visions as guides (Hazel & Mohatt, 2001). Promoting sobriety involves all four realms, strengthening individual development and family and community bonds. Mohatt et al. (2004) described how program developers worked with Native leaders to develop culturally appropriate evaluation methods.

CONCLUSION

In countries across the world, populations are becoming increasingly diverse. For example, in the United States, more than 30% of the U.S. population is composed of ethnic minorities (U.S. Census Bureau, 2009). Furthermore, population estimates suggest that people of color will constitute half of the U.S. population by the year 2050 if current immigration and birth rates continue. As we discussed, growing awareness of human diversity and social inequities in workplaces and community settings has led to new laws (e.g., fair housing and nondiscrimination on the basis of sexuality). Any work done in community settings requires an interest in learning about human diversity and conceptual tools that can guide this lifelong learning.

Two important overall questions remain. First, does this chapter's perspective on human diversity lead to moral relativism, endorsing all value systems (e.g., Nazism, religious intolerance, or oppression of women) as equally morally compelling?

Simply put, no. The perspective of this chapter is concerned with understanding human diversity in context. This involves comprehending other persons and cultures in their own terms, especially their strengths. This often leads to discerning one's own assumptions and values and to deeper awareness of both others and oneself. This process is not easy or simple, but only with such pluralistic, contextual understanding can informed, principled moral stances on human problems be built.

Overarching values, such as the seven values we have proposed for community psychology, help to address such issues. As we discussed in earlier sections, When Culture and Liberation Conflict" and "When Values of Diversity and Community Conflict, action based on principled values, such as social justice, by citizens acting collectively within their own culture can lead to personal and social transformation. Of course, the ways that community psychologists think about social justice or other values are rooted in their own cultural experiences. But community psychologists and others working for change (e.g., for empowerment of women) can ally themselves with members of other cultures or communities who hold similar values within their cultural context.

Second, with all our emphasis on how humans differ across cultural, racial, ethnic, gender, and other boundaries, how can we understand what humans have in common? On what shared basis can multicultural, diverse communities or societies be constructed and sustained?

This question requires some historical perspective. The question may presuppose the desirability of earlier times that seemed harmonious to members of privileged groups because both they and members of subordinated groups "knew their place." It is also important to note that Western social scientists often have assumed that their concepts and perspective were universal and later found those ideas were ethnocentric. Perspectives differ on how best to address this question (e.g., Fowers & Richardson, 1996; Hall, 1997; Sue, 2004). Searching for common ground on overarching values may help as long as we remember that each person's perspective is inevitably limited by his or her own cultural experiences.

Certainly, there is much that is universal in human experience, but we can understand it only if we also understand how others view that experience differently. As William James, one of psychology's founders, asserted: "There is very little difference between one person and another, but what little difference there is, is very important" (cited in Hall, 1997, p. 650).

CHAPTER SUMMARY

1. Important dimensions of human diversity for community psychology include culture, race, ethnicity, gender, sexual orientation, socioeconomic status or social class, ability/disability, age, and spirituality. These dimensions can be separated conceptually, but they converge in community life. Pluralism involves the assumption that everyone has a position somewhere on these dimensions and that each position is to be understood in its own terms. *Intersectionality* examines how these dimensions overlap.

2. Persons are socialized into cultural communities, and this socialization process strongly impacts who we are and how we understand ourselves and others. One important dimension of this socialization process across cultures

is *individualism-collectivism*. This includes conceptions of a more *independent self* or *interdependent self*. Individual and group thinking, emotions, and behavior are influenced by whether a culture is more individualistic or collectivistic, although all cultures must deal with tensions between individual and collective identities. However, the individualism-collectivism concept is useful only for describing broad themes of cultural differences, not for understanding any specific person, group, or culture well.

3. To understand more specific processes of socialization and identity development, *social identity development* models have been proposed. Most assume stages of identity that include an opening stage of unexamined identity, followed by stages of exploration, often within one's own group, and higher stages of forming a social (e.g., racial) identity and learning to relate to both one's own group and the wider world. Many people do not follow the stage sequence, so the "stages" might better be considered "states."

4. The *acculturation* perspective concerns individual adaptation to the interaction of two cultures or groups. Four acculturative strategies can be identified: *separation, assimilation, marginality,* and *biculturality* (or *integration*). (See Table 7.1.)

5. *Bicultural competence* refers to skills and conditions needed for effective adaptation to a second or dominant culture while retaining identification with one's culture of origin. Its eight factors are summarized in Table 7.2. Although evidence supports the value of the bicultural strategy in many circumstances, it is not always the wisest acculturative strategy.

6. Power and access to resources also create group differences. The *liberation perspective* describes social systems of oppression and aims of liberation. Oppression creates an inequality of power between a *dominant, privileged group* and an *oppressed, subordinated group*, often on grounds of factors such as gender or race that an individual cannot change. Oppression is more than prejudice; it is based in social systems that affect privileged and subordinated groups regardless of whether they like it or not. There are multiple systems of oppression (e.g., racism, sexism) working at multiple ecological levels (e.g., social myths, mass media stereotypes). Key elements of liberation theory are summarized in Table 7.3.

7. When culture and liberation conflict, attention to values is needed, and change needs to come from persons and values within the culture. Every culture has some diversity of values, and they change over time; these can be the bases for cultural challenge and transformation.

8. *Cultural competence* for community psychologists consists of qualities that promote genuine understanding and collaboration with members of a culture. Culturally sensitive community programs address the *surface structure* and *deep structure* of a culture.

9. Understanding and respecting human diversity does not mean moral relativism; one can hold strong values while seeking to understand other views. Better understanding of multiple forms of human diversity is needed.

RECOMMENDED READINGS

Bond, M., Hill, J., Mulvey, A. & Terenzio, M. (Eds.). (2000). Special issue part I: Feminism and community psychology. *American Journal of Community Psychology, 28*(5).

Freire, P. (1993). *Pedagogy of the oppressed*. New York: Continuum. (Original work published 1970.)

Trickett, E. J. (2009). Multilevel community-based culturally situated interventions and community impact: An ecological perspective. *American Journal of Community Psychology, 43,* 257–266.

Trickett, E. J., Watts, R. J. & Birman, D. (Eds.). (1994). *Human diversity: Perspectives on people in context*. San Francisco: Jossey-Bass.

Watts, R. & Serrano-Garcia, I. (Eds.). (2003). Special issue section: The psychology of liberation: Responses to oppression. *American Journal of Community Psychology, 31,* 73–204.

RECOMMENDED WEBSITES

American Psychological Association Public Interest Directorate:
http://www.apa.org/pi/

Information on Public Interest Directorate programs on psychological aspects of diversity topics.

Multicultural Pavilion:
http://www.edchange.org/multicultural

Information, exercises, and links to related sites on many dimensions of human diversity. Primarily education topics.

Understanding Prejudice:
http://www.understandingprejudice.org

Exercises, information and links, on a variety of prejudice and social justice issues.

8

Understanding Stress and Coping in Context

Photo provided by authors

OPENING EXERCISE

Think about an important stressful experience in your life. For example, it may have been a single event: a serious illness or injury or failing an important test. It may have been a life transition: beginning college or graduate school, divorce, loss of a job, loss of a loved one, or becoming a parent. It may be an ongoing or long-term situation: living on a low income, a chronic illness, harassment, or having to balance several demanding roles, such as mother, wife, student, and worker. It may be an experience that fits none of these categories well.

Consider the following questions about your experience:

- What was stressful about it for you?

- Was it a short-term or a long-term situation?

- What things did you do to cope with this experience?

- What resources helped you cope with this stressful experience? For example: support from others, your own coping or other skills, beliefs or practices that helped you persevere, money, time.

- How did the experience affect you as a person? What did you learn or how did you grow through this experience?

Box 8.1 contains reflections on personal stress and coping by two community psychologists.

B o x 8.1   Personal Experiences with Stress, Coping, Resources, and Thriving

The following accounts by two community psychologists illustrate some of the processes in this chapter.

Passage to Adulthood

When I was 21 in the summer between my junior and senior years of college, my mother died after long being ill with cancer. My father, sister, and I knew her death was coming—even welcomed it with relief; her cancer had been very painful. But it still came hard, with an emptiness and sense of great loss. Several things about that experience still stand out for me decades later.

Within hours, friends from our church and town began what is a bereavement tradition in many communities: delivering home-cooked food for us and the mourners who would join us. This and many other acts of kindness continued for days.

The next few days were a blur as we attended to the duties and rituals of bereavement in our culture. Some of those were not easy, but they were helpful— even inspiring. I felt I belonged—in extended family and community. I cannot count the ways that my family and I received support from others. Cultural and religious traditions and rituals helped make her life and death meaningful to me.

Sometime later that summer, while still recovering emotionally, I realized that I now had to grow up, especially to make decisions for myself. Like most mothers, mine had been a close personal guide, even

when I disregarded her advice. Her passing was a turning point for me. With the support of my family, friends, and my academic mentor and with spiritual support, the next year was a time of spiraling growth, a year of making choices, the beginning of adulthood. (Jim Dalton)

The End of the Road

It was dark and drizzling rain on a warm March night as I drove to spend the evening with my fiancé. There were few houses or landmarks on the rural county road I was traveling, but I felt reassured that I'd be warned of the approach of the T-shaped intersection by the rumble strips that signaled the stop ahead.

Suddenly, I was struck by the unexpected sight of another road crossing my path. I experienced a moment of disorientation and then realized that I'd missed the stop and was flying through the intersection. Resurfacing work had obliterated the rumble strips.

In the next moment, I was airborne as I sailed over the embankment at the end of the road. My thoughts raced as I quickly sized up the situation and my options. I concluded there was nothing that could be done until the car had landed and come to a stop. I marveled at how clear my thoughts were and vaguely wondered why my life wasn't flashing before me.

Finally, the car landed with a dull, bone-crushing thud and continued its forward motion into a grove of pine trees and scrub oaks. I prayed that I would not hit

---

STRESS AND COPING:
AN ECOLOGICAL-CONTEXTUAL MODEL

This chapter marks a transition point in the book. In our examples and discussion, we begin to apply the conceptual tools of community psychology that were introduced in the previous seven chapters to the prevention of life problems and the promotion of well-being. This chapter introduces a few more critical ways of thinking about how interventions might be developed and then presents examples of how they can be applied. Finally, we present how community psychology's understanding of intervention outcomes is broader than a traditional focus of avoiding illness or harm. This chapter reinforces the foundation in community psychology concepts that you have built over the first seven chapters and prepares you to discuss the models of intervention that are presented in Chapters 9–13.

one. I realized that the deeper the car was propelled into the forest, the less likely I would be found and the farther I'd have to make my way out. If my injuries were extensive, that might not be possible. The car finally came to a stop, slowed by the low scrubs and brush in the forest. I hadn't hit a tree, but once I had recovered my breath, I could quickly tell that I was too badly injured to move.

I don't know how long I sat there. I struggled to calm myself and deal with the intense feeling of fear that flooded me. Once I was calm, I began to consider what action—if any—I could take at this point. In spite of my circumstances, I was lucid and alert.

In what seemed like both an instant and an eternity, I heard a voice say, "Are you OK?" A man and his wife had been passing by when they saw my car cross the intersection. Realizing there was no road on the other side, they turned around to investigate. I quickly said a prayer of thanks before answering his question. I told him that I thought my back was broken and my ankles were fractured. He stayed there beside me while we waited for the ambulance, bolstering my courage with his steady presence and comforting words.

When at last the emergency medical personnel arrived, they spoke to me, did a cursory examination, then lashed me to a backboard and loaded me into the ambulance. I think I made a joke of some kind because I remember laughter, but I don't recall what was said. As we drove away, one EMT held my hand, softly speaking words of reassurance.

In the ambulance, I made a resolution that whatever adversity I might face, I would find a way to have a meaningful life. I remembered when I was a child seeing greeting cards created by a woman who was completely paralyzed, painted with a brush clenched in her teeth. I thought, "I'm artistic. I could do that."

During the weeks I lay in the hospital and the months of recovery that followed, I was fortified by an outpouring of support from family and friends. Fresh flowers were forbidden in the ICU, but a dear friend sent a small basket of artificial fruit held by a tiny elf. It was a strange little gift, but whenever I looked at it, I was reminded of the love of those who were thinking of me. When I was transferred from the ICU, the flowers, cards, visits, prayers, and small acts of kindness from family, friends, and even the hospital staff sustained me. My fiancé kept fresh roses in my room and stayed with me whenever he could to make sure my needs were met. My doctors, nurses, and physical therapists provided professional care and refused to give up on my recovery.

I did recover—beyond all expectations—and I mark this event as a key turning point in my life. Some of the chronic health repercussions have been challenging, but I've grown as a result of the experience. I have a deeper spiritual faith, a stronger belief in human goodness, and greater confidence in my own resiliency. I'm more determined now, and I'm much clearer about my priorities. Perhaps most important of all, I now believe that even the most difficult circumstances can be gifts in disguise. (Elise Herndon)

A community psychology view of stress, coping, coping resources, and possible outcomes emphasizes how persons are embedded in multiple contexts. We will show how community and clinical psychology can intersect and complement one another to create a more comprehensive approach to health care and promoting well-being. We highlight contextual and community processes in coping with stressors, leaving details of individual cognitive and emotional coping processes to more individually oriented textbooks and resources. However, we believe that both community-contextual and clinical-individual perspectives are needed for understanding the dynamic experiences and outcomes of stress and coping. In responding to stressful situations, individual and contextual processes are intertwined (Sandler, Gensheimer, & Braver, 2000).

To help introduce community psychology ways of thinking about intervention, Figure 8.1 illustrates the conceptual model of this chapter. It identifies key processes and outcomes, relationships among them, and points for constructive interventions. It is based on work of Barbara Dohrenwend, Rudolf Moos, and

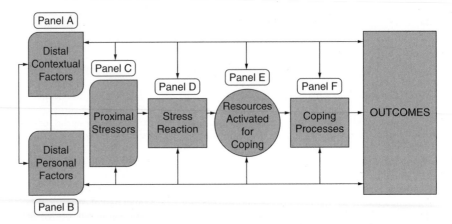

FIGURE 8.1 Potential relationships among ecological levels, stressors, and coping processes.

Abraham Wandersman and associates (Dohrenwend, 1978; Moos, 2002; Wandersman, 1990; Wandersman et al., 2002). We present the model to stimulate your own thinking about the stress and coping processes involved in responding to life's challenges. Causal pathways suggested in this figure are complex and often involve multiple processes that cannot be easily drawn. So, the figure is best used as a starting point for thinking about stressors, coping, and outcomes rather than a final statement about coping.

In this chapter, we draw case examples from our research and intervention work related to homelessness and natural disasters. However, as indicated in the opening exercise, this model can be a useful way of thinking about how people respond to a wide range of stressors and stressful situations. Stress and coping play out differently in different contexts and for different persons. Both can influence what stressors occur, how stress is understood and experienced, what resources are available and used, and what coping strategies the person chooses.

Risk and Protective Factors

In applying our ecological model to stress and coping, we distinguish between **risk factors** that are correlated with problem outcomes and **protective factors** that are associated with avoiding problems or promoting well-being (you may remember that we also used this distinction in Chapter 5 in discussing neighborhoods). We will also use our ecological model to conceptualize how risk and protective factors can exist at multiple levels of analysis—from individual qualities to macrosystem forces.

Risk factors are characteristics of individuals and situations that are thought to increase the likelihood that a person will experience problematic outcomes, such as personal distress, mental disorders, or behavior problems. For example, children who have a parent with a chronic illness could have multiple factors that put them at increased risk for developing their own problems. The ill parent may be unable to help the children with schoolwork, take the children to friends' houses, or go to school for activities or programs. The children may also receive less attention from a second parent who needs to attend to the sick parent's care and to work to cover the family's costs. Neither parent may be able to maintain regular contact with their children's teachers. The children's reactions may range from disappointment to frustration to anger and behavior problems. The children's learning and academic outcomes may suffer. Furthermore, the illness may affect the family's income and health care expenses. Older children may worry about their genetic vulnerability for contracting a similar illness. Thus, a parent's chronic illness, although only one of many factors in the family's life, may be related to academic or social problems for the children and to the family's economic and social well-being. Each of these factors may contribute to the development of specific risk processes that can be the focus of an intervention.

An accumulation of many risk factors can create situations that make people particularly vulnerable for developing problematic outcomes. In the example discussed above, if a parent's chronic illness leads to decreased support from parents, reduced income, and more distress in the family, it is not hard to imagine how this may make it hard for children to do well at school and may affect their coping. Of course, not all children whose parents have a chronic illness will develop mental health or academic problems. Risk factors do not always lead to processes that result in problematic situations. The same risk factors may affect children in each family differently, depending on their development, their access to social support outside of the family, or their relationships with peers. Thus, exposure to risk factors is not the whole story about stress and coping.

In contrast, protective factors provide resources for coping and often represent strengths of persons, families, and communities. Community psychologists examine potential strengths of individuals and situations that can buffer people from stressors rather than focusing only on potential risks. Protective factors may include *personal qualities* (such as a parent's optimism), *interpersonal resources* (such as friends who offer to help), *community resources* (such as support from religious congregations, school programs, or recreational opportunities), and *macrosystem resources* (such as access to affordable health care, child care, or home nursing). The availability of such protective factors can lead to protective processes where people use the resources to buffer the impact of stressors that they encounter. As presented in Chapter 6, a positive sense of community and social capital in neighborhoods and organizations can be protective factors for coping with stressful situations. Similarly, Bronfenbrenner (1979) asserted that the presence of an "irrationally caring" adult is the most essential protective factor for children. He meant that children benefit when they know someone unconditionally cares about them.

In our example of a family with a parent who has a chronic illness, suppose this family had several caring relatives or friends who were available to help the family and encourage the children. Add a caring school environment and a teacher who realizes these children need some special help. A flexible, well-paying job for the healthy parent could reduce economic hardship. With these protective influences, the risk of negative outcomes for these children may be significantly reduced.

Protective processes and the development of strengths can be a primary focus of intervention efforts themselves. For example, adolescents "at risk" for having academic problems often thrive as their personal strengths are identified, enhanced, valued, and linked to areas of difficulty (Brendtro, Brokenleg, & Van Bockern, 1990; Elias & Cohen, 1999). Community psychology has a long-standing interest in focusing on strengths of individuals and settings that can develop those strengths (Kelly, 1970; Rappaport, Davidson, Wilson, & Mitchell, 1974; Cowen & Kilmer, 2002). This interest shares similarities to work in the positive psychology movement (Seligman & Csikszentmihalyi, 2000a), positive youth development (Durlak, Taylor, Kawashima et al., 2007), and health promotion (O'Donnell, 2009). In community psychology, strengths are defined at multiple ecological levels beyond the individual, including those of cultural traditions, neighborhoods, organizations, and friendship networks (Maton, Schellenbach, Leadbeater, & Solarz, 2004). In addition, community and preventive interventions bolster abilities in social and emotional competencies (e.g., Weissberg & Kumpfer, 2003; Shinn & Yoshikawa, 2008)—particularly for those who have experienced social disadvantage. From a community psychology perspective, protective factors need to be conceptualized within an ecological model in which cultural traditions can be a protective resource. This can achieve a more complete understanding of how strengths of persons and communities can affect stress and coping outcomes.

How can knowledge about risk and protective factors be useful for interventions? Within this model, interventions may be designed (a) to reduce exposure to risk factors, (b) to boost protective factors and experiences, or (c) to be used in a combination of both strategies. Putting risks or strengths into context requires having a theory for how these factors may contribute to processes that can affect a person's life. It is not enough to note a statistical probability of increased vulnerability or protection. An intervention needs to have a plan for when, where, how, and with whom to intervene. These theories can be tested, researched, and refined for interventions rather than simply identifying a greater or less likelihood of having problems.

Distal and Proximal Factors

We begin explaining the theory behind Figure 8.1 by observing that factors affecting stress may be proximal or distal to lived experience—in addition to increasing risk for or protection from the development of problems.

Distal factors are more "distant" from a problem. They are *not* direct triggers of a problem but involve vulnerabilities that are indirectly linked to the problem. Much of what we have said in earlier chapters about levels of analysis identified *distal contextual* factors in societies, communities, and settings. These create vulnerabilities that are indirect causes of problems. For example, an economic recession is a distal factor (*macro-level*) that may reduce financial resources for employers (*organizational level*). In turn, these organizations lay off employees, directly affecting how their families cope (*micro-level*). With this increased stress, such problematic individual outcomes as increased substance abuse or developing depression may occur. However, distal factors also can also be *personal*, such as having a genetic vulnerability to depression. Many distal, predisposing factors for mental disorders are personal vulnerabilities. Figure 8.1 includes both contextual and personal distal factors.

Distal factors can involve risk or protection. Cultures, for instance, influence us in ways that may be risky (e.g., expectations for thinness that can lead to eating disorders) or protective (belief systems that help us cope with loss of a loved one). Personal traits may increase risk of stress or may be strengths that help prevent stress.

Proximal factors are "closer" to the individual or the problem, directly triggering or contributing to a problem or providing a resource that can be directly used for coping. In Figure 8.1, *proximal stressors* trigger stress and lead to coping efforts. Examples include a recent conflict with someone, losing your job, or bereavement. Proximal factors also can involve risk or protection. In Figure 8.1, *resources activated for coping* are proximal if the person turns directly to these for help in coping, such as seeking social support from friends.

Think of the distal-proximal distinction as a continuum, not two simple categories. It is useful to think of "more distal" and "more proximal" factors. A traumatic life experience that still affects you emotionally is more distal than a recent stressor but less distal than cultural or genetic factors. Problems involving stress and coping have many causes, which vary in how directly or indirectly they are related to stress that the person experiences.

Working Through the Ecological-Contextual Model

To help explain our ecological framework of stress and coping, we will take apart the model we presented earlier and build it up piece by piece. In Figure 8.1a, Panels A and B depict the distinct yet interrelated influences of distal contextual and personal factors.

Distal Contextual Factors   These include ongoing environmental conditions that may interact in various life domains. Cultural traditions, beliefs, practices or rituals, and institutions can provide meaning and strength in difficult times, as noted in Box 8.1. Yet they also can create stressors, for example, in the ways that many cultures' views about gender roles foster unequal workloads and limit opportunities for women. In a multicultural society, cultural influences include those from a dominant culture as well as those from other cultures. For example, immigrants need to negotiate cultural expectations from their culture of origin and that of where they live currently. Economic conditions at multiple levels, from global to local, also introduce both stressors and opportunities. Social and political forces affect individuals—for example, in the form of discrimination or through policies that limit it. An ongoing environmental hazard, such as toxic waste near a community, poses both biological and psychological risks. As we discussed in Chapters 5 and 6, neighborhood processes such as violence, sense of community, or informal neighboring can influence individual well-being.

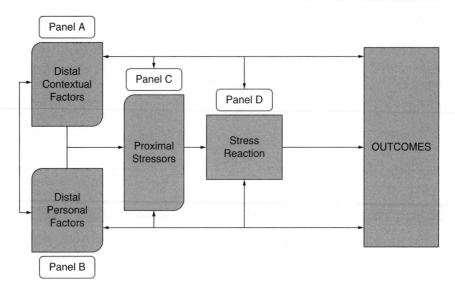

FIGURE 8.1a Potential relationships among ecological levels, stressors, and coping processes.

The social climate of a school, classroom, or workplace and the social regularities defined by social roles and power dynamics also shape individual lives. Finally, the dynamics of family life and of interpersonal relationships provide stressors and resources for individuals.

Distal contextual risk factors tend to be chronic stressors that involve long-term processes that can impact access to resources and accumulation of disadvantage over years and decades (Wandersman & Nation, 1998). Examples include poverty, environmental pollution, noise, crowding, neighborhood crime, lack of health care, and such family role demands as caregiving for a sick relative or parenting a challenging child (Dupre & Perkins, 2007; Evans, 2004; Rasmussen, Aber, & Bhana, 2004; Turner, 2007). Viewed as a prolonged and persistent situation of low resources to meet needs, poverty is often understood among many developmental psychologists as the biggest risk factor for problematic outcomes (Leventhal, Fauth, & Brooks-Gunn, 2005). (Note that within our model, income problems due to a sudden job loss would be labeled a proximal stressor.) The effects of chronic environmental conditions may be cumulative, such as the combined effects of poverty, crowding, and a chronic illness. Ongoing family conditions, such as parental alcoholism or chronic illness, may be both chronic stressors for the affected family member and contextual factors for the children in such families, which increase their risk of dysfunction (Barrera, Li, & Chassin, 1995).

Distal Personal Factors Distal personal factors are aspects of an individual and are generally not readily observable. They may include genetic and other biological factors; personality traits such as shyness, optimism, or extraversion; learned cognitive patterns, such as attributions about the source of problems;

TABLE 8.1 **Examples of Distal Factors in Coping**

Contextual	Personal
Cultural traditions and practices	Biological and genetic factors
Economic conditions	Personal temperaments and traits
Social and political forces	Patterns of thinking
Environmental hazards	Chronic illness or similar conditions
Neighborhood processes	Ongoing effects of prior life experiences
Setting social climates	
Social regularities	
Family dynamics	

and continuing effects of prior life experiences, such as child maltreatment. As with contextual factors, distal personal factors may act as stressors or resources and play a risk or protective role. For example, dispositional optimism promotes a positive appraisal of stressors and effective coping (Connor-Smith & Flachsbart, 2007; Scheier, Carver, & Bridges, 2001). Because these personal factors are well-covered in other sources about stress and coping, we do not review them in detail here. Our emphasis is on the contextual factors that have received less attention in stress and coping research (Dohrenwend, 1978).

We should note that the boundary between contextual and personal factors is permeable and fluid. A chronic illness, for example, is not only a personal issue. The personal impact of the illness is influenced by sociocultural interpretations of the illness, how disabling it is considered to be, and how individuals with that illness are expected to behave. Although family dynamics are contextual, they interact closely with a wide range of personal factors. The important point about this model is that we look at both contextual and personal factors in understanding the effects of stress and coping. See Table 8.1 for illustrative examples of distal factors.

Distinguishing between distal contextual and distal personal factors helps in designing interventions. For example, interventions to reduce the prevalence of bulimia nervosa might focus on distal contextual factors—such as mass media depictions of excessive thinness as always desirable for women—or use university-level social marketing approaches (e.g., a public service ad campaign in dorms and student organizations) to educate students about the risks of chronic, stringent dieting. Individual interventions would focus on reducing personal risk factors, including individual eating practices and body image.

Proximal Stressors

Panel C in Figure 8.1a represents proximal stressors. Stressors are events or situations that represent a threatened or actual loss of resources (Hobfoll, 1988, 1998; Lazarus & Folkman, 1984). Stressors are risk factors that vary in duration, severity, quantity, personal meaning, and point of impact. In addition, the boundary between proximal and distal-chronic stressors is not always simple. For instance,

T A B L E 8.2   Examples of Proximal Stressors

Major Life Events

Life Transitions

Daily Hassles

Disasters

traumatic events suchas rape or combat may evoke distress for years following the incident. Below we present four types of proximal stressors to illustrate our framework, recognizing that these categories overlap to some extent and that other useful categories exist.

In our model, stressors are first presented as antecedents prior to appraisal and coping. However, stressors and coping responses shape each other to some extent (see feedback arrows in Figure 8.1). For example, binge drinking to deal with a stressor can create additional stressors at work and in personal relationships. See Table 8.2 to review the major categories of proximal stressors.

Major Life Events   Holmes and Rahe (1967) pioneered the study of the impact of major life events. Their Social Readjustment Rating Scale is a standardized list of stressful life events such as grieving, divorce, and job loss. Based on empirical studies, each event is assigned a point value to estimate the amount of change or adjustment it requires of the individual. The sum of these points has been used to represent an individual's degree of exposure to stress. Similar to estimating how much stress a bridge can bear and not collapse, this approach to understanding proximal stressors expects that an accumulation of stressful events will likely lead to the development of psychological problems.

Correlations of life events scores and outcomes have been relatively modest, accounting for only 9%–10% of the variance (i.e., only 10% of negative outcomes are associated with major life events) (Hobfoll & Vaux, 1993; Zautra & Bachrach, 2000). Community psychology research has shown a number of shortcomings of the original life -events approach and potential advantages of refinements (Sandler et al., 2000). While stressors are defined as events requiring adaptive change, there are differences in the kinds of change that they demand. Life events lists typically include both"entrances" (such as marriage or the birth of a child that are usually seen positively) and "exits" (such as the death of a loved one or unemployment). Studies indicate that exits tend to have a stronger association with psychological distress and illness than entrances (Thoits, 1983; Vinokur & Selzer, 1975). Furthermore, standardized lists of life events are not sensitive to the cultural and personal meaning of those events to the individual (Mirowsky & Ross, 1989; Green, Chung, Daroowalla, Kaltman, & DeBenedictis, 2006). For example, divorce is given a single score, regardless of its cultural acceptability or the variability of its impact. Finally, uncontrollable and unpredictable events (e.g., major car accident) have been found to be particularly stressful, but these dimensions are not measured by most life events scales (Thoits, 1983). Continuing community psychology research will help understand how variation in major life event stressors can lead to different outcomes.

Life Transitions Within a stress and coping model, life transitions are expected to present challenges for coping. These transitions produce enduring changes in a person's life context, requiring the learning of new skills or assumption of new roles. Life transitions occur as part of regular human development (e.g., becoming an adolescent, an adult, or a senior) and as part of life circumstances (e.g., taking a job with new responsibilities or becoming a parent). Some transitions (e.g., losing a loved one) are also examined in a major life events inventory. This research approach requires a longer period of observation than counting whether an event happened. Recall the transition for you when you entered college or graduate school. What challenges did that life transition present to you? Perhaps you had to expand your academic, time management, or decision-making skills. Perhaps your network of friends changed or your relationships with loved ones. Did the transition lead to new insights about yourself or new insights about others? The impacts of a life transition are contextual. Each transition requires its own combination of coping skills; each has its own cultural-social meaning (e.g., attitudes about divorce), and persons bring different personal and social resources to the transition.

Some community psychologists focus on understanding regular life transitions as a point of intervention to promote healthy development of children. Transitions from elementary to middle and high school can be stressful, especially in large school systems that diminish individual contacts between students and staff. Seidman and associates studied multiracial samples of low-income adolescents in New York City, Baltimore, and Washington, D.C. After the transition to junior high school, grades, preparation for school, involvement in school activities, social support from school staff, and self-esteem all dropped. Engagement with peers increased, but this was not necessarily constructive because students reported that peers' values were becoming more antisocial (Seidman, Allen, Aber, Mitchell, & Feinman, 1994). At the transition to high school, similar but less negative effects occurred (Seidman, Aber, Allen, & French, 1996). Similar effects occurred among low-income, mainly Hispanic students in Chicago, where students moved directly from elementary school to high school. Decreases occurred in student grades, attendance, and perceptions of support from family, peers, and school staff (Gillock & Reyes, 1996). Declines in academic engagement are especially serious given the developmental importance of the early adolescent years (Seidman, Aber, & French, 2004). These studies document a loss of resources for many youth. Social support from adults, especially at school, decreases.

Daily Hassles A third strategy for documenting proximal stressors is to focus on challenges encountered in everyday experience. In contrast to a major life events approach, the study of daily hassles and uplifts applies the life events approach to short-term, smaller-scale events (Kanner, Coyne, Schaefer, & Lazarus, 1981; Kilmer, Cowen, Wyman, Work, & Magnus, 1998). Examples of daily hassles include family arguments, traffic jams, and conflicts at work. Although many daily hassles grow from environmental conditions or chronic stressors, daily hassles scales do not identify their larger causes. Scores are based on the frequency or intensity of the hassles themselves. Daily hassles scales do not address long-term causal factors; however, this method produces a more individualized understanding of the immediate antecedents of stress. Consistent with a community psychology approach that examines potential risks and protective processes, the approach of Kanner and colleagues also includes the measurement of daily uplifts. Uplifts are the small, commonplace, mood-lifting things that can occur day to day, such as the kind gesture of a coworker or a phone call from a friend.

Psychological research on racism shows how a distal contextual condition may create multiple specific proximal stressors. Harrell and associates studied racism-related stress among a multiracial sample of U.S. students and African American community members. They measured a variety of stressors. Specific racism-related life events, such as being harassed by police or being unfairly rejected for a loan, were infrequent but stressful. While major life events related to discrimination are certainly stressful, research has documented the cost of low-level hassles related to racism and discrimination. "Micro-aggressions" (similar to daily hassles)—such as being followed in stores, being avoided by others, and subtle expressions of disrespect or fear—were experienced almost daily by research participants. This research suggests that it is also stressful to witness racism that targeted others, such as seeing one's group blamed for problems, regularly encountering low expectations for youth of color, and chronic inequalities of income and material resources. Symptoms of depression, anxiety, and psychological trauma were correlated with each type of stressor, especially with daily microaggressions (Harrell, 1997; 2000; Prelow, Danoff-Burg, Swenson, & Pulgiano, 2004).

Disasters   The final type of proximal stressors regularly examined by community psychologists is disasters. These affect entire communities, regions, or nations. They include such natural disasters as hurricanes and floods, such technological disasters as an accident at a nuclear power plant, and such mass violence as terrorism and war (Norris, Friedman, Watson, Byrne, Diaz, & Kaniasty, 2002; Norris, Stevens, Pfefferbaum, Wyche, & Pfefferbaum, 2008). Reviewing 160 empirical studies involving 60,000 disaster victims, Norris and her colleagues found that the meaning of a disaster makes a difference; mass violence had more damaging psychological consequences than natural or technological disasters. Moreover, prior social context makes a difference; negative impacts of disasters were usually stronger among children, women, ethnic minorities, and people in developing nations rather than developed nations. Those exposed to more severe situations, those who had more prior problems and fewer resources reported greater problems.

Furthermore, Norris and colleagues found that in any disaster, problems are intertwined and tend to cluster together. Those who report mental health problems tend to also have problems related to physical health, family distress, fragmented social networks, property loss, and dislocation. How does this clustering of risk factors happen? We suggest that an ecological view is needed to understand such accumulation of risk factors and processes and potential points of intervention to promote healthy coping.

Vicious Spirals   Vicious spirals are cascading patterns among multiple stressors that compound the effects of risk factors. These spirals are set in motion when the loss of one resource triggers other losses (Hobfoll, 1998; Thorn & Dixon, 2007). Imagine the case of a single mother who loses her car because it was in an accident and she can't afford to repair it. Without transportation, she may be unable to get to work, which results in the loss of her job. She can no longer afford child care, which makes finding a new job even more difficult. Perhaps she cannot afford medications needed for herself or her children. These setbacks also undermine her self-esteem and belief in her ability to cope. If the loss of resources is profound, she may lose her housing and need shelter. Vicious spirals are particularly common for those with fewer material, social, or personal resources. In the example of our single mother, a vicious spiral might be interrupted by accessing one of several resources: an understanding employer, a community short-term loan fund, a relative who can provide child care, or a friend with car repair skills. An early intervention, such as the provision of child care, might stop the spiral long enough for her to get back on her feet.

Stress Reactions

The next component of our ecological model of stress and coping are the immediate reactions persons have when they encounter stressors. These reactions may range from mild irritation to serious health problems. The personal experience of stress includes physiological (e.g., racing heart, elevated cortisol, or elevated blood pressure), emotional (e.g., anxiety, agitation, or depression), behavioral (e.g., alcohol use or seeking help), cognitive (e.g., appraisal of threat and meaning of a stressor, or excessive worry), and social components (e.g., social withdrawal). These *stress reactions* are interdependent and often cyclical. When a dangerous threat is imminent, brain structures and neural pathways react instantaneously, allowing little time for rational consideration. In a less dangerous circumstance, there is more time for reflection and planning. As shown by Panel D in Figure 8.1a, the stress reaction will be more influenced by the proximal stressors and, in turn, will have a greater influence on outcomes. In some situations, an increase in proximal stressors may initiate stress responses that could be viewed as positive experiences, such as rising to meet a challenge. At higher levels of analysis, organizations and localities can be understood as having stress reactions that require changes in functioning when they encounter proximal stressors. While the analogy to individual stress does not exactly translate to organizations, they must also mobilize resources to respond to potential threats (e.g., a major factory will close in a small town—how do the businesses who depend on potential lost customers react to this stress). In response to stressors, organizations may also encounter impaired functioning (e.g., poor decision making, poor communication, disruption of relationships among coworkers, or isolation from other organizations) or rise to meet challenges that they face (e.g., creation of new working relationships by using bridging social capital, as discussed in Chapter 6).

A detailed description of stress reactions can be found in Folkman & Moskowitz, 2004; Goleman, 1995; and Somerfield & McCrea, 2000.

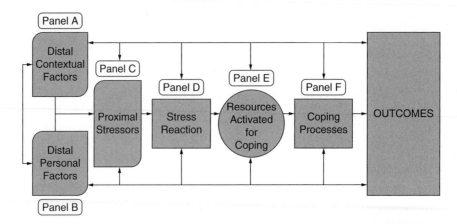

FIGURE 8.1b Potential relationships among ecological stressors, coping processes, and outcomes.

Resources Activated for Coping

The next component of our ecological stress and coping model includes resources that can be used to buffer the effect of stressors or to support the development of personal strengths. To handle stressors, individuals often mobilize available resources for coping (Panel E in Figure 8.1b). It is important to note that resources are involved at many points in our ecological model; contextual and personal protective factors are resources; stressors are defined by their threats to resources; interventions often provide resources. Simply having resources available does not lead to positive coping outcomes; a person needs to *activate* resources for coping. In this model, resources activated for coping are proximal resources. See Table 8.3 for an illustrative list of resources.

Material Resources   Material resources are tangible objects used to address personal needs and in daily life (e.g., money, car, shelter, food, or clothing). Many stressors are related to insufficient material resources, whose impact on psychological outcomes is greater than many realize. As discussed already, employment, transportation, and affordable housing are resources that can circumvent vicious

TABLE 8.3   Illustrative Resources for Coping

Material resources

Social-emotional competencies

Social settings

Cultural resources

Social support

Mutual help groups

Spiritual resources

spirals induced by job loss or divorce. In addition to meeting basic needs, material resources may provide opportunities for accomplishing goals. Material resources can create access to education (e.g., tuition, books, or labs) that helps students develop skills to obtain jobs and build careers.

Social-Emotional Competencies These personal competencies include self-regulation skills: managing emotions, motivations, cognitions, and other intrapersonal processes (Goleman, 1995). Social competencies are needed to connect with others and make use of the resources they offer. Empathy involves accurate understanding of the emotions of others. In a U.S. sample of highly stressed, low-income urban children, empathy was related to resilience and adjustment (Hoyt-Meyers et al., 1995). Making personal connections, building relationships, and managing conflicts are crucial among adults and children (Elias, Parker, Kash, & Dunkelblau, 2007). Assertiveness has been associated with a number of positive outcomes for children, including the ability to resist drug use (Rotheram-Borus, 1988). As discussed in Chapter 9, social and emotional competencies are a major focus of prevention-promotion programs in community psychology and related fields.

Social, Cultural, and Spiritual Resources Social resources often reflect the idea stated in the African proverb "It takes a village to raise a child." Such social settings as youth groups, mutual help organizations, and religious congregations can be coping resources. Cultural traditions, rituals, and beliefs provide systems of meaning for interpreting stressors, examples of skillful coping, and guides to coping choices. Religious writings, widely read stories, and folk sayings are examples of these. The rituals of bereavement in any culture provide resources to those who have lost loved ones. Later in this chapter, we discuss social support, mutual help, and social aspects of spiritual resources.

Coping Processes

In our ecological stress and coping model, Panel F of Figure 8.1b represents responses or strategies that a person uses to reduce stress (Moos, 2002). Coping is a dynamic process that fluctuates over time according to the demands of the situation, the available resources, and a person's ongoing appraisal and emotions. The literature on coping responses is extensive. Researchers have classified coping strategies and styles along a number of descriptive dimensions, such as approach-avoidance, cognitive-behavioral, and prosocial-antisocial (Folkman & Moskowitz, 2004; Hobfoll, 1998; Lazarus & Folkman, 1984; Moos, 1984, 2002; Shapiro, Schwartz, & Astin, 1996). Here, we briefly discuss a few key concepts.

Cognitive Appraisal During a stress reaction, appraisal is the ongoing process of constructing the meaning of a stressful situation or event (Lazarus & Folkman, 1984). The most relevant aspects of appraisal include the extent to which the situation is seen as challenging or threatening, expected or unexpected, and/or largely controllable or not. Appraisal of stressors or resources may change over time.

Reappraisal During coping processes, reappraising, or "reframing," a problem involves altering one's perception of the situation or its meaning (Lazarus & Folkman, 1984; Watzlawick et al., 1974). It may include changing one's view of the stressor's intensity, identifying unrecognized resources, or finding opportunities for growth or meaning in the situation. For example, you might reappraise a stressful circumstance as an opportunity to learn new skills or reframe an appraised threat as a challenge. People who have lost a job might reinterpret their situation as an opportunity for changing careers or seeking further education. Cultural values and social support influence which reappraisals are perceived as realistic or constructive.

Categories of Coping Empirically based studies have usually found three general categories of coping responses (Folkman & Moskowitz, 2004). **Problem-focused coping** involves addressing a problem situation directly, especially by making a plan to change the situation and then following that plan. Changing how one studies for tests, making a plan to improve one's diet, or learning interviewing skills to search for a new job would be examples. **Emotion-focused coping** addresses the feelings that accompany the stressors. Typically, this approach seeks to reduce anxiety or increase emotional support from friends or family. **Meaning-focused coping** involves finding significance in the stressor by reappraising it, especially if this leads to growth or learning important lessons. It may be based on deeper values, whether secular or spiritual, as when suffering is interpreted as leading to growth (see the accounts in Box 8.1). These categories may overlap, as when a person seeks emotional support from a friend.

From an ecological perspective, coping is contextual. Wise coping choices are based on the context and the person; there is no coping style or strategy that is always superior. Societal and cultural factors, gender and other forms of diversity, ecological level (e.g., community, neighborhood, and family), and the stressor itself must all be taken into account.

Virtuous Spirals Earlier, we noted how stressors may sometimes trigger each other in a vicious downward spiral. However, adaptive coping may initiate a very different cascade: a virtuous spiral in which resources are increased, successes build on each other, and the stressor is transformed into a catalyst for growth (Hobfoll, 1998). In a virtuous spiral, access to coping resources and the ability to utilize the resources can have a multiplicative effect, reducing risk and promoting functioning. Persons in long-term recovery from substance abuse who had hit rock bottom in a vicious spiral often describe how they were able to use coping resources and opportunities as a result from their steps to get sober, get support from peers and sponsors, and repair relationships. Many describe being thankful for "hitting bottom" because their lives are much better than they were before a vicious spiral associated with substance abuse consumed them. New opportunities for work, career, and a fulfilling life appear as virtuous spirals of opportunity and open doors to new resources.

Coping Outcomes

Traditionally, psychologists have studied coping outcomes with measures of maladaptive functioning. Problematic outcomes include psychological or physical disorders, raised levels of distress, or personal problems classified as dysfunction or clinical disorders (Folkman & Moskowitz, 2004). However, this perspective on coping is limited in two ways. First, it focuses on avoiding negative coping outcomes more than the possibility of promoting positive outcomes. Second, it tends to focus on individuals in isolation rather than also studying how individual functioning is related to broader ecological levels (families, organizations, communities, and societies). From a community psychology perspective, the promotion of well-being and positive outcomes is as important as avoiding negative outcomes. Thus, we refine our ecological model of stress and coping one more time to reflect two different sets of outcomes. In Figure 8.1c, Panel G concerns positive coping outcomes and their relationship to broader ecological levels, while Panel H concerns distress, dysfunction, and disorders.

Wellness is not simply the absence of symptoms of disorder or of distress; it is the experience of positive outcomes in health and subjective well-being (Cowen, 1994, 2000; Nelson & Prilleltensky, 2010). Life satisfaction, job satisfaction, positive affect, self-esteem, and academic achievement represent desired wellness outcomes that go beyond mere absence of symptoms (Cicchetti, Rappaport, Sandler, & Weissberg, 2000).

Resilience is an individual's capacity to adapt successfully and function competently despite exposure to stress, adversity, or chronic trauma (Bonanno, 2004; Masten, 2007). Resilience appears to be a common coping process. Many people experience distress due to a stressor (e.g., death of a loved one)

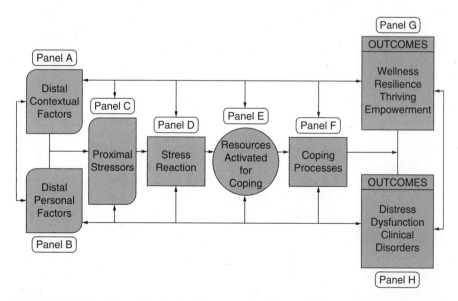

FIGURE 8.1c Potential relationships among stressors, coping processes, and outcomes.

but recover their prior level of functioning without clinical intervention. Some are able to maintain stable levels of healthy functioning in the face of stressors, with little or no emotional distress or physical symptoms at all. Resilience arises from the interplay of environmental and individual factors (Luthar, Cicchetti, & Becker, 2000). Resilience is typically viewed as a combination of individual and environmental processes (Luthar, Cicchetti, & Becker, 2000; Werner, 1993). Recognizing environmental influences, consistent with a community psychology perspective, suggests pathways for action involving multiple ecological levels, not just individuals. New work emerging from community psychology research on natural disasters has proposed that communities can have a capacity for resilience as well as individuals, such as a community that "bounces back" after a flood (Norris, Stevens, Pfefferbaum, Wyche, & Pfefferbaum, 2008).

Thriving   For some individuals, an encounter with adversity initiates a process of growth that takes them beyond their prior level of functioning. This positive outcome is referred to as thriving (Ickovics & Park, 1998). It may be thought of as "resilience plus"—in the face of stressors, not only holding one's ground but growing through the experience. For example, Abraido-Lanza, Guier, and Colon (1998) studied thriving among Latinas with chronic illness living in impoverished neighborhoods. Thriving in response to stressors often involves meaning-focused coping, access to coping resources, and the ability to mobilize scarce resources.

Empowerment   Wiley and Rappaport (2000) defined empowerment as gaining access to valued resources. We will discuss empowerment extensively in Chapter 11, but for now, it is important to recognize that empowerment involves actually gaining power in some way, not simply the feeling of being in control of one's life decisions (Zimmerman, 2000). For example, empowerment occurs when a person with a serious mental illness is able to understand and advocate for his rights, gain more control in treatment planning, and make decisions about where to live and work. Empowerment can also occur at multiple levels of analysis. For example, mutual help groups bring together persons with common challenges in coping with a specific problem, sharing their resources and promoting positive outcomes for individuals and the broader collective. The growing awareness of the group's empowerment can lead to effective advocacy and obtaining resources that support other positive outcomes of coping.

Distress, Dysfunction, and Clinical Disorders   Panel H includes problematic outcomes of coping. These outcomes range from symptoms of mental disorders to outcomes that are problematic but not considered clinical disorders. These include high levels of distress, irritability, or dysfunctional behaviors in family or work relationships, such as neglect, hostility, or even violence. Many psychological outcomes experienced by college students (e.g., anxiety about grades), by families (dissatisfaction with a marriage), and in workplaces (e.g., frustration over limited job opportunities) involve distress or dysfunction that is important and painful but are not considered mental disorders. Coping research related to clinical interventions has focused on avoiding symptoms of disorders (e.g., depression, anxiety, PTSD, and substance abuse) that can result from maladaptive coping, overwhelming exposure to stressors, and insufficient coping resources.

Coping Is Dynamic and Contextual   Look back at Figure 8.1c for a moment. Notice the feedback cycles and arrows. Outcomes are not end-states but simply one more step in the cyclical processes of coping. Outcomes can affect stressors and resources for future coping. Outcomes are best understood as snapshots in ongoing processes of living. Our coping processes and the stressors we encounter are dynamic, changing over time, and vary in the diverse contexts in which we live.

Interventions to Promote Coping

A primary purpose for developing the conceptual model presented in Figure 8.1 is to think about how and where community psychologists might work with others to improve coping outcomes and reduce exposure to risk factors. Community psychologists refer to actions taken to affect outcomes as interventions. Interventions can be targeted at each level of analysis and might be initiated by health, educational, or social service professionals, researchers, public leaders, or concerned citizens. Through the next five chapters, we will discuss in detail different interventions implemented and/or supported by community psychologists.

Using our ecological model of stress and coping, community psychologists can conceptualize a range of possibilities for better targeted and more holistic interventions (Yoshikawa & Shinn, 2002). As will be discussed in later chapters, interventions need to be selected to fit the definition of the problem, the level of analysis used for the problem definition, and available resources. The model also illustrates how community psychologists, clinical psychologists, and others who implement social interventions might work together to produce synergistic results.

Planning interventions requires considering several dimensions (Wandersman, 1990; Wandersman et al., 2002). *Timing* concerns the point of intervention in the ecological model: Is the goal to influence distal factors, proximal stressors, stress reactions, resource activation, and/or coping strategies? *Ecological levels* concern the intervention focus (e.g., individual, microsystem, organizational, locality, or macrosystem). *Content* goals of the intervention might include increasing awareness (a goal of many psychotherapies and of consciousness-raising in liberation movements), behavior change, skill building, social support, spiritual facilitation (as in 12-step groups), advocacy for individuals or families, changing social policy, or other goals. The value system inherent in the intervention is critical to its nature and effectiveness. For example, community efforts by expert helpers to reduce environmental stressors might not be as effective for neighborhood residents as an approach emphasizing their citizen participation and empowerment. A major point of this chapter is that many stressors cannot be addressed by individual coping alone (Somerfield & McCrea, 2000; Wong, Wong, & Scott, 2006). For example, job stress often is rooted in organizational and macrosystem

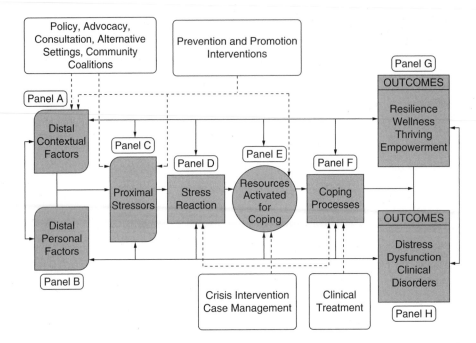

F I G U R E 8.2 Potential relationships among ecological levels, coping processes, and interventions.

conditions that require collective action. Improved individual coping skills alone cannot change these conditions.

In Figure 8.2, we have commented on the types of interventions that are most appropriate for addressing each component of our ecological model of stress and coping. From left to right, interventions range from more global to more individual in scope. The figure includes bothcommunity and clinical approaches to intervention. In our discussion to follow, we leave clinical treatments to other sources and focus on interventions most relevant to community psychology. As shown in Figure 8.2, community psychologists think broadly about the types of interventions that can support coping.

Social Policy and Advocacy   Improvements in the well-being of large numbers of persons involve changing laws, organizational practices, social programs, and funding decisions that affect resources for coping. These interventions can be understood as addressing stressors and distal factors in coping. Targets of advocacy may be government officials, private sector or community leaders, or media and the public. Advocacy may involve working to raise public awareness of an issue—for example, gaining media attention for the needs of homeless families in your community. It may involve social action—for example, protesting cuts in mental health or youth development programs or a Take Back the Night rally to call attention to violence against women.

Advocacy can be supported by community research. Community and developmental psychologists joined to promote a strengths-building perspective in

U.S. government policies regarding children, youth, and families (Maton et al., 2004). Furthermore, a group of community psychologists pooled their expertise to develop a resource guide for how communities can prepare for and respond to natural disasters (Norris, Olson, Berkowitz, et al., 2009). Not only was this guide created, but these community psychologists have built relationships with funders and government agencies to see that this guide is field-tested, refined, and then distributed among organizations that are early responders to natural disasters. We discuss approaches to community and social change in detail in Chapter 12.

Organizational Consultation   Human services, schools, and worksites are less effective when organizational problems create too many stressors. Community and organizational psychologists consult with these settings, seeking to change organizational policies and practices. These may include altering employees' roles, decision-making processes, or communication. Consultation may deal with issues such as work-family relationships, human diversity, and intergroup conflict. These interventions may lessen stress, increase social support, promote employee job satisfaction, or help make services more effective for clients (e.g., Bond, 1999; Boyd & Angelique, 2002; Shinn & Perkins, 2000; Trickett, Barone, & Watts, 2000).

Alternative Settings   At times, the shortcomings of an agency, clinic, or another setting may be so great that citizens or professionals decide to form an alternative setting to provide interventions. Charter schools and self-help organizations provide examples of citizens coming together to address distal factors and stressors that they felt were not being adequately addressed by conventional services. For example, when many community agencies failed to recognize the needs of battered women and rape victims, concerned women formed women's shelters and rape crisis centers. At first, these settings had very little funding or outside support, but they have grown into an established part of many communities. The Community Lodge (discussed in Chapters 2 and 5) and Oxford House (discussed in Chapter 1) are examples of alternative, supportive housing created by those concerned about the well-being of persons with mental illness or substance abuse problems. Alternative settings can provide citizens with important choices for services and values systems (Cherniss & Deegan, 2000; Reinharz, 1984).

Community Coalitions   This approach involves bringing together representatives from a local community to address such issues as preventing drug abuse or promoting health or youth development. Often, coalitions are created by bringing together and coordinating the work of groups already committed to addressing an issue but who had not been working together. An effective coalition brings together citizens from many walks of life to discuss community issues and work toward shared goals. It also builds collaboration among multiple agencies, whose separate funding streams and agendas often create a fragmented community service system. For example, community coalitions have increased rates of immunization of young children, affected community changes in drug abuse and domestic violence, and helped decrease levels of local gang violence (Allen,

2005; Butterfoss, Goodman, & Wandersman, 2001; Folayemi, 2001; Snell-Johns, Imm, Wandersman, & Claypoole, 2003; Wolff, 2001a). We discuss this approach in detail in Chapter 12.

Prevention and Promotion Programs   These are carefully designed interventions that seek to reduce the incidence of personal problems in living and illness or to promote health and personal development (see the box in the top center of Figure 8.2). Examples include school-based programs to promote social-emotional competence, family-based programs to strengthen parenting or promote resilience, and community-wide efforts to promote health or prevent drug abuse (Weissberg & Kumpfer, 2003). Many prevention/promotion programs have grown out of collaboration between community coalitions, schools, and researchers. These programs may strengthen coping skills or other protective factors also addressed in clinical treatment, but they focus on intervention before problems appear. We discuss these approaches in detail in Chapters 9–10.

Moving to the bottom-center of Figure 8.2, we next discuss community approaches more closely related to clinical treatments.

Crisis Intervention   After the September 11, 2001 terrorist attacks in the United States, more than one million New Yorkers received public education or individual counseling through Project Liberty, a public disaster mental health program (Felton, 2004). The most promising crisis intervention approaches immediately after traumatic events focus on providing emotional support, practical assistance, information about coping, and encouraging later use of one's own sources of support and treatment if needed (McNally, Bryan, & Ehlers, 2003). These are consistent with a community-ecological perspective. For mental health professionals, skills for responding to disasters include helping persons and families deal with multiple problems; working with community resources such as schools, workplaces, and religious congregations; and using mass media to provide information (Felton, 2004). Moreover, programs must be tailored to the specific cultures, needs, and resources of a community (Aber, 2005). Community psychologists have long advocated for the training of paraprofessionals and community members for similar outreach that might reduce the impact of stress reactions. Paraprofessionals can also promote the use of coping resources before dysfunction and the development of clinical symptoms (Rappaport, 1977; Center for Mental Health Services, 2000). As we discuss in Chapter 13, community psychologists also evaluate the effectiveness of programs, such as crisis intervention. While crisis intervention can be helpful (Jones, Allen, Norris, & Miller, 2009), in some cases, crisis intervention approaches have been found to increase long-term distress rather than ameliorate it (Gist & Lubin, 1989).

Case Management   To increase the availability of coping resources within agencies, professional treatment is often complemented with innovations in case management and client advocacy. These interventions focus on practical needs (e.g., housing) and psychological issues (e.g., decision making and social support). For example, community psychologists concerned about housing resources for persons who were homeless developed a new approach to providing housing. Rather than expecting persons to prove that they were ready to live in housing by working their way through a shelter system, Pathways to Housing in New York City developed a *"housing first"* program that put homeless persons with mental illness directly into apartments (Stefancic & Tsemberis, 2007; Tsemberis, Moran, Shinn, Asmussen, & Shern, 2003). The housing first approach makes available specialized case management and treatment options through Assertive Community Treatment (Bond et al., 1990) multidisciplinary teams (e.g., nurse, psychiatrist, case manager, vocational specialist, or substance abuse counselor) that visit tenants in their apartments to respond to a variety of needs. Housing First has demonstrated that helping homeless persons find suitable independent housing and develop a treatment plan once in housing is more effective than transitional housing approaches (e.g., have persons demonstrate their "housing readiness" by living in increasingly less supervised housing). Outcomes include more days housed, reduction in service use, and more cost-effective interventions (Gulcur, Stefanic, Tsemberis, Shinn, & Fischer, 2003; Tsemberis, Gulcur, & Nakae, 2004).

Our discussion of coping interventions is brief. Our purpose is to provide examples of the richness of intervention options and entry points available to address stress and coping. In the next three sections, we describe in detail three important community-based resources for coping: social support, mutual help organizations, and spirituality and religious settings. These areas of community psychology research and practice have implications for personal coping and professional services.

SOCIAL SUPPORT

Social support is a key resource for strengthening coping and well-being. Social support is an intuitive concept for many of us. As community psychologists understand social support, it represents a collection of social, emotional, cognitive, and behavioral processes occurring in relationships and social networks. Understanding how it works in our lives requires careful conceptualization and research. For this chapter, we provide a brief introduction to this naturally occurring resource for coping that can be bolstered or diminished by policy and interventions.

Interest in social support soared in the 1980s after research showed that it was associated with lower levels of personal distress and illness, even in the presence of stressful challenges. Research in a variety of disciplines found that social support was correlated with lesser anxiety, depression, distress, and physical illness among children, adolescents, and adults. It has also been correlated with stronger cardiovascular and immune functioning, academic performance, parenting skills, and job and life satisfaction. However, later research has indicated that its effects are complicated by many interacting factors, and some negative effects of supportive relationships have become clearer (Barrera, 2000; Cohen, 2004; Cohen, Underwood, & Gottlieb, 2000; Hobfoll & Vaux, 1993).

Generalized and Specific Support

Generalized support is sustained over time, providing the individual with a secure base for living and coping. It is not tailored to one specific stressor and does not necessarily involve behavioral helping in a specific situation. It is most clearly measured in terms of **perceived support**, in which research participants are asked about the general quality or availability of support in their lives (Barrera, 1986, 2000). Generalized support thus involves an assessment of the presence of meaningful others in one's life (Barrera, 2000; Cohen, 2004). It especially refers to experiences of caring and attachment in close personal relationships, such as a strong marriage, a parent-child relationship, or friendship. It is there in some form all the time.

Specific support or **enacted support** is behavioral help provided to people coping with a particular stressor. It may be emotional encouragement, information or advice, or tangible assistance, such as loaning money. Because it concerns distress already present in the recipient's life, specific support is discernible only when a person needs it and is tailored to a specific stressor (Barrera, 2000). This kind of support is received rather than only perceived.

Generalized and specific support can intertwine. Stressors such as job loss require both. A close relationship often provides both. Other relationships may involve less caring and more instrumental support, but that too is helpful. It is important to note that perceived support and specific support are different. For example, if you are having trouble in a demanding psychology course, a caring friend helps but so does a tutor. An empirical review of 23 research studies that compared perceived general and enacted specific support suggests that these types of support had an average correlation of 35% (Haber, Cohen, Lucas, & Baltes, 2007).

The meaning of specific support also depends on culture and context. Liang and Bogat (1994) found that specific, openly provided support was considered less helpful by mainland Chinese students than by U.S. students. Receiving support in a noticeable way may be embarrassing, especially in a collectivistic culture, where it might reflect poorly on one's family or another in-group. Even in Western cultures, receiving support from others may lead to feeling patronized or helpless. Consideration of what is supportive and what constitutes an additional source of stress requires an ecological examination of support interactions.

The Relationship Context of Support

Social support does not occur in a vacuum but within relationships with others. It is shaped by the dynamics in those relationships. In a number of studies, having close, confiding, reciprocal relationships has been linked to higher levels of social support and to less loneliness and greater life satisfaction (Hobfoll & Vaux, 1993; Barrera, 2000). Supportive relationships are central to both stories in Box 8.1. But it is also true that relationships can create stressors as well as provide support. Researchers have studied many support relationships; we will focus on a few examples.

Families and Contexts Family members, particularly parents and spouses, are important sources of support: generalized and specific. Compared with other sources, they often involve greater commitment and personal knowledge of the individual. However, they also involve greater obligation for reciprocity and greater potential for conflict, and they may not be useful for every stressor.

Pistrang and Barker (1998) studied the help provided to women with breast cancer by husbands and by fellow women patients, analyzing audiotaped 10-minute conversations. The women rated both conversations positively, but trained observers of the tapes rated the fellow patients more supportive, empathic, self-disclosing of feelings, and less critical than husbands. Marital satisfaction did not explain these differences, although other factors may have played a role: gender differences in helping styles, the firsthand experiential knowledge of the fellow patients, and husband fatigue with ongoing demands of caretaking.

Trotter & Allen (2009) studied the role of social support from family and friends for 45 women who experienced domestic violence in the past 12 months. Perhaps not surprisingly, the results of this qualitative study suggest that the reactions of families and friends were not always perceived as supportive. Only 22% of the women reported that responses from family and friends were uniformly supportive; these included assistance with obtaining a safe living situation, emotional support, and other practical aid. However, the majority of women experienced mixed support (78%) that included negative reactions of jeopardizing safety (25% of sample), limited or no emotional support (50% of sample), and limited practical help (33% of the sample). Trotter and Allen conclude that mobilizing support from families and friends can be instrumental in addressing stressors arising from domestic violence but that programs need to determine the nature of the perceived and specific support that families and friends will provide or else the programs may unintentionally put these women at greater risk.

Settings also influence sources of support. A study of first-year students at a suburban, primarily White university found differences in support for African American and European American students. For European Americans, peer support was the most important factor in commitment to college during the first year. Peer support for them was easily available on campus. In contrast, for African Americans, family support was a stronger predictor of commitment to college. Among high-achieving African American male students, family support was especially important (Maton et al., 1996; Maton, Hrabowski, & Greif, 1998). This example is discussed in more detail in Chapter 14.

Natural Helpers and Mentors Natural helpers and mentors are sources of informal support in a community. Some people become natural helpers because their jobs lead to conversations with personal-emotional meaning, such as beauticians and bartenders (Cowen, McKim, & Weissberg, 1981). Mentors are older or more experienced persons (other than one's parents) who support and guide younger, less experienced persons (Rhodes & DuBois, 2008; Sanchez, Esparza, & Colon, 2007). Mentors may occur naturally in one's social network or be provided through a program such as Big Brothers/Big Sisters. Reviews of research on mentoring programs for youth found only modest positive effects for mentoring but also identified characteristics of highly effective mentoring relationships that can be built into future mentoring programs (Dubois, Holloway, Valentine, & Cooper, 2002; Rhodes & Dubois, 2008). Mentoring programs were most helpful with youth in disadvantaged and risky environments. We discuss mentoring programs more fully in Chapter 13.

Relationships as Stressors   Of course, relationships can create stressors as well as support. Studies of HIV-positive persons revealed that depressive symptoms were associated with relationship conflicts with others (Fleishman et al., 2003; Siegel, Raveis, & Karus, 1997). A study of adolescent mothers found that depression was lower when more support was received but greater when those same relationships involved criticism, conflict, and disappointment (Rhodes & Woods, 1995). A study of Israeli women during the 1982 Israel-Lebanon war revealed "pressure cooker" effects (Hobfoll & London, 1986). These occurred because the women all experienced a simultaneous stressor, many individuals sought support, and the shared resources of the group were strained. In other contexts, if support is required over an extended time, for an illness or another chronic problem, conflict often occurs as supporters tire (Coyne, Ellard, & Smith, 1990; Kohn-Wood & Wilson, 2005). Providing support to others takes energy and time. Interventions have been developed to help promote social support among caregivers for whom old networks of support may not be sufficient for the stresses of caring for a loved one with a chronic illness (Dobrof, Ebenstein, Dodd, Epstein, Christ, & Blacker, 2006). Studying support in the context of relationships helps clarify its positive and negative effects.

Social Support Networks

Social support occurs within networks of relationships. Researchers analyze social networks in terms of many variables related to social support. We will focus on three: multidimensionality, density, and reciprocity.

Multidimensionality   Multidimensional relationships are those in which the two persons involved do a number of things together and share a number of role relationships. Multidimensional relationships exist when a coworker is also a friend that we see socially or when we share multiple interests and activities with neighbors. Unidimensional relationships are confined to one role: One sees a coworker only at work; neighbors are not friends. As a student, you have a multidimensional relationship with a classmate who is also a neighbor or who is involved in the same organization. With a person you know only in class, you share a unidimensional relationship.

Because a multidimensional relationship means we see the other person more often, forming and deepening friendships is easier. Multidimensional ties are more resilient. For example, the loss of a job effectively means the end of unidimensional relationships with coworkers, whereas multidimensional relationships would survive. However, unidimensional relationships are also valuable for linking with a broader number of people. (Recall the strength of weak ties and bridging social capital in Chapter 6.)

Density   Your social network contains relationships that your network members have with each other. A high-density network exists when many ties exist between network members—for example, when most network members are friends of each other. Residents of small towns and some urban neighborhoods often live in high-density networks. A low-density network exists when few of the members are closely connected to each other. A person with many friends in different settings—but whose friends do not know each other—has a low-density network. A high-density network and a low-density network could have the same number of persons, but those persons are more interconnected in the high-density network.

High-density networks usually offer greater consensus on norms and advice (Hirsch et al., 1990) and often quicker help in a crisis because the network members are more interconnected. However, low-density networks often hold a greater diversity of persons with a greater variety of skills and life experiences. Thus, they can provide a diversity of resources needed during life transitions such as divorce, bereavement, or entering college (Hirsch, 1980; Hobfoll & Vaux, 1993; Wilcox, 1981). In such transitions, too much density within one's network may inhibit the development of new roles and personal identities, or adaptation to changed circumstances.

Reciprocity   Social networks also vary in the extent to which the individual *both* receives support from others and provides it to others. Reciprocity of support may be the most important aspect of friendship across the life span (Hartup & Stevens, 1997).

In studies of self-help groups and of a religious congregation, Maton (1987, 1988) found that reciprocity of support was associated with greater psychological well-being. When individuals both provided and received support, well-being was higher. Among those who mostly provided or mostly received support and those who did little of either, well-being was lower. Maton's findings refer to overall reciprocity in the person's social network, not to reciprocity within each dyadic relationship. An individual may primarily provide support to one other person while primarily receiving support from another yet have an overall balance of providing and receiving.

What is the role of reciprocity in professional supportive relationships? When examining helping relationships, how important is reciprocity of support? Typically, relationships with doctors, therapists, or other health professionals do not have expectations of reciprocity. Some community psychologists have become concerned about small social support systems of persons with long histories of psychiatric treatment (Nelson et al., 2008; Nelson et al., 1998). Often, persons with serious and persistent mental illness have relied on the mental health system to meet many of their needs; typically, such resources as housing, transportation, employment, and even socializing with peers are managed by mental health workers. In such cases, persons with mental illness have a greatly reduced opportunity to give support as well as receive it.

In community psychology research and action, community psychologists are called to look for how their work can be collaborative and have elements of reciprocity in our professional relationships (see Chapters 1 and 3). Collaboration with mutual help organizations has been one approach advocated by community psychologists interested in promoting the availability of nonprofessional helping capacities in communities and changing professional systems of care (e.g., Davidson, Chinman, Kloos, et al., 1999).

MUTUAL HELP GROUPS

Mutual help, self-help, and mutual support groups are voluntary associations of persons who share a life situation or status that produce challenges for coping in their environments. In many cases, these groups are also alternative settings formed to address shortcomings in existing resources for addressing stressors. Examples include formal organizations—such as Alcoholics Anonymous (AA), an international support organization for persons who have problems with alcohol—or less formal groups of bereaved persons in a local community. Mutual help organizations have had tremendous growth across the world over the last 30 years (Borkman et al., 2005; Pistrang, Barker, & Humphreys, 2008). Over 1,200 mutual help organizations exist worldwide—each with a network of local groups (Chinman et al., 2002). Mutual help groups are usually affiliated with parent organizations and are not isolated microsystems (Borkman, 1991).

In a representative sample of U.S. citizens, 7% of adults reported attending a mutual help group within the past year, and 18% have done so within their lifetimes (Kessler, Mickelson, & Zhao, 1997). A smaller but significant portion of Canadians have reported using mutual help (Gottlieb & Peters, 1991). Twenty years ago, the proportion of the adult population in mutual help groups appears equal to that engaged in psychotherapy (Borkman, 1990). Today, the number of self-help initiatives outnumbers mental health agencies and organizations in the United States (Goldstrom et al., 2006). In just over 50 years, the first widely recognized mutual help organization, AA, has grown from the meeting of two founders to a worldwide organization with thousands of local groups. A majority of those seeking help for alcoholism in the United States attend AA meetings (Chinman et al., 2002). The newest developments in mutual help are online forms of mutual aid that have been expanding with greater accessibility to the Internet (Amichai-Hamburger, 2007; Madara, 1997).

Mutual help groups vary in the degree to which members direct the group. **Mutual assistance self-help** groups are facilitated by a person experiencing the focal concern and do not have professional involvement (e.g., groups like AA). Some **mutual support** groups are peer-led, with professionals assisting in supportive roles. Some professionals have sought to use distinctive features of mutual support to create professionally led peer support groups. (e.g., peer counseling groups in high schools and Reach to Recovery, a group for women with breast cancer) (Borkman, 1990; Salem, Reischl, & Randall, 2008). There is some debate about whether these professionally facilitated groups retain the critical ingredients of the mutual support experience (Davidson, Chinman, Kloos et al., 1999; Salem et al., 2008). However, self-help advocates had correctly predicted that collaboration between professionals and self-help groups will increase (Riessman & Banks, 2001). For simplicity and to focus on the communal aspect of these settings, we use the term *mutual help*, although readers should keep in mind the diversity of groups.

Distinctive Features of Mutual Help Groups

Mutual help groups have five distinctive features (Levy, 2000; Pistrang, Barker, & Humphreys, 2008; Riessman, 1990):

- A focal concern: A problem, life crisis, or issue common to all members
- Peer relationships rather than or in addition to a professional-client relationship
- Reciprocity of helping: Each member receiving and providing help
- Experiential knowledge used for coping
- A community narrative that embodies the experiences and wisdom of its members

Mutual help is based on peer relationships. It involves an exchange of helping based on interpersonal norms of reciprocity rather than a professional service provided for a fee. Each member both provides aid and receives help. Thus, the helping relationship is symmetrical, unlike the asymmetrical professional-client relationship. It also involves the **helper therapy principle** (Riessman, 1990): providing aid to others promotes one's own well-being. For instance, GROW— a mutual help group for persons with mental illnesses—emphasizes this principle: "If you need help, help others" (Maton & Salem, 1995, p. 641). In addition, needing and receiving aid for one's problems are less stigmatizing if everyone in the group shares similar concerns and if one expects to also provide aid.

Another distinctive element of mutual help is the type of knowledge that is most respected and used for helping. **Experiential knowledge** is based on the personal experiences of group members who have coped with the focal concern, often for years. This practical "insider" knowledge is shared in mutual help group meetings. Professional expertise is valuable in many contexts, but professionals usually do not have direct, daily, personal experience in coping with the focal problem.

Mutual help groups offer **community narratives**—expressing in story form a description and explanation of the focal problem—and an explicit guide to recovery or to coping. (We discussed these narratives in Chapter 6.) The group's belief system, rituals, and mutual storytelling provide ways to make meaning of life experiences, to transform one's identity, and to promote coping. As members become committed to the group, they interpret their own life stories and identities in terms similar to the community narrative. This is especially a concern of spiritually based 12-step groups (Humphreys, 2000; Rappaport, 1993, 1995).

Professional mental health treatment and mutual help can be complementary forms of helping (Chinman et al. 2002; Salem, D., Reischl, T.,& Randall, K., 2008). For example, professional treatment offers scientific and clinical knowledge of symptoms and treatments and is especially useful in assessing and treating complicated problems. Mutual help offers the benefits of peer relationships, helping others, and experiential-practical knowledge, at very low or no cost. Members of Schizophrenics Anonymous groups in Michigan clearly distinguished between expertise of group members and leaders and expertise of mental health professionals yet valued both (Salem, Reischl, Gallacher, & Randall, 2000). However, not all professionals are willing to support the use of mutual support to address life problems (Salzer, McFadden, & Rappaport, 1994). In a survey of mental health and rehabilitation professionals in Connecticut, those with more professional experience and those with personal or family experience with mental disabilities viewed mutual help groups more positively than other professionals and were more likely to refer clients to them (Chinman et al., 2002).

Mutual help groups are not helpful for everyone. Knowledge, personal contact, and discretion are helpful when professionals refer clients to specific mutual help groups. However, those caveats are also true for referrals to professionals. A consensus statement by leading researchers called for strengthening ties between drug abuse treatment professionals and self-help groups (Humphreys et al., 2004). Professionals or students can attend mutual help group meetings to initiate mutual understanding and collaboration (Chinman et al., 2002).

Online Mutual Help

Online mutual help groups provide a resource to those with privacy concerns or who cannot attend face-to-face groups (Madara, 1997; Kral, 2006; Ybarra & Eaton, 2005). Two studies of online mutual help groups—one for persons with depression (Salem, Bogat, & Reid, 1997) and another for problem drinkers (Klaw, Huebsch, & Humphreys, 2000)—found that online group interactions generally resembled interactions in face-to-face groups. Interestingly, both studies found gender involvement was different online. Unlike face-to-face groups, men more often used the online depression group and women the online problem drinking group. An online professionally moderated support group effectively engaged Asian American male college students in discussing ethnic identity issues, while face-to-face groups with similar aims had failed (Chang, Yeh, & Krumboltz, 2001). These findings indicate that persons reluctant to participate in face-to-face groups are more willing to join online groups and can receive similar benefits there. Although research on these interventions is still relatively new, several reviews have concluded that there are beneficial outcomes for adults who use Internet-based self-help (Kral, 2006; Ybarra & Eaton, 2005).

Online groups are more accessible for individuals who are less able to leave home. Dunham and associates (1998) developed a local computer mutual help network for low-income single mothers of young children. Each mother received a computer donated by local organizations and access to the network. A core group of mothers used the service intensively and experienced declines in parenting stress. Online groups are also helpful for persons with stressful illnesses. As we noted earlier, persons with health conditions that limit mobility may gain a particular benefit. In randomized experiments, online social support programs for HIV-positive persons, women with breast cancer, and adults with Type 2 diabetes were effective in providing support (Barrera, Glasgow, McKay, Boles, & Feil, 2002; Gustafson et al., 1999). In the diabetes study, the online support setting had a forum directed by persons with diabetes, where participants discussed day-to-day coping; a forum where professionals introduced topics and led discussion; and real-time chat rooms. In terms of policy, some researchers now argue that online mutual support needs institutional support, as it constitutes a medium that can reach "tens of millions of Americans ... and millions more abroad who are already seeking online mental health information" (Chang, 2005, p. 881).

Mutual Help Outcomes

Empirical evaluations of mutual help programs have documented their potential in helping members make changes in their lives (Kryouz et al., 2002; den Boer et al., 2004; Pistrang et al., 2008). For example, research with GROW found that weekly attendees of meetings experienced more positive changes in psychological, interpersonal, and community adjustment than infrequent attendees. Compared with matched controls, GROW members spent less than half as many days in psychiatric hospitalization over a 32-month period (Rappaport, 1993; Maton & Salem, 1995). In general, persons with psychiatric disabilities who participate in mutual help groups (not just GROW) have lower symptom levels and hospitalization rates, shorter hospital stays, and enhanced positive functioning and social networks (Chinman et al., 2002).

Studies of participants in AA and similar 12-step groups have generated similar findings (Kelly, 2003). Humphreys, Finney, and Moos (1994) followed 439 men and women with an alcohol abuse problem in the San Francisco area over three years. Those more involved with AA over the three-year period were more likely to develop active coping strategies, including less use of alcohol. AA participants also develop greater friendship resources, especially support from others committed to abstinence (Chinman et al., 2002; Humphreys & Noke, 1997).

It is important to note that mutual help groups are not for everyone. Dropout rates are significant (also an issue for professional treatment), and mutual help alone may not be enough for some especially complicated problems (Humphreys, 1997). Moreover, some mutual help groups welcome diverse members and address social injustices underlying some personal problems, whereas others do not (Rapping, 1997).

However, thinking of mutual help only as a treatment method overlooks much of its value (Humphreys & Rappaport, 1994). One joins a mutual help group for an extended period—perhaps for life. Membership incurs responsibility not only for working on one's own concerns but also for helping others. For example, Oxford Houses—a mutual help, self-governed, communal living arrangement for persons in substance abuse recovery—have counteracted neighbors' concerns about living near a halfway house by focusing on improving the community around them as well as themselves (Jason et al., 2008). Rappaport (1993) argued that a more revealing view of such groups is that they are normative communities, providing a sense of belonging, identification with the group, and mutual commitment: a psychological sense of community.

SPIRITUALITY AND COPING

Long before community psychology was organized, many people turned to spiritual practices and religious communities for support in times of stress. In times of suffering or loss but also in times of joy and of deeply felt commitment, people have used spiritual resources to understand their lives, to receive and give support, or to experience the transcendent. A spiritual perspective can help make sense of the incomprehensible, unfathomable, and uncontrollable (Pargament, 1997; 2008). This can be especially meaningful when one faces limitations in the ability to cope, such as when Western cultural and psychological assumptions about controlling outcomes in one's life fall short.

Spirituality and religion offer distinctive personal and social resources for coping. Personal resources include a spiritual relationship with God or another transcendent experience, a set of beliefs that provides meaning in life and may promote coping, and such specific coping methods as prayer and meditation. Social resources include membership and support within a religious congregation or another spiritual setting (including spiritually based mutual help groups) and shared spiritual practices and rituals (Fiala, Bjorck, & Gorsuch, 2002; Folkman & Moskowitz, 2004; Pargament, 2008; Pargament & Maton, 2000).

However, the personal and social impact of religion and spirituality can also be negative (Hebert et al., 2009). In a survey of U.S. battered women, one-half of respondents reported negative experiences with religion (Pargament, 1997). Spirituality and religion can create or worsen stressors, such as when the person interprets a stressor in a spiritual way that prevents helpful coping or when personal conflicts with a congregation are not resolved (Pargament, 1997). Among a sample of resilient African American single mothers, some found involvement in a religious community offered "protection and blessing" (Brodsky, 2000, pp. 213–214), while others found spiritual solace and strength outside religious congregations or avoided them.

Of course, religious beliefs, institutions, and cultural forms of spirituality have much larger purposes than existing solely as resources for coping. Their usefulness for coping must be understood within those larger aims. Spirituality involves a sense of transcendence—of going beyond oneself and daily life (Sarason, 1993; Hill, 2001; Kelly, 2002). Spiritual persons often view their relationship with God or a spiritual realm as distinct from other relationships. Spirituality cannot be simply reduced to coping resources (Mattis & Jagers, 2001). Our focus here on coping concerns only part of the meaning of spirituality.

Empirical Research on Spirituality and Coping

Empirically, how do spiritual and religious factors affect coping outcomes? Pargament's (1997) classic review of empirical studies of spirituality, religion, and coping has shaped how community psychologists think about spirituality and coping. Participants in these studies were mostly North American adults, including persons with chronic and terminal illnesses, bereaved widows and children, victims of automobile accidents and of floods, Whites and African Americans, heterosexuals and gays, and senior citizens. Most who indicated religious involvement were Christian. However, growing research literature has documented the benefits of religion and spirituality for coping of people across religious beliefs (e.g., Tarakeshwar et al., 2003, 2006; Rosmarin et al., 2009; Lee & Chan, 2009). Researchers measure a variety of coping outcomes, including psychological distress and well-being and health.

Spiritual-religious coping practices include prayer, a sense of a personal relationship with God or another transcendent experience, framing stressors in spiritual terms, engaging in spiritual practices and rituals, and seeking support from congregation members. Religious and nonreligious persons may use them in particular circumstances. Pargament's (1997) review documented five general findings about spiritual-religious coping:

- It was particularly important with stressful, largely uncontrollable situations.

- It was often empirically related to positive coping outcomes even after accounting for the influence of nonspiritual coping methods.

- Coping methods most related to positive outcomes included (a) the perception of a spiritual relationship with a trustworthy and loving God, (b) activities such as prayer, (c) religious reappraisal promoting the sense that growth can come from stressful events, and (d) receiving support from fellow members of a religious congregation. These findings have also been supported in more recent studies (Folkman & Moskowitz, 2004).

- While there are many positive relationships between religion, spirituality, and coping, studies are beginning to show patterns of negative religious coping. Negative effects included self-blame, a view of a harsh and severe deity, and lack of support from one's religious congregation.

- Persons with low incomes, the elderly, ethnic minorities, women, and the widowed were more likely to find religion and spirituality useful for coping than other groups. What these groups seem to have in common is less access to secular sources of power and resources that can be used to address their problems.

Pargament's reviews (1997, 2008) argue that religion and spirituality are important for understanding coping and community life. Their impact may be positive or negative. Their most distinctive coping contributions may occur when other resources are lacking or when stressors are uncontrollable. But this research is in its early stages, with much to be learned (Pargament & Maton, 2000; Folkman & Moskowitz, 2004). Community psychologists are beginning to develop an empirical foundation to understand stress and coping across diverse cultural contexts and religious experiences beyond African American and White Christians. For example, studies have examined the spiritual and religious experiences of engaged Buddhism, Chinese, Hindu, Jewish, Korean American, Mexican American, and Native Alaskan spirituality (Bjorck, Lee, & Cohen, 1997; Dockett, 1999; Hazel & Mohatt, 2001; Kress & Elias, 2001; Mattis & Jagers, 2001; Tarakeshwar et al., 2006; Leach et al., 2008; Dinh et al., 2009; Lee & Chan, 2009).

CONCLUSION

In this chapter, we provide an ecological model of the relationships between stress and coping. In particular, we examined the importance of understanding the context of stress and coping for selecting interventions that can prevent negative outcomes and promote positive outcomes. This model also outlines processes and resources relevant to coping, highlighting community-based resources. However, we do not assume that these concepts fully reflect the complex reality of coping or the diversity of resources and interventions that can be used. We encourage you to consider what else needs to be included and to diagram your own ecological model of coping.

CHAPTER SUMMARY

1. This chapter presents an ecological model for understanding the coping process. This model emphasizes the importance of social, cultural, and situational contexts and resources in coping. The model includes *risk factors* and *protective factors*.

2. *Distal factors* are predisposing situations or conditions indirectly related to stress and coping. They may involve risk factors or protective factors. Some are *contextual*; others are *personal*.

3. *Proximal stressors* represent a threatened or actual loss of resources, and they trigger stress. They include *major life events*, *life transitions*, *daily hassles*, and *disasters*. Multiple stressors can compound into *vicious spirals* of increasing stressors.

4. *Stress reactions* include cognitive appraisals, emotions, and physiological processes.

5. Persons need to activate potential resources for coping with stress. These include *material resources, social-emotional competencies,* and *social, cultural, and spiritual resources.*

6. Coping processes involve *reappraisal* and three types of coping: *problem-focused, emotion-focused,* and *meaning-focused.* Coping is contextual; the best approach depends on the situation and persons involved. Effective coping can create *virtuous spirals* of improved coping and less stress.

7. Coping outcomes refer to the psychological or health effects of coping. These include such positive outcomes as *wellness, resilience, thriving,* and *empowerment* and such problematic outcomes as *distress, dysfunction,* and *clinical disorders.*

8. Interventions to promote coping can occur at multiple ecological levels. Community interventions include *social and policy advocacy, organizational consultation, alternative settings, community coalitions, prevention and promotion programs, crisis intervention,* and *case management.* Interventions strategies need to match ecological understanding of the stressors and coping.

9. *Social support* is an important type of naturally occurring support that encompasses two basic types: *generalized* (or *perceived support*) and *specific* (or *enacted support*). Support occurs in relationships, including families and *natural helpers* or *mentors.* Relationships can be sources of stressors as well as support. Important qualities of *social support networks* include *multidimensionality, density,* and *reciprocity.*

10. *Mutual help groups* are also important community coping resources that offer support that professional forms of helping cannot provide. They have five key qualities: *focal concern, peer relationships, reciprocity of helping* (involving the *helper therapy principle*), *experiential knowledge,* and *community narratives of coping.* Online mutual help groups are a growing resource. Mutual help groups are not a cure-all but offer positive outcomes for many.

11. *Spirituality and religion* are a third type of naturally occurring community resources for coping. They can provide personal, social, and material resources. Positive outcomes of spiritual coping include usefulness with largely uncontrollable stressors, especially among groups with less access to secular resources. However, spiritual and religious coping and settings can also have negative effects, and research with more diverse spiritual traditions and populations is beginning to refine our understanding.

RECOMMENDED READINGS

Barrera, M. (2000). Social support research in community psychology. In J. Rappaport & E. Seidman (Eds.), *Handbook of community psychology* (pp. 215–246). New York: Kluwer Academic/Plenum.

Brown, L. D., Shepherd, M. D., Wituk, S. A. & Meissen, G. (2008). Special issue on mental health self-help. *American Journal of Community Psychology, 42*, 105–202.

Dohrenwend, B. (1978). Social stress and community psychology. *American Journal of Community Psychology, 6*, 1–14. Reprinted in T. Revenson et al. (Eds.) (2002). *A quarter century of community psychology* (pp. 103–117). New York: Kluwer Academic/Plenum.

Moos, R. (2002). The mystery of human context and coping: An unraveling of clues. *American Journal of Community Psychology, 30*, 67–88.

Pargament, K. I. (1997). *The Psychology of Religion and Coping: Theory, Research, Practice*, Guilford Publications, New York, NY.

RECOMMENDED WEBSITES

Mutual Help Clearinghouses

American Self-Help Clearinghouse: Self-Help Group Sourcebook Online:
http://mentalhelp.net/selfhelp

Lists local, face-to-face self-help groups and organizations. Also includes readings on self-help and how to start a group.

Fraternidad de Grupos de Autoayuda y Ayuda Mutua (Self-Help and Mutual Aid Group Fraternity):
http://www.ayudamutua.org

Clearinghouse of diverse self-help group materials in Spanish. Started by a Mexican psychologist.

National Mental Health Consumers' Self-Help Clearinghouse:
http://mhselfhelp.org

Consumer-run site with information on the mental health consumer movement and related organizations.

Self Help Nottingham:
www.selfhelp.org.uk

Links to self-help group research and listservs for group researchers.

Mental Health

American Psychological Association: Psychology Topics and Help Center:
http://www.apa.org/topics and http://www.apa.org/helpcenter

Information on topics related to coping and psychological interventions. The Help Center is consumer-oriented.

National Mental Health Association:
http://www.nmha.org

Information on this national advocacy organization with local chapters for the prevention and treatment of mental disorders.

U.S. Government Centers for Disease Control and Prevention:
http://www.cdc.gov

> Information on health and illness: prevention, treatment, health issues in the news; links to other health sites.

U.S. Government National Mental Health Information Center:
http://store.samhsa.gov/home

> Provides general and consumer-oriented information on mental health and federal programs.

9

Prevention and Promotion:
Key Concepts

HIRB/Index Stock/PhotoLibrary

OPENING EXERCISE: THE BROAD STREET PUMP

In 1854, a cholera epidemic struck London. Cholera was a relatively new (the first cholera pandemic began in 1816) and deadly disease. An outbreak in 1832 had killed more than 55,000 people in Great Britain, and in 1849, cholera claimed 14,137 victims in London alone. In 1852, the disease struck again. At the time, it was commonly believed that cholera, like other diseases, was spread through miasma (bad air). The mystery about the nature of the disease added to the fear and panic. The only way people knew to escape the disease was to flee the towns and cities in which it appeared. And for many people, especially the poor, leaving was not an option. A physician in London, John Snow, published a pamphlet disputing the miasma theory and suggested that cholera was reproduced in the human body and spread through food or water (he did not know which). Suppose you were John Snow in London in 1854. What could you do to stop the cholera epidemic? Could these deaths be prevented?

What Snow did was to develop a new approach to thinking about epidemics. He took a map of London and plotted the location of the homes in which 578 people had died from cholera. He went to those homes and spoke to the family members of the people who had died. He found that almost all the people who died had gotten their drinking water from the Broad Street pump. On his now famous map, he plotted the position of 13 water pumps, showing graphically the relationship between the pump on Broad Street and the cholera deaths. He took this information to a committee of city officials, who removed the handle from the Broad Street pump the next day. The cholera epidemic subsided (Johnson, 2006).

Snow is now considered one of the fathers of epidemiology, and his work in identifying the source of the 1854 London cholera epidemic is considered one of the founding events in the field of public health. This story also plays a central role in the development of community psychology because of what it teaches us about prevention. First, even if you do not know how to cure a problem, you may still be able to prevent it. Second, you do not need to know the cause of a problem to prevent it; you just need to understand something about the mechanisms through which the problem is transmitted or sustained. Third, you can often prevent a problem through changing some aspect of human behavior. And fourth, while individual behavior change can contribute to prevention, complete prevention of a problem often relies on public action.

These lessons have been fundamental to the development of prevention science and its application to emotional, behavioral, and cognitive disorders.

INTRODUCTION: PREVENTION AND PROMOTION ARE ALL AROUND YOU

In the previous chapters, we presented concepts that community psychologists use to understand individuals and communities. In this chapter and the next, we convey how community psychology values, concepts, and tools can be used in the context of preventing problem behaviors and mental health difficulties and promoting sound mental health and social competence. In this chapter, we outline key concepts and give some examples of prevention programming. In Chapter 10, we review in detail how to implement prevention/promotion innovations in a variety of contexts.

The concept of prevention has been explicitly valued in cultures around the world and throughout written history. Just take a moment to think of the proverbs you know that relate to prevention. Prevention and promotion are also fundamental concepts in the field of community psychology and are related to the core values of the field. The core values of individual and family wellness, respect for human diversity, citizen participation, collaboration and community strengths, and empirical grounding are central to the development and successful implementation of prevention and promotion programs.

Every day, parents and many others conduct prevention/promotion programs without the assistance of community psychologists. Prevention and promotion efforts are ubiquitous. Try this exercise: Think of examples in your own life of efforts (formal programs or informal actions) to prevent problem behaviors. Which efforts had a lasting effect? Why?

In addition, ask yourself this: Does it matter who developed or who implemented the prevention effort? The majority of prevention work is not done by community psychologists or by psychologists at all. It is conducted by teachers, nurses, social workers, police officers, and parents. As we mentioned in Chapter 1, community psychology has had a "peculiar success" in having its approaches widely adopted even though the field itself is not well known (Snowden, 1987). This is particularly true of prevention science. Since its founding, the field has been interdisciplinary and collaborative—so much so that its members and their work in prevention and promotion appear in many places, including law, education, government, public health, social work, the corporate world, and several fields of psychology (especially developmental, organizational, school, educational, and clinical). Furthermore, members of other disciplines often collaborate on research and interventions that appear as part of collections of work in community psychology. In this chapter, we help you recognize some of the work community psychologists are doing in prevention and promotion, alongside the work of practitioners in other disciplines and in various countries. We then discuss some successful prevention and promotion programs that illustrate the ideas we present in this chapter.

What Is Prevention?

Prevention is a commonsense concept that derives from Latin words meaning "to anticipate" or "before something to come." The language of prevention is found in all aspects of public endeavor. Parents try to prevent children from hurting themselves; police try to prevent crimes; the legal system is designed to prevent violation of certain rights; road signs are created and posted to prevent people from getting lost. While the idea of prevention can be found throughout the written history of humankind, the idea that prevention concepts could be systematically applied to mental disorders has a very recent history.

In 1959, George Albee looked at the number of people in the United States who could benefit from mental health counseling in a given year. Then, he looked at the number of mental health clinicians the country could produce. His analysis showed that there could never be a sufficient number of clinicians trained to provide all the needed mental health services for the population. Consider the implications of this extraordinary finding. Therapeutic resources were scarce and would realistically remain scarce. If we continued to rely on a one-on-one, professional-to-patient method for providing psychotherapy, the U.S. society would never be able to train enough professionals to provide therapy to everyone who needed it. And, not incidentally, we would not be able to pay for it.

Another issue raised by Albee's (1959) findings concerns how scarce treatment resources are distributed. A series of epidemiological studies (Hollingshead & Redlich, 1958; Myers & Bean, 1968) showed a strong relationship between socioeconomic status, ethnicity, and services received. Members of poor and minority groups were more likely to receive severe diagnoses, to receive medication rather than psychotherapy, and to be seen in groups rather than individually. The preferred clients were those most like the therapists—male, Caucasian, verbal, and successful.

Psychologists working in the 1950s saw research saying the following: 1) Psychotherapy may not work. 2) Even if it does work, we can't provide it to everyone who needs it. 3) Even if we could provide it, it is not equally available for all groups. These people looked at this research and said, "There has to be a better way."

Now we go back to our opening exercise: the story of John Snow and the beginning of the public health model. The public health model is based on the idea that no disease has ever been eradicated through the treatment of its victims. Snow did not develop a cure for cholera or even a more effective treatment. Instead, he prevented new occurrences of the disorder. Mental health professionals began thinking about what it would mean to apply this concept to cognitive, emotional, and behavior disorders. Our need for psychotherapy would be greatly decreased if we could prevent problems in living from arising to begin with.

Although community psychology has embraced the concept of prevention, there is another aspect of the concept that merits consideration. Think about these examples of everyday prevention efforts. Parents try to help children learn how to care for themselves safely; educators encourage learning in different forms; employers train and supervise employees to work effectively; road signs are posted to help people get to where they want to go. These examples focus on developing desired competencies, skills, and abilities. Overall health and quality of life become the goal, more than simply preventing psychiatric disorders or types of problem behaviors. Cowen (1991, 2000) championed the term *wellness* as a more fitting goal of preventive efforts. While wellness refers to life satisfaction or gratification in living, it is a transactional concept linked to the social ecology within which people live. Again, in Cowen's (1991) colorful words: "The pot-of-gold behind the pursuit of a wellness rainbow might be a genuine betterment of the human condition" (p. 408). Cowen's views have become central to how community psychologists think about prevention of disorder and promotion of competence and wellness.

CONCEPTS FOR UNDERSTANDING PREVENTION AND PROMOTION

In this section, we describe the historical progression of concepts from prevention of disorder, to promotion of competence, to ideas of strengths and thriving. In so doing, we define and illustrate key concepts in the contexts in which they are used.

Caplan: Primary, Secondary, and Tertiary Prevention

There is a rich history to the concept of prevention, rooted in the field of public health and the mental hygiene movement of the early 20th century (Heller, Price, Reinharz, Riger, & Wandersmann, 1984; Spaulding & Balch, 1983). However, Gerald Caplan is recognized as the individual whose use of the term *prevention* led to its becoming a part of the mental health lexicon. Caplan (1964) made a distinction between the following three types of prevention.

Primary Prevention   This is intervention given to entire populations when they are not in a condition of known need or distress. The goal is to lower the rate of new cases (from a public health perspective to reduce the incidence) of disorders. Primary prevention intervenes to reduce potentially harmful circumstances before they have a chance to create difficulty. Examples of this are such things as vaccinations, fluoridating water, and providing decision-making, problem solving, and skill-building programs to children in preschool. Similarly, primary prevention can also be thought of as being applied to all persons in a given setting, regardless of potential need (e.g., all fifth-graders in preparation for transition to middle school or all first-year college students).

Secondary Prevention   This is intervention given to populations showing early signs of a disorder or difficulty. Another term for this is *early intervention*. This concept is a precursor of current notions of being "at risk," which are discussed shortly. Examples of secondary prevention are programs targeted to children who are shy or withdrawn, those who are beginning to have academic difficulty, or adults who are getting into conflicts with coworkers on the job.

Secondary prevention presupposes some method of determining which individuals are at risk. Identifying such individuals creates a potential for stigmatization— both because they do not currently have a disorder and because they might never develop one. Improving methods of risk identification represents an important area of work in community psychology.

Tertiary Prevention   This is intervention given to populations who have a disorder, with the intention of limiting the disability caused by the disorder, reducing its intensity and duration, and thereby preventing future reoccurrence or additional complications. This type of effort when applied to individuals is referred to as **rehabilitation.** When these efforts are directed toward populations, they are labeled **tertiary prevention.**

If it strikes you that it is difficult to differentiate tertiary prevention from treatment, you are not alone. But Caplan had a purpose that is often forgotten by his critics today. A child psychiatrist by training, Caplan was trying to introduce a preventive way of thinking to the treatment-oriented medical, psychiatric, mental health, and social service fields. By emphasizing the similarities of prevention and treatment, he was able to link these concerns. Ultimately, he was successful in that the idea of prevention took hold, becoming a central tenet of such fields as community psychology and school psychology, and, increasingly, clinical and health psychology.

However, Caplan's (1964) framework appealed to those seeking resources for treatment. Some early prevention grants were given to programs designed for such things as the tertiary prevention of schizophrenia—a worthy goal but not exactly what Caplan had in mind. Prevention, even tertiary, is on a community level. As many have noted, prevention is a difficult concept to grasp. One is trying to keep away what is not (yet) there. Would it ever arrive if the prevention effort was not in place? Others have stated that if prevention is to be worthwhile, then one must specify what one is preventing. An emphasis on defining specific conditions such as suicide, depression, and conduct disorder as goals of prevention reflects this viewpoint.

Klein and Goldston (1977) were among a number of community psychologists who attempted to clarify the issues raised by Caplan's (1964) definitions and others' interpretations. Although agreeing with the definition of primary prevention, they felt it important to relabel secondary prevention as treatment given because of early identification and tertiary prevention as rehabilitation services. This helps to provide a clearer distinction between prevention and treatment for specific or severe problems. For example, debate still ensues over whether interventions given to shy children are best thought of as prevention or treatment. But other models have now risen to prominence, and thus, it pays little to dwell on past inconsistencies when current inconsistencies are available for examination.

The IOM Report: Universal, Selective, and Indicated Measures

A report by the U.S. Institute of Medicine (IOM; Mrazek & Haggerty, 1994) has had great influence on current thinking about prevention. Its main conceptual contribution is the idea of universal, selective, or indicated measures or methods for prevention.

Universal Preventive Measures   These interventions are designed to be offered to everyone in a given population group, and they are typically administered to populations that are not in distress. This is similar to primary prevention.

Selective Preventive Measures   These are designed for people at above-average risk for developing behavioral or emotional disorders. That risk may be based on their environment (e.g., low income or family conflict) or personal factors (e.g., low self-esteem, difficulties in school). These risk characteristics are associated with the development of particular disorders but are not symptoms of the disorder itself.

Indicated Preventive Measures   These are directed toward individual people who are considered at high risk for developing disorder in the future, especially if they show early symptoms of the disorder. However, they do not meet criteria for full-fledged diagnosis of mental disorder.

Interestingly, the IOM report places mental health promotion (including concepts related to competence and wellness) into a separate area, distinct from prevention. The editors viewed self-esteem and mastery as the main focus of mental health promotion, with *competence*, *self-efficacy*, and *individual empowerment* all terms commonly used in describing such efforts. The IOM report defined its focus in terms of whether an approach prevents a specific disorder, not in terms of competence enhancement.

Weissberg and Greenberg (1997) raised some thoughtful questions about the IOM framework. For example, should a violence prevention program be considered a universal intervention in a school with few incidents of violence yet selective in a school where violence is more common? Because depression is diagnosed more often among girls than boys, should a program for prevention of depression be considered universal if given to a troop of Boy Scouts but selective if given to a Girl Scout troop? For disorders such as conduct disorder, what is the boundary between predictors of a disorder (for selective prevention) and early symptoms (for indicated prevention)? Consider a program delivered to a class in which there is a diversity of students: (a) a student with conduct disorder and another with attention-deficit hyperactivity disorder; (b) several disaffected, underachieving, unmotivated students; and (c) others with no behavioral or emotional difficulty, some even with great strengths. Is the same program considered universal for the latter group, selective for the disaffected students, and indicated for the children with diagnosed disorders? Beneath these definitional questions is a fundamental concern for the direction in which preventive efforts should be headed—in terms of research and action. It is at this point that community psychologists would look to the fundamental values of our field to guide their prevention efforts.

Prevention of Disorder and Promotion of Wellness and Competence

Earlier in this chapter, we presented Cowen's view that the goal of intervention should not just be the prevention of disorder but rather the enhancement of wellness and competence. He and many others who share his viewpoint believed that the goal of merely preventing disorders was setting our sights too low. Rather than a goal of having people and families minimally functional, our goal should be to ensure that they are functioning to their fullest potential.

Among prevention scientists and public policymakers, there is a continuing debate about where the emphasis of time and resources is best placed: on prevention or promotion. In addition, within these areas, there are varying options for emphasis (e.g., based on age, socioeconomics, gender, and ethnicity). Convincing spokespersons of different viewpoints arise periodically, and this debate is ongoing. In general, the debate can be framed between proponents of prevention of disorder and those believing that promotion of wellness and social competence should be emphasized.

Advocates of the prevention view argue that we are learning a great deal about how to prevent such specific disorders as depression, suicide, conduct disorders, and schizophrenia. Research should be directed toward isolating and reducing the operation of risk factors most closely targeted with specific disorders. This view is most likely to be associated with selective and indicated interventions based on the IOM report.

Advocates for promotion note that many people are not in a state of sound psychological well-being despite not having specific disorders. We know a great deal about how to promote sound health and social competence, drawing in part from interventions in public health in such areas as the prevention of cardiovascular disease, from school settings in areas such as social and emotional skill building, and from workplace efforts to increase organizational effectiveness.

Research should be directed toward identifying and understanding the factors that promote health, wellness, and competence in daily living. These will differ in different living environments, cross-culturally and internationally.

In reality, it is often difficult to separate the two goals of health promotion and problem prevention. Several prevention scientists have argued that the distinction between prevention and promotion is particularly baseless when discussing child development. Children who do not drop out of school, do not abuse substances, are not involved in juvenile delinquency, and do not become pregnant as teenagers may still have problems developing into healthy, happy, well-functioning adults. So, programs that focus solely on preventing those negative outcomes will not be designed to ensure optimum development (Weissberg, Kumpfer, & Seligman, 2003). Programs that are aimed at the prevention of a specific problem may be focused on perceived deficits in the population, ignoring community psychology's focus on strengths and building competencies. In fact, strictly focused prevention programs may not be as effective as those with a broader health promotion focus. The distinction between the two types of programs becomes even more confused when you realize that health promotion programs are often evaluated in terms of specific prevention goals, basically because those types of goals are easier to specify and measure.

Issues of prevention and mental health have never been isolated from political and ideological considerations. As you learned in Chapter 2, in U.S. society, the social zeitgeist during conservative times favors individual, illness-oriented conceptions of mental health and other social problems. Prevention in those times tends to be understood in terms of preventing specific disorders. In more progressive times, an environmental focus supports a definition of prevention closer to the promotion of overall health and wellness and competence.

The United States has been experiencing a conservative social period, but at the time of this writing, there is some evidence that that may be changing. Research in recent years has focused on biological factors in mental health, and the mental health field is seeking to prove itself to be rigorous (at least as rigorous as medicine is perceived to be) and cost-conscious. Insurance companies and federal granting agencies prefer to pay for clear prevention outcomes rather than support efforts to improve health. However, such organizations as the World Federation of Mental Health and the World Health Organization tend not to share the view of the United States. Theirs is a more holistic view of health, in which mental health and physical well-being—which extends to basic issues of shelter, food, and freedom from war, societal anarchy, and enslavement—are essential parts of the overall picture. Many community psychologists embrace this broader view of health.

The goals of preventing specific disorders and promoting wellness and competence are not mutually exclusive, and the techniques used to pursue them may be the same in particular circumstances. There are strong parallels with physical health, where health-promoting activities such as a sound diet are valuable and may also serve to prevent problems such as cardiovascular disease—but also may not have specific preventive effects on specific conditions or illnesses. This issue may become a factor in the politics of prevention and promotion programs. Because the goals of prevention programs are generally easier to understand and evaluate than the goals of promotion programs, they may receive greater support among policymakers. However, as you will see later in this chapter, many programs that are designed as prevention programs actually end up having broader, health promotion effects.

Community psychologists try to keep a perspective on prevention that is best understood as an umbrella providing a common cover for both viewpoints or as a bridge linking them. Sometimes, community psychology knowledge is used to provide preventive interventions to specific populations to prevent specific disorders and at other times to general populations microsystems to promote overall wellness. The outcomes of these interventions are measured in terms of lowered incidence of a specific disorder and/or in terms of increased competence for coping, as appropriate.

PROMOTION OF WHAT? RISK AND RESILIENCY

In 1955, one of the most remarkable longitudinal studies in the history of developmental psychology began on the island of Kauai. Emmy Werner and her colleagues followed 698 children, every child born on the island that year, for 40 years. The children were multiracial, and a full 30% experienced one or more risk factors in their lives, such as prenatal or birth complications, poverty, family violence, divorce, or parents with psychopathology or low education. One of the first important findings to arise from this study was that two-thirds of the children who experienced four or more of these risk factors in the first two years of life developed learning disabilities, behavior disorders, delinquency, or mental health problems before adulthood (Werner, 1996; Werner, 2005). This finding and others like it helped to lead to the **cumulative-risk hypothesis** (Rutter, 1979). This hypothesis recognizes that almost all children can deal with one risk factor in their lives without it increasing their risk of negative outcomes. Most children can handle two risk factors. But when you get up to four risk factors, the chances of a negative outcome increase exponentially. It is not the presence of risk in a child's life that results in negative outcomes; it is the level of cumulative risk.

But in the more than 40 years since this study began, many people, including Emmy Werner, have decided that the findings on cumulative risk are not the only important thing we learned from this study. Instead, much of Werner's work has focused on the 30% of the children exposed to four or more risk factors who did not develop behavior or learning problems.

> ... one out of three of these children grew into competent, confident and caring adults. They did not develop any behavior or learning problems during childhood or adolescence. They succeeded in school, managed home and social life well, and set realistic educational and vocational goals and expectations for themselves. By the time they

reached age 40, not one of these individuals was unemployed, none had been in trouble with the law, and none had to rely on social services. Their divorce rates, mortality rates, and rates of chronic health problems were significantly lower at midlife than those of their same sex peers. Their educational and vocational accomplishment were equal to or even exceeded those of children who had grown up in more economically secure and stable home environments. (Werner, 2005, pp 11–12)

Werner termed these children who overcame multiple risk factors to become "competent, confident, caring adults" resilient, and the study of resiliency became the focus of her research. **Resiliency** refers to the ability of some individuals to overcome adverse conditions and experience healthy development. She and her colleagues identified factors that served to protect children exposed to multiple risk factors from negative outcomes. These protective factors (summarized in Table 9.1) have also been identified by other researchers (Garmezy, 1985; Masten & Powell, 2003; Rutter & Sroufe, 2000).

One of the important things to note about this table is the ways in which the factors interrelate and affect each other. Children with a positive outlook on life and an adaptable, social personality find it easier to form and maintain positive relationships. The presence of prosocial organizations in a community and the ability for children (or adults) to access those services provide opportunities for the development of positive relationships. The presence of high-quality health care and social services in a community might mean that there are programs that teach appropriate parenting skills (we will talk about some of those programs later). And the existence of strong, supportive relationships outside the family helps to support positive parenting.

T A B L E 9.1   **Examples of Attributes of Individuals and Their Contexts Often Associated with Resilience**

Individual Differences	Cognitive abilities (IQ scores, attentional skills, executive functioning skills)
	Self-perceptions of competence, worth, confidence (self-efficacy, self-esteem)
	Temperament and personality (adaptability, sociability)
	Self-regulation skills (impulse control, affect and arousal regulation)
	Positive outlook on life (hopefulness, belief that life has meaning, faith)
Relationships	Parenting quality (including warmth, structure and monitoring, expectations)
	Close relationships with competent adults (parents, relatives, mentors)
	Connections to prosocial and rule-abiding peers (among older children)
Community Resources and Opportunities	Good schools
	Connections to prosocial organizations (such as clubs or religious groups)
	Neighborhood quality (public safety, collective supervision, libraries, recreation centers)
	Quality of social services and health care

SOURCE: From Masten & Powell, 2003.

Before we leave the story of the Kauai Longitudinal Study, you might be interested in hearing about the 70% of the children exposed to four or more risk factors who did not display resiliency in childhood. These children all displayed significant behavioral or mental health problems by age 18. They experienced school failure, drug abuse, teen pregnancy, delinquency, and psychopathology. But when Werner and her colleagues followed up with these people at ages 32 and 40, they found that the majority were doing fine in middle age. They had stable employment, were happy with their relationships, and were productive members of their communities. What the researchers found, and what has been documented in other longitudinal studies of resiliency, is that for the majority of these troubled teens, the *opening of opportunities* in early adulthood led to significant improvement in functioning by middle age (Werner, 2005, p. 12). These opportunities included education, vocational and educational opportunities provided through the military, geographic relocation, a good marriage (often a second marriage), conversion to a religion that provided membership in a strong and active faith community, and surviving a life threatening experience.

Maston and Powell emphasize that resilience arises from what they term *ordinary magic* (Maston & Powell, 2003, p. 15). While these individuals are facing extraordinary adversity (think about what exposure to four or more risk factors means in the life of a child), they overcome that adversity through resources and relationships that are part of normal, everyday life. Professional intervention was found to play a very small role in the lives of resilient individuals (Werner, 2005).

The research on risk and protective factors, resiliency, and ordinary magic has resulted in a rich field devoted to exploring ways to decrease the presence of risk factors and increase the presence of protective factors in the lives of all children. The goal is not just to decrease the prevalence of disorders and problem behaviors but, rather, to develop strengths, support positive development, and promote resilience and thriving. Increasingly, this is becoming the goal of the majority of the programs described in this chapter and the next—even if the original intent of the program was narrowly defined as the prevention of a specific problem.

In Chapter 8, we presented a model of risk and protective processes in coping in which the positive outcomes are resilience, wellness, thriving, and empowerment. That model could easily be used to describe processes and intended outcomes in prevention and promotion. The goal is to use the research on specific risk and protective factors to ensure that everyone in a community has a chance to experience the ordinary magic that helps people to thrive.

Two examples of effective models for strengthening this ordinary magic in communities are the Communities That Care program and the Search Institute's Developmental Assets model. These models specifically address promoting healthy development of children and youth by changing the contexts of children's lives.

The Search Institute (2004) reviewed existing research and conducted extensive research of its own to develop a list of 40 developmental assets. **Developmental assets** are factors within the child, the child's family, or the child's school, neighborhood, or community that promote healthy child and youth development (Scales, Leffert, & Lerner, 2004). Internal assets include a strong commitment to learning, positive values, social competencies, and a positive identity. External assets include supportive relationships, opportunities for prosocial involvement, clear boundaries and expectations for behavior, and opportunities for constructive use of time. Many of the developmental assets identified in the research reflect the factors related to resiliency listed in Table 9.1.

The Search Institute has a survey available that coalitions can administer to youth in their communities to determine which developmental assets are strongly represented in their community and which are weak or absent. The coalition then uses the results of that assessment to develop an action plan to promote positive youth development. While the Search Institute is the organization most strongly identified with the developmental assets approach, there are other organizations, such as the Community Asset Development for Youth program at Michigan State University, which also uses this model.

The Communities That Care program was developed by David Hawkins and Richard Catalano (1992). Their materials can be downloaded directly from the website of the Substance Abuse and Mental Health Services Administration (SAMHSA). Communities That Care is similar to a developmental assets approach but includes both risk and protective factors in their assessment. Communities That Care also goes far beyond just the initial needs assessment in a community to make specific recommendations for evidenced-based approaches to address specific risk and protective factors. Large evaluation studies, including a study that randomly assigned 24 communities to either the Communities That Care intervention group or a control group, have found Communities That Care to be effective in reducing adolescent substance abuse and delinquency (Greenberg, Feinberg, Brendan, Gomez, & Osgood, 2005; Hawkins et al., 2009). A large scale evaluation of the Communities That Care model in Australia is currently under way.

Both of these programs begin with an assessment of the developmental assets/risk and protective factors currently existing in your community. The programs then guide you in selecting and implementing interventions that are targeted to the specific needs of your community. This holistic, strengths-based approach to community assessment and intervention clearly reflects the values and philosophy of community psychology.

THE PREVENTION EQUATIONS: INTEGRATIVE GUIDES FOR RESEARCH AND ACTION

To help you organize the prevention and promotion concepts that we have discussed so far, we are now going to introduce two prevention equations. These equations were formulated as a way of summarizing the factors that are linked to the development of behavioral and emotional disorders and to emphasize possible avenues for prevention and promotion efforts.

The first formula was developed by George Albee in 1982 to illustrate the factors leading to behavioral and emotional disorders.

$$\text{Incidence of disorders} = \frac{\text{physical vulnerability (1)} + \text{stress (2)}}{\text{coping skills (3)} + \text{social support (4)} + \text{self esteem (5)}}$$

The success of a prevention program can be measured by a decrease in the incidence of new occurrences of a disorder. Albee wanted to develop a formula that would capture the various factors involved in the development of disorders. The factors in his formula can be viewed as a guidebook of potential points for prevention interventions. Maurice Elias (1987) argued that Albee's equation could too easily be interpreted at an individual level (although this is not what Albee intended). Community psychology calls for ways of examining the risk and protective processes for populations and communities, not just for individuals. In order to reflect this emphasis, Elias extended Albee's formula to explicitly address the factors responsible for the incidence of behavioral and emotional disorders in populations rather than just in individuals. Elias refers to his formula as an environmental-level formula to emphasize that the formula is addressing these factors as they are exhibited in settings (e.g., families, schools, organizations, neighborhoods and societies) rather than in the lives of individuals.

$$\text{Incidence of disorders} = \frac{\text{risk factors in the environment (6)} + \text{stressors (7)}}{\substack{\text{positive socialization practices (8)} + \text{social support resources (9)} + \\ \text{opportunities for connectedness (10)}}}$$

Both formulas indicate that risk is increased as a function of stressors and risk factors in the environment and decreased to the extent to which protective processes are enhanced: positive socialization practices that support the development of coping skills, access to social support and socioeconomic resources, and opportunities for positive relatedness and connectedness of the kind that support the development of positive self-esteem and self-efficacy. Elias's equation specifies that these terms are attempts to denote properties of settings, not attributes of individuals. The interventions that are suggested by this equation are correspondingly focused on ecological levels that surround individuals. Taken together, these equations represent a refinement of the model presented in Chapter 8, which focused on conceptualizing potential risk and protective factors but was not as specific about how they combined to create problems.

You have probably learned about the *diathesis-stress model* of psychopathology. This is the idea that disorder arises through a combination of physical vulnerability and exposure to stress. Stress by itself does not have to lead to disorder, and neither do specific physical vulnerabilities. It is the interaction of the two that leads to disorder. The numerators and denominators of both equations are a reflection of the diathesis-stress model. In fact, as you look at these formulas, it might be helpful to consider that the numerators of each equation summarize the literature on risk processes and the denominators do the same for protective processes.

In the following sections, we will explore each element of these equations, giving examples of the factors and the types of interventions each factor suggests.

Risk Factors: The Numerators

Physical vulnerability (factor 1 in Albee's equation) and risk factors in the environment (factor 6 in Elias's equation) apply to the diathesis part of the diathesis-stress model. Physical vulnerability refers to organic factors that increase the risk for disorders. For example, we know that alcohol use during pregnancy is a major cause of mental retardation. Low birth weight is associated with a multitude of developmental problems. Lead poisoning, including the ingestion of lead-based paints, can also lead to brain damage and mental retardation. Programs that are designed to decrease alcohol consumption among pregnant women, decrease the incidence of low birth weight babies, or remove lead-based paints from residential buildings would logically reduce rates of brain damage and mental retardation in children.

Can you think of ways in which settings contribute to the incidence of physical vulnerabilities? This is what Elias is referring to when his equation highlights the risk factors in the environment that result in physical vulnerabilities. Elias' equation draws attention to the need to reduce these environmental risks in communities, not just in the lives of individuals. These risks include such conditions as lead in paint and water, malnutrition, and poor prenatal care, all of which create physical and psychological vulnerabilities that, in turn, hamper coping and development.

Stress (factor 2 in Albee's equation) and stressors (factor 7 in Elias' equation) refer to the stress aspect of the diathesis-stress model. Stress can be interpreted as events that impact the functioning of individuals, such as the loss of housing or jobs, family violence or discord, or traumatic events. What characteristics of settings might increase the likelihood that individuals in those settings would experience stressful events? Those characteristics are the stressors in Elias' equation; aspects of environments or contexts that engender stress in their inhabitants and are associated with dysfunction.

These are all factors that can be addressed successfully at the community level and, in fact, must be addressed at that level. Programs designed to increase access to prenatal care and decrease toxins in the environment would be interventions aimed at decreasing physical vulnerabilities. Programs designed to decrease poverty, community violence, and family violence would be interventions aimed at decreasing levels of stress.

Protective Factors: The Denominators

The first protective factor listed in the equations deals with coping skills (factor 3 in Albee's equation) and the socialization practices in microsystems that serve to support and develop those skills (factor 8 in Elias's equation). *Coping skills* is actually too narrow a term to encompass everything included here; a better term might be *social competencies*. For example, the Search Institute (mentioned earlier in this chapter) identifies such values as responsibility and restraint and such social competencies as planning and decision making, interpersonal competence, resistance skills, and conflict-resolution skills as developmental assets that help to promote healthy development in children and adolescents.

Think for a minute about the ways in which settings can promote the development of these social competencies. Factor 8, positive socialization practices, refers to the way in which microsystems fulfill their socializing functions. The term *socialization*, as it is used in this context, refers to how parents, teachers, and cultures teach children how to interact positively with the world around them (refer back to Chapter 7 for a discussion of how the socialization process reflects issues of cultural diversity). It includes such concepts as self-regulation of emotions and desires, the adoption of positive values, and how to recognize the motivations and feelings of other people and successfully adapt your behavior in relation to those people. All these skills are specifically defined by the cultural context in which the child is raised.

Because these skills are first learned at a very young age, when the lives of children are dominated by the influence of a few microsystems, the socializing functions of those microsystems are particularly important in child development. Are these systems designed to ensure that individuals are developing the coping skills and social competencies necessary to successfully negotiate the challenges of life? Later in this chapter, we will describe parenting programs designed to ensure that families work to promote these competencies in children, and in Chapter 10, we will discuss a set of programs designed to help schools instill social and emotional competency in children. These programs were developed specifically to address factor 8 in Elias' equation.

Social support (factor 4 in Albee's equation) refers to aspects of social networks that help to buffer individuals from the effects of stress. In general terms, social support is something that, when present, is a continual presence in a person's life. The basic question is, do you have a network of people that you can count on in your life? But research shows that the beneficial effects of social support are only obvious when someone is confronting significant stress. When life is going well, the presence of a solid social support network in your life has no significant effect on your overall happiness. It is when things go wrong, when you are forced to deal with serious problems, that social support becomes important. For those of you who actually enjoyed your statistics courses (and we know you are out there!), this is an example of an interaction effect. The presence of social support is a significant determinate of happiness during times of stress, but it does not affect happiness when things are going well.

Elias was drawing attention to the characteristics of settings, which promote the development of supportive networks. Social support resources (factor 9 in Elias' equation) refer not to the presence of social support in the lives of individuals but to whether social support resources are available and easily accessed by individuals during times of stress. Think about what you would do if you had just moved to a new city to pursue a great career opportunity. You love your job, but you left all your relationships behind, and you have not had time to develop new ones. Then, something horrible happens. There is a serious threat to your life or you experience an important loss. Who would you turn to? Elias' factor of social support resources refers to the availability of social networks when you need them. Can you find a support network for people experiencing bereavement or for those dealing with chronic physical or mental challenges?

Self-esteem (factor 5 in Albee's equation) and opportunities for connectedness (factor 10 in Elias's equation) are concepts with long-standing links to positive mental health outcomes. Rotter (1982) and Bandura (1982) showed that individuals with negative expectancies for their ability to impact their environments and a poor recognition and appreciation of their strengths are more likely to develop a variety of psychological disorders. Similarly, settings vary in the extent to which they provide opportunities for relatedness and connectedness and positive contributions by the people within them (Barker, 1968; Cottrell, 1976; Sarason, 1974; Wicker, 1979). Those settings that do provide such opportunities are likely to have more individuals who feel a positive sense of efficacy, and in turn, rates of disorder will be lower in them than in comparable types of settings that do not provide such opportunities.

For example, many colleges and universities work to ensure that there are social settings available for a wide variety of students and that students are aware of and can easily access those resources. Student clubs and organizations frequently serve this purpose by providing a clear opportunity for students to establish relationships soon after arriving at a new school. Colleges can provide structural support for this process by providing funding for student organizations, mentoring from staff and faculty, space on campus for student groups to meet, and opportunities for student groups to advertise their existence, particularly in the fall, when new students arrive.

DO PREVENTION PROGRAMS WORK?

The short answer to this question is yes, they do. But as with research regarding the efficacy of psychotherapy, research in prevention science has moved beyond the basic question "Does it work?" to sophisticated questions, such as "How well does it work, for whom, under what conditions, and what are the mechanisms that account for its effects?" Clear answers are a precursor to making sound decisions about prevention programming, policy, and funding. However, deriving such answers can be difficult.

One of the major tools in finding answers to those questions are meta-analytic techniques. Meta-analyses compare statistical findings of all quantitative studies done on a given topic that meet certain methodological criteria (e.g., comparison of parent training programs and control groups in randomized field experiments, all of which used similar dependent variables). For an experimental study of a prevention program, meta-analysis computes a statistical estimate of **effect size**: the strength of the effect of that intervention (independent variable) on the chosen outcomes (dependent variables). There are many ways of presenting information regarding effect sizes. For example, the statement "The children participating in the intervention demonstrated an increase of 10 percentage points on their test scores, while children in the control group demonstrated no such increase" is a description of the strength of the effect of the intervention. In meta-analyses the average effect size is computed for a set of similar programs tested in multiple studies and is generally presented as a statistic between zero and one. Although not without controversy (e.g., Trickett, 1997; Weissberg & Bell, 1997), meta-analysis is one useful tool for broad analyses of the effectiveness of prevention programs.

Another tool for deriving an understanding of what makes for effective prevention programming is the best practices approach. This approach includes qualitative analysis in addition to the quantitative approach taken by meta-analysis. In a best practice approach, the focus is on studying a specific type of program that has been empirically shown to be effective across multiple settings and gleaning from further studies of those settings the procedures that effective programs of that type have in common. Some best practice analyses are conducted through a review of the available research, while others involve actual site visits and qualitative research much more detailed and descriptive than is usually found in journal articles.

So, what does all this research tell us? There is a great deal of information generated by this research, and it is extremely difficult to summarize. We try to summarize it later in this section, but first, we would like to give you an idea of what some of the meta-analytic findings look like.

There have been many meta-analyses of prevention programs published in the literature. Generally, they focus on one area of prevention. For example, one of the earliest meta-analytic studies of prevention programs was conducted by Durlak and Wells in 1997. They examined 177 primary prevention programs directed at children and adolescents. Their conclusions, which have many qualifiers that are best read in the original study, are that from 59% to 82% of participants in a primary prevention program surpassed the average performance of those in control groups. This indicates clear superiority of prevention groups to controls. Durlak and Wells (1998) conducted a second meta-analysis on 130 secondary or indicated prevention programs for children who were experiencing such early signs of difficulty as persistent shyness, learning difficulties, and antisocial behavior. The average participant in these programs was better off than 70% of the control group members. These programs were especially effective for children whose externalizing behaviors put them at risk of conduct disorders and delinquency, for which later treatment is difficult.

Other meta-analytic studies have reviewed the following prevention areas and demonstrate significant effects for prevention programming:

- Prevention of childhood and adolescent depression (Horowitz & Garber, 2006; Stice, Shaw, Bohon, Marti, & Rohde, 2009)

- School bullying prevention programs (Merrell, Gueldner, Ross, & Isava, 2008; Smith, Schneider, Smith, & Ananiadou, 2004)

- Teen pregnancy and subsequent teen pregnancies (Corcoran & Pillai, 2007)

- Childhood obesity (Stice, Shaw, & Marti, 2006)

- Childhood and adolescent drug use (Brown, Guo, Singer, Downes, & Brinales, 2007; Tobler et al., 2000)
- Child sexual abuse (Davis & Gidycz, 2000)
- Programs implemented in infancy and early childhood (Manning, Homel, & Smith, 2010)
- Mentoring programs (DuBois, Holloway, Valentine, & Cooper, 2002)
- Social and emotional learning programs for children (Weissberg & Durlak, 2006)

While meta-analyses are and will continue to be an important part of our understanding of effective prevention programs, it can be difficult to translate their findings into clear guidelines for designing or implementing programs. For that, we need to add the qualitative piece provided by best practices analyses. The past decade has been extremely productive in combining information from these two approaches. Table 9.2 summarizes 10 principles for effective prevention and promotion programs. The table is adapted from work by Nation and colleagues (2003); Weissberg, Kumpfer, and Seligman (2003); and Zins, Weissberg, Wang, and Walberg (2004).

T A B L E 9.2   Principles of Effective Prevention/Promotion Programs

Principle	Definition
Theory-driven and evidence-based	Programs have a theoretical justification, address risk and protective factors identified in research, and have empirical support of efficacy.
Comprehensive	Programs provide multiple interventions in multiple settings to address interrelated goals.
Appropriately timed	Programs are provided before the onset of a disorder, at an appropriate development stage for the participants, or during important life transitions.
Socioculturally relevant	Programs are culturally sensitive and incorporate cultural norms when appropriate.
Behavioral and skills-based	Programs include a strong behavioral component that focuses on the acquisition of specific skills and ensures opportunities for practicing those skills.
Sufficient dosage	Programs are of a sufficient length and intensity to ensure the desired effects and have booster sessions when appropriate.
Positive relationships	Programs specifically promote the development of positive relationships to provide mentoring and social support.
Second-order change	Programs include a focus on changes in setting and communities, including changes in formal policies and specific practices and developing resources for positive development.
Support for staff	Programs provide appropriate training for staff and ongoing support to ensure effective implementation and evaluation.
Program evaluation	Programs have ongoing processes to ensure continual evaluation and improvement, assessment of outcomes, and assessment of community needs.

ARE PREVENTION PROGRAMS COST-EFFECTIVE?

When people are first presented with the data regarding the effectiveness of prevention programs, a common response is, "Sure. This all sounds good, but it must be expensive. We just can't afford it." Successfully implementing a prevention or promotion program requires significant human resources in terms of time, dedication, and effort. We will discuss these resources requirements in detail in the next chapter, but in this section, we want to specifically discuss monetary costs. While some prevention and promotion programs cost very little money to implement, many of them are quite expensive. Is the statement "We just can't afford it" a good reason for not implementing prevention programs?

Cost-effectiveness analyses essentially view prevention/promotion programs as an investment, and the analyses are trying to determine the return on that investment. Research on the cost-effectiveness of prevention programs has been ongoing for almost as long as the programs have been evaluated, but interest in this question has been particularly intense in recent decades. Even with this surge in interest and the intense need for information on cost-effectiveness to inform policy decisions, the body of good cost-effectiveness evaluations is still very small. The reason for this is clear: These evaluations are extremely complex and very hard to conduct.

One type of cost-effectiveness analysis compares several programs with similar goals to determine how economically efficient each program was in reaching that goal. The question is, if we have several programs that have each been shown to be effective in preventing a particular problem, which will lower the incidence of the problem for the least amount of money?

An example of this type of research was conducted by the Rand Corporation in an influential analysis of the California three strikes law. Three strikes laws are mandatory sentencing laws that send individuals convicted of a third felony to prison for life. California passed the United States' most sweeping three strikes law in 1994 (which was subsequently modified in 2000). In 1996, the Rand Corporation published an analysis of the cost-effectiveness of the three strikes law compared to four types of prevention programs: home visits and day care in early childhood; parenting training programs; monetary incentives for high-risk students to graduate from high school; and intensive supervision of delinquent juveniles. Their analysis consisted of estimating the number of serious crimes each initiative could be reasonably expected to prevent and then calculating the cost of each program per serious crime prevented. Programs with lower costs per crime prevented were more economically efficient. Their analysis showed that parent training and graduation incentives prevented serious crimes at a much lower cost than the three strikes law (Greenwood, Model, Rydell, & Chiesa, 1998). As the authors of the study point out, the three strikes law is more effective at preventing crime than are the prevention programs (the law is 100% effective in preventing "participants" from committing future crimes), but it does so at a much higher cost than the two prevention programs.

However, that type of analysis leaves out a great deal of information. For example, what about the money society saves by not having to incarcerate the successful graduates of the prevention programs? And what about the benefits to society of having those individuals become wage-earning (and taxpaying) members of society rather than prison inmates? The majority of cost-effectiveness studies are not just interested in the relative economic efficiency of different types of programs; they want to address the basic question of whether prevention programs result in an overall economic benefit for society. Are the economic benefits greater than the program costs? These types of analyses involve some type of **cost-benefit analysis**, and they are not easy to do. The evaluation of prevention programs overall is made difficult by the fundamental problem of measuring an event that did not occur. Cost-benefit evaluations are made even more complex because they must address this question: How much money was saved because an event did not occur?

Calculating the basic monetary costs of the cost-benefit equation often seems fairly simple. Most programs either publish or can easily compute program costs per person served (although even this can get quite challenging for many programs). Calculating the monetary benefits of prevention programs is much more difficult. Generally, these benefits fall into one of two categories: services the program participants will not need due the success of the program and monetary benefits to society in terms of wages earned and taxes paid by program participants that they otherwise would not have earned or paid. Services that prevention program participants may not need due to the success of the program include educational services, mental health services (including foster care and hospitalization), physical health services (such as treatment for health problems related to smoking, drug use, or obesity), criminal justice system costs, and welfare programs.

To illustrate these points, let us look at the High Scope/Perry Preschool Project, a program designed to prevent conduct disorder and other behavior disorders in adolescence. The original program provided high-quality, academically based day care to children born into poverty. The children were enrolled in the program starting at ages three and four. The 123 children were all African American and were randomly assigned to either the intervention group or a control group. The most recent results from the program were collected when the participants were 40 years old. Data were collected from 97% of the participants who were still living. A cost-benefits analysis found that the general public gained $12.90 for every $1 spent on the program (Belfield, Nores, Barnett, & Schweinhart, 2006). While other analyses have found a lower rate of return, the general finding that the program benefits outweigh program costs holds true over multiple analyses (Heckman, Moon, Pinto, Savelyev, & Yavitz, 2009; Schweinhart et al., 2005).

In addition to giving insight into questions such as which programs are most economically efficient at achieving the same outcomes and which programs generate economic benefits that outweigh the program costs, economic analyses can also shed insight on the selection of program components. If you look back at Table 9.2, you will see that one of the principles of effective prevention programming is that the program is comprehensive and provides multiple interventions across multiple settings. But just because multiple components increase positive effects does not necessarily mean the increased cost of those additional components is economically justified. We will present an analysis addressing this question later in this chapter when we discuss parent training programs.

A large and growing body of research demonstrates that not only do prevention programs work, but the ones that have demonstrated positive results generate economic benefits to society that far outweigh their costs. In general, targeted programs are more economically efficient than universal programs, and programs that are implemented in early childhood provide greater lifetime benefits. As a recent discussion of economic analyses of early childhood prevention programs concludes:

> The fundamental insight of economics when comparing early childhood policies with other social investments is that a growing body of program evaluations shows that early childhood programs have the potential to generate government savings that more than repay their costs and produce returns to society as a whole that outpace most public and private investments (italics in original). (Kilburn & Karoley, 2008, p. 11)

The great thing about cost-effectiveness analyses is that everyone who is serious about data-based decision making cares about them. Researchers and organizations spend a great deal of time and effort thinking about the complexities of these analyses and the best way to analyze the data so it can inform good public policies. The sad thing about cost-effectiveness analyses is that they so rarely actually have an effect on public policy. We will further discuss this sad phenomenon in Chapter 12.

EXAMPLES OF SUCCESSFUL PREVENTION AND PROMOTION PROGRAMS

In this section, we will present examples of prevention and promotion programs that have significant empirical evidence of success. We chose these programs to illustrate the ideas regarding prevention science that we covered in the first part of this chapter. Additional examples of successful programs will be presented in Chapter 10. We will also provide you with resources to help you locate other empirically supported programs that you may wish to consider for adaptation in your community.

First, we will review programs in HIV/AIDS prevention to illustrate some of the basic points of prevention science that we discussed at the beginning of this chapter. These programs are designed to change the behavior of individuals but are provided in community settings and have their major impact on the behavior of individuals in relationships. Then, we will discuss parent training programs, which were developed to prevent child and adolescent behavior disorders. These programs are designed to impact the microsystem of the family by improving parenting practices and parent-child relationships. While these programs focus on changing the behavior of parents, the goal is to change the microsystem of the family and the behavior of children. Finally, we will examine programs designed to prevent bullying in schools. These programs target the microsystem of the school as their level of intervention rather than individuals. While each of these programs was designed to prevent a specific problem (HIV infection, conduct disorder, and school bullying), as you shall see, in practice they all have clear promotion effects.

Prevention of HIV/AIDS Infection
(Promoting Healthy Sexual Behaviors)

For an explicit illustration of many of the concepts discussed in this chapter, let us take a look at the field of HIV/AIDS prevention. The story of HIV prevention began when public health officials first became aware that some strange things were occurring in the health of gay men in the United States in 1981. It is estimated that by this time, there were already at least 100,000 cases of HIV infection spread across five continents (Mann, 1989). This illustrates an important point of prevention science that we have not yet discussed: There must be public recognition of a problem before prevention efforts will begin.

In June 1982, the Centers for Disease Control published an article suggesting that the syndrome was caused by an infectious agent that was transmitted through sexual activity (CDC, June 1982). The name AIDS (Acquired Immune Deficiency Syndrome) was first suggested in July of that year, and in September, the CDC published the first proper description of AIDS (CDC, September, 1982). It was not until 1984 that HIV was identified as the virus that causes AIDS, and it was not until January 1985 that the first blood test for HIV was licensed.

But this lack of knowledge about the cause of AIDS did not stop the development of prevention efforts. By the end of 1982, a number of voluntary organizations had arisen, particularly in homosexual communities, to deal with the growing AIDS crisis. Several of these organizations began promoting safe sex practices as a way of stopping the spread of AIDS in their communities (Berridge, 1996). The first needle exchange program was established in Amsterdam in 1984 (National Institute on Drug Abuse, 1988). By 1988, the first descriptions of AIDS/HIV prevention programs were being published.

Remember John Snow and the lessons we learned from how he dealt with the cholera epidemic? 1) Even if you do not know how to cure a problem, you may still be able to prevent it. 2) You do not need to know the cause of a problem to prevent it; you just need to understand something about the mechanisms through which the problem is transmitted or sustained. 3) You can often prevent a problem through changing some aspect of human behavior. 4) While individual behavior change can contribute to prevention, complete prevention of a problem often relies on public action.

All these lessons are illustrated by the history of HIV prevention. While we now have better treatments for HIV infection, there is no "cure" or any vaccine. Effective prevention programs were being implemented even before the HIV virus was identified as the cause of AIDS. The reason this was possible was because it was known, very early on, that whatever was causing AIDS was most likely spread through sexual contact and probably through blood. We did not know the cause or have a cure, but we *did* have some ideas about the mechanism through which the disorder was transmitted, and this allowed effective prevention programs to be developed.

While modifying the behavior of individuals is obviously key to preventing the spread of HIV, managing the AIDS epidemic was heavily dependent upon public action. First, there had to be public recognition of the problem. This required public action to track the spread of the disease and to educate people and legislators about the epidemic. It also required public action to fund the research, medical services, public education programs, and prevention programs necessary to fight the disease.

A recent review of HIV/AIDS prevention programs by a group at the CDC identified 18 interventions as demonstrating "best evidence for efficacy for reducing HIV risk" (Lykes et al., 2007). We will describe one here: the Project SAFE program, which has had particularly good results and demonstrates many of the points of this chapter.

Project SAFE is a small group intervention that targets minority women who have been diagnosed with an STD in a public health clinic. The goals are to decrease risky sexual behaviors and subsequent STD infections. The intervention consists of three group sessions focusing on education regarding risky sexual behaviors, motivation to change those behaviors, and the development of specific skills needed to engage in protective sexual behaviors. For example, women are taught to identify barriers to condom use and how to talk to their partners about their sexual behavior. They learn new skills through watching videotapes and direct practice. They are also encouraged to talk to other people in their lives about what they are learning in order to help build a support network.

The original evaluation involved 775 Mexican American and African American women. The women were randomly assigned to either the intervention or a comparison group that received 15–20 minutes of STD counseling and testing by a nurse. Over two years of follow-up, women who received the intervention were significantly less likely to report having more than one sexual partner and were significantly less likely to acquire a new STD than were women in the comparison group (Shain et al., 1999; Shain et al., 2004). Evaluations of the program have also shown positive effects on unsafe and unprotected sexual behaviors. Since the initial evaluations, SAFE has been shown to be effective with teenagers and depressed women (both groups who have been shown to engage in a higher level of risky sexual behaviors than nondepressed adult women) (Holden et al., 2008; Thurman, Holden, Shain, Perdue, & Piper, 2008).

Take a minute to look back at Table 9.2, the principles of effective intervention programs. Although those principles were developed primarily through reviews of effective prevention programs with children and adolescents, many of the principles are reflected in the SAFE program, which was developed to work with adult women. The program is theoretically based. It was developed by using a theory called the *AIDS Risk Reduction Model* (Catania, Kegeles, & Coates, 1990). It is designed to address risky behaviors and protective factors that have been identified in the research, and it has been empirically supported. The program is timed to coincide with an important event (the diagnosis of an STD) but before the development of HIV infection. The program is also designed to be sensitive to the cultural norms of the minority women it serves, and it is behaviorally based, focusing on teaching specific skills. The program has clear implications for developing positive relationships. Through the use of standardized scripts for the sessions, flip charts, and random observations through one-way mirrors, SAFE provides ongoing training and supervision of staff. And the research team has conducted multiple evaluations of the program, including extensions of the program to groups in the community (teenagers and depressed women) that research indicates are prone to risky sexual behaviors.

One interesting result of the SAFE evaluations is that not one participant, either program participant or control, had been diagnosed with HIV at the time of the evaluation. This is not an unexpected finding because HIV infection is a relatively rare occurrence. But it does raise the interesting point that the program could not be evaluated on its effectiveness in preventing the spread of HIV, which was the explicit goal of the program when it was developed. Instead, the program has been evaluated on its ability to promote healthy sexual behaviors. So, what began as a program with an explicit prevention focus is actually functioning as a health promotion program. The promotion of healthy sexual behaviors obviously has effects far beyond the prevention of HIV.

HIV/AIDS continues to be an epidemic that affects all racial/ethnic groups in all parts of the world (CDC, 2007). As powerful medical interventions have changed the course of the disease, prevention efforts seem to have become routinized and driven by less urgency. Wolitski (2003) reports an upsurge of "safe sex fatigue" and "AIDS burnout." This leads prevention messages to be ignored, thereby increasing health risks and perpetuating the epidemic. This highlights the important point that there is never a single best response to a problem. Rather, a diversity of approaches, addressing different populations, cultures, and aspects of problem, along with an emphasis promoting overall healthy behavior, is needed to intervene in complex problems, such as HIV infection.

Prevention of Childhood Behavior Disorders
(Promoting Positive Parenting)

One of the clearest examples of effective prevention programming in the literature has to do with parenting practices. Research in developmental psychology, and particularly research on resiliency factors, has long emphasized the primary role that warm, accepting parenting behaviors, coupled with clear, consistent supervision and discipline, play in the development of happy, healthy children (Baumrind, 1991; Werner, 1996). Behaviorally based parent training programs have been shown in numerous reviews to be very effective in reducing problem behaviors in young children (including aggression, oppositional behaviors, and hyperactive behaviors). These reductions in early childhood are then empirically linked to the prevention of problems in adolescence, such as school failure, substance abuse, and delinquency (Center for Substance Abuse Prevention, 1998; Kumpfer & Alvarado, 2003).

It is important to note that these results do not apply to *parent education programs*, which have not been shown to result in measurable behavior change in children. Parent education programs typically focus on providing parents with information about child rearing, such as ideas for effective communication and information about normative behavior in childhood. While parents generally report feeling that the programs were helpful, evaluations of these programs fail to demonstrate any change in the behavior of the children of those parents (Kumpfer & Alvarado, 2003).

Behaviorally based parent training programs focus on specific skills training for parents. Information is presented, but the program's primary content centers on the acquisition of new parenting skills. The main emphasis is on improving parent-child interactions by teaching parents to engage in positive play with their children, give frequent reinforcement for good behavior, ignore most unwanted behavior, clearly communicate expectations, and set clear consequences.

One of these programs is The Incredible Years, developed by Carolyn Webster-Stratton and her colleagues (Webster-Stratton, 1984; Webster-Stratton, Mihalic, Fagan, Taylor, & Tingely, 2001). The program consists of 10 to 12 group sessions for parents of children ages three to eight. Generally, the program targets parents of children who are already displaying mild to severe levels of disturbed behavior at an early age because an extensive body of research supports the finding that children who display problem behaviors at an early age are at extremely high risk of developing multiple and severe problems by adolescence, including school failure, substance abuse, and involvement in the juvenile justice system. The sessions cover four general areas: play and attention, praise and reward, limit setting, and problem behaviors. The sessions are highly structured and include videos, discussion, direct practice, and feedback.

The Incredible Years has been evaluated in randomized trials over a dozen times (Webster-Stratton & Herman, 2008). It has been identified as a model evidence-based program by both the U.S. Office of Juvenile Justice and Delinquency Prevention and the Center for the Study of Prevention of Violence.

Since its initial inception, the developers have added a child-based component and a teacher-based component to The Incredible Years program. The child-based component can be given either in small groups (generally in conjunction with the parenting training program) or in the classroom. It is designed to help children acquire improved interpersonal skills and social competencies. The teacher-based component is designed to complement the parenting training program by helping teachers change the climate of their classrooms through the implementation of new ways of interacting with their students. The Incredible Years program provides significant training for implementers and resources to ensure fidelity to the program.

Referring to Table 9.2, you can see that The Incredible Years programs incorporate every principle of effective prevention programs, except perhaps for the program evaluation principle, although individual adopters of the program could ensure that principle is met also. This is not a coincidence. Over the years since its inception, The Incredible Years program, like other long-standing prevention programs, has both contributed to and benefitted from the growing research on best practices in prevention programming. The Incredible Years was one of the programs that helped to demonstrate that theory-based behavioral programs that focused on developing positive relationships can produce significant preventive effects. The developers also learned from the research about the importance of multiple interventions in multiple settings, hence the inclusion of the child-based and teacher-based components.

In the earlier section of this chapter related to cost-effectiveness, we mentioned an analysis of the economic benefits of adding components to a parent training program. That program was The Incredible Years. The researchers compared changes in child behavior among seven groups: child training only; parent training only; child-based and parenting training; parent training and teacher training; child training and teacher training; all three components; and a no treatment control. While there are many limitations to the study (most notably the small sample sizes in several groups), the researchers conclude that the data suggest that implementing multiple components is cost-effective (Foster, Olchowski, & Webster-Stratton, 2007). Because the cost per child for all three components was over $3,000 (in 2003 dollars), a relatively expensive intervention, additional analyses of this nature would be useful for formulating effective public policy.

While The Incredible Years is a strong example of an evidence-based, effective, parenting program, it is by no means the only one. For an example of a program that is designed specifically to reduce child abuse at the community level, see the Triple P Parenting Program (Prinz, Sanders, Shapiro, Whitaker, & Lutzker, 2009; Sanders, 2008).

Prevention of Bullying and School Violence (Promoting Safe School Climates)

For 2 years, Johnny, a quiet 13-year-old, was a human plaything for some of his classmates. The teenagers badgered Johnny for money, forced him to swallow weeds and drink milk mixed with detergent, beat him up in the rest room and tied a string around his neck, leading him around as a "pet." When Johnny's torturers were interrogated about the bullying, they said they pursued their victim because it was fun. (newspaper clipping cited in Olweus & Limber, 2010, p. 124).

Bullying-related behaviors are prevalent worldwide (Craig et al., 2009; World Health Organization, 2000). A recent cross-national study of school bullying surveyed 11-, 13-, and 15-year-old children during the 2005–2006 school year in 40 different countries in Europe and North America. The researchers found that up to 45.2% of boys and 35.8% of girls reported either being bullied, bullying someone else, or both. There was great variability among countries, with some countries (generally in Northern Europe) reporting rates as low as 8.6% for boys and 4.3% for girls. The two North American countries in the study, Canada and the United States, were both in the middle of the range, with rates of about 22% for boys and 17% for girls (Craig et al., 2009).

Just as there is a wide variation in school bullying rates across countries, rates also vary widely by schools. In some schools, these problems are far less frequent than others. Bullying can be conceptualized in ecological terms by using the individual and environmental-level prevention equations presented earlier. Key preventive influences on both of these problems are positive sources of relatedness and connectedness in both school and home life; supportive friends, family members, and other caring adults; and coping skills to deal with frustrations, setbacks, stress, conflict, and to accurately perceive emotional cues in oneself and others. Bullying prevention requires multilevel, ecological approaches to intervention (Ttofi, Farrington, & Baldry, 2008; Zins, Elias, & Maher, 2007).

Community psychologists are among those asking how it happens that certain schools are organized so their levels of violence are lower than those of other schools. The following conditions have been identified as conducive to low rates of school violence (Felner & Adan, 1988; Hawkins & Lam, 1987; Pepler & Slaby, 1994; Wager, 1993; Zins, Elias, & Maher, 2007):

- School courses are perceived as highly relevant to students' lives.
- School rules and structures allow students some control over what happens to them at school.
- School discipline policies are viewed as firm, fair, clear, and consistently enforced.
- A rational reward structure in the school recognizes students for their achievements.
- Strong and effective school governance exists, with strong principal leadership.
- Ongoing, positive contacts occur between students and adults.
- The curriculum includes education in social and emotional competencies.

These characteristics are the foci of a growing number of school-based prevention/promotion programs. The largest preventive effects with regard to bullying come from comprehensive school-wide efforts that create a climate of nonacceptance of bullying, a positive social norm of disclosure, a track record of effective action in response to threats and incidents, and curriculum-based training in social-emotional competencies (Elias & Zins, 2003; Zins, Elias, & Maher, 2007). Firm, clear, school-wide policies, referral procedures, and staff training must exist to deal effectively with student reports of problems. What follows is a discussion of one approach that has shown success in some contexts.

In 1983, three young boys committed suicide in northern Norway, most likely as a result of severe bullying. The Norwegian Ministry of Education started a national campaign to address bullying in schools. The Olweus Bullying

Prevention Program (BPP) was developed in response to that campaign (Olweus, Limber, & Mihalic, 1999; Olweus & Limber, 2010). It has been identified as a model program by the Center for the Study of Prevention of Violence. BPP has several core components, which have been identified by research as being central to the program's success. These include the use of a survey to identify the type and intensity of bullying in a school and to identify the areas and settings in the school where bullying is most likely to occur. After analysis of the survey data, the school holds a conference day with parents, teachers, and administrators to discuss the results of the survey and to decide how to use those results to implement the program in their school. Implementation is overseen by a coordinating committee composed of administrators, teachers, parents, and students.

A core component of intervention is increased teacher supervision of "hot spots" for bullying that were identified in the survey. These generally include the lunchroom and the playground. For example, because children generally take only 10 minutes to eat lunch but lunch lasts for 20 to 30 minutes, schools in the program often have board games available in the lunchroom, and teachers direct students to those games when they are finished eating. On the playground, teachers are supported in identifying and intervening in situations that could lead to bullying, such as "play fighting." Students are directed into prosocial, structured play and are provided with more games and play equipment. The intervention also involves regular class meetings with students, clear classroom and school-wide rules against bullying, and serious talks with students and parents when bullying occurs.

While the program does have core components, it also allows for a great deal of flexibility because each school determines the specifics of how the program will be implemented. Because of this flexibility, the program can be implemented with children in a variety of developmental stages and in different cultures. As with parenting programs, the main focus of BPP is on changing the behavior of adults (teachers) and changing the climate of the setting in order to change the behavior of the children. In essence, Olweus's approach creates a school with different patterns of social interaction and a different environmental "feel."

The first evaluations of the program in Norway demonstrated decreases in bullying of up to 50%, but subsequent evaluations found decreases of only 23% to 38% (Olweus, 1997; Olweus & Limber, 2010). There have also been major evaluations of the program conducted in England (Whitney, Rivers, Smith, & Sharp, 1994), Germany (Hanewinkel, 2004), and the United States, with varying levels of success. One recent implementation in the United States involved 13 inner-city schools over four years (Black, 2007). The program was evaluated on the number of observed instances of bullying, rates of reported bullying, and fidelity to the core components of the program. Overall, the schools saw an average decrease in bullying behaviors of 25.5% over the four years of the program.

The researchers found that only a few schools managed to implement the program, with a high degree of fidelity for four years, and that the success of the program was directly related to the degree of the fidelity of implementation. The main factor that assured fidelity was the existence of key people in the school (e.g., a principal, a school nurse, a group of teachers) who were strongly committed to the program. Schools that had difficulty maintaining fidelity or who could not maintain the program at all were marked by frequent changes in staffing and administration and other forms of internal change or crises.

We will discuss issues of program fidelity in detail in Chapter 10. We will also introduce you to another type of school-based prevention and promotion program called *social-emotional learning (SEL)*. While SEL programs have much broader aims than antibullying programs, the skills they teach and the changes in school climate that they promote should theoretically have the effect of reducing school violence.

THE IMPLEMENTATION AND SUSTAINABILITY OF PROGRAMS

As you have seen, answering the question "Does prevention work?" is much like answering the questions "Does surgery work?" or "Does education work?" The answer is "Yes," but it must be qualified by knowing how well interventions are implemented. More refined questions are appropriate: "Is this program being implemented as designed in accordance with theory and research?" and "How does it work with specific populations and contexts?"

Thus, a final, emerging area for research and action concerns actual implementation of prevention/promotion initiatives in local contexts. As we have noted throughout this chapter, ideas and approaches may work very well in one organization, locality, culture, or context but not be applicable in another. Interventions identified as effective by empirical research in multiple settings, even when backed by meta-analytic findings or best practices and supported by lessons learned in certain situations, must be adapted to the "local and particular" dynamics and resources of each setting. Community psychologists and other prevention advocates are continuously learning about the importance of carefully considering implementation plans in context. An equal concern now is how to sustain effective prevention/promotion initiatives even after they have been brought to the point of adequate implementation. We take up these matters in detail in Chapter 10.

CHAPTER SUMMARY

1. Prevention is an evolving field of study in community psychology and related disciplines. We began with the story of John Snow and the 1854 cholera epidemic in London. Dr. Snow's work is recognized as the beginning of the modern field of public health and illustrates much of the logic of prevention science.

2. Albee's (1959) work demonstrating that it was mathematically impossible to train enough mental health professionals in the United States to provide treatment to everyone who needed it helped to generate dissatisfaction with a treatment approach to dealing with mental health. Psychologists began considering the application of prevention to mental health problems.

3. Caplan's (1964) concepts of primary, secondary, and tertiary prevention were an early and highly influential conceptualization of prevention. In 1994, the IOM report defined prevention in terms of universal, selected, and indicated approaches.

4. Prevention has become a term that denotes two complementary processes: prevention of disorder and problem behavior and promotion of wellness and social competence. While some researchers view these as competing approaches, community psychologists tend to view this as false dichotomy. Prevention programs tend to have promotion effects, and promotion programs often have specific prevention goals.

5. Concepts for understanding and strengthening prevention and promotion efforts include risk, protection, and resilience. These dynamic processes are important topics for prevention and promotion.

6. Albee (1982) and Elias (1987) created two prevention equations useful for integrating the concepts presented.

7. The literature on prevention and promotion is constantly growing. Meta-analyses are a good way of evaluating the effectiveness of prevention programs, and these analyses show that prevention and promotion programs are effective in a number of areas. Ten principles for effective prevention programs are listed in Table 9.2.

8. Prevention and promotion are not only effective, but they are also cost-effective. We discussed several types of cost-effectiveness evaluations, including cost-benefit analysis.

9. Finally, we presented examples of programs that have shown effectiveness in the prevention of HIV/AIDS, childhood behavior disorders (parent-training programs), and school bullying. These examples were used to illustrate the main points of this chapter.

RECOMMENDED READINGS

Albee, G. (1982). Preventing psychopathology and promoting human potential. *American Psychologist, 37,* 1043–1050.

Elias, M. (1987). Establishing enduring prevention programs: Advancing the legacy of Swampscott. *American Journal of Community Psychology, 15,* 539–553.

Maton, K., Schellenbach, C., Leadbeater, B., & Solarz, A. (Eds.). (2004). *Investing in children, youth, families, and communities: Strengths-based research and policy*. Washington, DC: American Psychological Association.

Shinn, M. B., & Yoshikawa, H. (2008). *Toward positive youth development: Transforming schools and community programs*. New York: Oxford University Press.

Weissberg, R., & Kumpfer, K. (Eds.), (2003). Prevention that works for children and youth [special issue]. *American Psychologist*, 58.

RECOMMENDED WEBSITES

The Center for the Study of Prevention of Violence:
http://www.colorado.edu/cspv

National Institute on Drug Abuse: U.S. National Institutes of Health:
http://www.nida.nih.gov/drugpages/prevention.html

Prevention First:
http://www.prevention.org

Search Institute:
http://www.search-institute.org

10

Prevention and Promotion: Implementing Programs

HIRB/Index Stock/PhotoLibrary

OPENING EXERCISE: PREVENTION IN YOUR FUTURE

Imagine that you are working as the activities director for your local community center. And your boss tells you that as part of your job responsibilities, you will serve on a community board trying to address local health issues. When you attend your first meeting, you find that the board is currently focusing on teenage substance abuse, and by the time you leave your first meeting, you find that you are on a subcommittee charged with investigating ways of preventing adolescent substance abuse in your town.

Or imagine that you work as a school counselor in a middle school. One day, your principal calls you into her office and says that she thinks incidences of violence are increasing in the school, and she is concerned that the school staff members are increasingly relying on the police to deal with aggressive students. She wants you to investigate other ways of intervening in, or hopefully preventing, school violence.

Or maybe you are the president of the Parent-Teacher Association (PTA) at your child's school. The mayor calls you because the city was awarded a grant to investigate ways of preventing child abuse in your community. The first step in the grant is to set up a community board to oversee the process. They want a parent on the board, and someone gave him your name.

What would you do in these situations?

Everyday, people with no background in prevention work, community psychology, or even any aspect of mental health are finding themselves faced with preventing some problem in their community. Many of you reading this textbook will someday be in a situation like this, as a parent, community member, working professional, or community psychologist. The purpose of this chapter is to provide you with a guide for effectively addressing these situations.

INTRODUCTION: PROGRAM IMPLEMENTATION IS CHALLENGING

In this chapter, we will explore the question of how prevention science is implemented in real-life settings. As you will see, it is not easy. While the theory and research you read about in Chapter 9 form the basis of this chapter, they are not enough to guarantee successful replication of prevention and promotion programs.

This chapter is a summative chapter in the sense that information from every other chapter in this book can be applied to the material covered here. We will be making some of those links in this chapter, but we encourage you to make others yourself.

Community and preventive psychologists have learned a great deal about the art and science of implementing preventive efforts. Bringing good ideas and sound procedures of the kind you read about in Chapter 9 into high-quality, enduring practice is possible. The challenge can be likened to the difference between reviewing for a test in the library and actually taking the test or the difference between pitching in the bullpen and facing live batters in a stadium with a huge crowd roaring on every pitch. Performance in the "practice" situation does not always match what can be demonstrated under "real world" conditions. These challenges are made clear in the following study, which investigated the effectiveness of community-based substance abuse prevention programs.

In 2005, a group of researchers published a meta-analysis of results from 46 drug prevention programs funded by the U.S. Substance Abuse and Mental Health Services Administration (SAMHSA). A wide variety of programs were involved, but all were focused on the prevention of child and adolescent substance abuse and all targeted high-risk youth. Some programs focused on in-class instruction about substance abuse, others were designed to teach children specific skills, such as how to refuse offers of drugs and alcohol, and still others were recreation-oriented. The evaluations covered a total of five years over 46 sites around the United States. The meta-analysis included the computation of effect size, a statistic that, in most cases, ranges from 0 to 1. The results were extremely disappointing. The mean effect size over all the sites was only 0.02, almost zero. Even more discouraging, at 21 of the 46 sites, the effect sizes were negative, indicating that the comparison groups demonstrated less substance abuse than the participant groups after the intervention (Derzon, Sale, Springer, & Brounstein, 2005).

What happened? These programs all had displayed some kind of promising result in demonstration projects. That was why SAMHSA was willing to fund this large dissemination project. But when they tried to implement the programs in a variety of community contexts, those promising results disappeared. Or did they? Can you think of any reasons why the program failed to show positive results in real-world settings?

Some of the differences in effectiveness could be attributed to differences in the programs. For instance, the study found that programs that were behavioral and skills-based and those that were based on a coherent theory were among the most effective (refer back to Table 9.2 in Chapter 9). Programs that just provided information about substance abuse were not effective. But these programmatic differences did not completely explain the overall lack of positive results. Even the behavioral, theory-based programs showed a great deal of variability in effectiveness.

When the evaluators dug deeper, they discovered two things. First, at many of the sites, the control groups were not really control groups. Many of those children were actually being exposed to some sort of drug abuse prevention or intervention program; they were just not in the program being evaluated. And second, the programs were implemented in very different ways at the different sites. For example, the sites differed in how well the goals and procedures of the program were integrated into the day-to-day functioning of the organization. The researchers wanted to know how well the program would have worked if all the control groups had been true control groups and if the programs were implemented consistently across settings. When they statistically controlled for these factors, the estimated effect sizes across all 46 sites rose to a 0.24 and was statistically significant (Derzon, Sale, Springer, & Brounstein, 2005).

These discouraging results concerning attempts to disseminate promising prevention and promotion programs in real-life settings are not unique. But successful dissemination of prevention and promotion programs has taken place. What has been found is that program implementation itself must be the subject of serious research. While that research is still in its relative infancy, it does suggest some useful guidelines for successful implementation. The goal of this chapter is to provide you with the information you need to successfully implement prevention programs in your community. As we hope we showed in Chapter 9, there are many exciting and important advances in prevention science. In this chapter, we want to convince you that you can use those advances to benefit your community. But first, let us define exactly what we mean when we discuss implementation, and the evidence that shows implementation is important. Then, we will talk about the models that are being developed in the field of implementation research.

IT IS NOT JUST PROGRAM IMPLEMENTATION—IT IS PROGRAM INNOVATION

Historically, concepts of how best to transfer effective educational programs and adapt them to new host settings have evolved through four stages (RMC Research Corporation, 1995):

- **Cookbook:** In the 1970s, it was believed that programs had to be thoroughly documented, ideally in "kits" that could be followed precisely, step-by-step.

- **Replication:** Later, model programs were replicated by having staff trained in the methods used by program developers and then bringing these methods back to specific settings to be carried out as similarly as possible—but with some room for adaptation to the setting.

- **Adaptation:** By the late 1980s, models were understood to require adaptation to the unique context of the host site, ideally by having the developer serve as a consultant in making the necessary changes.

- **Invention/Innovation:** Recently, models have been seen as sources of ideas and inspiration rather than procedures to replicate or adapt. There is emphasis on creating a program tailored to the unique circumstances at a given time yet using ideas gleaned from best practices literature.

When we say that implementing prevention in real-life settings is as much an art as it is a science, we do not mean that one is more important than the other. Scientific methods must underlay implementation efforts; it will not just happen in the "cookbook" approach that was used in the 1970s. Prevention programs cannot just be replicated or even adapted to a local setting. There must be true innovation involved in every implementation. But that innovation must be based on real knowledge. Here is where an ecological understanding of settings, community, and diversity is so helpful. Adopting an action research model can help ensure that you are continually generating the knowledge needed to inform innovative implementation.

ISSUES IN IMPLEMENTATION

Implementation refers to how a program is actually delivered in a real-life setting. While everyone acknowledges the importance of implementation issues, in some respects, research on this issue is still in its infancy. The term *implementation* covers a wide range of practices. Durlak and Dupre (2008) discuss eight different aspects of implementation (five of which are based on work by Dane and Schneider, 1998). Those are:

- **Fidelity:** How closely is the design of the original program maintained?
- **Dosage/Intensity:** How often and how frequently is the program presented?
- **Quality:** How well are the components of the program presented?
- **Participant responsiveness:** How engaged are the participants?
- **Program differentiation:** Were there clear theoretical and practical distinctions between this program and other interventions?
- **Monitoring of control/comparison conditions:** Were the control participants exposed to any other type of intervention?
- **Program reach:** How many of the intended participants were actually enrolled in the program?

- **Adaptation:** What aspects of the program were adapted to fit the specific context of the setting?

Since our understanding of the science of implementation is still developing this list is only preliminary, and there could easily be important aspects of implementation that are not included. However, it is still a useful way of thinking about implementation issues that need to be addressed. Each of these aspects of implementation can be measured separately. For example, to measure program reach in a program designed for teen mothers, you could do two things. First, you could check to ensure that all the participants enrolled in the program are teen mothers. And second, you could look at public health data regarding the number of teen mothers in your area and compare that number to the number of participants in your program. To measure participant responsiveness, you could look at attendance in the program. (If participants are not actively involved in a program, they often will just stop attending.) You could also ask the participants to rate how enjoyable and interesting they found the program.

Unfortunately, even though all these aspects can be measured, all of them rarely are. Only a minority of programs monitor implementation issues at all (although that number is growing), and those that do tend to limit their focus to a few issues, such as fidelity, dosage/intensity, and program reach.

Research into how a program gets from experimental development to widespread implementation is a relatively small but growing field. Good sources for current summaries of this research include a special issue of the *American Journal of Community Psychology* (Saul et al., 2008) and a recent book collaboration between the National Research Council and the Institute of Medicine (O'Connell, Boat, & Warner, 2009). In the next section, we will present some of the implementation models developed by researchers active in this field.

Implementation Models

The process of going from original development of an innovation to its widespread implementation is sometimes referred to as **scaling up** (Schorr, 1997). That process represents the core of this chapter. Combining this work with a community psychology perspective, four stages of program development and implementation can be identified:

- **Experimental Development:** A program demonstrates its effectiveness under small-scale, optimal, highly controlled conditions compared to a control group.

- **Technological Application:** A program demonstrates effectiveness under real-world conditions, similar to the conditions for which it is eventually intended but still under the guidance of its developers.

- **Diffusion of Innovation:** A program is adopted by other organizations or communities and demonstrates effectiveness under real-world conditions when not under the direct scrutiny and guidance of its developers.

- **Widespread Implementation:** The diffusion stage brings the program to a few communities only. Implementation becomes widespread when a program continues to show its effectiveness in a wide variety of settings and is transferred from its developers to new implementers, who in turn conduct further program diffusion. The program has widespread impact only when this final stage occurs.

The term *diffusion of innovations* can actually refer to a broader theory of the processes through which new ideas, technology, and products spread through cultures. Interest in this topic is multidisciplinary, including sociology, anthropology, education, political science, and business and dates back to the end of the 17th century. In 1962, Everett Rogers published a textbook titled *Diffusion of Innovations*, which standardized some of the ideas in this area (also known as *technology transfer*). While this research is not specific to the dissemination of prevention programs, it is useful to summarize it here.

Rogers stated that in order for an organization or individual to adopt a new idea, a five-step process must occur. In his latest writings, he terms those stages **knowledge**, **persuasion**, **decision**, **implementation**, and **confirmation** (Rogers, 2003). In relation to the dissemination of prevention programming, the first two stages mean that potential adopters of the program need to be aware that the program exists, and they must be presented with sufficient evidence regarding the benefits of the program to persuade them to adopt it. After the decision to adopt is made, the program is then implemented. Rogers emphasized that the implementation stage was still in the nature of a "trial" of the program, and the adopter would need to see evidence that the program produces benefits in that setting before confirming a commitment to the program.

So, what exactly is happening when we try to diffuse our knowledge of successful prevention and promotion programs into widespread practice? Numerous researchers, funding sources, policy developers, and community members have tried to answer that question, with only partial success. Often, this is discussed in terms of the "gap" between prevention research and practice, and several models have been developed to explain that gap. The models generally have been of two types: research to practice models and community-centered models.

Research to practice models focus on the desire of researchers and policymakers to "push" communities and organizations to adopt evidenced-based programs. Program developers have put a great deal of effort and resources into demonstrating that their approach to dealing with a particular problem is effective, and now they want people to use it. Research to practice models ask the question "We know what works, but how do we get it successfully adopted in real-life settings?" **Community-centered models** come from a somewhat different perspective. Communities need to be able to answer the question "How do we find programs that will work for our issues in our community and then how do we successfully adopt them?"(Saul et al., 2008).

As we hope you will see in this chapter, this split between the two types of models is a bit of a false dichotomy. The primary goal of both types of models is to help generate information that will support the successful implementation of prevention research. Where they differ is on which perspective they take: that of the researcher or that of the community. In addition, both models assume that the development of new interventions begins with researchers. As Robin Miller and Marybeth Shinn point out, it is quite likely that communities have already developed effective prevention programs on their own (Miller & Shinn, 2005). They suggest that prevention scientists look for examples of these indigenous prevention efforts and learn from them. One major benefit from this approach is the fact that indigenous prevention efforts are likely to fit community capacity and community values in ways that programs developed under controlled research conditions cannot match.

As community psychologists, we emphasize the need to understand the community perspective, and in this chapter, we will emphasize that successful program implementation must be based on a participatory action research approach (see Chapter 3). Community members must be involved in every step, from defining the problem to deciding how well the program is working. But we also understand that the goals of researchers and community members often overlap.

An Integrative Model

There has been work done to integrate these two types of models, such as in the Interactive Systems Framework for Dissemination and Implementation (ISF), which attempts to describe the key elements and relationships involved in this process (Wandersman etal., 2008). The model describes three systems: the Prevention Synthesis and Translation System, the Prevention Support System, and the Prevention Delivery System. This model is not meant to describe the stages or processes involved in program dissemination and implementation; rather, it describes the systems that need to be in place in order for those processes to be successful.

The **Prevention Synthesis and Translation System** addresses the fact that information regarding promising prevention approaches is often difficult to access. It is published in multiple journal articles, often in specialized language and without the level of detail necessary for program adoption. This system acknowledges the need for someone to find all that information, synthesize it, and translate it into a form that is useful for potential adopters. Later in this chapter, we will introduce you to some organizations attempting to serve as this system.

The **Prevention Support System** addresses the capacity of organizations and communities to successfully adopt new innovations. This concept of capacity is so important that we will discuss it in detail later on in this section. One very important part of a good Prevention Support System is to provide significant training and technical support to adopters of a prevention program. This can help to develop the organization's capacity to successfully implement the program.

The **Prevention Delivery System** describes the systems (organizations, communities, or governmental agencies) that are actually implementing the new program or innovation. Are these systems able to apply the capacity they have to engaging in the activities necessary for successful implementation?

As shown in Figure 10.1, the three systems interact and inform each other and are influenced by such larger macrosystem forces as the existing theory and research, the availability of funding, and the social and political climate.

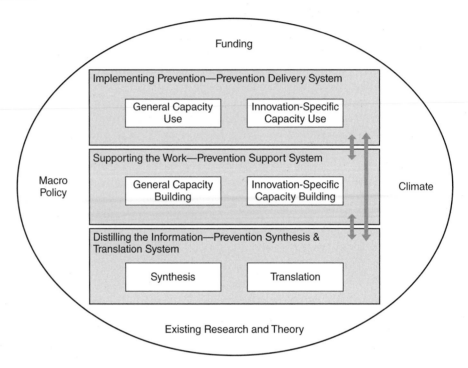

F I G U R E 10.1 The Interactive Systems Framework for Dissemination and Implementation

Support for some aspects of the ISF model comes from a very interesting meta-analysis specifically investigating the issue of program implementation. The authors hypothesized that elements of the Prevention Delivery System related to organizational capacity and two elements of the Prevention Support System (training and technical assistance) are key to successful implementation of prevention programs (Durlak & DuPre, 2008). The researchers were interested in evaluations of child and adolescent prevention and promotion programs that included information on implementation issues. The programs covered a wide variety of topic areas, including substance abuse, academic achievement, physical health, and violence. The research involved a review of five meta-analyses covering 483 studies and an additional 59 studies that specifically studied the impact of program implementation on program outcomes.

The basic result from this research is simple but profound. Sites that demonstrated better program implementation (specifically, closer fidelity to the original program and higher dosage levels) had effect sizes two to three times higher than sites demonstrating poorer program implementation. The researchers then went on to look specifically at which factors had the greatest effect on the implementation process. They list 23 factors that were each identified as impacting program implementation in at least five of the articles they reviewed. Those 23 factors were grouped into four categories. By far, the largest portion of the factors, 11 out of 23, related to the organizational capacity of the Prevention Delivery System. An abbreviated version of this list is included in Table 10.1.

T A B L E 10.1   Factors Affecting the Implementation Process

Community-Level Factors	The current state of prevention theory and research
	Politics, funding, and policy considerations
Provider Characteristics	Adopters' perceptions of the need for the program
	Adopters' assessment of their ability to implement the program
Innovation Characteristics	Compatibility of the program with the setting
	Degree to which the program can be adapted to the needs of the setting
The Prevention Delivery System: Organizational Capacity	Positive work climate
	Norms supporting change
	Sharing decision-making processes
	Open communication
	Strong leadership that is supportive of the program and the people directly implementing it

SOURCE: Adapted from Durlak and DuPre, 2008.

In the rest of this chapter, we will explain how you can use knowledge of all these concepts to guide successful implementations of prevention and promotion programs. To illustrate this process, we will use two examples of programs that have been successfully disseminated.

EXAMPLES OF SUCCESSFUL DISSEMINATION

In this section, we will introduce two types of prevention programming that have been widely disseminated with generally successful results: social-emotional literacy programs and home visiting programs. We will then use those programs as examples throughout the rest of this chapter of some general principles of program implementation, which we hope will serve as a guide in your own efforts to support effective prevention programming in your community.

Social-Emotional Learning Programs

Social-emotional learning (SEL) programs are school-based programs designed to foster social and emotional learning in children. The programs are based on research demonstrating that academic progress is supported by positive emotional development. In fact, academic progress is almost impossible to achieve for most children in settings that are characterized by aggression, incivility, and impulsive, destructive behaviors. The programs also reflect research showing that positive social and emotional behavior is based on a specific set of skills, which can be taught to children and can be supported through directed, school-wide organizational change (Elias et al., 1997).

Figure 10.2 gives a graphic display of the theory behind SEL programs and the mechanisms through which they work. Take a moment to compare it to the

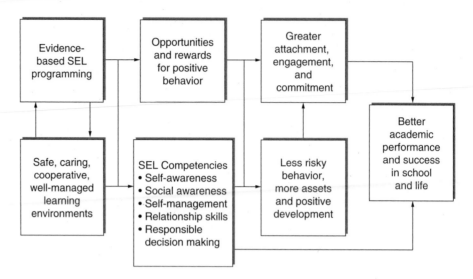

F I G U R E 10.2 School-Related Factors Predicting Academic Life and Success

prevention equations and the list of factors associated with resiliency in Chapter 9 (Table 9.1). As you can see, SEL programs are specifically designed to increase the strength and presence of protective factors in children's lives.

A wide variety of SEL programs are available. Most of these programs are directed at the classroom level, although many have components that extend to various other aspects of the school environment. Virtually all the most successful programs focus on building student skills in key areas. Their components and procedures have been carefully studied and identified. The Collaborative for Academic, Social, and Emotional Learning (CASEL) was established to promote the adoption of SEL programs from preschool through high school. CASEL provides extensive resources to help in the adoption of SEL programs at the organization's website (see the recommended websites at the end of this chapter).

SEL programs can make a difference. A recent report from CASEL summarized the findings of over 317 studies SEL programs involving 324,303 elementary and middle school children. The review included universal and indicated school-based programs and afterschool programs. Significant positive and negative outcomes in a wide variety of areas were found across all types of programs, including SEL skills, attitudes toward self and others, positive social behavior, emotional distress, conduct problems, and academic performance. The effect sizes were in the small to medium range (0.60 for SEL skills, 0.23 for conduct problems, and 0.28 for academic performance), but those numbers represent a significant change, and they remained significant at follow-up. To give you an idea of what those effect sizes mean, the report found that children's academic performance improved by 11 to 17 percentage points across all the studies reviewed (Payton et al., 2008).

For an example of one graduate student's interest in and experience with the complexities of implementing SEL programming, see Box 10.1.

Box 10.1   Community Psychology in Action

Social Emotional Learning

Amy Mart

M.Ed., University of Illinois at Chicago,
Department of Psychology - Community and Prevention Research Division,
Social and Emotional Learning Research Group

When I began reading the second edition of *Community Psychology: Linking Individuals and Communities* as a first-year doctoral student, I had only a vague notion of how I hoped to contribute to the field. The text helped me develop a deeper understanding of the history and values that form the foundation of community psychology, and it opened my thinking to consider the many areas of research and action in which community psychologists engage. In particular, my interest was piqued by discussion in Chapter 11 of the complexities of implementing programs in local contexts. Since then, much of my time has been devoted to learning more about the ways in which evidence-based prevention and promotion programs interact with the ecology of classrooms, schools, and districts. With this as my focus, CASEL and the SEL research group at the University of Illinois–Chicago have provided me with opportunities to investigate policies and processes that support successful, sustainable implementation of programs that promote healthy social and emotional development. I am hopeful that this work will contribute to community psychologists' ability to translate prevention research into action in schools and communities.

Home Visiting Programs

Home visiting programs involve having a trained staff person visit pregnant and new mothers in their homes. Generally, the programs are intensive, involving weekly to monthly visits for up to two to five years. Visits focus on providing parenting information and support for the mothers. The goals of the programs are to support healthy child development, increase positive parenting and parent–child interactions, and prevent child maltreatment. Home visiting programs are extremely popular. The programs exist in 40 states and provide services to about 2% of all children under six and their families in the United States (Astuto & Allen, 2009). The programs also exist in many other countries.

Two recent reviews give good overviews of these programs, including programs throughout the United States, New Zealand, Australia, and the Netherlands (Astuto & Allen, 2009; Howard & Brooks-Gunn, 2009). Two of these programs have been extensively disseminated and will be frequently referenced in this chapter. The Nurse-Family Partnership is a nonprofit agency that supports the dissemination of a program that grew out of David Olds' Prenatal/Early Infancy Project. Healthy Families America is a national program that initially developed as an extension of the Hawaii Healthy Start Program.

PARTICIPATORY ACTION RESEARCH
IN PROGRAM IMPLEMENTATION

Remember in Chapter 3 when we told you that community psychology blurs the distinction between research and practice? Well, program implementation is a perfect example of that. Effective program implementation requires that you understand the context in which you are working and that you are continually making program adaptations to fit the reality of your setting. But you cannot make those adaptations blindly. They must be based on empirical knowledge, not just of your setting and your chosen program but knowledge of the details of that ongoing interaction between the program and the setting. You gain that empirical knowledge through a participatory action research paradigm.

In alignment with the values of community psychology, we believe the process of successful program implementation and innovation must be participatory in nature. We will be discussing some specific program evaluation techniques that can be used as part of the participatory action research cycle in Chapter 13. For now, we want to give you a general overview of how the process can apply to successful program implementation and adaptation.

As we discussed in Chapter 13, there are many models for ensuring that research projects, including implementation projects, are participatory in nature. You can rely on an existing structure; develop new connections between existing organizations, committees, and individuals; or develop a completely new committee or board specifically to implement this program. However you choose to do it, keep in mind that developing some sort of structure and process to ensure that all key stakeholders have a collaborative role to play is central to successful program implementation and for developing the community capacity required for organizational or community change. True community work involves strengthening the community. After the intervention has been implemented successfully, the community members should have increased skills, and ideally, there should be formal and informal processes in place to pass these skills on to others. As one further point, remember that when you are discussing problems or settings involving children or adolescents, they should be viewed as key stakeholders and specifically have a role in the collaboration. (For examples of collaborative work with children and adolescents, see Langhout & Thomas, 2010; Miller, Kobes, & Forney, 2008; and Speer, 2008.)

Participatory action research is a collaborative cycle of activities in which research (assessment) continually informs action (implementation). The reverse is also true. Action informs research. Both of the programs highlighted in this chapter have benefitted extensively from knowledge gained during implementation. The organizing principles of a participatory action research cycle of program implementation can be generally summarized in the following activities:

- Identification and definition of a problem or area of concern
- Assessment of resources and community/organizational capacity
- Review of available research and potential programs or policies
- Assessment of fit between the innovation and the setting
- Training of personnel and development of supportive structures and processes
- Development of evaluation activities for implementation processes and outcomes

- Implementation of the program and adaptation based on information gained
- Repeat as appropriate

As suggested by the last point, the process of action research is cyclical and ongoing. Think back to the discussion of Kelly and Trickett's four ecological principles in Chapter 5. The last principle, succession, states that the first three principles will continually change over time. There will be multiple and ongoing changes in the relationships among the various aspects of the setting, the resources available, and the ways in which the setting and the innovation are continually adapting to each other. It is only through continual assessment processes that you can be aware of these changes and respond thoughtfully to them.

Remember that this is a general summary of activities that are part of the action research cycle in program implementation. How these activities are combined in a specific plan is going to look very different for different programs. This general description can be made very specific to the implementation of particular types of programs. For example, CASEL has specified an action research cycle for implementing SEL programs that involves 10 steps (See the CASEL website listed at the end of this chapter).

There are also models for program development, implementation, and evaluation that can be applied in any setting that is attempting to implement prevention activities. One of these models is called Getting To Outcomes, and we will describe that model in detail in Chapter 13. The activities described in this section, where they are discussed specifically in terms of program implementation, are closely aligned with the steps of the Getting To Outcomes approach (Wandersman, Imm, Chinman, & Kaftarian, 2000).

The rest of this chapter will be structured around these activities, but before we begin, we want to discuss one important aspect of evaluation that often gets overlooked: the need to evaluate for consequences you did not expect.

Evaluate for Unintended Consequences

Ongoing evaluation is important not only because it provides data for continual program innovation but also because even the best-designed programs can have unintended consequences, sometimes negative ones. These unintended, harmful consequences of what is planned as a helpful intervention are called **iatrogenic effects**.

An excellent example of a prevention program with unintended, negative consequences is the Scared Straight program. In the 1970s, inmates serving life sentences in Rahway State Prison in New Jersey began a program that they believed would help deter young people from a life of crime. Juvenile defenders were brought to the prison with the explicit intention of scaring them. They were given a brutal view of life in prison, including graphic stories of rape and murder. The program resulted in a documentary that claimed a 94% success rate, and as a result, the program was widely replicated.

The replications also reported success rates between 80% and 90%. Unfortunately, none of the evaluations included control groups or random assignment. In 1982, the program in Rahway was evaluated by using a control group and random assignment, and a different picture emerged. This evaluation found that juveniles who went through the program were actually more likely to be arrested than were those in the control group (Finckenauer, 1982). Instead of deterring juveniles from crime, it was increasing their risk. The program was having the opposite of the intended effect. Numerous other well-designed studies in multiple settings came to the same conclusion (Petrosino, Turpin-Petrosino, & Buehler, 2004; Schembri, 2009). Research suggests that the reason the program actually increases criminal behavior is because it reinforces attitudes and behaviors that are associated with criminality, such as the belief that aggression is an effective way to control other people.

Serious scientific investigation of negative effects from prevention programs (and other types of behavioral interventions) is still in the beginning stages, and there are no formal procedures for identifying safety concerns (such as the procedures monitored by the U.S. Food and Drug Administration to identifying potentially harmful medications). There are some preliminary reviews of potentially harmful therapies, with specific programs such as Scared Straight listed (Lilienfeld, 2007). But it is still largely up to practitioners to ensure that they are monitoring for negative effects.

The next section of this chapter will be organized according to the participatory action research activities listed previously.

Problem Identification and Definition

The first activity in our general model of participatory action research for program implementation is the identification and definition of the problem or area of concern. We say *problem* or *area of concern* to point out that prevention efforts do not always have to be directed toward a specific problem area. Communities may instead wish to work on strengthening existing resources and health promotion activities in their community or organization. As discussed in Chapter 9, these two goals often overlap.

Problems cannot be effectively addressed until they are widely identified as a problem. That may seem like a matter of common sense, but any review of the history of prevention science, or history in general, will give ample examples of the difficulty involved in achieving widespread recognition of a particular problem. The most common way of dealing with this issue is to wait until there is already widespread recognition of a problem before taking action. After all, there are plenty of recognized problems in our communities that are demanding our attention; we do not necessarily have to identify new ones.

But if you do wish to address something that the members of your community have not yet thought about, do not be discouraged. Form coalitions with like-minded individuals, do your research on the problem and its effects in your community, and then talk about it. Talk about it a lot. Write letters to the local newspapers, ask to speak to the city council and other legislative bodies, and present to as many groups as you can (e.g., church groups, PTAs, school boards, community groups, the chamber of commerce). The AIDS/HIV epidemic is a good example of this. It took a great deal of concentrated effort by scientists, the Centers for Disease Control and Prevention (CDC), community organizations, and individuals and their families to bring the HIV epidemic into public and political consciousness. And it takes effort to keep public attention focused on the epidemic.

Once there is some general level of agreement that the problem or area of concern is an important one, a common understanding of the problem needs to be developed. This is the process of problem definition. Think back to the discussion of problem definition in Chapters 1 and 3. How a problem is defined will directly affect how the problem is addressed. A fundamental example of this is the fact that a problem must be defined as something that *is preventable* before stakeholders will begin to consider prevention opportunities. There may be public recognition of a problem, but if that public recognition includes the belief that the problem is inevitable, then there will be no energy or resources available for prevention programming. Poverty is a good example of a societal problem that is considered by many to be inevitable. We will discuss this issue more in Chapter 12.

But the issue of problem definition goes beyond just instilling a general belief that a particular problem is preventable. The way the problem is defined has a huge impact on what possible interventions will be considered. SEL programming is a good example of this. Suppose there is a school district with high levels of disruptive behavior in the classrooms, high levels of bullying, violence, and vandalism, and low levels of academic achievement. There are many ways those problems could be understood. For example, if the problem is defined as being caused by aggressive, out of control children who are impossible to teach, then the chosen solution may be to increase police presence in the schools so those children can be arrested and removed when they cause trouble. If the problem is defined as being caused by poor teachers and inept administrators, then the obvious solution is to fire those poorly performing personnel. If the problem is defined as being caused by a lack of resources in the schools, then the preferred solution might be to funnel more money to the school district. But if the problem is defined in terms of school climate and a lack of opportunity for children to learn prosocial behaviors and self-regulatory skills, then SEL programming starts to seem like a good idea.

Obviously, such issues as local and national politics and the availability of resources are going to affect how problems are defined. (If you look back to Table 10.1, you will see that these are the community-level factors identified.) And in most cases, stakeholders are going to recognize that there are multiple causes to complex problems and that it could be useful to put several diverse approaches in place to deal with these problems. For example, most parents would endorse the idea that there needs to be better processes in place to evaluate and intervene with poorly performing teachers in public schools. But as community psychologists, we hope that when you are involved in these types of discussions that you will work to ensure that community problems are defined in such a way that they are seen as preventable and that risk and prevention factors that we know are amenable to intervention are included in the definition.

Assessment of the Setting

The next step in the action research cycle is to assess the resources and organizational capacity of the setting. This step is necessary to ensure that you understand the setting in which you are working. As we hope we have made abundantly clear in this chapter, prevention programs, no matter how well developed and researched, cannot just be forced on a setting like a patch ironed on a pair of torn jeans. They must be fully integrated into those settings, and both the programs and settings will be changed as a result.

From a community psychology perspective, there must be an ecological match, or fit, between the goals and methods of a program and the values and resources of the context in which the program is being implemented. **Context** is a complex concept. It refers to all aspects of the relevant setting, including cultural traditions and norms, the skills, goals, and concerns of the individuals, historical issues in that setting (e.g., prior experiences with similar innovations), and all the elements of community capacity. It would be difficult to overestimate the importance of community capacity in our discussion of program implementation. As stated earlier, 11 of the 23 factors identified as impacting program implementation by Durlak and Dupre (2008) were related to the organizational capacity of the Prevention Delivery System.

In a broad sense, **community and organizational capacity** refers to the resources present in a setting that would be available to help implement a new program or other types of innovation. Capacity can refer to individual-level resources (e.g., skills, education, motivation), organizational-level resources (e.g., clarity of mission, ability to attract funding, a cohesive staff), or community-level resources (e.g., strength of linkages among various groups, sense of community, history of other successful innovations). Community-level capacity can be seen as related to the concept of social capital we discussed in Chapter 6.

Discussions of capacity are often very general in nature, but there have been attempts in the literature to specify this concept. Many researchers differentiate between innovation-specific capacity and general capacity. **Innovation-specific capacity** refers to the motivation, skills, and resources that are necessary to implement a specific program. **General capacity** refers to the skills, characteristics, and overall level of functioning necessary to implement any type of program. Both types of capacity exist at individual, organizational, and community levels (Flaspohler, Duffy, Wandersman, Stillman, & Maras, 2008; Wandersman et al., 2008). An assessment of capacity should take place before the selection of any program.

For example, an assessment of a community's innovation-specific capacity might tell you that a home visiting program based on the Nurse-Family Partnership model will not work because your community is already experiencing a shortage of nurses, and it would be impossible to hire enough for the program. In this case, you might want to consider a different model of home visiting. An assessment of a community's innovation-specific capacity may also show that there is no need to identify an external program to prevent a problem; the community may already have existing programs that are working but need to be strengthened (Miller & Shinn, 2005).

Look back at Table 10.1. One element of organizational capacity that has repeatedly been found to be central to the organization process is strong leadership that is supportive of the program and the people who will be implementing it. In the CASEL study, they found that *strong, clear leadership* in the setting is key to successful implementation. Active administrative support for the program was critical for school commitment: for adopting and sustaining the program by teachers and other staff, for obtaining money and other resources, and for explaining the program to parents and community members (Elias et al., 1997). When administrative turnover occurred, programs with strong leadership proceeded with minimal disruption, usually because program developers engaged new administrators and offered program consultation to school staff. Sustainability can take a long-term emotional toll on even its most committed members if the program is in a constant state of reinvention or uncertainty.

There is one important point about community and organizational capacity that is becoming increasingly clear in the research on program implementation. When your assessment shows that existing capacity levels make it doubtful that a specific program can be successfully adopted, the most useful intervention may be to focus on increasing community capacity. Rather than focusing efforts on trying to address specific problems, some research suggests that the most beneficial approach is to focus on building community strengths (Miller & Shinn, 2005). Within an organization, effort could be placed on developing processes that have been linked to organizational capacity, such as shared decision-making processes and open communication. We will present examples of community organizations that have successfully accomplished this in Chapter 12.

Review of Available Programs

Once you have defined your problem and have a basic understanding of your setting, you have to select a program. In this chapter, we are encouraging you to follow certain steps: assess your setting, clarify goals, and review the available programs to select one appropriate for your goals and setting. Unfortunately, this recommended process of assessment, review, and selection is not always followed. A review of how various states select specific home visiting programs found that most states did not engage in any type of systemic evaluation of available programs. Generally, only one program was considered, and often, it was the program that was most popular nationally at the time (Wasserman, 2006). Think about that for a moment, reflecting back on the issues of context discussed previously. Do you think that a program selected based on popularity, with little consideration of how it would fit with a particular setting, has much chance of success?

Evidence-Based Programs   In most cases, there is no need for you to develop a program from scratch to address problems in your community. As you have seen in Chapter 9, there is a wealth of research on effective prevention programs and many, many organizations devoted to helping you choose an evidence-based prevention program that fits your goals and settings. In addition to the organizations we have already mentioned, such as CASEL, other highly regarded organizations include:

- Blueprints for Violence Prevention
- Substance Abuse and Mental Health Services Administration's (SAMHSA)
- National Registry of Evidence-Based Programs and Practices (NREPP)
- Office of Juvenile Justice and Delinquency Prevention Model Programs Guide

These organizations, as well as CASEL and other groups dedicated to providing information regarding evidence-based programs, are addressing the Prevention Synthesis and Translation System of the ISF model that we introduced at the beginning of this chapter. Their goal is to provide clear information regarding these programs to as wide an audience as possible. They want to help bridge the gap between research and practice by synthesizing the sometimes dense and complex information from research articles and presenting it in a useful format for the general public. This, of course, is also the goal of the program developers themselves.

The organizations mentioned at the beginning of this section are not trying to promote one specific program. They reflect a community-centered model of implementation by taking the community perspective. The websites do not assume that there is one "best" program to address any specific problem. Rather, the developers of these sites assume that only the members of the community can make an informed decision concerning what programs will best meet the needs of that community. The goal of those websites is to provide community members with as much information as possible about evidence-based prevention programs in order to ensure that the communities can make informed decisions.

This task is not an easy one. If you look at the Blueprints for Violence Prevention website and click on their Model Programs listing, you will see that the organization has reviewed over 800 violence prevention programs. At the time of this writing, only 11 met the organization's strict criteria to be identified as a model program, and another 20 met the criteria for promising programs. While we strongly recommend that you consider programs identified as model programs by one of these organization, we realize that the limited number of those programs may mean this is not feasible.

There could easily be a time when you are looking for an effective intervention of a type that is not evaluated by one of these sites. In that case, you need to have some basis for evaluating the available programs yourself. The Society for Prevention Research has published a guide titled *Standards of Evidence: Criteria for Efficacy, Effectiveness and Dissemination* (Society for Prevention Research, 2004). You should also be able to use the information in Table 9.2 to help you assess if the program fits what we know about best prevention practices.

These guidelines presented in the *Standards of Evidence* distinguish between the concepts of efficacy and effectiveness. **Efficacy** is defined as the beneficial effects delivered by the program under optimal conditions. This is distinguished from **effectiveness**, which is defined as the effects of the program when delivered in real-world settings. When selecting a program, it would obviously be best to select a program that has demonstrated both strong efficacy and strong effectiveness. But like much of the information in this chapter, that is just a guideline, not a hard and fast rule. There may be a problem in a community for which few programs have been developed or unique aspects of the community may make most of the available programs inappropriate. In those situations, it may make sense to select a program that has shown good efficacy, but perhaps it is too new to generate research on its effectiveness. If communities do select such a program, it is particularly important for them to have a good action research program that will provide them with ongoing information regarding how well the program is working in their setting.

As helpful as these organizations and guides are, they cannot determine what program is right for a particularsetting. As stated in Table 10.1, the community members must make a determination regarding the compatibility of the program with the setting and the degree to which the program can be adapted to the needs of the setting. In order to do that, community members must have a clear idea of the specific challenges and goals that exist in their setting. For example, there are a large number of evidence-based SEL programs, and they differ in important ways. Some focus on changing school climate; others on teaching specific skills. Some are designed for afterschool programs; many others are classroom based. Some have clear links to educational goals, such as literacy skills. And all of them have implicit cultural biases. Only through a collaborative assessment of the setting and the available programs can communities make a determination regarding what program is most likely to work for them.

Core and Adaptive Components   In order to successfully engage in program adaptation, those implementing the program must know what the core components of the program are and maintain fidelity to those; everything else is open to adaptation to the setting context. Developers of prevention/promotion programs understand the need to specify the key components of their programs, especially when they transfer their initiatives to new host settings. Two types of components have been identified. **Core components** are crucial to the identity and effectiveness of the program and need to be transferred with fidelity and care. **Adaptive components** may be altered to fit the social ecology or practical constraints of the new host setting (Price & Lorion, 1989). Some researchers also use the term **key characteristics** to refer to the adaptive components of the program. These include such things as specific activities or delivery methods (the exact videotapes used or the examples chosen to illustrate a point). For example, many major prevention programs, including both types highlighted in this chapter, specify that the presence of a structured curriculum of some sort is a core component for program success. But the details of what is covered in the curriculum can vary widely, even between programs of the same general type.

The need to be clear on the difference between core and adaptive components is illustrated by the research on home visiting programs. The programs differ greatly on such things as the goals of the program, the frequency and duration of home visits, the population served, the background of the home visitors, and whether the home visits are tied to other services, such as high-quality, center-based day care (Howard & Brooks-Gunn, 2009). Some programs begin home visits at birth; others begin prenatally. The visits can be weekly, biweekly, monthly, or at variable frequencies, and can last from as long as three months to five years. The visitors can be nurses, master's-level psychologists, college graduates, or paraprofessionals. So, how can you determine what the core components are?

Most organizations developed to support the implementation of specific programs are fully aware of the need to clarify core components, and they go to great lengths to ensure fidelity to those components. Home visiting programs are no exception. Although there is no widely recognized list of core components for home visiting programs in general, specific programs have worked to identify them, which can be seen on their websites.

Researchers have been working for decades to identify a set of core components common to general types of prevention programs, and they still have not completely succeeded. It is actually common in the literature to have a core component clearly specified for a general type of program, without specifying exactly what form that component should take. For example, as we have already mentioned, all home visiting programs agree that programs should have in place a method for assessing which families are most likely to benefit from the program. Home visitation, at least as it is implemented in the United States, is designed as a targeted intervention. But exactly who should be targeted in a specific community? The answer to that question varies depending on the goals of the program and the setting. Home visiting programs have been shown, in various studies, to demonstrate their strongest effects for specific populations, such as first-time teenage mothers, mothers with low psychological resources, and immigrant families, particularly Latino families (Astuto & Allen, 2009; Howard & Brooks-Gunn, 2009). Which program you choose would depend on whether you have a particular population you wish to target.

Another component of home visiting programs that may be considered adaptive is the issue of the qualifications necessary to be a home visitor. In general, the research supports the use of professional home visitors (nurses, social workers, or mental health counselors) rather than paraprofessionals for maximum beneficial effects (Howard & Brooks-Gunn, 2009). However, some evaluations have found positive effects with paraprofessionals (DuMont et al., 2008). Taking into account issues of context, there could easily be reasons why a community would chose to use paraprofessionals in a home visiting program. The community members may feel strongly that the program should employ individuals local to the community, which might make it difficult to hire enough visitors with professional degrees. There may also be important issues of cultural match between the visitors and the participant population that would make paraprofessionals a more appropriate choice for your community.

Another example of these points from the SEL literature is from a case study of an elementary school in the Chicago area: the Cossitt School. Starting in 1994, the school began researching SEL programs and eventually chose the Child Development Project (CDP) as the program they wished to implement in their school. CDP had over a decade of research supporting its effectiveness in a variety of school settings. The school made a long-term commitment to the program and dedicated a great deal of time and resources into training the teachers and educating the whole school community in the program. But the training and education was not limited to just that specific program. Teachers, administrators, and others began reading about multiple aspects of SEL, and as they did, their understanding of what they were doing and how they were doing it changed. As Cossitt School principal Mary Tavegia said, "We still do components of the program. But we've been trying to pull knowledge and best practices from everything we've read and learned about SEL" (CASEL, 2006).

As the school staff began to feel that they clearly understood the core components of SEL programs in general and could see that they were successfully implementing those components, they became comfortable in adapting other aspects of the program to better fit the needs of their school.

Assessing the Fit Between the Program and the Setting

While they are essential aspects, defining the problem and selecting a program with empirical evidence of preventing that problem are not enough to ensure successful adoption. Whatever the primary goals of the program, it must also clearly address the mission and most pressing goals of the setting and the people who inhabit that setting. Such settings as schools, workplaces, and governmental organizations face multiple pressures. They often have various constituent groups, with various needs that those groups expect the settings to address. These needs are often competing, leading to conflicting priorities for the setting. Sometimes, a regulatory agency or another constituency with authority over the setting will mandate that a particular goal become a priority for the setting. In order for a prevention program to be successful, it must adapt to the priorities of the setting.

Earlier, we said that the assessment of context includes recognition of the values of the community or organization. If the values espoused by the potential prevention program do not fit with the values of the setting (or the values of the funding organization), there is little chance that the program will be successfully implemented. However, before this determination is made, there should be a careful assessment of the core components of the program to see if those are actually in opposition to the values of the setting. If the core components are congruent with the values of the setting, other concerns with the program will probably be amenable to adaptation.

One aspect of context that must be taken seriously if a program is to be successfully disseminated is the skills and goals of the staff who implement it. Skilled staff members in any setting take pride in their craft and view their work with a sense of ownership. To gain their approval, an innovation must fit their values and identity: for instance, a police officer's sense of what police work involves. At the same time, an innovation must also offer something new that increases the staff's sense of effectiveness. Staff members of different ages, ranks in the organization, or levels of seniority may support or resist an innovation depending on how they understand their work and roles.

Almost all people have seen innovations come and go in their settings. And the longer they have been in that setting, the more experience they have with this process. That experience may be positive. They may have seen a problem in their community or organization effectively addressed through an innovation that was sustained over the long term. Or the experience may have been negative. They may have felt that a potentially positive innovation was not given enough support and died away. Or that an innovation was forced on them even though it was completely inappropriate for their setting. Some people may live or work in settings that have been subject to an almost continuous cycle of "innovations", none of which lasted for more than a year or two. These people in particular may be burned out on the whole idea of innovation and may be convinced that there is nothing truly different anyone can offer them.

The need to understand and meet the goals and priorities of the setting is illustrated by the experiences of the developers of the Social Decision Making and Social Problem Solving (SDM/SPS) program, a model SEL program. The organizers, from the Rutgers Social-Emotional Learning Lab, implemented the program in an urban, economically disadvantaged school setting. The district, in Plainfield, New Jersey, is an urban setting with a demographic profile that began as 95% African American and 5% Latino students, shifting to 70% and 30% over seven years. It was deemed a special-needs district by the state of New Jersey. The district is under unprecedented pressure to meet mandates to raise standardized test scores. These efforts have crowded out programs directed at social-emotional and character development (Elias & Kamarinos, 2003).

In order for SEL programs to be successfully adopted by such school districts, it is critical that the programs demonstrate a direct relationship to state and local mandates governing those schools. In Plainfield, these mandates are extensive. The success of the program implementation was based on the fact that the five skill areas of SEL (see Figure 10.2) are aligned with academic standards explicitly named and monitored in the district's goals.

Like most SEL programs, the SDM/SPS program has a set curriculum. To meet the needs of the Plainfield District, that curriculum had to be meshed with the various mandates the district was facing, especially concerning literacy. A series of topical modules to build readiness skills was created for grades K–1 as well as a supplemental small group intervention for young students with early reading difficulties (Elias & Kamarinos, 2003). This innovation demonstrated to the district that SEL programs could be used to address the academic mandates they will face.

Training and Support of Staff

One clear core component for any program is the need to provide significant training and ongoing support for the individuals implementing the program. Both areas of prevention programming highlighted in this chapter emphasize the need for significant training of the people who will be delivering the program. If you look at the model elements specified by the Nurse-Family Partnership and Healthy Families America home visiting programs (posted on their websites), you will see that both organizations emphasize the importance of training for the visitors. In addition, they both emphasize the need for significant supervision of the visitors, even going so far as to present guidelines regarding the number of visitors each supervisor should have on his or her caseload.

However, training by itself cannot ensure successful implementation. There must be planning before the beginning of the implementation of the program to develop processes to support the individuals involved in the day-to-day provision of the program. The developers of the SDM/SPS program make the point that support must be provided at multiple ecological levels. In successful implementations of the program, the superintendent assigned the areas of SEL and Character Education to a special projects coordinator, and she was designated the SEL Administrative Liaison. Site coordinators were also established in each school building to help with all aspects of implementation.

A Social Development Coordinating Committee determined overall direction, training, and resource allocation and included representation from the Rutgers SEL Lab Team. Initially, team members provided on-site assistance to teachers implementing the curriculum as well as site coordinators working with building-wide SEL initiatives; this support, which at its height included using as many as 50 trained undergraduates, faded gradually.

Training is only one aspect of support for program staff; they must also feel that their work is valuable and acknowledged. In the prevention equations in Chapter 9, we talked about the protective benefits of settings that provided opportunities for recognition of positive, prosocial behavior. This protective factor does not just apply to children. It is also important for adults and should be kept in mind while designing the structures that will support the implementation of a program. Processes need to be in place to recognize "small wins" so members of the setting can see and celebrate successes of the program early on.

Weick (1984) mustered evidence from social and cognitive psychology for the conclusion that when extensive changes are required of humans in organizations, their sense of being threatened rises, as does their resistance to change. When the proposed change seems smaller, the perceived threat is smaller, risks seem tolerable, allies are easier to attract, and opponents are less mobilized. **Small wins** is Weick's term for limited yet tangible innovations or changes that can establish a record of success and sense of momentum.

In a home visiting program that begins prenatally, one small win that could be tracked is the number of prenatal care appointments the clients successfully complete. This is a measure that has been shown to be positively impacted by these programs, it is data that should be kept as part of any program evaluation, and it is an achievement that the home visitors will recognize as important (particularly if they are health professionals). Progress on this measure should be extremely visible. For example, a chart could be put in a room where the program staff regularly meets, and each home visitor could indicate on the chart whenever a pregnant client keeps a prenatal care appointment. The chart may sound like an approach that would be used with children, but trust us: Adults need these visible celebrations of success too.

Developing the Evaluation Process

In Chapter 13, we will present a four-step model of program evaluation: 1) Identify goals and desired outcomes; 2) process evaluation; 3) outcome evaluation; and 4) impact evaluation. While we will discuss these activities in detail in Chapter 13, for now, we want to emphasize that process evaluations need to include questions regarding how well the program was implemented, including questions specific to model fidelity. Often, these questions center on the core components of the program. Did the participants match the intended target population? How much training did the people implementing the program receive? How much supervision did they receive during program implementation? If the program involved a set curriculum, was that curriculum accurately and consistently presented? Were other core components of the program implemented as intended?

Unfortunately, it is often these types of questions, the ones related to core components and model fidelity that are left unanswered in program implementations. Sometimes, they are not even asked. One of the major challenges in this field is that most programs and even evaluations of programs have not included an assessment of implementation fidelity. And the data we do have strongly suggests wide variations in how programs are implemented.

Part of the reason for a lack of assessment of core component fidelity is a shortage of funding for evaluation activities (Wasserman, 2006). Any time you find yourself involved in prevention program implementation, we strongly urge you to ensure that questions regarding fidelity to core components are included as part of your evaluation activities.

The developers of the programs can play a strong role in helping implementation sites maintain fidelity to core components. For example, in the area of home visitation programs, the Nurse-Family Partnership program is very specific regarding how the program should be implemented. The structure and content of home visits are clearly spelled out. In addition, sites seeking to adopt the program must first demonstrate that their settings have the capacity, including strong leadership and appropriate funding sources, to successfully implement the program. Organizations that wish to implement the model must sign a contract with the national organization, spelling out their commitment to maintain program fidelity and to participate in evaluation efforts.

Implementation, Adaptation, and Sustainability

In this chapter, we have emphasized the idea that to be successful, programs cannot be just *adopted* by a setting; they must be *adapted* to that setting. We are taking the specific position that successful program implementation must involve some level of program adaptation. This is still a matter of debate in the implementation literature. There are some researchers and program developers who still maintain that strict adherence to model programs is necessary to replicate positive results. However, we believe that the current state of the research supports the conclusion that while core components must be identified and adhered to, programs must be adapted to the specific context in which the program is being implemented.

Many of the challenges of implementation that we will discuss in this section relate back to concerns about core components, context, and program selection. This emphasizes again the need for a participatory action research approach to program implementation. If you do your groundwork in understanding your setting and understanding your program, implementation will be much easier. But it is never just a matter of doing the groundwork, implementing the program, and enjoying your success. You will not truly understand how the program interacts with the setting until you begin implementation. Issues that your groundwork suggested were going to be problematic may turn out to be easy, while there will almost certainly be unforeseen aspects of program/setting fit that turn out to be crucial. You must be continually collecting information and using that data to adjust and improve your program.

As we hope was clear from our discussion of the interaction between individuals and their environments in Chapter 5, adaptation is not a one-way street. While the program is adapting to the setting, the setting is also changing and adapting to the program. Program adaptation takes place over time; it must be **longitudinal** in nature. This idea is similar to Kelly's principle of succession. An innovation takes place in a setting with a history and culture. To be effective, it must change that setting in some way (Tornatzky & Fleischer, 1986). To be lasting, it must become part of that history and culture, not dependent on an influential leader or a few staff members, all of whom will eventually leave the setting. It must be **institutionalized**—made a part of the setting's routine functioning. Consider a youth group, a support group for senior citizens, or an organization at your college or university. How would it be different if a new, untrained leader runs it every year versus having a longer-term leader who, when he or she does leave, trains his or her successor well?

Moreover, any effective prevention/promotion innovation must be repeated or elaborated periodically for effect. One-shot presentations or activities seldom have lasting impact. Teaching a child to read is a multiyear effort, from identifying letters to reading novels (Shriver, 1992). Should it be any surprise that learning social-emotional skills or developing attitudes that limit risky behavior cannot be done quickly?

The institutionalization of the program should be an explicit goal of your action research program. Throughout the process, you should be collecting information and making modifications that will support eventual institutionalization. While it may seem that the three issues in this step, implementation, adaptation, and sustainability, should be addressed separately, we believe that all three issues are addressed through a good action research program. If you have done your work in the first six steps, this step, while comprising the bulk of your work with the program, should be much easier. The key is to continually assess your efforts through process and outcomes evaluation in order to identify potential problems and opportunities for strengthening your program.

In order for a program to be institutionalized, it must be integrated into the ongoing activities of the setting; it cannot be seen as something "extra." The CASEL evaluation of social and emotional learning programs found that sustained programs were integrated with other courses and into the mainstream of the school day and routine. This included use of the program in reading, health, and social studies as well as in school assemblies, school discipline and resolution of conflicts among students, and expectations for playground and lunchroom behavior. Integration takes place over a period of years and includes the program becoming a regular part of the school budget; external funding is often available only for a few years or can change over time (Elias et al., 1997).

The CASEL evaluation also found that sustained implementation required ongoing professional development about the program among teams of committed staff (teachers and others). This required some staff to become program advocates and role models. Sustainability is more likely when professional development is continual and implementers have a constantly deepening understanding of the theoretical principles and pedagogy on which the program is based. When teams of implementers with a deep commitment to the program work together, they can often maintain program momentum even during times of turnover. Most important, deep understanding of program principles allows implementers to adapt programs in response to changing circumstances yet maintain key program elements. While a surface understanding of the program may be sufficient for a setting to adopt it, in order for the program to be institutionalized, multiple members of the setting must have a deep understanding of the program and its core components and must be able to teach others about it.

McLaughlin and Mitra (2001) analyzed the staying power of school reforms over a five-year period and found that deep learning of theory and planned, proactive training of staff and administrators were important factors. Initial support for an innovation by administration and staff was less important than predicted if the innovation had a clear, feasible path of implementation and its benefits were soon apparent. Lessons about sustaining innovations in schools are similar to those in other workplaces. Administrative energy and direction are essential for sustainability, but overcoming turnover requires an educated, committed workforce. Administrative commitment, deep involvement of the workforce in ongoing change (especially at a face-to-face microsystem level), and innovations that address integral parts of the organization's mission foster sustainability (Elias & Kamarinos, 2003).

CULTURAL DIVERSITY IN PROGRAM IMPLEMENTATION

Throughout this chapter, we have emphasized the need to understand the community or setting in which you are working and to adapt programs to the values, strengths, and self-identified needs of the community. Program implementation and adaptation needs to proceed from an emic perspective and the process needs to be directed by the voices of the community members.

While this is true for all communities and settings, it is particularly true of communities where the culture is significantly different from the majority culture. Let us look at this issue in the context of a specific issue in a specific group of communities: suicide prevention in Native American/Alaskan Native communities.

As in so many of the discussions in this book, this one starts with the idea of problem definition. Problem definitions are rooted in historical perspective and cultural values. For Native American communities, many of the mental health problems seen on some reservations, such as substance abuse and depression, are the direct result of historical attempts by European Americans to destroy Native American cultures, traditions, and religions (Gone & Alcantara, 2007). From this perspective, there are clear problems with adopting interventions derived from European American culture.

> That's kind of like taboo. You know, we don't do that. We never did do that. If you look at the big picture—you look at your past, your history, where you come from—and you look at your future where the Whiteman's leading you, I guess you could make a choice: Where do I want to end up? And I guess a lot of people want to end up looking good to the Whiteman. Then it'd be a good thing to do: Go [to the] white psychiatrists in the Indian Health Service and say, "Rid me of my history, my past, and brainwash me forever so I can be like a Whiteman."—"Traveling Thunder" (Gone & Alcantara, 2007, p. 356)

The central role of problem definition is clear here. If substance abuse, depression, and suicide in Native American communities are defined by those communities as resulting from the decimation of their culture, values, and spirituality by the dominant American culture, then adopting an intervention from that dominant culture can never be seen as a solution. Rather, it would be a continuation of the problem (Gone, 2007; Gone & Alcantara, 2007).

From this perspective, any successful intervention or prevention program would have to be developed from the spiritual and cultural traditions of that specific community. Because the fundamental problem is not depression but rather the forced separation of community members from traditional approaches to understanding the world, then interventions should be judged by how well they attempt to address that fundamental problem.

The recognition that suicide prevention programming in Native American communities needs to be informed by this conceptualization of the problem is becoming widely recognized. In fact, the recent guide to suicide prevention among Native American and Alaskan Native youth, published by the U.S. Department of Health and Human Services (2010), lists historical trauma as a risk factor and cultural continuity as a protective factor.

However, this recognition does not mean that this culturally anchored definition of the problem has been reflected in evidence-based prevention programming. In fact, the whole concept of "evidence-based" programming can be seen in some communities as an attempt to force the dominant cultural values of science on communities that do not necessarily share those values (Gone & Alcantara, 2007). This means that every aspect of the participatory action research cycle, from definition and assessment, through implementation and evaluation, must be informed by and congruent with the values of the community. An example of this kind of work is the American Indian Life Skills Development curriculum. This is a high school–based suicide prevention curriculum that was originally developed in collaboration with the Zuni Pueblo community (LaFrombois & Howard-Pitney, 1995) and showed promising results when implemented in the high school there. The program was originally designed with a process for cultural adaptation built into the curriculum, and it has since been implemented with a number of different tribal communities and is considered a promising approach by the U.S. Department of Health and Human Services (2010).

These examples reflect the integration of cultural values at a deep structural level rather than just on a surface level. Including cultural references in a program is a surface level change that is likely to have little or no impact on the effectiveness or appropriateness of a program for a particular community. Integration on a deep level requires an in-depth understanding of a community's values, history, and practices and ensuring that those factors serve as a fundamental basis for the theory and implementation of a program. Deep integration of community values is difficult to achieve without a strong collaborative approach to program development, implementation, and evaluation. Community members need to be actively involved in each step of the process. The work of Gerald Mohatt and his colleagues on the issue of sobriety programming in Native American community discussed in Chapter 7 is another example of this type of deep structural integration of community values (Hazel & Mohatt, 2001; Mohatt et al., 2004).

PUTTING IT ALL TOGETHER

Perhaps you have read all this and concluded "But I want to do it all!" You want a home visiting program to promote healthy infant development and parent/child attachment, you want SEL programs in your local schools, and you want a community-wide, multilevel parenting program to reduce rates of child maltreatment. Plus you want some of the other programs you read about in Chapter 9.

In other words, you want to strengthen your whole community, not just address specific problems piecemeal. Well, first of all, the evidence supports you. All these programs have their largest effects when they are systematically applied in conjunction with other programs and services. For example, home visiting programs demonstrate some of their largest effects when they are offered in conjunction with high-quality day care and when they focus on connecting families with other services in the community (Astuto & Allen, 2009). In fact, one of the most serious criticisms of the Hawaii Healthy Start program was that the home visitors did not connect the families with other services, and this is considered to be an important factor in their poor program results (Howard & Brooks-Gunn, 2009).

While obviously impossible in a literal sense, doing it all is still not out of the collective reach of communities. In Chapter 12, we will talk about community change initiatives and the importance of community coalitions in ongoing community change. Community coalitions have their most positive effects when they are addressing issues in their community as a whole rather than specific problems. They also work longitudinally, engaging in a long-term process of community assessment and program implementation and adaptation. So, in the longterm, these community members are attempting to "do it all" for their communities.

After reading this chapter, you also may be wondering, if prevention and promotion programs are so effective, why do we not seem to see results on a national level? For example, if SEL programs are so effective and are implemented in so many schools, why is the American public school system still in such trouble? Why are things not getting better? The basic answer to that question is that such forces as poverty, politics, and state and federal policies have huge impacts on the functioning of schools. These large effects are going to affect evaluations of school performance on a national level much more than the implementation of SEL programming. (For a recent discussion of some of these issues, see Ravitch, 2010.) We will discuss efforts to address some of those macro-level factors in Chapter 12. But we would like to emphasize here that discouragement at a national level is no reason for discouragement at a local level. You may not be able to significantly improve the whole American public school system, but you can still improve the schools in your communities.

CHAPTER SUMMARY

1. Historically, our understanding of how to effectively implement prevention/ promotion programs has evolved from a *cookbook* approach, to *replication*, to *adaptation*, and, currently, to an *invention/innovation* approach. Successful implementation involves understanding the best practices and tailoring them to the unique circumstances of your setting.

2. While there is still much work to be done to understand the process of effective implementation, current research suggests that eight different aspects are key: *fidelity, dosage, quality, participant responsiveness, program differentiation, monitoring of control/comparison conditions, program reach,* and *adaptation.*

3. The process of spreading an effective program to many settings consists of four stages: *experimental development, technological application, diffusion of innovation,* and *widespread implementation.* This process is sometimes termed *scaling up.* Two general types of models have been developed to help explain the gap between prevention research (the first two stages) and practice (the last two stages). These are referred to as *research to practice models* and *community-centered models.*

4. The *Interactive Systems Framework for Dissemination and Implementation* (ISF) is an attempt to develop a comprehensive model of implementation, which integrates the two general types of models. The model describes three systems: the Prevention Synthesis and Translation System, the Prevention Support System, and the Prevention Delivery System. Table 10.1 summarizes research on factors affecting the implementation process that illustrates the importance of the Prevention Delivery System.

5. This chapter discussed two examples of types of programs that have been successfully disseminated: *social-emotional literacy programs* and *home visiting programs.*

6. *Participatory action research* is key to successful program implementation. Information gained from a continual process of assessment of the interaction between the program and the setting is necessary to design appropriate adaptations of the program. Kelly's ecological principle of succession emphasizes that the setting and the innovation will be continually adapting to each other. Eight steps of participatory action research in program implementation were presented, along with a specific action research model for implementing SEL programs. As part of the action research cycle, you must be sure to evaluate for unintended effects, including *iatrogenic effects* (unintended harmful effects of interventions).

7. *Identification and definition of a problem or area of concern* is the first step we have identified in the action research cycle. Something must be widely recognized as a problem before a community will be motivated to address it, and the definition of the problem must be framed in such a way that prevention activities are considered an appropriate response.

8. Assessment of resources and community/organizational capacity must include an assessment of community and organizational capacity. This includes an assessment of both innovation-specific capacity and general capacity. The presence of strong, clear leadership supportive of the innovation is an important part of organizational capacity.

9. Your review of available research and potential programs or policies should focus on *evidence-based programs*. There are a number of resources available on the Internet to help you do this. It is best to choose a program that has demonstrated both *efficacy* and *effectiveness*. It is very important to choose a program that has identified *core components* (which must be implemented with high fidelity) and *adaptive components* (which can be modified to fit the specific needs of your setting).

10. The final four steps in the action research cycle are: assessment of fit between the innovation and the setting; training of personnel and development of supportive structures and processes; development of evaluation activities for implementation processes and outcomes; and implementation of the program and adaptation based on information gained.

RECOMMENDED READINGS

Collaborative for Academic, Social, and Emotional Learning [CASEL]. (2003). *Safe and sound: An educational leader's guide to evidence-based social and emotional learning programs.* Retrieved from http://www.casel.org.

Wandersman, A., Duffy, J., Flaspohler, P., Noonan, R., Lubell, K., Stillman, L., Blachman, M., Dunville, R. & Saul, J. (2008). Bridging the gap between prevention research and practice: The Interactive Systems Framework for Dissemination and Implementation. *American Journal of Community Psychology, 41*(3–4), 171-181.

RECOMMENDED WEBSITES

The Collaborative for Academic, Social, and Emotional Learning (CASEL):
http://www.casel.org

The Nurse-Family Partnership:
http://www.nursefamilypartnership.org

Healthy Families America:
http://www.healthyfamiliesamerica.org

Blueprints for Violence Prevention:
http://www.colorado.edu/cspv/blueprints

Substance Abuse and Mental Health Services Administration National Registry of
    Evidence-Based Programs and Practices (SAMHSA):
http://nrepp.samhsa.gov

Office of Juvenile Justice and Delinquency Prevention Model Programs Guide:
http://www2.dsgonline.com/mpg

The Society for Prevention Research, Standards of Evidence: Criteria for Efficacy,
    Effectiveness and Dissemination:
http://www.preventionresearch.org/StandardsofEvidencebook.pdf

11

Empowerment and Citizen Participation

LRADAC, Abe Wandersman

OPENING EXERCISE

"If you have come to help me, you are wasting your time. But if you have come because your liberation is bound up with mine, then let us walk together...."

LILLA WATSON, Australian Aboriginal visual artist, activist, and educator, in response to mission workers

"There's a [Tennessee] mountain story ... of a traveling salesman here in the mountains. He gets lost and doesn't know which way to go. He found a little boy beside the road, and he said, "Hey there son, do you know the way to Knoxville?" The boy said, "No, sir." And he said, "Do you know the way to Gatlinburg?" "No, sir." Well, he said, "Do you know the way to Sevierville?" The boy said, "No, sir." And he said, "Boy, you don't know much, do you?" "No, sir, but I ain't lost!"

MYLES HORTON, founder of Highlander Folk School, as told in a conversation with Paolo Freire, in *We Make the Road by Walking*

In this chapter, we continue to elaborate the links between individual quality of life and ecological contexts as we focus on power dynamics in relationships, organizations, and communities. This chapter extends the section in Chapter 2 highlighting the concept of empowerment and its key role in defining the field of community psychology. Here, we examine *empowerment* in greater detail, beginning with definitions and concluding with a discussion of empowering practices and settings. We also focus on *power*, a concept at the root of empowerment, and *citizen participation* as a strategy for exercising power in community decision making. In Chapter 12, we will continue the discussion by focusing on processes of community and social change. However, keep in mind that this division is due to space limits. In the real world, engaging in empowering settings intertwines with changing communities and macrosystems. In Chapter 13, we consider how program evaluation methods can be used to empower individuals and communities—through developing and improving community programs.

To begin, let us look closely at this chapter's opening quotes and how they resonate for you. Take a minute to think about your response to each of the following questions:

- Why would Lilla Watson not want help in the form of services for her people?
- Why does the traveler discount the knowledge of the little boy?
- What are the stories that come to mind based on your own experiences of being helpful and of being helped?
- How is power working in each of the situations evoked in these quotes?
- What roles do you think Lilla Watson or the boy from rural Appalachia might envision for those who walk with them?

In this chapter, we will explore these key questions as we think about the roles and relationships that we engage—as community psychologists but also as students, teachers, parents, youth, elders, neighbors, social workers, researchers, health care professionals, and others—in trying to understand and improve quality of life in our communities. We will introduce concepts and tools that can be used to facilitate empowerment processes and outcomes, turning first to grounding definitions of key concepts.

WHAT IS EMPOWERMENT?

Empowerment is a term that has many meanings. It has become a buzzword with varying connotations—used by progressive and conservative forces in U.S. politics (Perkins, 1995). Corporations speak of empowering their employees— sometimes with no intent to actually share power (Klein, Ralls, Smith-Major, & Douglas, 2000). Nonprofit organizations frequently name empowerment as a major goal but do not often define how advocacy or services are empowering to clients (Kasturirangan, 2008). Physical exercise, meditation, and psychotherapy have been described as empowering; those are better understood in terms of personal growth or individual discipline, not empowerment as community psychologists use the term. Riger (1993) criticized varying, inconsistent usages of the term even within community psychology. A word that means everything also means nothing distinctive; sometimes, it seems that empowerment has suffered that fate.

However, let us look more closely. In community psychology, Rappaport (1981) originally suggested that empowerment is aimed toward enhancing the possibilities for people to control their own lives. He defined empowerment as "a process, a mechanism by which people, organizations, and communities gain mastery over their affairs" (1987, p. 122). Over time, Rappaport and others adopted a more elaborated, community-oriented definition proposed by the Cornell Empowerment Group (1989):

> an intentional, ongoing process centered in the local community,
> involving mutual respect, critical reflection, caring, and group partici-
> pation, through which people lacking an equal share of resources gain
> greater access to and control over those resources.

Empowerment in these definitions is accomplished with others, not alone. It involves gaining and exercising greater power (access to resources). At the individual level, it includes cognition (*critical reflection* in the Cornell definition) and emotion (caring) as well as the behavior of participation. At the setting level, it includes role relationships marked by mutual influence and reciprocal helping. Rappaport has intentionally sought to keep the definition of empowerment open, arguing that a simple definition is likely to limit understanding of its multiple forms.

Empowerment is a multilevel concept: individuals, organizations, communities, and societies can become more empowered (Rappaport, 1987). A person who becomes more skeptical of traditional authority, more willing to oppose injustice, and more involved in citizen participation is becoming empowered. A work organization may empower small teams to assume responsibility for day-to-day decisions. Through networking with other groups, a community organization may influence the wider locality. Through advocacy at higher levels of government, a locality may gain a greater control over its affairs. Empowerment also can concern dismantling or resisting oppressive systems of injustice—at macrosystem or other levels.

While empowerment may have radiating effects across levels, empowerment at one level does not necessarily lead to empowerment at other levels. Feeling empowered does not always lead to actual influence in collective decisions. Individuals with more power and control over their lives do not necessarily empower their organizations or communities. Empowering organizations may not be empowered to make changes in the larger community. A powerful organization in which leadership is tightly controlled does not empower its members. Successful empowerment efforts work across multiple levels (Perkins & Zimmerman, 1995; Zimmerman, 2000).

The Context and Limits of Empowerment

Empowerment is contextual: It differs across organizations, localities, communities, and cultures because of the differing histories, experiences, and environments of each (Rappaport, 1981). For example, in a civic group, a person may develop skills for influencing decisions through discussion, teamwork, and compromise. But that individual may find these skills ineffective for wielding power in a workplace that rewards directive, task-oriented decision making. The person is thus empowered in the first context but not the second. Even the nature of what empowerment means may be different in these two settings.

A focus on the context of empowerment is critical—not just because empowerment processes may be different across settings and cultural communities but because it leads us to ask key questions: Who is to be empowered? And for what purposes? (Berkowitz, 1990). As discussed previously, empowerment has often been understood in individualistic terms and used to promote personal self-advancement or individual entrepreneurship without regard for one's community or wider society. Empowerment also may be understood to mean strengthening the position and resources of one's in-group at the expense of other groups. Examples such as a White supremacy group come to mind. An ecological perspective helps us reflect on the complexities and dilemmas faced in working toward empowerment goals. For example, recall our discussion in Chapter 7 of issues of empowering women in patriarchal cultures (Brodsky, 2003; Ortiz-Torres, Serrano-Garcia, & Torres-Burgos, 2000). A special issue of the *American Journal of Community Psychology* provides studies of liberation in diverse contexts, and a number of the papers in that issue take up the relationship of empowerment to liberation and social change (Watts & Serrano-Garcia, 2003).

Thus, empowerment is a complex, dynamic process that develops in context and over time. It can deteriorate as well as grow, but it is not reversed by small setbacks (Zimmerman, 2000). It is often best understood by longitudinal and participatory research strategies, as we discussed in Chapters 3 and 4 and to which we will return in Chapter 13. Empowerment often occurs through engagement in settings in which help-giving roles and relationships are marked by reciprocity, and expertise is widely distributed. It often involves grassroots groups that are limited in size, possess a positive sense of community, involve members in decision making, and emphasize shared leadership and mutual influence (Rappaport, 1987; Maton & Salem, 1995). Empowerment also may involve linkages among organizations (Zimmerman, 2000) and collective action. To extend our discussion of collective decision making and action, we turn to citizen participation.

What Is Citizen Participation?

A useful definition of citizen participation is provided by Wandersman and colleagues (1984)—a process in which individuals take part in decision making in the institutions, programs, and environments that affect them (p. 339).

Let us unpack this definition. "Institutions, programs, and environments" include workplaces, hospitals or mental health centers, neighborhoods, schools, religious congregations, and society at large. They also include grassroots organizations formed for the purpose of influencing larger environments, including block associations, political action groups, or labor unions. It is a process that involves decision making. This does not necessarily mean holding the power to control all decisions but involves making one's voice heard and influencing decisions in democratic ways.

Think about the differences between being a *client* and being a *citizen*. Community psychologists seek guiding conceptual models that emphasize rights, competencies, and collaborative relationships rather than traditional medical models that emphasize needs, deficits, and hierarchical doctor-patient relationships. We draw on this distinction in our work with marginalized or stigmatized groups. For example, in efforts to reduce homelessness and integrate homeless persons with mental illness more fully into communities, practitioners have used a citizenship framework to encourage community members and organizations to rethink their relationship to homeless persons. In thinking about homeless persons as fellow citizens rather than simply as patients or clients who need services, we may place a greater emphasis on helping these individuals to contribute to their communities and find a valued niche in society (Rowe, Kloos, Chinman, Davidson, & Cross, 2001).

In this example, we see that the concept of citizenship is really useful to us as a way of describing persons and groups with whom we work, but citizenship as typically understood can also be used to exclude many people from full participation in their communities. Around the world, individuals and groups are too often displaced from their home countries because of violence, war, political upheaval, and economic distress; many of these people are not afforded formal citizenship in the places they live and work. Because of this, scholars have increasingly sought more inclusive notions of citizenship, including "cultural citizenship" and "global citizenship" as a way of understanding community belonging and civic participation (Flores & Benmayor, 1997; Berryhill & Linney, 2006). Many of us, in the United States and around the world, are recent immigrants ourselves or work with groups and communities that include many individuals facing challenges related to citizenship. (For example, remember the discussion in Chapter 6 of the controversies surrounding what it means to be Australian.) Expanded notions of citizenship help us work in diverse contexts; they may also help us to imagine children and youth with whom we work—not just as citizens in the making but as social agents capable of participating in civic life (Golombek, 2006; Langhout & Thomas, 2010). For example, in participatory action research with youth (as described in Chapter 3), children show that, with adult support, they are able to exercise the rights and responsibilities of full community members as they investigate real problems and work for meaningful change.

What about the concept of participation? Like empowerment, participation has become quite popular. An influential critique has suggested that in many arenas, from international development efforts to local community interventions, participation is merely a useful rhetoric, a fashionable way of speaking, rather

TABLE 11.1   Myths and Insights About Private Life and Public Life

Myth: Public life is for celebrities, politicians, and activists—people who like to be in the limelight or who want to make waves.

Insight: Every day, at school, where we work, where we worship, within civic or social groups, our behavior shapes the public world and is shaped by it. We are all in public life.

Myth: It is too depressing to get involved in public life—too easy to burn out.

Insight: Public life serves deep human needs—for example, to work with others or to make a difference. It is as essential as private life.

Myth: Public life is always nasty, cutthroat, all about conflict.

Insight: Public life involves encountering differences, but conflict does not have to be nasty. When understood and managed well, it can be lead to growth for individuals and groups.

Myth: Public life is about pursuing one's own selfish interests.

Insight: Selfishness and enlightened self-interest are not the same thing. Understanding how our true interests overlap with those of others comes only through involvement in public life.

Myth: Public life interferes with a private life.

Insight: Public life often enhances private life, making it more meaningful and enjoyable.

NOTE: Adapted from Lappe and DuBois (1994, pp. 21, 24, 29, 33, 39).

than an authentic practice (Cooke & Kothari, 2001). Community members are increasingly asked to participate in public forums, advisory boards, and so forth, but their voices may still not count when it comes to actual decision making. This caution seems useful in reminding us that citizen participation is not simply a process of consultation or gaining consent, whereby decision making remains in the hands of a small, powerful group. Participatory strategies require a shift in how decisions are made and a commitment to enact democratic values in meaningful practice (Hickey & Mohan, 2005).

Citizen participation is *not* simply volunteering or community service. For example, assisting with a school field trip is not citizen participation. Participation involves influence in making collective decisions, in groups, communities, or society. It occurs in a diversity of forms—for example, serving on a community coalition, writing a letter to the editor, debating the budget at a school board meeting, meeting with government officials to press for an action, testifying a public hearing, and voting in elections. Each of these forms involves acting in the public sphere—something that many people are hesitant to do. Perhaps that hesitancy comes from myths about engagement in public life (see Table 11.1).

Citizen Participation in Action

Acts of citizen participation are more effective when done collectively with others and when adequately supported over time (see Wandersman (2009) for a useful summary of keys to success as well as challenges). The following stories about the Waupun, Wisconsin, youth group and Alison Smith's growing role in community and state affairs illustrate ways of influencing decisions through collective actions.

"Some of the adults thought it might never happen. You could tell
by the way they looked they were just waiting for it to fail." (Cameron
Dary, quoted in Putnam & Feldstein, 2003, p. 143)

About 30 sixth-graders at the Waupun Middle School in Waupun, Wisconsin, met after class to choose projects they could take on to help their school and community. They divided into small groups to discuss possible service activities. Then, the groups presented their ideas to the meeting and the students voted on the list of possibilities. They agreed to take on the top three: raising money for a field trip fund for students whose families could not afford to pay the fees; getting new playground equipment for the school; and convincing authorities to install warning lights at a railroad crossing on Edgewood Street, a few blocks away. Only a small sign marked the crossing; brush and mounds of soil obscured the view down the tracks.

Cameron Dary, the sixth-grader who led the railroad crossing project, and his fellow students presented their idea to a meeting of the Waupun City Council. Told to collect evidence to support their ideas, they conducted a survey of residents near the crossing. Of 14 residents surveyed, 10 believed the crossing was unsafe, 12 had seen people not stopping, and 13 wanted a better warning device. Continued efforts by the youth for over a year eventually led to action: The railroad installed a series of warning signs and removed the debris to clear sight lines at the crossing (quoted and paraphrased from Putnam & Feldstein, 2003, pp. 142–144).

So I went to a town meeting of a couple hundred people, and …
I voiced my opinions as best I could, red-faced, hesitant, and
embarrassed.

That is how Alison Smith began to speak out about community issues. She soon joined the League of Women Voters and became active in environmental issues in her Connecticut town and later in Maine. "I was hesitant at first. I don't have a college degree. I'm more of a behind-the-scenes person. But I've always felt like someone who cares, even if I didn't always know what to do about it."

When the Maine League of Women Voters asked her to collect signatures for the Clean Elections statewide referendum, she did it. "I just sat at a table with a sign saying 'Do you want to take big money out of politics?' Almost everyone who came over responded and signed." Support for the initiative grew statewide, with Alison as one of over a thousand volunteers. "I felt nervous when the League asked me to do new things like speak at press conferences.… But I also found that as an ordinary person, I had more credibility than the political professionals."

The Clean Elections Act passed with 56% of the vote and became a national model for campaign finance reform. "It gave me a sense that I really can do something just by showing up to further a cause.… I'm in it, as I said, to challenge the cynicism and despair, both my own and that of our society." (Quoted and paraphrased from Loeb, 1999, pp. 63–66)

Participation: Means or End?

In these stories, citizen participation is both a means (a path to a goal) and an end (a goal in itself). As a means, participation is often encouraged to improve the quality of a plan or because citizens' commitment to a decision is often greater if they participated in making it (Bartunek & Keys, 1979; Wandersman & Florin, 2000). As an end, citizen participation is often seen as an essential quality of a democracy—regardless of whether it generates the practical benefits, such as better decisions or greater commitment.

This means-end distinction is not merely academic. Citizen participation is not always a means to better decisions, particularly if conflicts are not resolved or valid expertise is ignored. Nonetheless, citizen participation has many advantages. Reviews of field research in organizations show that participation by members usually (but not always) increases the quality of decisions and overall organizational effectiveness. This is especially true if disagreement is seen as a source of information rather than a threat. Studies of voluntary organizations indicate that participation promotes effective leadership and attaining goals (Bartunek & Keys, 1979; Fawcett et al., 1995; Maton & Salem, 1995; Wandersman & Florin, 2000).

Both empowerment and citizen participation involve exercising power in collective decision making. The principal distinction between them is that participation is a specific strategy or behavior, while empowerment is a broader process. Meaningful participation in civic life can be empowering, and the lack of opportunities for meaningful participation can be disempowering (Rich, Edelstein, Hallman, & Wandersman, 1995; Langhout & Thomas, 2010).

MULTIPLE FORMS OF POWER

Understanding empowerment and citizen participation requires considering different forms of power. We will introduce three types of power and then look more closely at how power works in social and community life. Our intent is to illuminate often-overlooked sources of power that may help to empower citizens and communities. Before reading this section, return to the opening quotes for this chapter, and consider these additional questions:

In settings and relationships in your own life, how do you exercise power? How do others exercise it? Is the use of power different in different settings or relationships? How? To what extent do your professors have power over you? Do you experience any differences in power in various classes? How? What forms of power can you exercise as a student? What are the limitations of these?

Now think more broadly about your communities and society. What forms of power exist here? How can someone like you exert power here?

Power Over, Power To, and Power From

One useful framework draws our attention to power in three forms (see Hollander & Offerman, 1990, p. 179; Riger, 1993; Rudkin, 2003; van Uchelen, 2000). **Power over** is the capacity to compel or dominate others—often through control of valued rewards or punishment (French & Raven, 1959). Power over may enforce a target person's behavioral compliance, but it also invites covert or overt resistance. It may be used in ways that seem gentle but carry a clear implication that if others do not comply, stronger means will follow. It is often rooted in social structures. For example, one form of power in organizations is "the ability to issue and enforce a command concerning the use of resources" (Levine, Perkins, & Perkins, 2005, p. 382). This ability is created by the organization's structure—regardless of the individuals involved. Also, in systems of oppression that we described in Chapter 7, the dominant group has power over—for example, when social customs and belief systems empower men more than women. Power over resembles classical sociological concepts of power (e.g., Giddens, Duneier, & Appelbaum, 2003). Use of power over involves a hierarchical, unequal relationship and can lead to injustice. But it also can be used collectively to promote justice, as when laws compel an end to racial discrimination.

Power to concerns the ability of individuals or groups to pursue their own goals and to develop one's capacities. Unlike power over, this can involve self-determination for each person. For example, Nussbaum's (2000, 2006) capabilities framework, which has been adopted by a number of international development and human rights organizations, emphasizes the power and freedom of individuals to engage in valued social activities and roles. This is also consistent with the goal of empowering practices—to which we will return later in this chapter—to enhance the possibility for people, organizations, and communities to author their own lives more fully. This sort of generative power may be shared, as it is not conceptualized as a limited commodity or zero-sum game.

Power from is an ability to resist the power or unwanted demands of others. It can be used to resist a dominant boss or friend or to resist wider forms of social oppression. Some feminist critiques of patriarchy (which involves power over) focus on how women often use power to and power from to resist domination (Hooks, 1984; Miller, 1976; van Uchelen, 2000).

Power "over," "to," and "from" occur in workplaces. For example, a manager may exercise power over by giving orders, by seeking to persuade employees to do what the manager wants, or by delegating decisions to workers (allowing them some power to). Individually or collectively, employees can exercise power to and power from. They can use various persuasive and negotiating strategies to impact managerial decisions and policies. They may circumvent the manager's orders when he or she is not looking or go "over the boss's head" to higher management. At the extreme, they can withdraw their labor (individually quit the job or collectively strike). This is not to say that the power of employers and employees is equal. Obstacles to employees' use of power (e.g., difficulties in organizing collective action) are greater than the obstacles employers face. However, because employers and employees both hold some forms of power, it is usually in the long-term interest of both to work together.

Integrative Power

Boulding (1989, p. 25) defined **integrative power** as the capacity to work together, build groups, bind people together, and inspire loyalty. This is sometimes termed *people power*; it is also a realization of power to and/or power from in the framework discussed previously. Mohandas Gandhi and others have often asserted that there exist forms of power stronger and more widespread than violence—powers without which human relationships (families, friendships, and communities) cannot exist.

People enact these forms of integrative power every day. In a sense, the social sources of integrative power are infinite—unlike finite sources, such as money (Katz, 1984). Some of the most remarkable forms of integrative power have been based on moral or spiritual principles. Gandhi proposed the concept of *satyagraha*—literally translated "clinging to truth" or more broadly as the power of truth (D. Dalton, 1993, p. 249). *Satyagraha* was the basis of Gandhi's nonviolent resistance to British colonialism, of the nonviolent demonstrations of the U.S. civil rights movement, and of more recent nonviolent resistance movements in Poland, South Africa, Chile, and elsewhere (Ackerman & DuVall, 2000; Boulding, 2000; Nagler, 2001). It is based on principled, active, openly expressed resistance to oppression—coupled with an appeal to a widely held sense of social justice.

Integrative power also exists in other forms. Labor unions have long used strikes as a form of people power. Boycotts are an exercise of integrative economic power: Colonial Americans boycotted tea to protest British policy, and Americans later boycotted cotton and sugar (made with slave labor) to protest slavery. In addition, many government officials will testify to the power of an organized citizens group demanding specific changes (e.g., the Clean Elections advocacy mentioned by Alison Smith at the beginning of this chapter). (We will discuss more examples in Chapter 12.) Block associations—to which we will turn later in this chapter—rely on integrative power, as do support networks and self-help groups.

Three Instruments of Social Power

Gaventa (1980), a social activist, used concepts of political science to describe three instruments of social power—or, in other words, three ways that power operates in community and social life (see also Speer & Hughey, 1995; Culley & Hughey, 2008). A story provides examples.

A corporation filed for a permit to use sludge containing human waste on their farm site, which produced grass sod in a rural area along the Wallkill River in upstate New York. Under a temporary permit granted by the state without any local input, sludge dumping began. Local citizens discovered the stench without warning and reacted with understandable anger. The state's Department of Environmental Conservation (DEC) held extensive public hearings on the company's application for a permanent permit before an administrative law judge. These hearings involved hours of testimony by technical experts and local citizens. In theory, all had full input into the DEC decision.

In practice, however, this formal process was distinctly one-sided. The local citizens were assigned seats in rows behind attorneys involved in the case. They did not have the legal training or technical background of the corporation's hired experts and knew neither the legal procedure nor the terminology used routinely during the hearings. They made a number of procedural errors until they hired their own attorney. When many of the local farmers became frustrated with their lack of real input, they used their tractors to block access to the sod farm. They were only temporarily successful.

Perhaps most telling, citizens' knowledge of local conditions was discounted. Years of accumulated practical experience had shaped their intuitive understanding of things such as the effects of rainwater runoff on streams and the Wallkill River. Yet expert testimony, by consultants who did not live or work in the community, primarily influenced the judge's decision. When that testimony revealed that the corporation's plans met all state regulations, the permit was granted.

Within five years, virtually every negative outcome predicted by the local citizens had occurred. Wastes had flowed into the Wallkill River, groundwater was contaminated with toxic cadmium, and illegal hazardous wastes had been stored at the site. The DEC sued the operators of the site for repeated violations and finally had to classify the property as a hazardous waste site for later cleanup. While unsuccessful in this case, local citizens came together to found Orange Environment (named for the county in New York where these events occurred). Orange Environment remains active in community organizing, legal action, and policy advocacy on environmental issues (adapted from Rich et al., 1995, pp. 660–662).

Let us look more closely at the ways that power operates in this story. Gaventa's first instrument of power is **controlling resources that can be used to bargain, reward, and punish**. This resembles power over. In the Wallkill River example, the company had the money to hire experts and attorneys, to use or circumvent the law, and to overwhelm local opposition. But in other contexts, an organized citizenry can effectively threaten such punishments as negative publicity or boycotts or offer attractive compromises.

The second instrument of social power is **controlling channels for participation in community decisions**. Speaking at public hearings, signing petitions, and voting are traditional forms of participation. However, Gaventa (1980) also refers to subtler mechanisms, such as controlling meeting agendas to exclude citizen comments and debate or requiring citizens to hire attorneys to advocate for them. Hidden "rules of the game" are used to systematically benefit one group over the other (Culley & Hughey, 2008). In the Wallkill River case, this instrument of power was used to limit citizen testimony. In theory, the DEC public hearings offered citizens the chance to participate in and influence a decision that would affect their health and livelihoods. In practice, legal procedures effectively prevented any meaningful citizen participation. But in other contexts, an organized opposition can open other channels of participation, such as public demonstrations or use of the media. Wallkill citizens founded Orange Environment in part to provide legal advocacy when needed for participating in decision making. Orange Environment also provided a site where residents could develop local knowledge and expertise through research and education. Residents learned that technical and legal experts were able to participate and influence decisions in a way that local community members were not. They realized that they needed to build and exercise **expert power**—a type of power based on the perceived knowledge, skill, or experience of a person or group.

It is important to note here that community psychologists have paid a great deal of attention to expert power and the role of the professional as expert (for example, the attorneys and scientists in the Wallkill River case). Community psychologists have drawn on expert power as researchers and professionals, but also have criticized the use of expert power to control channels of participation as well as constrain the agency and limit the freedoms of persons in distress (Rappaport, 1977; Ryan, 1971). For example, medical doctors and mental health professionals are considered experts in diagnosing and treating persons with psychological disorders. While a diagnosis of depression or attention deficit disorder can bring great relief to a person in distress and bring needed resources, it can also stigmatize and limit options. The power to define and treat what is (ab)normal can be part of a system of caring but also a system of social control and exclusion. For example, McDonald and Keys (2008) examined how research scientists on review boards exclude persons with disabilities from participation in research. They showed how the attitudes of key decision-makers limit community access for persons with disabilities. Yet expert power can also be used to offset power, as in mutual help groups, who also offer expertise on psychological difficulties and disorders. They provide a different perspective on illness and recovery for their members and different forms of participation in community. The participatory research methods that we discussed in Chapters 3 and 4 also can be a basis of expert power for communities. The Waupun youth group described earlier in this chapter conducted a survey that was instrumental in exerting pressure on city government and the railroad.

Often overlooked, the third instrument of power is **shaping the definition of a public issue or conflict**. Recall our discussions of problem definition throughout this text. We have emphasized the importance of looking across levels of analysis and examining values and assumptions implicit in different definitions of human and social problems. The power to define public problems or issues is often referred to as the power of "spin" or the ability to shape the terms of public debate on an issue (Gaventa, 1980). While this power may be used responsibly and different definitions of a public issue may arise from genuine disagreement and value differences, Lukes (2005) draws attention to how this power can be used to mislead—whether through outright censorship and disinformation or through various ways of discounting individual or group judgments. It is the power to make one perspective seem natural, normal, important, or rational while making another perspective seem strange, frightening, irrelevant, or unreasonable. For example, in the Wallkill River case, key decision-makers favored technical jargon and scientific expertise while discounting the local, practical knowledge of residents. In a more recent case recounted by Culley and Hughey (2008), powerful stakeholders tried to persuade the residents of Sugar Creek that there was no reason to get involved or worry about chronic oil refinery spills and the contaminants seeping into the area's soil and groundwater. They appealed to the community members' sense of themselves as residents of a "refinery town," with the refinery as a "good neighbor" and economic benefactor.

Communications media play a powerful role in shaping how social issues are defined, but the third instrument of power is not theirs alone. Behind the media are social institutions and interest groups with the money and perceived credibility to make their voices heard and to create the ideas of the media and the public. These dominant beliefs of a community or society—often shared in stories—shape how social issues are interpreted (Rappaport, 2000). An example is Tatum's (1997) metaphor of "breathing smog" for widely accepted social stereotypes (mentioned in Chapter 7). But in some situations, citizens who adroitly use the media or word-of-mouth channels also shape public opinion and social imagination (Christens, Hanlin, & Speer, 2007). Community members may also share persuasive counternarratives that challenge dominant stereotypes and help themselves and others envision how it could be otherwise (Greene, 1995; Rappaport, 1998). Orange Environment used this instrument of power in public advocacy regarding local environmental issues, as did the residents of Sugar Creek. Refer to Box 11.1 for a "Community Psychology in Action" feature describing Marci Culley's experience as an action researcher in Sugar Creek and how local citizens exercised their social power.

Summary Thoughts on Power

What is power, in terms useful to community psychologists?

Power is not a purely internal state, such as simply feeling powerful, inspired, or confident. Holding power involves the capacity to exert actual influence on decisions (Riger, 1993). Power is best understood as a dimension, not an all-or-none dichotomy. Seldom is a person or group all powerful or entirely powerless. Those who hold greater power will resist change, but others may be able to use alternative sources of power. Even small acts may reflect some degree of power. Persons and groups with little or no capacity to compel may find ways to resist the powerful. We do not discount the differences in power in oppressive systems but seek to call attention to sources of power that citizens can use.

Power is best understood in relationships (Gaventa, 1980; Serrano-Garcia, 1994). Power relationships in families, settings, communities, and societies are typically self-sustaining, resulting in stubborn social regularities (see Gruber & Trickett, 1987; Tseng et al., 2002; and recall Seidman, 1988, from Chapter 5). But they can change, shifting in both predictable and unpredictable ways. Power is also contextual; you may hold power in some circumstances (e.g., influencing decisions in a student group) but not elsewhere (e.g., in a job where you have little voice in decisions).

Exercising power or having an impact on decisions requires control of some resources and ultimately, at least, some capacity to compel those who resist so they go along or compromise. Many resources can empower communities, and personal willingness to get involved and work with others can help mobilize them (recall the examples that began this chapter or Debi Starnes in Chapter 1). Integrative power is demonstrated at a variety of levels—from neighbors coming together to create safer playgrounds to grassroots groups influencing international policies on climate change. But how does this "people power" develop over time?

B o x 11.1   Community Psychology in Action

Citizen Participation and Power: The Case of Sugar Creek

Marci R. Culley
Georgia State University

What does citizen participation "look like" as it unfolds in local communities? To learn more about this, I conducted a qualitative community case study to explore an environmental dispute that occurred in Sugar Creek, Missouri—a small town polluted by a BP refinery. Over decades, residents' concerns and outrage grew. One resident recalled: "People were mad. They'd been lied to for 40 or 50 years. Everything was 'fine,' everything was 'clean,' but yet ... there was over 200 million gallons of product underneath the neighborhood."

The study evolved from more than four years of my involvement as a participant-observer. I explored how federally mandated vehicles for citizen participation facilitated or undermined individual and collective decision making among stakeholders. Specifically, I examined the extent to which these vehicles, and stakeholders' experiences of the participatory processes initiated through them, were shaped by social power dynamics. Findings illustrated how participation was limited and how citizen influence could be manipulated via control of resources, barriers to participation, agenda setting, and shaping conceptions about what participation was possible. I learned a great deal from my work in this community. Three findings are particularly instructive for citizen participation efforts everywhere.

First, while participatory processes may on the surface appear open and collaborative, they can nonetheless contain significant power imbalances. In this case, subtle forms of power were often used by government and industry officials to marginalize community residents' views. As one regulator noted, existing environmental policy requires that regulators "pretty much work with the responsible party, in this case, BP." One federal health official lamented:

"Communities are given the wrong impression ... that they have more 'say' than they actually do."

Second, a profound disconnect often exists between stakeholders regarding the fairness and effectiveness of formal participatory processes. In this case, industry and government officials generally believed such processes worked well and that all stakeholders' views were considered fairly. As one regulator put it, such processes "allowed for a somewhat level playing field." However, citizens viewed these processes as mere window dressing, serving only to rationalize a preordained outcome. For example, citizens routinely characterized the formal public meetings as a "dog and pony show" that provided a way for government and industry officials to "get their propaganda out" and "feather their own bonnet."

Third, the most successful forms of community influence often exist beyond formal structures. Here, such influence emerged from "unofficial" avenues for citizen participation, (e.g., e-mail campaigns, use of news media, organized demonstrations). Such mechanisms were much more likely than formal avenues to result in desired outcomes and to leave citizens with the feeling that they had been "heard." As one community activist noted:

> We weren't participating in a function that was established and [where] perimeters were drawn ... and absolutely, we made a huge difference. It came down in the public's lap to affect change on this site.... [T]hose civil actions that we undertook are the single most important thing that's happened here as far as moving this [investigation] along.

Citizens everywhere can be inspired by their story.

HOW DO CITIZENS BECOME EMPOWERED LEADERS IN THEIR COMMUNITIES?

Use the following example to begin to think about how this might happen. What are key aspects of this change process?

At a community organizing meeting at her church, Virginia Ramirez raised her hand. "I have this problem. This neighbor lady of mine died because it was too cold and they wouldn't fix her house. I want someone to do something about it."

FIGURE 11.1 Sugar Creek resident's yard sign: Toxic spill

"What are *you* going to do about it?" the community organizer asked. Angered, Virginia left the meeting. A few days later, an organizer came to Virginia's home. Virginia let her in only because the organizer was a nun. The organizer asked only why Virginia was so angry. She responded with stories not only about her neighbor but also of poor schools and overt racism. Eventually, Virginia agreed to hold a meeting of neighbors in her home.

Virginia had never run a meeting, but the discussion quickly turned to neighborhood problems: poor housing, poor sewers, and few city services. Together, the group researched documents at city hall and discovered that city funds for repairing houses in their neighborhood had been diverted to build a street in an affluent area. When they went to a city council meeting to complain, Virginia froze. "I didn't remember my speech. I barely remembered my name. Then I … realized that I was just telling the story of our community. So I told it and we got our money back. It was hard…. But I began to understand the importance of holding people accountable…."

The community organizers encouraged Virginia to continue learning—to make her involvement in social causes more effective. They helped her reflect on each step of participation and learn new skills. Virginia earned her G.E.D. and eventually finished college. Her husband objected strenuously at first. When he yelled at her for studying instead of cleaning house and fixing supper, she trembled but told him, "I'm preparing for my future. If you don't like it, that's too bad because I'm going to do it. I'm sorry, but this is a priority."

Slowly and reluctantly, he accepted and even began to take pride in her accomplishments.

Virginia became a community organizer, supervising volunteers in health education outreach and training members of her church and community, especially women, to speak out. She has negotiated with politicians and business leaders to promote community development and better jobs and testified before the U.S. Senate about an innovative job training program she helped develop. Through it all, her faith has sustained her personally and directed her efforts (quoted and paraphrased from Loeb, 1999, pp. 15–20, 55).

One way to understand citizen participation and empowerment is to study how it develops over time, among individuals-in-communities like Virginia Ramirez. For example, Kieffer (1984) studied the development of a sample of 15 adult community activists. They included a working-class mother who had become the prime force in constructing a community health clinic, a migrant laborer who had become an organizer and boycott coordinator, a former junkie and gang leader who had become a leader in an urban homesteading program, and a retired laborer leading efforts against brown lung disease (Kieffer, 1984). From another perspective, Watts, Williams, and Jagers (2003) studied sociopolitical development among 24 African American youth and young adult activists. While Kieffer looked for similarities among activists in diverse cultural and social contexts, Watts and associates focused on the development of persons within African American culture. Both approaches used qualitative methods that allowed thick description of participants' experiences. While the processes and outcomes of development were different, some similarities emerged.

In both studies, individuals initially accepted the social and political status quo but increasingly recognized social injustice. They began to see how community and personal events involved power, which benefitted only members of dominant groups. For participants in the Watts et al. study, this involved experiences of racism. For Kieffer's participants, it involved varied, specific provocations: a dam that would flood a mountain community; a betrayal of trust by an employer; being assaulted in one's own yard. For Virginia Ramirez, the process began when she recognized the social injustice behind her neighbor's death. Events such as these can lead citizens, however reluctantly, to begin speaking out and confronting those they hold responsible. In both studies, participants passed through intermediate stages of development, leading to a transformed sense of self and to empowered participation in social action. Several themes ran through these participants' and researchers' words. Many of these also fit Virginia Ramirez's experiences.

- Conflict and growth were intertwined. Conflicts between competing family and community commitments and conflicts between citizens and powerful elites were typical.

- A cycle of practical experience and critical reflection led to insights and learning for the future.

- Social support from local organizations and a personal mentor who provided advice and support were key resources.

- Activists developed an awareness of power relationships in their communities and everyday lives and a sense that these relationships could be transformed if citizens worked together.

- An inspiring, shared vision of liberation helped define specific goals and sustain activists' personal commitment.

- Growth from uninvolved citizen to activist-leader took time. In Kieffer's sample, the process averaged four years, but there was much variability.

These developmental insights are useful, but are only one standpoint for understanding how participation, empowerment, and community intertwine. Another perspective is to study the qualities of empowered persons.

Personal Qualities for Citizen Participation and Empowerment

Empowerment appears not to be a spectator sport. (McMillan, Florin, Stevenson, Kerman, & Mitchell, 1995, p. 721)

In research that we reviewed, six personal qualities seem common among empowered persons engaged in citizen participation (see also reviews by Berkowitz (2000) and Zimmerman (2000)). But remember that empowerment is contextual. It develops in a specific setting, community, and culture and is strongly influenced by those contexts. Thus, the list of qualities that we subsequently describe is suggestive, but we do not expect it to be characteristic of empowered persons in all circumstances.

Critical Awareness   This is an understanding of how power and sociopolitical forces affect personal and community life (Freire, 1970/1993; Zimmerman, 2000). Serrano-Garcia (1994) listed two cognitive elements: "critical judgment about situations [and] the search for underlying causes of problems and their consequences" (p. 178). One form of critical awareness is understanding hierarchies of oppression, dominant and subordinated groups, and social myths that sustain such hierarchies of power (Moane, 2003; Watts et al., 2003). The feminist motto "The personal is political" is an expression of critical awareness.

Critical awareness emerges from three sources: life experiences with injustices, reflection on those experiences and lessons learned, and dialogue with others. It begins with questioning the legitimacy of existing social conditions and existing authority and learning to see problems as social practices that can be changed, not as the natural order of the world. It proceeds with answering questions such as: Who defines community problems? How are community decisions made? Whose views are respected, and whose are excluded? Who holds power, and how do they use it? How can these be challenged?

Consider the following story (told by Anderson Williams (2007, p. 813), program director at Community Impact! Nashville):

> In 2003, a 16-year-old high school sophomore had just begun to
> work with our organization. As I sat and talked with her, she began
> making broad generalizations about "black folk" (black herself) and her

frustrations with "their" behavior. She started throwing around the now popular adjective "project" (herself a public housing resident) to describe the negative behaviors of those around her. Knowing something of the history of the particular housing project where she lived, I sent her to the library to do some research on the history of that development. About 6 hours later, I called her and had to pick her up. She was so enthralled and excited because she found that many of the behaviors and actions she was complaining about had also been prevalent when "the projects" were completely full of White people. She was amazed. She presented this research to her peers, and thus we began the discussion of "systems" in the lives of our young people.

This story, along with the stories of Virginia Ramirez, Alison Smith, and the Waupun youth illustrate critical awareness. Remember how the research that Virginia Ramirez's group did, documenting that money had been diverted from services for their neighborhood, deepened their critical awareness of how a city decision had affected their lives and of where to focus their action. These stories also illustrate the role of collaborative change agents who support reflection and analysis of life experiences.

Participatory Skills   To be effective in citizen participation, the person also needs behavioral skills. Empirical research and other accounts suggest a variety of these (Balcazar, Seekins, Fawcett, & Hopkins, 1990; Berkowitz, 1987, 1996, 2000; Foster-Fishman, Berkowitz, Lounsbury, Jacobson, & Allen, 2001; Kieffer, 1984; Lappe & DuBois, 1994; Watts et al. 2003):

- Articulating community problems by using critical awareness
- Imagining and articulating visions of a better community
- Assertively and constructively advocating one's views
- Actively listening to others, including opponents
- Identifying and cultivating personal and community resources
- Relating well to people of diverse cultures and life experiences
- Building collaborative relationships and encouraging teamwork
- Identifying, managing, and resolving conflicts
- Planning strategies for community change
- Finding, using, and providing social support
- Avoiding burnout by finding ways to sustain commitment
- Sharing leadership and power

However, participatory competence is contextual; some of these skills are more important in one setting than another.

Skills for identifying and mobilizing resources are particularly important (Zimmerman, 2000). Resources include tangible factors such as time, money, skills, knowledge, and influential allies. They also include less tangible qualities such as legitimacy or status in the community, the talents and ideas of community members, their personal commitment to community change, and social support. Social resources include shared values and the shared rituals and stories that illustrate those values (Rappaport, 1995). Many of the psychological and social resources involved in empowerment (e.g., social support, commitment, knowledge) are not scarce but are multiplied through working together (Katz, 1984; Rappaport, 1987). These skills can be learned, as the stories of Alison Smith and Virginia Ramirez especially illustrate.

Sense of Collective Efficacy   This is the belief that citizens acting collectively can be effective in improving community life (Bandura, 1986, pp. 449–453; Perkins & Long, 2002, p. 295). Critical awareness and behavioral skills alone will seldom lead to action unless persons also believe that collective action will lead to constructive changes (Saegert & Winkel, 1996; Zimmerman, 2000).

Others defined this simply as collective efficacy. Our term *sense of* collective efficacy explicitly marks this as a belief or an individual cognition. Belief in collective efficacy usually arises along with personal experience in citizen participation. Sense of collective efficacy is contextual: A person may believe that citizens can collectively influence community decisions in one situation but not in another (Bandura, 1986; Duncan, Duncan, Okut, Strycker, & Hix-Small, 2003; Perkins & Long, 2002).

In quantitative studies of U.S. urban neighborhoods, citizens with stronger beliefs related to critical awareness, collective efficacy, or both, participated more in community organizations and experienced a stronger sense of community (Perkins, Brown, & Taylor, 1996; Perkins & Long, 2002; Speer, 2000). Neighborhoods with higher levels of collective efficacy had lower crime rates (Snowden, 2005). Kral and Idlout (2008) found that a sense of collective efficacy served as a foundation for mental health and wellness in rural Canadian indigenous communities. Suicide prevention and healing efforts were integrally tied to the collective power and intergenerational wisdom of local communities.

Sense of Personal Participatory Efficacy   This is the individual's belief that he or she personally has the capacity to engage effectively in citizen participation and influence community decisions. At its strongest, this includes confidence that one can be an effective leader in citizen action. This is not simply feeling empowered; it must also be connected to behavioral participation. It is a contextual belief; one can feel more effective in some situations than in others. It is thus a specific form of self-efficacy (Bandura, 1986). Virginia Ramirez and Alison Smith grew in sense of collective efficacy and sense of personal participatory efficacy.

Research has often concerned similar concepts of sociopolitical control, perceived control, and political efficacy (Zimmerman, 2000). (Again, we added *sense of* to make explicit the cognitive focus.) Such beliefs have been linked to citizen participation among residents of a neighborhood near a hazardous waste site, residents of urban neighborhoods, and in other circumstances (Speer, 2000; Zimmerman, 2000). However, context makes a difference: In one study, involvement in a community service experience led college students to

increased feelings of political commitment but a *decreased* sense of political efficacy (Angelique, Reischl, & Davidson, 2002). Perhaps these students discovered
community and social forces that were not as changeable as they had originally
expected.

Qualitative studies of community activists have found that long-term citizen participation was sustained by optimism: enjoyment of challenges, can-do
spirit, and excitement about the work (Berkowitz, 1987; Colby & Damon,
1992). In these studies, experienced citizen activists also attributed setbacks to
temporary or situational causes, not personal failures, and sought to learn from
them. They celebrated successes and accepted adversity with humor. These
optimistic ways of thinking seem related to personal efficacy beliefs about
participation.

Participatory Values and Commitment   Beliefs about efficacy are not enough
to motivate citizen action. Participation is often initiated and sustained by commitment to deeply held values. Qualitative studies and other accounts have often
found that spiritual or moral commitment sustained citizen participation and
empowerment (Berkowitz, 1987; Colby & Damon, 1992; Loeb, 1999; Moane,
2003; Nagler, 2001; Schorr, 1997). For some, this involved spiritual faith and
practices; for others, it centered on a secular commitment to moral principles,
such as social justice. Spiritual support for community involvement included a
sense of innate value within everyone, a sense of "calling" to the work, and a
certainty of the work's spiritual necessity. Beliefs that enabled taking risks
included a certainty that "God will provide" and a "willing suspension of fear
and doubt" as they began new challenges. A capacity for forgiveness in the
rough and tumble of community decision making was also important (Colby &
Damon, 1992, pp. 78–80, 189–194, and 296). Virginia Ramirez and others in
her church illustrate a spiritual basis for participatory commitment.

Moane's (2003) account of empowerment in the Irish women's liberation
movement included building personal strengths in creativity and spirituality and
a larger, positive vision of liberation. Berkowitz (1987, p. 323) found what he
called "traditional virtue" among many local activists: caring for others, integrity, persistence, and commitment. Colby and Damon (1992) found similar
commitments to justice, harmony, honesty, and charity. Schorr's (1997) review
of effective community organizations found that many promote a shared group
climate based on spiritual or secular ideals that provide shared meaning and
purpose related to community change.

Relational Connections   Empowerment and citizen participation do not occur
in a social vacuum. They involve a wide variety of relationships with others,
including both bonding and bridging ties (Putnam, 2000; recall these from
Chapter 6). They also include social support and mentoring for participation,
neighboring, and participating in community organizations (Kieffer, 1984;
Moane, 2003; Putnam & Feldstein, 2003; Speer & Hughey, 1995). Relational
connections were essential for Virginia Ramirez, Alison Smith, and the Waupun
youth in their development as citizen leaders.

T A B L E 11.2   Personal Qualities for Citizen Participation

Critical awareness

Participatory skills

Sense of collective efficacy

Sense of personal participatory efficacy

Participatory values and commitment

Relational connections

Table 11.2 lists the six qualities we have highlighted. Our list is merely suggestive; there is no single profile of empowered persons or citizen activists (Berkowitz, 2000; Zimmerman, 2000). Communities and settings also shape empowerment and citizen participation.

Sense of Community and Citizen Participation in Neighborhood Organizations

Neighborhood organizations illustrate how grassroots citizen participation and empowerment intertwine with sense of community (see also Chapter 6). For example, volunteer block associations offer many opportunities for participation in neighborhood decisions. (A "block" in this sense includes the two facing sides of a street one block long.) Block associations address a variety of such neighborhood issues as zoning, housing, neighborhood appearance, crime, traffic, and recreation. They form mediating structures between individual residents and city governments. In studies in New York City, resident perceptions of problems on the block decreased over time on blocks with an association and increased on those without one (Wandersman & Florin, 2000).

Community psychologists have studied citizen participation in block associations and larger neighborhood organizations in several U.S. cities: Nashville, New York City, Baltimore, and Salt Lake City. Citizen participation is usually measured as a variable ranging from attending meetings, to increasing involvement in association tasks, to association leadership. Samples in all four cities were multiracial, multiethnic, and of lower to middle income (Chavis & Wandersman, 1990; Florin, Chavis, Wandersman, & Rich, 1992; Florin & Wandersman, 1984; Perkins, Brown, & Taylor, 1996; Perkins, Florin, Rich, & Wandersman, 1990; Perkins & Long, 2002; Unger & Wandersman, 1983, 1985; Wandersman & Florin, 2000).

In general, these studies demonstrated the interrelationships of five key factors: sense of community for the neighborhood; informal neighboring, such as talking with neighbors or watching someone's house while they are away; initial dissatisfaction with neighborhood problems; sense of collective efficacy regarding working through the neighborhood organization; and extent of citizen participation in neighborhood organizations.

These findings suggest a pathway of citizen participation similar to the findings of the developmental studies (Kieffer, 1984; Watts et al. 2003) that we described earlier: embeddedness in a community, recognition of challenges there, a sense that these challenges can be addressed collectively, and a spiraling pattern of participation in a grassroots organization and strengthening sense of efficacy. While the process is often initiated by neighborhood problems, high levels of crime can inhibit participation (Saegert & Winkel, 2004). Longitudinal analyses of the New York City data indicated that participation led to increased feelings of efficacy (Chavis & Wandersman, 1990). More recent studies have also connected sense of community, social capital, and participation in grassroots organizations (Hughey, Speer, & Peterson, 1999; Peterson & Reid, 2003; Saegert & Winkel, 2004). Of course, not every person, organization, or locality follows this pattern, but these factors are often involved.

These studies demonstrate that sense of community, neighboring, and citizen participation are resources for communities—even those with fewer material resources. These resources involve not simply individuals but individuals-in-communities.

EMPOWERING PRACTICES AND SETTINGS

When I returned to Atlanta [after long involvement the civil rights movement, and serving as ambassador to the United Nations], I wanted nothing to do with politics. Some of the women in Ebenezer Baptist Church wanted me to run for mayor. I was very reluctant, but one of them told me, "We need for you to do this. And we *made* you." I told her, "That's funny, I thought Martin [Luther King Jr.] made me." "Oh, no" she replied. "We made him, too." (Andrew Young, speech to the Society for Community Research and Action, June 2001)

As this passage indicates, Ebenezer Baptist Church in Atlanta was a key setting in the civil rights movement (and as its members hoped, Andrew Young did become mayor of Atlanta). To fully understand citizen participation and empowerment, we must learn more about how community settings like this one empower citizens and foster citizen participation. We must understand better the empowering practices that transform role relationships within settings (Rappaport, 1995) and the conditions that help change disempowering and nonempowering settings into empowering ones (Maton, 2008).

This section on empowering practices and settings is intended to provide tools for observing and for acting with others in your community. Remember that collaborative change agents may be found in a variety of roles, including students, teachers, grandparents, youth leaders, scientists, artists, and (insert *your* most challenging roles here!). We begin this section with a brief discussion of empowering practices, provide a distinction between empowering and empowered settings, offer examples of empowering community practices and settings, and identify key features of these practices and settings. In Chapter 12, we will turn to a discussion of how empowered community settings and organizations can influence their communities and societies.

Empowering Practices

How can you or I—as people trying to work for change—collaborate with others to create more empowering settings and organizations? Community psychologists have sought to be facilitators who stay out of the spotlight in processes of organizational and community change. But this relative inattention to our role and how it is negotiated over time has often obscured how we do our work as researchers and practitioners. Leaders in the field have consistently argued that the "how" is often more important than the "what," and we are now beginning to articulate and fully value our work as practitioners. For example, D'Augelli (2006) examined his role as a community psychologist in empowering gay, lesbian, and bisexual people in a rural university community. He noted the challenge of organizing and gaining visibility when individuals had well-grounded fears about what would happen to them as they came together publicly and created new resources in the community. In examining successes over time, he found that those with more social power had to take the lead and take risks.

A number of community psychologists are currently exploring the role of community psychologists in empowering practice. The first ever Summit on Community Psychology Practice was held in 2007; a new community psychology practice journal was launched in 2009; and practitioners, researchers, and educators are working together to better articulate the theoretical and practical training needed to work as community psychologists in community settings (Francescato, 2007; Meissen, Hazel, Berkowitz, & Wolff, 2008).

While it is important to examine our own role as collaborative change agents, a focus on empowering practices is more generally a concern with the routine activities that maintain and/or transform role relationships within settings. It is a concern with the way professional helpers and experts approach their work—as facilitators and partners (Gone, 2007, 2008) and as teachers and learners (Horton & Freire, 1990). It leads us to an examination of the opportunities for reciprocal helping, for mutual influence, for collaboration, for decision making, and for creating change. An emphasis on empowering practices focuses our attention on how diverse experiences, strengths, and capacities are developed and affirmed in routine dialogue and communication (Ullman & Townsend, 2008). In other words, we begin to look closely at how the relational context across multiple levels serves as a foundation for empowering settings. We turn now to further discussion of these empowering settings and illustrations.

Empowering and Empowered Community Settings

Communities and community settings can be described as empowering or empowered (Zimmerman, 2000; Peterson & Zimmerman, 2004). **Empowering settings** foster member participation and sharing or power in group decisions and actions. They serve as viable and vital relational communities (Maton, 2008). **Empowered settings** exercise power in the wider community or society, influencing decisions and helping to create community and macrosystem change.

Becoming an empowered setting or organization often requires creating empowering opportunities for members and citizens (McMillan, Florin, Stevenson, Kerman, & Mitchell, 1995). But being empowering and empowered do not always go together. Organizations that exclude rank and file members from any real decision-making power may nonetheless be powerful forces in communities and societies. For example, Putnam (2000) noted the rise in the United States of national advocacy organizations, which rely on mail and online fundraising, use mass media and lobbying to exercise power, and lack active local chapters.

In addition, some organizations that empower their members choose not to seek wider influence. For example, a mutual help group or spiritual setting may empower its members to participate in decision making within the group. But many of these settings are not concerned with influencing communities or society. The individualistic focus of psychology—even community psychology— has meant that until recently, the study of empowerment focused on individual processes of empowerment. Thus, when settings or organizations were considered, researchers attended to factors that were empowering for individuals, not how citizen organizations gained and exercised power in community or society (Peterson & Zimmerman, 2004; Riger, 1993). That focus is now broadening to study how empowered community settings wield wider influence (Maton, 2008). This is consistent with Rappaport's (1987) original emphasis on empowerment at multiple levels (Zimmerman, 2000).

Next, we turn to stories that illustrate empowering community practices and settings. As you read about the Block Booster Project, the Highlander Research and Education Center, and Family Resource Centers, think about what makes them empowering to participants.

Block Booster: Capacity Building in Neighborhood Organizations

As you read earlier, residents in many urban neighborhoods across the United States have joined together to improve their communities. For example, block associations have formed to make safer places for children to play, to advocate for sidewalk and street repairs, or to fight against planned development that would increase traffic and noise pollution. But not all block associations survive. Why not? And how can block associations be strengthened? The Block Booster Project applied community psychology methods to strengthening block associations in New York City. The associations were in Brooklyn and Queens—areas where housing density is less than Manhattan and more typical of other U.S. cities. Neighborhoods were working-class and middle-class areas and were predominantly European American, predominantly African American, or racially diverse (Florin, Chavis, Wandersman, & Rich, 1992; Prestby, Wandersman, Florin, Rich, & Chavis, 1990; Wandersman & Florin, 2000).

Block associations flourish through citizen participation or lapse without it. In Block Booster studies, one-quarter to nearly one-half of block associations became inactive over time. Block associations that thrived differed from those that failed in a number of ways. They made more intensive efforts to recruit members, had more ways for individuals to become involved, provided more incentives and fewer barriers for participating, made decisions with more member participation, and carried out more activities.

The Block Booster Project applied these findings by providing organizational development assistance to block associations—to strengthen their capacity to involve citizens and implement community activities. First, Block Booster staff conducted surveys of each block's residents regarding attitudes about the block association, participation in block activities, and skills that might be useful for the neighborhood. Members of the block association were surveyed about group cohesiveness, leader support, group order and organization, and related concepts from social climate scales (Moos, 1994; recall these from Chapter 5). From these data, Block Booster Profiles were drawn up to describe each block and block association.

Block Booster staff then conducted training for block association leaders. Two leaders from each association participated in a workshop on strengthening block associations and in ongoing consultation with Block Booster staff. Training emphasized using member resources, decentralizing decisions and developing leaders, and linking with other organizations and external resources. Staff also explained specific strengths and areas for improvement for each block association as revealed in the Profiles. For example, if member surveys indicated that an association did not focus on tangible goals and tasks, leaders could learn ways to hold more organized meetings and set group goals. If residents indicated that lack of child care limited their meeting attendance, association leaders were encouraged to provide it. Block association leaders also developed action plans for their groups, put these into action, and evaluated their impacts.

An experimental evaluation of the Block Booster training found that 10 months after the workshops, associations that received the Block Booster training and consultation were significantly more active and more likely to still be in existence than a control group that received only limited assistance (Florin et al., 1992; Wandersman & Florin, 2000).

Highlander Research and Education Center

Many are familiar with the story of Rosa Parks, who helped to give birth to civil rights movements in the United States in the 1950s and 1960s. An African American woman, she refused to give up her seat on the bus to a White passenger, which was an act of civil disobedience during a time of legalized segregation and racial discrimination in the United States. Many of us are less familiar with the context of her action. Rosa Parks, along with Martin Luther King Jr. and many other civil rights leaders, had received extensive training in democracy education and community organizing at the Highlander Folk School, now known as the Highlander Research and Education Center, in Tennessee. There, civil rights organizers also learned what have become well-known freedom songs, such as "We Shall Overcome," which was adapted by Highlander staff from an old African American hymn. The songs were then sung at rallies, marches, and in jails across the South. They sustained and nurtured the nonviolent protestors who sang them; they also disconcerted those who used violence against them. Septima Clark, a civil rights organizer partici-pating in a training session, recalled a raid by local police at Highlander. Blacks and Whites were watching a film together when the police burst in. According to Clark (1986), one of the police "jerked the plug out of the wall, while one of the teenagers made up a new verse to 'We shall overcome.' She started sing-ing, and everyone followed: 'We are not afraid, we are not afraid tonight.' He say, '[Y]ou can sing, but don't sing too loud.' They had numbers of verses to it, and they sang them all. It made the police feel nervous." Clark was arrested for violating segregation laws and spent the night in jail. She recalled, "I had to sit up there, and the only thing I could think of was I'd sing, 'Michael row the boat ashore.' We had a workshop and Harry Belafonte had been there, teach-ing us 'Michael Row.' So I just sat up there and sang that, until they came to get me out of that room."

At Highlander, Clark and others also developed a successful strategy for voter education across the South. This strategy, known as Citizenship Schools helped many African Americans learn to read so they could pass the literacy tests required to become eligible voters in the South at the time. Originally founded in the 1930s to train labor organizers, Highlander continues to focus on democracy education and justice. Its current areas of focus are environmental justice in the Appalachian region and youth leadership development. It uses an empowerment approach, believing that the answers to the problems facing society lie in ordinary people, such as Clark and Rosa Parks, coming together to share their experiences and learn from one another. Those shared experiences—as they say, "so often belittled and denigrated in our society"—have grounded their empowering popu-lar education and research practices and continue to drive social change.

Family Resource Centers

Many of us have heard the adage, "It takes a village to raise a child," but what might this look like in practice? Visit a family resource or family support center in your area to find out. Family resource centers often focus on early learning, school readiness, and multilingual resources for parents, but in the community of one of your authors, you will also find an indoor play park, preventive health care screenings, counseling services, community celebrations, afterschool pro-grams for children and youth, clothing exchanges, art classes, referrals to social services, tax preparation help, and more. Family resource centers are grounded in 10 empowerment and strengths-based principles (see Table 11.3). They repre-sent a paradigm shift in human services, moving from clinically based, profes-sional service delivery designed to prevent poor child educational or developmental outcomes toward a focus on professionals, paraprofessional staff, and volunteers enabling families to solve problems, meet needs, achieve aspira-tions, share resources, and support one another in helping children thrive (Dunst, Trivette, & Deal, 1988, 1994; Kalafat, 2004).

My students and I (Elizabeth) worked with the family resource center in our community from "before the beginning," when it was a dream of many folks in our region. With the help of the school district, which provided space at a very

TABLE 11.3   Principles of Family Support

Staff and families work together in relationships based on equality and respect.

Staff enhance families' capacity to support the growth and development of all family members—adults, youth and children.

Families are resources to their own members, to other families, to programs, and to communities.

Programs affirm and strengthen families' cultural, racial, and linguistic identities and enhance their ability to function in a multicultural society.

Programs are embedded in their communities and contribute to the community-building process.

Programs advocate with families for services and systems that are fair, responsive, and accountable to the families they serve.

Practitioners work with families to mobilize formal and informal resources to support family development.

Programs are flexible and continually responsive to emerging family and community issues.

Principles of family support are modeled in all program activities, including planning, governance, and administration.

SOURCE: *Guidelines for Family Support Practice* (1996). Chicago: Family Resource Coalition.

low cost, and many community partners—including an organization created by local parents whose children have disabilities and a human service agency with experience in family support—the family center became a reality. We saw traditional helping roles and relationships transformed as program leadership and educational staff positions were filled by program participants, parents, and volunteers. We regularly experienced classes and events that were well attended and positively evaluated by families from a number of different cultural and linguistic communities because they were identified as a need by parents, designed in collaboration with parents, and marketed word of mouth by parents. Family resource centers represent one answer to Sarason's (1981) call for psychologists and other helping professionals to move away from medical models of helping to educational models of helping in which teachers and learners engage in collaborative change.

As consultants, we helped the organization think about how to put empowerment values into practice and provided technical support for participatory program evaluation, but we also vacuumed floors, cared for children, and led art classes. And we were learners much more often than we were teachers! An empowerment focus for consultation shifts our attention toward people within a setting that have little power and toward creating mechanisms for them to gain more (Juras, Mackin, Curtis, & Foster-Fishman, 1997). The consultant's role is assisting the setting participants in arriving at the best solution to their self-identified issues. Our role was not to define or decide but to help stakeholders decide what they wanted and needed from a family resource center.

Features of Empowering Practices and Settings

What qualities of community organizations empower their members? We have assembled key features of empowering practices and settings. These were identified in case studies of community settings, personal accounts of community psychologists, and reviews of research on effective neighborhood organizations, community coalitions, and organizational empowerment (Bond, 1999; Bond & Keys, 1993; Foster-Fishman, Berkowitz, Lounsbury, Jacobson, & Allen, 2001; Maton, 2008; Peterson & Zimmerman, 2004; Speer & Hughey, 1995; Wandersman & Florin, 2000; Wolff, 2001a). Some factors first identified as important in community settings focused on personal development (Maton & Salem, 1995) have also proven to be important in settings concerned with citizen participation in community decisions. Our list is suggestive; others might choose a different list from the many important factors.

Promoting a Strengths–Based Belief System   Empowering community settings promote principles or beliefs that define member and organizational goals, provide meaning and inspiration for action, develop strengths, and promote optimism in the face of setbacks. Shared community events, rituals, and narratives embody core values and strengthen sense of community as well as personal commitment to the group. The Highlander School is founded on a clear set of strengths-based values, including a belief in democracy. Myles Horton (1990), one of the founders of Highlander, put it this way: "If you believe in democracy, which I do, you have to believe that people have the capacity within themselves to develop the ability to govern themselves. You've got to believe in that potential, and to work as if it were true in the situation." Another clearly articulated principle is that the key to change is found in everyday people's experiences. These shared experiences as well as hopes and dreams for a better future are often given form at Highlander in storytelling, singing, and making art, as they take seriously the role of the arts in individual and social transformation (Greene, 1995; Sarason, 1990; Thomas & Rappaport, 1996).

Fostering Social Support   Empowering settings attend to the quality and nature of interpersonal relationships in a setting and promote exchange of social support among members (Brown, Shepherd, Merkle, Wituk, & Meisson, 2008; Maton, 2008). Social support is key to the work of family resource centers, where traditionally isolated parents of young children with disabilities, for example, share stories, learn from one another, and exchange information and resources (Dempsey & Keen, 2009). A case study of effective faith-based community advocacy organizations found that one-to-one meetings among members helped build mutual support and identified issues for action (Speer, Hughey, Gensheimer, & Adams-Leavitt, 1995). Social support and interpersonal ties among members also build organizational solidarity and power for influencing the wider community (Putnam & Feldstein, 2003; Speer & Hughey, 1995).

Developing Leadership   Empowering settings have committed leaders who articulate a vision for the organization, exemplify interpersonal and organizational skills, share power, and mentor new leaders (Maton, 2008; Maton & Salem, 1995). Mentoring was one of the key factors in the development of community activists in Kieffer's (1984) study. Sharing leadership and developing new leaders were also important in Block Booster. Leadership development is central to the mission and work of Highlander Folk School, where individuals continue to develop organizational and leadership skills in civil rights as well as economic and environmental justice.

Providing Participatory Niches and Opportunity Role Structures   Empowering organizations create roles and tasks that offer opportunities for members to become involved and assume responsibility: participatory niches (Speer & Hughey, 1995) or opportunity role structures (Maton, 2008; Maton & Salem, 1995). In Block Booster, effective block associations had more officers and committees in which individuals could actively work together (Wandersman & Florin, 2000). These tactics create underpopulated settings that promote member participation (Barker, 1968; Schoggen, 1989; recall this concept from Chapter 5). Participatory niches promote recruitment and training of individuals for roles needed by the setting, increase members' leadership skills, and strengthen their interpersonal ties within the group.

Members bring diverse skills to a community organization (e.g., assertion, emotional sensitivity, financial management, writing, planning events, securing volunteers, or remodeling dilapidated office space). Knowledge of cultures, languages, or community history may be useful. Social networks and connections, prestige or legitimacy as community leaders, and other social resources are important. An empowering organization has leaders and members who identify and engage such resources (Foster-Fishman et al., 2001; Peterson & Zimmerman, 2004).

In opportunity role structures, members also develop skills within an organization. Power comes not just from participation but also from opportunities to develop the necessary skills and competencies in order to be able to have real influence in settings. Evans (2007) reflects that many young people are waiting to be invited to join as full and active community participants but need adults in schools and youth-based organizations to support and challenge them to do so. Educational research supports this view that youth engagement is fostered in authentic learning experiences and positive relationships. Students become engaged when asked to participate in meaningful and valuable activities (Rahm, 2002). Community-based service learning illustrates this type of student engagement in authentic learning practices, which allows students to take what they need to become competent in a particular skill or way of thinking (Seely Brown & Duguid, 1993). Experienced leaders and peers can serve as skilled partners who scaffold learning and development within an organization (Lave & Wenger, 1991). They can also act as guides who introduce and model new ideas to newer members.

Keeping a Focus on Tasks and Goals   Many citizens prefer to become involved in community organizations that get things done, with clear goals and productive meetings (Wandersman & Florin, 2000). In addition, such organizational structure increases the capacity of the organization to make an impact in its community (Allen, 2005; Fawcett et al., 1995; Foster-Fishman et al., 2001; Wandersman, Goodman, & Butterfoss, 1997). This includes having organization goals and specific objectives for action, meeting agendas, time limits, and leaders who can summarize lengthy discussions and clarify choices to be made. The Block Booster training focused on strengthening this capacity.

Making Decisions Inclusively   This is the essence of citizen participation: widespread, genuine power and voice for citizens in making organizational decisions and plans. Block Booster research demonstrated that more inclusive decision making strengthened both citizen participation and organizational viability. Community coalitions function best when decisions are inclusive (Foster-Fishman et al., 2001). Allen (2005) studied 43 local domestic violence coordinating councils in one U.S. state. These councils included members from criminal justice, health, education, social services, and other community groups. The best predictor of council effectiveness (as perceived by its members) was an inclusive climate of shared decision making in which members from many community agencies and groups actively participated.

Rewarding Participation   Community groups rely on volunteers. If those volunteers do not find their involvement rewarding or if its personal costs are too high, they will leave. If they find involvement rewarding, they will often become more involved. Empowering community settings provide rewards for citizen participation that outweigh its costs (Prestby, Wandersman, Florin, Rich, & Chavis, 1990; see also Kaye, 2001; Kaye & Wolff, 1997). Lappe and DuBois (1994) found that rewards for U.S. citizens obtained from community involvement included taking pride in accomplishment, discovering how much one has to contribute, working with those who share concerns and hopes, learning new skills, knowing efforts will help create a better world, and enjoying better communities, schools, jobs, housing, and medical care.

Barriers to participation include competing demands on time and energy; finding child care; feeling out of place; and unpleasant meetings (e.g., rambling discussions or unproductive conflict). Family resource centers rely on participant-advisors to identify specific barriers to participation in program planning and evaluation. In the Block Booster Project, associations that fostered rewards and lowered barriers to participation had greater levels of member participation and were more likely to remain viable over time (Prestby et al., 1990).

Promoting Diversity   Empowering community organizations value member diversity, which can broaden the skills, knowledge, resources, legitimacy, and social connections available to the setting. For community coalitions and other organizations that seek to represent multiple parts of a community, seeking diversity is essential.

However, promoting diversity does not end with a diverse membership list. Often more difficult is the work of building an atmosphere of genuine inclusion of all viewpoints. When powerful community leaders or professionals (who are used to speaking out and being heeded) dominate discussion, the group must find ways to enable less powerful members to speak out, support each other, and influence decisions.

Promoting diverse participation includes having several members from a disenfranchised group, not just one token member. It also includes taking time to discuss issues of diversity and making organizational language inclusive (e.g., recognizing the presence of women or youth). Finally, diversity is not fully realized until the leadership, not simply the membership, is diverse (Foster-Fishman et al.,

2001; Goodkind & Foster-Fishman, 2002). For example, in nonprofit and educational settings, this means that teachers, case managers, and administrators reflect the diversity of participants.

Fostering Intergroup Collaboration   Promoting diversity can generate challenges for a setting. Community members share an overall sense of community but also have identifications with other groups within or outside the community (Wiesenfeld, 1996). This is also true of organizations. Diversity multiplies the number and types of groups to which individuals in an organization feel committed; this is often valuable for organizational learning, growth, and adaptation to changes in the environment. But a viable setting also needs commitment to the organization itself. So, the challenge may be framed as developing **bonding** ties while also promoting **bridging** ties (Putnam, 2000; recall this from Chapter 6). Bridging mechanisms—or **boundary spanning**, as it is understood in organizational psychology (Katz & Kahn, 1978)—refers to relationships that connect groups within an organization, helping each understand the other and building capacity for collaboration.

Organizations also need to develop practices and member skills in identifying, discussing, managing, and **resolving conflicts** (Chavis, 2001; Foster-Fishman et al., 2001). An important skill is recognizing when systems of oppression are involved, not simply interpersonal styles. Conflict is often a useful resource: for learning about problems and for creative ideas for action. It is often helpful to reframe conflicts as shared problems, not simply blame others, and search for shared values or goals based on the organizations belief system.

As a study aid, we suggest organizing these nine factors into three groups: those primarily concerned with group solidarity, with member participation, and with diversity and collaboration (see Table 11.4). Of course, these three functions overlap to some extent, and we encourage you to organize them in a way that makes sense to you.

T A B L E 11.4   Features of Empowering Practices and Settings

Solidarity
  Promoting a strengths-based belief system
  Fostering social support
  Developing leadership

Member participation
  Providing participatory niches and opportunity role structures
  Keeping a focus on tasks and goals
  Making decisions inclusively
  Rewarding participation

Diversity and collaboration
  Promoting diversity
  Fostering intergroup collaboration

Understanding and promoting citizen participation and empowerment is challenging. Verbal commitment to the principle of empowerment does not guarantee active individual or organizational commitment to empowering practices. Across a variety of employment, educational, and health care settings, disparities exist between organizational ideals and routine ways of accomplishing tasks and meeting goals (Gruber & Trickett, 1987).

Furthermore, citizen participation and empowerment are realized differently among diverse contexts and communities. Professional helpers and experts cannot assume that good intentions or well-designed programs will empower others. In making these assumptions, we more likely resemble the travelling salesman who finds himself lost in unfamiliar territory. Instead, as Lilla Watson suggests in the opening quote, we may walk with others as facilitators and partners, teachers and learners in a process of reciprocal helping, collaboration, and community change.

These processes are not simple. But as the stories throughout this chapter illustrate, they are deeply rewarding. In the next chapter, we take up how empowered organizations can foster social and community change.

CHAPTER SUMMARY

1. Empowerment and citizen participation are intertwining processes through which individuals and groups access valued resources and take part in community life.

2. *Empowerment* occurs when people lacking an equal share of resources gain greater access to and control over those resources. It refers to behavior, cognition, emotion, and development over time, and it involves gaining access to external resources or influencing collective decisions.

3. Empowerment occurs at multiple ecological levels: from individual to macrosystems. It is a process that develops over time and is different in different contexts. It involves collective efforts in relationships with others.

4. *Citizen participation* occurs when individuals take part in decision making in a community: group, organization, locality, or macrosystem. It is not the same as community service but involves exerting influence in collective decisions. It may be a means, a method of making decisions, or an end, a value about how to make decisions.

5. Power takes multiple forms. Power involves control of resources and influence in collective decision making, including at least some capacity to compel others. It is best understood in relationships between persons or groups and as a dimension rather than an all-or-none dichotomy.

6. Personal qualities associated with citizen participation and empowerment are listed in Table 11.2. These develop over time through citizen participation.

7. Citizen participation in neighborhood organizations is related to sense of community, neighboring, initial dissatisfaction with local problems, and sense of collective efficacy (that citizens together can address these problems effectively).

8. *Empowering* settings promote citizen participation and empowerment by their members. *Empowered* settings exert power and influence in wider community life. Characteristics of empowering community settings are summarized in Table 11.4.

RECOMMENDED READINGS

Berkowitz, B. (1987). *Local heroes*. Lexington, MA: D.C. Heath.

Horton, M. & Freire, P. (1990). *We make the road by walking*. Philadelphia: Temple University Press.

Maton, K. I. (2008). Empowering community settings: Agents of individual development, community betterment, and positive social change. *American Journal of Community Psychology, 41*, 4–21.

Rappaport, J. (1987). Terms of empowerment/exemplars of prevention: Toward a theory for community psychology. *American Journal of Community Psychology, 13*, 2, 121–148.

Wandersman, A., & Florin, P. (2000). Citizen participation and community organizations. In J. Rappaport & E. Seidman (Eds.), *Handbook of community psychology* (pp. 247–272). New York: Plenum.

RECOMMENDED WEBSITES

Community Tool Box:
http://ctb.ku.edu.

> Excellent site for learning about citizen participation and planning community change. Maintained by community psychologists. Includes tools and recommendations for planning, implementing, and evaluating community initiatives and links to many related sites.

Highlander Research and Education Center:
http://www.highlandercenter.org.

Innovation Center for Youth and Community Development:
http://www.theinnovationcenter.org.

> Excellent website on youth development and civic activism. Includes stories of youth impacts on communities, tools and resources for actions by young people, research on youth and community development, online surveys, and discussion forums.

12

Community
and Social Change

GrantPix/Index Stock/PhotoLibrary

OPENING EXERCISE

Ron Evans has lived in Camden, New Jersey, his whole life. Over the past 50 years, he has seen Camden undergo many changes, few for the better. Camden had the highest violent crime rate in the United States in 2009, over five times the national average. Over 40% of Camden residents have household incomes below the national poverty line. Evans says, "Demographically, the city has changed dramatically. Those who could afford to move, moved. Those who couldn't were left to suffer" (PICO, 2010a).

When Nilda Santana moved to Florida, she immediately started the process to enroll her kids in the state's health insurance system for children called Kid Care. She found the process extremely frustrating. "They would lose my paperwork. You would send them something and they wouldn't get it...I moved to Florida in November and my kids' health care didn't get approved until March." Her experience made her wonder about how other parents managed to navigate the system. "I mean, here I am, I'm computer literate, I speak English, and I still have all these problems. What about those who don't speak English?" (PICO, 2010b).

Virginia Munkelwitz was attending her local city council meeting when she learned that a businessman who was building a housing development on a local lake was reneging on his promise to include seven units of affordable housing. When she investigated how this happened, she was shocked. She says, "This was really an egregious betrayal of the public trust. The process was almost set up so as to let something like this happen" (PICO, 2010c).

What would you do if you were one of these people? All of us have had the experience of coming face-to-face with something in our communities, our societies, our nations that just makes us say, "This is wrong. We can do better than this." These people did something. They were associated with a national organization called the PICO Network, which supports faith-based community organizing in the United States. Each of them belonged to a religious congregation that had a community organizing group associated with PICO. They decided to do something about the problems they saw. And in the process, they changed their communities, their societies, and themselves.

WHY SHOULD WE ATTEMPT SOCIAL CHANGE?

Things alter for the worse spontaneously, if they be not altered for the better designedly.

FRANCIS BACON

Change is inevitable. Our world will change whether we want it to or not. In this book, we have tried to teach you to consciously examine and direct those change processes; to ensure that when change does occur, it results in stronger, healthier, and more effective organizations, neighborhoods, communities, and societies. These settings will then be better able to support healthy functioning in the people who live and work there. With this goal in mind, we want you to explicitly think about the concept of applying science to **social change**.

This concept is not without controversy. Concerns regarding the appropriateness of scientists becoming actively involved in efforts to change society are debated, even in community psychology. These concerns are focused on the idea of social engineers anxious to try out their pet theory on an unsuspecting community in which they have no personal stake. In no sense does the field of community psychology support the idea of an isolated intellectual dictating to a community what social policies or practices that community should adopt. That approach would constitute a violation of many of the fundamental values of the field, particularly the idea that communities have a basic right to self-determination.

However, we also strongly believe that science gains value through application. Community psychology is an applied field. As we hope we have emphasized throughout this book, science and practice inform each other. Scientific research is continually used to inform business practice and the political process, so why should it not be used to advance social change and justice?

Social change is a long-term process, and as such, it is useful to view it through the lens of the participatory action research cycle (as discussed in Chapters 3 and 10). Social change involves true second-order change in communities and societies, not just adding a new program or resource. Among other things, this means that resources and power are being redistributed (remember the discussion of ecological principles from Chapter 4). These changes can result in conflict and unintended effects.

The reality is that when you are discussing change at this level, the solutions you propose can easily generate new, unintended problems. There are always multiple, divergent solutions to a particular problem, each with its own costs and benefits. Communities are rarely homogenous, and the very presence of diversity in a community logically suggests that what might be good for one group in a community may actually be harmful for another. How you define the problem has a major impact on what you see as an appropriate solution, and part of your action research cycle should always involve periodically re-examining your problem definition (remember our discussion of this issue in Chapters 1 and 10).

We also need to question the assumption that change by itself is always necessary or good. There is no logical or philosophical reason for valuing change over other concepts, such as stability, the democratic process, or the right of a community to self-determination.

We are not bringing up any of these issues to discourage you from engaging in social change. Even no response is a response because it is support for the status quo. Particularly in relation to issues of social injustice, choosing not to react has clear consequences. The critical point we are raising here is that *how* people respond is important.

It sometimes seems to students of psychology that community and social change are exceedingly difficult—beyond their capabilities. To that concern, we have three initial responses. First, individual, community, and social change intertwine. All three are involved when members of a citizen coalition work together to promote positive youth development, when a woman leaves a violent relationship to pursue her own life, or when any disenfranchised person asserts his or her legitimate rights. Second, individual, community, and social change occur around us all the time. In every act of living, we involve ourselves in dynamic processes of change at many ecological levels. Third, community psychology presents an alternative paradigm to traditional psychological theories of human behavior and behavior change. Community psychology's different approach and scope provides tools to see where it is possible to institute change and skills to make those changes successfully. By chapter's end, we hope that you will see how often Margaret Mead's oft-quoted adage about changing the world comes true and how you can become involved.

> Never doubt that a small group of thoughtful, committed citizens can change the world. Indeed, it's the only thing that ever has.
>
> MARGARET MEAD

In this chapter, we are going to review several community organizing techniques, including community coalitions, consciousness raising, social action activities, community development work, organizational consultation, the development of alternative settings within communities, and the use of technology in community organizing. Then, we will turn to a discussion of a specific aspect of social change: public policy. We will discuss the relationship between prevention science and public policy by using crime policy in the United States as an example. Then, we will present two examples of problems that require that attention be paid to public policy, poverty, and homelessness. But first, let us revisit our opening exercise.

REVISITING THE OPENING EXERCISE: EXAMPLES OF COMMUNITY ORGANIZING

The three people described at the beginning of this chapter all decided that they wanted to do something about the problems they saw in their communities. They wanted to engage in social change. They did so with the help of an organization called the PICO Network. In this section, we will discuss what the PICO Network does, and we will describe what those three people eventually did about the problems they saw.

The PICO Network (originally the Pacific Institute for Community Organizing) is a national network of local faith-based groups in the United States. PICO organizations are based on religious congregations in low-income communities. The focus on religious congregations for community organizing is based on the fact that for many disadvantaged communities, religious organizations provide one of the few stable gathering places. In addition, congregations provide a means for gathering people based on shared positive values of social justice rather than anger regarding a specific local issue. PICO works with congregations of all faiths and denominations, and the local PICO organizations often develop relationships with other community organizations. PICO supplies intensive leadership training in using democratic processes to identify issues of concern to community residents and effectively address those issues.

While there are many community organizations that do the same type of work as PICO, we are focusing on PICO in this chapter because several community psychologists have written about them extensively. Paul Speer, Joseph Hughey, and their associates worked with community organizations and studied the processes and outcomes of PICO methods (Speer, 2008; Speer & Hughey, 1995; Speer, Hughey, Gensheimer, & Adams-Leavitt, 1995). PICO community organizing strategies combine building strong interpersonal and community relationships with "pressure-group tactics" to influence government and community leaders and institutions.

PICO community organizing proceeds through a **cycle of organizing**. In the initial phase—*assessment*—members of the community organization meet one-on-one with citizens to define community issues and to develop working partnerships that strengthen the group. This stage builds interdependence and mutual support.

In the second phase—*research*—organization members meet as a whole to identify the most pressing community issue for the group based on their conversations with citizens. Members gather further information on that issue via interviews, searching documents, or other sources. A key goal is to identify contradictions between stated policies and actual practices of government, business, and community services.

The third phase—*mobilization/action*—follows. Organization members meet to decide on an action plan and a person or office to be targeted to discuss community changes. If preparatory meetings with an official do not succeed, a public "accountability meeting" is arranged with that official. The key function of the meeting is to confront the target official, presenting the reality of the community problem and actions that citizens demand to resolve it. Meetings often have brought together city officials with large groups of well-informed citizens making clear, focused demands (due to the extensive groundwork conducted by the organization). They often result in commitments being made by the target official.

Especially for a public official, it is a potent experience of citizen power to face a unified crowd of hundreds of citizens who make clear demands for a policy change. Moreover, the community organization hosts the public meeting and carefully scripts its agenda, thus exercising the second and third instruments of power discussed in Chapter 11: channeling participation to maximize the strength of citizen voices and framing the issues for discussion.

The final phase—*reflection*—returns to the one-on-one relationships where the cycle began to evaluate outcomes and lessons learned. These themes are then discussed in meetings of the whole organization. PICO organizations also monitor the keeping of promises made by the target officials and institutions. The organization begins the cycle again with a new assessment phase.

As examples of how the PICO process works, let us revisit the stories of the three individuals at the beginning of this chapter. It might help if you took a minute to reread them.

Ron Evans has been involved in community development efforts in Camden, New Jersey, his whole adult life. He helped to found Camden Churches Organized for People (CCOP), the local PICO affiliate, and through his work with CCOP, he had been involved in many projects, such as limiting sewage dumping in the city. CCOP and other community organizations arranged a public meeting (called an *Action* in PICO terms), where 1,500 people met with the governor of New Jersey to push for legislation that eventually provided $175 million in recovery funds to Camden. Three years later, Ron helped to survey Camden residents to ask them how well they thought the recovery program was working. The answer was, not very well (Ott, 2005). The residents thought the majority of the recovery money was going to large-scale development projects rather than to efforts that would benefit long-term residents.

As Ron explains the situation, "We asked ourselves, 'How could we spend this money in a way that would benefit the people?' What we came up with is that the people who've committed to stay in Camden should be the ones who benefit."

Ron, the CCOP, and other Camden organizations (specifically, Concerned Black Clergy and the Camden Community Development Association) proposed a forgivable loan program that would allow residents up to $20,000 to rehab their homes. They then held another public Action that brought 500 people to meet with the New Jersey state treasurer to discuss their concerns and present their ideas. Since then, New Jersey has worked with CCOP on the Camden Home Improvement Program, which allocated $7.5 million for forgivable home improvement loans to long-term Camden residents. The program has been demonstrated to affect more than just the loan recipients. As neighbors of loan recipients see home improvement in their neighborhood, they tend to improve their homes too. An evaluation of the program found that as a result of the Camden Home Improvement Program, home values increased significantly in the neighborhoods targeted by the program (J. Chisholm, personal communication, April 23, 2010). By May 2010, the renovations were complete on 199 homes and another 110 were in progress, with 360 homeowners on a waiting list. In response to this success, the state awarded an additional $3.5 million to the program (Hirsch, 2010).

Nilda Santana did not believe she could take a leadership role in changing Florida's policies regarding Kid Care. "Usually, I'm the person who likes to do the behind the scenes work...so speaking out was a learning experience," she said. "But I learned that I need to speak up because there's other people out there who are also experiencing what I'm experiencing."

Nilda was a member of the local PICO affiliate in Orlando: the Federation of Congregations United to Serve (FOCUS). Nilda worked with other FOCUS members to ensure that the state of Florida streamlined and simplified the application process for Kid Care. Their efforts also resulted in an additional $1.1 million being allocated to the program. As Nilda say, "If you don't fight for your rights, who's going to do it?" (PICO, 2010b).

Like Nilda, Virginia Munkelwitz did not believe she, personally, could do anything about the problem that she saw. Her first thought after that city council meeting was that she had to tell the executive director of her local PICO chapter: Vermont Interfaith Action (VIA). Virginia thought VIA should write a letter to the housing review board, and the director asked her to take the lead doing that. This was a new role for Virginia, and at first, she was concerned. It meant doing a lot of research, much of it legal, and taking a leadership position. She says, "If you had asked me at the beginning if I could do this I would have said 'Forget it.' I'm the last person you'd think to be reading legal documents."

What she found was that the housing developer had used the promise of building seven affordable housing units to qualify for increased height and density bonuses on the lakefront hotel and market-rate condos that were part of the project. After building the hotel and condos, the developer stated that there were problems with building the seven affordable housing units and offered to pay the city $124,000 instead.

Virginia presented her research at an Action in February 2008, which was attended by over 300 people. VIA had developed specific recommendations regarding how they believed the city's affordable housing zoning laws should be changed. Those recommendations included a provision that developers would be fined $100,000 for every affordable unit promised but not built. The new ordinance was adopted, and as a result of the public Action, the city negotiated a $400,000 payment from the developer rather than the $124,000 offered. Virginia says, "Accurate research and public exposure are the keys to success" (V. Munkelwitz, personal communication, April 22, 2010).

The effectiveness of the PICO approach has been demonstration in more than these three communities. Speer and Hughey's (1995) studies of PICO organizations in one Midwestern U.S. city showed that they effectively mobilized citizens and produced specific changes in the policy and practices of city government and other organizations. Several psychological factors contribute to the effectiveness of PICO organizations: strong interpersonal networks, mutual support, an institutional and values base in religious congregations, participatory niches (recall this from Chapter 11) created by rotating offices and identifying emerging leaders, targeting specific issues and institutions for change, and mobilizing large meetings to make specific demands. With these tools, PICO organizations representing low-income communities can influence powerful private and public institutions. PICO's commitment to supporting the development of emerging community leaders can be seen in their current work with youth leaders (Speer, 2008).

The relationship between Paul Speer and his colleagues and PICO demonstrates the way in which research is informed by practice and vice versa. By developing a relationship with and observing organizations such as PICO, community psychologists learn a great deal about effective community organizations. They then can disseminate that information, and community organizers around the world can learn from the best practices of others working in the field.

In the next section, we will present some of what we have learned through working with community organizations such as PICO.

COMMUNITY ORGANIZING TECHNIQUES

In this section, we will discuss several techniques or tools that are often used by community organizers to achieve social change. All these techniques have at their core the development of social capital. If you remember from Chapter 6, social capital refers to the features of social life in a community (networks, norms, and relationships) that allow the members of the community to work together effectively to achieve shared goals. Increasing these tangible and intangible resources in a community serves to not only improve community life in the short term but to also strengthen the community's capacity to effectively address challenges in the future. This list is far from exhaustive, and not every technique is appropriate for every situation. Each technique has potential costs as well as benefits, and you need to be reflective about your specific circumstances before you decide to use a particular approach.

Community Coalitions

Community coalitions bring together a broad representation of citizens within a locality to address a community problem. Coalitions may involve citizens, community organizations (e.g., community agencies, schools, government, religious congregations, businesses, media, grassroots groups), or both. Coalitions agree on a mission and write and implement action plans. Those plans may involve action by the coalition itself or by affiliated organizations and may lead to changes in policies or to development of community programs. Coalitions have become a popular and often effective means for strengthening citizen participation and catalyzing community change (Allen, 2005; Brown, Feinberg, & Greenberg, 2010; Fawcett et al., 1995; Feinberg, Greenberg, & Osgood, 2004; Findley et al., 2008; McMillan, Florin, Stevenson, Kerman, & Mitchell, 1995; Wolff, 2010).

The Healthy Communities movement often uses community coalitions. The Healthy Communities model grew out of the recognition that environmental forces influence individual health and that prevention is needed in addition to treatment. For instance, asthma requires medical treatment and managing environmental factors. After a local Asthma Coalition pointed out that breathing engine exhaust can trigger asthmatic symptoms, a Connecticut school district changed its school bus contract to require that bus engines be turned off while waiting for riders at school (Wolff, 2004). In Massachusetts, local Healthy Communities coalitions have begun a mobile health van program, initiated a campaign to lessen sales of tobacco products to teens, hosted planning for economic and housing development, started a shelter for the homeless, developed a health outreach program for a low-income neighborhood, brought a dental clinic to an area without dental care, and developed health programs for children (Hathaway, 2001; Wolff, 2004).

The Communities That Care movement, which we introduced in Chapter 9, provides another example. Its mission is community-wide action to prevent drug abuse, foster positive youth development, and promote psychosocial competence, including many concepts that we emphasized in Chapters 9 and 10. The Communities That Care coalition model involves developing a local coalition to match prevention/promotion methods backed by empirical research with local community needs and resources (Brown, Feinberg, & Greenberg, 2010; Feinberg et al., 2004; Hawkins, Catalano et al., 1992).

Community coalitions have become popular for several reasons (Wolff, 2001, 2010). During times of economic recession and conservative political periods, funding for social services falls, increasing pressure on localities to do more with less. Agencies are given a deficits-oriented mission and are swamped by clients needing treatment, with little time for prevention or for considering community strengths. Categorical funding of government social services (e.g., separate funding streams for mental health, public health, education, child protective services, and criminal justice) complicates coordination among agencies. Community coalitions bring organizations together to coordinate action, create or coordinate preventive programs, and engage the resources of nongovernmental community institutions, such as religious congregations, philanthropic foundations such as United Way, and civic and business groups.

Let us take a look at how one coalition worked to address the issues of substance abuse in the community. After their teenage son was killed in an alcohol-related boating accident on Lake Murray in South Carolina, a family wanted to do something to prevent similar tragedies from happening again. They asked the Lexington/Richland Drug and Alcohol Abuse Coalition to help prohibit boating under the influence of alcohol. The coalition grew out of state and local initiatives to reduce the social and personal costs of drug abuse (including alcohol and tobacco). The coalition worked with the family, state legislators, and others to promote public awareness of the problem, draft the proposed law and testify in the legislature, and organize grassroots support. In 1999, the bill was signed into law. A public awareness campaign for boating safety also began at Lake Murray. Alcohol-related boating accidents there have dropped 30% (Snell-Johns, Imm, Wandersman, & Claypoole, 2003).

Other projects of the coalition included helping to develop a no-smoking policy for Richland County schools and a no-drug-use (including alcohol and tobacco) policy for county recreation fields, implemented by the recreation authority. The coalition also organized a merchant education program to decrease sales of alcohol and tobacco to minors. In 1995, research in Richland County stores found that 77% of minors who attempted to purchase tobacco products were offered a sale. The 2003 rate was only 8%.

Snell-Johns et al. (2003) concluded that these efforts succeeded for several related reasons. The coalition included broad community representation and worked to develop relationships with other community groups. It was persistent in pursuit of its goals. Its core values regarding drug use and abuse were clearly stated and attracted wide support, but the coalition was not perceived as having an overtly political or one-sided agenda. The coalition also had paid staff and some outside funding and was able to act quickly when opportunities occurred. But the coalition's successes also rested on the volunteer efforts of a broad representation of citizens.

Community coalitions need to put a lot of work into deciding how they will function. A community coalition must make choices about its mission, whether it will have a narrow or broad focus, who the members will be, how decisions will be made, whether the coalition will work within existing social structures or attempt to engage in social change, how the coalition will be funded, and how conflict will be negotiated. Community psychologist Tom Wolff, a leader in the community coalition movement, has summarized much of the existing practitioners' wisdom about them in various sources (Wolff, 2001, 2004, 2010). The Community Toolbox website (http://ctb.ku.edu), developed by community psychologists, contains valuable, practical guidance and resource materials for community coalitions and similar organizations. Empirical research on the qualities of effective community coalitions is growing. One point to remember is that coalitions are settings in themselves and benefit from the same characteristics as other settings, such as a shared sense of values, a sense of collective self-efficacy, and meaningful roles for all members, which allow them influence over the coalition as a whole. Coalitions also seem to benefit from an effective strategic planning process, strong leaders with an inclusive leadership style, strong internal and external relationships, and significant technical assistance and support in both coalition building and program implementation and support (Allen, 2005; Brown et al., 2010; Foster-Fishman et al., 2001; Feinberg et al., 2004; Fujimoto, Valente, & Pentz, 2009; Watson-Thompson, Fawcett, & Schultz, 2008; Wells, Ward, Feinberg, & Alexander, 2008).

Consciousness Raising

Consciousness raising involves increasing citizens' critical awareness of social conditions that affect them and energizing their involvement in challenging and changing those conditions. For instance, Paulo Friere's (1970/1993) *Pedagogy of the Oppressed* and many branches of the feminist movement embody this approach. Consciousness is raised as women and men become aware of personal experiences with systematic oppression of any sort, such as racism, classism, or ageism. These experiences can take place in the family, workplace, communities, or societies. However, consciousness raising is not solely cognitive or emotional. New personal understanding is connected to working with others and actions for change. Action and reflection feed each other. Actions may include other social change approaches, but consciousness raising distinctively emphasizes personal *and* social transformation.

Consciousness raising is reflected in some persons we described in Chapter 11: Virginia Ramirez, Alison Smith, Kieffer's (1984) community activists, and African American youth leaders (Watts, Williams, & Jagers, 2003). Life experiences, personal reflections and discussions with others led them to critical awareness of social injustice. They questioned the credibility of community and corporate leaders and began to oppose injustice and insist on citizen participation. In all the case examples described so far in this chapter, consciousness raising occurs but to differing degrees. In the community-building process of PICO, citizens meet to identify and analyze community problems and their causes. The Lexington/Richland coalition achieved changes in public views, which began with the personal commitment of their members.

Of all the approaches we discuss here, consciousness raising most directly addresses personal values, awareness, and commitment. It often precedes or accompanies use of the other approaches in cycles of deepening critical awareness, supportive relationships, and liberatory actions. As a community organizing technique, consciousness raising must be used in a respectful manner. There is an inherent power differential in any consciousness raising attempt. One group is actively trying to change another group's perception of its community, its relationships, and its lives. Even though this is done with laudatory goals, it is important to remember that the only person truly in a position to interpret a life is the person living it. This means that consciousness raising should always be attempted in the spirit of hypothesis testing. Consciousness-raising interpretations should be offered as suggestions, not as truths that the recipient must adopt. You must always keep in mind that your understanding of a situation may be incomplete or incorrect.

Consciousness raising can be extended to whole communities. The concept of **community readiness** refers to how much a locality recognizes a problem and takes steps to address or prevent it. Action researchers at the Tri-Ethnic Prevention Research Center in Colorado proposed a nine-stage model of community readiness, especially for substance abuse and health issues (Edwards, Jumper-Thurman, Plested, Oetting, & Swanson, 2000). In their model, readiness involves knowledge of the problem and of methods to address it, existing efforts to address it, strength of community leadership on that issue, presence of other resources for action, and overall community climate of attitudes and commitment on the issue. Their nine stages are:

- No awareness of the problem
- Denial that it is a local problem, even if a problem elsewhere
- Vague awareness of the problem but without local efforts to address it
- Preplanning and local information gathering about the problem
- Preparing strategies for community change, led by a local team
- Initiating programs or policy changes to address the problem
- Establishing them to stay within local organizations, such as schools, with local resources
- Evaluating, improving, and expanding them over time
- Maintaining strong program support, evaluation, and excellence

Strategies for moving through the stages include identifying and influencing opinion leaders in the community, gathering and disseminating information in focus groups and the media, focusing on local examples and statistics regarding the problem, fostering local leadership, planning everything within the local cultural context, integrating programs or policies within local organizations, and evaluation to promote ongoing program or policy improvement. While outside consultants can provide assistance, moving through the stages requires local leadership, resources, and commitment. The community readiness model has been validated in research and used to develop culturally valid health interventions in Native American, Mexican American, and Anglo communities (Engstrom, Jason, Townsend, Pokorny, & Curie, 2002; Jumper-Thurman, Edwards, Plested, & Oetting, 2003; Oetting, Jumper-Thurman, Plested, & Edwards, 2001).

Social Action

Grassroots groups use social action to offset the power of organized money with the power of organized people (integrative power, as discussed in Chapter 11) (Alinsky, 1971). Social action identifies specific obstacles to empowerment of disadvantaged groups and creates constructive conflict to remove these obstacles through direct, nonviolent action.

Social action has a long history that is reflected by labor movements in many countries, Gandhi's movement to free India, and the U.S. civil rights movement. Social action was also used in East Germany in 1989 to bring about the reunification of Germany, in Poland in the 1980s to defy and ultimately help to bring down an unjust communist state, in Chile to help end a murderous dictatorship, and in South Africa to help bring a relatively peaceful transformation to democracy when many expected widespread violence (Ackerman & Duvall, 2000). The effectiveness of social action methods in attaining their immediate goals depends on the context, but in the right circumstances, they can lead to surprising changes.

Saul Alinsky's classic *Rules for Radicals* (1971) delineated social action principles. To effectively oppose organized, powerful interests, citizens must identify their capacities (the strengths of community group members and their potential to act together) and the capacities of the opposing group or community institution. In addition, they need to identify a situation that dramatizes the need for change and that calls forth citizens' strengths. It is best if that situation is something their opponents have never encountered before and that they cannot dominate.

Social action involves power and conflict. If powerful elites limit citizen participation in a decision, adroit choice of a social action can assert citizen views and frame the issue in their terms. For these reasons, social action can be an important tool when addressing issues of social justice. The following example from the civil rights movement aptly illustrates the uses of people power to create a situation that the opponent had never experienced (adapted from Alinsky, 1971, pp. 146–148).

> A large, prominent department store in a U.S. city traditionally hired African Americans only in very menial positions, and was more discriminatory in its hiring than its competitors. The store had resisted appeals to halt these practices. Boycotts called by African American community groups had failed, due to the prestige of the store. African American community groups met and decided to plan a "shop-in."
>
> The plan called for busloads of African American customers to arrive at the store at its opening on a busy Saturday. In small groups they would shop every department in the store, carefully examining merchandise, asking sales clerks for help, doing nothing illegal yet occupying the store's space. These groups would rotate through the various departments in the store. Regular customers would arrive only to find the store crowded, and if they were hurried or uncomfortable with being in largely Black crowds they might go to another store. Finally, shortly before closing, customers would begin purchasing everything they could, to be delivered on Monday, with payment due on delivery. They planned to refuse these deliveries, causing even more expense for the store.
>
> The community groups deliberately leaked these plans to the store, while going ahead with arrangements. The next day, officials of the store called to ask for an urgent meeting with African American groups to plan new hiring practices, before the Saturday of the shop-in. The shop-in never had to be carried out.
>
> The shop-in had several elements that mark effective social action (Alinsky, 1971). The goal was clear and tangible: specific changes in

hiring policy and practices. Shopping was something that protesters knew how to do; it would even be enjoyable. Social action generates more participation if it asks citizens to do familiar things. At the same time, the situation was outside the experience of their opponents. Store management had ignored boycotts and public appeals, but they had never faced a shop-in. The tactic would cause disruption, potential bad publicity, and increased expenses for the store, yet it was entirely legal; store security or police would have little recourse to stop it. The threat was credible because the African American community was organized and willing to act. The threat of competition from other retailers not being targeted increased the pressure on the targeted store. The goal was just and the tactic shrewd; its power was revealed when the store quickly capitulated (Alinsky, 1971).

The "accountability meetings" of the PICO approach are another example of social action. In fact, the PICO Network calls these events public Actions and they are an integral part of their work. They draw power from an organized community making specific demands on specific targets.

From a community psychology perspective, this piece of social action (making specific demands of specific targets) is a necessary one. Social action involves highly visible, emotionally charged events that generally require some level of public risk on the part of the participants. If all that occurs without some tangible result, the participants can become discouraged with the whole idea of community involvement. Their sense of personal and collective efficacy is damaged. Having a clear expectation for the outcome of the social action event, one that is based upon sound research and for which specific individuals can be held accountable, greatly increases the probability that the event will be successful in the eyes of the participants. And when a social action event is perceived as successful, that builds a collective sense of self-efficacy and social capacity.

Community Development

At its core, community development is concerned with increasing community resources. Those resources could be jobs, infrastructure, strengthened relationships among individuals and organizations, or increased access to the political process. Community development efforts can increase tangible resources in communities (good jobs, schools, parks, health facilities), but they also increase less tangible but equally important resources such as social capital.

Community development approaches often bring together the resources of multiple groups in a locality, such as neighborhood and civic organizations, religious congregations, businesses, schools, youth groups, libraries, and other community resources (Kaye & Wolff, 1997; Kretzmann & McKnight, 1993; Lappe & DuBois, 1994; Nation, Wandersman, & Perkins, 2002; Putnam, Feldstein, & Cohen, 2003; Saegert, Thompson, & Warren, 2001). Perkins, Crim, Silberman, and Brown (2004) give a useful overview.

Community development can focus on one or more of four domains (Perkins et al., 2004):

- Economic development (e.g., of businesses and jobs)
- Political development (e.g., of community organizations to influence decisions in the community and at wider levels)
- Improving social environment (e.g., health, education, policing, promoting youth development)
- Improving physical environment (e.g., housing, transportation, city services, parks, public spaces)

The Block Booster Project we described in Chapter 11 exemplifies locality-based community development. One block association in New York City initiated crime watch patrols, improved street lighting, encouraged property cleanup, discouraged illegal drug sales, sponsored outdoor parties and recreational trips, and met regularly to discuss block activities and problems. These collective acts lowered crime, increased neighboring, and strengthened the sense of community. Effective locality-based community development often leads to such outcomes (Wandersman & Florin, 2000).

As with just about every other issue discussed in this book, particularly intervention techniques, specific approaches to community development are hotly debated and have undergone significant changes over the past half century. An example of these changes can be seen in community development work in Bangladesh. The Bangladesh Rural Advancement Committee (BRAC) was established in 1971 with the specific goal of alleviating the extreme poverty in Bangladesh. It is currently one of the largest nongovernmental organizations (NGOs) in the world.

The approach of BRAC has evolved significantly over the 40 years of its existence (Reza & Ahmmed, 2008). The original focus was on straight relief work, alleviating the most horrendous effects of extreme poverty through the direct provision of such things as food, housing, education, and health care. However, it became clear that efforts to *alleviate* poverty generally did little to *eradicate* poverty. BRAC then began to focus on community development, with a major focus on collective action and microfinancing. It was at this stage that the Grameen Bank was begun. But this approach did little to recognize the structural forces and public policies affecting and sometimes supporting the continued existence of poverty. So, BRAC began a policy of supporting political education and political activism among the people it serves. Most recently, in recognition of the global nature of poverty, BRAC has expanded its efforts to include establishing affiliates in other countries facing extreme poverty.

BRAC's structure is based on Village Organizations. As of December 2008, there were 293,016 Village Organizations, with 8.09 million members (Bangladesh Rural Advancement Committee, 2008). These organizations meet once a month to discuss BRAC initiatives in their communities and to plan for future needs and objectives. The Village Organizations provide a basis for political education and activism. Subcommittees of the Village Organizations may meet more frequently to discuss specific projects. The Village Organizations serve as the mechanism for BRAC's microfinance program, exemplified by the Grameen Bank.

The Grameen Bank movement blends economic development with microsystem cooperatives. The program began in rural Bangladesh to provide small loans to more than a million landless poor women for their own small businesses. Loans are made to small groups of four to seven women, who are then responsible for repayment as a group and must have a business plan approved by the bank. The Grameen idea has spread internationally, in urban and rural settings, with women and men as borrowers, helping to create working businesses among the poor, with very low default rates (Lappe & DuBois, 1994, pp. 99–100). In a similar effort in rural West Virginia, a coalition of churches and community groups provided the loan that began Wellspring, a crafts cooperative run by women in isolated communities (Kretzmann & McKnight, 1993, p. 308).

Organizational Consultation

This approach involves professionals working as consultants with workplaces, for-profit or nonprofit, to make changes in the organization's policies, structure, or practices. To qualify as community or social change, this must alter the organization, not simply individual workers, and be connected to wider changes in community or society. In other words, the consultation must result in second-order changes, not just surface-level changes. Organizational consulting may change organizational policies; alter roles, decision making, or communication in the organization; or deal with organizational such issues as work–family relationships, understanding human diversity, and intergroup conflict.

As conceptualized in community psychology, organizational consultation is grounded in an ecological and contextual understanding of the specific organizations involved (Trickett, Barone, & Watts, 2000). For this reason, all the ecological principles discussed in Chapter 5 are fundamental to consultative work. Issues of power and empowerment (see Chapter 11) are also key to organizational change, and helping an organization become empowered could be a specific goal of the consultation process.

The consultative relationship goes both ways, as we hope we have made clear throughout our discussions. While organizations are learning from consultants, the consultants are also learning through their work with the organizations. Consultants can then play a role in disseminating that information so others can learn from it.

The Block Booster Project is a good example of this reciprocal relationship. The project involved community psychologists in consultation with community organizations. The goal of the consultation was to help the organizations become more effective in changing communities. The psychologists could offer this consultation because of what they had learned working with community organizations, and that knowledge base was continually expanded through their work (Wandersman & Florin, 2000). Reviews of organizational concepts and approaches in community psychology include Boyd and Angelique (2002); Shinn and Perkins (2000); Trickett, Barone, and Watts (2000).

Alternative Settings

What do these settings have in common: women's shelters, rape crisis services, alternative schools, mutual help groups, community gardens, a street health clinic bus that operates at night to distribute HIV prevention information and condoms, self-governing cooperative housing for low-income residents, and consumer-run mental health organizations, such as Oxford Houses and Community Lodges?

All of these are alternative settings that grew out of dissatisfaction with mainstream services to provide an alternative to those services (Brown, 2009; Brown, Shepherd, Wituk, & Meissen, 2008; Cherniss & Deegan, 2000; Reinharz, 1984). Women dissatisfied with conventional mental health and social services created their own settings for battered women and rape victims. Those settings not only help clients but also promote public awareness of sexism. Mental health consumer-run organizations (CROs) provide powerful new roles for mental health consumers. Rather than the dependent roles generally assigned to them in traditional mental health service centers, CROs allow mental health consumers to assume helper roles, which can help shape their identities in powerful and therapeutic ways (Brown, 2009; Brown, Shepherd, Wituk, & Meissen, 2008).

Alternative settings can promote such values as sense of community, social justice, respect for human diversity, and citizen self-governance in ways that conventional organizations often do not. Their organizational structures are often less bureaucratic or hierarchical. They usually foster a spirit of mutual commitment that formal organizations do not. Alternative settings have a centuries-long history, including many spiritually-based settings, women's organizations, and utopian communities. Alternative settings may be politically progressive, conservative, or apolitical. The Harlem Children's Zone and Fairweather's Community Lodge (described in Chapter 5) are examples of alternative settings.

Alternative settings provide a fertile ground for social change. Instead of "working within the system" to reform mainstream institutions or using social action and conflict to demand changes in those institutions, this approach goes around the mainstream institutions to create new settings. Alternative settings provide a choice for citizens or consumers of services. They can provide a safe haven and support for individuals experiencing discrimination and injustice. They often develop settings or services that later become widely accepted, such as some mutual help groups and women's services.

However, alternative settings encounter characteristic dilemmas (Cherniss & Deegan, 2000; Reinharz, 1984). They often begin with few resources other than the ideals and commitment of their founders. That can lead to burnout among their workers. Their values focus and lack of resources can lead to resisting evaluation and improvement of services (Wandersman et al., 2004). Alternative settings founded to empower the disenfranchised may also encounter dilemmas of who exactly is to be empowered (we discussed these in Chapter 11; see Riger, 1993). Finally, the existence of an alternative setting may paradoxically reduce the pressure on mainstream services to change because an alternative is available. However, many alternative settings have found ways to overcome these obstacles and have pioneered constructive, lasting changes in communities and societies. Cherniss and Deegan (2000) reviewed processes that contribute to their effectiveness and longevity.

Use of Technology

From of the viewpoint of a community psychologist, one of the most exciting things about the development of new information and communication technologies (ICTs) is their potential to enhance community organizing. They can contribute to community development efforts, social action efforts, community consultation across geographic boundaries, and the development of alternative settings. ICTs are all about communication, both in the sense of sharing information and in developing relationships. In Chapter 6, we discussed bonding and bridging forms of relationships and the ways in which both are forms of social capital. The Internet in particular has been embraced by people and organizations involved in community work, serving both as a source for resources and as a means of connection and communication. Most of the organizations mentioned in this chapter and throughout this book have websites, and we encourage you to visit them to learn more about their work.

Because technology and its applications for community organizing change so quickly, we will not attempt to conduct any type of systematic review of the available technological tools. To truly take advantage of ICTs requires ongoing education, and at the end of this section, we will give you some resources dedicated to helping community organizations and nonprofits stay informed of advances in this area. First, though, we would like to present an example of how traditional organizing work is interacting with ICTs to provide a flexible and exciting tool for community development and activism. The example we have chosen is called *crowdsourcing*.

Crowdsourcing is a very grassroots, community organizing approach that collects information directly from community members regarding their own experiences in their communities. While this is the fundamental basis of all community work, crowdsourcing takes advantage of such ICTs as texting and the internet to quickly collect, analyze, and distribute information for immediate use.

In December 2007, Ory Okolloh was living in South Africa but went home to Kenya to vote in the national elections. Immediately after the election, violence broke out throughout Kenya, triggered by widespread concerns about the legitimacy of the election results. There was a three-day news blackout, but Ory ran a blog on Kenyan politics, and as friends and acquaintances texted her messages regarding what they were seeing, she put the information on the blog. Ory asked her blog readers if they could help her map the information she was receiving on Google Maps. Within a few days, Ushahidi ("testimony" in Swahili) was born. Since then, Ushahidi has been used by a number of organizations for a number of purposes, including mapping reports of trapped survivors and fires during the 2009 Haitian earthquake and tracking the availability of pharmaceuticals in Zambia (Bahree, 2008).

Crowdsourcing is also being utilized for needs assessment and program evaluation efforts. For example, the Peer Water Exchange (PWX) uses the same basic technology as Ushahidi, essentially, mobile phones, mapping software, and a website. PWX is dedicated to using volunteers to fund, evaluate, and share information regarding the successes and failures of clean water projects. The premise is that clean water projects must be small scale and tailored to the needs of each particular community. They also need to be evaluated and modified over time in order to continue to meet the needs of the community. This process has been extremely hard to achieve under traditional philanthropic approaches, which are geared to large-scale projects with intensive evaluations. The necessary small-scale projects do not get funded, but if they do get funded, the funding agencies never see any sort of evaluation. PWX relies on a brief, easy funding application, which receives an open peer review. Information on the success of the project is sent to PWX, which then maps the information on its website. They also promote the use of volunteers who visit projects and send information back to PWX (Peer Water Exchange, n.d.).

At the time of this writing, the home page of the PWX website proclaimed "Welcome to the Approach That Will Enable Us to Solve Humanity's Crises." While the evaluation data are obviously still out on that claim, the statement does accurately reflect the excitement people feel regarding the potential for ICTs to transform community developing, organizing, and action. These technologies allow for the rapid collection and analysis of information, often provided by the direct observations of community members; extensive communication and relationship building among people and organizations that may never actually interact face-to-face; flexible responses to rapidly changing situations; and, at least potentially, increased utilization of nonhierarchal and consensus-building organizational processes. Some observers believe we may be seeing a fundamental change in the culture of activism (Juris & Pleyers, 2009). While it is too soon to decide if this is taking place, it is true that ITCs offer the opportunity to respond to the competing demands of keeping community work local while still recognizing and dealing with the global nature of the problems communities face.

Since 1987, a nonprofit organization named TechSoup has been providing free information, training, and support on the use of technology for nonprofit agencies, libraries, and community organizations. TechSoup also solicits donations from corporations, which allow them to provide free and discounted software and hardware to nonprofit organizations. You can find them at www.techsoup.com.

ELEMENTS OF EFFECTIVE COMMUNITY CHANGE INITIATIVES

What qualities promote effective community-level change? How do top-down and bottom-up approaches differ in community change? Do effective efforts for community change have common elements? What processes promote social change? Just as we used reviews of best practices to help determine what works in prevention programming, researchers have reviewed the work of community organizations to determine what elements support effective community change. In this section, we give a summary of what they have found.

Efforts to promote community change can adopt a **community betterment** approach. These are attempts to improve specific aspects of community functioning and often involve a primarily top-down approach in which the work is initiated and directed by professionals. While these approaches can be useful, it may be more useful to adopt a **community empowerment** model. These models use a primarily bottom-up approach in which members or residents of a community are involved in initiating the effort, and they retain primary influence and control. Empowerment efforts are more likely than community betterment approaches to benefit from local wisdom and result in increased community capacity through the development of local leaders, strengthened community relationships, and increased social capital (Himmelman, 2001; Kaye & Wolff, 1997; Kretzmann & McKnight, 1993). They can also result in strengthening the **sense of community** among the members, an important aspect of social capital in itself.

Empowered community organizations effectively exert power in community decisions, policies, and practices (Peterson & Zimmerman, 2004). They may directly **implement actions** (e.g., directly influencing decisions or providing community programs). They may also **disseminate information** to influence decision-makers or the public in more generalized ways (Peterson & Zimmerman, 2004). The effectiveness of community actions can be assessed in terms of their influence on actual policy and decisions; on creation of alternative settings, community programs, and similar initiatives; and on deployment of resources in the community and wider society (Peterson & Zimmerman, 2004).

Effective change initiatives must address **multiple areas of action** (Caughey, O'Campo, & Brodsky, 1999; Schorr, 1997; Wolff, 2001). A community cannot address all things at once. But it can develop a comprehensive perspective in which linkages are recognized (Schorr, 1997, p. 361). While it may seem simpler to focus on only one issue, research suggests that it is only through this comprehensive approach that wider community change occurs.

Effective community initiatives have substantial **local control** of planning and implementing changes (Peterson & Zimmerman, 2004). At the same time, they work on developing **external linkages and resources**. Few communities facing serious problems can make significant headway completely on their own. Thus, although community change is best controlled locally, it often requires resources from outside the community, such as funding, expert knowledge, and political influence (Schorr, 1997, p. 363). Communities can cultivate these resources through **interpersonal networks** with persons outside the community and **organizational alliances** with other organizations (Peterson & Zimmerman, 2004).

As is the case with effective prevention programming, to be successful, a community change initiative needs to be guided by a **plausible theory of community change** (Nation et al., 2003; Schorr, 1997, p. 364). Theory can be based on social science research but also on citizen practical experience. Initiatives for community change must be of an **effective intensity**, involving changes that are strong enough to make a detectable difference in everyday life. There is a threshold for effective response to a community problem; initiatives below that threshold will not be effective. Again, think back to the discussion of effective prevention programs and the need for an appropriate level of intensity.

Finally, effective community change initiatives must take a **long-term perspective** (Schorr, 1997). The community initiatives described in this chapter are often the products of years of effort. When decisions are made through genuine citizen participation, time is a necessary resource. But initiatives that build slowly and steadily and have citizen input are likely to be sustained even if conditions change because their participatory base is solid.

There are no exact formulas for community change (Alinsky, 1971). These elements described above are best understood as rules of thumb, with many possible ways to apply them in practice. Each community and community issue involves a unique mix of resources, obstacles, allies and opponents, means and ends, intentions, and unanticipated consequences. Community change initiatives are an art, but a collective art that involved personal relationships and shared successes and failures.

PUBLIC POLICY

The definition of public policy used in this chapter is a broad one, including such things as tax policy, traffic laws, local ordinances, and the regulations regarding how those policies are carried out. The dress code at the local public school is a public policy, as is the policy of a state's child health care program to only accept typed applications submitted in person. By this definition, all the PICO members in our opening examples were engaged in public policy work.

Public policy work involves conducting research and seeking to influence public decisions, policies, or laws. To develop recommendations regarding public policy and to act on those recommendations draws upon all the aspects of community and prevention science discussed in this book and all the community organizing techniques presented previously. It often involves persuading government officials but may influence leaders in the private sector, journalists, or others. It especially involves framing how a social issue is understood. Remember the importance of problem definition when you are doing public policy work. This work generally seeks to persuade with information (especially research findings) and reasoned arguments but may also involve more confrontational approaches, such as public action.

Policy research and advocacy may be focused on legislative, executive, or judicial branches of government at local, state or provincial, national, or international levels. Examples of policy advocacy by community psychologists include expert testimony in public interest lawsuits, filing "friend of the court" briefs in court cases, serving on advisory commissions (e.g., the Federal Interagency Council on Homelessness), contacts with lawmakers or government officials, testimony in legislative hearings on proposed bills, interviews or writing for mass media, working with advocacy organizations (e.g., the Children's Defense Fund or the National Mental Health Association), working as a staff member for legislators or in executive or judicial branches of government, and even serving as an elected official, from the local school board to wider office (Mayer & Davidson, 2000; Melton, 1995, 2000; Meyers, 2000; Phillips, 2000; Shinn, Baumohl, & Hopper, 2001; Solarz, 2001; Toro, 1998). The community research we have cited in this book offers many examples of policy-relevant studies and findings. Several qualities of community psychology equip it especially for policy concerns: concern with both research and action, emphasis on multiple ecological levels, and participatory approaches to working with citizens (Melton, 1995; Perkins, 1988; Phillips 2000).

Box 12.1 presents an account by community psychologist Leonard Jason of his appearance in a congressional committee hearing during consideration by Congress of a national settlement of tobacco lawsuits. (The full version appears in Jason [1998].) His team's research on youth access to tobacco appears in Jason, Berk, Schnopp-Wyatt, and Talbot (1999) and in Jason and colleagues (2009).

Policy advocacy is often based on policy research, which is conducted to provide empirical information on social issues. An early instance of research-based public advocacy was the use of social science research findings in the 1954 Supreme Court desegregation case *Brown vs. Board of Education*. Psychological

---

B o x   12.1   Community Psychology in Action

"Dr. Jason Goes to Washington": Advocacy Testimony

Leonard Jason, Ph.D. DePaul University, Center for Community Research

On Tuesday, December 2, I was called by a staff member of the House Commerce Committee, Subcommittee on Health and Environment, and was asked to testify about behavioral aspects of teenage tobacco use. He mentioned that I had three days to prepare my testimony, and I naïvely agreed to this request.

I religiously read dozens of new bills on the tobacco settlement being introduced into Congress and sought consultation from American Psychological Association (APA) staff. By Monday morning, after spending the weekend with different drafts of the testimony, I finally had a document, although I continued to incorporate new ideas into it until I boarded the plane to Washington.

There were television cameras from CSPAN and chairs for about 100 people. As people began filtering in, the tension began to rise. Faithfully, I practiced my deep breathing exercises. Various speakers gave their testimony, and I was the last person to present my views.

I stressed that it is possible to reduce the number of young people who smoke. I next indicated that it is possible to appreciably reduce the percent of vendors that sell to youth and that school prevention programs can effectively reduce the percentage of children who

later smoke. I then talked about how children will be exposed to imagery-laden tobacco advertisements and that to deal with this, we need a ratio of antismoking ads to cigarette ads to be 1:4 or greater. I would have preferred saying that all ads should be banned, but I knew that this would raise First Amendment rights issues.

One congressperson asked me if I thought that smoking should be completely banned. He kept using the terms "ban" and "restricting youth access to tobacco" interchangeably, and I had to constantly point out the differences in these two concepts.

So, what do I make of this experience? First, it is great fun to be able to testify in Congress and actually have policymakers interested in your research and viewpoints. To do this type of work, one needs to be able to relatively quickly develop a position that addresses key points and reduces the cognitive complexity of a particular topic. Working collaboratively with other organizations, in this case APA, are key attributes for reaching these types of audiences. Keeping a sense of humor and being diplomatic are prudent.

research was also used for community mental health reforms and early childhood programs, such as Head Start (Phillips, 2000).

The idea of promoting community change through the adoption of specific public policies (often legislation) can be a controversial one. Many people hold the personal philosophy that government should interfere as little as possible in the daily lives of people and the daily functions of communities and organizations. In fact, the statement "that government is best which governs least" is a central belief in American culture and forms the basis for the philosophical and political position of libertarianism (the quote is from Henry David Thoreau in 1849).

But just as change is inevitable, so is public policy. Even the most extreme libertarian representations of society still postulate the existence of rules that everyone in a community is required to follow or else face consequences. Societies seem to require formal policies in order to survive. Just imagine what would happen if everyone decided they wanted to ignore stop signs? And public policy, along with community norms and resources, shape the structure of the world in which we live.

Those of you who have taken sociology, and particularly those who have taken a class specifically in social stratification, should be well aware of the effect of social forces on individual well-being. Structural forces shape who you are, what you believe, how you behave, and what opportunities you have. As a quick example of this, just imagine how different your life would have been if you have been born in poverty, to HIV infected parents, in a part of Ethiopia stricken by famine. But this recognition of the power of structural forces does not mean we are mere robots. We can consciously examine those structural forces, and we can change them.

Let us start with an example of prevention research that has specific policy implications.

Crime Policy: Punishment vs. Prevention

Crime policy may be the clearest example of why it is important to systematically examine our public policies. All modern societies have laws defining criminal behavior and procedures for enforcing those laws. We also have a large and long-standing body of research regarding the effects of crime policies. So, for example, we know that:

- Moderate punishments consistently enforced have the greatest deterrent effects.
- Increased education leads to decreased recidivism.
- Any type or length of incarceration can increase the chances of recidivism when compared to such diversion programs as community service and restorative justice programs.
- Treatment for drug abusers is a more cost-effective approach to dealing with drug-related offenses than incarceration.

Each of these specific statements is related to some basic research findings (see Sherman et al., 1998; and Wright, 1996, for reviews). First, incarceration is damaging to individuals, leaving them alienated, with few positive social supports and limited economic resources. Even individuals who are incarcerated for extremely short time periods experience increased alienation and recidivism compared to individuals who committed the same offenses but were not incarcerated. Second, increasing the severity of punishment does little to increase deterrent effects. When you are aware of these basic research findings, it gives you a starting point to evaluate proposed or existing crime policy.

In our discussion of cost-benefit analyses in Chapter 9, we said that the sad thing about cost-effectiveness analyses is that they so rarely actually have an effect on public policy. This depressing point is particularly salient when discussing crime policy. Recently, a major cost-benefit analysis in Pennsylvania evaluated an effort on the part of the state to invest in evidence-based prevention programs (largely through the Communities That Care model). The state had dedicated over $60 million over a 10-year period to support these programs in 120 Pennsylvania communities. The evaluation addressed seven programs, including Big Brothers/Sisters, the Nurse-Family Partnership (a home visiting program), two substance abuse prevention programs, and three early intervention programs for children demonstrating significant behavioral problems, which are generally considered forms of secondary prevention. The researchers concluded that:

> Using conservative and widely-accepted methodology, we determine that these programs not only pay for themselves, but represent a potential $317 million return to the Commonwealth in terms of reduced corrections costs, welfare and social services burden, drug and mental health treatment, and increased employment and tax revenue. The programs described in this report produce returns of between $1 and $25 per dollar invested, and can generate cost savings as much as $130 million for a single program. (Jones, Bumbarger, Greenberg, Greenwood, & Kyler, 2008, p. 3)

Now, that is obviously good news. The depressing news is that, at the same time this report was written, the Pennsylvania Department of Corrections had asked for over $700 million to construct new prisons. This would only be a stop-gap measure, as even with those new prisons, the state would be dealing with overcrowded prisons again within five years.

Between 1985 and 2010, Pennsylvania's spending on prisons increased nearly 650%. This increase in spending on incarceration has continued even though in recent years the state has seen decreases in both overall population and crime rates. In contrast, state spending for evidence-based prevention programming has been cut by 93% since 2002. This is despite the fact that those programs have been shown to save the state up to $25 for every $1 spent (Jones et al., 2008). And remember, those figures are not derived from a controlled evaluation of a small-scale, experimental pilot program. They are based on the actual implementation of programs in the communities of Pennsylvania.

We do not mean to pick on Pennsylvania. In fact, the only reason this analysis is possible is because the state made a significant commitment to statewide prevention programming. But that commitment occurred during a time of relative economic prosperity. And even though that commitment was extremely successful, it has not resulted in any long-term change in public policy.

This example illustrates an important point about policy advocacy. The impact of social science research on policymaking is generally much broader than just advocating for a specific regulation (Phillips, 2000). Instead, policy advocacy often involves educating policymakers, influencing their overall perspective on an issue. The researchers at Penn State University cited previously do make specific policy recommendations, but their main goal is to use the results of prevention science to shift the general perspective of lawmakers to a consideration of the importance of prevention. This shift of perspective can take years of work.

Crime policy has specific social justice implications. Minority populations in the United States, particularly African American populations, are disproportionately represented in prison populations, far beyond what would be expected given differences in criminal offenses between different ethnic groups. While there are obviously pragmatic, economic, and social welfare reasons for being concerned about the state of crime policy, the serious social justice implications add urgency to the situation.

Macro-Level Change: Public Policy Regarding Poverty

Poverty is another issue with pragmatic, economic, social welfare, and social justice implications. We (the authors) chose this topic deliberately for this book because we know that, at least in America, there is a prevalent societal belief that poverty is an inevitable fact of existence.

The fact that poverty is correlated with almost every conceivable negative outcome humans can face is well established. People who live in poverty have poorer nutrition, poorer health, less education, and shorter life spans than people who are not living in poverty. This is true even in wealthy, developed countries where poverty is defined relative to the median income. For a recent review of the effects of poverty on child development, see Huston & Bentley (2010).

It is difficult to find anyone that does not agree that poverty is a serious problem, but there is little agreement on what to do about it. In fact, there are many people who argue that there is little a society can or should do about poverty in developed countries. In fact, all developed countries have a long history of public policy efforts to decrease poverty, decrease income inequality, and support the development of a middle class. In the United States, those policies include the public school system (starting in the early 1800s), public funding of land grant colleges and universities (starting in 1854), the Homestead Act of 1862, antitrust legislation (starting in at the end of the 19th century), the first progressive income tax in 1913, the New Deal legislation of the 1930s (including the Social Security System and unemployment insurance), the GI Bill of Rights (starting after WWII), and the Great Society programs (starting in 1964), including instituting health insurance (in the form of Medicare and Medicaid) for the elderly and the poor.

These programs worked. The U.S. Census Bureau first began collecting data on poverty rates in 1959. That year, the U.S. poverty rate was 22.4%. In 2008 (the last year for which data was available at the time of this writing), it had gone down to 13.2% (U.S. Census Bureau, 2009a). However, just looking at the overall decrease in the poverty rate masks some important differences among groups of Americans.

In 1959, the poverty rate for Americans less than 18 years of age was 27.3%. The rate for Americans 65 and older was 35.2%, and the rate for Americans ages 18 to 64 was 17%. Poverty disproportionately affected children and the elderly. Rates for all three groups declined from 1959 until about 1969, when the Great Society programs were in place. By child poverty was at 14%, poverty in the elderly was at 25.3%, and poverty for non-elderly adults was 8.7%. Since then, poverty among the elderly has continued to show a general decline and in 2008 was 9.7%. In contrast, after sharp decreases in the 1960s and early 1970s, child poverty began to rise again and is currently 19% (see Figure 12.1).

Poverty in general and child poverty in particular are serious public problems in the United States. These concerns are related to the even larger, overarching issue of income inequality. Income inequality is measured by the difference between the households with the highest income and those with the lowest income. In the United States, income inequality decreased significantly after WWII, with households at all levels experiencing relatively equal gains in income. That trend changed in the late 1970s, and the United States is currently ranked 42 out of 134 in its level of income inequality, according to the *CIA World Factbook*.

Since 1979, the gap between the wealthiest 1% of American households and those in the bottom 20% more than tripled. There is more income concentrated

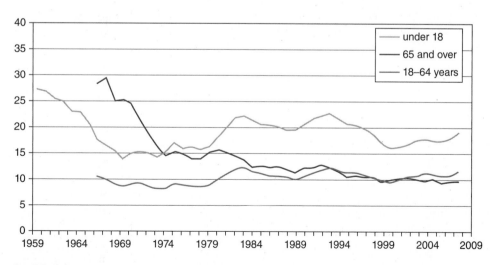

FIGURE 12.1 U.S. Poverty Rates by Age

SOURCE: U.S. Census Bureau, Historical Poverty Tables, Table 3. Poverty Status of People, by Age, Race, and Hispanic Origin: 1959 to 2008.

TABLE 12.1   **Average After-Tax Income by Income Group 1979–2007 (in 2007 dollars)**

Income Category	1979	2007	Percent Change 1979–2007	Dollar Change 1979–2007
Lowest fifth	$15,300	$17,700	16%	$2,400
Second fifth	$31,000	$38,000	23%	$7,000
Middle fifth	$44,100	$55,300	25%	$11,200
Fourth fifth	$57,700	$77,700	35%	$20,000
Top fifth	$101,700	$198,300	95%	$96,600
Top 1%	$346,600	$1,319,700	281%	$973,100

SOURCE: Table from the Center on Budget and Policy Priorities, 2010, based on data from the Congressional Budget Office, *Effective Federal Tax Rates: 1979–2007*, June 2010.

in the highest-earning American households now than at any time since 1928 (Sherman & Stone, 2010) (see Table 12.1).

How wealth is distributed in a society is a function of many factors; most importantly, the basic structure of the economy and the tax system. As with social change and social policy, the distribution and redistribution of wealth is occurring and will continue to occur regardless of our actions. We encourage you to consciously examine these processes in your society.

Policy Approaches: What Can We Do?   Before we can answer this question, we much go back to the issue of problem definition. What approach you chose to take to deal with the problem of income inequality depends very much on how you define the problem. For example, if your understanding of child poverty is that poverty is correlated with increased risk factors and decreased protective factors in children's lives, then your answer will be to focus on ameliorating the effects of poverty on the lives of children. In this case, you might work to implement prevention and wellness-promotion programs, such as the home visiting and SEL programs discussed in Chapters 9 and 10 and Head Start, which have the goal of enhancing the development of children living in poverty.

If your understanding of the problem is that families with young children are particularly vulnerable to poverty, then you might focus your efforts on providing supports for those families. For example, such programs as the Supplemental Nutrition Assistance Program (what used to be food stamps) and housing vouchers have the goal of reducing the numbers of children living in poverty by providing increased resources to families with children.

Finally, if your understanding of the problem is that increased income inequality in a country leads to increased numbers of people living in poverty, then your answer might be to promote economic policies that result in the reduction income inequality and thus decrease the incidence of poverty throughout a society. An example of this type of policy in the United States is the Earned Income Tax Credit (EITC).

In the rest of this section, we will discuss examples of these last two groups of policies and the effect on poor families. First, let us get a picture of what one of these families might look like.

In 2009, the poverty threshold for a single parent with two children in the United States was $17,285 (U.S. Census Bureau, 2009b). The minimum wage is $7.25 (with no scheduled increases in the future). If a single mother with two children worked full-time (40 hours a week for 52 weeks a year), her gross income would be $15,080—not enough to lift her and her children above poverty. And she would even make even less if she or her children get sick and she must miss work. Let us assume that our single mom is lucky enough to have a job that pays $8.31 an hour—more than a dollar an hour over the federal minimum wage and the lowest salary that she needs to earn more than the federal poverty level.

While this woman would most probably not be liable for any income tax, she would still have to pay 7.65% of her gross income for Social Security and Medicaid (FICA). The U.S. Department of Agriculture estimates that a thrifty mother of two young children (ages two and four) could feed all three of them for about $82.53 a week, assuming that all meals are prepared at home (USDA, 2009). The 2010 Fair Market Rent for a two-bedroom apartment in the United States is $959. This includes rent and utilities and varies widely depending on geographic location (DeCrappeo, Pelletiere, Crowley, & Teater, 2010). In 2006, the last year for which data is available, the average weekly child care expenses of families with mothers who worked outside the home in the United States was $115 a week (U.S. Census Bureau, 2006).

We are assuming that this family will qualify for some sort of public health insurance program; her children certainly will. And she will probably qualify for food stamps (now called the Supplemental Nutrition Assistance Program [SNAP]). SNAP is a federal program that is administered by the states, so benefits can vary a great deal according to geographic location. In 2009, the average SNAP participant received $124.45 a month per person, which would result in this family receiving $373.35 a month, or $4,480.20 a year (U.S. Department of Agriculture, 2010).

Put all this together, and here is how it works out (see Table 12.2).

TABLE 12.2

Gross income	$17,285
Food stamps	$4,480
Total income	$21,765
FICA	$1,323
Rent and utilities	$11,508
Food	$4,292
Child care	$5,980
Total expenses	$23,102
Income minus expenses	−$1,337

So, even without spending a penny on transportation, clothes, or such necessary items as toilet paper and soap, this woman is already facing a deficit of $1,337. This is why many economists calculate that for a family to live safely while meeting their basic needs, they need an income that is twice the federal poverty level (Mishel, Bernstein, & Shierholz, 2009). Many families are in the same situation as our single mother of two. In 2008, 27% of American family households with children had incomes at or below twice the poverty threshold for a parent with two children.

Unfortunately, as you can see from our example, for many American families, working full-time is no guarantee that they can lift their families out of poverty. In 2007, a full-time, year-round worker needed to earn $10.20 an hour to keep a family of four above the poverty level. In that year, over 25.4% of all workers in the United States earned less than that amount (Mishel, Bernstein, & Shierholz, 2009, p. 139).

Preventing Homelessness   Perhaps you looked at the estimated housing costs for our family and thought that unless they could find cheaper housing, they were in danger of homelessness. This is a valid concern. In Chapter 1, we used the issue of homelessness to illustrate the conceptual shift we would hope you would make while reading this book. We asked you to accept that while individualistic explanations of homelessness had some validity (such issues as mental illness, substance abuse, and domestic violence), structural issues that exist only at the community and societal level had much more explanatory power. We asked you to shift from an individual to a community understanding of homelessness, and we specifically asked you to accept that the fundamental cause of homelessness in a society had nothing to do with the characteristics of individuals; it was a lack of affordable housing.

Homelessness presents a powerful example of the role community psychologists and all those who believe in community change can play in public policy and human welfare. Community psychologist Marybeth Shinn has joined many other social scientists in advocating, with research supporting their contentions, that homelessness must be understood fundamentally as a problem of access to affordable housing. While these researchers do support specific types of legislation, their message has focused fundamentally on this shift in problem definition. Policy makers, at local, state, and national levels are increasingly speaking and acting from this perspective. This shift in perspective is occurring after years of work, and the "influence is more on ways of thinking" about policy issues than on particular research findings or programs (M. Shinn, personal communication, September 22, 2004).

As the collective research on homelessness has become more conclusive, the recommendations from social scientists have become more specific. The first conclusion is that the single most effective policy approach to eliminating homelessness is to provide affordable housing (generally in the form of subsidized housing) for every family. The second conclusion is a matter of perspective, related to the shift in defining homelessness as a community-level rather than an individual-level issue. Research has increasingly supported the idea that if you want to intervene successfully in the multiple problems faced by people and families who are without a stable residence, then meeting their housing needs must come first.

The Section 8 program is an example of a subsidized housing program. The program determines the local Fair Market Rent (calculated annually by the U.S. Department of Housing and Urban Development) and then provides vouchers to cover the difference between 30% of a participants' income and the local rental costs. The program can be linked to specific housing projects or the renter can use the voucher to find housing anywhere in the community. Allowing the renter to find housing anywhere in a community or having public housing policies that require new units of affordable housing to be spread throughout the community are approaches that can help to eliminate areas of concentrated poverty. The program requires participants to spend 30% of their income because most economists agree that housing costs (rent plus utilities) that total less than 1/3 of a family's income are affordable.

Housing subsidy programs such as Section 8 are an amazingly effective way of ending family homelessness. In a recent report for the National Alliance to End Homelessness, Shinn says, "In every study that examined this issue, subsidized housing—with or without any additional services—has helped families to leave shelters and stay out" (Shinn, 2009). One study she cites looked at families who were first-time users of shelters. Five years later, 97% of the families that received subsidies were in their own apartments, and more than 80% had been in that apartment for at least a year. Among families that did not receive a subsidy, only 38% were in their own apartments (Shinn et al., 1998). Not surprisingly, subsidized housing has also been shown to be extremely effective in preventing homelessness from even occurring (Wood, Turner, & Mills, 2008).

The second homeless policy point on which there is widespread agreement has to do with the order in which services should be supplied to the homeless. As a group, homeless families have fewer serious and chronic problems than individuals who are homeless. In fact, homeless families are essentially identical to poor families who have housing (Shinn, 2009). However, there are subsets of poor families and an even larger group of homeless individuals who have a wide variety of such problems as mental illness and substance abuse. Traditional approaches to working with these people were based on the idea that these problems needed to be dealt with before stable housing could be achieved. A large body of research now supports the opposite perspective; if stable housing is provided first, it becomes easier to address the other problems.

Even among homeless persons with serious mental illness, programs that "put housing first" are more effective and less costly. These programs place homeless persons with mental illness in subsidized housing first and then offer other treatment and support services rather than requiring them to receive mental health treatment in transitional housing programs before becoming eligible for their own housing (Gulcur, Stefancic, Shinn, Tsemberis, & Fischer, 2003).

Research alone is not enough to influence policy. Shinn has written reports with recommendations for the Federal Interagency Council on Homelessness and the Homelessness Research Institute, co-chaired a New York City

TABLE 12.3

Gross income	$17,285
Food stamps	$4,480
Total income	$21,765
FICA	$1,323
Rent and utilities	$5,185
Food	$4,292
Child care	$5,980
Total expenses	$16,780
Income minus expenses	$4,985

government task force that wrote a multiyear plan for how the city will address homelessness, and helped to found a research advisory panel for the City Department of Homeless Services (M. Shinn, personal communication, September 22, 2004; Shinn, 2009). Another community psychologist, Paul Toro, has worked with homeless persons and advocates in policy research and advocacy. Toro and associates have surveyed homeless persons themselves to determine needs for services, studied homelessness issues and policies across the United States and internationally, and helped develop local services for homeless persons in Detroit (Acosta & Toro, 2000; Tompsett et al., 2003; Toro & Warren, 1999). As we described in Chapter 1, Debi Starnes (2004) has been a leader in developing city policy and funding for services for the homeless in Atlanta. They and others have brought a community psychology perspective to discussions of public policy on homelessness: recognizing multiple ecological levels, attending to the voices of the diversity of homeless persons, cultivating collaborative relationships with policymakers and citizens, developing innovative research methods, and translating findings into policy.

Let us look at the effect of a housing voucher on the circumstances of our family. A voucher would reduce her expenses for rent and utilities to 30% of her income, or $5,185. This significantly improves her financial situation (see Table 12.3).

While this situation looks better, think about all the things we expect that mother to do with $4,985 a year. Not only does she need to pay for clothes, transportation, and basic household expenses (such as soap), we also expect her to be saving for her retirement, her children's education, emergency expenses, and perhaps a down payment on her own home. Next, we will discuss a program designed not to decrease our family's expenses but rather to increase their income: the Earned Income Tax Credit.

Getting Work to Pay: The Earned Income Tax Credit (EITC) In 1996, the United States implemented comprehensive changes to federal welfare programs. Before this point, most policies were designed to give direct aid to poor families. The largest of these programs was Aid to Families with Dependent Children

(AFDC). The 1996 reform was called the Personal Responsibility and Work Opportunity Reconciliation Act (PRWOR). Under PRWOR, the AFDC program was replaced by the Temporary Assistance for Needy Families (TANF) program. The primary goal of the new program was to move families off of welfare programs by moving them into the labor market. It does this by implementing strict work requirements, sanctions for failing to work or engage in job training programs, and time limits for receiving benefits (Ziliak, 2009). Evaluations of the program have been complex, but most agree that TANF has been successful in the goal of increasing employment, at least up until the beginning of the current recession. However, as we saw in our discussion of our single mother with two children, having a full-time job in the United States most certainly does not guarantee that a family will be lifted out of poverty.

The EITC is designed to address this situation by "making work pay" for even low income workers. This federal income tax program, first initiated in the United States in 1975, is quite possibly the single most effective tax policy designed to reduce poverty (and income inequality) the country has ever implemented. The program works by providing low-income families a refundable tax credit. The size of the credit is substantial. For example, in 2009, the credit could be up to $5,028 for a single parent with two children, with earnings up to $40,295, or married couples earning up to $42,295. The credit is refundable, which means that any amount left over after it is used to offset income tax owed is refunded to the families. The credit is designed to "make work pay" by supplementing the income of those working in low-paying jobs to ensure they actually earn enough to support their families. Because the credit only applies to earned income, it is designed to encourage employment, and there is evidence that it has worked that way. Studies have repeatedly concluded that expansions of the federal EITC have reduced welfare use among single mothers by increasing employment and earnings (Gao, Kaushal, & Waldfogel, 2009; Lim, 2009; Ziliak, 2009).

The EITC improves the circumstances of our family a great deal. The mother would receive the maximum credit of $5,028, and because with her low income she would probably owe no income tax, all that money would be refunded. As of 2007, 17 states had implemented their own refundable ETIC, which operate in addition to the federal program and which have been shown to have their own positive effects (Lim, 2009). But for simplicity's sake, let us assume this family does not live in one of those states. This leaves her with $10,013 to pay for all her family's other expenses for the year—a much more reasonable situation than the previous scenarios (see Table 12.4).

One problem with the TANF program is that increased work participation results in significantly increased expenses, such as transportation, clothes, child care, and purchasing food outside of the home. TANF does provide for some additional supports, such as child care subsidies for some participants, but these additional supports are not always available for everyone who qualifies for them. While TANF is a federal program, it is implemented at the state level, and specifics of the program differ significantly from state to state. At the time of this writing, some states were cutting back significantly on aspects of the

TABLE 12.4

Gross income	$17,285
Food stamps	$4,480
EITC	$5,028
Total income	$26,793
FICA	$1,323
Rent and utilities	$5,185
Food	$4,292
Child care	$5,980
Total expenses	$16,780
Income minus expenses	$10,013

program, such as child care vouchers. Likewise, even though our family qualified for a housing voucher, demand for these vouchers exceeds the supply, and long wait times are common (U.S. Department of Housing and Urban Development, n.d.). Coupled with the economic recession, this results in a situation where fewer single parents are able to find work that pays them enough to support their families, and they end up leaving work and relying on cash welfare assistance.

An interesting aspect of the EITC, and tax credits for low and middle income families in general, is the effect these programs have had on current public discussions of tax policy in the United States. An article by the Associated Press, which ran in April 2010, started off with this sentence "Tax Day is a dreaded deadline for millions, but for nearly half of U.S. households it's simply somebody else's problem." The article was based on a report by the Tax Policy Center that calculated that about 47% of U.S. households would owe no income tax in 2009, largely because of programs such as the EITC. The article correctly points out that households at all income levels had benefitted from reductions in income taxes in recent years and that the "vast majority" of the households that paid no income tax still paid significant amounts in other taxes. But those points do not stop the writer from quoting an analyst from the Heritage Foundation, who says, "We have 50 percent of people who are getting something for nothing" (Ohlemacher, 2010).

Think about this statement. Do you think it is an accurate description of programs that are designed to ensure that full-time workers can adequately support their families? What impact do you think articles such as that one (which was widely reported) have on the public perception of programs such as the EITC and on other efforts to reduce income inequality?

As we saw with crime policy, the process of policy decision making is not always about what works. Rather, it is often driven by what ideas (and problem definitions) are most popular at a particular time. Money also plays a role, particularly in crime policy. Building new prisons and ensuring that those prisons are

RECOMMENDED WEBSITES

Community Toolbox:
http://ctb.ku.edu.

> Excellent site for learning about citizen participation and planning community change; maintained by community psychologists. Includes tools and recommendations for planning, implementing, and evaluating community initiatives and links to many related sites. The best practical resource for community and social change initiatives.

Psychologists for Social Responsibility:
http://www.psysr.org.

> An organization of psychologists concerned with international and U.S. social issues, including peace and war, ethnopolitical violence, conflict resolution, social justice, and other issues. Includes entries on scholarly works and action initiatives and links to other organizations.

13

Program Evaluation
and Program Development

LRADAC, Abe Wandersman

OPENING EXERCISE

If you or your children went to public school in the United States in the past 30 years, there is a good chance you have experience with a substance abuse prevention program called DARE (Drug Abuse Resistance Education). DARE involves police officers going to classrooms in local schools to present a curriculum over several weeks. Officers present information on the dangers of drug use and teach refusal skills to help participating students resist peer pressure to use drugs. The program was originally based on a zero-tolerance policy regarding drug use, and students were encouraged to sign pledges stating that they would not use drugs. Students who complete the program receive certificates, T-shirts, and other materials that promote a "just say no to drugs" message.

If you participated in a DARE program, take a moment to think back. What do you remember about the program? Did you enjoy it? Did you think it was effective? Do you think it helped to prevent substance abuse in your school or community? Have your thoughts about the program changed in the years since your participation?

DARE was begun in 1983 by the Los Angeles Police Department in cooperation with the Los Angeles Unified School District. Over the years, it has developed a number of different curricula targeting different grades and topics (such as prescription drug abuse). It continues to be the most popular school-based drug-use prevention program in the United States. According to the organization's website, DARE is taught in all 50 states and most school districts and in 43 countries, reaching millions of school children (DARE, 2009).

But a number of evaluations of school curricula delivered by DARE have provided only limited evidence of its effectiveness. For example, results from a longitudinal evaluation of the program in 36 schools in Illinois showed only a small impact on students' drug use immediately following the intervention and no evidence of impact on drug use one or two years after receiving DARE instruction. In addition, evaluations indicated that DARE programs had only limited positive effects on such variables as self-esteem and no effect on such social skills variables as resistance to peer pressure (Enett et al., 1994, p. 113). Negative evaluations continued to pile up over the years. By 1998, a report to the National Institute of Justice concluded that DARE was ineffective (Sherman et al., 1998), and in 2001, the Surgeon General of the United States placed DARE in the "Does Not Work" category of prevention programs (Satcher, 2001).

Do these negative results fit with your experience of the program? What do you think might have caused these negative results?

In this chapter, we are going to discuss how program evaluation is used to help develop, improve, and evaluate the effectiveness of programs such as DARE. One of the goals of this chapter is to provide you some very specific models and skills that you can use to conduct these types of evaluations. We will come back to DARE, but we first want to make the point that you already know a great deal about program evaluation.

EVALUATION IN EVERYDAY LIFE

Evaluation is not just an activity performed by social scientists. We all engage in what is essentially program evaluation, and we do it basically every day. When you go to a new restaurant or watch your favorite sports team, you are engaged in evaluation. In a restaurant, you think about the quality of the service, the quality of the food, the cost, and the atmosphere. If the service was slow, the food was nothing special, and the cost was high, you probably will not go there again. And you will probably "disseminate your results." If a friend asks you about your experience with the restaurant, you will give your data (poor service, mediocre food, and high price) and your overall evaluation (do not bother going there).

When you watch your favorite sports team, you are thinking about the individual performance of the players (in that game, over the season, and in previous seasons), the team's performance against the opposing team in the past, the quality of the coaching, and perhaps the cost to the team of recruiting individual players. You will also probably consider the context in which the game is being played. Some contextual factors you might consider are the weather, if the team is playing at home or away, whether the team has had a chance to rest since their last game, and popular opinion about the team's chances of winning. With a sports team, your evaluation and the data you consider will probably depend a great deal on your goals for the team. If the team is performing much better than the previous season, with a number of talented new players and a new coach, your evaluation is likely to be positive, even if the team does not have an outstanding season. If you are evaluating your child's soccer team and your goal is to have the players learn to get along well and have fun, with every child having an opportunity to play, the team's actual performance may have little to do with your evaluation of the success of the team.

While evaluation activities can sometimes result in a yes or no decision (as in the case of the restaurant when you decide not to return there), they are more likely to result in decisions regarding steps to take to foster improvement (as with your favorite sports team). Most sports fans do not give up on their favorite teams just because they have a losing season and coaches and owners certainly do not. Instead, they spend a great deal of time reviewing their evaluation data to decide how to help the team improve.

It Seemed Like a Good Idea, But Is It Really Working?
(Results-Based Accountability)

The DARE program illustrates the importance of comprehensive program evaluation. DARE used a great deal of public resources (its main funding sources were state and federal agencies) and a relatively large amount of classroom time that could have been used for other educational purposes. Perhaps more importantly, school districts that implemented DARE were *not* implementing other available programs, which had been proven to successfully prevent teen substance abuse (e.g., Botvin & Tortu, 1988; Greenberg et al. 2003; Hawkins, Catalano et al., 1992). Regardless, many school systems have continued to use the DARE approach, in part because it is familiar and sometimes because law enforcement and other funds have been used so a school system can spend less of its own money.

Each year, billions of dollars in tax money, charitable contributions, and grants by philanthropic foundations are spent to do good things in communities. Millions of citizens volunteer time and effort to promote these goals. Even paid staff members in community organizations often choose to work for a low salary in order to promote those goals. Is that time, effort, and money making a difference? Government, nonprofit, and private sectors are being challenged to show results (see the U.S. Government Accounting Office at http://www.gao. gov and the United Way at http://liveunited.org/pages/about-united-way-worldwide). This is commonly referred to as **results-based accountability**. At first, this can be a frightening prospect to people who run programs. Here are some common complaints and fears about program evaluation (compiled by the Northwest Regional Educational Laboratory, 1999):

- Evaluation can create anxiety among program staff.
- Staff members may be unsure how to conduct evaluation.
- Evaluation can interfere with program activities or compete with services for scarce resources.
- Evaluation results can be misused and misinterpreted, especially by program opponents.

Imagine yourself as a board member of a foundation who has to make funding decisions about community programs. You get many more requests for funding than you could possibly fund. It makes sense to ask grantees, "How can we know if your program, supported by our grant money, actually accomplishes its goals?" Schorr (1997) described several types of responses to this question often given by nonprofit organizations and government agencies.

Trust and Values   "Trust us. What we do is so valuable, so complex, so hard to document, so hard to judge, and we are so well intentioned that the public should support us without demanding evidence of effectiveness. Don't let the bean counters who know the cost of everything and the value of nothing obstruct our valiant efforts to get the world's work done" (Schorr, 1997, p 116).

A potential problem with this answer: If program funding is based on trust, citizens and decision-makers do not know the process of how the program works and do not know whether there are any results.

Process and Outputs   "Our agency sees 200 eligible clients yearly in the 20 parent education programs we offer with our 2 licensed staff members who are funded by your grant." This is probably the most typical answer, with detailed documentation of programs or services provided and resources expended.

A potential problem: Simply providing services does not mean that those services are effective. Services may be misdirected, thus not addressing the real problem. They may be wellplanned but not strong or wellfunded enough to make a difference. They may have unintended side effects. Hopeful but undocumented expectations underlie many community programs.

Results-Based Accountability   Using program evaluation, agency staff and evaluators can show that a specific program achieved its intended effects. They can also modify it to become even more effective. Potential problems: Often, agency staff members are not trained to do evaluation. Also, what happens if the evaluation shows that the program does not have its intended results? Will the program be given a chance to improve and the resources it needs to do so?

Program evaluation and desire for improvement   You can see a number of these themes in the responses of the DARE directorship to the negative evaluation results. The 1998 report from the National Institute of Justice states that, "DARE proponents challenge the results of the scientific DARE evaluations. Officials of DARE America are often quoted as saying that the strong public support for the program is a better indicator of its utility than scientific studies" (Sherman et al., 1998). Rather than using the evaluation results to strengthen the program, DARE proponents initially rejected the validity of the results.

But that is not the end of the DARE story. Even with the disappointing evaluation results, there were good reasons not to just eliminate the DARE program. DARE has something other programs do not have: extremely successful national and international prevention support and delivery systems. Remember our discussion of these systems as part of the Interactive Systems Framework for Dissemination and Implementation in Chapter 10? DARE has shown for decades that police officers can be successfully trained to provide the program as designed (officers receive a minimum of 80 hours of training) and that schools and police departments working together can implement the program with high fidelity to the intended audience (Merrill et al., 2006). As you might recall from Chapter 10, effective, large-scale prevention support and delivery systems are something that many evidence-based programs have not been able to develop, and the fact that DARE has managed to develop them is an important finding.

In addition, the full DARE program includes curricula developed for elementary through high school students. The elementary school curriculum is the one most often evaluated, but prevention scientists agree that a comprehensive, developmentally appropriate approach is recommended. Finally, remember our discussion of efficacy vs. effectiveness studies in Chapter 9? Efficacy studies are generally conducted under controlled conditions while the program is still under development and are designed to test whether the program is capable of producing positive results. Effectiveness studies are done in a variety of settings, often with much less control, and are designed to test whether the program can produce positive results under real-life conditions. Many programs that have been successful in efficacy studies have failed to replicate those results in effectiveness studies. Because of the unique circumstances around its development, DARE essentially never had any efficacy studies and basically went straight to the harder standard of effectiveness.

DARE officials did begin to acknowledge that there were problems with their program, and they began making modifications and developing new programs. Even these new programs often resulted in disappointing results (Sloboda et al., 2009). More recently, DARE has adopted a new evidence-based middle school curriculum developed by researchers at Penn State University and Arizona State University. The program, called keepin' it REAL, has been included in the SAMSHA National Registry of Evidence-Based Programs and Practices (http://www.nrepp.samhsa.gov/ViewIntervention.aspx?id=133). At the time of this writing, DARE is just beginning its use of this new program. It will be very interesting to see what happens when an evidence-based program is combined with DARE's proven program support and delivery systems.

The DARE story illustrates some important themes in this chapter: 1) Evaluations about the effectiveness of a program can lead to program improvement efforts, and 2) whether programs work and for whom should influence data-informed decision making in communities (e.g., while early substance abuse prevention education is a good idea, follow-up booster approaches in high-risk years should also be considered). In sum, program evaluation and program development need to be linked so data can inform decisions. Without that linkage, decisions about community programs are made with much misinformation and wishful thinking about what the actual effects of the program are. If program evaluation and program development are linked, even initially disappointing results might lead to systematic improvements in a program and to data-informed decisions about what strategies to implement with whom.

Program evaluation does not have to be frightening. Results-based accountability requires us to understand program evaluation and how programs can be improved to achieve their goals. When evaluation is done well, it can strengthen a program's quality as well as its ability to resist critics.

THE LOGIC OF PROGRAM EVALUATION

For DARE, as for many community programs, evaluation studies were initially designed to yield a final verdict on the program's effectiveness, not to provide specific information on how to improve it. Such studies often compare an intervention group that received a program with a comparison group that did not. Whether the groups differ significantly or not, such an outcome study does not tell us specifically why the intervention worked (or did not work) or what to do to improve outcomes. Without such information, program staff and community members have little guidance for their decisions about the future of the program.

In program evaluation, we are often concerned with two major points: 1) Did it work? and 2) Why or why not? How can we analyze a program to see whether it is working (outcomes) and why it is working or not working (process)?

There are at least two reasons why programs do not work: **theory failure** and **implementation failure**. Theory failure concerns program theory: the rationale for why a particular intervention is considered appropriate for a particular problem with a specific target population in a particular cultural and social context. Program theory also helps choose appropriate measurements or methods to study the effects of the program. Let us return to the research on DARE described at the beginning of this chapter. In the case of DARE, the program theory is: Presenting students information on the harmful effects of drug use, along with peer pressure refusal skills, will result in less adolescent drug abuse. Implementation failure concerns quality of program implementation. You may have an excellent program theory that has been demonstrated elsewhere to work with your target population, but the implementation in your location may be weak due to a lack of resources, inexperienced personnel, insufficient training, or other reasons (see Chapter 10). See logic of DARE in Table 13.1

Since the 1960s, the field of program evaluation has developed concepts and methods based on the methods of the social sciences to study program theory and implementation. This chapter uses many of these basic program evaluation concepts. However, we focus on approaches that make program evaluation

TABLE 13.1   Logic of DARE

Needs	Activities	Outcomes
▪ Preventing teen drug abuse ▪ Throughout a whole community ▪ Using a collaboration of local police departments and schools	▪ Seventeen weeks of an in-school curriculum ▪ Presenting information on the dangers of drugs ▪ Providing training in peer pressure refusal skills ▪ Soliciting a commitment from students not to use drugs	▪ Very little evidence of decreased drug use among participants ▪ Strong support for program among police departments, school districts, and community members

user-friendly and accessible to a wider audience. (For a more detailed review, see Patton, 2008; Rossi, Lipsey, & Freeman, 2004.)

Professional evaluators are trained to think causally. They recognize that an intervention or prevention activity should be based on using a theory or model of variables that cause the problem (model of the problem) and a program theory of the strategies that would change these variables to produce an improvement (model of the solution) (see Goodman & Wandersman, 1994). These models may be clearly stated by the program's developers or the program may only be based on implicit assumptions. The desired effects are not likely to occur if:

- The underlying assumptions of the program theory are not appropriate for the program's context.
- The program is implemented well yet does not affect the variables specified by program theory.
- The activity or program is not adequately implemented.

For social scientists, this type of thinking becomes so automatic that it is easy to forget it is not universal. Agency staff members often need a "critical friend" to help them identify their underlying assumptions about their program theory, goals, and implementation.

For example, a common community prevention activity is sponsoring a Red Ribbon Awareness Campaign. A local group wants to significantly reduce alcohol, tobacco, and other drug (ATOD) use by getting citizens to display red ribbons. Why would wearing a red ribbon lead to reductions in ATOD use? For example, the logic may be that a red ribbon stimulates awareness of the hazards of alcohol use, which then either reduces one's own consumption of alcohol or at least stimulates a sober friend to drive. Questioning the connections between the display of red ribbons and the ultimate outcome of reduction of drunk driving requires critical thinking about cause and effect. It is important for school and community practitioners to use causal thinking and, as much as possible, to develop a causal model for a community program. That "logic model" can then indicate questions for evaluation of program process and outcome, which will help demonstrate program effectiveness.

The principal purpose of a causal logic model is to show in a simple, understandable way the logical connections between the conditions that contribute to the need for a program in a community, the activities aimed at addressing these conditions, and the outcomes and impacts expected to result from the activities (e.g., http://toolkit.childwelfare.gov/toolkit).

The logic model is a graphic representation of how the program works. Figure 13.1 illustrates a four-step logic model that can be applied to program evaluation. Its top row consists of four circles, representing program conditions, activities, outcomes, and impacts. The circles are linked together with lines that show the expected logical relationships among them based on the program theory. These relationships among circles also show the sequence of intended events that occur as a result of program activities.

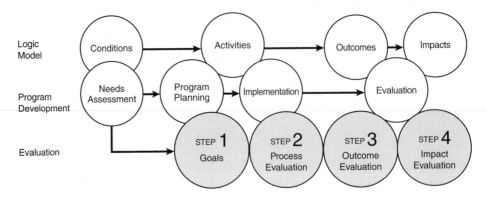

FIGURE 13.1 Causal Logic Model

In the first circle, **conditions** include risk factors or processes, community problems, or organizational difficulties that the program seeks to address. The second circle includes the **activities** that address each condition; one or more activities can aim at solving each of the conditions. The third circle contains the immediate **outcomes** that result from the activity (e.g., changes in knowledge or attitudes of program participants or changes in local laws or organizational policy). The fourth circle concerns the eventual **impacts** of the program on the community at large. For example, impacts in ATOD might include lowering alcohol and other drug abuse in a community as well as related consequences, such as lower crime and better personal health.

In Figure 13.1, the middle row illustrates the steps in program development and their relationships to the logic model. A program developer assesses the need for a program (often with community surveys or interviews), plans a program to address the need, implements the program, and evaluates whether the program has been successful. The bottom row of Figure 13.1 shows how a four-step model of program evaluation relates to the logic model and to program development.

In 1996, the United Way network of community philanthropy organizations began to promote a workbook on outcome measurement, which has revolutionized evaluation among many nonprofit community organizations in the United States. While the United Way model differs in some terminology from our four-step model (detailed in the next section), its essence is similar. The United Way model provides an example of a logic model often used in community practice (United Way, 1996).

A FOUR-STEP MODEL OF PROGRAM EVALUATION

Linney and Wandersman (1991) sought to design materials that would stimulate analytical thinking about the ways in which prevention programs might affect outcomes, realistic thinking about the effect of any one preventive effort, and careful planning for implementation. Their volume, *Prevention Plus III*, was developed to teach people at the local level the basics about evaluation and how to do elementary evaluations of their own programs. The book boils program evaluation down to four basic steps (goals and desired outcomes, process evaluation, outcome evaluation, and impact evaluation) that relate to the logic model (see Figure 13.1, row three).

Step 1: Identify Goals and Desired Outcomes

Starting with goals sets the project's sights. Goals represent what a project is striving for (e.g., children who have positive social relationships and are well-educated so they will be productive members of society). Goals tend to be ambitious and set a framework for outcomes. Outcomes are more specific and represent what the project is accountable for. Goals can be general; outcomes must be specific and measurable (Schorr, 1997).

If a community program has prevention/promotion aims (see Chapter 9 of this book), goals and outcomes concern problems to be prevented or competencies and health outcomes to be promoted. Alternatively, if a community initiative addresses a wider community issue (see Chapter 12), the changes it seeks to create indicate its goals and desired outcomes.

In Step 1, program developers describe the program's:

- **Primary goals**, such as increasing parent involvement in the schools or reducing drug use.

- **Target group(s)**, such as teachers, children of a specific age, parents, or general public. Target groups can be described by demographic characteristics (e.g., age, sex, race, socioeconomic status), developmental transitions (e.g., entering middle school, divorce, bereavement), risk processes (e.g., low grades, multiple conduct incidents in school), locality, or other criteria.

- **Desired outcomes**, such as increases in attitudes rejecting smoking or decreases in school absences. Well-formulated outcomes are clearly defined and specific, realistic and attainable, and measurable.

Table 13.2 illustrates the four-step evaluation method with worksheets adapted from *Prevention Plus III* (Linney & Wandersman, 1991). Step 1 in that table shows the questions that program planners need to ask themselves to specify program goals, target groups, and desired outcomes.

Step 2: Process Evaluation

In Step 2, the activities designed to reach the desired outcome are described. They answer the question "What did the program actually do?"

Purposes of Process Evaluation   Process evaluation has several purposes. First, monitoring program activities helps organize program efforts. It helps ensure that

T A B L E 13.2　　Specific Questions in Four-Step Program Evaluation

Step 1: Identify Goals and Desired Outcomes

A. Make a list of the primary goals of the program.

　　Ask yourself: "What were we trying to accomplish?"

1.

2.

3.

B. What groups did you want to involve?

　　Ask yourself: "Whom were we trying to reach?"

　　For each group, how many persons did you want to involve?

1.

2.

3.

C. What outcomes did you desire?

　　Ask yourself: "As a result of this program, how would we like participants to change? What would they learn? What attitudes, feelings, or behaviors would be different?"

1.

2.

3.

Step 2: Process Evaluation

A. What activities were implemented?

　　Ask yourself: "What did we actually do to implement this program?" Form a chronology of events.

　　Date　　Description of Activity

1.

2.

3.

　　For each activity above, indicate the following:

　　Activity Length (hours)　　Percentage of Activity Time Goal　　Attendance　　Percentage of Attendance Goal

Total duration of all activities (in hours) =

Total attendance at all activities =

Other services delivered:

B. What can you learn from this experience?

　　What topics or activities were planned but not delivered? What happened that these were not accomplished?

　　Activity　　　　　　　　　　　　　　　　　　　　　　Problem

Who was missing that you had hoped to have participate in the program?

What explanations can you give for any discrepancy between the planned and actual participation?

What feedback can be used to improve the program in the future?

Step 3: Outcome Evaluation

Desired Outcome	Measure
1.	1.
2.	2.
3.	3.

Step 4: Impact Evaluation

Desired Outcome	Measure
1.	1.
2.	2.
3.	3.

NOTE: Adapted from Linney and Wandersman (1991, pp. 44–51).

all parts of the program are conducted as planned. It also helps the program use resources where they are needed—for example, not spending most of its money on only one activity or target group. Furthermore, it provides information to help manage the program and modify activities, leading to midcourse corrections that enhance the project's outcomes.

Second, information in a process evaluation provides accountability that the program is conducting the activities it promised to do. This can be provided to administration, funding sources, boards of directors, or other stakeholders.

Third, after a later evaluation of outcomes and impacts, the process evaluation can provide information about why the program worked or did not work. By providing information on what was done and who was reached, program planners can identify reasons for achieving outcomes or not achieving them. Process evaluation information also can provide information for future improvements and for sharing practical tips with others planning similar programs.

Fourth, process evaluation can help you decide whether you are ready to assess the effects of your program. For example, if a program has been in existence for only a short time and you have implemented only the third activity of a seven-activity program, then it is premature to assess program outcomes.

Fifth, conditions sometimes change and what was planned is not what actually happens. Process evaluation helps keep track of such changes. Answering process evaluation questions before, during, and after the planned activities documents what actually happened.

Conducting a Process Evaluation   A process evaluation centers on two related questions: What were the intended and actual activities of the program? After it was implemented, what did program planners and staff members learn from their experiences? (See Table 13.2 Parts A and B, Step 2.)

Regarding activities, process evaluation asks: *Who* was supposed to do *what* with *whom* and *when* was it to be done? (See Table 13.2.)

Who refers to the staff delivering the services. How many staff members? What kinds of qualifications and training do they need?

What refers to what the staff are asked to do (e.g., hold classes, show movies, model behavior).

Whom refers to the target groups for each activity.

When refers to the time and setting of the activity (e.g., during school assemblies, after school).

The more clearly the questions are answered, the more useful the process evaluation will be (see Table 13.2, Step 2, for specific questions). All the information gathered in the process evaluation can be used to improve (or discard) the activity in the future (see Table 13.2, Part B of Step 2).

Step 3: Outcome Evaluation

Outcome evaluation assesses the immediate effects of a program. The "bottom line" of program evaluation concerns these immediate effects (see Table 13.2, Step 3) and ultimate program impacts (Step 4). (Note that the field of program evaluation uses the terms *outcomes* and *impacts* as they are described in this chapter. The field of public health reverses these terms and uses the term *outcomes* to mean long-term indicators and *impacts* to mean short-term indicators.)

Outcome evaluation, as the term is used in program evaluation and community psychology, is concerned with measuring the short-term or immediate effects of a program on its participants or recipients. It attempts to determine the direct effects of the program, such as the degree to which a drug-use prevention program increased knowledge of drugs and the perceived risk of using drugs.

Basically, Step 3 looks at the desired outcomes described in Step 1 and seeks evidence regarding the extent to which those outcomes were achieved (see Table 13.2, Step 3). Evidence of program outcomes for a drug-abuse prevention program could include increased awareness of drug dangers or improved scores on a measure of social skills for resisting pressure to use drugs. Planning how to collect this data or evidence is best begun along with planning program goals and outcomes.

Outcome Measures   These should be closely linked to goals but more specific. There are several potential ways to measure outcomes.

Self-report questionnaires are commonly used to measure outcomes. As you probably know from prior methodology courses, they must be chosen with care, and their reliability and validity should be considered. The test/retest reliability (stability) of a measure is a particular concern if it is to be given before and after an intervention. Construct validity, the extent to which a questionnaire measures what it claims to measure, also is an important concern. Does a particular measure of problem-solving skills actually measure those skills? Predictive validity is also a concern. Does a measure of attitudes about drug use predict actual drug use one year later? Program developers and evaluators need to consider these questions in light of their program theory. What measures of what constructs will best reflect the true outcomes of the program? (A measure of self-esteem useful for adults may not work well for adolescents or for drug-related outcomes.)

Self-report questionnaires are not the only means of collecting outcome data. For some purposes, it is useful to obtain information from other sources about a participant, such as ratings of a child by a parent or ratings of students by teachers. Persons completing questionnaires who are not reporting on themselves are termed **key informants**. In-depth interviews with key informants or participants are excellent sources of qualitative data. *Behavior observation* ratings may be useful, although they are often challenging to collect and analyze.

Step 4: Impact Evaluation

Impact evaluation is concerned with the ultimate effects desired by a program. In alcohol and other drug prevention programs, the ultimate effects might include reduction in overall drug use (prevalence), reduction in rate of new students starting drug use (incidence), decreases in drunk-driving arrests, and decreases in school disciplinary actions for drug or alcohol offenses (see Table 13.2, Step 4).

Outcomes (Step 3) are immediate or short-term results of a program, whereas impacts (Step 4) are longer-term effects of the program.

Archival data, based on records often collected for other purposes, help assess impacts. Examples include medical records, juvenile court or police records, or school grades and attendance records.

Summary Illustration of the Four-Step Evaluation Model

Suppose a coalition in your community implemented a prevention program to reduce adolescents' use of alcohol, tobacco, and other drugs. The four-step *Prevention Plus III* evaluation model would be applied as follows. Table 13.3 presents each step by using adaptations of *Prevention Plus III* forms (Linney & Wanderman, 1991).

Step 1: Identifying Goals This step involves specifying program goals, objectives, and target groups. The overall program goals are to reduce overall drug use and drug-related arrests, accidents, and illnesses among youth (and, eventually, adults). Two specific program objectives are to increase citizen knowledge of drug-related issues and their commitment to action on those issues. Additional objectives are to increase adolescents' skills in resisting pressure from peers and media to use drugs and to decrease local sales of tobacco to minors. Specific target groups include the community, parents of adolescents, students in grades 7 to 9, and local stores that sell tobacco products (see Table 13.3, Step 1).

T A B L E 13.3   Four-Step Program Evaluation Example

Step 1: Identify Goals and Desired Outcomes

A. Make a list of the primary goals of the program.

Ask yourself: "What were we trying to accomplish?"

1. Decrease adolescent use of alcohol, tobacco, and other drugs.

2. Decrease rates of accidents, illness, and other drug-related conditions and drug-related arrests.

B. What groups did you want to involve?

Ask yourself: "Whom were we trying to reach?"

For each group, how many persons did you want to involve?

1. Local citizens (all residents of locality)

2. Parents in training course (20 families in first year)

3. Adolescents in grades 7–9 (500 in first year)

4. Local stores selling tobacco (25 stores)

C. What outcomes did you desire?

Ask yourself: "As a result of this program, how would we like participants to change? What would they learn? What attitudes, feelings or behaviors would be different?"

1. Increase citizen knowledge of drug-related issues and problem.

2. Increase citizen commitment to action on these issues.

3. Increase parent skills in communicating with children about drug use.

4. Increase teens' skills in resisting pressure to use drugs.

5. Decrease local sales of tobacco to minors.

Step 2: Process Evaluation Worksheet

A. What activities were implemented?

Ask yourself: "What did we actually do to implement this program?" Form a chronology of events.

Date	Description of Activity
1.	Public awareness campaign: TV, radio, newspapers (ads, letters, columns, brochures, interviews)
2.	Public meetings: schools, religious congregations, etc.
3.	Curriculum and materials in school health classes
4.	Dramatic skits in schools by student team
5.	Parent communication skills training (six sessions)
6.	Intervention to test and reduce store willingness to sell tobacco to teens (modeled on Biglan et al. [1996])

For each activity above, indicate the following:

Activity Length (hours)	Percentage of Activity Time Goal	Attendance	Percentage of Attendance Goal
1. 46 hours	92%	250	50%
2. 100 hours	80%	400	80%
3. 10 hours	100%	400	80%
4. 12 hours	100%	18	90%
5. 25 hours	25%	25 store visits	25%

Total duration of all activities (in hours) = 293 hours

Total attendance at all activities = 1,068 persons

Other services delivered:

1. One hundred total actions to increase community awareness, involving media campaigns (Activity #1)
2. Guest lectures in community college classes

B. What can you learn from this experience?

What topics or activities were planned but not delivered? What happened that these were not accomplished?

Activity	*Problem*
Tobacco sales testing not completed	Training, logistics took longer than planned
Who was missing that you had hoped to have participate in the program?	Youth, parents from high-risk family and neighborhood environments
	Not enough business, civic, and religious leaders
What explanations can you give for any discrepancy between the planned and actual participation?	Competing news events overshadowed some media campaigns
	Courses, materials for youth need to be more appealing
What feedback can be used to improve the program in the future?	Improve "teen appeal" of course materials. Skits were a hit; use that format more. Identify potential student and community leaders and involve them. Involve youth and parents from high-risk environments in planning.

Step 3: Outcome Evaluation

Desired Outcome	*Measure*
1. Increased citizen knowledge of drug abuse issues	Scores on survey of knowledge
2. Increased citizen commitment to action to prevent drug abuse	Number of volunteers for antidrug activities
3. Increased parent communication skills with teens re: drug abuse	Self-report survey of parent skills before and after training sessions
4. Increased student resistance	Teacher ratings, student questionnaires on student resistance skills before and after training
5. Decreased sales of tobacco	Number of times clerks were willing to sell when teen assessment teams attempted purchases before and after behavioral intervention

Step 4: Impact Evaluation

Desired Impact	*Measure*
1. Decreased drug-related traffic accidents, arrests	Police records: number of drug-related accidents, arrests before and after program
2. Decreased school disciplinary actions related to drug use	School records: number of drug-related disciplinary actions before and after program
3. Decreased incidence of drug-related conditions, accidents	Hospital records: number of drug-related emergency room visits, number of admissions for drug-related conditions before and after program

NOTE: Adapted from Linney and Wandersman (1991).

Step 2: Process Evaluation   The program is to be implemented in several ways. A media campaign and public meetings will be conducted to raise public awareness of drug-related issues. School classes (grades 7–9), including exercises and dramatic skits, and school assemblies will be conducted on drug-related issues, including skills for resisting drug use. A parent training course will focus on communications skills with adolescents. A behavioral intervention for testing stores' willingness to sell tobacco products to minors and reinforcing their refusals to sell will be implemented. To conduct the process evaluation, the following will be recorded: the number of meetings, classes, assemblies, and training workshops planned and actually held, the staff time spent on each, and attendance at each session. The time and persons involved in training student testers and implementation of the behavioral intervention for testing stores would also be recorded (see Table 13.3, Part A of Step 2). After each program component is implemented, the process evaluation will include a discussion of what program staff and planners learned from the experience (see Table 13.3, Part B of Step 2).

Step 3: Outcome Evaluation   Before and after public meetings and in surveys of community members conducted before and after the media campaign, a questionnaire would assess changes in citizens' knowledge of drug abuse issues and the number of volunteers for coalition activities. A questionnaire measuring parenting skills for communicating with adolescents would be given before and after the parent training course to measure changes in these areas among course participants. In the schools, questionnaires completed by students and teachers would measure students' gains in skills for resisting drug use (measured before and after the classroom intervention). Student questionnaires could also be used to measure changes in attitudes and behavior regarding drug use. Finally, behavioral tests of store clerks' willingness or refusal to sell tobacco to minors would be conducted and recorded (see Table 13.3, Step 3).

Step 4: Impact Evaluation   For example, long-term effects of the program could be measured by changes in drug-related school disciplinary actions, police arrest and accident records for youth, and hospital records of drug-related treatment (see Table 13.3, Step 4).

Although the four-step program evaluation method in *Prevention Plus III* was initially developed for evaluation in the alcohol, tobacco, and other drug abuse domain, it is adaptable to any program area, such as community-based mental health prevention programs (McElhaney, 1995).

MENTORING: A PROGRAM EVALUATION PERSPECTIVE

In this section, we further illustrate program evaluation concepts by applying them to mentoring programs. The material for this section was primarily written by Bernadette Sanchez of DePaul University.

The term *mentoring* comes from Greek mythology, where Mentor was a trusted friend of Odysseus and served as a guardian and tutor to Odysseus's son when Odysseus was away (Haskell, 1997). Mentoring relationships generally involve an older, more experienced person (the mentor) and a younger, less experienced person (the mentee). The mentor helps develop the character and competence of the mentee or assists the mentee in reaching goals while also displaying trust, confidence, empathy, and companionship, modeling positive behavior, and serving as an advocate for the mentee (DuBois & Karcher, 2005; Rhodes, 2002; Rhodes & DuBois, 2008; Rhodes, Spencer, Keller, Liang, & Noam, 2006; Spencer, 2006).

Studies show that mentoring was related to adolescents' increased positive social and psychological development (e.g., DuBois & Silverthorn, 2005; Karcher, 2008), school achievement (e.g., DuBois & Silverthorn, 2005; Sanchez, Esparza, & Colon, 2008), career development (e.g., Klaw & Rhodes, 1995), and to less substance use and delinquency (e.g., Zimmerman, Bingenheimer, & Notaro, 2002). However, the evaluations show that the effects of mentoring are actually modest. Two reviews of mentoring programs have supported these findings of positive but modest effects in relation to a wide variety of outcomes, including improved behavioral, health-related, and career outcomes and decreased juvenile delinquency, compared to individuals who were not mentored (Eby et al., 2007; Jolliffe & Farrington, 2007).

Many of these evaluations focus on whether mentoring works. In other words, does mentoring make a difference in the lives of young people? Although these evaluations suggest that mentoring promotes positive youth development, it is important to consider the processes that are taking place in these mentoring programs to understand what contributes to these outcomes.

How Does Mentoring Work?

To understand how mentoring promotes positive youth development, researchers have examined the characteristics of these relationships. Relationship duration, frequency of contact, amount of time spent together, and relationship quality have been shown to be important (Herrera et al., 2007; Jolliffe & Farrington, 2007). Our interpretation of these results is that it is the mentoring relationship (one that is characterized by trust, empathy, mutuality, respect, etc.) that ultimately promotes positive youth outcomes. There is evidence to suggest that youth mentoring leads to greater benefits when it is complemented with other support services (Kuperminc et al., 2005). In fact, Jolliffe and Farrington's (2007) evaluations of mentoring programs targeting youth recidivism showed that mentoring was more successful in reducing reoffending when it was part of a variety of interventions in which youth participated. Complementary interventions included employment programs, educational programs, counseling, and behavioral modification. Next, we describe an evaluation of a mentoring program using the four-step method from *Prevention Plus III* as a guide.

Mentoring: Applying the Four-Step Evaluation Method

GirlPOWER! is an innovative mentoring program for ethnic minority, low-income, young adolescent girls, who are paired with women adult volunteers. This program is part of Big Brothers Big Sisters of Metropolitan Chicago (BBBSMC), and it supplements the one-on-one mentoring relationship model that is typical in BBBS. In GirlPOWER!, girls and their female mentors meet regularly (at least monthly) in a group with several other female mentoring pairs for one year. Mentor-mentee pairs are also expected to meet regularly on their own outside the GirlPOWER! program. (GirlPOWER! is described in more detail in DuBois et al. (2008); the researchers were involved with the development and evaluation of GirlPOWER!)

A number of steps were taken in program development. First, the researchers interviewed various stakeholders, including parents, youth, mentors and staff members, to determine the goals and topics that should be addressed in the mentoring program as well as how the program should be implemented. Second, the researchers reviewed the relevant theoretical, empirical, and intervention literature. Third, a pilot program was implemented based on the previous two steps and then the program was revised based on feedback from participants.

The overarching goal of GirlPOWER! is to facilitate the development of strong and lasting mentoring relationships that empower girls to grow into healthy and successful women. The program has more specific measurable goals in the areas of health promotion (e.g., exercise, nutrition), risk behavior prevention (e.g., substance use, violence), education (e.g., academic success, career exploration), and positive youth development (e.g., self-esteem, problem solving, ethnic identity).

In order to assess the degree to which the program was successfully achieving its goals and desired outcomes, process and outcome evaluation components were conducted. Several different stakeholders in the program were surveyed in an attempt to get their feedback about satisfaction with the current program and suggestions for improvement. These stakeholders included mentors, mentees, parents, and the staff who ran the program. In addition, worksheets were completed to document important program components (e.g., mentor recruitment, training, supervision).

Process evaluation results showed that mentors and youth found Girl-POWER! to be generally fun and helpful. Participants provided feedback on the strengths and areas of improvement. For example, some reported that they enjoyed the structured opportunities for mentors and youth to interact, and they liked that the topics in the GirlPOWER! sessions served as seeds for further discussion in their own time. They also liked spending time with other mentors and youth during the sessions. Participants also provided suggestions for program improvement. They stated that they wanted more time during the GirlPOWER! sessions to engage in activities and explore topics in-depth to allow for spontaneous and creative interactions between mentors and youth. Furthermore, in the beginning of the program, attendance was on average about 50%, so efforts were made by staff members to increase attendance.

An outcome evaluation was conducted by using an experimental design. Twenty mentor-youth pairs were randomly assigned to GirlPOWER! while 20 mentor-youth pairs were randomly assigned to the traditional one-on-one mentoring program provided by BBBS. All mentors and youth were surveyed at the beginning of the program, three months into the program, and at the end of the program. Mentoring relationship quality and a variety of youth developmental outcomes were measured. Comparisons of the two groups showed that, overall, participants in the GirlPOWER! mentoring program had better quality mentoring relationships than their counterparts in the traditional mentoring program. Furthermore, GirlPOWER! youth reported more health knowledge, more parental support, better peer self-esteem, and higher academic aspirations and motivation than their peers. However, there were no differences between the two groups in other outcomes, such as grades, ethnic identity, other self-esteem areas, and aggression. Longer-term impacts (Step 4) were not assessed.

LINKING PROGRAM EVALUATION TO PROGRAM DEVELOPMENT

Some of the outcome results of the GirlPOWER mentoring program were disappointing. This can provide clues for program development and program improvement. Because GirlPOWER! targeted a wide array of youth outcomes, perhaps more concentrated efforts in areas that did not achieve results need to be made in the program. For example, if increasing grades is a goal, then tutoring services might have been necessary to change grades. Another example is that ethnic identity was covered in only one component of a workshop. Perhaps spending more time on this topic would have made a difference in girls' ethnic identity. Furthermore, each monthly workshop was focused on a specific topic (e.g., culture, self-esteem). It might be that effects were not observed in some of the outcomes because the workshop had taken place months before the evaluation of that outcome was conducted. It is possible that the timing of the workshop in relation to the evaluation influenced the findings. (This might be an example of evaluation failure.)

The big picture on evaluation of programs is that the measured outcomes of many treatment, prevention, and educational programs are often disappointing (e.g., the results from DARE). The frequent occurrence of disappointing results has spurred strong movements for accountability and for program improvement in community and social programs. Traditionally, program evaluation has been concerned with whether a program already developed is working and why. However, the traditional program evaluation approach does not study how to develop an effective program in the first place.

Continuous quality improvement (CQI) of programs relies on the use of evaluation data to plan and implement program modifications. Many barriers prevent program planners and staff from using such feedback well. First, programs may use an outside evaluator, a person with no stake in the success or failure of the program (thus, presumably more objective). Such an approach can set up an "us vs.

them" relationship that can limit the quality and usefulness of the evaluation findings. (Recall from Chapter 3 the importance of relationships between researchers and communities studied.) But program practitioners often believe that they do not have the time, resources, or expertise to conduct their own evaluation. Second, program evaluation usually provides feedback at the end of program implementation, without opportunities for midcourse corrections. Therefore, program staff members often view evaluation as an intrusive process that results in a report card of success or failure but no useful information for program improvement. A third, related barrier is the general perception of evaluation research and findings as too complex, theoretical, or not user-friendly.

Program evaluation can and should provide important information about processes and outcomes. This information is important but is much more meaningful if community program staff members and participants understand how and why the program outcomes were or were not produced. If the outcomes were positive, stakeholders can pinpoint some of the processes that led to program success. Conversely, if the outcomes were less than expected, they can identify what needs to be improved.

EMPOWERMENT EVALUATION

In this section, we will describe empowerment evaluation in terms of 1) a definition, 2) principles (values), and 3) a "how-to"—Getting To Outcomes. The four-step model (pp. 435–438) describes some of the basic logic of evaluation and tries to demystify what evaluation is. In this section, we will show how expanding this logic can be helpful to practitioners (e.g., teachers, staff of afterschool programs) for planning and implementing effective programs as well as evaluating programs. An innovative approach to program evaluation, called *empowerment evaluation* (EE), grew out of discussions of "new" and evolving roles for evaluators, designed to encourage the self-determination of program practitioners (e.g., Fetterman, 2001; Fetterman & Wandersman, 2005; Linney & Wandersman, 1991). EE breaks down barriers inherent in traditional evaluation methods and values, promoting an empowerment and citizen participation perspective (Fetterman, 1996).

The definition of **empowerment evaluation** (EE) is:

> An evaluation approach that aims to increase the probability of achieving program success by: (a) providing program stakeholders with tools for assessing the planning, implementation, and self-evaluation of their program, and (b) mainstreaming evaluation as part of the planning and management of the program/organization. (Wandersman et al., 2005, p. 28)

Empowerment evaluators collaborate with community members and program practitioners to determine program goals and implementation strategies, serve as facilitators or coaches, provide technical assistance to teach community members and program staff to do self-evaluation, and stress the importance of using information from the evaluation in ongoing program improvement. In sum, empowerment evaluation helps program developers and staff to achieve their program goals by providing *them* with tools for assessing and improving the planning, implementation, and results of their own programs.

EE Principles

EE shares some values and methods with other approaches to evaluation, including traditional evaluation and EE's close relatives: collaborative evaluation, participatory evaluation, and utilization-focused evaluation. However, it is the set of EE principles (see Table 13.4) considered in their entirety that distinguishes EE from other evaluation approaches. The numbering of the principles does not reflect any type of hierarchy or prioritization of one principle over another. Instead, the principles are to be considered as a set of core beliefs that, as a whole, communicate the underlying values of EE and guide the work

T A B L E 13.4   The Why, What, When, Where, How, and Who of Empowerment Evaluation*

Why was EE developed?
There is a commonly held perception that many program evaluations tend to show few—if any—outcomes. This has led to tremendous dissatisfaction and disappointment with programs and with program evaluation. There are many reasons EE was developed. However, a major motivation for the creation of EE was to offer an alternative approach to program evaluation that is sensitive enough to detect and document program outcomes and that helps programs work better.

What is EE?
EE aims to increase the probability of achieving program success by (a) providing program stakeholders with tools for assessing the planning, implementation, and self-evaluation of their program and (b) mainstreaming evaluation as part of the planning and management of the program/organization.

When is EE appropriate?
EE is well suited as an evaluation approach when the primary goal of the evaluation is to help place evaluation tools in the hands of program participants and staff members to help programs achieve results. EE is particularly appropriate if the stakeholders are interested in having the evaluators involved at the beginning with program planning and implementation. If the primary goal of the evaluation is to examine whether a program worked according to a predetermined theory and without influence from the evaluator, then the hands-off stance of traditional evaluation is more likely to be a suitable approach.

Where is EE used?
EE is used in health and human service programs, nonprofits, education, businesses, foundations, churches and synagogues, and government. It is also used at multiple levels, including program, organization, municipality, state, national, and international levels. The EE approach can be useful in a variety of settings as long as the evaluation needs fit the why and when of EE.

How is EE practiced?
The application of the principles of EE (improvement, community ownership, inclusion, democratic participation, social justice, community knowledge, evidence-based strategies, capacity building, organizational learning, and accountability) guides the practice of EE. Multiple methods—including traditional evaluation methodology, Fetterman's three-step approach (Fetterman, 2001), and the Getting To Outcomes 10-step approach (see below)—can be used to implement the values of the approach. EE is not defined by its methods but by the collaborative manner in which methods are applied according to the EE principles.

Who uses EE?
EE involves key program stakeholders, including funders, practitioners, program staff members, participants, and evaluators. These stakeholders hold each other accountable to an interdependent, results-based approach.

*Adapted from Wandersman and Snell-Johns, 2005.

of empowerment evaluators; these principles are compatible with and overlap with some of the values of community psychology (Chapter 1) and participatory research (Chapter 3). The description of the principles is an abbreviated description excerpted from Wandersman et al. (2005, pp. 29–38).

Principle 1: Improvement   Empowerment evaluators want programs to succeed. Toward that end, EE values improvement in people, programs, organizations, and communities.

Principle 2: Community Ownership   Empowerment evaluators also believe that evaluation is most likely to lead to program improvement when the community is empowered to exercise its legitimate authority to make decisions that direct the evaluation process. In EE, the stakeholders, with the assistance of the empowerment evaluators, conduct the evaluation and put the evaluation findings to use.

Principle 3: Inclusion   Empowerment evaluators believe the evaluation of a program or organization benefits from having stakeholders and staff from a variety of levels involved in planning and decision making. Being inclusive is distinct from how people make their decisions as a group, such as democratic forms of participation (see Principle 4).

Principle 4: Democratic Participation   The definition of EE assumes that stakeholders have the capacity for intelligent judgment and action when supplied with appropriate information and conditions. Democratic participation also (1) underscores the importance of deliberation and authentic collaboration as a critical process for maximizing use of the skills and knowledge that exist in the community and (2) emphasizes that fairness and due process are fundamental parts of the EE process.

Principle 5: Social Justice   Empowerment evaluators believe in and have a working commitment to social justice: a fair, equitable allocation of resources, opportunities, obligations, and bargaining power (Prilleltensky, 1999). EE is well suited for most programs and populations that are interested in improving their performance. Not all programs identify directly with social justice as part of their mission. However, EE advocates believe that almost any program that is designed to help people and communities at any level (individuals, families, neighborhoods) and domain (e.g., education, health, economic) ultimately contributes to the larger goal of social justice.

Principle 6: Community Knowledge   In EE, community-based knowledge and wisdom are also valued and promoted. EE embraces local community knowledge and believes that people typically know their own problems and are in a good position to generate their own solutions.

Principle 7: Evidence-Based Strategies   EE values the role of science and evidence-based strategies and believes that a review of relevant evidence-based or best practice interventions is important to consider early in the process of designing and/or selecting a program to address a community need. Just as EE respects the work of the community and its knowledge base, it also respects the knowledge base of scholars and practitioners who have provided empirical information about what works in particular areas (e.g., prevention, treatment).

Principle 8: Capacity Building   Patton (2008) defines capacity building as individual changes in thinking and behavior and program or organizational changes in procedures and culture that result from the learning that occurs during the evaluation process (p. 90). Empowerment evaluators believe that when stakeholders learn the basic steps and skills involved in conducting program evaluation, they are in a better position to shape and improve their lives and the lives of those who participate in their programs.

Principle 9: Organizational Learning   Improvement is enhanced when there is a process that encourages learning (organizational learning) and an organizational structure that encourages learning (a learning organization). There is a vast amount of information on organizational learning and learning organizations in organization and management literature (e.g., Ang & Joseph, 1996; Argyris & Schon, 1978; Argyris, 1999; Senge, 1990).

Principle 10: Accountability   EE provides an innovative vehicle for helping programs be accountable to themselves and to the public by generating process and outcome-oriented data within an evaluation framework that heightens an organization's sensitivity to its responsibility to the public and to itself (R. Miller, personal communication).

Case Examples of Empowerment Evaluation

Foundation For the Future (FFF)   The FFF empowerment evaluation was described in Keener, Snell-Johns, Livet, and Wandersman (2005). Realizing that the youth they served were exposed to multiple risk factors (e.g., poverty, lack of family support), the Boys & Girls Club of Metro Spartanburg, South Carolina, created a community partnership: the Foundation For the Future (FFF). FFF would provide additional services to families of Boys & Girls Club members while simultaneously increasing the capacity of other existing agencies to reach populations their programs typically did not serve. The FFF partnership was founded on the belief that existing organizations and programs in the community could achieve more working together than they each could operating independently. Those programs include five arts programs, a Junior Achievement program, a Parents as Teachers program for parents of young children, and a Parent University program for parents of Boys & Girls Club members. A major FFF component was an enhanced afterschool program. Although each agency had its own unique set of desired outcomes, the partnership was unified around the overall goal of increasing families' sense of belonging, usefulness, influence, and competence.

The FFF initiative capitalized on evidence-based programs that already existed in the Spartanburg area. The evaluation contract stated that the first objective of the evaluation team was to help establish and maintain an effective self-evaluation system. To fulfill this task, the evaluation team worked closely with FFF member organizations to develop individual evaluation plans and products. However, the major responsibility for the evaluation belonged to FFF (not the evaluators). This is consistent with EE principles of community ownership, inclusion, democratic participation, and capacity building.

A portion of the evaluation findings gives a sense of the FFF approach. One FFF objective was to improve student scores on standardized tests in schools, to be accomplished by afterschool programs at the Boys & Girls Clubs. Those programs included a daily homework completion hour and a program for educational and career development. Local Boys & Girls Clubs committed to having over one-third of their weekly programs in these areas, and staff prepared weekly tracking reports on programs. An outcome evaluation compared 334 program participants in multiple FFF programs, with a group of 836 similar students from the same schools, on a yearly standardized test in schools. In English, math, social studies, and science, FFF participants outperformed the comparison group. The largest program effects were moving students from the lowest-scoring category into the basic proficiency category, although positive effects were seen at multiple levels.

We asked Greg Tolbert, the executive director of the Boys & Girls Club that led the FFF project, to provide an update (2010), which is provided in Box 13.1. His update provides a useful description of the use of evaluation data for accountability and improvement and a description of issues around sustaining a program after the initial grant ends.

Evaluating Empowerment Evaluation   Campbell et al. (2004) conducted an evaluation of the EE approach, studying all state-funded rape prevention and victim services programs in Michigan. The state wanted to build the evaluation capacity of each agency so staff members could evaluate their own programs. The authors were involved in using an empowerment evaluation approach with all the organizations that included training, technical assistance, and manuals. They then studied what happened and found that 90% of the prevention programs and 75% of the victim services programs successfully developed and launched program evaluations and 90% sustained evaluation processes one year after the formal program funding ended. Campbell et al. also measured increases in evaluation capacity and found significant increases over time. The study provides empirical support for a number of key concepts in empowerment evaluation.

Controversies and Dialogues About Empowerment Evaluation   Ever since EE began, lively debates and dialogues have taken place about issues involving EE, including (a) conceptual ambiguity, methodological specificity, and outcomes; (b) empowering others; (c) bias; (d) social agenda; and (e) differences between collaborative, participatory, and empowerment evaluation (Alkin & Christie, 2004; Brown, 1997; Cousins, 2005; Miller & Campbell, 2006; Scriven, 1997, 2005; Sechrest, 1997; Stufflebeam, 1994; Patton, 1997a, 2005). Fetterman and Wandersman (2007) responded to these issues. For example, a number of critiques were concerned that empowerment evaluators might be biased and promote a

B o x 13.1   Community Psychology in Action

A Community-Based Organization Director's Perspective on Empowerment Evaluation
Greg Tolbert
CEO of the Boys & Girls Club of the Upstate, Spartanburg, SC

When the grant funding for FFF ended, we had to rely on other funding for programs. Our education in empowerment evaluation by Dr. Wandersman and his team enabled us to easily write and win a 21st Century Community Learning Centers (21st CCLC) grant from the South Carolina Department of Education (a federal pass-through grant program). The grant sought to fund exactly the kind of afterschool program that FFF had helped us develop—educationally enhanced and enriched by partnerships. While these grants are tailor-made for schools, many of our local school districts have been repeatedly unsuccessful. Since then, we have written and won six 21st CCLC grants, which grew our operations from four to 13 clubs in 10 years. Here are updates on three FFF program initiatives.

ARTS is the great story. Pre-FFF Spartanburg had great arts for such a small town, but with the exception of Colors (an inner-city youth art studio), the arts in Spartanburg were not accessible or welcoming to the poor or minority populations. Post-FFF, the arts partners kept up their end of the deal as best I could have hoped. They kept doing programs and events on their own dime. It became a regular thing for our kids and parents to attend Twitchel Auditorium in their jeans and regular shirts. Our partnerships with the various arts groups have continued through thick and thin. For the past 12 months, as the economy hit them particularly hard, we have been able to funnel excess grant funds and contracted grant funds into enhanced and programmatically focused programs conducted by various groups and buy advanced tickets to many shows, including theater and ballet.

The Parents As Teachers program was owned by the school district. We are on our fourth school superintendent since FFF's inception. That program has limped along with trickling funding, but there was no district dedication to the FFF partnership. Our partnership with the program ended with the grant.

Parent University originated with another charity specializing in parent programming. During FFF grant funding, we took it over due to leadership problems with that partner. We partnered with the Urban League to keep operating the Parent University. However, at the end of the FFF grant, we had to find new partners and new resources to keep it operating. We created Parent Advisory Boards (PAB) at each site and put each club director in charge of their PAB and its annual fundraising campaign. This effort was mainly focused on tapping the tremendous overlooked resource of parents in high-poverty schools and helping sustain our clubs. Our parents contributed $10,000 the first year we tried. Parent fundraising has continually raised $10,000 or more.... Combined with our 21st Century grants, we have provided some form of family literacy programming as part of the initiative over the past five years. The fruit is a stronger partnership between the club and its host school for reaching the parents of students with effective programming and relationship-building events.

The Boys & Girls Club initiatives have been able to sustain and improve upon positive outcomes. For example, on standardized tests in the year 2008–2009, Boys & Girls Club members improved 6.2 points in reading, 5.7 points in math, and 6.8 points in language on the MAP (standardized test). Also, Boys & Girls Club members had 62% fewer school discipline referrals than nonclub members at their school and had 50% fewer absences than nonclub members at their school.

biased outcome evaluation. Fetterman and Wandersman answer this concern by noting that the aim of empowerment evaluation is to help programs achieve outcomes and that the outcomes are the same as those that are measured in a traditional evaluation. Therefore, if the outcomes are objective measures (e.g., standardized tests, number of cases of AIDS in a population), they are assessed the same way in an empowerment evaluation or in a traditional evaluation. The discussions have been illuminating and may be of interest to readers who want to delve deeper into important issues in the field of evaluation (and also to see how controversies among academics are played out).

GETTING TO OUTCOMES

Empowerment evaluation sounds good and is attractive to many funders and practitioners. How can you actually do EE? How can you achieve accountability? Using the empowerment evaluation philosophy, Wandersman, Imm, Chinman, and Kaftarian (1999, 2000) developed a 10-step approach to results-based accountability called Getting To Outcomes® (GTO®). (Getting To Outcomes and GTO are trademarks registered by the University of South Carolina and RAND.) By asking and answering 10 key questions, interventions can be guided to results-based accountability and program improvement.

The 10 GTO Accountability Questions

GTO is a straightforward approach that demystifies evaluation and accountability, and demonstrates to program practitioners the value of evaluation in implementing quality prevention programs. Whether beginning a new program or continuing an existing one, program practitioners can start thinking about program effectiveness and program improvement by answering the 10 GTO accountability questions, which serve as a beginning guide to successfully planning, implementing, and evaluating programs. Each question involves a number of self-assessment steps. The answers to each question lead to the next question—this is a form of what is called *data-informed decision making*. With careful consideration of each question and its answers, an organization should significantly increase the likelihood that it will achieve desired outcomes and demonstrate that it is acting with accountability.

T A B L E 13.5   The 10 Accountability Questions and How to Answer Them

Accountability Questions	Strategies for Answering the Questions
1. What are the needs and resources in your organization/school/community/state?	Needs assessment Resource assessment
2. What are the goals, target population, and desired outcomes (objectives) for your school/ community/state?	Goal setting
3. How does the intervention incorporate knowledge of science and best practices?	Science and best practices literature
4. How does the intervention fit with other programs already being offered?	Collaboration Cultural competence
5. What capacities do you need to put this intervention into place with quality?	Capacity building
6. How will this intervention be carried out?	Planning
7. How will the quality of implementation be assessed?	Process evaluation
8. How well did the intervention work?	Outcome and impact evaluation
9. How will continuous quality improvement strategies be incorporated?	Total quality management Continuous quality improvement
10. If the intervention (or a component) is successful, how will it be sustained?	Sustainability Institutionalization

Table 13.5 presents the 10 GTO questions and strategies for answering them. In the table, these are presented in chronological order for a project that is just beginning its planning stage. However, GTO questions can be used at any stage in the life cycle of a program (e.g., if you have already chosen a program, you can pick ideas that will help you implement it with quality). The questions serve as a useful teaching device to demonstrate to program practitioners and funders the relevance and importance of evaluation and program accountability (Wandersman, Imm, Chinman, & Kaftarian, 2000).

In Table 13.5, questions 2, 6, 7, and 8 contain the four steps of *Prevention Plus III* (discussed earlier in this chapter). What Wandersman et al. realized was that the *Prevention Plus III* approach can help program developers conduct their programs better, but it did not help them ask whether they were doing the right program. Thus, using only *Prevention Plus III* would be like tuning up your car engine and filling your tires so your car runs better and you could drive at 70 mph instead of chugging along at 30: but you might just be going down the wrong road faster. Questions 1 to 5 in the GTO questions help the program staff plan, members choose the right program, while questions 6 to 10 help the program staff implement and improve the program and keep it going.

Question 1: What are the needs and resources in your organization/school/ community/state?   How do you know you need a program? Often, programs are selected because they are popular or have been implemented at other local sites rather than because they have been demonstrated to effectively prevent a specified problem in your setting. For example, Kaskutas, Morgan, and Vaeth (1992) described the experience of a guidance counselor who was working on a project as part of an interagency collaboration; after two months of planning a drug group for the senior high school kids in the project who were nonworking, he discovered that there were no senior high kids in the project who did not have jobs (p. 179)! Therefore, there was no need for the program.

In order to determine which types of programs are needed in a given community, school, or another agency, a planning strategy called a *needs assessment* is often used (Soriano, 1995; Altschuld, 2010). This assessment is designed to gather information about the issues most in need of improvement or intervention in a community or organization (e.g., youth violence, alcohol and drug abuse). A good needs assessment also includes a resource assessment and identification of individual, organizational, and community strengths that can be used to address community needs. Assets may include individual talents, microsystems that can offer social support systems for persons involved in the program, or organizations that can provide funding, a meeting space, or a venue for public discussion of program goals. Resource assessment also provides a counterpoint to needs assessment. The identification of community problems involved in needs assessment is balanced by an assessment of community strengths (Kretzmann & McKnight, 1993).

Question 2: What are the goals, target population, and desired outcomes (objectives) for your organization/school/community/state?   After the needs and resources for a program have been determined, it is essential to specify the goals of the program, the specific target group(s) of the program, and the desired outcomes. (This is Step 1 of the *Prevention Plus III* four-step evaluation method covered earlier in this chapter.)

Question 3: Which evidence-based interventions can be used to reach your goal?   Once program personnel have decided that there is a need to address a specific program and have developed their goals and desired outcomes, how will they achieve them? Strategies will need to be put in place to achieve the goals and desired outcomes. Decisions need to be made on which program or intervention to use. For example, administrators of school and community programs are showered with glossy mailings advertising multimedia curriculum products for such programs as violence prevention, sex education, and substance abuse prevention. How should they decide which program to choose? This decision is frequently based on convenience or availability. Does one rely on the program used last year, regardless of success, or use the program that can be borrowed for free from another source or maybe use the program advertised at the last convention? It is important to keep in mind that although convenience and availability are important, they do not ensure program effectiveness.

A goal of prevention science is to provide two kinds of information. One is empirical findings (usually quantitative) about the effectiveness of programs in attaining identified goals. Another is information (usually qualitative) about best practices, the elements and methods of programs that work best for a particular type of problem within a particular type of population (recall this idea from Chapters 9 and 10). These types of knowledge are useful in answering the question of which program to select. To be effective, programs need to be based on a theory of the target problem and be tied to current and relevant research (Buford & Davis, 1995; Goodman & Wandersman, 1994; Green & Lewis, 1986; Leviton, 1994; Nation et al., 2003; Weiss, 1995). Science and best practices knowledge helps not only in program selection but also in program planning and implementation. Several federal agencies, such as the Center for Substance Abuse Prevention and the U.S. Department of Education, have websites with information about evidence-based programs (see the end of Chapters 9 and 10).

Question 4: How does the intervention fit with other programs already being offered?   Will this program enhance, interfere with, or be unrelated to other programs that are already offered? Will it be part of a comprehensive and coordinated package or just a new program in a long list of programs?

When designing a new program, it is important to be sure that it fits well with the community's needs as well as the available services already in place (Elias, 1995). When a new program is to be implemented in a school or another community setting, a primary consideration should be to make sure that the new intervention will enhance existing efforts. To reduce duplication, practitioners should be familiar with the programs already existing in their school or community. In order to prevent overlap of programs or the implementation of a program that does not fit with overall agency or community goals, a process called *program mapping* can be used.

Program mapping is an assessment of how well a proposed program's goals and methods will fit with the broader goals or motivating philosophy of the sponsoring organization. Programs can fit into an organization in three basic ways: They can have an add-on effect (one program adds to another), a synergistic effect (one program multiplies the effect of another), or an interference effect (one program diminishes another).

Question 5: What capacities do you need to put this intervention into place with quality?   Organizational capacity consists of the resources the organization possesses to direct and sustain the prevention program (Flaspohler et al., 2008). Some model programs may be too difficult or resource-intensive for an organization to deliver. In GTO, organizational capacities to assess include having (a) adequate numbers of staff, with appropriate credentials and experience to implement the program; (b) clearly defined staff roles and strong staff commitment to the program; (c) strong program leadership by leaders who understand the program; (d) adequate funding and technical resources for the program or a plan to get them.

Question 6: How will this intervention be carried out?   What are the steps that program personnel will take to carry it out? During this planning stage, program developers must identify how they will implement the program. Outlining how a program will be implemented includes determining specific steps to carry out the program, identifying and training personnel to carry out each of these steps, and developing a timeline or schedule for this plan. Program staff should specify what will happen during scheduled program activities and where these activities will take place. All these components must be clearly defined in order to plan and implement a program effectively.

Question 7: How will the quality of implementation be assessed?   Was the program actually implemented as planned? Was the entire program delivered? If not, which components were not delivered? What went right, and what went wrong? Evaluating how a program was implemented is called *process evaluation* (Step 2 of the *Prevention Plus III* method discussed earlier).

Question 8: How well did the intervention work?   Did the program have the desired effects and proposed outcomes? Were there any unanticipated consequences? (Evaluating outcomes and impacts comprise Steps 3 and 4 of the *Prevention Plus III* method discussed earlier).

Question 9: How will continuous quality improvement (CQI) strategies be incorporated?   Many programs are repeated. Given that no program is perfect, what can be done to improve the program's effectiveness and efficiency in the future? If the process and outcomes of a program are well-documented, the opportunity to learn from previous implementation efforts is enormous. Keeping track of program components that worked well ensures that such components will be included in the future. Assessing what program components did not work provides the opportunity for improvement.

Lessons about what went well with a program and what areas can use improvement come from such informal sources as personal observations and verbal reports from participants and staff members or such formal sources as participant satisfaction measures and evaluations of the program process and outcomes. However gathered, information for program improvement is obtained from the answers to questions 1 to 8.

Program staff members who are open to learning from the results of evaluation can continuously improve their programs. Instead of seeing evaluation as purely a documentation/report to funders, it should be viewed as a feedback mechanism that can guide future planning and implementation.

Question 10: If the intervention (or a component) is successful, how will the intervention be sustained?   After service providers have gone through the time, energy, and money to develop a successful program, what will they do to see it continued? Unfortunately, this is an often neglected question in prevention programming. Even when programs have successful outcomes, they often are not continued due to a lack of funding, staff turnover, or loss of momentum. Lerner's (1995) review of prevention programs for youth development concluded that there are numerous effective programs to prevent risks and problem behaviors, but unfortunately, these programs were rarely sustained over time.

Goodman and Steckler (1987) defined institutionalization as developing community and organizational supports for health promotion and prevention programs so they remain viable in the long term. They identified factors related to successful institutionalization, such as identifying resources and making program components accessible and user-friendly to host organization staff. Johnson et al. (2004) reviewed the literature on sustainability and developed a model that identified factors related to sustaining programs *and* to sustaining the organization that implements the program (e.g., a coalition).

Optimally, GTO is a never-ending process. Even for an effectively implemented, thoroughly institutionalized program, its staff members start over again with question 1. Figure 13.2 illustrates that GTO is 1) continuous, 2) results-oriented, and 3) amenable tobeing used at any stage of the life cycle of a program (it is like a merry-go-round—you get on at whatever stage you are at).

An Example of GTO in Action: Preventing Underage Drinking

This section is excerpted from "Preventing Underage Drinking Using Getting To Outcomes™ with the SAMHSA Strategic Prevention Framework to Achieve Results" by Pamela Imm, Matthew Chinman, Abraham Wandersman, David Rosenbloom, Sarah Guckenburg, and Roberta Leis (RAND, 2007). Permission granted by RAND for use.

Why is underage drinking a problem? Should we really worry so much about this "rite of passage"? In a word, yes. Alcohol is the primary contributor to

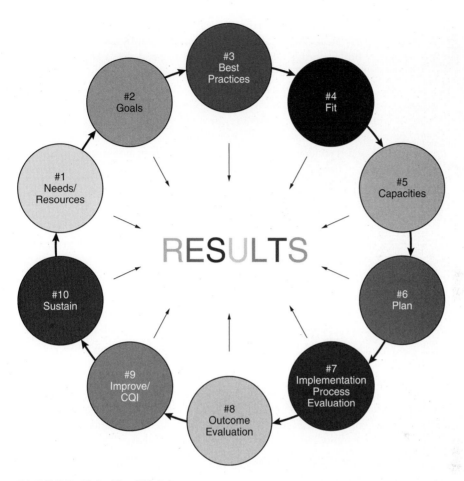

FIGURE 13.2 The GTO Palette

the leading causes of adolescent deaths (NIAAA, 2003). Between 12 percent and 20 percent of all the alcohol consumed in the United States is drunk by people who are legally too young to drink at all and there are real, preventable, negative consequences (Foster et al., 2003). For many people, the heaviest drinking period in their life is before they reach the age of 21. Some youth will emerge in their twenties, reduce their drinking, and be fine. For others, drinking will lead to injury or death, sexual assaults, violence, and diminished life chances. Research shows that over 95 percent of the adults in the United States who are alcohol-dependent started drinking before they were 21 years of age (SAMHSA, 2004).

To demonstrate how communities can use the GTO process in their work, an abbreviated case study of a community that used the 10 GTO accountability questions is presented below. The case study, the South Carolina Alcohol Enforcement Team (AET), began as a result of the following situation.

South Carolina Alcohol Enforcement Team   A female high school student was hosting a party at her house after the Homecoming football game. A deputy came upon her house during a normal patrol and noticed that a large number of cars surrounded the house. The deputy called for back-up and entered the house. Tickets were issued to approximately 40 high school students. Some students managed to escape and hid in the woods or got into vehicles and left. A number of parents were concerned about the way the incident was handled, and it became a point of major public controversy in the community.

As a result of this incident there was a great deal of discussion in the community about the role of police in underage drinking. A small group of concerned parents, school administrators, teachers, law enforcement and community leaders developed an initial working group that evolved into a larger community coalition to combat underage drinking as a community problem. The community coalition utilized the GTO accountability questions in order to plan, implement, and evaluate their comprehensive plan to reduce underage drinking.

Community Mobilization   Following the prom party where law enforcement become involved, the chairperson of the school district convened an initial group of key stakeholders, including members of law enforcement agencies, teachers, guidance counselors, parents, and members of the local alcohol and drug abuse agency (see Chapter 12 for more on coalitions). The group continued to organize by developing a regular meeting schedule, forming subcommittees, and formalizing procedures to become a structured community coalition. This included mechanisms for establishing by-laws, determining membership on subcommittees, conflict resolution procedures, and strategies for communication and coordination. In addition, the coalition recognized that in order to understand the genuine underlying needs and conditions of their school district and surrounding neighborhoods, they needed to begin a formal assessment process.

1) Needs/Resources   One of the first activities of the newly formed coalition was to conduct needs and resources assessments in the school district that included input from youth, merchants, and law enforcement. Members of the local alcohol and drug abuse agency conducted several focus groups of middle and high school youth. One clear result was that alcohol was very easy for the youth to obtain, and they had little fear that law enforcement, their parents, or school administrators would catch them. As a result, law enforcement and local merchants were surveyed to gather some additional information. The results indicated that neither group knew the South Carolina underage drinking laws very well, law enforcement did not believe that enforcing underage drinking laws was really worth their time, and the merchants had little knowledge about how to properly conduct ID checks for alcohol sales. Additional results included the following:

- Approximately 28 percent of minors could buy alcohol in convenience stores in the targeted areas.
- 64 percent of 12- to 18-year-old students said that it would be "very easy" or "fairly easy" to get beer or malt liquor in the targeted areas.

- The majority of youth questioned believed that they would be "very unlikely" to be caught by law enforcement for underage drinking.

Results of surveys from law enforcement and local merchants included the following:

- The majority of officers (N = 23) answered only 20 percent of the questions about laws related to underage drinking correctly.

- Merchant groups (e.g., bartenders, cashiers) reported a need for additional training in proper identification and the legal responsibility for alcohol sales by merchants.

- Most merchants reported that they would attend a free training on alcohol sales, if offered.

One major resource was the community coalition, which was becoming larger and more representative of the population. In addition, the school board and school district personnel (e.g., school nurse, teachers) were interested in considering what actions the school board might take to address related needs. Law enforcement agencies faced issues regarding jurisdiction, interpretation of laws, and uninformed magistrates. Fortunately, the community coalition was able to secure funding through the South Carolina State Incentive Grant (funded by the Center for Substance Abuse Prevention) to begin addressing the needs identified.

2) Goals   The community coalition decided that the goal should be an effort to reduce youth access to alcohol by targeting the attitudes and behavior of law enforcement officials and merchants. To achieve the outcomes in reducing access, there would need to be changes in the behaviors of law enforcement and merchants. For example, merchant knowledge of laws regarding underage drinking would increase by 20% after merchant training, as measured by a pre–post survey.

3) Best Practices   A review of evidence-based literature was conducted and the following research-based findings were used to plan and implement an initiative to address underage alcohol use. Information was obtained from the Pacific Institute of Research and Evaluation and its Underage Drinking Enforcement and Training Center. The following summary reviews evidence-based principles related to underage drinking:

- Environmental strategies targeted at availability, accessibility, and social norms have shown to be the most effective at reducing underage alcohol use

- The most effective strategies create environments in which the opportunities to drink are fewer and the temptations weaker. Some of these include

  - policy-level changes, including consequences for the youth attempting to buy and the merchants selling to youth

  - laws against adults who buy for minors or allow them to drink in their homes

  - enforcement of laws that is consistent and representative of adequate sanctions and punishment

■ settings that promote a strong normative message that excessive drinking is not typical or widely accepted behavior.

A variety of environmental strategies was selected as part of the community's comprehensive plan. Several of the strategies used were:

■ Compliance checks (underage youth attempt to buy alcohol)

■ Party patrols (patrolling of neighborhoods where parties are suspected or have been held in the past)

■ Traffic stops (establishing probable cause for traffic violations)

■ Traffic safety checkpoints (checking for drivers' licenses, open container violations, or other safety violations)

■ Casual contact (making contact with the community—merchants, students, parents, community groups)

■ Merchant education (free of charge until July 2004)

■ Distribution of the merchant messenger quarterly

4) Fit   Prior to finalizing the underage drinking plan primarily designed to reduce underage access to alcohol, the community coalition examined how its potential strategies fit with existing interventions to reduce underage alcohol use among youth. Data from the resource assessment indicated that there were some individually oriented programs for youth (e.g., health classes in school); however, there were no systematic environmental interventions designed to influence behaviors of law enforcement officials and merchants. Because key members of the community (e.g., law enforcement, community coalitions, business, etc.) were involved early in the process, they became strong supporters of the plan to reduce underage drinking (i.e., good key partners fit). This assisted with issues around community readiness and ensuring that the strategies would be pursued in a culturally competent manner. The coalition easily determined that the fit was a good one because the community wanted a solution to the problem (i.e., a good values fit) and the involvement of law enforcement was viewed as advantageous. The coalition also knew that there were some strategies in the underage drinking plan that might be controversial (e.g., sobriety checkpoints) but they decided to move forward with pursuing these activities because law enforcement was such a strong ally.

5) Capacity   The community coalition examined what capacities they possessed to develop a comprehensive plan that would help to reduce youth access to alcohol. Because they knew that the goals were to reduce youth access to alcohol and that law enforcement and merchants would be the primary target populations, they considered their current capacities and what needed to be strengthened.

■ Human: Continued buy-in from school personnel, undercover cooperating informants, merchant educators, project coordinators, and law enforcement coordinators

- Fiscal: Funding was adequate, but continued state and national training opportunities were needed

- Technical: Best practice resources, access to evaluation expertise, law enforcement expertise (including surveillance), and public awareness efforts

- Structural: Continued efforts to gain buy-in from the community and champions in law enforcement who would remain committed to the effort over a long period of time

6) Plan   Compliance Check Component Only—Officers would receive training on how to conduct compliance checks from the Pacific Institute for Research and Evaluation. Prior to beginning any compliance checks, a clear protocol had to be established for what to do when a clerk sold alcohol to a minor. The five-person AET team and volunteer undercover youth planned to conduct approximately 20 compliance checks per month for a ten month time period. The plan was endorsed by the AET liaison, a lead officer who serves as a liaison between the AET team, the sheriff's department, and the ATOD agency. The AET liaison is ultimately responsible for overall operations, including planning, coordination of efforts, and documentation.

7) Implementation Process/Evaluation   A process evaluation was conducted to monitor implementation of the plan. The process evaluation included a schedule of completion, a tool to measure implementation, and the person responsible for carrying out each task. An example of careful monitoring revealed that although the average number of compliance checks for the ten months was at 125 percent (more than anticipated), it is note-worthy that no compliance checks were conducted during two months (December 2003 and April 2004). The holiday season, including vacation time for the AET officers, contributed to the lack of compliance checks in December. In April 2004, issues of financial obligations emerged, so officers could not perform their duties without knowing how they would be paid. These issues were resolved fairly quickly, but they did result in no operations done in April 2004.

8) Outcome   A number of desired outcomes were achieved. For example, rates of underage youth who were able to "buy" liquor in the compliance checks was reduced from 38% before the strategies (steps 3, 4, and 5) were implemented to 10% after one year (a 73% decrease). Clearly youth were less able to purchase alcohol.

9) CQI   The coalition members used the CQI tool (see Table 13.6) to organize all the feedback from the evaluation to facilitate changes. Their completed CQI tool is reprinted below. The feedback included information from law enforcement, merchants, and youth.

10) Sustain   To ensure sustainability, emphasis was placed on obtaining positive outcomes and securing additional funding. Utilizing the Getting To Outcomes method ensured that the staff planned, implemented, and evaluated the initiative in a way that increased the likelihood of achieving positive results for future

TABLE 13.6   CQI

Summary of Main Points from GTO Questions 1–9	How Will This Information Be Used to Improve Implementation Next Time?
Is there a need to increase organization/mobilization of members of the coalition and/or policy panel? Yes, there is a need to gather more support, especially from merchants who need training.	Better marketing plan to target merchants so they enroll in program
Have the needs of the target group/resources in the community changed? No, there is still a need for the underage drinking plan.	No need to change the strategies based on this question
Have the goals/desired outcomes/target population changed? No, the goals, desired outcomes, and target population are still the same.	No need to change the strategies based on this question
Have the capacities to address the identified needs changed? Yes, there is less funding available from the state department of alcohol and drug abuse. One additional law enforcement team would like to replicate the AET in its jurisdiction.	Given the success of the AET, we will apply to local and federal sources for additional funding as well as private foundations.
Are new and improved evidence-based/best practice technologies available? Not at this time.	No need to change the strategies based on this question
Does the underage drinking plan continue to fit with the values of the coalition (philosophically and logistically) and the community? Yes, the plan fits with the values of the coalition and the community.	No need to change the strategies based on this question
How well was the plan implemented? What suggestions are there for improvement? There needs to be a concerted effort to recruit merchants into RBS. The coalition needs to be more active in recruiting merchants for training.	We will examine evidence-based strategies for recruitment of merchants. The coalition will work with the marketing director at the local ATOD commission to determine a plan for recruitment. In addition, the coalition will develop a plan for legislative change to mandate server training when underage sales are successful.
How well was the underage drinking plan implemented? What were the main conclusions from the process evaluation? The law enforcement piece (including compliance checks, sobriety checkpoints, and other activities) went very well. Law enforcement had some complaints about paperwork. The plan to recruit merchants needs to be revised.	Work with law enforcement to determine the most efficient way to deal with paperwork; consider alternative recruitment strategies for merchants.
How well did the strategies reach the outcomes? What were the main conclusions from the outcome evaluation for different types of participants? Youth access to alcohol decreased as measured through compliance checks.	More compliance checks need to be done in rural areas because the rate did not decrease as dramatically as it did in the city. This will require a discussion about the cost of travel because the stores are much more spread out.

funding opportunities. Specifically, LRADAC managed to secure funding for the AET through a state incentive grant. This funding allowed the continued functioning of the AET initiative. The likelihood of continued sustainability of the AET initiative was also increased as a result of several recognitions and awards received by the AET teams. In August 2004, the AET received "exemplary" status for innovative programs at the National Prevention Network Conference in Kansas City, Missouri. This award, presented to only five programs in the nation, is awarded by several national agencies, including the Center for Substance Abuse Prevention, the National Association of State Alcohol and Drug Abuse Directors, and the Community Anti-Drug Coalitions of America. In addition, the AET team was presented with the Law Enforcement Partnership of the Year Award, a national recognition presented by their law enforcement peers. These awards led to increased ownership of and commitment to the AET model, thereby contributing to sustainability efforts. The positive outcomes led to various funding and acknowledgements, including a $100,000 Drug-Free Communities grant awarded by ONDCP and administered by SAMHSA. In addition, various in-kind donations, including space and meeting times from the Lexington police department and the Lexington school district, were obtained. In addition, the state of South Carolina adopted the model and is awarding funds to additional counties to replicate the AET model.

More About GTO

The Getting to Outcomes workbook for substance abuse prevention won the 2008 Outstanding Publication Award from the American Evaluation Association. Chinman et al. (2008) conducted a quasi-experimental study, funded by CDC, comparing programs that received the GTO manuals, technical assistance, and training vs. programs that did not receive GTO on their prevention capacity and program quality over time. Standardized ratings of program quality show that GTO helped the program staff improve in the various prevention activities known to be associated with outcomes more than the comparison programs. As a result of GTO, all the programs either started new ongoing program evaluations where before there were none or significantly improved their current designs. The data collected— although on a small number of programs—suggests that GTO builds capacity of local practitioners and helps to improve the quality of performance in planning, implementation, and evaluation of prevention programs. The programs that used GTO showed greater outcomes. Whether these results were due to a greater ability to evaluate and report outcomes or to actually achieving greater outcomes could not be determined from the data and await future studies.

The GTO approach has been applied to a number of public health domains, including underage drinking prevention (Imm et al., 2007), teen pregnancy and STD prevention (Lesesene et al., 2008), and positive youth development (Fisher et al., 2006). Early work in the areas of mental health and substance abuse treatment are taking place.

CONCLUSION

Chelimsky (1997) described three purposes of evaluation:

- Program development (e.g., information collected to strengthen programs or institutions)

- Accountability (e.g., measurement of results or efficiency)
- Broader knowledge (e.g., increasing understanding about factors underlying public problems)

Traditional evaluation is primarily oriented to the second purpose. The methods explained in this chapter expand the focus to include the first and second purposes and can inform research concerning the third (Wandersman et al., 2004). However, this does not preclude more traditional evaluation approaches (Fetterman, 2001). The value of any evaluation approach depends on the purpose of the evaluation (Chelimsky, 1997; Patton, 1997). Table 13.4 presents a summary of the why, what, when, where, how, and who of empowerment evaluation (Wandersman & Snell-Johns, 2005).

As we have seen in this chapter, program evaluation concepts can be incorporated into program planning and program implementation. When this is done, the boundaries between program development and program evaluation are blurred for the sake of improving the program and increasing the probability of successful results. GTO is an example of this approach. Although the GTO emphasis so far has been on the accountability of practitioners who receive money for prevention (or treatment or education), Wandersman (2003) noted that the accountability questions also apply to funders and to researchers or evaluators. For example, when funders consider developing a new initiative, the questions of how do they know they need a new initiative, how will it use science and best practices, how does it fit with other initiatives, and so on, should be asked and answered. For evaluators, the same questions would concern whether a new or intensified evaluation process is needed or justified, how well it fits with existing evaluation procedures, and how best practices for program evaluation will be used in planning this evaluation.

As societies, funders, and citizens become more concerned about accountability and results for schools, health care, human services, and related areas, evaluation can lead to fear and resistance or to openness, honesty, empowerment, and improvement. Evaluation and accountability need not be feared—if we work together for results.

CHAPTER SUMMARY

1. Program success depends on having a good theory of why something works and implementing it with quality. Logic models link community needs or conditions with activities, outcomes, and impacts. Program development and program evaluation thus have similar components.

2. A four-step program evaluation model (from *Prevention Plus III*) boils program evaluation down to identifying goals and desired outcomes, process evaluation, outcome evaluation, and evaluation of impacts. Tables 13.2 and 13.3 illustrate this approach. Mentoring is described, including the use of the four-step approach.

3. Accountability involves linking *program evaluation* to *program development*. While the four-step evaluation model helps improve an existing program, it does not address what program is needed or whether a program is the best one for the context. Methods of Empowerment Evaluation (EE) and Getting To Outcomes (GTO) were described as ways to help interventions reach results-based accountability, which does address these issues. Table 13.5 summarizes the 10 EE principles. Table 13.6 summarizes the 10 accountability questions of GTO. An example of applying GTO to prevent underage drinking was presented.

RECOMMENDED READINGS

Fetterman, D., & Wandersman, A. (Eds.). (2005). *Empowerment evaluation: Principles in practice*. New York: Guilford.

Rossi, P. H., Lipsey, M., & Freeman, H. E. (2004). *Evaluation: A systematic approach* (7th ed.). Thousand Oaks, CA: Sage.

Imm, P., Chinman, M., Wandersman, A., Rosenbloom, D., Guckenburg, S., & Leis, R. (2007). *Preventing underage drinking: Using Getting to Outcomes with the SAMHSA strategic prevention framework to achieve results*. RAND, TR-403-SAMHSA. Santa Monica, CA: RAND Corporation. Full manual: http://www.rand.org/pubs/technical_reports/TR403 (available for free).

RECOMMENDED WEBSITES

American Evaluation Association:
http://www.eval.org.

Listings and links for a variety of program evaluations resources and networks.

Community Tool Box:
http://ctb.ku.edu.

The Community Toolbox website, mentioned in previous chapters, includes excellent sections on program planning and evaluation—suitable for citizen groups and others.

Evaluation Exchange:
http://www.hfrp.org/evaluation/the-evaluation-exchange/.

Online evaluation journal

Getting To Outcomes 2004 workbook (Chinman, Imm, & Wandersman, 2004):
http://www.rand.org/pubs/technical_reports/TR101.html.

Step-by-step instructions for each of the GTO accountability questions. Free for downloading.

14

Looking Ahead

HIRB/Index Stock/PhotoLibrary

In the first chapter, we presented how community psychology represents an alternative paradigm for understanding and addressing social problems. In each of the subsequent chapters, we considered how community psychology perspectives can lead to defining social problems in ways that examine relationships between ecological levels of analysis rather than only looking for individuals' deficits or individual explanations for social problems (e.g., people who are homeless have an addiction or are lazy). Furthermore, by defining problems differently, community psychology considers a wider array of possible interventions—not only seeking to address problems but considering ways to prevent them and to promote well-being. These changes in perspective encourage community stakeholders to look for resources within their communities and possibilities for collaborative action to address problems. We have emphasized the pragmatism of community psychology by considering problems across levels of analysis, involving local stakeholders, and appreciating the potential resources of human diversity in addressing social problems. Even though engaging a number of stakeholders can be challenging, it is more likely to lead to a comprehensive solution than social change efforts that overlook or exclude a wide variety of community perspectives. Balancing commitments to empiricism and action, community psychology's approaches to social intervention can lead to a variety of intervention strategies as well an assessment of their effectiveness: community organizing, creating and improving prevention programs, health promotion strategies, changing public policy. These chapters document that there are many ways to do community psychology.

For this final chapter, we consider the future of community psychology. We start by discussing some emerging directions and challenges for community psychology research and action. Next, we consider opportunities for using community psychology perspectives as an engaged citizen and in human service careers. For those of you who are interested, we describe opportunities for training in community psychology that can prepare you for social change careers. We present a few examples of recent successful interventions that demonstrate the promise of community psychology. We conclude by inviting you to consider different ways that you might use your insights from studying community psychology to promote well-being in your communities.

EMERGING TRENDS IN COMMUNITY PSYCHOLOGY

Commentators on contemporary life often remark on the tremendous changes taking place in many communities. Some of these include the changing demographics all around the world, the increasing globalization in workplaces and markets, and the necessity of learning new technologies to navigate daily life. These transformations present challenges and opportunities for community psychology in promoting individual and community well-being. Above all, they call for an increased use of community psychology paradigms and skills to understand how communities are changing.

An Emerging Science of Community

Wandersman (2003) proposed the term *community science* for an interdisciplinary field that would bridge gaps between empirical research and development of programs and policy and everyday practice in communities. While his focus was primarily on prevention and promotion, much of his definition of community science also fits efforts for broader policy advocacy and social change. A special issue of the *American Journal of Community Psychology* (Wandersman, Kloos, Linney, & Shinn, 2005) provided specific examples of methods and issues involved in community science.

Articulating a community science approach was necessary to address the shortcomings of the prevention science research and development approach advocated by the Institute of Medicine (IOM) (Mrazek & Haggerty, 1994). In the IOM approach, research identifies a disorder or behavior problem and its associated risk and protective factors. Preventive interventions are developed to address the risk and protective factors and refined through research. The most promising are tested in intervention and effectiveness trials with experimental designs, ultimately including large-scale replications in multiple sites. Finally, experts promote generalization and implementation of the effective programs in many communities in forms as close as possible to the proven intervention.

There are some critical differences between this approach and the approaches of many community psychologists. Decades of experience in efforts for change in localities and community settings have shown the wisdom of being highly sensitive to community and cultural context (especially community strengths), of collaborative and participatory approaches that involve citizen control and commitment, and of developing or adapting interventions for the local context and local organizational capacity to implement a program (e.g., Miller & Shinn, 2005; Wandersman & Florin, 2003). The effectiveness of a prevention program (or a social policy) developed in a few selected communities will not necessarily generalize everywhere. This perspective is the basis of Chapters 10 and 13 in this book. Wandersman (2003, p. 229) argued that prevention science is useful but not sufficient for meeting these challenges. A new field—community science—is needed.

Community science as defined by Wandersman (pp. 236-237) incorporates many concepts we have discussed in this book. It involves:

- Clear core values that help guide goals for change and processes of working in communities

- Understanding historical, cultural, community, and other contexts and incorporating this awareness in research and action

- A participatory approach that enables citizens to be active shapers of community programs and policies and that builds the community's capacity for initiating and sustaining its own processes of innovation and change

- Recognizing multiple ecological levels of analysis and targeting multiple social and community systems for change

- Empirical, contextual research involving multiple methods of inquiry, practical as well statistical significance, and longer timelines for longitudinal and community research

- Interdisciplinary collaboration to address community issues at multiple levels

- Using knowledge for community change, including local self-evaluation for continuous improvement over time

While Wandersman was thinking at a collective level for the field, Biglan and Smolkowski (2002) proposed a role description for community psychologists at the local level, involving elements of collaboration, citizen participation, and empirical research. It represents what could become a local base for community science. In their conception, a local community psychologist or human service worker would facilitate strategic planning and implementing of programs and policies by local citizens for promoting community well-being. This would include four general tasks.

Monitoring local community well-being involves collecting information from surveys, archival information sources, and other local resources on behavioral and community problems (e.g., health, drug abuse, juvenile crime, personal and family problems). A community psychologist would also need skills in effectively presenting these findings to large, diverse citizen audiences.

Facilitating planning includes helping to organize community coalitions to address local issues and fostering a planning process in which citizens identify specific goals and strategies for community change. As we discussed in Chapter 12, coalitions need to truly represent community diversity. As part of this process, the community psychologist would also provide research findings from the previously mentioned monitoring activities.

For a problem or goal that citizens have chosen, the community psychologist also would *articulate what works*: identifying community interventions and policies that have been empirically demonstrated to be effective elsewhere. This would not assume that any empirically supported intervention would automatically succeed in the local context, but such support does indicate its potential value there.

Through *consultation, training*, and *evaluation*, community psychologists would assist communities and organizations in implementing and evaluating programs and policies. This will require attention to the process of intervention and to the capacity of the community to sustain it. An interesting application of these ideas can be found in school-community partnerships to promote social change. Helm and Flaspohler (2008) organized a discussion of articles focused on bridging the gap between research and practice in promoting social change in schools. These efforts include community-university partnerships to articulate new research questions and explore new partnerships and resources for programming. This resembles the approaches to implementation in Chapter 10 and evaluation in Chapter 13 of this book.

Biglan and Smolkowski's approach describes one local role for community psychologists. However, this is only one of many possible roles for community psychologists to promote community and social change at multiple ecological levels. For example, advocacy for social justice involves skills and roles that go beyond the Biglan and Smolkowski list (e.g., Nelson & Prilleltensky, 2010; Tseng et al., 2002). However, the diversity of approaches in community psychology share a value for grounding action in empirical research. Thus, they all embody the role proposed at the Swampscott conference: the participant-conceptualizer.

Growing Awareness of the Global Diversity of Communities

There is growing awareness of the diversity of community psychology across the world. Over half of the members of community psychology professional organizations now live outside the United States. Given community psychology's emphasis on understanding the ecology of settings (remember Chapter 5), it is not too surprising that different regions will emphasize different aspects of community psychology (e.g., social justice, social intervention, or research). As was discussed in Chapter 2, the development of community psychology in each country has its own unique story. Some community psychologies are aligned with providing alternatives to mental health systems, while others are focused on social conditions and social action. This is also not surprising. We have found that different regions have different demands, different social conditions, and different resources to address them. Reviews of international community psychology suggest a diversity of approaches and intervention traditions that are tailored for the local ecologies of a region's communities. Interestingly, there appears to be substantial overlap in core values of these community psychologies across countries as well as a variety of emphases in community psychology research and action that are suited for local conditions (Reich et al., 2007). The development of community psychology around the world can be seen in the regular community psychology conferences that occur in Australia/New Zealand, Europe, Japan, and Latin America. There are community psychology textbooks and journals developed specifically for these different regions: Italian, Japanese, Portuguese, Latin American Spanish, European Spanish, and different English media for Australia, British Isles, Canada, New Zealand, and the United States.

Within the United States and Canada, there is also growing awareness of the diversity of community psychology in different regions. In the last 10 years, the Society for Community Research and Action (SCRA)—the professional organization for community psychologists in the United States and many from Canada—has created new working groups based on awareness of the diversity of interests among community psychologists, including the SCRA Task Force on Disaster, Community Readiness, and Recovery; Environmental Justice; Lesbian, Gay, Bisexual, and Transgender Interest Group; Indigenous Interest Group; and Organization Studies. The proportion of the SCRA members who identify themselves as ethnic minorities (23%) has been steadily growing and is now more than four times the proportion of such members in the American Psychological Association (Toro, 2005). The focus of community psychology practitioners and researchers varies greatly by their location. Although the majority of community psychologists have focused on urban areas, there is awareness of the value of community psychology approaches to addressing problems of rural areas; more than 25% of the U.S. population lives in rural areas (Heflinger & Christens, 2006; Mulder, Jackson, & Jarvis, 2010). Rural community psychology interventions focus on barriers to participation in services, such as access to resources, less developed service systems, higher costs, and lack of transportation (Mulder et al., 1999). Development of Internet resources has potential for overcoming some of these barriers (Ybarra & Eaton, 2005).

Demands of work settings influence the focus of community psychologists' work. Many community psychologists work in clinical, health-, or medical-related settings. Some specialize in organizational work, such as schools. Many focus on collaborating with coalitions and consulting with community groups.

Community psychology journals increasingly contain culturally anchored research and interventions (Langhout & Thomas, 2010). We have highlighted a number of these throughout this book. These trends in published work and in membership are examples of a growing trend in the field, in which community psychology is (belatedly) recognizing how its values and perspective lead to including the voices of diverse persons in the field. Ten years after the founding of community psychology in the United States, the students and teachers were still primarily male and primarily White (Moore, 1977; Gridley et al., 2010). However, entering the second decade of the 21st century, many more women and persons of color have held leadership positions in professional organizations and in training programs. Like much of social change, it has been the participation of persons of color and women that have been instrumental in making these changes happen. Greater inclusion of diverse perspectives has had transformative effects on how community psychologists conduct research, collaborate with community members, design interventions, and conceptualize their work. Greater representation of the diversity of experiences and perspectives in community psychology is a work in progress in which day-to-day practices and published works must continue to develop toward our ideals (Martin, Lounsbury, & Davidson, 2004).

In addition to the increasing diversity of community psychology around the world, community psychology will be confronting the challenge of addressing social change in an increasingly "globalized" world. Marsella (1998) proposed developing initiatives for a "global-community psychology" to study the links between economic and political forces of globalization, the development and destruction of diverse cultures and local communities, and how these are related to the psychological functioning of families and individuals. In particular, he was concerned about the tension between two opposing viewpoints: "globalization from above and indigenization from below" (Marsella, 1998). Within his framework, **globalization** refers to the centralizing effects of market capitalism, advertising, mass media, and values of individualism and economic output. **Indigenization** refers to consciousness of traditional collective values and community bonds of indigenous ethnic cultures and local communities (see also Friedman, 2000; Stiglitz, 2003). Of course, there exists a diversity of local peoples, with a diversity of responses to the different aspects of globalization. But the interface of globalizing markets and traditional cultures does influence individual and community life across the world. Indigenous resistance to globalization is increasing as local communities seek to conserve their identities and values. It is not yet clear what roles community psychology might play in helping individuals and communities address the tensions between indigenization and globalization.

Most contemporary globalization proponents have emphasized economic advantages of interdependent markets but have not developed many initiatives consistent with community psychology values, such as social justice, well-being, empowerment, and prevention (Reich et al., 2007). There is a need for community psychology's perspectives to recognize and promote the diversity of world cultures, to seek to understand them on their own terms, and to accept that Western psychological principles are only one form of psychology among many. Increased connectivity between distant parts of the world creates opportunities for community psychology to engage in dialogues and action that support social change. However, that poses several challenges for the field: increased understanding of the experiences of diverse peoples, even more participatory approaches to research, learning from community psychologists outside the United States, and careful consideration of how to apply core community psychology values in action.

As we observed in Chapter 7, attending to the values of diversity and community can require the need for new approaches to intervention and collaboration. Townley and colleagues (2011) have argued that a *community-diversity dialectic* forms a creative tension for the field that will be critical for its development in the next decade. Both concepts are needed to understand human communities, but each may require different levels of attention in different settings. For community psychology, it is important to foster genuine understanding and respect for the many forms of human diversity and to conduct careful research to deepen that understanding. There is much to learn. At the same time, it is also important to articulate widely shared human ideals and to articulate the particular ideals of our field so that in conversations with diverse persons and communities, we can understand both ourselves and others.

Broadening Concern with Social Justice

In community psychology, many trends are coalescing to bring increased energy to advocacy for social justice, liberation, and social transformation. As we discussed in Chapter 2, community psychology has long had a concern with addressing conditions that were perceived as unjust or unfair (e.g., Ryan, 1971). However, the field is building more sophisticated understandings of how social justice theory can inform its interventions. For example, social justice has been particularly important in choices of *with whom* prevention and health promotion interventions are conducted; these have emphasized a *distributive justice* concerned with access to resources and how community psychology interventions might be used to connect people with resources (Rappaport, 1977; Fondacaro & Weinberg, 2002). Empowerment initiatives emphasize understandings of procedural justice focusing on how interventions are carried out and participation by persons who have often been left on the margins of society (Rappaport, 1981; Fondacaro & Weinberg, 2002). Social justice concerns have begun to be incorporated into evaluative criteria of scientific work by critical community psychologists (e.g., Prilleltensky & Nelson, 1997; Nelson & Prilleltensky, 2010). From this perspective, the merit of science and intervention needs to reflect on assumptions about power and legitimacy of knowledge and action within the work. Critical community psychologists encourage the field to examine these power assumptions in light of social justice values (e.g., distributive justice and procedural justice) rather than assuming that scientific discoveries are absolute truths that do not have implications for social justice.

The example of social psychologist and Jesuit priest Ignacio Martin-Baro's work in El Salvador has been influential in broadening social justice concerns of community psychology across the world. Martin-Baro worked to promote mental health and well-being by confronting oppression before he was murdered in 1989 on account of his social activism. Martin-Baro persuasively argued that an emphasis on a social justice perspective reminds us to identify oppressive conditions and work toward creating access to resources (material, social, and personal) for all citizens. Understanding many forms of human diversity and many communities requires understanding issues of social justice—both historical and current (Prilleltensky, 2008). Moreover, it requires an understanding of macrosystems—even global forces.

The variety of social justice informed interventions that can be created have been documented in community psychology articles and conferences. For example, at the 2005 SCRA conference, Lykes (2005) gave a keynote address about her 20 years of involvement in liberatory action research with local communities in Guatemala, South Africa, Northern Ireland, and the United States. Community psychology researchers and practitioners have applied these concepts to address issues of poverty and homelessness (Israel & Toro, 2003). These included increasing awareness in psychology courses of the psychological effects of economic inequalities, working with homeless parents to empower them to speak out for their children's interests with schools, and creating ways for businesses and community groups to provide resources for homeless children. Similarly, Degirmencioglu (2003) described efforts to promote better Greek-Turkish youth relations and to improve the lives of street children in Turkey. In a special section of *The Community Psychologist* (http://www.scra27.org/resources/scrapublic/tcp), Bothne and Olson (2006) organized a special section to feature how human rights perspectives were being used by community psychologists to clarify ethical decisions for research and action about women's issues, social services, integration of child soldiers in countries with prolonged armed conflicts, and psychologists involved interrogation.

The involvement of psychologists in interrogation is an important example of the need for psychologists, including community psychologists, to be critical of their own profession. In June 2005, the board of the American Psychological Association (APA) authorized the participation of psychologists in the interrogation of detainees held in military prisons and other sites outside the United States. This authorization was extremely disturbing given that many organizations, such as the International Red Cross, were condemning the interrogation techniques used at those sites as cruel and inhuman punishment and, in the case of techniques such as waterboarding, as torture. In response to the APA's actions, a group of psychologists, including community psychologist Brad Olson, formed the Coalition for an Ethical Psychology and Psychologists for an Ethical APA in 2006. Thanks to the sustained, strenuous efforts of these groups and with the support of many other psychologists, the APA has adopted a series of resolutions detailing increasingly clear and specific ethical standards to limit the role of psychologists in interrogations at these sites.

Of course, an emphasis on social justice in community psychology is not new. Many community psychologists dedicate themselves to working toward social justice through their community science. In fact, the efforts of community psychologists were selected as the most outstanding examples of psychology in the public interest for the entire American Psychological Association for the three years prior to the writing of this book. Here are excerpts of their nominations for this award.

Gary W. Harper won the 2007 Award for Distinguished Early Career Contributions to Psychology in the Public Interest for

... leadership and commitment to applying psychological principles and
social justice values to the development of innovative community health
promotion programs. Gary W. Harper has dedicated his career to the
prevention of HIV among gay/bisexual youths, young women, and
homeless youths in the United States, as well as among youths in Kenya.
His action research involves active community collaboration and
provides an excellent framework for ensuring that the social problem
solving work of psychologists is grounded in the needs and concerns
of communities. The great impacts of his work are reflected in the
respect he has earned among community activists and academics alike.
(Harper, 2007, p. 803)

Rebecca Campbell won the 2008 Award for Distinguished Early Career
Contributions to Psychology in the Public Interest for her work that

... has made substantial theoretical, empirical, and practical contributions
in the area of violence against women. Her goal is to understand the
real-life experiences of victimized women and uncover solutions to the
problems they face. She examines innovative, socioculturally sensitive,
coordinated multisystemic approaches to serving women who have been
victimized. Her research—which includes a cohesive combination of
multivariate statistical approaches and qualitative inquiry—is significantly
improving the quality and effectiveness of the nation's community
services for women. (Campbell, 2008, pp. 699–700)

Keith Humphreys won the 2009 Award for Distinguished Early Career
Contributions to Psychology in the Public Interest for

... his work as a program evaluator and policy analyst has informed
important legislation that has enhanced access to and quality of mental
health services for U.S. veterans within the Department of Veterans
Affairs. Moreover, he has been a prime mover in shaping the Iraqi
Ministry of Health's effort to create a modern and equitable system of
mental health care for the Iraqi community. (Humphreys, 2009, p. 710)

A broadening focus on social justice has led to the organization of several
initiatives to advance social justice within community psychology and related disciplines. Conway, Evans, and Prilleltensky (2003) created Psychologists Acting
with Conscience Together (Psy-ACT), a network of psychologists advocating
for social justice, initially through local efforts such as letters to newspaper editors
to raise awareness of poverty issues. Sloan, Anderson, and Fabick (2003) reported
on Psychologists for Social Responsibility, which since 1982 has involved psychologists in promoting social justice. Two of their current projects concern
public education about group conflicts and developing approaches to helping
victims of trauma due to political violence. These are only some illustrations of
how community psychologists can enact concerns for social justice. Participatory
research, policy research, and empowerment evaluation provide additional examples of how community research can be concerned with social justice (see Chapters 3, 12, and 13).

Collaborative, Participatory Research, and Action

One of the most distinctive contributions of community psychology to the social sciences is our development of concepts and practical strategies for culturally anchored, truly collaborative action research that promotes genuine citizen participation in making decisions. Throughout this book, especially in Chapters 3, 11, and 13, we have highlighted examples of collaborative, participatory work (see also Jason et al., 2004). Not all participatory-collaborative approaches are the same. Even within community psychology and closely related fields, such approaches as community coalitions, empowerment evaluation, participatory action research, and various approaches to culturally anchored research are based on differing values and worldviews (Trickett & Espino, 2004). This diversity of ideals and practices provides many rich resources and options for promoting community collaboration and participation. It also provides the basis for many future conversations about their differences, strengths, and limitations as applied in real-life community contexts. Because communities are diverse, it also is likely that different conceptions of collaboration and citizen participation will be useful in different communities.

Like recent development of more sophisticated frameworks for advancing social justice in community psychology, more detailed frameworks are beginning to be articulated for collaborative approaches to research and action. For example, Schensul and Trickett (2009) pushed the field to consider how collaborative action can be conceptualized across levels of analysis. Research can help identify the conditions under which different types of intervention may have greater effects and be more sustainable. Furthermore, they propose that intervention activities be coordinated across levels of analysis to facilitate empowerment of collaborative partners. Models for collaboration and participatory action research are being re-examined and adapted to fit the contexts of the projects. The application of collaborative and participatory methods with different populations will require adaptation and evaluation of methodological assumptions. Langhout and Thomas (2010) devoted a special issue of the *American Journal of Community Psychology* to the examination of how frameworks for participatory action research and collaboration need to be adapted to work with children. They suggest that several assumptions need to be re-examined to facilitate participatory action research with children: children's capabilities and likely expansion of expectations for children as social actors; the kinds of research deemed "appropriate" to do with children if an understanding of their capabilities is expanded; and the epistemological frameworks used for learning about children's lives. Finally, limitations of participatory and collaborative methods will likely vary by context and need to be explicitly examined. For children, limitations will likely be encountered when considering the realities of the social structures in which they live, the time needed to build collaborative relationships, and the deeply embedded power and ethical issues that can converge when children are viewed as social actors in domains outside traditional children's settings (e.g., public policy deliberations).

The importance and usefulness of participatory approaches has now been reflected in many fields (e.g., public health, anthropology, social work). Increasingly, it is expected that community members have active roles in research and intervention efforts in their communities. There is still a need for wider acceptance of the concept that community members have a central role to play throughout the action research cycle—from program conceptualization through implementation and evaluation—but progress has been made. In addition, there is growing awareness across disciplines that programs must be adapted to local contexts and that "cookbook" implementation of model programs is not an effective approach.

The Promise of Community Psychology Practice

The action arm of community psychology has been part of the field in the United States since its founding (Chavis, 1993), but roles for community psychology practitioners have not always been prominent in presentations of community psychology. However, over the past few years, community psychology practitioners have helped raise community psychology practice to a new level of emphasis. In 2007, community psychology practitioners organized a Community Psychology Practice Summit to devote a day of a conference to examining how community psychology practice could be better specified and promoted. Like other formative conferences in the field (e.g., Swampscott in 1965 and Austin in 1975), this summit included discussion of the role of graduate training to advance the field (Meissen, Hazel, Berkowitz, & Wolff, 2008). However, this summit also included explicit consideration of how awareness of the skills and knowledge base of community psychologists can be more widely distributed. Unlike some fields (e.g., public health, nursing), there are relatively few settings that are dedicated explicitly for community psychologists. The wide-ranging skills of community psychologists and the alternative perspectives that the field advocates can be applied in a wide variety of settings.

The Community Psychology Practice Summit fostered much discussion about community practice and the development of practice skills. It should be noted that a robust dialogue about community psychology practice had begun before the Practice Summit in *The Community Psychologist*. Julian (2006) initiated recent discussion about definitions of community psychology practice. Scott (2007) expanded the discussion with a proposal for specific community psychology competency skills, which was followed by Hazel's (2007) articulation of frameworks for greater focus on practice skills in community psychology education. It is also noteworthy that these articles were used to engage other community psychologists in dialogues and written commentaries. In other words, community psychology practitioners organized and built coalitions to bring increasing attention to community practice.

These efforts have resulted in the creation of a Practice Council within the Society for Community Research. As stated on the SCRA website, "[t]he Practice Council's purpose is to promote the role of practice in all aspects of SCRA and Community Psychology. Our primary goal is to produce concrete benefits for communities and community groups ..." (http://www.scra27.org/practice). This marks the first time that the formal SCRA organizational structure has explicitly designated a component to promote community psychology practice. The council has also placed an emphasis on better developing a knowledge base of community psychology intervention skills. A collaboration between the SCRA Practice Council and the SCRA Council for Education Programs has resulted in an ongoing dialogue about community practice in graduate training in the quarterly publication of SCRA: *The Community Psychologist*. Discussions at the 2007 Practice Summit also contributed to the creation of an electronic journal dedicated to community practice. The *Global Journal of Community Psychology Practice* provides articles of community interventions, case studies, and video links of practitioners discussing their work.

The prominence of community psychology practice also has caught the attention of publishers. *The Power of Collaborative Solutions: Six Principles and Effective Tools for Building Healthy Communities* (Wolff, 2010) draws on Tom Wolff's 30-year career in community practice to provide examples of successful collaboration and coalition building. Consistent with community psychology values, the book is written to be accessible to citizens who may be interested in learning about the field. Finally, the Practice Council provides mentoring and training opportunities for students interested in community practice careers rather than a primary emphasis on research. At the time of the publication of this book, the council is launching initiatives to educate employers about the wide range of contributions that community psychologists can make to organizations (see Box 14.1). Through these efforts, community psychology practitioners are creating resources for students interested in developing a community psychology practice career. There appears to be many opportunities for entrepreneurial students to create careers in community psychology practice.

PROMOTING COMMUNITY AND SOCIAL CHANGE

This book has provided an introduction into the rationale and methods of community change. We take the position that these topics are relevant for citizen participation in our communities and professional careers in human services as well as careers as community psychologists.

Opportunities for Citizens

We see great promise in citizens using community psychology ideas to address the concerns of their communities. Based in our North American contexts, democratic forms of government are designed to balance power among diverse, competing interests, with systems of checks and balances often divided among branches and levels of government. For this to work effectively, citizens need to be informed about issues and have avenues for addressing them. When such avenues are unavailable, there is a tradition in the United States of creating new settings to address

B o x 14.1   **Introducing Community Psychology**

Al Ratcliffe Ph.D. (alratcliffe@gmail.com)
Bill Neigher Ph.D. (william.neigher@atlantichealth.org)
For the Community Psychology Practice Council

Community psychology is a distinctive approach to understanding and solving community, organizational, and societal problems. While others are also concerned with community welfare, what makes community psychologists distinctive is that we apply well-established psychological principles and techniques—tested and proven in practice—to improve well-being and effectiveness at individual, organizational, and community levels. We do so with an explicit concern for social justice, inclusiveness and participation, the value of diversity, collaboration, and a focus on strengths.

What Do Community Psychologists Do?
Community psychologists work collaboratively with others to help strengthen systems, provide cost-effective services, increase access to resources, and optimize quality for individuals, private and governmental organizations, corporations, and community groups. Community psychologists build on existing strengths of people, organizations, and communities to create sustainable change.

Community psychologists work as consultants, educators, grant writers, professors, human service managers, program directors, policy developers, service coordinators, evaluators, planners, trainers, team leaders, and researchers in all sectors, including government, for profit, and nonprofit organizations.

In addition to a solid grounding in the science of psychology, most community psychologists can:

- **Locate, evaluate, and apply information** from diverse information sources to new situations.
- **Incorporate psychological, ecological, and systems-level understanding** into community development processes.
- **Contribute to organizational decision making** as part of a collaborative effort.
- **Evaluate programs/services:** Develop evaluation designs and collect, analyze, report, and interpret evaluation data.

- **Plan and conduct community-based applied research.**
- **Translate policy** into community and organizational plans and programs with observable outcomes.
- **Provide leadership, supervisory, and mentoring skills** by organizing, directing, and managing services offered.
- **Communicate effectively** in technical and lay language with diverse stakeholder groups.
- **Build and maintain collaborations** with a network of clients, communities, organizations, and other involved professions. Negotiate and mediate between different stakeholder groups around a particular issue.
- **Demonstrate and teach** cultural competence and other key relationship skills to a wide range of constituencies.
- **Develop social marketing and other media-based campaigns.**

Where Do Community Psychologists Work or Consult? (Examples)

Academic settings	Foundations
Health and human service agencies Education systems	Community development, architectural, planning, and environmental organizations
Corporations and for-profit and nonprofit organizations Government systems— legislative and executive branches	Research centers, independent consulting groups, evaluation firms
Community-based organizations, advocacy groups, religious institutions, and neighborhood groups	Public policy and community planning and development organizations

concerns and work toward action (e.g., the U.S. Revolutionary War, U.S. civil rights and women's liberation movements). Conceptualizing citizen action across levels of analysis, there are roles at neighborhood, local, and higher levels of government. As a citizen, you can help redefine problems, push for evidence of effectiveness of intervention strategies, and demand a place at the table in deciding how problems are addressed. Recall the examples of the schoolchildren in Wisconsin described in Chapter 11 who changed local policy and the neighbors in Camden, New Jersey, related in Chapter 12 who changed how community development money was distributed.

While a decentralized democratic structure has many strengths, a challenge is that it makes it difficult to muster sufficient agreement that a social problem exists, much less on how to respond. To gain wide attention, a social issue (e.g., homelessness, drug abuse, poverty, or racism) often must assume crisis proportions. Community psychology seeks to address these challenges as opportunities so citizens and decision-makers consider long-term solutions rather than quick fixes. However, examples in this book suggest that we be prepared for the difficulties in sustaining long-term changes, especially within short political election cycles (Heller, 1984; Marris & Rein, 1973; Riger, 1993; Schorr, 1997). Citizen action on community issues requires a balance of acting when opportunities arise, being creative and persistent when encountering resistance, and having a long-term commitment to action.

The history of social and community change illustrates the value of two seemingly contradictory ideas about time in relation to intervention: **seizing the day** and **taking the long view**. Early in the history of community psychology, Kelly (1970b) articulated the importance of both for citizens and community psychologists.

For citizens, **seizing the day** means applying community psychology concepts and action skills to today's social and community problems. That usually involves taking advantage of opportunities for learning: community events, processes, and resources (Kelly, 1970b). It can also often involve building partnerships with persons that you do not know but who have common experiences and purposes. It means speaking out and acting as a group of citizens and communities whenever possible.

Taking a long view also involves recognizing the ongoing, dynamic nature of social and community change (Tseng et al., 2002). In a world of instant messaging and 24-hour news cycles, it is easy to conclude that nothing can be done about complex social or community problems that do not change quickly. However, this view misses a fundamental reality: Social change occurs all around us every day. Don Klein, a founder of community psychology in the United States, mused in a 1995 interview that when he began his career in the 1950s, it was inconceivable that smoking would someday be widely considered a health problem and banned in many public places. But that is today's reality (Klein, 1995). In the 1950s and 1960s, African American college students took practical steps to resist segregation and (soon learning to work with others in their communities) conducted sit-ins, voter registration, and other actions of the civil rights movement—doing so against violent opposition and seemingly insurmountable odds (Lewis, 1998). Their highest aims have yet to be realized, but substantial changes took place. Women's movements are transforming societies around the world. Berkowitz (1987) interviewed 22 community activists who had played leadership roles in sustained community and social changes. Some were famous and their initiatives well known; many were not, but their contributions were valuable nonetheless—even if only at a local level.

These and other examples illustrate that social change, while not easy, is pervasive (Ackerman & DuVall, 2000; Loeb, 2004). Recall the discussion in Chapter 12 of the social change that PICO congregation members are doing all around the United States.

Prospects for Community Psychologists

For community psychologists, *seizing the day* means finding settings and partners where they can apply their perspectives, knowledge of research, and skills to today's social and community problems. This may involve building relationships for collaboration or becoming directly involved as a participant. Community psychology encourages its practitioners to be involved and engaged in community life (Kelly, 1970b, 1979b): participating in community organizations, addressing local issues, attending community events, and helping to develop or organize local resources. It also often involves calling attention to the views and experiences of those who are powerless and ignored, through research and advocacy (Price, 1989; Rappaport, 1981). Seizing the day means speaking out and taking action alongside citizens and organizations, with views grounded in empirical research whenever possible.

Taking a long view means understanding historical swings of perspective and power, which influence how social and community issues are addressed (Levine & Levine, 1992). It also means learning the histories of communities and attempts to address the social concern; those histories influence the issues of the day (Tseng et al., 2002). Moreover, taking a long view on social change involves sustained commitment and involvement—perhaps for years—attending carefully to the process (e.g., personal-emotional relationships and power dynamics) of that work (Elias, 1994; Kelly, 1970b, 1990; Primavera & Brodsky, 2004). Taking the long view can mean devising, implementing, evaluating, and refining community interventions that can offer sound, scientific evidence of effectiveness in addressing clearly defined objectives. By doing that, we can provide empirically supported approaches that are not only tailored to local context but are also more likely to weather the changes of social, political, and economic climates (Heller, 1984, p. 47) than interventions that have popular appeal but little efficacy. Finally, it means articulating core values in ways that sustain persons and communities through setbacks and challenges (Tseng et al., 2002; Kelly, 2010). In these ways, community psychologists can continue to pursue community and social transformation despite changes in the current social context.

Another dimension of time concerns the need for community psychology to listen to its youth—including students—and its seniors—including those whose involvement stretches back to its emergence as a distinct field (Olson, 2004). Youthful community psychologists bring passion and a sense of immediacy to the field. Their concerns are often not based on the traditions (and limitations) of the field. This is a strength; it promotes questioning assumptions, enables fresh perspectives and innovative practices to emerge, and helps to focus on the issues of the day. At the same time, seasoned community psychologists—if they are willing to listen and share their views in collaborative ways—can offer the wisdom of personal experience and growth over time. Nuances and lessons to learn can be difficult to understand at first, but awareness of them emerges in the rough and tumble of community action—sometimes through dealing with misunderstandings, opponents, painful experiences, and failures (Sarason, 2003a). In understanding the complexities of community and social life, all community psychologists are students. Both the visions of youth and the wisdom of experience are too valuable to overlook.

In this book, we have presented many examples of roles for community psychologists, which involve the core values of the field. It is important to note that a community psychologist cannot play every role and cannot focus in equal depth on every value. Some may primarily pursue individual/family wellness and sense of community. Others might primarily pursue social justice, empowerment, and citizen participation. Some may focus on building the empirical knowledge base for action, while others involve themselves in community or wider social action itself. Through collaborations with other community psychologists, human service professionals, and citizens, more complete implementation of community psychology values and interventions can be realized.

As the variety of concepts and action approaches in this book indicates, community psychology is a "big tent," bringing together psychologists and others with shared values but also with many ways of acting on those values in communities (Toro, 2005). That variety can be a strength. Its contradictions foster discussions that deepen understanding. Another useful metaphor for community psychology is a conversation in which multiple views are articulated, considered, modified through consideration of other views, and developed over time. Perhaps the field comprises a conversation in a big tent, with diverse participants and views and illustrating Rappaport's Rule: "When everyone agrees with you, worry" (Jozefowicz-Simbeni, Israel, Braciszewski, & Hobden, 2005; Olson, 2003, 2004; Toro, 2005).

Qualities for a Community Psychologist

Soon after the outset of the field of community psychology, James Kelly (1971) described seven desirable personal qualities for community psychologists. These qualities remain an insightful, useful summary for today's community psychologists (Rudkin, 2003). They address many themes of the field and of this book.

A Clearly Identified Competence   The community psychologist must demonstrate skills useful to a community—whether as a participatory researcher, program evaluator, policy analyst, advocate, grant writer, clinical helper, consultant, workshop leader, or other role. This competence must also be taught in some way to community members, sharing it as a resource, not simply being an expert.

Creating an Eco-Identity   This involves immersing oneself in a community, identifying with it, and caring about it (Kelly, 2006). This emotional engagement with a community supports enduring commitment, deeper understanding, and respecting its members' choices.

Tolerance for Diversity   This actually goes well beyond passive tolerance to understanding and embracing diversity. It involves relating to people who may be very different from oneself and understanding how those differences are resources for the community even when they involve conflict. It also involves understanding differences among community members and looking for ways to use those resources.

Coping Effectively with Varied Resources   All community members are or have resources, but these may not be visible in community life. It becomes essential to identify hidden skills, knowledge, and other resources and to draw on them while working together. This often involves stepping out of the professional-expert role to collaborate with citizens as true partners, respecting their skills and insights.

A Commitment to Risk Taking   This involves being an advocate for a real cause or person, seeking positive community change. This will often involve taking sides with a marginal, unpopular, low-status person or group against more powerful interests. It may involve risking failure, advocating a course of action before knowing if it will succeed. This risk taking is not impulsive but is a careful expression of one's values for the community.

A Metabolic Balance of Patience and Zeal   To remain engaged in a community, one needs to feel passionate about the values and goals of one's work but also be patient with the time required for community change. Knowing when to speak out and when to be silent is an art to be learned, as is finding ways to sustain oneself through successes and failures.

One element for this is supportive relationships with people who promote learning about the community and taking risks in one's work. That may be a network of personal relationships or a community setting or group.

A second element is awareness of emotions involved in community work. Videos of interviews with early community psychologists in the United States reveal emotions not visible in journal articles or books (Kelly, 2003). These included anger that propelled advocacy, pride and sense of personal connection with a community setting, glee when injustice was confronted, the excitement of finding like-minded allies, the ability to laugh about the ironies of community work, and a mixture of pride and loss when a community was ready to pursue its own future, saying goodbye to the psychologist. Emotions can express values, energize commitment, and strengthen community solidarity. Community psychology can be passionate.

Giving Away the Byline   The goals are to strengthen community resources, work with community partners, and accomplish positive community change. Seeking or basking in personal recognition interferes with the long-term pursuit of those goals. It is important to celebrate successes but share the credit.

Training in Community Psychology

After taking this course, some of you may be interested in specializing in community psychology. Of course, you do not need an advanced degree in community psychology to be involved in efforts to improve your community. Graduate training in community psychology can provide focused experiences in how you assess problems and resources, choose or develop interventions, and evaluate evidence about the need for and the effectiveness of social interventions. For many professional positions in human services, policy, or government or academic positions, an advanced degree is required. Similarly, an advanced degree is expected for those involved in research careers. To test your interest in a research career, it is possible to work as a research assistant as a student or after you have graduated with a B.A. In fact, working in a research lab and supervised community interventions are good ways to get experience for your graduate school applications.

Several universities across the United States and Canada offer graduate training. A listing of community psychology training programs is periodically updated at the SCRA website (http://www.scra27.org/resources/educationc/academicpr). Master's programs typically take two years to complete for full-time students, although evening part-time courses are often available for those completing a degree while working a full-time job. Ph.D. programs typically take five to six years to complete and place more emphasis on research. Psy.D. programs also take about five years to complete but have more of an emphasis on community psychology practice. In most programs, there is a combination of coursework, practica, and community placements to develop your skills. There is much diversity in community psychology training programs. It is important to find a good match for your interests. There are master and doctoral programs that emphasize training in clinical-community, interdisciplinary approaches to community intervention, and community psychology focused programs. In addition, training programs may specialize in addressing the concerns of particular populations (e.g., children, families, ethnic minorities, or persons with disabilities) or particular concerns (e.g., substance abuse, prevention of health problems, or working with community coalitions). For doctoral study, the match between your interests and those of an advisor is particularly important. If you are considering graduate study of any type, we encourage you to talk with your professors to learn how you can better prepare for your applications.

SIGNS FOR HOPE AND EXAMPLES OF CHANGE

To close, we will describe four hopeful, empirically grounded examples of tangible change in communities. These examples are directly linked to the efforts of citizens and community psychologists. There are certainly many other success stories in community psychology—some of which we have highlighted in prior chapters. Three examples here concern education, which is one of the multiple social systems where community psychologists work. But they illustrate some of the overarching themes and values of community psychology. The last example shows the potential of the field to work together to bring community psychology perspectives to addressing community responses to natural disasters. Each example illustrates many of Kelly's skills in their own efforts to seize the day while taking a long view of their relationships and their work.

Social-Emotional Literacy/Character Education

Exciting changes are happening in the United States in social-emotional learning (SEL) and character education (CE), which we discussed in Chapters 9 and 10. In response to strong empirical evidence that these programs affect positive outcomes for children and growing concern with addressing prosocial values and social responsibility as part of K–12 education, support for SEL and CE programs is growing at the district, state, and federal levels and also internationally. Research and action by community psychologists are ensuring that initiatives not only spread to increasing numbers of schools but also involve long-term commitments to developing, implementing, and sustaining effective prevention and promotion practices.

While establishing a firm empirical grounding for SEL and CE, community psychologists have also devoted attention to investigating and supporting effective program implementation, ensuring that students and teachers reap the full benefits of high-quality programming. Maurice Elias has been instrumental in establishing the New Jersey Center for Character Education (NJCCE), an action-research and technical assistance center for the schools of New Jersey as they implement SEL and CE. A major concern of the NJCCE is how to help schools coordinate different, well-established programs, such as a K–5 curriculum, a middle school curriculum, and modules for high school courses. The school districts involved represent a range of sizes, locations, and socioeconomic profiles of students, and the goal is creating approaches applicable in diverse contexts.

Roger Weissberg leads the Collaborative for Academic, Social, and Emotional Learning (CASEL, www.CASEL.org), a Chicago-based not-for-profit organization committed to the advancement of SEL science, practice, and policy. CASEL has synthesized research on SEL to create documents and materials that guide practitioners in selecting, planning, implementing, and sustaining evidence-based programs. In the past several years, CASEL has trained and supported hundreds of schools in effective implementation of school-wide SEL programming. CASEL also brings together experts in psychology, education, and prevention science to investigate such issues as assessment, dissemination, and public policy—all with the goal of ensuring that all children have the opportunity to benefit from advances in SEL. Moving forward, CASEL is working to support a nationwide initiative in SEL, with a growing focus on federal and state education policy and collaboration with districts on system-wide SEL implementation.

Recall the excitement with which Amy Mart described seeing how her efforts to promote SEL were making a difference in community settings (Chapter 10, Box 10.1). Many municipalities and individual schools are including SEL and CE as part of their local educational goals and policies, including large school districts that have made this work a district-wide priority. Noteworthy among large school districts that are planning or have made significant progress in effective implementation of SEL and CE are Louisville, Anchorage, and Cleveland. A number of states, including New Jersey, Illinois, Ohio, Iowa, Rhode Island, New York, and Georgia, have adopted and implemented state-level policies, mandates, and/or guidelines for educators with regard to carrying out SEL and CE in schools. In addition, many states are promoting or requiring service learning as an educational experience with similar goals. CASEL is currently studying state standards and policies throughout the United States, with the goal of improving structural support for SEL and related initiatives. Coordination of SEL, CE, service learning, positive youth development, and other prevention and promotion programming is an important area for future development.

At the federal level, the Academic, Social, and Emotional Learning Act (H.R. 4223) was introduced with bipartisan support in the U.S. House of Representatives in December 2009. This legislation would allocate resources for training, technical assistance, and evaluation of evidence-based SEL programming in schools across the country. The bill has received support from Democrats and Republicans who are working to include it in the reauthorization of the Elementary and Secondary Education Act (ESEA).

Interest in SEL and CE has also grown in countries across the world. Since 2006, the Ministry of Education in Singapore has been engaged in a nationwide implementation of SEL, adopting standards for SEL education and integrating SEL principles into teacher preparation programs. The Department of Education and Skills in the United Kingdom has adopted a variety of programs to address the "social and emotional aspects of learning." Approaches to education that address social, emotional, and character development have also become prominent in Latin America, Finland, Sweden, the Netherlands, Spain, Israel, Australia, and many other countries.

Empowerment Evaluation in Schools

As noted in Chapter 10, the U.S. No Child Left Behind Act of 2001 was a centerpiece of President George W. Bush's efforts to improve K–12 education. It was "designed to change the culture of America's schools by closing the achievement gap." Schools whose students test below national standards must first provide supplemental services such as tutoring, and if this does not raise scores, they must "make dramatic changes in the way the school is run" (U.S. Department of Education, n.d.). Those "dramatic changes" can include firing principals and teachers or diverting public school funds into private schools. Clearly, the act's intent to improve student performance is noteworthy, but the reliance on standardized tests and punitive remedies has created many problems (Sadker & Zittleman, 2004). Moreover, as implemented under federal and state standards, schools face penalties but often receive little or no additional funding to address these problems. In a prosperous locality, local funding can be used for this purpose, but in a low-income area, money is simply not present. These were some of the challenges facing two rural and impoverished school districts in the

Arkansas Delta, which had been classified as "academic distressed" by the state (Fetterman, 2005).

David Fetterman, a pioneer of the empowerment evaluation approach described in Chapter 13, was asked to apply empowerment evaluation in these districts. Arkansas law defines "academic distress" as having over 40% of students scoring at or below the 25th percentile on the Arkansas state assessment of grade-level student achievement (a standardized test mandated by the state). One district had been in academic distress for over six years, beginning under Arkansas requirements that predated the federal No Child Left Behind law. By law, the state has the right to take over schools in "academic distress" status and to replace the entire staff (Fetterman, 2005).

Firing all the principals and teachers was not an appropriate or a realistic option. First, as is true in many rural and inner-city areas, the schools were the largest local employer. Second, these remote, impoverished communities found it difficult to recruit credentialed teachers. Evaluators and state and local school officials therefore worked collaboratively to strengthen the existing capacity of the local schools to improve student learning, raise test scores, and exit the "distressed" status. As reported by the evaluators:

> An initial needs assessment documented that there was potential for improvement. The aim was to build individual, program, and school district capacity in order to construct a firm foundation for future improvements. Everyone was focused on improvement in critical areas (which they identified as a group). Specifically, we focused on improving test scores, discipline, parental involvement, and administrative support and follow-through. School district teachers, administrators, staff members, and community members documented their improvement or progress using the taking stock (baseline) data and comparing the baseline data with a second data point (a post-test following the intervention of improved teaching and discipline). (Fetterman, 2005, pp. 107, 109)

The schools made tangible improvements in each of these areas, including raising student test scores. Arkansas state education officials considered the empowerment evaluation, with its focus on building local capacity and documenting processes and outcomes, to be instrumental in producing these improvements (Fetterman, 2005). For example, at the beginning of the intervention in fall 2001, 59% of students in one school district scored below the 25th percentile on standardized tests. By the end of the empowerment evaluation intervention in spring 2003, only 38.5% of students scored below the 25th percentile. This 20% improvement was very significant in practical terms and removed the schools from the "distressed" list. Similar results were obtained in another school district (Fetterman, 2005, p.116). As of 2010, the schools remain out of academic distress and in some areas have appreciably improved (Fetterman, personal communication, August 2010). The success of these efforts was publically recognized by the Arkansas State Board of Education and aired on a state educational news program. Empowerment evaluation was applied to additional schools in academic distress as a result of these successful demonstrations. In both districts, efforts are continuing to further improve student learning. Empowerment evaluation addressed a pressing issue for these schools and communities but also helped develop a process for continuous improvement of learning over the long term.

Moreover, the leaders of tobacco prevention initiatives in the state adopted an empowerment evaluation approach based on these school-based results (Fetterman & Wandersman, 2007, p. 192). Empowerment evaluation's capacity to effectively enhance evaluation skills and produce outcomes in schools and tobacco prevention was also recognized by the Arkansas State Legislature. Based on the results in education and tobacco prevention, Rep. Stephanie Flowers and Sen. Henry Wilkins drafted a bill that passed the House and Senate to create the Arkansas Evaluation Center (State of Arkansas, S.B. 951, 2007). The center is guided by empowerment evaluation and designed to build evaluation capacity and improve program performance. The center has already provided training in evaluation, formal academic programs for evaluation students, and workshops participants from across the United States. These initiatives have also helped form the Arkansas Group of Evaluations, chaired by Linda Delaney, which is dedicated to facilitate capacity building in the field of evaluation and networking to support the work of evaluators.

Meyerhoff Scholars

While individual African Americans have attained visible success in U.S. life, the overall proportion of African Americans in some professions remains low. This is especially true in the natural sciences, technology, engineering, and mathematics (STEM) fields. At the University of Maryland at Baltimore County, a predominantly European American university, the Meyerhoff Scholars program successfully prepares a largely African American student group for graduate study and careers in STEM fields. It reflects a strengths-based approach: Instead of focusing on deficits to be remedied, it identifies strengths to be built upon and enhanced. These include personal talents, family and community resources, and university settings that promote learning and achievement. Community psychologists Ken Maton and Anne Brodsky have been involved in evaluating and refining the Meyerhoff program (Maton & Hrabowski, 2004; Maton, Hrabowski, Ozdemir, & Wimms, 2008; Maton & Brodsky, 2011).

Meyerhoff Scholars combines several components that research has shown to be critical to academic success in STEM and other fields: financial aid to allow a focus on studies; high standards for performance in classes; program values that emphasize achievement and support; community building among program members; peer study groups; individualized academic advising and personal support; faculty involvement outside the classroom; mentoring by STEM professionals; summer research internships; family involvement; and community service (Maton & Hrabowski, 2004).

Research on Meyerhoff Scholars has compared the academic careers of its participants to a comparison group of similar students who were offered admission to the program but chose to attend other universities (where they may or may not have had access to resources similar to what Meyerhoff Scholars offers). Since 1989, over 800 scholars have participated in the program. Nearly 30% of Meyerhoff Scholars graduates have enrolled in or graduated from Ph.D. programs in STEM fields—*five times* the rate for the comparison group. Seventy-one percent of Meyerhoff Scholars graduates were enrolled in or graduated from Ph.D., M.D., and master's STEM programs, compared to 56% of the comparison group. Surveys and interviews with graduates indicated the importance of these factors in student achievement: sense of community in the Meyerhoff Scholars program, peer study groups, the involvement of program staff in advising and counseling, faculty accessibility, research and mentoring opportunities, and financial aid. Because the comparison group included similarly talented students, these program elements appear to have been critical factors in the graduates' success (Maton & Hrabowski, 2004; Maton & Brodsky, 2010). African American students participating in the Meyerhoff Scholars program arrived at college with considerable family support. Research on this support showed these particular family strengths: persistent engagement in the child's schooling, child-focused love and support, strict discipline and limit setting, and connectedness with outside community resources, including extended family, religious congregations, and extracurricular activities at school (Maton & Hrabowski, 2004). Interestingly, the executive director of the program, Earnestine Baker, has observed how the program has created a strong sense of community for students and alumni of the program (Baker, n.d.). Before and during college, these resources complemented the support offered in the program. The strengths perspective and multiple resources of Meyerhoff Scholars can be adapted for a diversity of students of many interests and backgrounds. In fact, the success of the program has supported larger, university-wide social transformations to enhance representation, retention, and achievement of minority students (Maton et al., 2008). The Meyerhoff Scholars program was instrumental in promoting discussions that led to an in-depth understanding of the value of the program and its approach for a public university.

Preparing Responses to Disasters

In the United States and around the world, there seems to be an increasing awareness of the challenges posed to individuals and communities after large-scale disasters. Hurricanes, earthquakes, oil spills, toxic waste sites, and war regularly rip the social fabric of many communities, with adverse affects on the health and well-being of community members. Like many citizens, community psychologists have asked themselves what they could do to respond to such overwhelming individual and community needs. After Hurricane Katrina devastated New Orleans and much of the U.S. Gulf Coast, SCRA president Carolyn Swift convened a group of community psychologists to see what the field might offer to addressing the needs of the persons affected. While a few community psychologists have specialized in addressing natural disasters, (e.g., Kilmer & Gil-Rivas, 2010; Norris et al., 2002; Norris, Tracy, & Galea, 2009) or environmental disasters (e.g., Culley & Hughey, 2008), there was a sense that the field as a whole had something more to offer this unique disaster. Fran Norris, Bill Berkowitz, and Brad Olson agreed to lead an initiative that would produce a resource to assist communities responding to natural disasters. They decided to survey experts across community psychology to create a manual that could be used in the long-term recovery efforts of individuals, groups, and communities. They made a strategic decision to focus efforts on the period after major attention leaves the immediate aftermath of disasters or during slowly developing disasters that are particular difficult for communities (Cline et al., 2010).

The SCRA Task Force on Disaster, Community Readiness, and Recovery was formed to produce a community resource manual. This task force drew upon the expertise of 25 community psychologists from 18 U.S. states in this collaboration. Collectively, this group had expertise ranging from community development, mutual help, policy, and dissemination of interventions to trauma responses of children, older adults, and disaster programs. It is interesting to note that only five of these 25 community psychologists were specialists in how individuals or communities responded to disasters. In creating the task force and manual, they have created another model of how community psychologists can collaborate to respond to needs of communities. It is unlikely that many of these community psychologists would have been involved in using their skills on a national level if this unique collaboration was not created. Refer to Box 14.2 for a "Community Psychology in Action" feature about how community psychologists worked together in a unique collaboration to produce this resource.

The manual was created "for any community member (or organization) who has the interest, inclination, and potential for action and leadership" (Olson & Kloos, 2010). The manual shares specific information about "managing different stakeholder interests, particularly when they are in competition with one another, to make your own voice heard, to negotiate and navigate through difficulties, and to marshal the social and tangible resources around you." Task force members used their expertise to gather evidence from research and best practices so community members using the manual could make the best decisions possible in promoting community members strengths and addressing challenges. However, the manual should not be viewed as offering easy solutions to the challenges of disaster response. Rather, it was designed to provide resources that community members can use in best meeting the needs that they identify over the course of recovery efforts. The manual includes sections on the effects of disasters, individual and community responses, and resilience. In providing recommendations that can promote resilience, it offers practical advice on assessing needs, making action plans, reaching out to diverse groups, creating structures to work together, utilizing community-based approaches to intervention, and tracking results. The manual also includes appendices with information about particular interventions (e.g., how to start a self-help group). The SCRA task group views the manual as a living document that will change as it is used. The task group is currently disseminating the manual to disaster response organizations where feedback has been encouraging. They actively solicited feedback from disasters response professionals and citizens. Box 14.2 gives more detail about the creation of

---

B o x 14.2   Community Psychology in Action

The Society for Community Research and Action (SCRA) as a Community:
The Disaster Task Force

Brad Olson
National-Louis University

As community psychologists, we can be so heavily concentrated on outside communities that we forget we are also a community—one that needs cross collaboration and one that must be responsive to real-world problems. Groups can feel most like a cohesive community through large-scale events. This happened to the SCRA after Hurricane Katrina. Following the event, the SCRA listserv received multiple posts asking, "What can we, as community psychologists who are supposed to know something about action, do together?"

Carolyn Swift, a longtime community practitioner, was SCRA's incoming president. She formed a disaster task force. Carolyn asked Fran Norris, a community psychologist and expert on disasters, to be co-chair. I was asked to be the other co-chair. We started by inviting approximately 20 psychologists to join. Most were community psychologists. Many had interests in disasters; others in schools, action research, or evaluation. Most had never worked together, but now, the SCRA Task Force on Disaster, Community Readiness, and Recovery had been formed. The group had rich intellectual resources. How to combine them in such a large group and in a completely pragmatic way was less clear.

We decided to write a manual that in a "giving psychology away" way would present useful principles of community psychology that could be used by anyone in any community. A strong willingness to help one's community was the only requirement. Every task force member participated in a team of two, writing

multiple sections. Fran assigned the teams, and they worked out well. We struggled. All of us did—particularly in trying to put research and theoretical ideas in clear, practical terms. A steering committee on writing and dissemination emerged: Bill Berkowitz, Jessica Goodkind, Ryan Kilmer, and Judah Viola. As a subgroup, we all worked to refine the language into a straightforward voice.

Eventually, we gave a "completed" draft to four independent community members. The four individuals had much firsthand experience on the ground in disasters. Their revisions were extensive, humbling, and transformative. It was a good sign they were so honest and thorough, although they almost felt guilty giving so much feedback. One critique began: "I hope this is helpful and not seen as too critical. I believe you are developing a great tool here, you just have a ways to go before it is very useable...." Another stated: "I hope I am not overstepping the task you assigned me...." We gave close attention to the participatory feedback. It added experiential expertise to our existing informational expertise. The manual is now complete and dissemination has begun, although it will continually be revised as a living document. At this writing, we have received additional positive feedback from Haiti to the Philippines.

As community psychologists, we can work as a "community" toward other challenges. We are optimistic about the manual, but the best way to tell is to see it yourself on the SCRA website at http://www. scra27.org/disaster_recovery_manual.

---

the manual. You can obtain a copy of the manual from the SCRA website (http://www.scra27.org/disaster_recovery_manual).

A FINAL EXERCISE: WHERE WILL YOU USE
COMMUNITY PSYCHOLOGY?

As you pause at the end of this book, briefly reflect on what you have learned in this course and how it might be useful for you. Think about a specific domain of your life and the community-based challenges that you may encounter (e.g., family life/interpersonal relationships, home/neighborhood, work/school, or health care). If you do not currently see challenges for yourself, what challenges do you observe as you move around your community? Choose one challenge to focus on and then consider these questions:

- How do you define this challenge?
- What is your understanding at different ecological levels of analysis?
- What resources are available for addressing this challenge?
- How would you choose and implement an intervention strategy?
- What type of change are you seeking to make?
- How would you decide if the intervention was effective?
- What more do you want to know?

After working through the material presented in these chapters, we hope that you have a better understanding of community psychology. In particular, we expect that you have a greater appreciation of how individual, family, organizational, community, and society levels of analysis are intertwined in the development of social issues. We hope that you have a willingness to consider the many sides of social issues respecting the value of empirical inquiry and the perspectives of human diversity in understanding better and addressing these issues. We imagine that many of you have a greater awareness of your own values at the end of this course. Furthermore, we hope that this book has played a role in preparing you to embrace opportunities for citizen engagement that can change your communities for the better. We came to community psychology because it engaged our minds, our values, and our lives. We hope that this book did that for you too.

CHAPTER SUMMARY

1. We identified and described emerging directions in community psychology: a developing science of community; growing awareness of the global diversity of communities; broadening concern with social justice; collaborative, participatory research and action; and the promise of community psychology practice.

2. We outlined opportunities for promoting community and social change as citizens and as community psychologists. In particular, we argued that community psychology approaches presented in this book can help anyone engage in social change. We described how *seizing the day* and *taking the long view* are important time orientations for social interventions.

3. We discussed seven qualities for the community psychologist, first identified by James Kelly in 1971 but still apt today. They are *demonstrate a clearly identified competence; create an eco-identity; understand and embrace diversity;*

collaborate effectively with community resources; cultivate a commitment to taking risks; continuously balance patience and zeal; and give away the byline.

4. We provided four examples of successful community change illustrating these themes: social-emotional literacy and character education programs in schools, empowerment evaluation to promote student learning in "distressed" schools, the Meyerhoff Scholars program for African American students in STEM fields, and a model for how community psychologists can work together to create resources for individuals and communities affected by disasters.

5. Finally, we asked you to envision how you will use community psychology ideas to address challenges that affect your communities.

RECOMMENDED READINGS

Aber, M., Maton, K., & Seidman, E. (Eds.). (2011). *Empowering settings and voices for social change.* New York: Oxford University Press.

Nelson, G., & Prilleltensky, I. (Eds.). (2010). *Community psychology: In pursuit of well-being and liberation* (2nd ed.). London: MacMillan.

Shinn, M., & Thaden, E. (Eds.). (2010). *Current directions in community psychology (Association for Psychological Science).* Boston: Allyn & Bacon.

Wolff, T. (2010). *The power of collaborative solutions: Six principles and effective tools for building healthy communities.* San Francisco: Jossey-Bass.

RECOMMENDED WEBSITES

Community Toolbox:
http://ctb.ku.edu.

Global Journal of Community Psychology Practice:
http://www.gjcpp.org/en.

Society for Community Research and Action:
http://www.scra27.org.

Psychologists for Social Responsibility:
http://www.psysr.org.

References

Abdul-Adil, J. K., & Jason, L. A. (1991, Fall). Community psychology and Al-Islam: A religious framework for social change. *The Community Psychologist, 24*, 28–30.

Aber, J. L. (2005, June). *Children's exposure to war and violence: Knowledge for action*. Keynote address presented at the Biennial Meeting of the Society for Community Research and Action, Champaign-Urbana, IL.

Abraido-Lanza, A., Guier, C., & Colon, R. (1998). Psychological thriving among Latinas with chronic illness. *Journal of Social Issues, 54*, 405–424.

Ackerman, P., & DuVall, J. (2000). *A force more powerful: A century of nonviolent conflict*. New York: Palgrave.

Acosta, O., & Toro, P. A. (2000). Let's ask the homeless people themselves: A needs assessment based on a probability sample of adults. *American Journal of Community Psychology, 28*, 343–366.

Alaimo, K., Reischl, T. M., & Allen, J. O. (2010). Community gardening, neighborhood meetings, and social capital. *Journal of Community Psychology, 38*(4), 497–514.

Albee, G. W. (1959). *Mental health manpower trends*. New York: Basic Books.

Albee, G. W. (1982). Preventing psychopathology and promoting human potential. *American Psychologist, 37*, 1043–1050.

Albee, G. W. (1995). [Untitled videotape interview]. In J. G. Kelly (Ed.), *The history of community psychology: A video presentation of context and exemplars*. Chicago: Society for Community Research and Action.

Albee, G. W. (2000). The future of primary prevention. *Journal of Primary Prevention, 21*(1), 7–9.

Albee, G. W., & Gullotta, T. (Eds.). (1997). *Primary prevention works*. Thousand Oaks, CA: Sage.

Alegria, M., Takeuchi, D., Canino, G., Naihua, D., Shrout, P., Meng, X. I., et al. (2004). Considering context, place, and culture: The national Latino and Asian American Study. *International Journal of Methods in Psychiatric Research, 13*(4), 208–220.

Alinsky, S. (1971). *Rules for radicals: A practical primer for realistic radicals*. New York: Random House.

Alkin, M., & Christie, C. (2004). An evaluation theory tree. In M. Alkin (Ed.), *Evaluation roots: tracing theorists' views and influences* (pp. 381–392). Thousand Oaks, CA: Sage.

Allen, N. E. (2005). A multi-level analysis of community coordinating councils. *American Journal of Community Psychology, 35*, 49–64.

Allen, N., Watt, K., & Hess, J. (2008). A qualitative study of the activities and outcomes of domestic violence coordinating councils. *American Journal of Community Psychology, 41*, 63–73.

Altschuld, J. (2010). *The needs assessment kit*. Beverly Hills, CA: Sage.

American Anthropological Association. (1998). *Statement on "race."* Retrieved July 28, 2005, from http://www.aaanet.org/stmts/racepp.htm

American Psychological Association (2006). *Report of the APA Task Force on Socioeconomic Status.* Washington, DC, American Psychological Association. Retrieved February 4, 2011 from http://www.apa.org/pi/ses/resources/publications/task-force-2006.pdf

American Psychological Association. (2010). *Resolution on poverty and SES [per website].* Retrieved February 2, 2011, from http://www.apa.org/about/governance/council/policy/povertyresolution.aspx

Amichai-Hamburger, Y. (2007). Internet and well-being. *Computers in Human Behavior, 23,* 893–897.

Ang, S., & Joseph, D. (1996, August 9–12). Organizational learning and learning organizations: Triggering events, processes and structures. *Proceedings of the Academy of Management Meeting,* Cincinnati, OH.

Angelique, H., & Culley, M. (2003). Feminism found: An examination of gender consciousness in community psychology. *Journal of Community Psychology, 31,* 189–209.

Angelique, H., Reischl, T., & Davidson, W. S. (2002). Promoting political empowerment: Evaluation of an intervention with university students. *American Journal of Community Psychology, 30,* 815–835.

Argyris, C. (1999). *On organizational learning.* Malden, MA: Blackwell Business.

Argyris, C., & Schon, D. (1978). *Organizational learning.* Reading, MA: Addison-Wesley.

Astuto, J., & Allen, L. (2009). Home visitation and young children: An approach worth investing in? *Social Policy Report, 23,* 3–21.

Bahree, M. (2008, December 8). Citizen voices. *Forbes.* Retrieved February 5, from http://www.forbes.com/free_forbes/2008/1208/083.html

Baker, E. (n.d.). *Meyerhoff Scholars executive director on the sense of community in the program.* Retrieved August 30, 2010, from http://www.umbc.edu/meyerhoff/videogallery.php?movie=Baker.flv

Baker, E. J. (1970, December). *Developing community leadership.* Taped interview with Gerda Lerner. Retrieved February 5, from http://us.history.wisc.edu/hist102/pdocs/baker_leadership.pdf

Balcazar, F., Seekins, T., Fawcett, S. B., & Hopkins, B. (1990). Empowering people with physical disabilities through advocacy skills training. *American Journal of Community Psychology, 18,* 281–296.

Balcazar, F. E., Suarez-Balcazar, Y., & Taylor-Ritzman, T. (2009). Cultural competence: Development of a conceptual framework. *Disability and Rehabilitation, 31,* 1153–1160.

Bandura, A. (1982). Self-efficacy mechanisms in human agency. *American Psychologist, 37,* 122–147.

Bandura, A. (1986). *Social foundations of thought and action: A social cognitive theory.* Englewood Cliffs, NJ: Prentice Hall.

Bangladesh Rural Advancement Committee (2008). *Annual Report, 2008.* Retrieved February 5, from http://brac.net/oldsite/useruploads/files/BRAC%20Annual%20Report%20-%202008.pdf

Barker, R. (1965). Explorations in ecological psychology. *American Psychologist, 20,* 1–14.

Barker, R. (1968). *Ecological psychology.* Stanford, CA: Stanford University Press.

Barker, R. (1978). Behavior settings. In R. Barker & Associates (Eds.), *Habitats, environments, and human behavior* (pp. 29–35). San Francisco: Jossey-Bass.

Barker, R., & Associates. (1978). *Habitats, environments and human behavior.* San Francisco: Jossey-Bass.

Barker R., & Gump, P. (Eds.). (1964). *Big school, small school.* Stanford, CA: Stanford University Press.

Barker, R., & Schoggen, P. (1973). *Qualities of community life: Methods of measuring environment and behavior applied to an American and an English town.* San Francisco: Jossey-Bass.

Barker, R., & Wright, H. (1955). *Midwest and its children.* New York: Harper & Row.

Barker, R., & Wright, H. (1978). Standing patterns of behavior. In R. Barker & Associates (Eds.), *Habitats, environments and human behavior* (pp. 24–28). San Francisco: Jossey-Bass. (Original work published 1955)

Barrera, M. (1986). Distinctions between social support concepts, measures, and models. *American Journal of Community Psychology, 14,* 413–445.

Barrera, M. (2000). Social support research in community psychology. In J. Rappaport & E. Seidman (Eds.), *Handbook of community psychology* (pp. 215–246). New York: Kluwer/Plenum.

Barrera, M., Glasgow, R., McKay, H., Boles, S., & Feil, E. (2002). Do Internet-based support interventions change perceptions of social support?: An experimental trial of approaches for supporting diabetes self-management. *American Journal of Community Psychology, 30,* 637–654.

Barrera, M., Jr., Li, S. A., & Chassin, L. (1995). Effects of parental alcoholism and life stress on Hispanic and Non-Hispanic Cacausian adolescents: A prospective study. *American Journal of Community Psychology, 23,* 479–507.

Bartunek, J. M., & Keys, C. B. (1979). Participation in school decision-making. *Urban Education, 14,* 52–75.

Bateman, H. V. (2002). Sense of community in the school: Listening to students' voices. In A. Fisher, C. Sonn, & B. Bishop (Eds.), *Psychological sense of community: Research, applications and implications* (pp. 161–180). New York: Kluwer/Plenum.

Bathum, M. E., & Baumann, L. (2007). A sense of community among immigrant Latinas. *Family & Community Health, 30,* 167–177.

Baum A., & Fleming, I. (1993). Implications of psychological research on stress and technological accidents. *American Psychologist, 48,* 665–672.

Baumrind, D. (1991). Parenting styles and adolescent development. In R. M. Lerner, A. C. Peterson, & J. Brooks-Gunn (Eds.), *Encyclopedia of adolescence* (Vol. 11), 746–758. New York: Garland.

Belenky, M., Clinchy, B., Goldberger, N., & Tarule, J. (1986). *Women's ways of knowing: The development of self, voice and mind.* New York: Basic Books.

Belfield, C. R., Nores, M., Barnett, W. S., & Schweinhart, L. J. (2006). The high/scope perry preschool program: Cost-benefit analysis using data from the age-40 follow-up. *The Journal of Human Resources, 41,* 162–190.

Bellah, R., Madsen, R., Sullivan, W., Swidler, A., & Tipton, S. (1985). *Habits of the heart: Individualism and commitment in American life.* New York: Harper & Row.

Benjamin, L. T., Jr., & Crouse, E. M. (2002). The American Psychological Association's response to *Brown v. Board of Education*: The case of Kenneth B. Clark. *American Psychologist, 57,* 38–50.

Bennett, C., Anderson, L., Cooper, S., Hassol, L., Klein, D., & Rosenblum, G. (1966). *Community psychology: A report of the Boston Conference on the Education of Psychologists for Community Mental Health.* Boston: Boston University.

Berger, P., & Neuhaus, R. (1977). *To empower people.* Washington, DC: American Enterprise Institute.

Berkowitz, B. (1987). *Local heroes.* Lexington, MA: Lexington Books.

Berkowitz, B. (1990, Summer). Who is being empowered? *The Community Psychologist, 23,* 10–11.

Berkowitz, B. (1996). Personal and community sustainability. *American Journal of Community Psychology, 24,* 441–460.

Berkowitz, B. (2000). Community and neighborhood organization. In J. Rappaport & E. Seidman (Eds.), *Handbook of community psychology* (pp. 331–358). New York: Kluwer/Plenum.

Bernal, G., & Enchautegui-de-Jesus, N. (1994). Latinos and Latinas in community psychology: A review of the literature. *American. Journal of Community Psychology, 22,* 531–558.

Bernal, G., Trimble, J., Burlew, A. K., & Leong, F. (Eds.). (2003). *Handbook of racial and ethnic minority psychology.* Thousand Oaks, CA: Sage.

Bernard, J. (1973). *The sociology of community.* Glenview, IL: Scott, Foresman.

Berridge V. (1996). *AIDS in the UK, the making of policy 1981–1994.* Oxford: Oxford University Press.

Berrigan, D., & McKinnon, R. (2008). Built environment and health. *Preventive Medicine, 47*(3), 239–240.

Berry, J. (1994). An ecological perspective on cultural and ethnic psychology. In E. Trickett, R. Watts, & D. Birman (Eds.), *Human diversity: Perspectives on people in context* (pp. 115–141). San Francisco: Jossey-Bass.

Berry, J. (2003). Conceptual approaches to acculturation. In K. Chun, P. Organista, & G. Marin (Eds.), *Acculturation: Advances in theory, measurement and applied research* (pp. 17–38). Washington, DC: American Psychological Association.

Berry, J., & Sam, D. (1997). Acculturation and adaptation. In J. W. Berry, M. Segall, & C. Kagitçibasi (Eds.), *Handbook of cross-cultural psychology. Vol. 3: Social behavior and applications* (pp. 291–325). Needham Heights, MA: Allyn & Bacon.

Berryhill, J. C., & Linney, J. A. (2006). On the edge of diversity: Bringing African Americans and Latinos together in a neighborhood group. *American Journal of Community Psychology, 37,* 247–255.

Bess, K., Fisher, A., Sonn, C., & Bishop, B. (2002). Psychological conceptions of community: Theory, research and application. In A. Fisher, C. Sonn, & B. Bishop (Eds.), *Psychological sense of community: Research, applications and implications* (pp. 3–22). New York: Kluwer/Plenum.

Bess, K., Prilleltensky, I., Perkins, D., & Collins, L. (2009). Participatory organizational change in community-based health and human services: From tokenism to political engagement. *American Journal of Community Psychology, 43,* 134–148.

Betancourt, H., & Lopez, S. R. (1993). The study of culture, ethnicity, and race in American psychology. *American Psychologist, 48,* 629–637.

Bhana, A., Petersen, I., & Rochat, T. (2007). Community psychology in South Africa. In S. M. Reich, M. R. Riemer, I. Prilleltensky, & M. Montero (Eds.), *International community psychology: History and theories.* New York: Springer. 377–391.

Bierman, K., & the Conduct Problems Prevention Research Group. (1997). Implementing a comprehensive program for the prevention of conduct problems in rural communities: The Fast Track experience. *American Journal of Community Psychology, 25,* 493–514.

Biglan, A., Ary, D., Koehn, V., Levings, D., Smith, S., Wright, Z., et al. (1996). Mobilizing positive reinforcement in communities to reduce youth access to tobacco. *American Journal of Community Psychology, 24,* 625–638.

Biglan, A., & Smolkowski, K. (2002). The role of the community psychologist in the 21st century. *Prevention & Treatment, 5,* Article 2.

Birman, D. (1994). Acculturation and human diversity in a multicultural society. In E. J. Trickett, R. J. Watts, & D. Birman (Eds.), *Human diversity: Perspectives on people in context* (pp. 261–283). San Francisco: Jossey-Bass.

Birman, D. (1998). Biculturalism and perceived competence of Latino immigrant adolescents. *American Journal of Community Psychology, 26,* 335–354.

Birman, D., Trickett, E. J., & Buchanan, R. (2005). A tale of two cities: Replication of a study on the acculturation and adaptation of immigrant adolescents from the former Soviet Union in a different community context. *American Journal of Community Psychology, 35,* 83–102.

Birman, D., Trickett, E. J., & Vinokurov, A. (2002). Acculturation and adaptation of Soviet Jewish refugee adolescents: Predictors of adjustment across life domains. *American Journal of Community Psychology, 30,* 585–607.

Bishop, B., Coakes, S., & D'Rozario, P. (2002). Sense of community in rural communities: A mixed methodological approach. In A. Fisher, C. Sonn, & B. Bishop (Eds.), *Psychological sense of community: Research, applications and implications* (pp. 271–290). New York: Kluwer/Plenum.

Bjorck, J., Lee, Y., & Cohen, L. (1997). Control beliefs and faith as stress moderation for Korean American versus Caucasian American Protestants. *American Journal of Community Psychology, 25,* 61–72.

Black, S. (2007). Evaluation of the Olweus Bullying Prevention program: How the program can work for inner city youth. *Proceedings of Persistently Safe Schools: The 2007 National Conference on Safe Schools.* OJJDP-Sponsored, NCJ 226233.

Bonanno, G. (2004). Loss, trauma, and human resilience: Have we underestimated the human capacity to thrive after extremely aversive events? *American Psychologist, 59,* 20–28.

Bond, G., Witheridge, T., Dincin, J., Wasmer, D., Webb, J., & De Graaf-Kaser, R. (1990). Assertive community treatment for frequent users of psychiatric hospitals in a large city: A controlled study. *American Journal of Community Psychology, 18,* 865–892.

Bond, L. A., Belenky, M. F., & Weinstock, J. (2000). The Listening Partners program: An initiative toward feminist community psychology in action. *American Journal of Community Psychology, 28,* 697–730.

Bond, M. A. (1989). Ethical dilemmas in context: Some preliminary questions. *American Journal of Community Psychology, 17,* 355–360.

Bond, M. A. (1990). Defining the research relationship: Maximizing participation in an unequal world. In P. Tolan, C. Keys, F. Chertok, & L. Jason (Eds.), *Researching community psychology* (pp. 183–185). Washington, DC: American Psychological Association.

Bond, M. A. (1999). Gender, race and class in organizational contexts. *American Journal of Community Psychology, 27,* 327–356.

Bond, M. A., & Harrell, S. P. (2006). Diversity challenges in community research and action: The story of a special issue of *AJCP. American Journal of Community Psychology, 37,* 157–166.

Bond, M. A., Hill, J., Mulvey, A., & Terenzio, M. (Eds.). (2000a). Special issue part I: Feminism and community psychology. *American Journal of Community Psychology, 28*(5).

Bond, M. A., Hill, J., Mulvey, A., & Terenzio, M. (Eds.). (2000b). Special issue part II: Feminism and community psychology. *American Journal of Community Psychology, 28*(6).

Bond, M. A., & Keys, C. B. (1993). Empowerment, diversity, and collaboration: Promoting synergy on community boards. *American Journal of Community Psychology, 21*, 37–58.

Bond, M. A., & Mulvey, A. (2000). A history of women and feminist perspectives in community psychology. *American Journal of Community Psychology, 28*, 599–630.

Borkman, T. (1990). Self-help groups at the turning point: Emerging egalitarian alliances with the formal health care systems? *American Journal of Community Psychology, 18*, 321–332.

Borkman, T. (Ed.). (1991). Self-help groups [Special issue]. *American Journal of Community Psychology, 19*(5).

Borkman, T., Karlsson, M., Munn-Giddings, C., & Smith, C. (2005). *Self-help organizations and mental health: Case studies.* Skondal, Sweden: Skondal Institute and University.

Bothne, N., & Olson, B. (2006). Tools for community psychologists: Human rights. *The Community Psychologist, 39*(4), 40–57.

Botvin, G., & Tortu, S. (1988). Preventing adolescent substance abuse through life skills training. In R. Price, E. Cowen, R. Lorion, & J. Ramos-McKay (Eds.), *Fourteen ounces of prevention* (pp. 98–110). Washington, DC: American Psychological Association.

Boulding, E. (2000). *Cultures of peace: The hidden side of history.* Syracuse, NY: Syracuse University Press.

Boulding, K. (1989). *Three faces of power.* Newbury Park, CA: Sage.

Boyd, N., & Angelique, H. (2002). Rekindling the discourse: Organization studies in community psychology. *Journal of Community Psychology, 30*, 325–348.

Bradford, H. D. (2001, Spring). *What went wrong with public housing in Chicago? A history of the Robert Taylor homes.* Illinois State Historical Society.

Bradford, L., Gibb, J., & Benne, K. (1964). *T-group theory and laboratory method: Innovation in re-education.* New York: Wiley.

Bradley, R., & Corwyn, R. (2002). Socioeconomic status and child development. *Annual Review of Psychology, 53*, 371–399.

Braveman, P., Cubbin, C., Egerter, S., Williams, D., & Pamuk, E. (2010). Socioeconomic disparities in health in the United States: what the patterns tell us. *American Journal of Public Health, 100*(Suppl, 1), 189–196.

Brendtro, L., Brokenleg, M., & Van Bockern, S. (1990). *Reclaiming youth at risk: Our hope for the future.* Bloomington, IN: National Educational Service.

Brewer, M. (1997). The social psychology of intergroup relations: Can research inform practice? *Journal of Social Issues, 53*, 197–211.

Brewer, M. B., & Chen, Y. R. (2007). Where (Who) Are Collectives in Collectivism? Toward Conceptual Clarification of Individualism and Collectivism. *Psychological Review, 114*(1), 133–151.

Bringle, R., & Hatcher, J. (2002). Campus-community partnerships: The terms of engagement. *Journal of Social Issues, 58*, 503–516.

Brodsky, A. (1996). Resilient single mothers in risky neighborhoods: Negative psychological sense of community. *Journal of Community Psychology, 24*, 347–364.

Brodsky, A. (2000). The role of spirituality in the resilience of urban, African American, single mothers. *Journal of Community Psychology, 28*, 199–220.

Brodsky, A. (2001). More than epistemology: Relationships in applied research with underserved communities. *Journal of Social Issues, 57*, 323–336.

Brodsky, A. (2003). *With all our strength: The Revolutionary Association of the Women of Afghanistan.* New York: Routledge.

Brodsky, A. (2009). Multiple psychological senses of community in Afghan context: Exploring commitment and sacrifice in an underground resistance community. *American Journal of Community Psychology, 44*, 176–187.

Brodsky, A., & Faryal, T. (2006). No matter how hard you try, your feet still get wet: Insider and outsider perspectives. *American Journal of Community Psychology, 37*, 311–320.

Brodsky, A., Loomis, C., & Marx, C. (2002). Expanding the conceptualization of PSOC. In A. Fisher, C. Sonn, & B. Bishop (Eds.), *Psychological sense of community: Research, applications and implications* (pp. 319–336). New York: Kluwer/Plenum.

Brodsky, A., & Marx, C. (2001). Layers of identity: Multiple psychological senses of community within a community setting. *Journal of Community Psychology, 29*, 161–178.

Brodsky, A., O'Campo, P. J., & Aronson, R. E. (1999). PSOC in community context: Multi-level correlates of a measure of psychological sense of community in low-income, urban neighborhoods. *Journal of Community Psychology, 27,* 659–680.

Brodsky, A., Senuta, K., Weiss, C., Marx, C., Loomis, C., Arteaga, S., et al. (2004). When one plus one equals three: The role of relationships and context in community research. *American Journal of Community Psychology, 33,* 229–242.

Bronfenbrenner, U. (1979). *The ecology of human development: Experiments by nature and design.* Cambridge, MA: Harvard University Press.

Brown, H., Guo, J., Singer, L. T., Downes, K., & Brinales, J. (2007). Examining the effects of school-based drug prevention programs on drug use in rural settings: Methodology and initial findings. *The Journal of Rural Health, 23,* 29–36.

Brown, J. (1997). Review of the book *Empowerment evaluation: Knowledge and tools for self-assessment and accountability. Health Education & Behavior, 24*(3), 388–391. Retrieved February 5, from http://www.davidfetterman.com/BrownBookReview1.htm.

Brown, L. (2009). How people can benefit from mental health consumer-run organizations. *American Journal of Community Psychology, 43,* 177–188.

Brown, L., Feinberg, M., Greenberg, M. (2010). Determinants of community coalition ability to support evidence-based programs. *Prevention Science, 11,* 287–297.

Brown, L. D., Shepherd, M. D., Merkle, E. C., Wituk, S. A., & Meisson, G. (2008). Understanding how participation in a consumer-run organization relates to recovery. *American Journal of Community Psychology, 42,* 167–178.

Brown, L., Shepherd, M., Wituk, S., & Meissen, G. (Eds.). (2008). Introduction to Mental health self-help [Special issue]. *American Journal of Community Psychology, 42*(2), 105–109.

Brydon-Miller, M., & Tolman, D. (Eds.). (1997). Transforming psychology: Interpretive and participatory methods [Special issue]. *Journal of Social Issues, 53*(4), 597–603.

Buford, B., & Davis, B. (1995). *Shining stars: Prevention programs that work.* Louisville, KY: Southeast Regional Center for Drug-Free Schools and Communities.

Bullock, H., Wyche, K., & Williams, W. (2001). Media images of the poor. *Journal of Social Issues, 57,* 229–246.

Burlew, A. K. (2003). Research with ethnic minorities: Conceptual, methodological, and analytical issues. In G. Bernal, J. Trimble, A. K. Burlew, & F. Leong (Eds.), *Handbook of racial and ethnic minority psychology* (pp. 179–197). Thousand Oaks, CA: Sage.

Burman, E. (1997). Minding the gap: Positivism, psychology, and the politics of qualitative methods. *Journal of Social Issues, 53,* 785–802.

Butterfoss, F., Goodman, R., & Wandersman, A. (2001). Citizen participation and health: Toward a psychology of improving health through individual, organizational and community involvement. In A. Baum, T. Revenson, & J. Singer (Eds.), *Handbook of health psychology.* Mahwah, NJ: Erlbaum.

Caldwell, C., Kohn-Wood, L., Schmeelk-Cone, K., Chavous, T., & Zimmerman, M. (2004). Racial discrimination and racial identity as risk or protective factors for violent behaviors in African American young adults. *American Journal of Community Psychology, 33,* 91–106.

Camic, P., Rhodes, J., & Yardley, L. (2003). *Qualitative research in psychology: Expanding perspectives in methodology and design.* Washington, DC: American Psychological Association.

Campbell, R. (2002). *Emotionally involved: The impact of researching rape.* New York: Routledge.

Campbell, R. (2008). The psychological impact of rape victims. *American Psychologist, 63*(8), 702–717.

Campbell, R., Dorey, H., Naegeli, M., Grubstein, L., Bennett, K., Bonter, F., et al. (2004). An empowerment evaluation model for sexual assault programs: empirical evidence of effectiveness. *American Journal of Community Psychology, 34,* 251–262.

Campbell, R., & Salem, D. (1999). Concept mapping as a feminist research method: Examining the community response to rape. *Psychology of Women Quarterly, 23,* 67–91.

Campbell, R., Sefl, T., Wasco, S., & Ahrens, C. (2004). Doing community research without a community: Creating safe space for rape survivors. *American Journal of Community Psychology, 33,* 253–260.

Campbell, R., & Wasco, S. (2000). Feminist approaches to social science: Epistemological and methodological tenets. *American Journal of Community Psychology, 28,* 773–792.

REFERENCES **495**

Caplan, G. (Ed.). (1961). *Prevention of mental disorders in children.* New York: Basic Books.

Caplan, G. (1964). *Principles of preventive psychiatry.* New York: Basic Books.

Caplan, N., & Nelson, S. (1973). On being useful: The nature and consequences of psychological research on social problems. *American Psychologist, 28,* 199–211.

Carli, L. (1999). Gender, interpersonal power, and social influence. *Journal of Social Issues, 55,* 81–100.

Carli, L. (2003). Gender and social influence. *Journal of Social Issues, 57,* 725–742.

Carling, P. J. (1995). *Return to the community: Building support systems for people with psychiatric disabilities.* New York: The Guilford Press.

Carter, R. T., Helms, J. E., & Juby, H. L (2004). The relationship between racism and racial identity for White Americans: A profile analysis. *Journal of Multicultural Counseling and Development, 32,* 2–17.

Castro, F. G., Barrera, M. & Martinez, C. R. (2004). The cultural adaptation of prevention interventions: Resolving tensions between fidelity and fit. *Prevention Science, 5,* 41–45.

Catania, J., Kegeles, S., & Coates T. (1990). Towards an understanding of risk behavior: An AIDS risk reduction model (ARRM). *Health Education Quarterly, 17,* 53–72.

Caughey, M. O., O'Campo, P., & Brodsky, A. (1999). Neighborhoods, families and children: Implications for policy and practice. *Journal of Community Psychology, 27,* 615–633.

Center for Substance Abuse Prevention. (1998). *Preventing substance abuse among children and adolescents: Family-centered approaches—Prevention Enhancement Protocol System (PEPS)* (DHHS Publication No. SMA 3223). Washington, DC: U.S. Government Printing Office.

Center for Mental Health Services. (2000). *Training manual for mental health and human services workers in major disasters* (2nd ed.). (DHHS Publication No. ADM 90-538). Washington, DC: D. J. DeWolf.

Centers for Disease Control. (1982, June). A cluster of Kaposi's sarcoma and pneumocystis carinii pneumonia among homosexual male residents of Los Angeles and Orange counties, California. *Morbidity and Mortality Weekly Report, 23,* 305–307.

Centers for Disease Control. (1982, September). Current trends update on acquired immune deficiency syndrome (AIDS)—United States. *Morbidity and Mortality Weekly Report, 31,* 507–508, 513–514.

Centers for Disease Control and Prevention. (2003). *HIV/AIDS surveillance report, 13*(2), 1–44. Retrieved 6 March, 2011, from http://www.cdc.gov/hiv/surveillance/resources/reports/2001report_no2/index.htm

Centers for Disease Control. (2007). *HIV/AIDS surveillance report, 19*(2), 1–44. Retrieved March 6, 2011, from http://www.cdc.gov/hiv/topics/surveillance/resources/reports/2007report/pdf/2007SurveillanceReport.pdf.

Chang, T. (2005). Online counseling: Prioritizing psychoeducation, self-help, and mutual help for counseling psychology research and practice. *The Counseling Psychologist, 33,* 881–890.

Chang, T., Yeh, C., & Krumboltz, J. (2001). Process and outcome evaluation of an on-line support group for Asian American male college students. *Journal of Counseling Psychology, 48,* 319–329.

Chataway, C. (1997). An examination of the constraints on mutual inquiry in a participatory action research project. *Journal of Social Issues, 53,* 747–766.

Chavis, D. M. (1993). A future for community psychology practice. *American Journal of Community Psychology, 21,* 171–184.

Chavis, D. (2001). The paradoxes and promise of community coalitions. *American Journal of Community Psychology, 29,* 309–320.

Chavis, D. M., Hogge, J., McMillan, D. W., & Wandersman, A. (1986). Sense of community through Brunswik's lens: A first look. *Journal of Community Psychology, 14,* 24–40.

Chavis, D. M., Stucky, P., & Wandersman, A. (1983). Returning basic research to the community: A relationship between scientist and citizen. *American Psychologist, 38,* 424–434.

Chavis, D. M., & Wandersman, A. (1990). Sense of community in the urban environment: A catalyst for participation and community development. *American Journal of Community Psychology, 18,* 83–116. Reprinted in T. Revenson, A. D'Augelli, S. E. French, D. Hughes, D. Livert, E. Seidman, M. Shinn, & H. Yoshikawa (Eds.), (2002), *A quarter century of community psychology* (pp. 265–292). New York: Kluwer Academic/Plenum.

Chelimsky, E. (1997). The coming transformation in evaluation. In E. Chelimsky & W. Shadish (Eds.), *Evaluation for the 21st century: A handbook* (pp. 1–26). Thousand Oaks, CA: Sage.

Cheng, S. K., Chan, A. C. M., & Philllips, D. R. Quality of life in old age: An investigation of well older persons in Hong Kong. *Journal of Community Psychology, 32,* 309–326.

Cheng, S. K. & Heller, K. (2009). Global aging: Challenges for community psychology. *American Journal of Community Psychology, 44,* 161–173.

Cherniss, C., & Deegan, G. (2000). The creation of alternative settings. In J. Rappaport & E. Seidman (Eds.), *Handbook of community psychology* (pp. 359–378). New York: Kluwer/Plenum.

Chesir-Teran, D. (2003). Conceptualizing and assessing heterosexism in high schools: A setting-level approach. *American Journal of Community Psychology, 31,* 267–280.

Chinman, M., Hunter, S. B., Ebener, P., Paddock, S. M., Stillman, L., Imm, P., et al. (2008). The Getting To Outcomes demonstration and evaluation: An illustration of the Prevention Support System. *American Journal of Community Psychology, 41*(3–4), 206–224.

Chinman, M., Imm, P., & Wandersman, A. (2004). *Getting To Outcomes 2004: Promoting accountability through methods and tools for planning, implementation, and evaluation.* Santa Monica, CA: RAND Corporation. Retrieved March 6, 2011, from http://www.rand.org/pubs/technical_reports/TR101.html

Chinman, M., Kloos, B., O'Connell, M., & Davidson, L. (2002). Service providers' views of psychiatric mutual support groups. *Journal of Community Psychology, 30*(4), 349–366.

Chipuer, H. M., & Pretty, G. M. H. (1999). A review of the Sense of Community Index: Current uses, factor structure, reliability, and further development. *Journal of Community Psychology, 27,* 643–658.

Chirowodza, A., van Rooyen, H., Joseph, P., Sikotoyi, S., Richter, L., & Coates, T. (2009). Using participatory methods and geographic information systems to prepare for an HIV community-based trial in Vulindela, South Africa. *Journal of Community Psychology, 37,* 41–57.

Christens, B. D., Hanlin, C. E., & Speer, P. W. (2007). Getting the social organism thinking: Strategy for systems change. *American Journal of Community Psychology, 39,* 229–238.

Cicchetti, D., Rappaport, J., Sandler, I., & Weissberg, R. P. (2000). *The promotion of wellness in children and adolescents.* Washington, DC: Child Welfare League of America.

Clark, K. (1953). Desegregation: An appraisal of the evidence. *Journal of Social Issues, 9*(4), 2–76.

Clark, K., Chein, I., & Cook, S. (1952). The effects of segregation and the consequences of desegregation. [Appendix to the appellants' briefs in *Brown v. Board of Education of Topeka, Kansas; Briggs v. Elliot;* and *Davis v. Prince Edward County, Virginia.* Signed by 29 other social scientists. September 22, 1952.] Reprinted in *American Psychologist, 59,* 495–501 (2004).

Clark, S. (1986). *Ready from within: Septima Clark and the civil rights movement.* Navarro, CA: Wild Trees Press.

Cline, R. W., Orom, H., Berry-Bobovski, L., Hernandez, T., Black, C., Schwartz, A. G., et al. (2010). Community-level social support responses in a slow-motion technological disaster: The case of Libby, Montana. *American Journal of Community Psychology, 46*(1–2), 1–18.

Coalition for Community Living, (n.d.) Retrieved February 4, 2011, from http://www.theccl.org/

Cohen, S. (2004). Social relationships and health. *American Psychologist, 59,* 676–684.

Cohen S., Underwood, L., & Gottlieb, B. (2000). *Social support measurement and intervention.* New York: Oxford University Press.

Collaborative for Academic, Social, and Emotional Learning. (2006). *Cossitt school case study.* Retrieved March 7, 2011, from http://www.casel.org/downloads/cossitt_casestudy.pdf

Colby, A., & Damon, W. (1992). *Some do care: Contemporary lives of moral commitment.* New York: Free Press.

Collier-Thomas, B., & Franklin, V. P. (Eds.). (2001). *Sisters in the struggle: African-American women in the civil rights–Black power movement.* New York: NYU Press.

Coleman, J., & Hoffer, T. (1987). Public and private schools: The impact of communities. New York: Basic Books.

Collaborative for Academic, Social, and Emotional Learning. (2006). *CASEL practice rubric for schoolwide*

SEL implementation. Retrieved March 7, 2011, from http://www.casel.org/downloads/Rubric.pdf

Collins, F. S. & Mansoura, M. K. (2001). The human genome project: Revealing the shared inheritance of all humankind. *Cancer, 91,* 221–225.

Comas-Diaz, L., Lykes, M. B., & Alarcon, R. (1998). Ethnic conflict and the psychology of liberation in Guatemala, Peru, and Puerto Rico. *American Psychologist, 53,* 778–792.

Community Toolbox. (2005). Retrieved July 28, 2005, from http://ctb.ku.edu

Connor-Smith, J. K., & Flachsbart, C. (2007). Relations between personality and coping: A meta-analysis. *Journal of Personality and Social Psychology, 93,* 1080–1107.

Conway, P., Evans, S., & Prilleltensky, I. (2003, Fall). Psychologists acting with conscience together (Psy-ACT): A global coalition for justice and well-being. *The Community Psychologist, 36,* 30–31.

Cooke, B., & Kothari, U. (2001). *Participation: The new tyranny?* New York: Zed Books.

Coppens, N., Page, R., Thow, T. (2006). Reflections on the evaluation of a Cambodian youth dance program. *American Journal of Community Psychology, 37,* 321–332.

Corcoran, J., & Pillai, V. (2007). Effectiveness of secondary pregnancy prevention programs: A meta-analysis. *Research on Social Work Practice, 17,* 5–18.

Cornell Empowerment Group, (1989). Empowerment and Family Support. *Cornell Empowerment Group Networking Bulletin, 1,* 2.

Cortes, D. E., Rogler, L. H., & Malgady, R. G. (1994). Biculturality among Puerto Rican adults in the United States. *American Journal of Community Psychology, 22,* 707–721.

Cosgrove, L., & McHugh, M. (2000). Speaking for ourselves: Feminist methods and community psychology. *American Journal of Community Psychology, 28,* 815–838.

Cottrell, L. S. (1976). The competent community. In B. H. Kaplan, R. N. Wilson, & A. H. Leighton (Eds.), *Further explorations in social psychiatry* (pp. 195–209). New York: Basic Books.

Coulton, C., Korbin, J., Chan, T., & Su, M. (2001). Mapping residents' perceptions of neighborhood boundaries: A methodological note. *American Journal of Community Psychology, 29,* 371–383.

Cousins, J. B. (2005). Will the real empowerment evaluation please stand up? A critical friend perspective. In D. M. Fetterman & A. Wandersman (Eds.), *Empowerment evaluation principles in practice* (pp. 183–208). New York: Guilford.

Cowen, E. L. (1973). Social and community interventions. *Annual Review of Psychology, 24,* 423–472.

Cowen, E. L. (1977). Baby steps toward primary prevention. *American Journal of Community Psychology, 5,* 1–22.

Cowen, E. L. (1991). In pursuit of wellness. *American Psychologist, 46,* 404–408.

Cowen, E. L. (1994). The enhancement of psychological wellness: Challenges and opportunities. *American Journal of Community Psychology, 22,* 149–180. Reprinted in T. Revenson, A. D'Augelli, S. E. French, D. Hughes, D. Livert, E. Seidman, M. Shinn, & H. Yoshikawa (Eds.), (2002), *A quarter century of community psychology* (pp. 445–475). New York: Kluwer Academic/Plenum.

Cowen, E. L. (2000a). Community psychology and routes to psychological wellness. In J. Rappaport & E. Seidman (Eds.), *Handbook of community psychology* (pp. 79–100). New York: Kluwer/Plenum.

Cowen, E. L. (2000b). Prevention, wellness enhancement, Y2K and thereafter. *Journal of Primary Prevention, 21*(1), 15–19.

Cowen, E. L. (2000c). Psychological wellness: Some hopes for the future. In D. Cicchetti, J. Rappaport, I. N. Sandler, & R. P. Weissberg (Eds.), *The promotion of wellness in children and adolescents* (pp. 477–503). Washington, DC: Child Welfare League of America Press.

Cowen, E. L., Hightower, A. D., Pedro-Carroll, J., Work, W., Wyman, P., & Haffey, W. (1996). *School-based prevention for children at risk: The Primary Mental Health Project.* Washington, DC: American Psychological Association.

Cowen, E. L., & Kilmer, R. (2002). "Positive psychology": Some plusses and some open issues. *Journal of Community Psychology, 30,* 449–460.

Cowen, E. L., McKim, B. J., & Weissberg, R. P. (1981). Bartenders as informal, interpersonal help-agents. *American Journal of Community Psychology, 9,* 715–729.

Cowen, E. L., Pedersen, A., Babigian, H., Izzo, L. D., & Trost, M. A. (1973). Long-term follow-up of early detected vulnerable children. *Journal of Consulting and Clinical Psychology, 41,* 438–446.

Coyne, J., Ellard, J., & Smith, D. (1990). Social support, interdependence, and the dilemmas of helping. In B. R. Sarason, I. G. Sarason, & G. Pierce (Eds.), *Social support: An interactional view* (pp. 129–148). New York: Wiley.

Craig, W., Harel-Fisch, Y., Fogel-Grinvald, H., Dostaler, S., Hetland, J., Simons-Morten, B., et al. (2009). *International Journal of Public Health, 54,* 216–224.

Crosby, F., Iyer, A., Clayton, S., & Downing, R. (2003). Affirmative action: Psychological data and the policy debates. *American Psychologist, 58,* 93–115.

Culley, M. R., & Hughey, J. (2008). Power and public participation in a hazardous waste dispute: A community case study. *American Journal of Community Psychology, 41,* 99–114.

D'Augelli, A. R. (1994). Lesbian and gay male development: Steps toward an analysis of lesbians' and gay men's lives. In B. Greene and G. Herek (Eds.), *Contemporary perspectives in gay and lesbian psychology* (Vol. 1, pp. 118–132). Newbury Park, CA: Sage.

D'Augelli, A. R. (2006). Coming out, visibility, and creating change: Empowering lesbian, gay, and bisexual people in a rural university community. *American Journal of Community Psychology, 37,* 203–210.

Dahl, T. Ceballo, R., & Huerta, M. (2010). In the eye of the beholder: mothers' perceptions of poor neighborhoods as places to raise children. *Journal of Community Psychology, 38*(4), 419–434.

Dalton, D. (1993). *Mahatma Gandhi: Nonviolent power in action.* New York: Columbia University Press.

Dan, A., Campbell, R., Riger, S., & Strobel, M. (2003). Feminist panel: Discussing "Psychology constructs the female." In J. G. Kelly (producer, director), (2003), *Exemplars of community psychology* [DVD set]. Society for Community Research and Action. (Available from SCRA Membership Office, 4440 PGA Blvd. #600, Palm Beach Gardens, FL 33410 (561-623-5323). E-mail: office@scra27.org.)

Dane, A., & Schneider, B. (1998). Program integrity in primary and secondary prevention: Are implementation effects out of control. *Clinical Psychology Review, 18,* 23–45.

DARE (2008). *2008 Annual report.* Retrieved March 7, 2011, from http://www.dare.org/home/documents/2008AnnualReport.pdf

Davidson, L., Chinman, M., Kloos, B., Weingarten, R., Stayner, D., & Tebes, J. K. (1999). Peer support among individuals with severe mental illness: A review of evidence. *Clinical Psychology: Science and Practice, 6*(2), 165–187.

Davidson, W. B., & Cotter, P. (1989). Sense of community and political participation. *Journal of Community Psychology, 17,* 119–125.

Davidson, W. B., & Cotter, P. (1993). Psychological sense of community and support for public school taxes. *American Journal of Community Psychology, 21,* 59–66.

Davis, K., & Gidycz, C. (2000). Child sexual abuse prevention programs: A meta-analysis. *Journal of Clinical Child Psychology, 29,* 257–265.

DeCrappeo, M., Pelletiere, D. Crowley, S., & Teater, E. (2010). Out of reach, 2010. Report of the National Low Income Housing Coalition. Retrieved March 7, 2011, from http://www.nlihc.org/oor/oor2010

Degirmencioglu, S. M. (2003, Fall). Action research makes psychology more useful and more fun. *The Community Psychologist, 36,* 27–29.

Dempsey, I., & Keen, D. (2009). A review of process and outcomes for family-centered services for children with a disability. *Topics in Early Childhood Special Education, 28,* 42–52.

Den Boer, P. C. A. M., Wiersma, D., & van den Bosch, R. J. (2004). Why is self-help neglected in the treatment of emotional disorders? A meta-analysis. *Psychological Medicine, 34,* 971.

Denzin, N., & Lincoln, Y. (Eds.). (1994). *Handbook of qualitative research.* Thousand Oaks, CA: Sage.

Derzon, J., Sale, E., Springer, J. F., & Brounstein, P. (2005). Estimating intervention effectiveness: Synthetic projection of field evaluation results. *The Journal of Primary Prevention, 26,* 321–343.

Dickinson, T. (2008). The machinery of hope. *Rolling Stone, 1048,* 36–42.

Dinh, K. T., & Bond, M. A. (2008). Introduction to Special Section—The Other Side of Acculturation: Changes among Host Individuals and Communities in their Adaptation to Immigrant Populations. *American Journal od Community Psychology, 42,* 283–285.

Dinh, K. T., González Castro, F., Tein, J., & Kim, S. Y. (2009). Cultural predictors of physical and mental health status among Mexican American women: A mediation model. *American Journal of Community Psychology, 43,* 35–48.

Dobrof, J., Ebenstein, H., Dodd, S., Epstein, I., Christ, G., & Blacker, S. (2006). Caregivers and professionals partnership Caregiver Resource Center: Assessing a hospital support program for family caregivers. *Journal of Palliative Medicine, 9,* 196–205.

Dockett, K. H. (1999, June). Engaged Buddhism and community psychology: Partners in social change. In J. Kress (Chair), *Bringing together community psychology and religion/spirituality towards an action research agenda for SCRA.* Symposium conducted at the Biennial Meeting of the Society for Community Research and Action, New Haven, CT.

Dohrenwend, B. S. (1978). Social stress and community psychology. *American Journal of Community Psychology, 6,* 1–14. Reprinted in T. Revenson, A. D'Augelli, S. E. French, D. Hughes, D. Livert, E. Seidman, M. Shinn, & H. Yoshikawa (Eds.), (2002), *A quarter century of community psychology* (pp. 103–117). New York: Kluwer Academic/Plenum.

Dokecki, P. R., Newbrough, J. R., & O'Gorman, R. T. (2001). Toward a community-oriented action research framework for spirituality: Community psychological and theological perspectives. *Journal of Community Psychology, 29,* 497–518.

Domhoff, G. W. (2010). *Who rules America?: Challenges to corporate and class dominance.* Boston: McGraw-Hill.

Dooley, D., & Catalano, R. (2003). Underemployment and its social costs: New research directions [Special issue]. *American Journal of Community Psychology, 32*(1).

Drew, N., Bishop, B., & Syme, G. (2002). Justice and local community change: Towards a substantive theory of justice. *Journal of Community Psychology, 30,* 623–634.

DuBois, D. L., Holloway, B. E., Valentine, J. C., & Cooper, H. (2002). Effectiveness of mentoring programs for youth: A meta-analytic review. *American Journal of Community Psychology, 30,* 157–197.

DuBois, D. L., & Karcher, M. J. (2005). Youth mentoring: Theory, research, and practice. In D. L. DuBois & M. J. Karcher (Eds.), *Handbook of youth mentoring* (pp. 2–11). Thousand Oaks, CA: Sage Publications.

DuBois, D. L., & Silverthorn, N. (2005). Natural mentoring relationships and adolescent health: Evidence from a national study. *American Journal of Public Health, 95,* 518–524.

DuBois, D. L., Silverthorn, N., Pryce, J., Reeves, E., Sánchez, B., Silva, A., et al. (2008). Mentorship: The GirlPOWER! program. In C. W. Leroy & J. E. Mann (Eds.), *Handbook of preventive and intervention programs for adolescent girls.* Hoboken, NJ: Wiley.

DuBois, W. E. B. (1986). The souls of black folk. In N. Huggins (Ed.), *W. E. B. DuBois: Writings* (pp. 357–548). New York: Library of America. (Original work published 1903)

Dudgeon, P., Mallard, J., Oxenham, D., & Fielder, J. (2002). Contemporary Aboriginal perceptions of community. In A. Fisher, C. Sonn, & B. Bishop (Eds.), *Psychological sense of community: Research, applications and implications* (pp. 247–269). New York: Kluwer/Plenum.

Duffy, K. G., & Wong, F. (2003). *Community psychology* (3rd ed.). Boston, MA: Allyn & Bacon.

Dumka, L., Gonzales, N., Wood, J., & Formoso, D. (1998). Using qualitative methods to develop contextually relevant measures and preventive interventions: An illustration. *American Journal of Community Psychology, 26,* 605–637.

DuMont, K., Mitchell-Herzfeld, S., Greene, R., Lee, E., Lowenfels, A., Rodriguez, M., et al. Healthy Families New York (HFNY) randomized trial: Effects on early child abuse and neglect. *Child Abuse and Neglect, 32,* 295–315.

Duncan, T., Duncan, S., Okut, H., Strycker, L., & Hix-Small, H. (2003). A multilevel contextual model of neighborhood collective efficacy. *American Journal of Community Psychology, 32,* 245–252.

Dunst, C., Trivette, C., & Deal, A. (1988). *Enabling and empowering families: Principles and guidelines for practice.* Cambridge, MA: Brookline Press.

Dunst, C., Trivette, C., & Deal, A. (1994). *Supporting and strengthening families.* Cambridge, MA: Brookline Press.

Dupéré, V., & Perkins, D. (2007). Community types and mental health: A multilevel study of local environmental stress and coping. *American Journal of Community Psychology, 39*(1), 107–119.

Durkheim, E. (1893/1933). *The division of labor in society.* New York: The Free Press.

Durlak, J., & DuPre, E. (2008). Implementation matters: A review of research on the influence of implementation on program outcomes and the factors affecting implementation. *American Journal of Community Psychology, 41,* 327–350.

Durlak, J. A., Taylor, R. D., Kawashima, K., Pachan, M. K., DuPre, E. P., Celio, C. I., et al. (2007). Effects of positive youth development programs on school, family, and community systems. *American Journal of Community Psychology, 39,* 269–286.

Durlak, J. A., & Wells, A. M. (1997). Primary prevention mental health programs for children and adolescents: A meta-analytic review. *American Journal of Community Psychology, 25,* 115–152.

Durlak, J., & Wells, A. (1998). Evaluation of indicated preventive intervention (secondary prevention) mental health programs for children and adolescents. *American Journal of Community Psychology, 26,* 775–802.

Eagly, A. H. & Carli, L. L. (2007). *Through the labyrinth: The truth about how women become leaders.* Cambridge, MA: Harvard Business School Press.

Eby, L. T., Allen, T. D., Evans, S. C., Ng, T., & DuBois, D. L. (2007). Does mentoring matter? A multidisciplinary meta-analysis comparing mentored and non-mentored individuals. *Journal of Vocational Behavior, 72,* 254–267.

Edgerton, J. W. (2000). [Untitled videotape interview]. In J. G. Kelly (Ed.), *The history of community psychology: A video presentation of context and exemplars.* Chicago: Society for Community Research and Action.

Edwards, R., Jumper-Thurman, P., Plested, B., Oetting, E., & Swanson, L. (2000). Community readiness: research to practice. *Journal of Community Psychology, 28,* 291–307.

Elias, M. J. (1987). Establishing enduring prevention programs: Advancing the legacy of Swampscott. *American Journal of Community Psychology, 15,* 539–553.

Elias, M. J. (1994). Capturing excellence in applied settings: A participant conceptualizer and praxis explicator role for community psychologists. *American Journal of Community Psychology, 22,* 293–318.

Elias, M. J. (1995). Primary prevention as health and social competence promotion. *Journal of Primary Prevention, 16,* 5–24.

Elias, M. J. (2002). Education's 9/11 report card. *Education Week, 22*(1), 47.

Elias, M. J. (2004). The connection between social-emotional learning and learning disabilities: Implications for intervention. *Learning Disability Quarterly, 27*(1), 53–63.

Elias, M. J., Bryan, K., Patrikakou, E., & Weissberg, R. P. (2003). Challenges in creating effective home-school partnerships in adolescence: Promising paths for collaboration. *The School Community Journal, 13*(1), 133–153.

Elias, M. J., & Clabby, J. (1992). *Building social problem-solving skills: Guidelines from a school-based program.* San Francisco: Jossey-Bass.

Elias, M. J., & Cohen, J. (1999). *Lessons for life: How smart schools build social, emotional, and academic intelligence.* Bloomington, IN: National Education Service/ National Center for Innovation and Education. www.communitiesofhope.org

Elias, M. J., Gara, M. A., Schuyler, T. F., Branden-Muller, L. R., & Sayette, M. A. (1991). The promotion of social competence: Longitudinal study of a preventive school-based program. *American Journal of Orthopsychiatry, 61,* 409–417.

Elias, M. J., Gara, M. A., Ubriaco, M., Rothbaum, P., Clabby, J., & Schuyler, T. F. (1986). Impact of preventive social-problem-solving intervention on children's coping with middle school stressors. *American Journal of Community Psychology, 14,* 259–275.

Elias, M. J., & Kamarinos, P. (2003, August). *Sustainability of school-based preventive social-emotional programs: A model site study.* Presentation at the meeting of the American Psychological Association, Toronto, Canada.

Elias, M. J., Parker, S. J., Kash, V. M., & Dunkelblau, E. (2007). Social-emotional learning and character and moral education in children: Synergy of fundamental divergence in our schools? *Journal of Research in Character Education, 5,* 167–181.

Elias, M. J., & Tobias, S. E. (1996). *Social problem-solving interventions in the schools.* New York: Guilford.

Elias, M. J., & Zins, J. (Eds.). (2003). *Bullying, peer harassment, and victimization in the schools: The next generation of prevention.* New York: Haworth.

Elias, M. J., Zins, J., Weissberg, R. P., Frey, K., Greenberg, M., Haynes, et al. (1997). *Promoting social and emotional learning: Guidelines for educators.* Alexandria, VA: Association for Supervision and Curriculum Development.

Ellis, L., Marsh, H., & Craven (2009). Addressing the challenges faced by early adolescents: A mixed-method evaluation of the benefits of peer support. *American Journal of Community Psychology, 44,* 54–75.

Ellison, N., Steinfield, C., & Lampe, C. (2007). The benefits of Facebook "friends": Social capital and college students use of online social network sites. *Journal of Computer-Mediated Communication, 12,* 203.

Enett, S., Rosenbaum, D., Flewelling, R., Bieler, G., Ringwalt, C., & Bailey, S. (1994). Long-term evaluation of drug abuse resistance education. *Addictive Behaviors, 19,* 113–125.

Engstrom, M., Jason, L. A., Townsend, S., Pokorny, S., & Curie, C. (2002). Community readiness for prevention: Applying stage theory to multi-community interventions. *Journal of Prevention and Intervention in the Community, 24,* 29–46.

Evans, G. W. (2004). The environment of childhood poverty. *American Psychologist, 59,* 77–92.

Evans, S. (2007). Youth sense of community: Voice and power in community contexts. *Journal of Community Psychology, 35,* 693–709.

Evans, S., Hanlin, C., & Prilleltensky, I. (2007). Blending ameliorative and transformative approaches in human service organizations: A case study. *Journal of Community Psychology, 35,* 329–346.

Fairweather, G. W. (1967). *Methods for experimental social innovation.* New York: Wiley.

Fairweather, G. W. (1979). Experimental development and dissemination of an alternative to psychiatric hospitalization. In R. Munoz, L. Snowden, & J. G. Kelly (Eds.), *Social and psychological research in community settings* (pp. 305–342). San Francisco: Jossey-Bass.

Fairweather, G. W. (1994). [Untitled videotape interview]. In J. G. Kelly (Ed.), *The history of community psychology: A video presentation of context and exemplars.* Chicago: Society for Community Research and Action.

Fairweather, G. W., Sanders, D., Cressler, D., & Maynard, H. (1969). *Community life for the mentally ill: An alternative to institutional care.* Chicago: Aldine.

Farrell, S., Aubry, T., & Coulombe, D. (2004). Neighborhoods and neighbors: Do they contribute to personal well-being? *Journal of Community Psychology, 32,* 9–26.

Fawcett, S. B., Paine-Andrews, A., Francisco, V., Schulz, J., Richter, K., Lewis, R., et al. (1995). Using empowerment theory in collaborative partnerships for community health and development. *American Journal of Community Psychology, 23,* 677–698.

Fawcett, S. B., White, G., Balcazar, F., Suarez-Balcazar, Y., Mathews, R., Paine-Andrews, A., Seekins, T., & Smith, J. (1994). A contextual-behavioral model of empowerment: Case studies involving people with physical disabilities. *American Journal of Community Psychology, 22,* 471–496.

Feinberg, M., Greenberg, M., & Osgood, D. W. (2004). Readiness, functioning and perceived effectiveness in community prevention coalitions: A study of Communities That Care. *American Journal of Community Psychology, 33,* 163–176.

Felner, R., & Adan, A. (1988). The School Transition Environment Project: An ecological intervention and evaluation. In R. Price, E. Cowen, R. Lorion, & J. Ramos-McKay (Eds.), *Fourteen ounces of prevention* (pp. 111–122). Washington, DC: American Psychological Association.

Felton, B., & Berry, C. (1992). Groups as social network members: Overlooked sources of social support. *American Journal of Community Psychology, 20,* 253–262.

Felton, B., & Shinn, M. (1992). Social integration and social support: Moving "social support" beyond the individual level. *Journal of Community Psychology, 20,* 103–115.

Felton, C. (2004). Lessons learned since September 11th 2001 concerning the mental health impact of terrorism, appropriate response strategies and future preparedness. *Psychiatry, 67,* 147–152.

Ferrari, J., Jason, L., Olson, B., Davis, M., & Alvarez, J. (2002). Sense of community among Oxford House residents recovering from substance abuse: Making a house a home. In A. Fisher, C. Sonn, & B. Bishop (Eds.), *Psychological sense of community: Research, applications, and implications* (pp. 109–122). New York: Kluwer Academic/Plenum.

Fetterman, D. (1996). Empowerment evaluation: An introduction to theory and practice. In D. Fetterman, S. Kaftarian, & A. Wandersman (Eds.), *Empowerment evaluation: Knowledge and tools for self-assessment and accountability* (pp. 3–46). Thousand Oaks, CA: Sage.

Fetterman, D. (2001). *Foundations of empowerment evaluation.* Thousand Oaks, CA: Sage.

Fetterman, D. (2002). Empowerment evaluation: Building communities of practice and a culture of learning. *American Journal of Community Psychology, 30,* 89–102.

Fetterman, D. M. (2005). Empowerment evaluation: from the digital divide to academic distress. In D. Fetterman & A. Wandersman, (Eds.), *Empowerment evaluation principles in practice* (pp. 107–121). New York: Guilford.

Fetterman, D., & Wandersman, A. (Eds.). (2005). *Empowerment Evaluation Principles in Practice.* New York: Guilford Press.

Fetterman, D. M., & Wandersman, A. (2007). Empowerment evaluation: yesterday, today, and tomorrow. *American Journal of Evaluation, 28*(2), 179–198.

Fiala, W., Bjorck, J., & Gorsuch, R. (2002). The religious support scale: Construction, validation, and cross-validation. *American Journal of Community Psychology, 30,* 761–786.

Field, J. (2003). *Social capital.* New York: Routledge.

Fields, A. M., Swan, S., & Kloos, B. (2010). "What it means to be a woman": Ambivalent sexism in female college students' experiences and attitudes. *Sex Roles, 62,* 554–567.

Finckenauer, J. (1982). *Scared Straight and the panacea phenomenon.* Englewood Cliffs, NJ: Prentice Hall.

Findley, S., Irigoyen, M., Sanchez, M., Stockwell, M., Mejia, M., Guzman, L., et al. (2008). Effectiveness of a community coalition for improving child vaccination rates in New York City. *American Journal of Public Health, 98,* 1959.

Fine, M., & Burns, A. (2003). Class notes: Toward a critical psychology of class and schooling. *Journal of Social Issues, 59,* 841–860.

Fisher, A., & Sonn, C. (2002). Psychological sense of community in Australia and the challenges of change. *Journal of Community Psychology, 30,* 597–609.

Fisher, A., Sonn, C., & Bishop, B. (Eds.). (2002). *Psychological sense of community: Research, applications and implications.* New York: Kluwer/Plenum.

Fisher, D., Imm, P., Chinaman, M., & Wandersman, A. (2006). *Getting To Outcomes with developmental assets: Ten steps to measuring success in youth programs and communities.* Minneapolis: Search Institute.

Fisher, P., & Ball, T. (2003). Tribal participatory research: Mechanisms of a collaborative model. *American Journal of Community Psychology, 32,* 207–217.

Fitzgerald, F. S. (1995). *The great Gatsby.* New York: Simon & Schuster. (Original work published 1925)

Flad, H. (2003, April 30). *Sense of places, senses of place.* Spring convocation address, Vassar College, Poughkeepsie, NY.

Flaspohler, P., Duffy, J., Wandersman, A., Stillman, L., & Maras, M. A. (2008). Unpacking capacity: An intersection of research-to-practice models and community-centered models. *American Journal of Community Psychology, 41,* 182–196.

Fleishman, J., Sherbourne, C., Cleary, P., Wu, A., Crystal, S., & Hays, R. (2003). Patterns of coping among persons with HIV infection: Configurations, correlates, and change. *American Journal of Community Psychology, 32,* 187–204.

Flores, W. V., & Benmayor, R. (1997). *Latino cultural citizenship: Claiming identity, space, and rights.* Boston: Beacon Press.

Florin, P., Chavis, D., Wandersman, A., & Rich, R. (1992). A systems approach to understanding and enhancing grassroots organizations: The Block Booster Project. In R. Levine & H. Fitzgerald (Eds.), *Analysis of dynamic psychological systems: Methods and applications* (Vol. 2, pp. 215–243). New York: Plenum.

Florin, P., & Wandersman, A. (1984). Cognitive social learning and participation in community development. *American Journal of Community Psychology, 12,* 689–708.

Folayemi, B. (2001). Case story #1: Building the grassroots coalition. *American Journal of Community Psychology, 29,* 193–197.

Folkman, S., & Moskowitz, J. (2004). Coping: Promises and pitfalls. *Annual Review of Psychology, 55,* 745–774.

Fondacaro, M., & Weinberg, D. (2002). Concepts of social justice in community psychology: Toward a social ecological epistemology. *American Journal of Community Psychology, 30,* 473–492.

Foster, S. E., Vaughan, R. D., Foster, W. H., & Califano, J. A. (2003). Alcohol consumption and expenditures for underage drinking and adult excessive drinking. *The Journal of the American Medical Association [JAMA], 289,* 989–995.

Foster-Fishman, P., & Behrens, T. (2007). Systems change reborn: Rethinking our theories, methods, and efforts in human services reform and community-based change. *American Journal of Community Psychology, 39,* 191–196.

Foster-Fishman, P., Berkowitz, S., Lounsbury, D., Jacobson, S., & Allen, N. (2001). Building collaborative capacity in community coalitions: A review and integrative framework. *American Journal of Community Psychology, 29,* 241–262.

Foster-Fishman, P., Nowell, B., Deacon, Z., Nievar, M. A., & McCann, P. (2005). Using methods that matter: The impact of reflection, dialogue, and voice. *American Journal of Community Psychology, 36,* 275–291.

Foster, M., Olchowski, A., & Webster-Stratton, C. (2007). Is stacking intervention components cost effective? An analysis of the Incredible Years program. *Journal of the American Academy of Child and Adolescent Psychiatry, 46,* 1414–1424.

Foster-Fishman, P., Nowell, B., & Yang, H. (2007). Putting the system back into systems change: A framework for understanding and changing organizational and community systems. *American Journal of Community Psychology, 39,* 197–215.

Fowers, B., & Richardson, F. (1996). Why is multiculturalism good? *American Psychologist, 51,* 609–621.

Frable, D. (1997). Gender, racial, ethnic, sexual and class identities. *Annual Review of Psychology, 48,* 139–162.

Francescato, D. (2007). Community psychology core competencies taught at the undergraduate and master's level in some Italian universities and in most non-academically based master's programs. *The Community Psychologist, 40*(4), 49–52.

Francescato, D., Arcidiacono, C., Albanesi, C., & Mannarini, T. (2007). Community psychology in Italy: Past developments and future perspectives. In S. M. Reich, M. Riemer, I. Prilleltensky, & M. Montero (Eds.), *International community psychology. History and theories* (pp. 263–281). New York: Springer.

Frankl, V. (1984). *Man's search for meaning: An introduction to logotherapy* (3rd ed.). New York: Simon & Schuster. (Original work published 1959.)

Freeman, H., Fryers, T., & Henderson, J. (1985). *Mental health services in Europe 10 years on.* Copenhagen: WHO.

Freire, P. (1993). *Pedagogy of the oppressed* (Rev. ed.). New York: Continuum. (Original work published 1970)

French, J. R. P., & Raven, B. (1959). The bases of social power. In D. Cartwright, (Ed.), *Studies in social power* (pp. 150–167). Ann Arbor, MI: Institute for Social Research.

Friedman, T. (2000). *The Lexus and the olive tree.* New York: Random House.

Fryer, D., & Fagan, R. (2003). Toward a critical community psychological perspective on unemployment and mental health research. *American Journal of Community Psychology, 32,* 89–96.

Fujimoto, K., Valente, T., & Pentz, M. A. (2009). Network structural influences on the adoption of evidence-based prevention in communities. *Journal of Community Psychology, 37,* 803–845.

Gallimore, R., Goldenberg, C., & Weisner, T. (1993). The social construction and subjective reality of activity settings: Implications for community psychology. *American Journal of Community Psychology, 21,* 537–559.

Gao, Q., Kaushal, N., & Waldfogel, J. (2009). How have expansions in the earned income tax credit affected family expenditures? In J. Ziliak (Ed.), *Welfare reform and its long-term consequences for America's poor.* Cambridge, UK: Cambridge University Press.

Garbarino, J., & Kostelny, K. (1992). Child maltreatment as a community problem. *Child Abuse and Neglect, 16,* 455–464.

Garcia, I., Giuliani, F., & Weisenfeld, E. (1999). Community and sense of community: The case of an urban barrio in Caracas. *Journal of Community Psychology, 27,* 727–740.

Garmezy, N. (1985). Stress resistant children: The search for protective factors. In J. E. Stevenson (Ed.), *Recent research in developmental psychology* (book supplement to the *Journal of Child Psychology and Psychiatry, No. 4*). Oxford: Pergamon.

Gatz, M., & Cotton, B. (1994). Age as a dimension of diversity: The experience of being old. In E. J. Trickett, R. J. Watts, & D. Birman (Eds.), *Human diversity: Perspectives on people in context* (pp. 334–355). San Francisco: Jossey-Bass.

Gaventa, J. (1980). *Power and powerlessness: Quiescence and rebellion in an Appalachian valley.* Urbana, IL: University of Illinois Press.

Gergen, K. (1973). Social psychology as history. *Journal of Personality and Social Psychology, 26,* 309–320.

Gergen, K. (2001). Psychological science in a postmodern context. *American Psychologist, 56,* 803–813.

Gershuny, J., & Fisher, K. (1999). *Leisure in the UK across the 20th century.* Institute for Social and Economic Research, University of Essex.

Giddens, A., Duneier, M., & Appelbaum, R. (2003). *Introduction to sociology* (4th ed.). New York: Norton.

Gilens, M. (1996). Race and poverty in America: Public misperceptions and the American news media. *Public Opinion Quarterly, 60,* 515–541.

Gilliam, F., & Iyengar, S. (2000). Prime suspects: The influence of local television news on the viewing public. *American Journal of Political Science, 44,* 560–574.

Gillock, K. L., & Reyes, O. (1996). High school transition-related changes in urban minority students' academic performance and perceptions of self and school environment. *Journal of Community Psychology, 24,* 245–262.

Gist, R., & Lubin, B. (1989). *Psychosocial aspects of disaster.* Oxford, England: John Wiley & Sons.

Glidewell, J. (1994). [Untitled videotape interview]. In J. G. Kelly (Ed.), *The history of community psychology: A video presentation of context and exemplars.* Chicago: Society for Community Research and Action.

Glidewell, J., Gildea, M., & Kaufman, M. (1973). The preventive and therapeutic effects of two school mental health programs. *American Journal of Community Psychology, 1,* 295–329.

Glover, M., Dudgeon, P., & Huygens, I. (2005). Colonization and racism. In G. Nelson & I. Prilleltensky (Eds.), *Community psychology: In pursuit of liberation and well-being* (pp. 330–347). New York: Palgrave Macmillan.

Goldston, S. (1994). [Untitled videotape interview]. In J. G. Kelly (Ed.), *The history of community psychology: A video presentation of context and exemplars.* Chicago: Society for Community Research and Action.

Goldstrom, I. D., Campbell, J., Rogers J. A., Lambert, D. B., Blacklow, B., Henderson M. J., et al. (2006). National estimates for mental health mutual support groups, self-help organizations, and consumer-operated services. *Administration and Policy in Mental Health & Mental Health Services Research, 33,* 92–103.

Goleman, D. (1995). *Emotional intelligence.* New York: Bantam.

Gone, J. P. (2006). Research, reservations: Response and responsibility in an American Indian community. *American Journal of Community Psychology, 37,* 333–340.

Gone, J. P. (2007). "We never was happy living like a Whiteman": Mental health disparities and the post-colonial predicament in American Indian communities. *American Journal of Community Psychology, 40,* 290–300.

Gone, J. P., & Alcantra, C. (2007). Identifying effective mental health interventions for American Indians and Alaska Natives: A review of the literature. *Cultural Diversity and Ethnic Minority Psychology, 13,* 356–363.

Gone, J. P. (2008). Encountering professional psychology: Re-envisioning mental health services for Native North America. In L. J. Kirmayer & G. G. Valaskakis (Eds.), *Healing traditions: The mental health of Aboriginal Peoples in Canada* (pp. 419–439). Vancouver: UBC Press.

Gonsiorek, J. C., & Weinrich, J. D. (1991). The definition and scope of sexual orientation. In J. C. Gonsiorek & J. D. Weinrich (Eds.), *Homosexuality: Research implications for public policy* (pp. 1–12). Newbury Park, CA: Sage.

Gonzales, N. A., Cauce, A. M., Friedman, R. J., & Mason, C. A. (1996). Family, peer, and neighborhood influences on academic achievement among African-American adolescents: One-year prospective effects. *American Journal of Community Psychology, 24,* 365–388. Reprinted in T. Revenson, A. D'Augelli, S. E. French, D. Hughes, D. Livert, E. Seidman, M. Shinn & H. Yoshikawa (Eds.), (2002), *A quarter century of community psychology* (pp. 535–556). New York: Kluwer Academic/Plenum.

Gonzalez, N., Moll, L. C., & Amanti, C. (2005). *Funds of knowledge: Theorizing practices in households, communities, and classrooms.* Malwah, NJ: Lawrence Erlbaum Associates.

Goodkind, J., & Deacon, Z. (2004). Methodological issues in conducting research with refugee women: Principles for recognizing and re-centering the multiply marginalized. *Journal of Community Psychology, 32,* 721–740.

Goodkind, J., & Foster-Fishman, P. (2002). Integrating diversity and fostering interdependence: Ecological lessons learned about refugee participation in multiethnic communities. *Journal of Community Psychology, 30,* 389–410.

Goodman, R. M., & Steckler, A. (1987). A model for the institutionalization of health promotion programs. *Family and Community Health, 11,* 63–78.

Goodman, R. M., & Wandersman, A. (1994). FORE-CAST: A formative approach to evaluating community coalitions and community-based initiatives. In S. Kaftarian & W. Hansen (Eds.), *Journal of Community Psychology Monograph Series,* Center for Substance Abuse Prevention [Special issue], 6–25.

Goodstein, L., & Sandler, I. (1978). Using psychology to promote human welfare: A conceptual analysis of the role of community psychology. *American Psychologist, 33,* 882–891.

Gottlieb, B. H., & Peters, L. A. (1991). A national demographic portrait of mutual aid participants in Canada. *American Journal of Community Psychology, 19,* 651–666.

Gould, S. J. (1981). *The mismeasure of man.* New York: Norton.

Granovetter, M. (1973). The strength of weak ties. *American Journal of Sociology, 78,* 1360–1380.

Green, B. L., Chung, J. Y., Daroowalla, A., Kaltman, S., & DeBenedictis, C. (2006). Evaluating the cultural validity of the stress life events screening questionnaire. *Violence Against Women, 12,* 1191–1213.

Green, L., & Lewis, M. (1986). *Measurement and evaluation in health education and health promotion.* Palo Alto: Mayfield.

Greenberg, M. T., Feinberg, M., Brendan, J., Gomez, B., & Osgood, D. (2005). Testing a community prevention focused model of coalition functioning and sustainability: A comprehensive study of Communities That Care in Pennsylvania. In T. Stockwell, P. Gruenewald, J. Toumbourou, & J. Loxley (Eds.), *Preventing harmful substance use: The evidence base for policy and practice* (pp. 129–142). London: Wiley.

Greenberg, M. T., Weissberg, R., O'Brien, M., Zins, J., Fredericks, L., Resnik, H., et al. (2003). Enhancing school-based prevention and youth development through coordinated social, emotional, and academic learning. *American Psychologist, 58,* 466–474.

Greene, M. (1995). *Releasing the imagination: Essays on education, the arts, and social change.* San Francisco: Jossey-Bass.

Greenfield, P., Keller, H., Fuligni, A., & Maynard, A. (2003). Cultural pathways through universal development. *Annual Review of Psychology, 54,* 461–490.

Greenfield, T., Stoneking, B, Humphreys, K., & Bond, J. (2008). A randomized trial of a mental health consumer-managed alternative to civil commitment for acute psychiatric crisis. *American Journal of Community Psychology, 42,* 135–144.

Greenwood, P., Model, K., Rydell, C. P., & Chiesa, J. (1998). *Diverting children from a life of crime: Measuring costs and benefits.* Santa Monica, CA: Rand Corporation.

Griffith et al., 2007

Gridley, H., & Turner, C. (2010). Gender, power, and community psychology. In G. Nelson, & I. Prilleltensky (Eds.), *Community psychology: In pursuit of well-being and liberation* (2nd ed., pp. 389–406). London: MacMillan.

Gruber, J., & Trickett, E. J. (1987). Can we empower others? The paradox of empowerment in the governing of an alternative public school. *American Journal of Community Psychology, 15,* 353–371.

Guerra, N. G., & Knox, L. (2008). How culture impacts the dissemination and implementation of innovation: A case study of the families and schools together program (FAST) for preventing violence with immigrant Latino youth. *American Journal of Community Psychology, 42,* 304–313.

Gulcur, L., Stefanic, A., Shinn, M., Tsemberis, S., & Fischer, S. N. (2003). Housing, hospitalization and cost outcomes for homeless individuals with psychiatric disabilities participating in continuum of care and housing first programmes. *Journal of Community and Applied Social Psychology, 13,* 171–186.

Gustafson, D., Hawkins, R., Boberg, E., Pingree, S., Serline, R., Graziano, F., & Chan, C. (1999). Impact of a patient-centered, computer-based health information/support system. *American Journal of Preventive Medicine, 16,* 1–9.

Haber, M., Cohen, J., Lucas, T., & Baltes, B. (2007). The relationship between self-reported received and perceived social support: A meta-analytic review. *American Journal of Community Psychology, 39*(1), 133–144.

Haertl, K. (2005). Factors influencing success in a Fairweather model mental health program. *American Journal of Psychiatric Rehabilitation, 28*(4), 370–377.

Haertl, K. (2007). The Fairweather mental health housing model—a peer supportive environment: Implications for psychiatric rehabilitation. *American Journal of Psychiatric Rehabilitation, 10*(3), 149–162.

Hall, C. C. I. (1997). Cultural malpractice: The growing obsolescence of psychology with the changing U.S. population. *American Psychologist, 52,* 642–651.

Hall, P. (1999). Social capital in Britain. *British Journal of Political Science, 29,* 417–461.

Hamby, S. (2000). The importance of community in a feminist analysis of domestic violence among American Indians. *American Journal of Community Psychology, 28,* 649–670.

Hanewinkel, R. (2004). Prevention of bullying in German schools: An evaluation of an anti-bullying approach. In P. Smith, D. Pepler, & K. Rigby (Eds.), *Bullying in schools: How successful can interventions be?* (pp. 81–97). Cambridge, UK: Cambridge University Press.

Harlem Children's Zone. (n.d.). Retrieved August 9, 2010, from http://www.hcz.org/our-results

Harper, G. W. (2007). Sex isn't that simple: Culture and context in HIV prevention interventions for gay and bisexual male adolescents. *American Psychologist, 62*(8), 806–819.

Harper, G. W. (2010). A journey towards liberation: Confronting heterosexism and the oppression of lesbian, gay, bisexual and transgendered people. In G. Nelson & I. Prilleltensky (Eds.), *Community psychology: In pursuit of liberation and well-being, 2nd Edition* (pp. 407–431). New York: Palgrave Macmillan.

Harper, G. W., Bangi, A., Contreras, R., Pedraza, A., Tolliver, M., & Vess, L. (2004). Diverse phases of collaboration: Working together to improve community-based HIV interventions for adolescents. *American Journal of Community Psychology, 33,* 193–204.

Harper, G. W., Lardon, C., Rappaport, J., Bangi, A., Contreras, R., & Pedraza, A. (2004). Community narratives: The use of narrative ethnography in participatory community research. In L. A. Jason, C. Keys, Y. Suarez-Balcazar, R. Taylor, & M. Davis (Eds.), *Participatory community research: Theories and methods in action* (pp. 199–217). Washington, DC: American Psychological Association.

Harrell, S. P. (1997, May). *Development and initial validation of scales to measure racism-related stress.* Poster presentation at the Biennial Conference of the Society for Community Research and Action, Columbia, SC.

Harrell, S. P. (2000). A multidimensional conceptualization of racism-related stress: Implications for the well-being of people of color. *American Journal of Orthopsychiatry, 70,* 1–16.

Harrell, S. P., Taylor, S., & Burke, E. (Eds.). (1999, Winter). Cultural competence in community research and action [Special section]. *The Community Psychologist, 32,* 22–54.

Hartup, W. W., & Stevens, N. (1997). Friendships and adaptation in the life course. *Psychological Bulletin, 121,* 355–370.

Haskell, I. (1997). *The effectiveness of character education and mentoring: An evaluation of the Troopers school-based program.* Unpublished manuscript, University of South Carolina.

Hathaway, B. (2001). Case story #2: Growing a healthy community: A practical guide. *American Journal of Community Psychology, 29,* 199–204.

Hawkins, J. D., Catalano, R. F., & Associates. (1992). *Communities That Care: Action for drug abuse prevention.* San Francisco: Jossey-Bass.

Hawkins, J. D., & Lam, T. (1987). Teacher practices, social development, and delinquency. In J. D. Burchard & S. N. Burchard (Ed.), *Prevention of delinquent behavior* (pp. 241–274). Newbury Park, CA: Sage.

Hawkins, J., Oesterle, S., Brown, E., Arthur, M., Abbott, R., Fagan, A., et al. (2009). Results of a Type 2 translational research trial to prevent adolescent drug use and delinquency: A test of Communities That Care. *Archives of Pediatric and Adolescent Medicine, 163,* 789–798.

Hazel, K. (2007). Infusing practice into community psychology graduate education. *The Community Psychologist, 40,* 2, 81–86.

Hazel, K. L., & Mohatt, G. V. (2001). Cultural and spiritual pathways to sobriety: Informing substance abuse prevention and intervention for Native American communities. *Journal of Community Psychology, 29,* 541–562.

Hazel, K., & Onanga, E. (2003). Experimental social innovation and dissemination [Special issue]. *American Journal of Community Psychology, 32*(4).

Hebert, R., Zdaniuk, B., Schulz, R., & Scheier, M. (2009). Positive and negative religious coping and well-being in women with breast cancer. *Journal of Palliative Medicine, 12*(6), 537–545.

Heckman, J. J., Moon, S. H., Pinto, R., Savelyev, P. A., & Yavitz, A. Q. (2009). *The rate of return to the High Scope Perry Preschool program* (NBER Working Paper No. 15471). Retrieved March 7, 2011, from http://www.nber.org.

Heflinger, C. A., & Christens, B. (2006). Rural behavioral health services for children and adolescents: An ecological and community psychology analysis. *Journal of Community Psychology, 34,* 379–400.

Heilman, M. (2001). Description and prescription: How gender stereotypes prevent women's ascent up the organizational ladder. *Journal of Social Issues, 57,* 657–688.

Heller, K. (1984). Historical trends in mental health beliefs and practices. In K. Heller, R. Price, S. Reinharz, S. Riger, & A. Wandersman (Eds.). *Psychology and community change* (2nd ed., pp. 26–48). Homewood, IL: Dorsey.

Heller, K., & Monahan, J. (1977). *Psychology and community change.* Homewood, IL: Dorsey.

Heller, K., Price, R. H., Reinharz, S., Riger, S., & Wandersman, A. (1984). *Psychology and community change: Challenges of the future.* Homewood, IL: Dorsey Press/Pacific Grove, CA: Wadsworth.

Helms, J. E. (1994). The conceptualizations of racial identity and other "racial" constructs. In E. J. Trickett, R. J. Watts, & D. Birman (Eds.), *Human diversity: Perspectives on people in context* (pp. 285–310). San Francisco: Jossey-Bass.

Helm, S. (2003, June). Rural health in Molokai: Land, people and empowerment. In C. O'Donnell (Chair), *Interdisciplinary training and rural capacity.* Symposium at the Biennial Meeting of the Society for Community Research and Action, Las Vegas, NM.

Helm, S., & Flaspohler, P. (2008). Systems change through school-community partnerships [Special section]. *The Community Psychologist, 41,* 2.

Hebert, R., Zdaniuk, B., Schulz, R., & Scheier, M. (2009). Positive and negative religious coping and well-being in women with breast cancer. *Journal of Palliative Medicine, 12*(6), 537–545.

Hermans, H., & Kempen, H. (1998). Moving cultures: The perilous problems of cultural dichotomies in a globalizing society. *American Psychologist, 53,* 1111–1120.

Herrera, C., Grossman, J. B., Kauh, T. J., Feldman, A. F., & McMaken, J. (2007). *Making a difference in schools: The Big Brothers Big Sisters school-based mentoring impact study.* Philadelphia: Public Private Ventures.

Hickey, S., & Mohan, G. (2005). *Participation: From tyranny to transformation? Exploring new approaches to participation in development.* New York: Zed Books.

Hill, J. (1996). Psychological sense of community: Suggestions for future research. *Journal of Community Psychology, 24,* 431–438.

Hill, J. (2000). A rationale for the integration of spirituality into community psychology. *Journal of Community Psychology, 28,* 139–150.

Hill, P., & Pargament, K. (2003). Advances in the conceptualization and measurement of religion and spirituality: Implications for physical and mental health research. *American Psychologist, 58,* 64–74.

Hillier, J. (2002). Presumptive planning: From urban design to community creation in one move? In A. Fisher, C. Sonn, & B. Bishop, (Eds.), *Psychological sense of community: Research, applications and implications* (pp. 43–68). New York: Kluwer/Plenum.

Himmelman, A. (2001). On coalitions and the transformation of power relations: Collaborative betterment and collaborative empowerment. *American Journal of Community Psychology, 29,* 277–284.

Hirsch, B. J. (1980). Natural support systems and coping with life changes. *American Journal of Community Psychology, 8,* 159–172.

Hirsch, B. J., Engel-Levy, A., DuBois, D. L., & Hardesty, P. (1990). The role of social environments in social support. In B. R. Sarason, I. G. Sarason, & G. Pierce (Eds.), *Social support: An interactional view* (pp. 367–393). New York: Wiley.

Hirsch, D. (2010, April 30). Program has $3.5 million more to fix homes. *Courier Post.* Retrieved September 15, 2010, from http://www.courierpostonline.com/article/20100430/NEWS01/4300334/1006/news01

Hirschi, T. (1969). *Causes of delinquency.* Berkeley, CA: University of California Press.

Hobfoll, S. E. (1988). *The ecology of stress.* New York: Hemisphere.

Hobfoll, S. E. (1998). *Stress, culture and community: The psychology and philosophy of stress.* New York: Plenum.

Hobfoll, S. E., & London, P. (1986). The relationship of self-concept and social support to emotional distress among women during war. *Journal of Social and Clinical Psychology, 4,* 189–203.

Hobfoll, S. E., & Vaux, A. (1993). Social support: Social resources and social context. In L. Goldberger & S. Breznitz (Eds.), *Handbook of stress: Theoretical and clinical aspects* (2nd ed., pp. 685–705). New York: Free Press.

Hochschild, J. (2003). Social class in public schools. *Journal of Social Issues, 59,* 821–840.

Holahan, C. J., & Spearly, J. (1980). Coping and ecology: An integrative model for community psychology. *American Journal of Community Psychology, 8,* 671–685.

Holahan, C. J., Moos, R. H., & Bonin, L. (1997). Social support, coping, and psychological adjustment: A resources model. In G. Pierce, B. Lakey, I. G. Sarason, & B. R. Sarason (Eds.), *Sourcebook of social support and personality* (pp. 169–186). New York: Plenum.

Holden, A., Shain, R., Miller, W., Piper, J., Perdue, S., Thurman, A., & Korte, J. (2008). The influence of depression on sexual risk reduction and STD infection in a controlled, randomized intervention trial. *Sexually Transmitted Diseases, 35,* 898–904.

Hollander, D., & Offerman, L. (1990). Power and leadership in organizations: Relationships in transition. *American Psychologist, 45,* 179–189.

Hollingshead, A., & Redlich, F. (1958). *Social class and mental illness: A community study.* New York: Wiley.

Holmes, T. H., & Rahe, R. H. (1967). The social readjustment rating scale. *Journal of Psychosomatic Research, 11,* 213–218.

Hooks, B. (1984). *Feminist theory: From margin to center.* Boston, MA: South End Press.

Horton, M. (1990). *The long haul: An autobiography.* New York: Doubleday.

Horton, M., & Freire, P. (1990). *We make the road by walking: Conversations on education and social change.* Philadelphia: Temple University Press.

Horowitz, J., & Garber, J. (2006). The prevention of depressive symptoms in children and adolescents: A meta-analytic review. *Journal of Consulting and Clinical Psychology, 74,* 401–415.

Howard, K., & Brooks-Gunn, J. (2009). The role of home-visiting programs in prevention child abuse and neglect. *The Future of Children, 19,* 119–146.

Hoyt-Meyers, L., Cowen, E. L., Work W. C., Wyman P. A., Magnus, K., Fagen, D. B., & Lotyczewski, B. S.

(1995). Test correlates of resilient outcomes among highly stressed second- and third-grade urban children. *Journal of Community Psychology, 23,* 326–338.

Hughes, D., & DuMont, K. (1993). Using focus groups to facilitate culturally anchored research. *American Journal of Community Psychology, 21,* 775–806. Reprinted in T. Revenson, A. D'Augelli, S. E. French, D. Hughes, D. Livert, E. Seidman, M. Shinn, & H. Yoshikawa (Eds.), (2002), *Ecological research to promote social change: methodological advances from community psychology* (pp. 257–289). New York: Kluwer Academic/Plenum.

Hughes, D., & Seidman, E. (2002). In pursuit of a culturally anchored methodology. In T. Revenson, A. D'Augelli, S. E. French, D. Hughes, D. Livert, E. Seidman, M. Shinn, & H. Yoshikawa (Eds.), (2002), *Ecological research to promote social change: methodological advances from community psychology* (pp. 243–255). New York: Kluwer Academic/Plenum.

Hughey, J., & Speer, P. (2002). Community, sense of community, and networks. In A. Fisher, C. Sonn, & B. Bishop, (Eds.), *Psychological sense of community: Research, applications and implications* (pp. 69–84). New York: Kluwer/Plenum.

Hughey, J., Speer, P. W., & Peterson, N. A. (1999). Sense of community in community organizations: Structure and evidence of validity. *Journal of Community Psychology, 27,* 97–113.

Hughey, J., & Whitehead, T. (2003, June). Institutions and community: Where power and ecology meet. In P. Speer (Chair), *Power and empowerment: Institutions, organizations and the grass-roots.* Symposium at the biennial meeting of the Society for Community Research and Action, Las Vegas, NM.

Humphreys, K. (1996). Clinical psychologists as psychotherapists: History, future, and alternatives. *American Psychologist, 51,* 190–197.

Humphreys, K. (1997, Spring). Individual and social benefits of mutual aid self-help groups. *Social Policy, 27,* 12–19.

Humphreys, K. (2000). Community narratives and personal stories in Alcoholics Anonymous. *Journal of Community Psychology, 28,* 495–506.

Humphreys, K. (2009). Responding to the psychological impact of war on the Iraqi people and U.S.

veterans: Mixing icing, praying for cake. *American Psychologist, 64*(8), 712–723.

Humphreys, K., Finney, J. W., & Moos, R. H. (1994). Applying a stress and coping framework to research on mutual help organizations. *Journal of Community Psychology, 22,* 312–327.

Humphreys, K., & Noke, J. M. (1997). The influence of posttreatment mutual help group participation on the friendship networks of substance abuse patients. *American Journal of Community Psychology, 25,* 1–16.

Humphreys, K., & Rappaport, J. (1993). From the community mental health movement to the war on drugs: A study in the definition of social problems. *American Psychologist, 48,* 892–901.

Humphreys, K., & Rappaport, J. (1994). Researching self-help/mutual aid groups and organizations: Many roads, one journey. *Applied and Preventive Psychology, 3,* 217–231.

Humphreys, K., Wing, S., McCarty, D., Chappel, J., Gallant, L., Haberle, B., et al. (2004). Self-help organizations for alcohol and drug problems: Toward evidence-based practice and policy. *Journal of Substance Abuse Treatment, 26,* 151–158.

Hunsberger, B. (1995). Religion and prejudice: The role of religious fundamentalism, quest and right-wing authoritarianism. *Journal of Social Issues, 51,* 113–130.

Hunter, A., & Riger, S. (1986). The meaning of community in community mental health. *Journal of Community Psychology, 14,* 55–70.

Hurtado, A. (1997). Understanding multiple group identities: Inserting women into cultural transformations. *Journal of Social Issues, 53,* 299–328.

Huston, A., & Bentley, A. (2010). Human development in societal context. *Annual Review of Psychology, 61,* 411–437.

Ickovics, J., & Park, C. (Eds.). (1998). Thriving: Broadening the paradigm beyond illness to health [Special issue]. *Journal of Social Issues, 54*(2).

Imm, P. Chinman, M., Wanderman, A., Rosenbloom, D., Guckenburg, S., Leis, R. (2007). *Preventing underage drinking using Getting To Outcomes™ with the SAMHSA strategic prevention framework to achieve results.* Santa Monica, CA: Rand Corporation. Retrieved March 8, 2011, from http://www.rand.org/pubs/technical_reports/TR403.html

Inequality.org. (2004). An inequality briefing book: July 2004. Retrieved July 17, 2004, from http://www.inequality.org/facts.html

Internet World Stats (2010). Retrieved June 15, 2010 from http://www.internetworldstats.com/stats.htm

Iscoe, I. (1974). Community psychology and the competent community. *American Psychologist, 29,* 607–613.

Iscoe, I., Bloom, B., & Spielberger, C. (Eds.). (1977). *Community psychology in transition: Proceedings of the national conference on training in community psychology.* Washington, DC: Hemisphere.

Isenberg, D. H., Loomis, C., Humphreys, K., & Maton, K. (2004). Self-help research: Issues of power-sharing. In L. A. Jason, C. Keys, Y. Suarez-Balcazar, R. Taylor & M. Davis (Eds.), *Participatory community research: Theories and methods in action* (pp. 123–138). Washington, DC: American Psychological Association.

Israel, N., & Toro, P. (2003, Fall). Promoting local action on poverty. *The Community Psychologist, 36,* 35–37.

Jacobs, J. (1961). *The death and life of great American cities.* New York: Random House.

Jahoda, M. (1958). *Current conceptions of positive mental health.* New York: Basic Books. (Reprinted in 1980. New York: Arno Press.)

Jahoda, M., Lazarsfeld, P., & Zeisel, H. (1971). *Marienthal: The sociography of an unemployed community.* London: Tavistock. (Originally published in German, 1933.)

James, S., Johnson, J., Raghavan, C., Lemos, T., Smith, M., & Woolis, D. (2003). The violent matrix: A study of structural, interpersonal and intrapersonal violence among a sample of poor women. *American Journal of Community Psychology, 31,* 129–142.

Janzen, R., Nelson, G., Hausfather, N., & Ochocka, J. (2007). Capturing system level activities and impacts of mental health consumer-run organizations. *American Journal of Community Psychology, 39,* 287–299.

Jason, L. A. (1998, February). Dr. Jason goes to Washington. *The Community Psychologist, 31,* 27–30.

Jason. L. A., Berk, M., Schnopp-Wyatt, D. L., & Talbot, B. (1999). Effects of enforcement of youth access laws on smoking prevalence. *American Journal of Community Psychology, 27,* 143–160.

Jason, L. A., Ferrari, J., Davis, M., & Olson, B. (2006). *Creating communities for addiction recovery: The Oxford House model.* New York: Haworth. [Also published as

Journal of Prevention and Intervention in the Community, 31(1/2).]

Jason, L. A., Groh, D., Durocher, M., Alvarez, J., Aase, D., & Ferrari, J. (2008). Counteracting "not in my backyard": The positive effects of greater occupancy within mutual-help recovery homes. *Journal of Community Psychology, 36*(7), 947–958.

Jason, L. A., Keys, C., Suarez-Balcazar, Y., Taylor, R., & Davis, M. (Eds.). (2004). *Participatory community research: Theories and methods in action.* Washington, DC: American Psychological Association.

Jason, L. A., Olson, B. D., Ferrari, J. R., Lo Sasso, A. T. (2006). Communal housing settings enhance substance abuse recovery. *American Journal of Public Health, 96,* 1727–1729.

Jason, L., Porknoy, S., Adams, M., Topliff, A., Harris, C., Hunt, Y. (2009). Effects of youth tobacco access and possession policy interventions on heavy adolescent smokers. *International Journal of Environmental Research and Public Health, 6,* 1–9.

Johnson, K., Hays, C., Center, H. and Daley, C., (2004). Building capacity and sustainable prevention innovations: a sustainability planning model. *Evaluation and Program Planning, 27,* 135–149.

Johnson, S. (2006). *The ghost map: The story of London's most terrifying epidemic—and how it changed science, cities and the modern world.* New York: Riverhead Books.

Joint Commission on Mental Health and Mental Illness. (1961). *Action for mental health: Final report.* New York: Basic Books.

Jolliffe, D., & Farington, D. P. (2007). *A rapid evidence assessment of the impact of mentoring on re-offending: A summary.* Cambridge University: Home Office Online Report 11/07. Retrieved March 8, 2011, from http://www.crimereduction.gov.uk/ workingoffenders/work ingoffenders069.htm

Jones, D., Bumbarger, B., Greenberg, M., Greenwood, P., & Kyler, S. (2008). *The economic return on PCCD's investment in Research-based programs: A cost-benefit assessment of delinquency prevention in Pennsylvania.* Philadelphia, PA: The Prevention Research Center for the Promotion of Human Development, Penn State University.

Jones, K., Allen, M., Norris, F. H., & Miller, C. (2009). Piloting a new model of crisis counseling: Specialized crisis counseling services in Mississippi after Hurricane Katrina. *Administration and Policy in Mental Health and Mental Health Services Research, 36,* 195–205.

Jones, J. M. (1994). Our similarities are different: Toward a psychology of affirmative diversity. In E. J. Trickett, R. J. Watts, & D. Birman (Eds.), *Human diversity: Perspectives on people in context* (pp. 27–45). San Francisco: Jossey-Bass.

Jones, J. M. (1997). *Prejudice and racism* (2nd ed.). New York: McGraw-Hill.

Jones, J. M. (1998). Psychological knowledge and the new American dilemma of race. *Journal of Social Issues, 54,* 641–662.

Jones, J. M. (2003). Constructing race and deconstructing racism: A cultural psychology approach. In G. Bernal, J. Trimble, K. Burlew, & F. Leong (Eds.), *Handbook of racial and ethnic minority psychology* (pp. 275–290). Thousand Oaks, CA: Sage.

Jordan, L., Bogat, A., & Smith, G. (2001). Collaborating for social change: The Black psychologist and the Black community. *American Journal of Community Psychology, 29,* 599–620.

Jozefowicz-Simbeni, D., Israel, N., Braciszewski, J., & Hobden, K. (2005). The "big tent" of community psychology: Reactions to Paul Toro's 2004 presidential address. *American Journal of Community Psychology, 35,* 17–22.

Julian, D. A. (2006). A community practice model for community psychologists and some examples of the application of community practice skills from the partnerships for success initiative in Ohio. *American Journal of Community Psychology, 37*(1–2), 21–27.

Jumper-Thurman, P., Edwards, R., Plested, B., & Oetting, E. (2003). Honoring the differences: Using community readiness to create culturally valid community interventions. In G. Bernal, J. Trimble, K. Burlew, & F. Leong (Eds.), *Handbook of racial and ethnic minority psychology* (pp. 589–607). Thousand Oaks, CA: Sage.

Juras, J. L., Macklin, J. R., Curtis, S. E., & Foster-Fishman, P. G. (1997). Key concepts of community psychology: Implications for consulting in educational and human service settings. *Journal of Educational and Psychological Consultation, 8,* 111–133.

Juris, J., & Pleyers, G. (2009). Alter-activism: emerging cultures of participation among young global justice activists. *Journal of Youth Studies, 12,* 57–75.

Kagitçibasi, C. (1997). Individualism and collectivism. In J. W. Berry, M. Segall, & C. Kagitçibasi (Eds.), *Handbook of cross-cultural psychology: Vol. 3: Social behavior and applications* (pp. 1–50). Needham Heights, MA: Allyn & Bacon.

Kalafat, J. (2004). Enabling and empowering practices of Kentucky's school-based family resource centers: A multiple case study. *Evaluation and Program Planning, 27,* 65–78.

Kamenetz, A. (2005, September 5–11). Talking about my generation: There's passion among today's youth—if only people would pay attention. *Washington Post Weekly Edition,* p. 22.

Kaniasty, K., & Norris, F. H. (1995). In search of altruistic community: Patterns of social support mobilization following Hurricane Hugo. *American Journal of Community Psychology, 23,* 447–478.

Kanner, A., Coyne, J., Schaefer, C., & Lazarus, R. S. (1981). Comparison of two modes of stress measurement: Daily hassles and uplifts versus major life events. *Journal of Behavioral Medicine, 4,* 1–37.

Karcher, M. J. (2008). The study of mentoring in the learning environment (SMILE): A randomized evaluation of the effectiveness of school-based mentoring. *Prevention Science, 9*(2), 99–113.

Kaskutas, L., Morgan, P., & Vaeth, P. (1992). Structural impediments in the development of community-based drug prevention programs for youth: Preliminary analysis from a qualitative formative evaluation study. *International Quarterly of Community Health Education, 12,* 169–182.

Kasturirangan, A. (2008). Empowerment and programs designed to address domestic violence. *Violence Against Women, 14,* 1465–1475.

Katz, D., & Kahn, R. L. (1978). *The social psychology of organizations.* New York: Wiley.

Katz, R. (1984). Empowerment and synergy: Expanding the community's healing resources. In J. Rappaport, C. Swift, & R. Hess (Eds.), *Studies in empowerment: Steps toward understanding and action* (pp. 210–226). New York: Haworth Press.

Kaye, G. (2001). Grassroots involvement. *American Journal of Community Psychology, 29,* 269–276.

Kaye, G., & Wolff, T. (Eds.). (1997). *From the ground up: A workbook on coalition building and community development.* Amherst, MA: AHEC/Community Partners.

Kawachi, I., & Kennedy, B. (2006). *The health of nations: Why inequality is harmful to your health* (2nd ed.). New York: New Press.

Keener, D., Snell-Johns, J., Livet, M., & Wandersman, A. (2005). Lessons that influenced the current conceptualization of empowerment evaluation: Reflections from two evaluation projects. In D. Fetterman & A. Wandersman (Eds.), *Empowerment evaluation principles in practice* (pp. 73–91). New York: Guilford Press.

Kelly, J. F. (2003). Self-help for substance-use disorders: History, effectiveness, knowledge gaps, and research opportunities. *Clinical Psychology Review, 23,* 639–663.

Kelly, J. G. (1966). Ecological constraints on mental health services. *American Psychologist, 21,* 535–539.

Kelly, J. G. (1970). Antidotes for arrogance: Training for community psychology. *American Psychologist, 25,* 524–531.

Kelly, J. G. (1971). Qualities for the community psychologist. *American Psychologist, 26,* 897–903.

Kelly, J. G. (Ed.). (1979a). *Adolescent boys in high school: A psychological study of coping and adaptation.* Hillsdale, NJ: Erlbaum.

Kelly, J. G. (1979b). "Tain't what you do, it's the way you do it." *American Journal of Community Psychology, 7,* 244–258.

Kelly, J. G. (1986). Context and process: An ecological view of the interdependence of practice and research. *American Journal of Community Psychology, 14,* 581–605.

Kelly, J. G. (1990). Changing contexts and the field of community psychology. *American Journal of Community Psychology, 18,* 769–792.

Kelly, J. G. (1997). [Untitled videotape interview]. In J. G. Kelly (Ed.), *The history of community psychology: A video presentation of context and exemplars.* Chicago: Society for Community Research and Action.

Kelly, J. G. (2002a). The spirit of community psychology. *American Journal of Community Psychology, 30,* 43–63.

Kelly, J. G. (Producer, Director). (2003). *Exemplars of community psychology* [DVD set]. Society for Community Research and Action. (Available from SCRA Membership Office, 4440 PGA Blvd. #600, Palm Beach Gardens, FL 33410 (561-623-5323). E-mail: office@scra27.org)

Kelly, J. G. (2006). *Becoming ecological: An expedition into community psychology.* New York: Oxford University Press.

Kelly, J. G. (2010). More thoughts: On the spirit of community psychology. *American Journal of Community Psychology, 45*(3–4), 272–284.

Kelly, J. G., Azelton, S., Burzette, R., & Mock, L. (1994). Creating social settings for diversity: An ecological thesis. In E. J. Trickett, R. J. Watts & D. Birman (Eds.), *Human diversity: Perspectives on people in context* (pp. 424–450). San Francisco: Jossey-Bass.

Kelly, J. G., Azelton, S., Lardon, C., Mock, L., Tandon, S. D., & Thomas, M. (2004). On community leadership: Stories about collaboration in action research. *American Journal of Community Psychology, 33*, 205–216.

Kelly, J. G., Ryan, A. M., Altman, B. E., & Stelzner, S. P. (2000). Understanding and changing social systems: An ecological view. In J. Rappaport & E. Seidman (Eds.), *Handbook of community psychology* (pp. 133–160). New York: Kluwer Academic/Plenum.

Keppel, B. (2002). Kenneth B. Clark in the patterns of American culture. *American Psychologist, 57*, 29–37.

Kessler, R. C., Mickelson, K. D., & Zhao, S. (1997, Spring). Patterns and correlates of self-help groups membership in the United States. *Social Policy, 27*, 27–46.

Keys, C., McMahon, S., Sanchez, B., London, L., & Abdul-Adil, J. (2004). Culturally-anchored research: Quandaries, guidelines, and exemplars for community psychology. In L. A. Jason, C. Keys, Y. Suarez-Balcazar, R. Taylor & M. Davis (Eds.), *Participatory community research: Theories and methods in action* (pp. 177–198). Washington, DC: American Psychological Association.

Kieffer, C. (1984). Citizen empowerment: A developmental perspective. In J. Rappaport, C. Swift, & R. Hess (Eds.), *Studies in empowerment: Steps toward understanding and action* (pp. 9–36). New York: Haworth.

Kilburn, R., & Karoly, L. (2008). *The economics of early childhood policy: What the dismal science has to say about investing in children.* Santa Monica, CA: The Rand Corporation. Retrieved March 8, 2011, from http://www.rand.org/pubs/occasional_papers/2008/RAND_OP227.pdf

Kilmer, R. P., Cowen, E. L., Wyman, P. A., Work, W. C., & Magnus, K. B., (1998). Differences in stressors experienced by urban African American, White, and Hispanic children. *Journal of Community Psychology, 26*, 415–428.

Kilmer, R. P., & Gil-Rivas, V. (2010). Exploring posttraumatic growth in children impacted by Hurricane Katrina: Correlates of the phenomenon and developmental considerations. *Child Development, 81*, 1211–1227.

Kim, I. J. & Lorion, R. P. (2006) Introduction to special issue: Addressing mental health disparities through culturally competent research and community-based practice. *Journal of Community Psychology, 34*, 117–120.

Kim, J., & Ross, C. E. (2009). Neighborhood-specific and general social support: Which buffers the effect of neighborhood disorder on depression? *Journal of Community Psychology, 37*(6), 725–736.

Kim, U., & Berry, J. (Eds.). (1993). *Indigenous psychologies: Research and experience in cultural context.* Newbury Park, CA: Sage.

Kim, U., Triandis, H., Kagitçibasi, C., Choi, S.-C., & Yoon, G. (Eds.). (1994). *Individualism and collectivism: Theory, method, and applications.* Thousand Oaks, CA: Sage.

King, M. L., Jr. (1968). The role of the behavioral scientist in the civil rights movement. *American Psychologist, 23*, 180–186.

Kingry-Westergaard, C., & Kelly, J. G. (1990). A contextualist epistemology for ecological research. In P. Tolan, C. Keys, F. Chertok, & L. Jason (Eds.), *Researching community psychology* (pp. 23–32). Washington, DC: American Psychological Association.

Kitayama, S. & Marcus, H. R. (1994). *Emotion and culture: Empirical studies of mutual influence.* Washington, DC: American Psychological Association.

Kitayama S., Karasawa M., Curhan K. B., Ryff C. D. & Markus, H. R. (2010). Independence and interdependence predict health and well-being: Divergent patterns in the United States and Japan. *Frontiers in Psychology 1*(163). Retrieved March 8, 2011, http://www.frontiersin.org/cultural_psychology/10.3389/fpsyg.2010.00163/full

Klaw, E., Huebsch, P., & Humphreys, K. (2000). Communication patterns in an on-line mutual help group. *Journal of Community Psychology, 28*, 535–546.

Klein, D. (1987). The context and times at Swampscott: My story. *American Journal of Community Psychology, 12*, 515–517.

Klein, D. (1995). [Untitled videotape interview]. In J. G. Kelly (Ed.), *The history of community psychology: A video presentation of context and exemplars.* Chicago: Society for Community Research and Action.

Klein, D. C., & Goldston, S. E. (1977). Primary prevention: An idea whose time has come. *Proceedings of the Pilot Conference on Primary Prevention,* April 24, 1976 (Department of Health, Education, and Welfare Pub. No. ADM 77–447). Washington, DC: U.S. Government Printing Office.

Klein, D., & Lindemann, E. (1961). Preventive intervention in individual and family crisis situations. In G. Caplan (Ed.), *Prevention of mental disorders in children* (pp. 283–306). New York: Basic Books.

Klein, K., Ralls, R. S., Smith-Major, V., & Douglas, C. (2000). Power and participation in the workplace. In J. Rappaport & E. Seidman (Eds.), *Handbook of community psychology* (pp. 273–300). New York: Kluwer Academic/Plenum.

Kloos, B. (2010). Creating new possibilities for promoting liberation, well-being, and recovery: Learning from experiences of psychiatric consumers/survivors. In G. Nelson, & I. Prilleltensky, (Eds.), *Community psychology: In pursuit of well-being and liberation* (2nd ed., pp. 453–476). London: MacMillan.

Kloos, B., & Moore, T. (Eds.). (2000a). Spirituality, religion, and community psychology [Special issue]. *Journal of Community Psychology, 28*(2).

Kloos, B., & Moore, T. (2000b). The prospect and purpose of locating community research and action in religious settings. *Journal of Community Psychology, 28,* 119–138.

Kloos, B., & Moore, T. (Eds.). (2001). Spirituality, religion, and community psychology II: Resources, pathways, and perspectives [Special issue]. *Journal of Community Psychology, 29*(5).

Kloos, B., & Shah, S. (2009). A social ecological approach to investigating relationships between housing and adaptive functioning for persons with serious mental illness. *Journal of Community psychology, 44*(3–4), 316–326.

Kohn-Wood, L. P., & Wilson, M. N. (2005). The context of caretaking in rural areas: Family factors influencing the level of functioning of serious mentally ill patients living at home. *American Journal of Community Psychology, 36,* 1–13.

Kral, G. (2006). Online communities for mutual help: Fears, fiction, and facts. In M. Murero & R. E. Rice (Eds.), *The Internet and health care: Theory, research, and practice* (pp. 215–232). Mahwah, NJ: Lawrence Erlbaum Associates.

Kral, M. J., & Idlout, L. (2008). Community wellness and social action in the Canadian Arctic: Collective agency as subjective well-being. In L. J. Kirmayer & G. G. Valaskakis (Eds.), *Healing traditions: The mental health of Aboriginal peoples in Canada* (pp. 315–336). Vancouver: UBC Press.

Kraut, R., Patterson, M., Lundmark, V., Kiesler, S., Mukopadhyay, T., & Scherlis, W. (1998). Internet paradox: A social technology that reduces social involvement and psychological well-being? *American Psychologist, 53,* 1017–1031.

Kraut, R., Kiesler, S., Boneva, B., Cummings, J., Helgeson, V., & Crawford, A. (2001). Internet paradox revisited. *Journal of Social Issues, 58,* 49–74.

Kress, J. S., & Elias, M. J. (2000). Infusing community psychology and religion: Themes from an action-research project in Jewish identity. *Journal of Community Psychology, 28,* 187–198.

Kessler, R. C., Mickelson, K. D., & Zhao, S. (1997, Spring). Patterns and correlates of self-help groups membership in the United States. *Social Policy, 27,* 27–46.

Kretzmann, J. P., & McKnight, J. L. (1993). *Building communities from the inside out: A path toward finding and mobilizing a community's assets.* Chicago: ACTA Publications.

Kroeker, C. J. (1995). Individual, organizational and societal empowerment: A study of the processes in a Nicaraguan agricultural cooperative. *American Journal of Community Psychology, 23,* 749–764.

Kroeker, C. J. (1996). The cooperative movement in Nicaragua: Empowerment and accompaniment of severely disadvantaged persons. *Journal of Social Issues, 52,* 123–137.

Kyrouz, E. M., Humphreys, K., & Loomis, C. (2002). A review of research on the effectiveness of self-help mutual aid groups. In B. J. White & E. J. Madera (Eds.), *The self-help source book* (7th ed.). Cedar Knolls, NJ: American Self-Help Group Clearinghouse.

Kumpfer, K., & Alvarado, R. (2003). Family-strengthening approaches for the prevention of youth problem behaviors. *American Psychologist, 58,* 457–465.

Kuo, F., & Sullivan, W. (2001). Environment and crime in the inner city. Does vegetation reduce crime? *Environment and Behavior, 33,* 343–367.

Kuo, F. E., Sullivan, W. C., Coley, R. L., & Brunson, L. (1998). Fertile ground for community: Inner-city neighborhood common spaces. *American Journal of Community Psychology, 26,* 823–852.

Kuperminc, G., Emshoff, J. G., Reiner, M. N., Secrest, L. A., Niolon, P., & Foster, J. D. (2005). Integration of mentoring with other programs and services. In D. L. DuBois & M. J. Karcher (Eds.), *Handbook of youth mentoring* (pp. 314–334). Thousand Oaks, CA: Sage.

LaFromboise, T., Coleman, H. L. K., & Gerton, J. (1993). Psychological impact of biculturalism: Evidence and theory. *Psychological Bulletin, 114,* 395–412.

LaFrombois, T., & Howard-Pitney, B. (1995). The Zuni life skills development curriculum: Description and evaluation of a suicide prevention program. *Journal of Counseling Psychology, 42,* 479–486.

Lal, S. (2002). Giving children security: Mamie Phipps Clark and the racialization of child psychology. *American Psychologist, 57,* 20–28.

Langhout, R. D. (2003). Reconceptualizing quantitative and qualitative methods: A case study dealing with place as an exemplar. *American Journal of Community Psychology, 32,* 229–244.

Langhout, R. D., & Thomas, E. (2010). Imagining participatory action research in collaboration with children: An introduction [Special issue]. *American Journal of Community Psychology, 46,* 60–66

Lappe, F. M., & DuBois, P. M. (1994). *The quickening of America: Rebuilding our nation, remaking our lives.* San Francisco, CA: Jossey-Bass.

Lave, J., & Wenger, E. (1991). *Situated learning: Legitimate peripheral participation.* New York: Cambridge University Press.

Lavee, Y., & Ben-Arit, A. (2008). The association of daily hassles and uplifts with family and life satisfaction: Does cultural orientation make a difference? *American Journal of Community Psychology, 41,* 89–98.

Lazarus, R. S., & Folkman, S. (1984). *Stress, appraisal, and coping.* New York: Springer.

Leach, M., Martin, P., Bowles, T., & Taliaferro, J. (2008). Our Souls look back in wonder: The spirituality of African American families surviving Hurricane Katrina. In Singleton, D. (Ed.), *The Aftermath of Hurricane Katrina: Educating traumatized children pre-K through college.* Maryland: University Press of America.

Lee, C. (Ed.). (2000). Australian indigenous psychologies [special issue]. *Australian Psychologist, 35*(2).

Lee, E., & Chan, K. (2009). Religious/spiritual and other adaptive coping strategies among Chinese American older immigrants. *Journal of Gerontological Social Work, 52*(5), 517–533.

Lee, S. J. (2009). Online communication and adolescent social ties: Who benefits more from Internet use? *Journal of Computer-Mediated Communication, 14,* 509–531.

Lee, W., & Kuo, E. C. Y. (2002). Internet and displacement effects: Children's media use and activities in Singapore. *Journal of Computer-Mediated Communication, 7*(2). Article first published online: 23 JUN 2006. doi: 10.1111/j.1083-6101.2002.tb00143.x

Lehavot, K., Balsam, K., & Ibrahim-Wells, G. (2009). Redefining the American quilt: Definitions and experiences of community among ethnically diverse lesbian and bisexual women. *Journal of Community Psychology, 37,* 439–458.

Lehrner, A., & Allen, N. (2008). Social change movements and the struggle over meaning-making: A case study of domestic violence narratives. *American Journal of Community Psychology, 42,* 220–234.

Lenhart, A., Madden, M, & Hitlin, P. (2005). *Teens and technology: Youth are leading the transition to a fully wired and mobile nation.* Washington, DC: Pew Internet & American Life Project.

Lerner, R. M. (1995). *America's youth in crisis: Challenges and options for programs and policies.* Thousand Oaks, CA: Sage.

Lesesne, C. A., Lewis, K. M., White, C. P., Green, D., Duffy, J., & Wandersman, A. (2008). Promoting science-based approaches to teen pregnancy prevention: Proactively engaging the three systems of the Interactive Systems Framework. *American Journal of Community Psychology, 41,* 379–392.

Leventhal, T., Fauth, R. C., & Brooks-Gunn, J. (2005). Neighborhood poverty and public policy: A 5-year follow-up of children's educational outcomes in New York City moving to opportunity demonstration. *Developmental Psychology, 41,* 933–952.

Levine, A. (1982). *Love Canal: Science, politics, and people.* Lexington, MA: Heath.

Levine, M. (1981). *The history and politics of community mental health.* New York: Oxford University Press.

Levine, M., & Levine, A. (1970). *A social history of helping services.* New York: Oxford University Press.

Levine, M., & Levine, A. (1992). *Helping children: A social history.* New York: Oxford University Press.

Levine, M., Perkins, D. D., & Perkins, D. V. (2005). *Principles of community psychology: Perspectives and applications* (3rd ed.). New York: Oxford University Press.

Levine, M., & Perkins, D. V. (1987). *Principles of community psychology: Perspectives and applications*. New York: Oxford University Press.

Leviton, L. C. (1994). Program theory and evaluation theory in community-based programs. *Evaluation Practice, 15,* 89–92.

Levy, L. H. (2000). Self-help groups. In J. Rappaport & E. Seidman (Eds.), *Handbook of community psychology* (pp. 591–613). New York: Kluwer/Plenum.

Lewin, K. (1935). *A dynamic theory of personality.* New York: McGraw-Hill.

Lewis, J. (1998). *Walking with the wind: A memoir of the movement.* New York: Simon & Schuster.

Liang, B., & Bogat, G. A. (1994). Culture, control, and coping: New perspective on social support. *American Journal of Community Psychology, 22,* 123–147.

Liang, B., Glenn, C., & Goodman, L. (2005, Summer). Feminist ethics in advocacy relationships: A relational vs. rule-bound approach. *The Community Psychologist, 38,* 26–28.

Liegghio, M., Nelson, G., & Evans, S. (2010). Partnering with children diagnosed with mental health issues: Contributions of a sociology of childhood perspective to participatory action research. *American Journal of Community Psychology, 46,* 84–99.

Lilienfeld, S. (2007). Psychological treatments that cause harm. *Perspectives on Psychological Science, 2,* 53–70.

Lim, Y. (2009). Can "refundable" state Earned Income Tax Credits explain child poverty in the American states? *Journal of Children and Poverty, 15,* 39–53.

Lincoln, Y., & Guba, E. (1985). *Naturalistic inquiry.* Newbury Park, CA: Sage.

Lindemann, E. (1957). The nature of mental health work as a professional pursuit. In C. Strother (Ed.), *Psychology and mental health* (pp. 136–145). Washington, DC: American Psychological Association.

Linney, J. A. (1986). Court-ordered school desegregation: Shuffling the deck or playing a different game. In E. Seidman & J. Rappaport (Eds.), *Redefining social problems* (pp. 259–274). New York: Plenum.

Linney, J. A. (1989). Optimizing research strategies in the schools. In L. A. Bond & B. E. Compas (Eds.), *Primary prevention in the schools* (pp. 50–76). Newbury Park, CA: Sage.

Linney, J. A. (1990). Community psychology into the 1990's: Capitalizing opportunity and promoting innovation. *American Journal of Community Psychology, 18,* 1–17.

Linney, J. A. (2000). Assessing ecological constructs and community context. In J. Rappaport & E. Seidman (Eds.), *Handbook of community psychology* (pp. 647–668). New York: Kluwer/Plenum.

Linney, J. A., & Reppucci, N. D. (1982). Research design and methods in community psychology. In P. Kendall & J. Butcher (Eds.), *Handbook of research methods in clinical psychology* (pp. 535–566). New York: Wiley.

Linney, J. A., & Wandersman, A. (1991). *Prevention plus III: Assessing alcohol and other drug prevention programs at the school and community level: A four-step guide to useful program assessment.* Rockville, MD: U.S. Department of Health and Human Services, Office for Substance Abuse Prevention.

Lipsey, M., & Cordray, D. (2002). Evaluation methods for social intervention. *Annual Review of Psychology, 51,* 345–375.

Loeb, P. (1999). *Soul of a citizen: Living with conviction in a cynical time.* New York: St. Martin's Press.

Loeb, P. R. (2004). *The impossible will take a little while: A citizen's guide to hope in a time of fear.* New York: Basic Books.

Lohmann, A., & McMurran, G. (2009). Resident-defined neighborhood mapping: Using GIS to analyze phenomenological neighborhoods. *Journal of Prevention & Intervention in the Community, 37,* 66–81.

Long, D., & Perkins, D. D. (2003). Confirmatory factor analysis of the Sense of Community Index and development of a Brief SCI. *Journal of Community Psychology, 31,* 279–296.

Lonner, W. (1994). Culture and human diversity. In E. J. Trickett, R. J. Watts, & D. Birman (Eds.), *Human diversity: Perspectives on people in context* (pp. 230–243). San Francisco: Jossey-Bass.

Loomis, C., Dockett, K., & Brodsky, A. (2004). Change in sense of community: An empirical finding. *Journal of Community Psychology, 32,* 1–8.

Lott, B. (2001). Low-income parents and the public schools. *Journal of Social Issues, 57,* 247–260.

Lott, B., & Bullock, H. (2001). Who are the poor? *Journal of Social Issues, 57,* 189–206.

Lounsbury, D. W. & Mitchell, S. G. (2009). Introduction to special issue on social ecological approaches to community health research and action. *American Journal of Community Psychology, 44,* 213–220.

Lounsbury, J., Leader, D., Meares, E., & Cook, M. (1980). An analytic review of research in community psychology. *American Journal of Community Psychology, 8,* 415–441.

Lounsbury, J., Loveland, J., & Gibson, L. (2003). An investigation of psychological sense of community in relation to Big Five personality traits. *Journal of Community Psychology, 31,* 531–542.

Luke, D. (2005). Getting the big picture in community science: Methods that capture context. *American Journal of Community Psychology, 35,* 185–200.

Luke, D., Rappaport, J., & Seidman, E. (1991). Setting phenotypes in a mutual help organization: Expanding behavior setting theory. *American Journal of Community Psychology, 19,* 147–168. Reprinted in T. Revenson, A. D'Augelli, S. E. French, D. Hughes, D. Livert, E. Seidman, M. Shinn & H. Yoshikawa (Eds.), (2002), *Ecological research to promote social change: Methodological advances from community psychology* (pp. 217–238). New York: Kluwer Academic/Plenum.

Lukes, S. (2005). *Power: A radical view* (2nd ed.). New York: Palgrave Macmillan.

Luthar, S., Cicchetti, D., & Becker, B. (2000). The construct of resilience: A critical evaluation and guidelines for future work. *Child Development, 71,* 543–562.

Lykes, C., Kay, L., Crepaz, N., Herbst, J., Passin, W., Kim, A., et al. (2007). Best-evidence interventions: Findings from a systematic review of HIV behavioral interventions for US populations at high risk, 2000–2004. *American Journal of Public Health, 97,* 133–143.

Lykes, M. B. (2005). Narratives and representations of survival: The politics and praxis of action research and liberatory community psychology in a post-9/11 world. Keynote address, Biennial Conference of Society for Community Research and Action, Champaign-Urbana, IL.

Lykes, M. B., Blanche, M. T., & Hamber, B. (2003). Narrating survival and change in Guatemala and South Africa: The politics of representation and a liberatory community psychology. *American Journal of Community Psychology, 31,* 79–90.

Madara, E. (1997, Spring). The mutual aid self-help online revolution. *Social Policy, 27,* 20–26.

Mahan, B., Garrard, W., Lewis, S., & Newbrough, J. R. (2002). Sense of community in a university setting: Campus as workplace. In A. Fisher, C. Sonn, & B. Bishop (Eds.), *Psychological sense of community: Research, applications and implications* (pp. 123–140). New York: Kluwer/Plenum.

Mankowski, E. S., & Maton, K. I. (2010). A community psychology of men and masculinity: Historical and conceptual review. *American Journal of Community Psychology, 45,* 73–86.

Mankowski, E., & Rappaport, J. (Eds.). (2000). Qualitative research on the narratives of spiritually-based communities [Special section]. *Journal of Community Psychology, 28*(5).

Mankowski, E., & Thomas, E. (2000). The relationship between personal and collective identity: A narrative analysis of a campus ministry community. *Journal of Community Psychology, 28,* 517–528.

Mann, J. M. (1989). AIDS: A worldwide pandemic. In M. Gottlieb, D. Jeffries, D. Mildvan, A. Pinching, & T. Quinn (Eds.), *Current topics in AIDS* (Vol. 2). Hoboken, NJ: John Wiley & Sons.

Manning, M., Homel, R., & Smith, C. (2010). A meta-analysis of the effects of early developmental prevention programs in at-risk populations on non-health outcomes in adolescence. *Children and Youth Services Review, 32,* 506–519.

Marecek, J., Fine, M., & Kidder, L. (1997). Working between worlds: Qualitative methods and social psychology. *Journal of Social Issues, 53,* 631–643.

Markus, H. T., & Kitayama, S. (1991). Culture and the self: Implications for cognition, emotion, and motivation. *Psychological Review, 98,* 224–253.

Marris, P., & Rein, M. (1973). *Dilemmas of social reform* (2nd ed.). Chicago: Aldine.

Marrow, A. J. (1969). *The practical theorist.* New York: Basic Books.

Marsella, A. (1998). Toward a "global-community" psychology. *American Psychologist, 53,* 1282–1291.

Martin, P., Lounsbury, D., & Davidson, W. (2004). AJCP as a vehicle for improving community life: An historic-analytic review of the journal's contents. *American Journal of Community Psychology, 34,* 163–174.

Martin-Baro, I. (1990). Religion as an instrument of psychological warfare. *Journal of Social Issues, 46,* 93–107.

Martin-Baro, I. (1994). *Writings for a liberation psychology.* [Eds. A. Aron & S. Corne.] Cambridge, MA: Harvard University Press.

Mason, C., Chapman, D., & Scott, K. (1999). The identification of early risk factors for severe emotional disturbances and emotional handicaps: An epidemiological approach. *American Journal of Community Psychology, 27,* 357–381.

Masten, A. S. (2007). Resilience in developing systems: Progress and promise as the fourth wave rises. *Development and Psychopathology, 19,* 921–930.

Masten, A., & Powell, J. (2003). A resilience framework for research, policy, and practice. In S. Luthar (Ed.), *Resilience and vulnerability: Adaptation in the context of childhood adversities* (pp. 1–25). New York: Cambridge University Press.

Maton, K. I. (1987). Patterns and psychological correlates of material support within a religious setting: The bidirectional support hypothesis. *American Journal of Community Psychology, 15,* 185–207.

Maton, K. I. (1988). Social support, organizational characteristics, psychological well-being, and group appraisal in three self-help group populations. *American Journal of Community Psychology, 16,* 53–77.

Maton, K. I. (1989). Community settings as buffers of life stress? Highly supportive churches, mutual help groups, and senior centers. *American Journal of Community Psychology, 17,* 203–232. Reprinted in T. Revenson, A. D'Augelli, S. E. French, D. Hughes, D. Livert, E. Seidman, M. Shinn, & H. Yoshikawa (Eds.), (2002), *A quarter century of community psychology* (pp. 205–235). New York: Kluwer Academic/Plenum.

Maton, K. I. (1993). A bridge between cultures: Linked ethnographic empirical methodology for culture anchored research. *American Journal of Community Psychology, 21,* 747–774.

Maton, K. I. (2000). Making a difference: The social ecology of social transformation. *American Journal of Community Psychology, 28,* 25–58.

Maton, K. I. (2001). Spirituality, religion, and community psychology: Historical perspective, positive potential, and challenges. *Journal of Community Psychology, 29,* 605–613.

Maton, K. I. (2008). Empowering community settings: Agents of individual development, community betterment, and positive social change. *American Journal of Community Psychology, 41,* 4–21.

Maton, K. I., & Brodsky, A. E. (2011). Empowering community settings: Theory, research and action. In M. Aber, K. I. Ma-ton, & E. Seidman (Eds.), *Empowering settings and voices for social change.* Oxford University Press.

Maton, K. I., Hrabowski, F. A., Özdemir, M., & Wimms, H. (2008). Enhancing representation, retention, and achievement of minority students in higher education: A social transformation theory of change. In M. Shinn, H. Yoshikawa, M. Shinn, & H. Yoshikawa (Eds.), *Toward positive youth development: Transforming schools and community programs* (pp. 115–132). New York: Oxford University Press.

Maton, K. I., & Hrabowski, R. A. (2004). Increasing the number of African American PhDs in the sciences and engineering: A strengths-based approach. *American Psychologist, 59,* 547–556.

Maton, K. I., Hrabowski, R. A., & Greif, G. L. (1998). Preparing the way: A qualitative study of high achieving African American males and the role of the family. *American Journal of Community Psychology, 26,* 639–668.

Maton, K. I., & Salem, D. A. (1995). Organizational characteristics of empowering community settings: A multiple case study approach. *American Journal of Community Psychology, 23,* 631–656.

Maton, K., Schellenbach, C., Leadbeater, B., & Solarz, A. (Eds.). (2004). *Investing in children, youth, families and communities: Strengths-based research and policy.* Washington, DC: American Psychological Association.

Maton, K. I., Teti, D. M., Corns, K. M., Vieira-Baker, C. C., Lavine, J. R., Gouze, K. R., et al. (1996). Cultural specificity of support sources, correlates and contexts: Three studies of African-American and Caucasian youth. *American Journal of Community Psychology, 24,* 551–587.

Maton, K. I., & Wells, E. A. (1995). Religion as a community resource for well-being: Prevention, healing, and empowerment pathways. *Journal of Social Issues, 51,* 177–193.

Mattis, J., & Jagers, R. (2001). A relational framework for the study of religiosity and spirituality in the lives of African Americans. *Journal of Community Psychology, 29,* 519–540.

Mayer, J., & Davidson, W. S. (2000). Dissemination of innovation as social change. In J. Rappaport &

E. Seidman (Eds.), *Handbook of community psychology* (pp. 421–443). New York: Kluwer Academic/Plenum.

McChesney, K. Y. (1990). Family homelessness: A systemic problem. *Journal of Social Issues, 46*(4), 191–205.

McDonald, K., Keys, C., & Balcazar, F. (2007). Disability, race/ethnicity and gender: themes of cultural oppression, acts of individual resistance. *American Journal of Community Psychology, 39,* 145–161.

McDonald, K. E., & Keys, C. B. (2008). How the powerful decide: Access to research participation by those at the margins. *American Journal of Community Psychology, 42,* 79–93.

McDonald, M. (2008a). 2000 general election turnout rates. *United States Elections Project.* Retrieved March 5, 2011, http://elections.gmu.edu/Turnout_2000G.html

McDonald, M. (2008b). 2004 general election turnout rates. *United States Elections Project.* Retrieved March 5, 2011, from http://elections.gmu.edu/Turnout_2004G.html

McDonald, M. (2010). 2008 general election turnout rates. *United States Elections Project.* Retrieved March 5, 2011, fromhttp://elections.gmu.edu/Turnout_2008G.html

McElhaney, S. (1995). *Getting started: NMHA guide to establishing community-based prevention programs.* Alexandria, VA: National Mental Health Association.

McIntosh, P. (1998). White privilege and male privilege: A personal account of coming to see correspondences through work in women's studies. In M. Andersen & P. H. Collins (Eds.), *Race, class and gender: An anthology* (pp. 94–105). Belmont, CA: Wadsworth.

McLaughlin, M., & Mitra, D. (2001). Theory-based change and change-based theory: Going deeper, going broader. *Journal of Educational Change, 2*(4), 301–323.

McLoyd, V. (1998). Socioeconomic disadvantage and child development. *American Psychologist, 53,* 185–204.

McMahon, S., & Watts, R. (2002). Ethnic identity in urban African American youth: Exploring links with self-worth, aggression and other psychosocial variables. *Journal of Community Psychology, 30,* 411–432.

McMillan, B., Florin, P., Stevenson, J., Kerman, B., & Mitchell, R. E. (1995). Empowerment praxis in community coalitions. *American Journal of Community Psychology, 23,* 699–728.

McMillan, D. W. (1996). Sense of community. *Journal of Community Psychology, 24,* 315–326.

McMillan, D. W., & Chavis, D. M. (1986). Sense of community: Definition and theory. *Journal of Community Psychology, 14,* 6–23.

McNally, R., Bryant, R., & Ehlers, A. (2003). Does early psychological intervention promote recovery from posttraumatic stress? *Psychological Science in the Public Interest, 4,* 45–79.

Meissen, G., Hazel, K., Berkowitz, B., & Wolff, T. (2008). The story of the first ever Summit on Community Psychology Practice. *The Community Psychologist, 41*(1), 40–41.

Melton, G. B. (1995). Bringing psychology to Capitol Hill: Briefings on child and family policy. *American Psychologist, 50,* 766–770.

Melton, G. B. (2000). Community change, community stasis, and the law. In J. Rappaport & E. Seidman (Eds.), *Handbook of community psychology* (pp. 523–540). New York: Kluwer Academic/Plenum.

Menec, V. H., Shooshtari, S., Nowicki, S., & Fournier, S. (2010). Does the relationship between neighborhood socioeconomic status and health outcomes persist into very old age? A population-based study. *Journal of Aging and Health, 22*(1), 27–47.

Merrell, K., Gueldner, B., Ross, S., & Isava, D. (2008). How effective are school bullying intervention programs? A meta-analysis of intervention research. *School Psychology Quarterly, 23,* 26–42.

Merrill, J., Pinsky, I., Killeya-Jones, L., Sloboda, Z., & Dilascio, T. (2006). Substance abuse prevention infrastructure: A survey-based study of the organizational structure and function of the D.A.R.E. program. *Substance Abuse Treatment, Prevention, and Policy.* Retrieved March 5, 2011, from http://www.substanceabuse policy.com/content/1/1/25

Meyers, J. (2000). A community psychologist in the public policy arena. In J. Rappaport & E. Seidman (Eds.), *Handbook of community psychology* (pp. 761–764). New York: Kluwer/Plenum.

Miles, M., & Huberman, A. (1994). *Qualitative data analysis* (2nd ed.). Thousand Oaks, CA: Sage.

Miller, J. B. (1976). *Toward a new psychology of women.* Boston: Beacon Press.

Miller, K. (2004). Beyond the frontstage: Trust, access, and the relational context in research with refugee communities. *American Journal of Community Psychology, 33,* 217–228.

Miller, K., & Banyard, V. (Eds.). (1998). Qualitative research in community psychology [Special issue]. *American Journal of Community Psychology, 26*(4).

Miller, R. L., & Campbell, R. (2006). Taking stock of empowerment evaluation: An empirical review. *American Journal of Evaluation, 27,* 296–319.

Miller, R. L., Kobes, S., & Forney, J. (2008). Building the capacity of small community-based organizations to better serve youth. In M. Shinn & H. Yoshikawa (Eds.), *Toward positive youth development: Transforming schools and community programs.* New York: Oxford University Press.

Miller, R. L., & Shinn, M. (2005). Learning from communities: Overcoming difficulties in dissemination of prevention and promotion efforts. *American Journal of Community Psychology, 35,* 169–184.

Mirowsky, J., & Ross, C. (1989). *Social causes of psychological distress.* New York: Aldine de Gruyter.

Mishel, L., Bernstein, J., & Shierholz, H. (2009). *The state of working America 2008/2009.* Economic Policy Institute. Ithaca, NY: Cornell University.

Moane, G. (2003). Bridging the personal and the political: Practices for a liberation psychology. *American Journal of Community Psychology, 31,* 91–102.

Mock, M. (1999, Winter). Cultural competency: Acts of justice in community mental health. *The Community Psychologist, 32,* 38–41.

Mohatt, G., Hazel, K., Allen, J., Stachelrodt, M., Hensel, C., & Fath, R. (2004). Unheard Alaska: Culturally anchored participatory action research on sobriety with Alaska Natives. *American Journal of Community Psychology, 33,* 263–274.

Molock, S. D., & Douglas, K. B. (1999, Summer). Suicidality in the Black community: A collaborative response from a womanist theologian and a community psychologist. *The Community Psychologist, 32,* 32–36.

Montero, M. (1996). Parallel lives: Community psychology in Latin America and the United States. *American Journal of Community Psychology, 24,* 589–606.

Montero, M. (Ed.). (2002). Conceptual and epistemological aspects in community social psychology [Special issue.] *American Journal of Community Psychology, 30*(4).

Montero, M., & Varas-Díaz, N. (2007). Latin American community psychology: Development, implications, and challenges within a social change agenda. In S. M. Reich, M. Riemer, I. Prilleltensky, & M. Montero (Eds.), *International community psychology: History and theories* (pp. 63–98). New York: Springer.

Moore, T. (1977). Social change and community psychology. In I. Iscoe, B. Bloom, & C. D. Spielberger (Eds.), *Community psychology in transition* (pp. 257–266). Washington, DC: Hemisphere.

Moore, T., Kloos, B., & Rasmussen, R. (2001). A reunion of ideas: Complementary inquiry and collaborative interventions of spirituality, religion and psychology. *Journal of Community Psychology, 29,* 487–496.

Moos, R. (1973). Conceptualizations of human environments. *American Psychologist, 28,* 652–665.

Moos, R. (1974). *Evaluating treatment environments: A social ecological approach.* New York: Wiley.

Moos, R. (1975). *Evaluating correctional and community settings.* New York: Wiley.

Moos, R. (1984). Context and coping: Toward a unifying conceptual framework. *American Journal of Community Psychology, 12,* 5–25.

Moos, R. (1994). *The social climate scales: A user's guide* (2nd ed.). Palo Alto, CA: Consulting Psychologists Press.

Moos, R. (2002). The mystery of human context and coping: An unraveling of clues. *American Journal of Community Psychology, 30,* 67–88.

Moos, R. (2003). Social contexts: Transcending their power and their fragility. *American Journal of Community Psychology, 31,* 1–14.

Moos, R. H., & Holahan, C. S. (2003). Dispositional and contextual perspectives on coping: Toward an integrative framework. *Journal of Clinical Psychology, 59,* 1387–1403.

Moos, R., & Trickett, E. J. (1987). *Classroom environment scale manual* (2nd ed.). Palo Alto, CA: Consulting Psychologists Press.

Mrazek, P., & Haggerty, R. (1994). *Reducing risks for mental disorders: Frontiers for preventive intervention research.* Washington, DC: National Academy Press.

Muehrer, P. (Ed.). (1997). Prevention research in rural settings [Special issue]. *American Journal of Community Psychology, 25*(4).

Mulder, P. L., Jackson, R., & Jarvis, S. (2010). Services in rural areas. In B. L. Levin & M. A. Becker (Eds.), *A public health perspective on women's mental health* (pp. 313–333). New York: Springer.

Mulder, P. L., Shellenberger, S., Streiegel, R., Jumper-Thurman, P., Danda, C. E., Kenkel, M. B., et al. (1999). *The behavioral healthcare needs of rural women.* A report of the Rural Women's Work Group of the Rural Task Force of the American Psychological Association and the American Psychological Association's Committee on Rural Health. Retrieved August 30, 2010, from http://www.apa.org/pubs/info/reports/rural-women.pdf.

Mulvey, A. (1988). Community psychology and feminism: Tensions and commonalities. *Journal of Community Psychology, 16,* 70–83.

Mulvey, A. (2002). Gender, economic context, perceptions of safety, and quality of life: A case study of Lowell, Massachusetts (U.S.A.), 1982–96. *American Journal of Community Psychology, 30,* 655–680.

Mulvey, A., Bond, M. A., Hill, J., & Terenzio, M. (2000). Weaving feminism and community psychology: An introduction to a special issue. *American Journal of Community Psychology, 28,* 585–598.

Mulvey, A., Gridley, H., & Gawith, L. (2001). Convent girls, feminism and community psychology. *Journal of Community Psychology, 29,* 563–584.

Murray, H. (1938). *Explorations in personality.* New York: Oxford University Press.

Murrell, S. (1973). *Community psychology and social systems.* New York: Behavioral Publications.

Myers, J. K., & Bean, L. L. (1968). *A decade later: A follow-up of "Social class and mental illness."* New York: Wiley.

Myers, L. J., & Speight, S. (1994). Optimal theory and the psychology of human diversity. In E. J. Trickett, R. J. Watts, & D. Birman (Eds.), *Human diversity: Perspectives on people in context* (pp. 81–100). San Francisco: Jossey-Bass.

Nagler, M. (2001). *Is there no other way? The search for a nonviolent future.* Berkeley, CA: Berkeley Hills Books.

Nation, M., Crusto, C., Wandersman, A., Kumpfer, K., Seyboldt, D., Morriessey-Kane, E., et al. (2003). What works in prevention: Principles of effective prevention programs. *American Psychologist, 58,* 449–456.

Nation, M., Wandersman, A., & Perkins, D. D. (2002). Promoting healthy communities through community development. In D. Glenwick & L. Jason, (Eds.), *Innovative strategies for preventing psychological problems* (pp. 324–344). New York: Springer.

National Institute on Drug Abuse. (1988). *Needle sharing among intravenous drug abusers: National and international perspectives* (NIDA Research Monograph Series 80). Retrieved March 5, 2011, from http://archives.drugabuse.gov/pdf/monographs/download80.html

Neigher, W., & Fishman, D. (2004, Spring). Case studies in community practice. *The Community Psychologist, 37,* 30–34.

Neilsen, D. (n.d.) Do something spotlight: Daniel Kent and Senior Connects. Retrieved March 5, 2011, from http://money.howstuffworks.com/do-something-spotlight-daniel-kent-senior-connects.htm

Nelson, G., Janzen, R., Trainor, J., & Ochocka, J. (2008). Putting values into practice: Public policy and the future of mental health consumer-run organizations. *American Journal of Community Psychology, 42*(1), 192–201.

Nelson, G., Lavoie, F., & Mitchell, T. (2007). The history and theories of community psychology in Canada. In S. M. Reich, M. Reimer, I. Prilleltensky, & M. Montero (Eds.), *The history and theories of community psychology: An international perspective* (pp. 13–36). New York: Springer.

Nelson, G., Ochocka, J., Griffin, K., & Lord, J. (1998). "Nothing about me, without me": Participatory action research with self-help/mutual aid organizations for psychiatric consumer/survivors. *American Journal of Community Psychology, 26*(6), 881–912.

Nelson, G., & Prilleltensky, I. (Eds.). (2005). *Community psychology: In pursuit of liberation and well-being.* New York: Palgrave Macmillan.

Nelson, G., & Prilleltensky, I. (Eds.). (2010). *Community psychology: In pursuit of liberation and well-being.* New York: Palgrave Macmillan.

Nelson, G., Prilleltensky, I., & MacGillivray, H. (2001). Building value-based partnerships: Toward solidarity with oppressed groups. *American Journal of Community Psychology, 29,* 649–678.

New Freedom Commission on Mental Health. (2003). *Achieving the Promise: Transforming Mental Health Care* in America. *Final Report*. DHHS Pub. No. SMA-03-3832. Rockville, MD.

Newbrough, J. R. (1995). Toward community: A third position. *American Journal of Community Psychology, 23*, 9–38.

Newbrough, J. R. (Ed.). (1996). Sense of community [Special issue]. *Journal of Community Psychology, 24*(4).

Newbrough, J. R., & Chavis, D. M. (Eds.). (1986a). Psychological sense of community: I. Theory and concepts [Special issue]. *Journal of Community Psychology, 14*(1).

Newton, L., Rosen, A., Tennant, C., Hobbs, C., Lapsley, H. M., & Tribe, K. (2000). Deinstitutionalisation for long-term mental illness: An ethnographic study. *The Australian and New Zealand Journal of Psychiatry, 34*, 484–490.

Nicotera, N. (2007). Measuring neighborhood: A conundrum for human service researchers and practitioners. *American Journal of Community Psychology, 40*, 26–51.

Nisbet, R. (1953). *The quest for community: A study in the ethics of order and freedom*. Oxford University Press.

Norris, F. H., Friedman, M., & Watson, P. (2002). 60,000 disaster victims speak: Part II. Summary and implications of the disaster mental health research. *Psychiatry: Interpersonal and Biological Processes, 65*, 240–260.

Norris, F. H., Friedman, M., Watson, P., Byrne, C., Diaz, E., & Kaniasty, K. (2002). 60,000 disaster victims speak: Part I. An empirical review of the empirical literature, 1981–2001. *Psychiatry: Interpersonal and Biological Processes, 65*, 207–239.

Norris, F. H., Tracy, M., & Galea, S. (2009). Looking for resilience: Understanding the longitudinal trajectories of responses to stress. *Social Science & Medicine, 68*, 2190–2198.

Norris, F., Olson, B., Berkowitz, B., Goodkind, J. R., Haber, M., Kilmer, R. P., et al. (2009, June). Town Hall Meeting for SCRA Task Force on Disaster, Community Readiness, and Recovery at the 12th biennial meeting of the Society for Community Research and Action, Montclair, NJ.

Norris, F. H., Stevens, S., Pfefferbaum, B., Wyche, K., & Pfefferbaum, R. (2008). Community resilience as a metaphor, theory, set of capacities, and strategy for disaster readiness. *American Journal of Community Psychology, 41*(1), 127–150.

Northwest Regional Educational Laboratory (National Mentoring Center). (1999). *Making the case: Measuring the impact of your mentoring program* (p. 41). Retrieved March 5, 2011, from http://www.mentoring.org/program_resources/library/category/all

Novaco, R., & Monahan, J. (1980). Research in community psychology: An analysis of work published in the first six years of the *American Journal of Community Psychology*. *American Journal of Community Psychology, 8*, 131–145.

Nussbaum, M. C. (2000). *Women and human development: The capabilities approach*. Cambridge: Cambridge University Press.

Nussbaum, M. C. (2006). *Frontiers of justice: Disability, nationality, and species membership*. Cambridge, MA: Harvard University Press.

Obst, P., & White, K. (2004). Revisiting the Sense of Community Index: A confirmatory factor analysis. *Journal of Community Psychology, 32*, 691–706.

Obst, P., Zinkiewicz, L., & Smith, S. (2002). Sense of community in science fiction fandom. Part 2: Comparing neighborhood and interest group sense of community. *Journal of Community Psychology, 30*, 105–118.

O'Connell, M. E., Boat, T., & Warner, K. (Eds.). (2009). Preventing mental, emotional, and behavioral disorders among young people: Progress and possibilities. Washington, DC: National Academies Press.

O'Donnell, C. R. (2005, June). Beyond diversity: Toward a cultural community psychology. Presidential address at the Biennial Meeting of the Society for Community Research and Action, Urbana-Champaign, IL.

O'Donnell, C. R., Tharp, R. G., & Wilson, K. (1993). Activity settings as the unit of analysis: A theoretical basis for community intervention and development. *American Journal of Community Psychology, 21*, 501–520.

O'Donnell, C. R., & Yamauchi, L. (Eds.). (2005). *Culture and context in human behavior change: Theory, research, and applications*. New York: Peter Lang.

O'Donnell, M. P. (2009). Integrating health promotion into national health policy. *American Journal of Health Promotion, 23*, iv–vi.

Oetting, E., Jumper-Thurman, P., Plested, B., & Edwards, R. (2001). Community readiness and health services. *Substance Use and Misuse, 36,* 825–843.

Ohlemacher, S. (2010, April 17). Nearly half of US households escape fed income tax. Associated Press. Retrieved March 5, 2011, from http://finance. yahoo.com/news/Nearly-half-of-US-households-apf-1105567323.html?x=0&.v=1

Olson, B. (2003, Fall). Ten primary notions for the SCRA community action interest group. *The Community Psychologist, 36,* 34–35.

Olson, B. (2004, Fall). Thoughts on attending SCRA at the APA convention this year. *The Community Psychologist, 37,* 48–49.

Olson, B., & Kloos, B. (2010, June). The SCRA Task Force on Disaster, Community Readiness, and Recovery: Creating a grassroots manual based on principles and practical advice from community psychology. Roundtable presentation at the 3rd International Conference on Community Psychology, Puebla, Mexico.

Olweus, D. (1997). Bully/victim problems in school: Facts and intervention. *European Journal of Psychology of Education, 12,* 495–510.

Olweus, D., & Limber, S. (2010). Bullying in school: Evaluation and dissemination of the Olweus bullying prevention program. *American Journal of Orthopsychiatry, 80,* 124–134.

Olweus, D., Limber, S., & Mihalic, S. (1999). *The Bullying Prevention program: Blueprints for violence prevention* (Vol. 10). Boulder, CO: Center for the Study and Prevention of Violence.

O'Neill, P. (1989). Responsible to whom? Responsible for what? Some ethical issues in community intervention. *American Journal of Community Psychology, 17,* 323–342.

O'Neill, P. (2005). The ethics of problem definition. *Canadian Psychology, 46,* 13–20.

Ortiz-Torres, B., Serrano-Garcia, I., & Torres-Burgos, N. (2000). Subverting culture: Promoting HIV/AIDS prevention among Puerto Rican and Dominican women. *American Journal of Community Psychology, 28,* 859–882.

Ostrove, J., & Cole, E. (2003). Privileging class: Toward a critical psychology of social class in the context of education. *Journal of Social Issues, 59,* 677–692.

Ott, D. (2005, July 19). Revitalization efforts gets failing grade, survey says. *The Philadelphia Inquirer,* pp. B1, B6.

Oxley, D., & Barrera, M. (1984). Undermanning theory and the workplace: Implications of setting size for job satisfaction and social support. *Environment and Behavior, 16,* 211–234.

Pager, D. (2003). The mark of a criminal record. *American Journal of Sociology, 108,* 937–975.

Paradis, E. (2000). Feminist and community psychology ethics in research with homeless women. *American Journal of Community Psychology, 28,* 839–858.

Pargament, K. I. (1997). *The psychology of religion and coping: Theory, research and practice.* New York: Guilford.

Pargament, K. I. (2008). The sacred character of community life. *American Journal of Community Psychology, 41,* 22–34.

Pargament, K. I., & Maton, K. I. (2000). Religion in American life: A community psychology perspective. In J. Rappaport & E. Seidman (Eds.), *Handbook of community psychology* (pp. 495–522). New York: Kluwer/Plenum.

Park, R. (1952). *Human communities: The city and human ecology.* New York: Free Press.

Patton, M. Q. (1997). Toward distinguishing empowerment evaluation and placing it in a larger context. *Evaluation Practice, 15*(3), 311–320. Retrieved March 5, 2011, from http://www.davidfetterman.com/pattonbkreview1997.pdf

Patton, M. Q. (2005). Toward distinguishing empowerment evaluation and placing it in a larger context: Take two. *American Journal of Evaluation, 26,* 408–414.

Patton, M. Q. (2008). *Utilization-focused evaluation* (4th ed.). Beverly Hills, CA: Sage

Paxton, K. C., Guentzel, H., & Trombacco, K. (2006). Lessons learned in developing a research partnership with the transgendered community. *American Journal of Community Psychology, 37,* 349–356.

Paxton, P. (1999). Is social capital declining in the United States? A multiple indicator assessment. *American Journal of Sociology, 105,* 88–127.

Paxton, P. (2002). Social capital and democracy: An interdependent relationship. *American Sociological Review, 67,* 254–277.

Paxton, P. (2007). Association membership and generalized trust: A multilevel model across 32 countries. *Social Forces, 86,* 47–76.

Payne, C. (1995). *I've got the light of freedom: The organizing tradition and the Mississippi freedom struggle.* Berkeley, CA: University of California Press.

Payton, J., Weissberg, R., Durlak, J., Dymnicki, A., Taylor, R., Schellinger, K., et al. (2008). *The positive impact of social and emotional learning for kindergarten to eighth-grade students: Findings from three scientific reviews.* Retrieved March 5, 2011, from http://www.lpfch.org/sel/PackardES-REV.pdf

Peer Water Exchange. (n.d.). Retrieved March 5, 2011, from http://peerwater.org.

Pepler, D., & Slaby, R. (1994). Theoretical and developmental perspectives on youth and violence. In L. Eron, J. Gentry, & P. Schlegel (Eds.), *Reason to hope: A psychosocial perspective on violence and youth* (pp. 27–58). Washington, DC: American Psychological Association.

Perkins, D. D. (1988). The use of social science in public interest litigation: A role for community psychologists. *American Journal of Community Psychology, 16,* 465–486.

Perkins, D. D. (1995). Speaking truth to power: Empowerment ideology as social intervention and policy. *American Journal of Community Psychology, 23,* 765–794.

Perkins, D. D., Brown, B. B., & Taylor, R. B. (1996). The ecology of empowerment: Predicting participation in community organizations. *Journal of Social Issues, 52,* 85–110.

Perkins, D. D., Crim, B., Silberman, P., & Brown, B. (2004). Community development as a response to community-level adversity: Ecological theory and strengths-based policy. In K. Maton, C. Schellenbach, B. Leadbeater, & A. Solarz (Eds.), *Investing in children, youth, families and communities: Strengths-based research and policy* (pp. 321–340). Washington, DC: American Psychological Association.

Perkins, D. D., Florin, P., Rich, R., Wandersman, A., & Chavis, D. (1990). Participation and the social and physical environment of residential blocks: Crime and community context. *American Journal of Community Psychology, 18,* 83–116.

Perkins, D. D., & Long, D. A. (2002). Neighborhood sense of community and social capital: A multi-level analysis. In A. Fisher, C. Sonn, & B. Bishop (Eds.), *Psychological sense of community: Research, applications and implications* (pp. 291–318). New York: Kluwer/Plenum.

Perkins, D. D., & Taylor, R. (1996). Ecological assessments of community disorder: Their relationship to fear of crime and theoretical implications. *American Journal of Community Psychology, 24,* 63–108.

Reprinted in T. Revenson, A. D'Augelli, S. E. French, D. Hughes, D. Livert, E. Seidman, M. Shinn, & H. Yoshikawa (Eds.), (2002), *Ecological research to promote social change: Methodological advances from community psychology* (pp. 127–170). New York: Kluwer Academic/Plenum.

Perkins, D. D., & Zimmerman, M. (1995). Empowerment theory, research and application. *American Journal of Community Psychology, 23,* 569–580.

Perkins, D. V., Burns, T., Perry, J., & Nielsen, K. (1988). Behavior setting theory and community psychology: An analysis and critique. *Journal of Community Psychology, 16,* 355–372.

Peterson, N. A., & Reid, R. (2003). Paths to psychological empowerment in an urban community: Sense of community and citizen participation in substance abuse prevention activities. *Journal of Community Psychology, 31,* 25–38.

Peterson, N. A., & Zimmerman, M. (2004). Beyond the individual: Toward a nomological network of organizational empowerment. *American Journal of Community Psychology, 34,* 129–146.

Petrosino, A., Turpin-Petrosino, C., & Buehler, J. (2003). *"Scared Straight" and other juvenile awareness programs for preventing juvenile delinquency.* http://campbellcollaboration.org/lib/download/13

Phillips, D. (2000). Social policy and community psychology. In J. Rappaport & E. Seidman (Eds.), *Handbook of community psychology* (pp. 397–420). New York: Kluwer/Plenum.

Phinney, J. (1990). Ethnic identity in adolescents and adults: Review of research. *Psychological Bulletin, 108,* 499–514.

Phinney, J. (2003). Ethnic identity and acculturation. In K. Chun, P. Organista, & G. Marin (Eds.), *Acculturation: Advances in theory, measurement and applied research* (pp. 63–94). Washington, DC: American Psychological Association.

Pickren, W., & Tomes, H. (2002). The legacy of Kenneth B. Clark to the APA: The Board of Social and Ethical Responsibility. *American Psychologist, 57,* 51–59.

PICO. (2010a). *A commitment to get things done in Camden.* PICO National Network. Retrieved March 7, 2011, from http://www.piconetwork.org/leaders?id=0007

PICO. (2010b). *Learning that there are others out there with the same experience.* PICO National Network.

Retrieved March 7, 2011, from http://www.piconetwork.org/leaders?id=0001

PICO. (2010c). *In Vermont, realizing what it means to be a leader.* PICO National Network. Retrieved March 7, 2011, from http://www.piconetwork.org/leaders?id=0009

Pistrang, N., & Barker, C. (1998). Partners and fellow patients: Two sources of emotional support for women with breast cancer. *American Journal of Community Psychology, 26,* 439–456.

Pistrang, N., Barker, C., & Humphreys, K., (2008). Mutual help groups for mental health problems: A review of effectiveness studies. *American Journal of Community Psychology, 42,* 110–121.

Plas, J. M., & Lewis, S. E. (1996). Environmental factors and sense of community in a planned town. *American Journal of Community Psychology, 24,* 109–144.

Pokorny, S., Baptiste, D., Tolan P., Hirsch, B., Talbot, B., Ji, P., et al. (2004). Prevention science: Participatory approaches and community case studies. In L. A. Jason, C. Keys, Y. Suarez-Balcazar, R. Taylor, & M. Davis (Eds.), *Participatory community research: Theories and methods in action* (pp. 87–104). Washington, DC: American Psychological Association.

Pool, B. (2009, October 16). Woman, 97, has a front seat to homelessness. *Los Angeles Times.* Retrieved March 7, 2011, from http://articles.latimes.com/2009/oct/16/local/me-bessie16.

Potts, R. (Ed.). (1999, Summer). The spirit of community psychology: Spirituality, religion, and community action [Special section]. *The Community Psychologist, 32.*

Potts, R. (2003). Emancipatory education versus school based prevention in African American communities. *American Journal of Community Psychology, 31,* 173–185.

Prelow, H. M., Danoff-Burg, S., Swenson, R., & Pulgiano, D. (2004). The impact of ecological risk and perceived discrimination on psychological adjustment of African American and European American youths. *Journal of Community Psychology, 32,* 375–389.

Prestby, J., Wandersman, A., Florin, P., Rich, R., & Chavis, D. (1990). Benefits, costs, incentive management and participation in voluntary organizations: A means to understanding and promoting empowerment. *American Journal of Community Psychology, 18,* 117–150.

Pretty, G. M. H. (2002). Young people's development of the community-minded self: Considering community identity, community attachment, and sense of community. In A. Fisher, C. Sonn, & B. Bishop (Eds.), *Psychological sense of community: Research, applications and implications* (pp. 183–203). New York: Kluwer/Plenum.

Pretty, G. M. H., Andrewes, L., & Collett, C. (1994). Exploring adolescents' sense of community and its relationship to loneliness. *Journal of Community Psychology, 22,* 346–358.

Pretty, G. M. H., Conroy, C., Dugay, J., Fowler, K., & Williams, D. (1996). Sense of community and its relevance to adolescents of all ages. *Journal of Community Psychology, 24,* 365–380.

Prezza, M., Amici, M., Roberti, T., & Tedeschi, G. (2001). Sense of community referred to the whole town: Its relations with neighboring, loneliness, life satisfaction, ad area of residence. *Journal of Community Psychology, 29,* 29–52.

Price, R. (1989). Bearing witness. *American Journal of Community Psychology, 17,* 151–167.

Price, R., Cowen, E., Lorion, R., & Ramos-McKay, J. (Eds.). (1988). *Fourteen ounces of prevention: A casebook for practitioners.* Washington, DC: American Psychological Association.

Price, R., & Lorion, R. (1989). Prevention programming as organizational reinvention: From research to implementation. In D. Shaffer, I. Phillips, & N. Enzer (Eds.), *Prevention of mental disorders, alcohol and other drug use in children and adolescents* (pp. 97–123). Office of Substance Abuse Prevention, Prevention Monograph No. 2 (Department of Health and Human Services Publication No. ADM 89–1646). Washington, DC: U.S. Government Printing Office.

Prilleltensky, I. (1997a). *Community psychology: Reclaiming social justice.* Thousand Oaks, CA: Sage Publications.

Prilleltensky, I. (1997b). Values, assumptions, and practices: Assessing the moral implications of psychological discourse and action. *American Psychologist, 52,* 517–535.

Prilleltensky, I. (1999). Critical psychology foundations for the promotion of mental health. *Annual Review of Critical Psychology, 1,* 95–112.

Prilleltensky, I. (2001). Value-based praxis in community psychology: Moving toward social justice and social action. *American Journal of Community Psychology, 29,* 747–778.

Prilleltensky, I. (2003). Understanding, resisting, and overcoming oppression: Toward psychopolitical validity. *American Journal of Community Psychology, 31,* 195–202.

Prilleltensky, I. (2008). The role of power in wellness, oppression, and liberation: the promise of psycho-political validity. *Journal of Community Psychology, 36,* 116–136.

Prilleltensky, I., & Gonick, L. (1994). The discourse of oppression in the social sciences: Past, present, and future. In E. J. Trickett, R. J. Watts, & D. Birman (Eds.), *Human diversity: Perspectives on people in context* (pp. 145–177). San Francisco: Jossey-Bass.

Prilleltensky, I., & Nelson, G. (2002). *Doing psychology critically: Making a difference in diverse settings.* New York: Palgrave Macmillan.

Primavera, J. (2004). You can't get there from here: Identifying process routes to replication. *American Journal of Community Psychology, 33,* 181–191.

Primavera, J., & Brodsky, A. (2004). Process of community research and action [Special issue]. *American Journal of Community Psychology, 33*(3/4).

Prinz, R., Sanders, M., Shapiro, C., Whitaker, D., & Lutzker, J. (2009). Population-based prevention of child maltreatment: The U.S. Triple P system population trial. *Prevention Science, 10,* 1–12.

Putnam, R. D. (1996). The strange disappearance of civic America. *The American Prospect, 7.* http://epn.org/prospect/24/24putn.html

Putnam, R. (2000). *Bowling alone: The collapse and revival of American community.* New York: Simon & Schuster.

Putnam, R., & Feldstein, L., with Cohen, D. (2003). *Better together: Restoring the American community.* New York: Simon & Schuster.

Rahm, J. (2002). Emergent learning opportunities in an inner-city youth gardening program. *Journal of Research in Science Teaching, 39,* 164–184.

Rapley, M., & Pretty, G. (1999). Playing Procrustes: The interactional production of a "psychological sense of community." *Journal of Community Psychology, 27,* 695–714.

Rappaport, J. (1977a). *Community psychology: Values, research, and action.* New York: Holt, Rinehart and Winston.

Rappaport, J. (1977b). From Noah to Babel: Relationships between conceptions, values, analysis levels, and social intervention strategies. In I. Iscoe, B. L. Bloom, C. D. Spielberger (Eds.), *Community psychology in transition: Proceedings from the national conference on training in community psychology* (pp. 174–184). New York: John Wiley & Sons.

Rappaport, J. (1981). In praise of paradox: A social policy of empowerment over prevention. *American Journal of Community Psychology, 9,* 1–25. Reprinted in T. Revenson, A. D'Augelli, S. E. French, D. Hughes, D. Livert, E. Seidman, M. Shinn, & H. Yoshikawa (Eds.), (2002), *A quarter century of community psychology* (pp. 121–145). New York: Kluwer Academic/Plenum.

Rappaport, J. (1987). Terms of empowerment/exemplars of prevention: Toward a theory for community psychology. *American Journal of Community Psychology, 15,* 121–144.

Rappaport, J. (1990). Research methods and the empowerment social agenda. In P. Tolan, C. Keys, F. Chertok, & L. Jason (Eds.), *Researching community psychology* (pp. 51–63). Washington, DC: American Psychological Association.

Rappaport, J. (1993). Narrative studies, personal stories, and identity transformation in the mutual help context. *Journal of Applied Behavioral Science, 29,* 239–256.

Rappaport, J. (1995). Empowerment meets narrative: Listening to stories and creating settings. *American Journal of Community Psychology, 23,* 795–808.

Rappaport, J. (1998). The art of social change: Community narratives as resources for individual and collective identity. In X. B. Arriaga & S. Oskamp (Eds.), *Addressing community problems: Psychological research and interventions* (pp. 225–246). Thousand Oaks, CA: Sage.

Rappaport, J. (2000). Community narratives: Tales of terror and joy. *American Journal of Community Psychology, 28,* 1–24.

Rappaport, J., Davidson, W. S., Wilson, M. N., & Mitchell, A. (1975). Alternatives to blaming the victim or the environment: Our places to stand have not moved the earth. *American Psychologist, 29,* 525–528.

Rappaport, J., & Seidman, E. (Eds.). (2000). *Handbook of community psychology.* New York: Plenum.

Rapping, E. (1997, Spring). There's self-help and then there's self-help: Women and the recovery movement. *Social Policy,* 56–61.

Rasmussen, A., Aber, M., & Bhana, A. (2004). Adolescent coping and neighborhood violence: Perceptions, exposure, and urban youths' efforts to deal with danger. *American Journal of Community Psychology, 33*(1), 61–75.

Ratcliffe, A., & Neigher, B. (n.d.). *Introducing community psychology*. http://www.scra27.org/practice/documents/value_proposition.pdf

Ravitch, D. (2010). *The death and life of the great American school system: How testing and choice are undermining education*. New York: Basic Books.

Raviv, A., Raviv, A., & Reisel, E. (1990). Teachers and students: Two different perspectives?! Measuring social climate in the classroom. *American Educational Research Journal, 27,* 141–157.

Raynes-Goldie, K., & Walker, L. (2008). Our space: Online civic engagement tools for youth. In W. L. Bennett (Ed.), *Civic life online: Learning how digital media can engage youth* (pp. 161–188). Cambridge, MA: MIT Press.

Reason, P., & Bradbury, H. (Eds.). (2001). *Handbook of action research: Participative inquiry and practice*. London: Sage.

Reich, S. M., Riemer, M., Prilleltensky, I., & Montero, M. (Eds.). (2007). *International community psychology: History and theories*. New York: Springer Science + Business Media.

Reid, T. R. (1999). *Confucius lives next door*. New York: Random House.

Reinharz, S. (1984). Alternative settings and social change. In K. Heller, R. Price, S. Reinharz, S. Riger, & A. Wandersman (Eds.), *Psychology and community change* (2nd ed., pp. 286–336). Homewood, IL: Dorsey.

Reinharz, S. (1994). Toward an ethnography of "voice" and "silence." In E. J. Trickett, R. J. Watts, & D. Birman (Eds.), *Human diversity: Perspectives on people in context* (pp. 178–200). San Francisco: Jossey-Bass.

Repetti, R., & Cosmas, K. (1991). The quality of the social environment at work and job satisfaction. *Journal of Applied Social Psychology, 21,* 840–854.

Resnicow, K., Braithwaite, R., Ahluwalia, J., & Baranowski, T. (1999). Cultural sensitivity in public health: Defined and demystified. *Ethnicity and Disease, 9,* 10–21.

Revenson, R., & Seidman, E. (2002). Looking backward and moving forward: Reflections on a quarter century of community psychology. In T. Revenson, A. D'Augelli, S. E. French, D. Hughes, D. Livert, E. Seidman, M. Shinn, & H. Yoshikawa (Eds.), *A quarter century of community psychology* (pp. 3–32). New York: Kluwer Academic/Plenum.

Revenson, T., D'Augelli, A., French, S., Hughes, D., Livert, D., Seidman, E., et al. (Eds.). (2002a). *Ecological research to promote social change: Methodological advances from community psychology*. New York: Kluwer Academic/Plenum.

Revenson, T., D'Augelli, A., French, S., Hughes, D., Livert, D., Seidman, E., et al. (Eds.). (2002b). *A quarter century of community psychology: Readings from the American Journal of Community Psychology*. New York: Kluwer/Plenum.

Reza, H., & Ahmmed, F. (2008). Structural social work and the compatibility of NGO approaches: A case analysis of Bangladesh Rural Advancement Committee (BRAC). *International Journal of Social Welfare, 18,* 173–182.

Rheingold, H. (2000). *The virtual community: Homesteading on the electronic frontier*. Cambridge, MA: MIT Press.

Rhodes, J. E. (2002). *Stand by me: The risks and rewards of mentoring today's youth*. Cambridge, MA: Harvard University Press.

Rhodes, J. E., & DuBois, D. L. (2008). Mentoring relationships and programs for youth. *Current Directions in Psychological Science, 17*(4), 254–258.

Rhodes, J. E., Spencer, R., Keller, T. E., Liang, B., & Noam, G. (2006). A model for the influence of mentoring relationships on youth development. *Journal of Community Psychology, 34*(6), 691–707.

Rice, J. (2001). Poverty, welfare, and patriarchy: How macro-level changes in social policy can help low-income women. *Journal of Social Issues, 57,* 355–374.

Rich, R. C., Edelstein, M., Hallman, W., & Wandersman, A. (1995). Citizen participation and empowerment: The case of local environmental hazards. *American Journal of Community Psychology, 23,* 657–676.

Rickard, K. (1990). The effect of feminist identity level on gender prejudice toward artists' illustrations. *Journal of Research in Personality, 24,* 145–162.

Ridgeway, C. (2001). Gender, status, and leadership. *Journal of Social Issues, 57,* 637–656.

Riessman, F. (1990). Restructuring help: A human services paradigm for the 1990's. *American Journal of Community Psychology, 18,* 221–230.

Riessman, F., & Banks, E. (2001). A marriage of opposites: Self-help and the health care system. *American Psychologist, 56,* 173–174.

Riger, S. (1989). The politics of community intervention. *American Journal of Community Psychology, 17,* 379–385.

Riger, S. (1990). Ways of knowing and organizational approaches to community research. In P. Tolan, C. Keys, F. Chertok, & L. Jason (Eds.), *Researching community psychology* (pp. 42–50). Washington, DC: American Psychological Association. Reprinted in S. Riger, (2000), *Transforming psychology: Gender in theory and practice* (pp. 72–80). New York: Oxford University Press.

Riger, S. (1992). Epistemological debates, feminist voices: Science, social values and the study of women. *American Psychologist, 47,* 730–740. Reprinted in S. Riger, (2000), *Transforming psychology: Gender in theory and practice* (pp. 7–22). New York: Oxford University Press.

Riger, S. (1993). What's wrong with empowerment? *American Journal of Community Psychology, 21,* 279–292. Reprinted in T. Revenson, A. D'Augelli, S. E. French, D. Hughes, D. Livert, E. Seidman, M. Shinn, & H. Yoshikawa (Eds.), (2002), *A quarter century of community psychology* (pp. 395–408). New York: Kluwer Academic/Plenum. Also reprinted in S. Riger (2000), *Transforming psychology: Gender in theory and practice* (pp. 97–196). New York: Oxford University Press.

Riger, S. (2001). Transforming community psychology. *American Journal of Community Psychology, 29,* 69–81.

Rivers, I., & D'Augelli, A. R. (2001). The victimization of lesbian, gay, and bisexual youths. In A. R. D'Augelli & C. J. Patterson (Eds.), *Lesbian, gay and bisexual identities and youth: Psychological perspectives* (pp. 199–223). New York: Oxford.

RMC Research Corporation. (1995). *National Diffusion Network schoolwide promising practices: Report of a pilot effort.* Portsmouth, NH: Author.

Roberts, L., Smith, L., & Pollock, C. (2002). MOOing till the cows come home: The search for sense of community in virtual environments. In A. Fisher, C. Sonn, & B. Bishop (Eds.), *Psychological sense of community: Research, applications and implications* (pp. 223–246). New York: Kluwer Academic/Plenum.

Roberts, L. J., Luke, D., Rappaport, J., Seidman, E., Toro, P., & Reischl, T. (1991). Charting uncharted terrain: A behavioral observation system for mutual help groups. *American Journal of Community Psychology, 19,* 715–738.

Roberts, L. J., Salem, D., Rappaport, J., Toro, P. A., Luke, D., & Seidman, E. (1999). Giving and receiving help: Interpersonal transactions in mutual-help meetings and psychosocial adjustment of members. *American Journal of Community Psychology, 27,* 841–868.

Robertson, N., & Masters-Awatere, B. (2007). Chapter 6: Community Psychology in Aotearoa/New Zealand: Me tiro whakamuri a kia hangai whakamua. In S. M. Reich, M. Riemer, I. Prilleltensky, & M. Montero (Eds.), *International community psychology: History and theories* (pp. 140–163). New York: Springer.

Robinson, W. L. (1990). Data feedback and communication to the host setting. In P. Tolan, C. Keys, F. Chertok, & L. Jason (Eds.), *Researching community psychology* (pp. 193–195). Washington, DC: American Psychological Association.

Rogers, E. (2003). *Diffusion of innovations* (5th ed.). New York: Free Press.

Rogoff, B. (2003). *The cultural nature of human development.* Oxford: Oxford University Press.

Roosa, M., Jones, S., Tein, J.-Y., & Cree, W. (2003). Prevention science and neighborhood influences on low-income children's development: Theoretical and methodological issues. *American Journal of Community Psychology, 31,* 55–72.

Rosario, M., Hunter, J., Maguen, S., Gwadz, M., & Smith, R. (2001). The coming-out process and its adaptational and health-related associations among gay, lesbian, and bisexual youths: Stipulation and exploration of a model. *American Journal of Community Psychology, 29,* 133–160.

Rosmarin, D., Pargament, K., Krumrei, E., & Flannelly, K. (2009). Religious coping among Jews: Development and initial validation of the JCOPE. *Journal of Clinical Psychology, 65*(7), 670–683.

Ross, L. (1977). The intuitive psychologist and his shortcomings. In L. Berkowitz, (Ed.), *Advances in experimental social psychology* (Vol. 10, pp. 173–220). New York: Academic Press.

Rossi, P., Lipsey, M., & Freeman, H. (2004). *Evaluation: A systematic approach* (7th ed.). Newbury Park, CA: Sage.

Rotheram-Borus, M. J. (1988). Assertiveness training with children. In R. Price, E. Cowen, R. Lorion, & J. Ramos-McKay (Eds.), *Fourteen ounces of prevention* (pp. 83–97). Washington, DC: American Psychological Association.

Rotter, J. B. (1954). *Social learning and clinical psychology.* Englewood Cliffs, NJ: Prentice Hall.

Rotter, J. B. (1966). Generalized expectancies for internal versus external control of reinforcement. *Psychological Monographs, 80* (Whole No. 609).

Rotter, J. B. (1982). *The development and application of social learning theory.* New York: Praeger.

Rotter, J. B. (1990). Internal versus external control of reinforcement: A case history of a variable. *American Psychologist, 45,* 489–493.

Rowe, M., Kloos, B., Chinman, M., Davidson, L., & Cross, A. B. (2001). Homelessness, mental illness, and citizenship. *Social Policy and Administration, 35,* 14–31.

Rudkin, J. K. (2003). *Community psychology: Guiding principles and orienting concepts.* Upper Saddle River, NJ: Prentice Hall.

Rudman, L., & Glick, P. (2001). Prescriptive gender stereotypes and backlash toward agentic women. *Journal of Social Issues, 57,* 743–762.

Rutter, M. (1979). Protective factors in children's responses to stress and disadvantage. In M. W. Kent & J. E. Rolf (Eds.), *Primary prevention of psychopathology: Social competence in children* (Vol. 3). Hanover: University of New England.

Rutter, M., Moffitt, T. E., & Caspi, A. (2006). Gene–environment interplay and psychopathology: multiple varieties but real effects. *Journal of Child Psychology and Psychiatry, 47*(3–4), 226–261.

Rutter, M., & Sroufe, A. (2000). Developmental psychopathology: Concepts and challenges. *Developmental Psychopathology, 12,* 265–296.

Ryan, W. (1971). *Blaming the victim.* New York: Random House.

Ryan, W. (1981). *Equality.* New York: Pantheon.

Ryan, W. (1994). Many cooks, brave men, apples, and oranges: How people think about equality. *American Journal of Community Psychology, 22,* 25–36.

Saegert, S. (1989). Unlikely leaders, extreme circumstances: Older Black women building community households. *American Journal of Community Psychology, 17,* 295–316.

Saegert, S., Thompson, J. P., & Warren, M. (2001). *Social capital and poor communities.* New York: Russell Sage.

Saegert, S., & Winkel, G. (1990). Environmental psychology. *Annual Review of Psychology, 41,* 441–477.

Saegert, S., & Winkel, G. (1996). Paths to community empowerment: Organizing at home. *American Journal of Community Psychology, 24,* 517–550.

Saegert, S., & Winkel, G. (2004). Crime, social capital and community participation. *American Journal of Community Psychology, 34,* 219–234.

Salem, D., Bogat, G. A., & Reid, C. (1997). Mutual help goes on-line. *Journal of Community Psychology, 25,* 189–208.

Salem, D., Reischl, T., Gallacher, F., & Randall, K. (2000). The role of referent and expert power in mutual help. *American Journal of Community Psychology, 28,* 303–324.

Salem, D., Reischl, T., & Randall, K. (2008). The effect of professional partnership on the development of a mutual-help organization. *American Journal of Community Psychology, 42*(1), 179–191.

Salina, D., Hill, J., Solarz, A., Lesondak, L., Razzano, L., & Dixon, D. (2004). Feminist perspectives: Empowerment behind bars. In L. A. Jason, C. Keys, Y. Suarez-Balcazar, R. Taylor, & M. Davis (Eds.), *Participatory community research: Theories and methods in action* (pp. 159–176). Washington, DC: American Psychological Association.

Salzer, M. S., McFadden, L., & Rappaport, J. (1994). Professional views of self-help groups. *Administration and Policy in Mental Health & Mental Health Services Research, 22,* 85–95.

Sanchez, B., Esparza, P., & Colon, Y. (2008). Natural mentoring under the microscope: An investigation of mentoring relationships and Latino adolescents' academic performance. *Journal of Community Psychology, 36,* 468–482.

Sanders, M. (2008). Triple P-Positive Parenting program as a public health approach to strengthening parenting. *Journal of Family Psychology, 22,* 506–517.

Sandler, I. N., Gensheimer, L., & Braver, S. (2000). Stress: Theory, research and action. In J. Rappaport & E. Seidman (Eds.), *Handbook of community psychology* (pp. 187–214). New York: Kluwer/Plenum.

Sandler, J. (2007). Community-based practices: Integrating dissemination theory with critical theories of power and justice. *American Journal of Community Psychology, 40,* 272–289.

Santiago-Rivera, A., Morse, G. S., Hunt, A., & Lickers, H. (1998). Building a community-based research partnership: Lessons from the Mohawk Nation of Akwesasne. *Journal of Community Psychology, 26,* 163–174.

Sarason, S. B. (1972). *The creation of settings and the future societies.* San Francisco: Jossey-Bass.

Sarason, S. B. (1974). *The psychological sense of community: Prospects for a community psychology.* San Francisco: Jossey-Bass.

Sarason, S. B. (1976). Community psychology and the anarchist insight. *American Journal of Community Psychology, 4,* 243–261.

Sarason, S. B. (1978). The nature of problem-solving in social action. *American Psychologist, 33,* 370–380.

Sarason, S. B. (1981). An asocial psychology and a misdirected clinical psychology. *American Psychologist, 36,* 827–836.

Sarason, S. B. (1982). *The culture of the school and the problem of change* (2nd ed.). Boston: Allyn & Bacon.

Sarason, S. B. (1988). *The making of an American psychologist: An autobiography.* San Francisco: Jossey-Bass.

Sarason, S. B. (1990). *The challenge of art to psychology.* New Haven, CT: Yale University Press.

Sarason, S. B. (1993). American psychology and the needs for the transcendence and community. *American Journal of Community Psychology, 21,* 185–202.

Sarason, S. B. (1994). The American worldview. In S. B. Sarason (Ed.), *Psychoanalysis, General Custer, and the verdicts of history, and other essays on psychology in the social scene* (pp. 100–118). San Francisco: Jossey-Bass.

Sarason, S. B. (1995). [Untitled videotape interview]. In J. G. Kelly (Ed.), *The history of community psychology: A video presentation of context and exemplars.* Chicago: Society for Community Research and Action.

Sarason, S. B. (2002). *Educational reform: A self-scrutinizing memoir.* New York: Teachers College Press.

Sarason, S. B. (2003a). The obligations of the moral-scientific stance. *American Journal of Community Psychology, 31,* 209–212.

Sarason, S. B. (2003b). American psychology and the schools: A critique. *American Journal of Community Psychology, 32,* 99–106.

Sasao, T. (1999, Winter). Cultural competence promotion as a general prevention strategy in urban settings: Some lessons learned from working with Asian American adolescents. *The Community Psychologist, 32,* 41–43.

Sasao, T., & Sue, S. (1993). Toward a culturally anchored ecological framework of research in ethnic-cultural communities. *American Journal of Community Psychology, 21,* 705–728.

Sasao, T., & Yasuda, T. (2007). Historical and theoretical orientations of community psychology practice and research in Japan. In S. M. Reich, M. Riemer, I. Prilleltensky, & M. Montero (Eds.), *International community psychology: History and theories* (pp. 164–179). New York: Springer.

Saul, J., Wandersman, A., Flashpohler, P., Duffy, J., Lubell, K., & Noonan, R. (Eds.). (2008). Research and action for bridging science and practice in prevention [Special issue]. *American Journal of Community Psychology, 41.*

Scales, P., Leffert, N., & Lerner, R. (2004). *Developmental assets: A synthesis of the scientific research on adolescent development.* Minneapolis, MN: Search Institute Press.

Scheier, M. F., Carver, C. S., & Bridges, M. W. (2001). Optimism, pessimism, and psychological well-being. In E. C. Chang (Ed.), *Optimism and pessimism: Implications for theory, research, and practice* (pp. 189–216). Washington, DC: American Psychological Association.

Schembri, A. (2009). *Scared Straight programs: Jail and detention tours: Lessons gained from research.* Florida Department of Juvenile Justice White Paper. Retrieved March 7, 2001, from http://www.djj.state.fl.us/Research/Scared_Straight_Booklet_Version.pdf.

Schensul, J. J., & Trickett, E. (2009). Introduction to multi-level community based culturally situated interventions. *American Journal of Community Psychology, 43,* 232–240.

Schneider, M., & Harper, G. (2003). Lesbian, gay, bisexual and transgendered communities: Linking theory, research and practice [Special issue]. *American Journal of Community Psychology, 31*(3/4).

Schoggen, P. (1988). Commentary on Perkins, Burns, Perry & Nielsen's "Behavior setting theory and community psychology: An analysis and critique." *Journal of Community Psychology, 16,* 373–386.

Schoggen, P. (1989). *Behavior settings.* Stanford, CA: Stanford University Press.

Schoggen, P., & Schoggen, M. (1988). Student voluntary participation and high school size. *Journal of Educational Research, 81,* 288–293.

Schorr, L. (1997). *Common purpose: Strengthening families and neighborhoods to rebuild America.* New York: Anchor Books.

Schwartz, S. H. (1994). Are there universal aspects in the structure and contents of human values? *Journal of Social Issues, 50*(4), 19–46.

Schweinhart, L. J., Montie, J., Xiang, Z., Barnett, W. S., Belfield, C. R., & Nores, M. (2005). *Lifetime effects: The HighScope Perry Preschool study through age 40.* (Monographs of the HighScope Educational Research Foundation, 14) Ypsilanti, MI: HighScope Press.

Scott, J., & Leonhardt, D. (2005, May 15). Class matters: Shadowy lines that still divide. *New York Times.* Retrieved June 1, 2005, from http://www.nytimes.com

Scott, R. L. (2007). Establishing core competencies for students in community psychology. *The Community Psychologist, 40,* 1–11.

Scottham, K. M., Cooke, D. Y., Sellers, R. M., Ford, K. (2010). Integrating process with content in understanding African American racial identity development. *Self and Identity, 9,* 19–40.

Scriven, M. (1997). Empowerment evaluation examined. *Evaluation Practice, 18*(2), 165–175. http://www.davidfetterman.com/scrivenbkre view1997.pdf

Scriven, M. (2005). Review of the book *Empowerment evaluation principles in practice. American Journal of Evaluation, 26*(3), 415–417.

Search Institute. (2004). *40 developmental assets.* Retrieved October 21, 2005, from http://www.search-institute.org/assets.

Seaton, E. K., Scottham, K. M., & Sellers, R. M. (2006). The status model of racial identity development in African American adolescents: Evidence of structure, trajectories, and well-being. *Child Development, 77,* 1416–1426.

Seaton, E. K., Yip, T. & Sellers, R. M. (2009). A longitudinal examination of racial identity and racial discrimination among African American adolescents. *Child Development, 80,* 406–417.

Sechrest, L. (1997). Review of the book *Empowerment evaluation: Knowledge and tools for self-assessment and accountability. Environment and Behavior, 29*(3), 422–426. Retrieved March 7, 2001, from http://www.davidfetterman.com/SechrestBookReview.htm

Seedat, M. (1997). The quest for a liberation psychology. *South African Journal of Psychology, 27,* 261.

Seely Brown, J., & Duguid, P. (1993). Stolen knowledge. *Educational Technology, 33*(3), 10–15.

Seidman, E. (1988). Back to the future, community psychology: Unfolding a theory of social intervention. *American Journal of Community Psychology, 16,* 3–24. Reprinted in T. Revenson, A. D'Augelli, S. E. French, D. Hughes, D. Livert, E. Seidman, M. Shinn, & H. Yoshikawa (Eds.), (2002), *A quarter century of community psychology* (pp. 181–203). New York: Kluwer Academic/Plenum.

Seidman, E. (1990). Pursuing the meaning and utility of social regularities for community psychology. In P. Tolan, C. Keys, F. Chertok, & L. Jason (Eds.), *Researching community psychology* (pp. 91–100). Washington, DC: American Psychological Association.

Seidman, E. (2003). Fairweather and ESID: Contemporary impact and a legacy for the twenty-first century. *American Journal of Community Psychology, 32,* 371–375.

Seidman, E., Aber, J. L., Allen, L., & French, S. E. (1996). The impact of the transition to high school on the self-system and perceived social context of poor urban youth. *American Journal of Community Psychology, 24,* 489–516.

Seidman, E., Aber, J. L., & French, S. E. (2004). The organization of schooling and adolescent development. In K. Maton, C. Schellenbach, B. Leadbeater, & A. Solarz (Eds.), *Investing in children, youth, families, and communities* (pp. 233–250). Washington, DC: American Psychological Association.

Seidman, E., Allen, L., Aber, J. L., Mitchell, C., & Feinman, J. (1994). The impact of school transitions in early adolescence on the self-system and perceived social context of poor urban youth. *Child Development, 65,* 507–522.

Seidman, E., & Rappaport, J. (1974). The educational pyramid: A paradigm training, research, and manpower utilization in community. *American Journal of Community Psychology, 2,* 119–130.

Seidman, E., & Rappaport, J. (Eds.). (1986). *Redefining social problems.* New York: Plenum.

Seligman, M., & Csikszentmihalyi, M. (Eds.). (2000a). Positive psychology [Special issue]. *American Psychologist, 55*(1).

Sellers, R. M., Caldwell, C. H., Schmeelk-Cone, K. H., & Zimmerman, M. A. (2003). Racial identity, racial discrimination, perceived stress, and psychological distress among African American young adults. *Journal of Health and Social Behavior, 44,* 302–317.

Sellers, R. M., Copeland-Linder, N., Martin, P. P., & Lewis, R. L. (2006). Racial identity matters: The relationship between racial discrimination and psychological functioning in African American adolescents. *Journal of Research on Adolescence, 16,* 187–216.

Sellers, R. M. & Shelton, J. N. (2003). The role of racial identity in perceived racial discrimination. *Journal of Personality and Social Psychology, 84,* 1079–1092.

Sellers, R. M., Smith, M., Shelton, J. N., Rowley, S., & Chavous, T. (1998). Multidimensional model of racial identity: A reconceptualization of African American racial identity. *Personality and Social Psychology Review, 2,* 18–39.

Senge, P. (1990). *The fifth discipline: The art and practice of organizational learning.* New York: Doubleday.

Serrano-Garcia, I. (1994). The ethics of the powerful and the power of ethics. *American Journal of Community Psychology, 22,* 1–20.

Serrano-García, I., Figueroa-Rodríguez, M., & Pérez-Jiménez, D. (Eds.). (2008). *Dos décadas de desarrollo de la psicología social-comunitaria: De Puerto Rico al mundo* [CD]. San Juan, PR: Publicaciones Puertorriqueñas.

Shadish, W., Cook, T., & Campbell, D. (2002). *Experimental and quasi-experimental designs for generalized causal inference.* Washington, DC: American Psychological Association.

Shain, R., Piper, J., Holden, A., Champion, J., Perdue, S. T., Korte, J. E., et al. (2004). Prevention of gonorrhea and Chlamydia through behavioral intervention: Results of a two-year controlled randomized trial in minority women. *Sexually Transmitted Diseases, 31,* 401–408.

Shain, R., Piper, J., Newton, E., Perdue, S., Ramos, R., Champion, J. D., et al. (1999). A randomized, controlled trial of a behavioral intervention to prevent sexually transmitted disease among minority women. *New England Journal of Medicine, 340,* 93–100.

Shapiro, D. H., Schwartz, C. E., & Astin J. (1996). Controlling ourselves, controlling our world: Psychology's role in understanding positive and negative consequences of seeking and gaining control. *American Psychologist, 51,* 1213–1230.

Shaw, C., & McKay, H. (1969). *Juvenile delinquency and urban areas.* Chicago: The University of Chicago Press.

Sherman, A., & Stone, C. (2010). *Income gaps between the very rich and everyone else more than tripled in last three decades, new data show.* Center for Budget and Policy Priorities. Retrieved March 7, 2011, from http://www.cbpp.org/files/6-25-10inc.pdf

Sherman, L., Gottfredson, D., MacKenzie, D., Eck, J., Reuter, P., & Bushway, S. (1998). *Preventing crime: What works, what doesn't, what's promising.* National Institute of Justice, Research in Brief. Retrieved March 7, 2011, from http://www.ncjrs.gov/pdffiles/171676.PDF

Shinn, M. (1990). Mixing and matching: Levels of conceptualization, measurement, and statistical analysis in community research. In P. Tolan, C. Keys, F. Chertok, & L. Jason (Eds.), *Researching community psychology* (pp. 111–126). Washington, DC: American Psychological Association.

Shinn, M. (1992). Homelessness: What is a psychologist to do? *American Journal of Community Psychology, 20,* 1–24. Reprinted in T. Revenson, A. D'Augelli, S. E. French, D. Hughes, D. Livert, E. Seidman, M. Shinn, & H. Yoshikawa (Eds.), (2002), *A quarter century of community psychology* (pp. 343–366). New York: Kluwer Academic/Plenum.

Shinn, M. (Ed.). (1996). Ecological assessment [Special issue]. *American Journal of Community Psychology, 24*(1).

Shinn, M. (2009). *Ending homeless for families: The evidence for affordable housing.* Retrieved March 7, 2011, from http://www.endhomelessness.org/content/article/detail/2436

Shinn, M., Baumohl, J., & Hopper, K. (2001). The prevention of homelessness revisited. *Analyses of Social Issues and Public Policy,* 95–127.

Shinn, M., & Perkins, D. N. T. (2000). Contributions from organizational psychology. In J. Rappaport & E. Seidman (Eds.), *Handbook of community psychology* (pp. 615–641). New York: Kluwer Academic/Plenum.

Shinn, M., & Rapkin, B. (2000). Cross-level research without cross-ups in community psychology. In J. Rappaport & E. Seidman (Eds.), *Handbook of community psychology* (pp. 669–696). New York: Kluwer/Plenum.

Shinn, M., & Toohey, S. (2003). Community contexts of human welfare. *Annual Review of Psychology, 54,* 427–459.

Shinn, M., & Yoshikawa, H. (Eds.). (2008). *Toward positive youth development: Transforming schools and community programs.* New York: Oxford University Press.

Shriver, T. (1992). Video segment in *The world of abnormal psychology: An ounce of prevention* (T. Levine, Producer). New York: A. H. Perlmutter. (Available from Annenberg/CPB Collection, 1-800-LEARNER)

Siegel, K., Raveis, V. H., & Karus, D. (1997). Illness-related support and negative network interactions: Effects on HIV-infected men's depressive symptomatology. *American Journal of Community Psychology, 25,* 395–420.

Silka, L., & Tip, J. (1994). Empowering the silent ranks: The Southeast Asian experience. *American Journal of Community Psychology, 22,* 497–530.

Simons, R., Johnson, C., Beaman, J., Conger, R., & Whitbeck, L. (1996). Parents and peer group as mediators of the effect of community structure on adolescent problem behavior. *American Journal of Community Psychology, 24,* 145–172.

Sloan, T., Anderson, A., & Fabick, S. (2003, Fall). Psychologists for social responsibility. *The Community Psychologist, 36*(4), 37–39.

Sloboda, Z., Stephens, R., Stephens, P., Grey, S., Teasdale, B., Hawthorne, R., et al. (2009). The adolescent substance abuse prevention study: A randomized field trial of a universal substance abuse prevention program. *Drug and Alcohol Dependence, 102,* 1–10. Retrieved March 7, 2011, from http://dare.procon.org/sourcefiles/2009Sloboda.pdf

Smedley, A., & Smedley, B. (2005). Race as biology is fiction, racism as social problem is real: Anthropological and historical perspectives on the social construction of race. *American Psychologist, 60,* 16–26.

Smith, J. (2006). At a crossroad: Standing still and moving forward. *American Journal of Community Psychology, 38,* 23–27.

Smith, J., Schneider, B., Smith, P., & Ananiadou, K. (2004). The effectiveness of whole-school antibullying programs: A synthesis of evaluation research. *School Psychology Review, 33,* 547–560.

Smith, R. S. (2008). The case of a city where 1 in 6 residents is a refugee: Ecological factors and host community adaptation in successful resettlement. *American Journal of Community Psychology, 42,* 328–342.

Snell-Johns, J., Imm, P., Wandersman, A., & Claypoole, J. (2003). Roles assumed by a community coalition when creating environmental and policy-level changes. *Journal of Community Psychology, 31,* 661–670.

Snow, D., Grady, K., & Goyette-Ewing, M. (2000). A perspective on ethical issues in community psychology. In J. Rappaport & E. Seidman (Eds.), *Handbook of community psychology* (pp. 897–918). New York: Plenum.

Snowden, L. (2005). Racial, cultural and ethnic disparities in health and mental health: Toward theory and research at community levels. *American Journal of Community Psychology, 35,* 1–8.

Snowden, L. R. (1987). The peculiar successes of community psychology: Service delivery to ethnic minorities and the poor. *American Journal of Community Psychology, 15,* 575–586.

Society for Prevention Research. (2004). *Standards of evidence: Criteria for efficacy, effectiveness and dissemination.* Retrieved March 7, 2011, from http://www.preventionresearch.org/StandardsofEvidencebook.pdf

Solarz, A. L. (2001). Investing in children, families and communities: Challenges for an interdivisional public policy collaboration. *American Journal of Community Psychology, 29,* 1–14.

Somerfield, M. R., & McCrea, R. R. (2000). Stress and coping research: Methodological challenges, theoretical advances, and clinical applications. *American Psychologist, 55,* 620–625.

Sonn, C. (2002). Immigrant adaptation: Understanding the process through sense of community. In A. Fisher, C. Sonn, & B. Bishop (Eds.), *Psychological sense of community: Research, applications and implications* (pp. 205–221). New York: Kluwer/Plenum.

Sonn, C., & Fisher, A. (1996). Psychological sense of community in a politically constructed group. *Journal of Community Psychology, 24,* 417–430.

Sonn, C., & Fisher, A. (1998). Sense of community: Community resilient responses to oppression and change. *Journal of Community Psychology, 26,* 457–472.

Sonn, C., & Fisher, A. (2003). Identity and oppression: Differential responses to an in-between status. *American Journal of Community Psychology, 31,* 117–128.

Sonn, C., & Fisher, A. (2010). Immigration and settlement: Confronting the challenges of cultural diversity. In G. Nelson & I. Prilleltensky (Eds.), *Community psychology: In pursuit of liberation and well-being* (2nd ed., pp. 371–388). London: Palgrave Macmillan.

Soriano, F. (1995). *Conducting needs assessments: A multidisciplinary approach.* Thousand Oaks, CA: Sage.

Spanierman, L. B., Neville, H. A., Liao, H. Y., Hammer, J. H., & Wang, Y. F. (2008). Participation in formal and informal campus diversity experiences: Effects on students' racial democratic beliefs. *Journal of Diversity in Higher Education, 1,* 108–125.

Spanierman, L. B., Todd, N. R., & Anderson, C. J. (2009). Psychosocial costs of racism to Whites: Understanding patterns among university students. *Journal of Counseling Psychology, 56,* 239–252.

Spaulding, J., & Balch, P. (1983). A brief history of primary prevention in the twentieth century: 1908 to 1980. *American Journal of Community Psychology, 11,* 59–80.

Speer, P. (2000). Intrapersonal and interactional empowerment: Implications for theory. *Journal of Community Psychology, 28,* 51–62.

Speer, P. (2008). Altering patterns of relationships and participation: Youth organizing as a setting-level intervention. In M. Shinn & H. Yoshikawa (Eds.), *Toward positive youth development: Transforming schools and community programs.* New York: Oxford University Press.

Speer, P., Dey, S., Griggs, P., Gibson, C., Lubin, B., & Hughey, J. (1992). In search of community: An analysis of community psychology research from 1984–1988. *American Journal of Community Psychology, 20,* 195–210.

Speer, P., & Hughey, J. (1995). Community organizing: An ecological route to empowerment and power. *American Journal of Community Psychology, 23,* 729–748.

Speer, P., Hughey, J., Gensheimer, L., & Adams-Leavitt, W. (1995). Organizing for power: A comparative case study. *Journal of Community Psychology, 23,* 57–73.

Spencer, R. (2006). Understanding the mentoring process between adolescents and adults. *Youth & Society, 37*(3), 287–315.

Stack, C. (1974). *All our kin: Strategies for survival in a Black community.* New York: Harper.

Stanley, J. (2003). An applied collaborative training program for graduate students in community psychology: A case study of a community project working with lesbian, gay, bisexual, transgender, and questioning youth. *American Journal of Community Psychology, 31,* 253–266.

Stark, W. (2009). Community psychology in Europe: Potentials and challenges. Plenary presentation at the 7th European Congress of Community Psychology, Paris.

Starnes, D. (2004). Community psychologists—get in the arena! *American Journal of Community Psychology, 33,* 3–6.

State of Arkansas. (2007). Senate Bill 951: An Act to Create the Arkansas Evaluation Center. Retrieved March 7, 2011, from http://homepage.mac.com/profdavidf/sb951arkevalcenterbill.pdf

Steele, C. (1997). A threat in the air: How stereotypes shape intellectual identity and performance. *American Psychologist, 52,* 613–629.

Stefancic, A., & Tsemberis, S. (2007). Housing first for long-term shelter dwellers with psychiatric disabilities in a suburban county: A four-year study of housing access and retention. *Journal of Primary Prevention, 28,* 265–279.

Stein, C. H., & Mankowski, E. S. (2004). Asking, witnessing, interpreting, knowing: Conducting qualitative research in community psychology. *American Journal of Community Psychology, 33,* 21–36.

Stein, C. H., Ward, M., & Cislo, D. A. (1992). The power of a place: Opening the college classroom to people with serious mental illness. *American Journal of Community Psychology, 20,* 523–548.

Stein, C. H., & Wemmerus, V. (2001). Searching for a normal life: Personal accounts of adults with schizophrenia, their parents and well-siblings. *American Journal of Community Psychology, 29,* 725–746.

Steinman, K., & Zimmerman, M. (2004). Religious activity and risk behavior among African American adolescents: Concurrent and developmental effects. *American Journal of Community Psychology, 33,* 151–161.

Sternberg, R. J., Griorenko, E. L., & Kidd, K. K. (2005). Intelligence, race, and genetics. *American Psychologist, 60,* 46–59.

Stewart, E. (2000). Thinking through others: Qualitative research and community psychology. In J. Rappaport & E. Seidman (Eds.), *Handbook of community psychology* (pp. 725–736). New York: Kluwer/Plenum.

Stice, E., Shaw, H., Bohon, C., Marti, C. N., & Rohde, P. (2009). A meta-analytic review of depression prevention programs for children and adolescents: Factors that predict magnitude of success. *Journal of Consulting and Clinical Psychology, 77,* 486–503.

Stice, E., Shaw, H., & Marti, C. N. (2006). A meta-analytic review of obesity prevention programs for children and adolescents: The skinny on interventions that work. *Psychological Bulletin, 132,* 667–691.

Stiglitz, J. (2003). *Globalization and its discontents.* New York: Norton.

Stimpson, J. P., Ju, H., Mukaila, R. A., & Eschbach, K. (2007). Neighborhood deprivation and health risk behaviors in NHANES III. *American Journal of Health Behavior, 31*(2), 215–222.

Stone, R. A., & Levine, A. G. (1985). Reactions to collective stress: Correlates of active citizen participation at Love Canal. *Prevention in Human Services, 4,* 153–177.

Strother, C. (1987). Reflections on the Stanford Conference and subsequent events. *American Journal of Community Psychology, 15,* 519–522.

Stuber, S. (2000). The interposition of personal life stories and community narratives in a Roman Catholic religious community. *Journal of Community Psychology, 28,* 507–516.

Stufflebeam, D. (1994). Empowerment evaluation, objectivist evaluation, and evaluation standards: Where the future of evaluation should not go and where it needs to go. *Evaluation Practice, 15*(3), 321–338. Retrieved March 7, 2011, from http://www.davidfetterman.com/stufflebeambkreview.pdf

Suarez-Balcazar, Y. (1998, July). Are we addressing the racial divide? *The Community Psychologist, 31,* 12–13.

Suarez-Balcazar, Y., Davis, M., Ferrari, J., Nyden, P., Olson, B., Alvarez, J., et al. (2004). University-community partnerships: A framework and exemplar. In L. Jason, C. Keys, Y. Suarez-Balcazar, R. Taylor, & M. Davis (Eds.), *Participatory community research: Theories and methods in action* (pp. 105–120). Washington, DC: American Psychological Association.

Substance Abuse and Mental Health Services Administration (SAMHSA), Office of Applied Studies. (2004, April 30). *Graduated driver licensing and drinking among young drivers.* The National Survey on Drug Use. Samhsa in Washington, DC.

Sue, D. W. (2004). Whiteness and ethnocentric monoculturalism: Making the "invisible" visible. *American Psychologist, 59,* 761–769.

Sue, S. (1999). Science, ethnicity, and bias. *American Psychologist, 54,* 1070–1077.

Sullivan, C. (2003). Using the ESID model to reduce intimate male violence against women. *American Journal of Community Psychology, 32,* 295–304.

Sum, S., Mathews, M., Pourghasem, M., & Hughes, I. (2009). Internet use as a predictor of sense of community in older people. *CyberPsychology & Behavior, 12,* 235–239.

Sundstrom, E., Bell, P., Busby, P., & Asmus, C. (1996). Environmental psychology, 1989–1994. *Annual Review of Psychology, 47,* 485–512.

Swift, C., Bond, M., & Serrano-Garcia, I. (2000). Women's empowerment: A review of community psychology's first twenty-five years. In J. Rappaport & E. Seidman (Eds.), *Handbook of community psychology* (pp. 857–896). New York: Kluwer/Plenum.

Sykes, C. (1992). *A nation of victims: The decay of the American character.* New York: St. Martin's Press.

Tandon, S. D., Azelton, L. S., Kelly, J. G., & Strickland, D. A. (1998). Constructing a tree for community leaders: Contexts and processes in collaborative inquiry. *American Journal of Community Psychology, 26,* 669–696.

Tarakeshwar, N., Pargament, K. I. & Mahoney, A. (2003). Initial development of a measure of religious coping among Hindus. *Journal of Community Psychology, 31,* 607–628.

Tarakeshwar, N., Vanderwerker, L. C., Paulk, E., Pearce, M. J., Kasl, S. V., & Prigerson, H. G. (2006). Religious coping is associated with quality of life of patients with advanced cancer. *Journal of Palliative Medicine, 9,* 646–657.

Tatum, B. (1997). *Why are all the Black kids sitting together in the cafeteria?* New York: Basic Books.

Tatum, B. (2004). Family life and school experience: Factors in the racial identity development of Black youth in White communities. *Journal of Social Issues, 60,* 117–136.

Taylor, A., Wiley, A., Kuo, F., & Sullivan, W. (1998). Growing up in the inner city: Green spaces as places to grow. *Environment and Behavior, 30,* 3–27.

Taylor-Ritzler, T., Balcazar, F., Dimpfl, S., Suarez-Balcazar, Y., Willis, C. & Schiff, R. (2008). Cultural competence training with organizations serving people with disabilities from diverse cultural backgrounds. *Journal of Vocational Rehabilitation, 29,* 77–91.

Tebes, J. (2000). External validity and scientific psychology. *American Psychologist, 55,* 1508–1509.

Tebes, J. (2005). Community science, philosophy of science, and the practice of research. *American Journal of Community Psychology, 35,* 213–230.

Thoits, P. A. (1983). Multiple identities and psychological well-being: A reformulation and test of the social hypothesis. *American Sociological Review, 48,* 174–187.

Thomas, E., & Rappaport, J. (1996). Art as community narrative: A resource for social change. In M. B. Lykes, A. Banuazizi, R. Liem, & M. Morris, (Eds.), *Myths about the powerless: Contesting social inequalities* (pp. 317–336). Philadelphia: Temple University Press.

Thorn, B. E., & Dixon, K. E. (2007). Coping with chronic pain: A stress-appraisal coping model. In E. Martz & H. Livneh (Eds.), *Coping with chronic illness and disability: Theoretical, empirical, and clinical aspects.* New York: Springer Science.

Thurman, A., Holden, A., Shain, R., Perdue, S., & Piper, J. (2008). Preventing recurrent sexually transmitted diseases in minority adolescents: A randomized trial. *Obstetrics and Gynecology, 111,* 1417–1425.

Timko, C. (1996). Physical characteristics of residential psychiatric and substance abuse programs: Organizational determinants and patient outcomes. *American Journal of Community Psychology, 24,* 173–192.

Tobler, N. S., Roona, M. R., Ochshorn, P., Marshall, D. G., Streke, A. V., & Stackpole, K. M. (2000). School-based adolescent drug prevention programs: 1998 meta-analysis. *Journal of Primary Prevention, 20,* 275–337.

Todd, N. R., Spanierman, L. B., & Aber, M. S. (2010). White students reflecting on whiteness: Understanding emotional responses. *Journal of Diversity in Higher Education, 3,* 97–110.

Tolan, P., Keys, C., Chertok, F., & Jason, L. (Eds.). (1990). *Researching community psychology: Issues of theory and methods.* Washington, DC: American Psychological Association.

Tolman, D., & Brydon-Miller, M. (Eds.). (2001). *From subjects to subjectivities: A handbook of interpretative and participatory methods.* New York: NYU Press.

Tompsett, C., Toro, P., Guzicki, M., Schlienz, N., Blume, M., & Lombard, S. (2003). Homelessness in the US and Germany: A cross-national analysis. *Journal of Community and Applied Social Psychology, 13,* 240–257.

Tonnies, F. (1988). *Community and society.* [Translation of *Gemeinschaft und Gesellschaft*]. New Brunswick, NJ: Transaction Publishers. (Original work published 1887)

Tornatzky, L., & Fleischer, M. (1986, October). *Dissemination and/or implementation: The problem of complex socio-technical systems.* Paper presented at the meeting of the American Evaluation Association, Kansas City, MO.

Toro, P. (1998, February). A community psychologist's role in policy on homelessness in two cities. *The Community Psychologist, 31,* 25–26.

Toro, P. (1999). Homelessness [Special issue]. *Journal of Community Psychology, 27*(2).

Toro, P. (2005). Community psychology: Where do we go from here? *American Journal of Community Psychology, 35,* 17–22.

Toro, P., Rappaport, J., & Seidman, E. (1987). Social climate comparison of mutual help and psychotherapy groups. *Journal of Consulting and Clinical Psychology, 55,* 430–431.

Toro, P., Reischl, T., Zimmerman, M., Rappaport, J., Seidman, E., Luke, D., et al. (1988). Professionals in mutual help groups: Impact on social climate and members' behavior. *Journal of Consulting and Clinical Psychology, 56,* 631–632.

Toro, P., & Warren M. (1999). Homelessness in the United States: Policy considerations. *Journal of Community Psychology, 27,* 119–136.

Tough, P. (2008). *Whatever it takes: Geoffrey Canada's quest to change Harlem and America.* New York: Houghton Mifflin Harcourt.

Townley, G., Kloos, B., Green, E. P., & Franco, M. (2011). Reconcilable differences? Human diversity, cultural relativity, and sense of community. *American Journal of Community Psychology, 47*(1–2), 69–85.

Triandis, H. C. (1994). *Culture and social behavior.* New York: McGraw-Hill.

Trickett, E. J. (1984). Toward a distinctive community psychology: An ecological metaphor for the conduct of community research and the nature of training. *American Journal of Community Psychology, 12,* 261–279.

Trickett, E. J. (1996). A future for community psychology: The contexts of diversity and the diversity of contexts. *American Journal of Community Psychology, 24,* 209–234. Reprinted in T. Revenson, A. D'Augelli, S. E. French, D. Hughes, D. Livert, E. Seidman, M. Shinn, & H. Yoshikawa (Eds.), (2002), *A quarter century of community psychology* (pp. 513–534). New York: Kluwer Academic/Plenum.

Trickett, E. J. (1997). Ecology and primary prevention: Reflections on a meta-analysis. *American Journal of Community Psychology, 25,* 197–206.

Trickett, E. (2009). Community psychology: Individuals and interventions in community context. *Annual Review of Psychology, 60,* 395–419.

Trickett, E. J., Barone, C., & Watts, R. (2000). Contextual influences in mental health consultation: Toward an ecological perspective on radiating change. In J. Rappaport & E. Seidman (Eds.), *Handbook of community psychology* (pp. 303–330). New York: Kluwer/Plenum.

Trickett, E. J., & Espino, S. L. R. (2004). Collaboration and social inquiry: Multiple meanings of a construct and its role in creating useful and valid knowledge. *American Journal of Community Psychology, 34,* 1–70.

Trickett, E. J., Kelly, J. G., & Todd, D. M. (1972). The social environment of the school: Guidelines for individual change and organizational redevelopment. In S. Golann & C. Eisdorfer (Eds.), *Handbook of community mental health* (pp. 331–406). New York: Appleton-Century-Crofts.

Trickett, E. J., Trickett, P., Castro, J., & Schaffner, P. (1982). The independent school experience: Aspects of the normative environments of single sex and coed secondary schools. *Journal of Educational Psychology, 74,* 374–381.

Trickett, E. J., Watts, R. J., & Birman, D. (Eds.). (1994). *Human diversity: Perspectives on people in context.* San Francisco: Jossey-Bass.

Trimble, J., Helms, J., & Root, M. (2003). Social and psychological perspectives on ethnic and racial identity. In G. Bernal, J. Trimble, K. Burlew, & F. Leong (Eds.), *Handbook of racial and ethnic minority psychology* (pp. 239–275). Thousand Oaks, CA: Sage.

Trotter, J., & Allen, N. (2009). The good, the bad, and the ugly: Domestic violence survivors' experiences with their informal social networks. *American Journal of Community Psychology, 43*(3), 221–231.

Trout, J., Dokecki, P., Newbrough, J. R., & O'Gorman, R. (2003). Action research on leadership for community development in West Africa and North America: A joining of liberation theology and community psychology. *Journal of Community Psychology, 31,* 129–148.

Tsemberis, S., Gulcur, L., & Nakae, M. (2004). Housing first, consumer choice, and harm reduction for homeless individuals with a dual diagnosis. *American Journal of Public Health, 94,* 651–656.

Tsemberis, S., Moran, L., Shinn, M., Asmussen, S., & Shern, D. (2003). Consumer preference programs for individuals who are homeless and have psychiatric disabilities: A drop-in center and a supported housing program. *American Journal of Community Psychology, 32,* 305–318.

Tseng, V., Chesir-Teran, D., Becker-Klein, R., Chan, M., Duran, V., Roberts, A., et al. (2002). Promotion of social change: A conceptual framework. *American Journal of Community Psychology, 30,* 401–427.

Tseng, V., & Yoshikawa, H. (2008). Reconceptualizing acculturation: Ecological processes, historical contexts, and power inequities commentary for AJCP special section on "The other side of acculturation: changes among host individuals and communities in their adaptation to immigrant populations." *American Journal of Community Psychology, 42,* 355–358.

Ttofi, M., Farrington, D., & Baldry, A. (2008). *Effectiveness of programmes to reduce school bullying.* Retrieved March 7, 2011, from http://www.bra.se/extra/measurepoint/? module_instance=4&name=Effectiveness_of_ programmes_to_reduce_school_bullying_webb. pdf&url=/dynamaster/file_archive/081023/ 04395cbc5720 1c39fa6c7f78319ea2ab/Effectiveness% 255fof%255fprogrammes%255fto%255freduce% 255fschool%255fbullying%255fwebb.pdf

Turner, H. (2007). The significance of employment for chronic stress and psychological distress among rural single mothers. *American Journal of Community Psychology, 40*(3), 181–193.

Tyler, F. (2001). *Cultures, communities and change.* New York: Kluwer/Plenum.

Tyler, F., Pargament, K., & Gatz, M. (1983). The resource collaborator role: A model for interactions involving psychologists. *American Psychologist, 38,* 388–398.

Ullman, S. E., & Townsend, S. M. (2008). What is an empowerment approach to working with sexual assault survivors? *Journal of Community Psychology, 36,* 299–312.

Unger, D., & Wandersman, A. (1983). Neighboring and its role in block organizations: An exploratory report. *American Journal of Community Psychology, 11,* 291–300.

Unger, D., & Wandersman, A. (1985). The importance of neighbors: The social, cognitive and affective components of neighboring. *American Journal of Community Psychology, 13,* 139–170.

Unger, R. (2001). Marie Jahoda [obituary]. *American Psychologist, 56,* 1040–1041.

U.S. Bureau of Labor Statistics. (2010). *Volunteering in the United States, 2010.* Retrieved March 8, 2011, from http://www.bls.gov/news.release/volun.nr0.htm

U.S. Census Bureau. (2005, August 30). *News conference: 2004 income, poverty and health insurance estimates from the Current Population Survey.* Retrieved September 19, 2005, from http://www.census.gov/hhes/www/income/income04.html

U.S. Census Bureau. (2006). *Who's minding the kids? Child care arrangements: Summer 2006,* Table 6. Retrieved March 8, 2011, from http://www.census.gov/population/www/socdemo/child/tables-2006.html

U.S. Census Bureau. (2009a). *Income, poverty and health insurance coverage in the United States: 2008.* http://www.census.gov/prod/2009pubs/p60-236.pdf

U.S. Census Bureau. (2009b). *Poverty thresholds for 2009 by size of family and number of related children under 18 years.* http://www.census.gov/hhes/www/poverty/threshld/thresh09.html

U.S. Census Bureau. (n.d.). *Frequently asked questions about income statistics from the Current Population Survey.* Retrieved July 14, 2004, from http://www.census.gov/hhes/income/incfaq.html

U.S. Census Bureau. (n.d.). *Historical poverty tables: Table 3. Poverty status of people, by age, race, and Hispanic origin: 1959 to 2008.* http://www.census.gov/hhes/www/poverty/histpov/perindex.html

U.S. Conference of Majors. (2009). *Hunger and homelessness survey.* http://www.usmayors.org/pressreleases/uploads/USCMHungercomplete WEB2009.pdf

U.S. Department of Agriculture. (2009). *Official USDA food plans: Cost of food at home at four levels, U.S. average, June 2009.* http://www.cnpp.usda.gov/Publications/FoodPlans/2009/Costof FoodJun09.pdf

U.S. Department of Agriculture. (2010). *Supplemental nutrition assistance program participation and costs, May 3, 2010.* http://www.fns.usda.gov/pd/SNAPsummary.htm

U.S. Department of Education. (n.d.). *No Child Left Behind Act: Accountability.* Retrieved July 28, 2005, from http://www.ed.gov/nclb/accountability/index.html

U.S. Department of Health and Human Services. (1999). *Mental health: A report of the Surgeon General.* Rockville, Md, Center for Mental Health Services, Substance Abuse and Mental Health Services Administration, NIMH, NIH.

U.S. Department of Health and Human Services. (2001). *Mental Health: Culture, Race, and Ethnicity, Supplement to Mental Health: A Report of the Surgeon General.* Rockville, Md, Center for Mental Health Services, Substance Abuse and Mental Health Services Administration, NIMH, NIH.

U.S. Department of Health and Human Services. (2010). *To live to see the great day that dawns: Preventing suicide by American Indian and Alaska Native youth and young adults.* DHHS Publication SMA (10)-4480, CMHS-NSPL-0196. Rockville, MD: Center for Mental Health Services, Substance Abuse and Mental Health Services Administration (SAMHSA).

U.S. Department of Housing and Urban Development. (2010). *2009 Annual homeless assessment report to Congress.* http://www.huduser.org/publications/pdf/5thHomelessAssessmentReport.pdf

U.S. Department of Housing and Urban Development. (n.d.). *HUD's public housing program.* http://portal.hud.gov/portal/page/portal/HUD/topics/rental_assistance/phprog

Valenzuela, S., Park, N., & Kee, K. (2009). Is there social capital in a social network site?: Facebook use and college students' life satisfaction, trust, and participation. *Journal of Computer-Mediated Communication, 14,* 875–901.

Vanden-Kiernan, M., D'Elio, M. A., O'Brien, R., Banks Tarullo, L., Zill, N., & Hubbell-McKey, R. (2010). Neighborhoods as a developmental context: A multilevel analysis of neighborhood effects on Head Start families and children. *American Journal of Community Psychology, 45,* 68–72.

Van Egeren, L., Huber, M., & Cantillon, D. (2003, June). *Mapping change: Using geographic information systems for research and action.* Poster presented at the biennial meeting of the Society for Community Research and Action, Las Vegas, NM.

van Uchelen, C. (2000). Individualism, collectivism and community psychology. In J. Rappaport & E. Seidman (Eds.), *Handbook of community psychology* (pp. 65–78). New York: Kluwer/Plenum.

Varas-Diaz, N., & Serrano-Garcia, I. (2003). The challenge of a positive self-image in a colonial context: A psychology of liberation for the Puerto Rican experience. *American Journal of Community Psychology, 31,* 103–116.

Venkatesh, S. (2002). *American project: The rise and fall of a modern ghetto.* Harvard University Press, Cambridge, MA.

Ventis, W. L. (1995). The relationships between religion and mental health. *Journal of Social Issues, 51,* 33–48.

Vincent, T., & Trickett, E. (1983). Preventive intervention and the human context: Ecological approaches to environmental assessment and change. In R. Felner, L. Jason, J. Moritsugu, & S. Farber (Eds.), *Preventive psychology: Theory, research, and practice* (pp. 67–86). New York: Pergamon.

Vinokur, A. D., & Selzer, M. L. (1975). Desirable vs. undesirable life events: Their relationship to stress and mental distress. *Journal of Personality and Social Psychology, 32,* 329–337.

Vivero, V., & Jenkins, S. (1999). Existential hazards of the multicultural individual: Defining and understanding "cultural homelessness." *Cultural Diversity and Ethnic Minority Psychology, 5,* 6–26.

Wager, C. (1993). Toward a shared ethical culture. *Educational Leadership, 50*(4), 19–23.

Waldo, C. R., Hesson-McInnis, M. S., & D'Augelli, A. R. (1998). Antecedents and consequences of victimization of lesbian, gay, and bisexual young people: A structural model comparing rural university and urban samples. *American Journal of Community Psychology, 26,* 307–334.

Walsh, R. (1987). A social historical note on the formal emergence of community psychology. *American Journal of Community Psychology, 15,* 523–529.

Walsh-Bowers, R. (2000). A personal sojourn to spiritualize community psychology. *Journal of Community Psychology, 28,* 221–236.

Wandersman, A. (1984). Citizen participation. In K. Heller, R. Price, S. Reinharz, S. Riger, & A. Wandersman (Eds.), *Psychology and community change* (2nd ed., pp. 337–379). Homewood, IL: Dorsey.

Wandersman, A. (1990). Prevention is a broad field: Toward a broad conceptual framework of prevention. In P. Mueherer (Ed.), *Conceptual research models for preventing mental disorders* (pp. 48–59). Rockville, MD: National Institute of Mental Health.

Wandersman, A. (2003). Community science: Bridging the gap between science and practice with community-centered models. *American Journal of Community Psychology, 31,* 227–242.

Wandersman, A. (2009). Four keys to success (theory, implementation, evaluation, and resource/system support): High hopes and challenges in participation. *American Journal of Community Psychology, 43,* 3–21.

Wandersman, A., Coyne, S., Herndon, E., McKnight, K., & Morsbach, S. (2002, Summer). Clinical and community psychology: Case studies using integrative models. *The Community Psychologist, 35,* 22–25.

Wandersman, A., Duffy, J., Flaspohler, P., Noonan, R., Lubell, K., Stillman, L., et al. (2008). Bridging the gap between prevention research and practice: The interactive systems framework for dissemination and implementation. *American Journal of Community Psychology, 41,* 171–181.

Wandersman, A., & Florin, P. (1990). Citizen participation, voluntary organizations and community development: Insights for empowerment and research [Special section]. *American Journal of Community Psychology, 18*(1), 41–177.

Wandersman, A., & Florin, P. (2000). Citizen participation and community organizations. In J. Rappaport & E. Seidman (Eds.), *Handbook of community psychology* (pp. 247–272). New York: Plenum.

Wandersman, A., & Florin, P. (2003). Community interventions and effective prevention. *American Psychologist, 58,* 441–448.

Wandersman, A., & Hallman W. (1993). Are people acting irrationally? Understanding public concerns about environmental threats. *American Psychologist, 48,* 681–686.

Wandersman, A., Imm, P., Chinman, M., & Kaftarian, S. (2000). Getting to outcomes: A results-based approach to accountability. *Evaluation and Program Planning, 23,* 389–395.

Wandersman, A., Keener, D., Snell-Johns, J., Miller, R., Flaspohler, P., Livet-Dye, M., et al. (2004). Empowerment evaluation: Principles and action. In L. Jason, C. Keys, Y. Suarez-Balcazar, R. Taylor, & M. Davis (Eds.), *Participatory community research: Theories and methods in action* (pp. 139–156). Washington, DC: American Psychological Association.

Wandersman, A., Kloos, B., Linney, J. A., & Shinn, M. (Eds.). (2005). Science and community psychology: Enhancing the vitality of community research and action [Special issue]. *American Journal of Community Psychology, 35*(3/4).

Wandersman, A., & Nation, M. (1998). Urban neighborhoods and mental health: Psychological contributions to understanding toxicity, resilience and interventions. *American Psychologist, 53,* 647–656.

Wandersman, A., & Snell-Johns, J. (2005). Empowerment evaluation: Clarity, dialogue and growth. *American Journal of Evaluation, 26,* 421–428.

Wandersman, A., Snell-Johns, J., Lentz, B., Fetterman, D., Keener, D., Livet, M., et al. (2005). The principles of empowerment evaluation. In D. Fetterman & A. Wandersman (Eds.), *Empowerment evaluation principles in practice* (pp. 27–41). New York: Guilford Press.

Wasco, S., Campbell, R., & Clark, M. (2002). A multiple case study of rape victim advocates' self-care routines: The influence of organizational context. *American Journal of Community Psychology, 30,* 731–760.

Wasserman, M. (2006). *Implementation of home visitation programs: Stories from the states.* Chapin Hall Center for Children: Issue Brief #109.

Watson-Thompson, J., Fawcett, S., & Schultz, J. (2008). Differential effects of strategic planning on community changes in two urban neighborhood coalitions. *American Journal of Community Psychology, 42,* 25–38.

Watts, R. J. (1994). Paradigms of diversity. In E. J. Trickett, R. J. Watts, & D. Birman (Eds.), *Human diversity: Perspectives on people in context* (pp. 49–79). San Francisco: Jossey-Bass.

Watts, R. J. (2010). Advancing a community psychology of men. *American Journal of Community Psychology, 45,* 201–211.

Watts, R. J., & Serrano-Garcia, I. (2003). The psychology of liberation: Responses to oppression [Special issue]. *American Journal of Community Psychology, 31* (1/2).

Watts, R. J., Williams, N. C., & Jagers, R. (2003). Sociopolitical development. *American Journal of Community Psychology, 31,* 185–194.

Watzlawick, P., Weakland, J., & Fisch, R. (1974). *Change: Principles of problem formation and problem resolution.* New York: Norton.

Weber, L. (2010). *Understanding race, class, gender, and sexuality: A conceptual framework.* London, Oxford University Press.

Webster-Stratton, C. (1984). A randomized trial of two parent-training programs for families with conduct-disordered children. *Journal of Consulting and Clinical Psychology, 52,* 666–678.

Webster-Stratton, C., & Herman, K. C. (2008). The impact of parent behavior management training on child depressive symptoms. *Journal of Counseling Psychology, 55,* 473–484.

Webster-Stratton, C., Mihalic, S., Fagan, A., Taylor, T., & Tingely, C. (2001). *Blueprints for violence prevention: Book eleven: The incredible years: Parents, teachers, and children training series.* Boulder, CO: Center for the Study and Prevention of Violence.

Weick, K. (1984). Small wins: Redefining the scale of social issues. *American Psychologist, 39,* 40–49.

Weinstein, R. (2002a). Overcoming inequality in schooling: A call to action for community psychology. *American Journal of Community Psychology, 30,* 21–42.

Weinstein, R. (2002b). *Reaching higher: The power of expectations in schooling.* Cambridge, MA: Harvard University Press.

Weinstein, R. (2005, June). *Reaching higher in community psychology.* Seymour Sarason Award address, biennial meeting of the Society for Community Research and Action, Champaign-Urbana, IL.

Weinstein, R., Gregory, A., & Strambler, M. (2004). Intractable self-fulfilling prophecies: Fifty years after *Brown v. Board of Education. American Psychologist, 59,* 511–520.

Weinstein, R., Soule, C., Collins, F., Cone, J., Mehlhorn, M., & Simontacchi, K. (1991). Expectations and high school change: Teacher-researcher collaboration to prevent school failure. *American Journal of Community Psychology, 19,* 333–364.

Weiss, C. H. (1995). Nothing as practical as good theory: Exploring theory-based evaluation for comprehensive community initiatives for children and families. In J. P. Connell, A. Kubisch, L. Schorr, & C. H. Weiss (Eds.), *New approaches to evaluating community initiatives: Concepts, methods, and contexts* (pp. 65–92). Washington, DC: Aspen Institute.

Weissberg, R. P., & Bell, D. N. (1997). A meta-analytic review of primary prevention programs for children and adolescents: Contributions and caveats. *American Journal of Community Psychology, 25,* 207–214.

Weissberg, R. P., & Durlak, J. (2006). *Meta-analysis of the effect of social-emotional learning and positive youth development programs on academic achievement and problem behaviors.* Retrieved March 8, 2011, from www.CASEL.org

Weissberg, R. P., & Greenberg, M. T. (1997). School and community competence-enhancement and prevention programs. In I. Sigel & K. Renninger (Eds.), *Handbook of child psychology. Vol. 4: Child psychology in practice* (5th ed., pp. 877–954). New York: Wiley.

Weissberg, R. P., & Kumpfer, K. (Eds.). (2003). Prevention that works for children and youth [Special issue]. *American Psychologist, 58*(6/7).

Weissberg, R. P., Kumpfer, K., & Seligman, M. (2003). Prevention that works for children and youth: An introduction. *American Psychologist, 58,* 425–432.

Weisstein, N. (1993). Psychology constructs the female: Or, the fantasy life of the male psychologist (with some attention to the fantasies of his friends, the male biologist and the male anthropologist). *Feminism and Psychology, 3,* 195–210. (Originally published 1971. Boston: New England Free Press.)

Wells, R., Ward, A., Feinberg, M., & Alexander, J. (2008). What motivates people to participate in community-based coalitions? *American Journal of Community Psychology, 42,* 94–104.

Werner, E. E. (1993). Risk, resilience, and recovery: Perspectives from the Kauai Longitudinal Study. *Development and Psychopathology, 5,* 503–515.

Werner, E. E. (1996). Vulnerable but invincible: High risk children from birth to adulthood. *European Journal of Child and Adolescent Psychiatry, 5,* 47–51.

Werner, E. E. (2005). Resilience and recovery: Findings from the Kauai Longitudinal Study. *Research, Policy, and Practice in Children's Mental Health, 19,* 11–14.

White, G. (2010). Ableism. In G. Nelson & I. Prilleltensky, (Eds.), *Community psychology: In pursuit of liberation and well-being* (pp. 431–452). New York: Palgrave Macmillan.

White Johnson, R. L., Ford, K. R., & Sellers, R. M. (2010). Parental racial socialization profiles: Association with demographic factors, racial discrimination, childhood socialization and racial identity. *Cultural Diversity and Ethnic Minority Psychology, 16*(2) 237–247.

Whitney, I., Rivers, I., Smith, P., & Sharp, S. (1994). The Sheffield project: Methodology and findings. In P. Smith & S. Sharp (Eds.), *School bullying: Insights and perspectives* (pp. 20–56). London: Routledge.

Wicker, A. (1969). Size of church membership and members' support of church behavior settings. *Journal of Personality and Social Psychology, 13,* 278–288.

Wicker, A. (1973). Undermanning theory and research: Implications for the study of psychological and behavioral effects of excess populations. *Representative Research in Social Psychology, 4,* 185–206.

Wicker, A. (1979). Ecological psychology: Some recent and prospective developments. *American Psychologist, 34,* 755–765.

Wicker, A. (1987). Behavior settings reconsidered: Temporal stages, resources, internal dynamics, and context. In D. Stokols & I. Altman (Eds.), *Handbook of environmental psychology* (Vol. 1, pp. 613–653). New York: Wiley.

Wicker, A., & Sommer, R. (1993). The resident researcher: An alternative career model centered on community. *American Journal of Community Psychology, 21,* 469–482.

Wiesenfeld, E. (1996). The concept of "we": A community social psychology myth? *Journal of Community Psychology, 24,* 337–346.

Wilcox, B. L. (1981). Social support in adjusting to marital disruption: A network analysis. In B. Gottlieb (Ed.), *Social networks and social support* (pp. 97–116). Beverly Hills, CA: Sage.

Wiley, A., & Rappaport, J. (2000). Empowerment, wellness, and the politics of development. In D. Cicchetti, J. Rappaport, I. Sandler, & R. Weissberg (Eds.), *The promotion of wellness in children and adolescents* (pp. 59–99). Washington, DC: CWLA Press.

Williams, A. (2007). Support, expectations, awareness and influence: Reflections on youth and democracy articles. *Journal of Community Psychology, 35,* 811–814.

Williams, D. R., & Jackson, P. B. (2005). Social sources of racial disparities in health. *Health Affairs, 24,* 325–334.

Williams, D. R., & Williams-Morris, R. (2000). Racism and mental health: The African American experience. *Ethnicity and Health, 5,* 243–268.

Wilson, B. D. M., Harper, G. W., Hidalgo, M. A., Jamil, O. B., Torres, R. S., Fernandez, I., & Adolescent Medicine Trials Network for HIV/AIDS

Interventions. (2010). Negotiating dominant masculinity ideology: Strategies used by gay, bisexual, and questionng male adolescents. *American Journal of Community Psychology, 45,* 169–185.

Wilson, B. D. M., Hayes, E., Greene, G., Kelly, J. G., & Iscoe, I. (2003). Community psychology. In D. Freedheim (Ed.), *Handbook of psychology. Vol. 1: History of psychology* (pp. 431–449). New York: John Wiley.

Wingenfeld, S., & Newbrough, J. R. (2000). Community psychology in international perspective. In J. Rappaport & E. Seidman (Eds.), *Handbook of community psychology* (pp. 779–810). New York: Kluwer/Plenum.

Winkel, G., Saegert, S., & Evans, G. W. (2009). An ecological perspective on theory, methods, and analysis in environmental psychology: Advances and challenges. *Journal of Environmental Psychology, 29*(3), 318–328.

Wolff, T. (1987). Community psychology and empowerment: An activist's insights. *American Journal of Community Psychology, 15,* 151–166.

Wolff, T. (1994, Summer). Keynote address given at the fourth biennial conference. *The Community Psychologist, 27,* 20–26.

Wolff, T. (Ed.). (2001). Community coalition building: Contemporary practice and research [Special section]. *American Journal of Community Psychology, 29,* 165–329.

Wolff, T. (2004, Fall). Collaborative solutions: Six key components. *Collaborative Solutions Newsletter.* Retrieved March 8, 2011, from http://www.tomwolff.com

Wolff, T. (2010). *The power of collaborative solutions: Six principles and effective tools for building healthy communities.* San Francisco: Jossey-Bass.

Wolff, T., & Lee, P. (1997, June). *The Healthy Communities movement: An exciting new area for research and action by community psychologists.* Workshop presented at the meeting of the Society for Community Research and Action, Columbia, SC.

Wolitski, R. J. (2003, Fall). What do we do when the crisis does not end? *The Community Psychologist, 36,* 14–15.

Wollman, N., Lobenstine, M., Foderaro, M., & Stose, S. (2005). *Principles for promoting social change: Effective strategies for influencing attitudes and behaviors* (booklet). Ann Arbor, MI: Society for the Psychological Study of Social Issues.

Wong, P. T. P., Wong, L. C. J., & Scott, C. (2006). Beyond stress and coping: The positive psychology of transformation. In P. T. P. Wong & L. C. J. Wong (Eds.),

Handbook of multicultural perspectives on stress and coping. (pp. 1–26). Dallas, TX: Spring Publications.

Wood, L., Giles-Corti, B., Bulsara, M., & Bosch, D. (2007). More than a furry companion: The ripple effect of companion animals on neighborhood interactions and sense of community. *Society and Animals, 15,* 43–56.

Wood, M., Turnham, J., & Mills, G. (2008). Housing affordability and family well being: Results from the housing voucher evaluation. *Housing Policy Debate, 19,* 367–412.

World Health Organization. (2000). *Preventing suicide: A resource guide for general physicians.* Geneva: Author, Department of Mental Health.

Wright, P., & Kloos, B. (2007). Housing environment and mental health outcomes: A levels of analysis perspective. *Journal of Environmental Psychology, 27,* 79–89.

Wright, R. (1996). The missing or misperceived effects of punishment: The coverage of deterrence in criminology textbooks, 1956 to 1965 and 1984 to 1993. *Journal of Criminal Justice Education, 7,* 6–8.

Wuthnow, R. (1994). *Sharing the journey: Support groups and America's new quest for community.* New York: Free Press.

Xu, Q., Perkins, D., & Chow, J. C. (2010). Sense of community, neighboring, and social capital as predictors of local political participation in China. *American Journal of Community Psychology, 45,* 259–271.

Ybarra, M. L., & Eaton, W. W. (2005). Internet-based mental health interventions. *Mental Health Services Research, 7,* 75–87.

Yip, T., Sellers, R. M., & Seaton, E. K. (2006). African American racial identity across the lifespan: Identity status, identity content, and depressive symptoms. *Child Development, 77,* 1504–1517.

Yoshikawa, H., & Shinn, M. (2002). Facilitating change: Where and how should community psychology intervene? In T. A. Revenson, A. R. D'Augelli, S. E. French, D. L. Hughes, D. Livert, E. Seidman, M. Shinn, & H. Yoshikawa (Eds.), *A quarter century of community psychology: Readings from the American Journal of Community Psychology* (pp. 33–49). New York: Plenum Publishers.

Yoshikawa, H., Wilson, P., Hseuh, J., Rosman, E., Chin, J., & Kim, J. (2003). What front-line CBO staff can tell us about culturally anchored theories of behavior change in HIV prevention for Asian/Pacific Islanders. *American Journal of Community Psychology, 32,* 143–158.

Zander, A. (1995). [Untitled videotape interview]. In J. G. Kelly (Ed.), *The history of community psychology: A video presentation of context and exemplars.* Chicago: Society for Community Research and Action.

Zautra, A., & Bachrach, K. M. (2000). Psychological dysfunction and well-being: Public health and social indicator approaches. In J. Rappaport & E. Seidman (Eds.), *Handbook of community psychology* (pp. 165–186). New York: Kluwer/Plenum.

Ziliak, J. (Ed.). (2009). *Welfare reform and its long-term consequences for America's poor.* Cambridge, UK: Cambridge University Press.

Zimmerman, M. A. (2000). Empowerment theory: psychological, organizational and community levels of analysis. In J. Rappaport & E. Seidman (Eds.), *Handbook of community psychology* (pp. 43–63). New York: Kluwer/Plenum.

Zimmerman, M. A., Bingenheimer, J. B., & Notaro, P. C. (2002). Natural mentors and adolescent resiliency: A study with urban youth. *American Journal of Community Psychology, 30,* 221–243.

Zimmerman, M. A., Reischl, T. M., Seidman, E., Rappaport, J., Toro, P. A., & Salem, D. A. (1991). Expansion strategies of a mutual help organization. *American Journal of Community Psychology, 19,* 251–278.

Zins, J., Elias, M. J., & Maher, C. A. (Eds.). (2007). *Bullying, victimization and peer harassment: A handbook of prevention and intervention.* New York: Haworth Press.

Zins, J. E., Weissberg, R. P., Wang, M. C., & Walberg, H. J. (Eds.). (2004). *Building academic success on social and emotional learning: What does the research say?* New York: Teachers College Press.

Zuckerman, M. (1990). Some dubious premises in research and theory on racial differences: Social, scientific and ethical issues. *American Psychologist, 45,* 1297–1303.

Name Index

Guckenburg, S., 450
Gueldner, B., 303
Guentzel, H., 215
Guerra, N. G., 238, 239
Guier, C., 266
Gulcur, L., 271, 413
Gump, P., 151, 152
Guo, J., 304
Gustafson, D., 279
Gwadz, M., 222

H
Haber, M., 272
Haertl, K., 165, 166
Haffey, W., 47
Haggerty, R., 77, 292, 462
Hall, C. C., 196, 245
Hallman, W., 154, 358
Hamber, B., 30, 63
Hamby, S., 91
Hamer, F. L., 48
Hanewinkel, R., 314
Hanlin, C. E., 114, 363
Harper, G. W., 93, 94, 117, 216, 243, 468–469
Harrell, S. P., 90, 212, 238, 260
Hartup, W. W., 275
Haskell, I., 437
Hatcher, J., 81, 82, 84
Hathaway, B., 392
Hausfather, N., 133
Hawkins, J. D., 298, 313, 392, 423
Hayes, E., 42
Hazel, K. L., 82, 89, 94, 123, 164, 170, 200, 201, 243, 244, 282, 346, 373, 471
Hebert, R., 280
Heckman, J. J., 306
Heflinger, C. A., 465
Heilman, M., 235
Heller, K., 51, 216, 290, 474, 475
Helm, S., 26, 98, 243, 464
Helms, J. E., 90, 213, 214, 222, 224
Henderson, M. J., 44
Herman, K. C., 311
Hermans, H., 221
Herndon, E. J., 8, 251
Herrera, C., 437
Hess, J., 121
Hickey, S., 356

Hidalgo, M. A., 216
Hightower, A. D., 47
Hill, J., 30, 79, 82, 178, 183, 199, 200, 214, 231, 280
Hillier, J., 155
Himmelman, A., 403
Hirsch, B. J., 275, 390
Hitlin, P., 204
Hix-Small, H., 369
Hobden, K., 476
Hobfoll, S. E., 257, 258, 261, 263, 264, 271, 272, 274, 275
Hochschild, J., 235
Hoffer, T., 186
Hogge, J., 183
Holahan, C. J., 145
Holden, A., 309
Hollander, D., 358
Hollingshead, A., 289
Holloway, B. E., 274, 304
Holmes, T. H., 258
Homel, R., 304
Hooks, B., 359
Hopkins, B., 368
Hopper, K., 5, 405
Horowitz, J., 303
Horton, M., 373, 378
Howard, K., 329, 337, 338, 346
Howard-Pitney, B., 345
Hoyt-Meyers, L., 263
Hrabowski, R. A., 273, 482, 483
Huber, M., 122
Huberman, A., 107
Huebsch, P., 278
Huerta, M., 161
Hughes, D., 29, 82, 90, 91, 112, 114, 205
Hughey, J., 98, 114, 122, 182, 183, 186, 188, 194, 202, 360, 361, 362, 370, 372, 378, 379, 388, 391, 483
Humphreys, K., 25, 43, 53, 59, 81, 125, 200, 201, 202, 276, 277, 278, 279, 469
Hunsberger, B., 200
Hunt, S. B., 94
Hunter, A., 192, 194, 222
Hurtado, A., 222
Huston, A., 408
Huygens, I., 63

I
Ibrahim-Wells, G., 114, 216
Ickovics, J., 266
Idlout, L., 369
Imm, P., 270, 331, 393, 447, 450
Inequality.org, 230
Institute of Medicine (IOM), 77, 292–293, 323, 462
Internet World Stats, 203
Isava, D., 303
Iscoe, I., 42, 60
Isenberg, D., 25, 81, 84, 89
Israel, N., 468, 476
Iyengar, S., 234
Iyer, A., 235

J
Jackson, R., 218, 465
Jacobs, J., 155
Jacobson, S., 368, 378
Jagers, R., 199, 200, 201, 231, 236, 281, 282, 366, 394
Jahoda, M., 39, 40, 44
James, S., 233
Jamil, O. B., 216
Janzen, R., 133
Jarvis, S., 465
Jason, L. A., 16, 33, 79, 81, 82, 85, 86, 109, 200, 280, 395, 405, 470
Jeffries, D., 214
Jenkins, S., 227
Johnson, K., 160, 288, 450
Joint Commission on Mental Health and Mental Illness, 44
Jolliffe, D., 437
Jones, D., 162, 213, 214, 229, 235, 236, 238, 270, 407
Jordan, L., 243
Joseph, D., 122, 131, 443
Jozefowicz-Simbeni, D., 476
Ju, H., 160
Juby, H. L., 224
Julian, D. A., 89, 471
Jumper-Thurman, P., 243, 395
Juras, J. L., 377
Juris, J., 402

K
Kaftarian, S., 331, 446, 447
Kagitçibasi, C., 220

Subject Index

A

Academic, Social, and Emotional Learning Act, 480

Accountability, 443, 446–450
results-based, 423–425

Acculturation, 224–227
contextual perspective in, 228–230
identity development and, 221–224

Action research, 45–46, 81

Action skills, 61–62

Activity settings approach, 153–154, 171
contributions of, 153–154
limitations of, 153–154

Acts of qualitative methods, 107–110
asking, 107–108
interpreting, 108–109
knowing, 109–110
witnessing, 108

Adaptation, 143, 171, 322, 337–339, 342–344

Adolescents, mixed-method evaluation of peer support for, 132–133

Advocacy, 125, 268–269

Africa, community psychology in, 65–66

Age, as dimensions of human diversity for community psychology, 216

AIDS Risk Reduction Model (Catania, Kegeles & Coates), 310

Aid to Families with Dependent Children (AFDC), 414–415

Akwesasne Task Force on the Environment, 94–95

Alaska Natives, spirituality and sobriety of, 243–244

Alcohol, Drug Abuse, and Mental Health Administration, 53

Alcohol, tobacco, and other drug (ATOD), 427, 455

Alcoholics Anonymous (AA), 16, 276, 279

Alternative settings, 163–169, 400–401
Community Lodge movement, 164–165
Harlem Children's Zone, 167–169
as intervention, for promoting coping, 269

American Indian Life Skills Development curriculum, 345

American Journal of Community Psychology, 51, 323, 462, 470

American Psychological Association (APA), 49, 468

Annual Review of Psychology (Cowen), 51

Archival data, 114, 433

Arkansas Evaluation Center, 482

Asia, community psychology in, 65–66

Asking (Act One of qualitative research), 107–108

Assertive Community Treatment, 271

Assertiveness, 263

Assimilation, 225, 226

Asthma Coalition, 392

Attending to unheard voices approach, 78

Attentiveness, 106

Australia, community psychology in, 64–65

B

Bangladesh Rural Advancement Committee (BRAC), 398–399

Behavior observation ratings, 433

Behavior setting, 150–151, 171

Belonging and identification, 181

Between-group designs, 92

Bicultural competence, 227–228, 246
bicultural efficacy, 228
communication competence, 228
social support networks, 228
strong cultural identity, 227
strong individual identity, 227

Bicultural efficacy, 228

features of, 377–382

Highlander Research and Education Center, 375–376

maintenance of, 145

neighborhood organizations, capacity building in, 374–375

optimally populated, 151, 171

for prevention and promotion programs, assessment of, 333–335

underpopulated, 151–152, 171

Sexual behavior, promotion of healthy, 308–310

Sexual orientation, as dimension of human diversity for community psychology, 216

Shaping the definition of a public issue or conflict instrument of power, 362

Shared assumptions, 172

Shared emotional connection, 182

Skills

action, 61–62

design, 61

participatory, 368–369

social, 62

Small wins, 341

Sobriety, of Alaska Natives, 243–244

Social action, 395–397

Social capital, 186–190

bonding, 187

bridging, 187–188

community psychology and, 190

Social change

defined, 386

movements for, 47–49

promoting, 472–478

purpose of, 386–388

Social class, as dimension of human diversity for community psychology, 215

Social climate approach

dimensions of, 144–146

use of, in research and community practice, 146–147

Social competencies, 300

Social Decision Making and Social Problem Solving (SDM/SPS) program, 340

Social Development Coordinating Committee, 341

Social Disorganization Theory, 14

Social-emotional competencies, 263

Social-emotional learning (SEL) programs, 315, 327–329, 479–480

Social environments, mapping, 122

Social identity development models, 246

Social inequalities, as dimension of human diversity for community psychology, 217–218

Social issues of community psychology research. *See also* cultural and social contexts of community psychology research

bottom-up approaches to, 57–58

change in, limits of, 17–18

divergent reasoning and, 58–59

and equality, 55–57

in progressive and conservative eras, 54–55

shifting, 52–60

top-down approaches to, 57–58

viewpoints on, opposing, 58–59

Socialization, 301. *See also* human diversity for community psychology

in cultural communities, 219–230

Social justice, 169, 442

concern with, broadening, 467–469

as core value in community psychology, 29–30

distributive justice, 29

procedural justice, 29

Social myths, 233–234

Social policy, 268–269

Social power, instruments of, 360–363

Social psychology, concept of, 11

Social Readjustment Rating Scale, 258

Social regularities, 147–149, 171

contributions of, 148–149

limitations of, 148–149

Social relationships, 145

Social resources activated for coping with stress, 263

Social Security and Medicaid (FICA), 411

Social Security System, 408

Social skills, 62

Social support networks, 96–97, 185, 228, 274–276, 378

for coping with stress, 271–276

enacted support, 272

generalized support, 272

high-density networks, 275

multidimensionality, 274–275

perceived support, 272

reciprocity, 275–276

relationship context of, 272–274

social support networks, 274–276

specific support, 272

Social support resources, 301–302

Society for Community Research and Action (SCRA), 13, 61, 62, 465, 471–472, 483–484

Society for Prevention Research, The, 336

Society for the Psychological Study of Social Issues (SPSSI), 45, 48

Socioeconomic status (SES), 215

South Carolina Alcohol Enforcement Team (AET), 451–452, 455

Specific support, 272

Spiritual communities

in community life, 200–202

defined, 200

identity in, 202–203

meaning-making in, 202–203

narratives in, 202–203

Spirituality, 199–200

of Alaska Natives, 243–244

coping with stress and, 280–282

human diversity for community psychology, as dimension of, 216–217

Spiritual realm of living, 244

Spiritual resources, activated for coping with stress, 263

Staff, training and support of, 340–341